IN SEARCH OF OURSELVES

An Introduction to Physical Anthropology
Third Edition

Frank E. Poirier
The Ohio State University

Burgess Publishing Company
Minneapolis, Minnesota

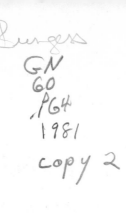
Editorial: Jeff Holtmeier, Marta Reynolds, Mary Vail, Gary Phillips
Art: Judy Vicars
Cover Photography: Dennis Tasa
Production: Morris Lundin, Pat Barnes

Burgess Publishing Company
7108 Ohms Lane
Minneapolis, Minnesota 55435

Credits

Art when not otherwise cited was drawn by Mary Dersch, Shirley Hoeman, or Don Beimborn. Figure 17-19 courtesy of Richard E. Leakey, National Museums of Kenya. Figures 10-1, 10-2, and 11-7 through 11-15 by Frank E. Poirier. Photo sequences on pages 224, 255, and 261 by Wendy Lawrence.

Figures 17-11 and 17-15 are after W. Le Gros Clark, *The Fossil Evidence for Human Evolution*, copyright © 1955, 1964 by The University of Chicago, and Figure 17-5 is adapted from M. D. Leakey, "Preliminary summary of the cultural material from Beds I and II, Olduvai Gorge, Tanzania," in *Background to Evolution in Africa*, edited by W. Bishop and J. Clark, copyright © 1967 by the Wenner-Gren Foundation for Anthropological Research, Inc. Used by permission of the University of Chicago Press. Photo sequence on page 259 by D. C. Johanson.

Chapter 2. *Figures 2-2 and 2-3*. Racle, F., *Introduction to Evolution*, 1979, pp. 101, 102. Reprinted by permission of Prentice-Hall, Inc., Englewood Cliffs, New Jersey. *Figure 2-4*. Courtesy of the American Museum of Natural History. *Figures 2-5 and 2-6*. From M. Cartmill, *Primate Origins*. Burgess Publishing Company, Minneapolis, 1975.

(continued on page 517)

Preface

This book is about life, our collective lives: past, present, and future. An unhealthy intellectual arrogance has recently been created by our scientific successes, our flights to the moon, medical discoveries, and our ability to create and destroy life. The finality of this last property, the ability to destroy life, emphasizes the need to replace this arrogance, this know-it-allness, with a new humility based on expanding knowledge of the complexity of life, of which we are but one part. Kierkegaard once stated that life can only be understood backward, but it must be lived forward. However, it can only be lived forward with knowledge and appreciation of the past.

In these next few pages we examine our evolutionary history, noting the major signposts along the way. Time and our own blindnesses have erased some of the signs; but the path is not yet obscure. Prepare for the journey; for some for whom this is all new, it is as rewarding and as dangerous as any new, unexplored, uncharted venture.

Many things were taken into consideration in producing this new edition. User suggestions inspired rewriting and reorganization in the section on human variation. New information on Mendelian, molecular, and biochemical genetics has been added to give students a better feeling for some of the biological aspects of evolution. The discovery of new fossils in East Africa or elsewhere occasioned the rewriting of the section on the fossil evidence for evolution. The section on primate behavior has been expanded.

Users of the first two editions will notice rewriting and reorganization throughout the text. The bibliography has been enlarged considerably, and gender references have been removed except in direct quotations. The objective of the book remains the same, however, namely, to provide a comprehensive review of current information on primate evolution—and specifically human evolution—for students with little or no background in anthropology or biology. The attempt to integrate biology, behavior, and culture is of key importance as we look at human evolution, nonhuman primate behavior, and human diversity. I hope the readers will enjoy this introduction to physical anthropology as much as I have enjoyed putting it together.

Many authors write books because they have a particular theoretical perspective they wish to champion. This has been particularly true of the scholarship in paleoanthropology. As you will note in your reading, many alternatives have been offered to study the primate fossil record. Many new finds, many new investigative techniques have appeared since the first edition. In some cases views expressed in the first edition have been modified, and in other cases, have been deleted. I have, however, been hesitant to delete controversial viewpoints, for who knows what turn of events will occur. This book may be and has been criticized on that score; nevertheless it has taken a very conscious effort to prevent this author's viewpoints from being the focal point of the book. Students do not need to be told that one viewpoint is gospel; what is needed is a perspective of all possible scenarios. I have attempted to provide this scenario by describing as many feasible alternatives as possible. In a true learning situation, students should be helped to form their own opinions based on the current evidence. I hope that enough evidence for conflicting viewpoints has been presented for students to begin this process.

The presentation of different viewpoints is particularly germane to the discussions about the early primates, the role of the dryopithecines in subsequent hominoid evolution, the evolutionary role of *Ramapithecus,* the interpretation of the diversity of the Pliocene-Pleistocene hominid fossil record, and the divergence of opinion as presented by the fossil and the biochemical evidence. In the first and second editions of this book the dryopithecines were presented as a group with clear affinities to later pongids and hominids. Now, however, there is mounting evidence to challenge that perspective. In this, the third edition, evidence is presented both pro and con as to the place of the dryopithecines in the hominid evolutionary scheme. Recent evidence suggests that the dryopithecines may not have had a place in hominid evolutionary history; nevertheless, the case is surely not closed. In the first edition *Ramapithecus* was presented as the first probable hominid; in the second edition, the case was presented that the issue is not so clear. By the third edition evidence has mounted suggesting that *Ramapithecus* had little to do with the hominid evolutionary line, and the evidence on this score is rather strong.

Some paleontologists, however (i.e., Elwyn Simons), still argue for the inclusion of *Ramapithecus* in the hominid evolutionary line. Although this perspective is rapidly losing support, it is presented herein. The amount of hominid fossil material in the Pliocene and early Pleistocene has greatly increased since the first edition of this book. With the increased evidence there have been increasing numbers of interpretive frameworks, some of which have superseded earlier interpretations. Taxonomic assignments have been reshuffled, deleted, and one new taxon (*Australopithecus afarensis*) has been established. The interpretive frameworks are conflicting, confusing, and numerous. A number of such schemes have been presented for your consideration. Surely, they all cannot be correct; I have, however, attempted not to take a stand on this issue in this edition.

In the first and second editions of this book the phylogenetic framework proposed by the biochemical (protein) clock was given rather short shrift, reflecting its nonacceptance by a majority of paleontologists. Unfortunately, this brief discussion also reflected my prejudices at the time. Now, however, the time spans proposed by the protein clock have been somewhat refined and have received greater credence. This edition reflects that changing position. This latter case is a prime example of what would have happened had the author exercised an option and chosen not to mention a scheme out of tune with his own thoughts. Although readers were unfortunately biased against this theme in earlier presentations, they were presented with an opportunity to learn about this possibility, which now enjoys wider support.

Other factors have changed since earlier editions of this work and these have been presented. The current edition has been updated as new material appeared. The readers must be cautioned, however, that discoveries occurred as this book was being revised and while the work was in print. This is the frustrating, yet fascinating, aspect of this material. New frameworks emerge as the fossils themselves emerge and as schemes based upon earlier materials are refined. In this sense, the book must always be somewhat out-of-date.

Acknowledgments

Few people can write a book or teach a course without the help of others. I wish to acknowledge the help of those many undergraduate students and teaching assistants who took the time to comment on my teaching, to provide constructive criticism, and to buoy my spirits when they were low. I am grateful to the users of the original edition as well as reviewers of drafts of the present and past editions for their insightful comments and suggestions. It is primarily because of their interest that much of the book has taken new form.

My family always suffers when I work hard on a project, but without their support I couldn't finish. I thank my wife Darlene and our two children, Alyson and Sevanne. Special thanks are due to the C. V. Mosby Company, St. Louis, for kindly granting permission to use material from my 1981 publication entitled *Fossil Evidence: The Human Evolutionary Journey*. I wish to thank Paul Sciulli for his helpful criticisms and Mary Lalley for her help.

As was true in the two previous editions, I received unstinting support from the publisher, Burgess Publishing Company. Throughout the development of this book I have been fortunate to work with many fine people at Burgess. Regrettably, one of those with whom I enjoyed working during the revision of the second edition, Ms. Dora Stein, has passed away. Four people at Burgess are closely associated with this third edition: Ms. Marta Reynolds, Ms. Mary Vail, Mr. Jeffrey Holtmeier, and Dr. Gary Phillips. To them I owe a debt of gratitude. Mr. Holtmeier has been particularly instrumental in the change of this book since we began working on the second edition. Not only have I benefited greatly from his insights and his editorial help, I have enjoyed his friendship over the years.

Thanks are due also to all publishers and individuals that have allowed us to use photographs, drawings, and tables. Where not shown in the text, credits will be found in a separate list at the end of the book.

As is perhaps true of many who have researched a topic for many years and who have had the good fortune of being able to present this research to interested audiences, be they students or others, it soon becomes difficult to differentiate your own ideas from those which you have read and which belong rightfully to others. The task of a synthesizer, to take the ideas which many have labored to produce and attempt to put them together into some comprehensive format, is fascinating. If I have succeeded in doing this, my debt lies with so many who have worked so hard to produce the original ideas. In fact, it may be very close to the truth to state that, in what follows, there is little which is purely original with this author. I trust that I have repaid my debt for many enjoyable hours by acknowledging the sources. If I have erred even once in this process I hope I may be forgiven by the researcher whose work I have discussed. If there are places where the reader recognizes his or her own hand in what I have said, I hope that I have been gracious enough to say that I acknowledge my debt. Should

I have failed, I hope it is enough to say that I have attempted to do my best to record your achievements. I thank you for providing the material giving me the opportunity to do so. To paraphrase a line from Tennyson's *Ulysses:* This work is part of all I have read, of all those I have had the good fortune of knowing, and of all I have been privileged to see.

If I knew as much about one thing as some claim to know about many, I would be very wise indeed.

Columbus, Ohio
February 1981

F. E. P.

Contents

Part Three—Reconstructing the Past: Behavioral Studies   107

Part Four—The Fossil Record: Recovering the Past   189

Part Five—Human Diversity   409

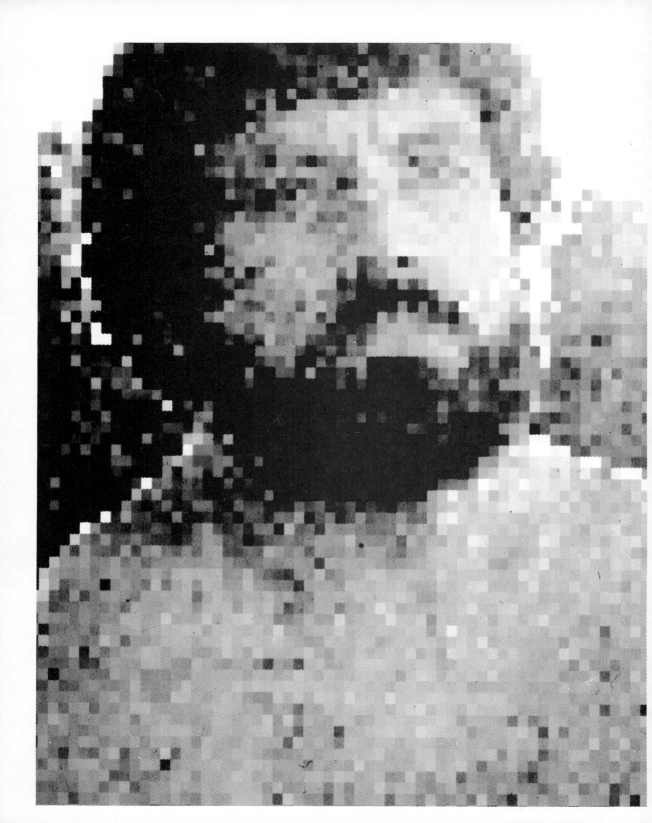

Part One

Introduction

If today you can take a thing like evolution and make it a crime to teach it in the public schools, tomorrow you can make it a crime to teach it in the private schools. . . . At the next session you may ban books and the newspaper. Soon you may set Catholic against Protestant, and Protestant against Protestant, and try to foist your own religion upon the minds of men.

After a while, your Honor, it is the setting of man against man and creed against creed, until with flying banners and beating drums we are marching backward to the glorious ages of the sixteenth century when bigots lighted fagots to burn the men who dared to bring any intelligence and enlightenment and culture to the human mind.

From Clarence Darrow, "Statement for the Defense from the Scopes Trial."

Chapter 1

Brief History of Physical Anthropology

Preevolutionary thought was dominated by the Biblical injunction, God created heaven and earth, which since remained stable. We reconstruct our history of physical anthropology by drawing on general reviews of the history of science. Physical anthropology is merely part of this larger process. Prior to Charles Darwin the scientific world had absorbed the thoughts of such individuals as Aristotle, da Vinci, and Linnaeus. The Darwinian evolutionary scheme altered the picture of life by allowing that change occurred and that organisms evolve one from another.

Prior to the 1950s what became known as physical anthropology was a field of study dominated primarily by technique and lacking an integrating theoretical stance. In the early 1950s S. L. Washburn suggested a realignment of priorities and helped popularize the term "new physical anthropology" to describe a new outlook and new subject matter.

The Biblical Injunction

Until the end of the fourteenth century the written record suggests that most intellectuals accepted the Genesis version of Creation as truth. Most writers of the period had a static view of life. We were God's supreme handiwork, made in His image, first appearing on the sixth day of the universe's creation, and possessing a soul distinguishing us from all other animals. Early thinkers were quick to note our bipedal, erect posture and free hands. Thomas Aquinas noted, for example, "He has reason and hands whereby he can make himself arms and clothes, and other necessaries of life, of infinite variety." Aristotle called the hand "the organ of organs."

Renaissance Thought

The rise of commercial capitalism stirred the thought of the fifteenth and sixteenth centuries. Colonial exploration led to numerous explorers' accounts attesting to the diversity of cultures and peoples and, in the intellectual community, the Renaissance produced a naturalistic empiricism as opposed to the theological authoritarianism preceding it. As the theological grip began to erode, scientists dared human dissection and drew behavioral and anatomical comparisons between human and nonhuman animals.

Leonardo da Vinci was among those who led this scientific thrust. His dissections and anatomical illustrations laid a base for comparative anatomy. During the early years of the sixteenth century, Vesalius taught that physicians should study the human body by dissection. He was the first to suggest such practical experience, which theologians still considered sacrilege.

Most writers in this early period considered humans distinct from, and higher creations than, the rest of the animal kingdom. Many early volumes attempting to classify the animal kingdom excluded humans from their schemes. One exception was a series of volumes by Edward Wooton entitled *De differentiis animalium*. One whole volume of this series is devoted to the human animal.

Seventeenth Century

The seventeenth century generated much discussion as to the differences between the human and nonhuman animal. Pierre Charron made one of the most interesting attempts to catalogue these differences, and thus perhaps by implication show that we were God's supreme gift to the world. Of the many traits available for comparative purposes, Charron was impressed by our faculty for speech, our erect posture, our hand, the nakedness and smoothness of our skin (see Morris, *The Naked Ape*), and the ability to laugh and cry. Many of these are still cited as evidence of our distinctiveness from the rest of the animal world.

One of the best known accomplishments of this period was Edward Tyson's work in comparative primate anatomy. In 1699, his work was published under the title of "Orang Outang, sive Homo Sylvestris: or, the Anatomy of a Pygmie compared with that of a Monkey, an Ape and a Man." Tyson found that his ape (a young chimpanzee), or "pygmie" as he called it, resembled a human (Figure 1-1). He reasoned that this animal was an intermediate link between human and nonhuman primates. Despite the importance of Tyson's work, his fellow scientists did not pursue Tyson's ideas, perhaps because in contrast to the efforts of Vesalius and later Charles Darwin, Tyson's work did not stir controversy. The seventeenth-century outlook was also dominated by the concept that development was static, that species were unchanging. That is, all forms of life as witnessed in the seventeenth century had resulted from the original creation and had always looked the same.

Eighteenth Century

Eighteenth-century scientific inquiry was characterized by a concept known as naturalism. Humans were viewed as a natural phenomenon, as a part of the universe governed by its laws. During the eighteenth century there was a good deal of work in the areas of comparative anatomy and systematics. Humans were now considered part of the natural order. As early as 1732, the systematist Linnaeus wrote about the relationship between the human and nonhuman primate. In the first edition of *Systema Naturae* (1735) he included the human primate in the category of "Anthropomorpha." This group included the other known primates.

Although Linnaeus appreciated the similarity between human and nonhuman primates, we do not know if he believed in what later became known as evolution. His writings are unclear or deliberately defensive and ambiguous on this issue as he was cautious in his expression of

Figure 1-1. Tyson's "pygmie" or "orang outang" was actually an immature chimpanzee.

heresies (remember a doctrine of evolution would have been diametrically opposed to theological doctrine and could have been dangerous to anyone expressing it). In some passages he argues for the **fixity of species**[1,2] (i.e., divine creation); in others he advocates the doctrine of mutability. In some passages Linnaeus seems to have accepted the possibility that organisms change over time according to the pressures exerted by nature; such a process is now labeled adaptation and natural selection. His exact position remains unknown.

Another eighteenth-century scientist contributing to the history of physical anthropology was not so circumspect. James Burnett, better known as Lord Monboddo, insisted that the orangutan (a tree-living ape that lives in the jungles of Borneo and Sumatra) was actually a human being. ". . . the Orang Outangs . . . are of our species, and though they have made some progress in the arts of life, they have not advanced as far as to invent a language." Lest it be thought that Monboddo was simply naive, it should be mentioned that anatomically we share a large number of similarities with the Great Apes (chimpanzees, gorillas, and orang-

---

[1]The concept that every species was originally divinely created and that the first individual served as a model for its descendants.

[2]Boldfaced terms are defined in the glossary, which begins on p. 509.

utans), and Monboddo was reacting to this similarity, calling upon the little knowledge available at that time.

Erasmus Darwin (Charles Darwin's grandfather) seems to have had an evolutionary view of human development. In one of his poems he stated

> Imperious man, who rules the bestial crowd,
> Of language, reason, and reflection proud,
> With brow erect who scorns this earthly sod,
> And styles himself the image of his God:
> Arose from rudiments of form and sense,
> An embryon paint, or microscope lens!

Erasmus Darwin believed in the mutability (capability to change) of **species.** This belief is seen in the following quote: ". . . the great globe itself, and all that it inhabit, appear to be in a perpetual state of mutation and improvement, . . . animals seem to have undergone great changes, as well as the inanimate parts of the earth and are probably still in a state of gradual improvement." Despite his belief in change, however, Erasmus Darwin still differentiated between the human and nonhuman animal.

Nineteenth Century

The nineteenth-century scientists who probably had the greatest impact on later scientific development were Charles Darwin and Gregor Mendel. In contrast to Darwin's work, which had an immediate impact on the intellectual community, Mendel's discoveries of the mechanisms of inheritance languished in total obscurity only to be discovered years after his death. Some of the works of most importance to Darwin's theory are discussed in Chapter 3 and Mendel's contributions are discussed in Chapter 4.

Twentieth Century

Twentieth-century physical anthropology underwent two distinct phases of development separated from one another by their outlook, technique, and subject matter. During the first half of the twentieth century, prior to 1951, physical anthropology was primarily a field whose outlook was dominated by techinque. This period is often labeled the "romantic" phase and was dominated by measurement and description of body form. The major concerns of early twentieth-century physical anthropologists fall into categories called **osteometry** (measurement of defleshed bone) and **anthropometry** (study and comparison of human body measurements). Prior to the 1950s, physical anthropology was 80 percent measurement of bones and teeth.

Formation of racial taxonomies was another major concern of early twentieth-century physical anthropologists. While much attention focused on fossil populations, living populations were placed into any one of a number (varying from five to several dozen) of "racial types." Early classification attempts often proceeded on the premise that some populations are more highly evolved than others. Since such classification was done primarily by European scientists, Europeans and those of European descent were commonly the apex of this scale. A scheme recognizing "higher" and "lower" races seems to have been a natural outgrowth of colonialism.

Another characteristic of early twentieth-century physical anthropology was a heavy use of statistics. Some academic positions in physical anthropology, especially those in Europe, were

---

Table 1-1. Intellectual Influences on Development of Physical Anthropology

---

The Fifteenth and Sixteenth Centuries—Renaissance Thought

Leonardo da Vinci	Scientific dissections and anatomical illustrations laid basis for comparative anatomy.
Edward Wooton	Wrote *De differentiis animalium,* which was a scientific attempt to classify the animal world. One volume of the series was devoted to the human animal.

The Seventeenth Century

Pierre Charron	Tried to catalogue differences between the human and nonhuman animal.
Edward Tyson	Worked with comparative primate anatomy. First to dissect a chimpanzee.

The Eighteenth Century—Naturalism in Scientific Inquiry

Carolus Linnaeus	Taxonomy.
Lord Monboddo (James Burnett)	Dissection and comparative anatomy.
Erasmus Darwin	Natural history, defended the doctrine of the modifiability of the species.

The Nineteenth Century

Charles Darwin	Promoted the theory of evolution, theory of natural selection.
Gregor Mendel	The founder of modern genetics.

The Twentieth Century

Prior to 1951 the major concerns were measurement of the body (osteometry and anthropometry). Constructing racial classifications consumed a good deal of the time of the anthropologists of the early 1900s.

The "new" physical anthropology is based on the concept of population genetics and the synthetic theory of evolution, as well as changes in technique and outlook in other fields of scientific endeavor.

---

staffed with statisticians and biometricians lacking biological training. This tradition, a reliance on quantification, often without analysis, had the lasting effect of discrediting physical anthropology in the minds of many.

In 1951 S. L. Washburn delivered a short speech entitled "The New Physical Anthropology" and provided a major catalyst for change. In this speech, he suggested a realignment of priorities. Washburn suggested that we study human populations instead of solely measuring fossil bones. Instead of sitting in laboratories poring over mathematical formulae, he suggested that physical anthropologists become field oriented, that is, get out and work with the subjects where they are. Instead of merely measuring bone or muscle, he suggested that we concern ourselves with experimental anatomy and functional anatomical research. Washburn's speech stands as a convenient point for distinguishing the "old" from the "new" physical anthropology. It should be noted, however, that similar changes in outlook and technique also characterized other scientific fields at this time.

Physical anthropology has moved from a collecting to an experimental stage. The "new" physical anthropology is firmly based in the biological and natural sciences. In fact, physical anthropologists are often unsure of what academic department is best suited to their concerns. Many see physical anthropology as an amalgamation of such disciplines as biology, zoology, genetics, chemistry, physiology, anatomy, psychology, and still others. Physical anthropology has carved itself a niche among its better financially endowed relatives by proclaiming itself the font of knowledge about human evolution. Physical anthropologists are the interpretors and curators of human evolutionary history from the appearance of the primates approximately 55 million to 60 million years ago until today.

Much of what is the "new" physical anthropology is actually a new philosophical approach to evolution. This new approach has been greatly assisted by assimilation of knowledge of population genetics, by new geological dating techniques, and by computerization of rapidly increasing reams of data. It should also be noted that physical anthropology received a boost from the "rediscovery" of Darwinian evolution. There was a movement away from mere classification of data toward understanding the processes of natural selection and adaptation as the key to understanding evolutionary change. Research interests, especially measurement of the living and nonliving form, cultivated before 1950 have not disappeared. They have, however, been refined by taking into account causal relationships. To reconstruct our evolutionary history, physical anthropologists study the blood groups and chromosomes of human and nonhuman primates and the behavior as well as anatomy of the nonhuman primates, and have adopted a comprehensive approach for interpreting fossil evidence (Table 10-1).

These processes are discussed in the chapters that follow, which are witness to the fruitfulness of this new integrative approach, the new synthetic theory of evolution. The "new" physical anthropology is concerned with living populations and with physically, culturally, and behaviorally reconstructing their ancestors. The "new" physical anthropology is a field science buoyed by laboratory research. Above all, the "new" physical anthropology is a challenge—a challenge for us to reconstruct our past and thus perhaps assist in structuring the future.

We have traced the history of physical anthropology from a nonevolutionary documentation of life to an evolutionary approach for understanding life. Today's physical anthropology is concerned with understanding life's diversity, especially among human and nonhuman primates. Today's physical anthropology is concerned with documenting and understanding primate evolution through the fossil record, through the study of nonhuman animals, and through the study of modern populations.

Bibliography

Clark, W. Le Gros. 1958. Re-orientations in physical anthropology. In *The scope of physical anthropology and its place in academic studies,* edited by D. F. Roberts and F. S. Weiner, pp. 1-6. Oxford: Church Army Press.

Morris, D. 1967. *The naked ape: a zoologist's study of the human animal.* New York: McGraw-Hill.

Morris, D., and Morris, R. 1968. *Men and apes.* New York: McGraw-Hill.

Slotkin, J. 1965. *Readings in early anthropology.* New York: Wenner-Gren Foundation.

Washburn, S. 1951. The new physical anthropology. *Transactions of the New York Academy of Sciences* 13:298.

Chapter 2

Our Place in the Animal Kingdom

Within the scientific classificatory system, we, *Homo sapiens sapiens,* occupy certain categories: Kingdom Animalia, Class Mammalia, Order Primates, Suborder Anthropoidea, Family Hominidae, Genus *Homo,* Species *sapiens,* and Subspecies *sapiens.* Here we discuss our mammalian heritage by briefly tracing the evolutionary history of mammalian groups, especially placentals. Although we trace our primate origins perhaps as far back as about 60 million years ago, we differ from other primates in a number of anatomical and behavioral traits. Some similarities and differences are discussed in this chapter.

Our Place in the Taxonomic System

As will be discussed later, there has been an attempt to relate living forms to one another scientifically in an evolutionary sequence. This chapter discusses our place within the animal kingdom. We are members of the Kingdom Animalia, the Class Mammalia, the Order Primates, and the Genus *Homo.* To appreciate our relationship with the rest of the animal kingdom, and specifically to the other primates, we will briefly present some of the evidence for that relationship.

A novel way of presenting our place within the animal kingdom was suggested by B. S. Kraus (1964). Increasing numbers of individuals struggle through years of secondary and higher educational institutions to achieve the distinction of appending a set of initials after their name. From the moment of birth, however, without one day of schooling, each of us could legitimately print a calling card with the following legend:

Jane Doe, K.A., S.K.M., P.C., S.P.V., C.M., O.P., S.O.A., S.F.H., F.H., G.H., S.S., S.S.S.

We "achieve" these initials by virtue of our place within the zoological classification system. Perhaps as much as half a billion years of evolution were invested in the attainment of these honors, by which we "earned" the right to append the following "degrees" to our name:

Kingdom Animalia	(K.A.)
Subkingdom Metazoa	(S.K.M.)
Phylum Chordata	(P.C.)
Subphylum Vertebrata	(S.P.V.)
Class Mammalia	(C.M.)
Order Primates	(O.P.)
Suborder Anthropoidea	(S.O.A.)
Superfamily Hominoidea	(S. F.H.)
Family Hominidae	(F.H.)
Genus *Homo*	(G.H.)
Species *sapiens*	(S.S.)
Subspecies *sapiens*	(S.S.S.)

Vertebrate Evolution

The Paleozoic Era (520 million to 200 million years ago) witnessed the rise of the invertebrates and the Mesozoic Era (200 million to 70 million years ago) witnessed the proliferation of three major vertebrate groups: fish, amphibians, and reptiles. Each group evolved different survival strategies that enabled it to diversify in its respective niche. By the end of the Precambrian Era and the first stages of the Paleozoic, invertebrates were the dominant animal forms in the waters of the world. However, the sudden appearance of a great variety of invertebrate forms in the early Paleozoic strata, plus the lack of fossils representing the transition from form to form, makes reconstruction of their evolutionary history difficult.

Vertebrates may have evolved from primitive starfishlike forms during the Cambrian Period (520 million to 435 million years ago). This suggestion is based on the fishlike nature of the larvae of starfishes and on similarities of proteins between starfishes and vertebrates. The first vertebrates may have resembled the sea lancelet (amphioxus), a small animal that presently inhabits coastal regions around the world (Figure 2-1). One trait of the sea lancelet is the presence of a **notochord** and a dorsal nerve cord. The notochord, a rodlike structure

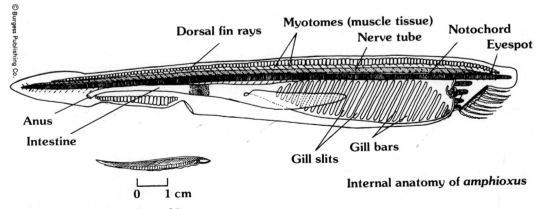

© Burgess Publishing Co.

External appearance of *amphioxus*

Internal anatomy of *amphioxus*

Figure 2-1. Sea lancelet.

running the length of the body, provides both strength and support and appears in some stage of the life cycle of all vertebrates. The first true vertebrate fossils appear in rocks dating to the Ordovician Period (435 million to 335 million years ago). These were jawless fishes (Ostracoderms) that had a true spinal column enclosing the nerve cord and an internal skeleton composed of soft cartilage rather than bone.

A number of factors led to terrestrial habitation by the vertebrates. In all likelihood, changing environmental patterns made semiaquatic life impossible. Extensive droughts during the Devonian Period (from about 335 million to 280 million years ago) caused many streams and lakes to dry and the sea level to fall. Rainfall during this time appears to have been concentrated in particular seasonal patterns of alternating moderately moist to very dry seasons. Many plants and animals were stranded on drying mud flats. Although many of these organisms perished, a few possessed traits allowing short-term survival out of water. These plants and animals gradually accumulated traits allowing them to survive for ever longer periods out of water, and they slowly adapted to terrestrial life.

All the animals that successfully adjusted to terrestrial life were confronted with the twin problems of respiration and reproduction. Solutions to these problems differed as each animal group met these problems with different physiological and anatomical adaptations. The immediate problem to be solved if vertebrates were to survive on land was that of obtaining oxygen. Fish gills cannot function in air and fishes lack a protective covering to prevent water loss; thus, fishes soon dehydrate when placed in the relative dryness of the atmosphere.

Among the many species of fishes populating the Devonian seas were the lobefins, or crossopterygians, bony fishes with an unusual combination of structures that favored survival along the drying margins of the oceans. Lobefins were able to make a successful transition from an aquatic to a terrestrial habitat because they had two important characteristics: (1) the unique structure of their lateral fins (Figure 2-2) and (2) the presence of primitive lungs. The lobefin's fin structure permitted it to "walk" for short distances. This ability was important, for example, when the lobefin needed to move from a pool that was drying or becoming stagnant (thus low in oxygen) to a more favorable location. The ability to move short distances on land meant the difference between survival and extinction.

Given its structure, the lobefin was able to obtain oxygen by its gills from water and from its primitive lungs while on land. The ability to store air in its lungs aided survival out of water. With gradual modification of these structures into specialized organs capable of breathing air the lobefins greatly extended the period of time they could spend terrestrially.

Lobefins had other traits aiding their terrestrial adaptation: (1) the skin was thick, helping to reduce water loss, (2) the spine, shoulder girdle, and limbs were strengthened and modified, (3) there were changes in the skull and teeth for feeding, and (4) the senses of smell and hearing, both important in a terrestrial environment, were improved. The cumulative effect of these changes was the origin of the first group of terrestrial vertebrates, the amphibians (Figure 2-3).

Amphibians were a successful group during the Carboniferous Period (280 million to 225 million years ago), a time when the continental plates were low and rainfall was plentiful. Such conditions provided an abundant food source and shelter in the marshes and swamps covering much of the land surface. The amphibians quickly spread in this environment. Amphibians were not completely terrestrial—they retained the external reproductive system of their ancestors and had to return to water to reproduce. Female amphibians lay their eggs in or near water, and in most species eggs are fertilized externally by the male. Water is the

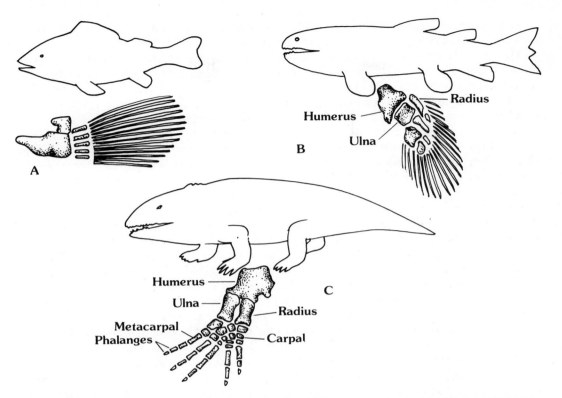

Figure 2-2. Evolution of the amphibian forelimb. (A) Bone structure of perch fin. (B) Bone structure of lobe fin. (C) Bone structure of forelimb of the amphibian *Seymouria*.

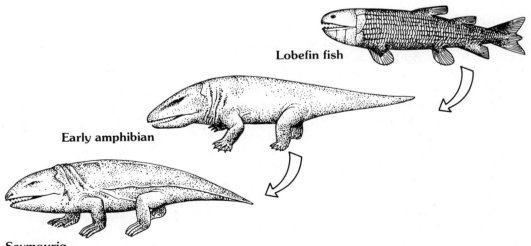

Figure 2-3. Stages in the evolution of amphibians.

essential medium in amphibian reproduction. Amphibian eggs lack a hard shell and, when exposed to air, dry rapidly. This method of reproduction cannot function on land.

The generally warm and wet climates of the Carboniferous Period ended with a change to cooler and dryer weather. This climatic shift was accompanied by elevation of the land masses, causing the drainage of wetland areas and the creation of dry upland habitats. The water-oriented amphibians began to decline with reduction of favorable habitats. Their decline was accelerated by the rise of a new vertebrate group, the reptiles.

Because of changes in the reproductive system, principally the evolution of an internal reproductive system, reptiles were no longer required to return to land for reproduction. They colonized dry upland regions and invaded the swamps and marshes occupied by amphibians. The first reptiles were the primitive cotylosaurs, the stock from which all other reptilian forms evolved.

Reptiles were the first completely terrestrial vertebrates, evolving from an amphibian stock during the later Carboniferous Period. Reptiles rose to dominance during the Permian Period (225 million to 200 million years ago). They showed several advances over the amphibian line; the most important was the development of the amniotic (amnion-containing) egg. Reptiles evolved an internal reproductive system in which the sperm is introduced into the female's body and fertilization occurs in the moist environment of the female's reproductive tract. After fertilization, the embryo is enveloped by a membranous sac, the amnion, which maintains a moist environment for the developing embryo. A second sac, the allantois, surrounds the amnion and receives and stores the waste products of metabolism. The entire structure is surrounded by a limelike shell that permits exchange of oxygen and carbon dioxide while preventing water loss. The egg also contains membranous structures that allow exchange of oxygen and carbon dioxide through the shell and for storing wastes from the embryo, and a food supply, the yolk. These structures allow the reptile to develop into a nearly full-formed miniature adult at the time of hatching. This eliminates both the larval stage of the amphibian life cycle and the necessity to return to a water environment. The amniotic egg is an adaptation to a terrestrial life style.

Mammalian Evolution

The first true mammalian fossils appear in rocks dating to the Jurassic Period (180 million to 145 million years ago) and were descendants of the therapsid line of reptiles. Therapsids exhibited several mammalian traits and were, in all probability, representative of the evolutionary transition between reptiles and mammals.

The first mammals were small and inconspicuous compared with most dinosaurs that dominated the landscape (Figure 2-4). The reptiles, however, especially the large ones, found survival increasingly difficult. Mountains were rising, causing major changes in the earth's surface. The food supply was changing. As the food supply of the large reptiles dwindled, reptiles became more restricted in their distribution.

A number of factors led to the demise of the reptiles and an increase in mammals. Among these factors were internal control of body temperature in mammals, which allowed them to inhabit a wider range of environments than reptiles. Mammals are also far more intelligent than reptiles; even the large dinosaurs possessed only small brains in relation to their body size. The mammalian mode of reproduction was significant. The reproductive system of one group of mammals, the placentals, allowed for an extensive period of development, particularly neural development, prior to birth. The developmental period is extended further by nursing the

Figure 2-4. *Tyrannosaurus rex*, a large, flesh-eating dinosaur.

young. Nursing means that the young need not begin to feed or defend themselves immediately after birth. A number of anatomic differences separated mammals and reptiles, some of which allowed for more efficient use of the terrestrial habitat. Finally, mammals evolved an immune response that was advantageous in resisting such infectious diseases that must have been evolving along with terrestrial animal populations.

With the extinction of many reptiles, mammals had vast evolutionary opportunities. Mammals began to move into and exploit the new, relatively unoccupied habitat, resulting in rapid diversification, expansion, and proliferation of members of the Class Mammalia. This process is known as adaptive radiation, and is one of the first stages in the evolution of new taxonomic groups. The Order Primates, the mammalian subdivision to which we belong, is one product of this evolutionary expansion.

Mammalian Subclasses. Certain reproductive specialties are important as differentiating mechanisms among the three subclasses of mammals. The first subclass, the Monotremata (monotremes), includes the duck-billed platypus and the spiny anteater. In common with birds and reptiles, monotremes lay eggs as their mode of reproduction.

The second subclass is the Marsupialia (marsupials). This group is more widespread than the monotremes and includes the opposum, kangaroo, and koala bear. Marsupials are **viviparous,** that is, they give birth to their young rather than laying eggs. Marsupials do, however, lack a placenta. Their young are born at a very immature stage and migrate to the mother's pouch where they attach themselves to her nipples. They remain within the pouch until they are adequately developed and then emerge.

The third subclass is the placental mammals, the Eutheria. Placentals develop by a special process in which the egg is expelled from the mother's ovary, is then fertilized, and implants itself within the walls of the mother's womb. The early stage of the organism's development is termed the embryo. The embryo produces a tissue, the placenta, on the wall of the womb. The placenta permits interchange of fluid between the mother and developing offspring. Whereas the bird's or reptile's egg must contain enough yolk to nourish the embryo until it is hatched, as well as storing waste products, placental mammals use the mother's physiological mechanisms for these functions and for supplying oxygen to the tissues of the embryo. In this way the offspring are protected until they are more fully developed than the offspring of egg-laying animals.

Mammalian Traits. Only with difficulty can we differentiate the earliest mammals from their reptilian ancestors. The most significant traits distinguishing mammals from reptiles do not fossilize. Four major traits differentiated early mammals from their reptilian ancestors: warm-bloodedness (or **homoiothermy,** the maintenance of a constant body temperature),[1] **heterodontism** (differentiation of teeth for different functions), reproductive economy (few births per parturition and a long growth period), and **effectance motivation** (investigatory behavior not serving an immediate end, such as sexual and feeding behavior). The fossil evidence is helpful primarily in regard to the second trait, heterodontism. The oldest undoubted mammalian fossil remains are teeth, jaw fragments, and rare skulls of small, shrewlike creatures embedded in rocks dating to about 170 million years ago. Throughout the period of dinosaur domination, mammals remained small and inconspicuous animals, making rare fossil appearances. The earliest mammals were generally mouselike animals that fed on seeds and insects. Most were evolutionary dead ends.

---

[1]There is now evidence suggesting that the dinosaurs may have been warm-blooded (de Ricqles, 1974).

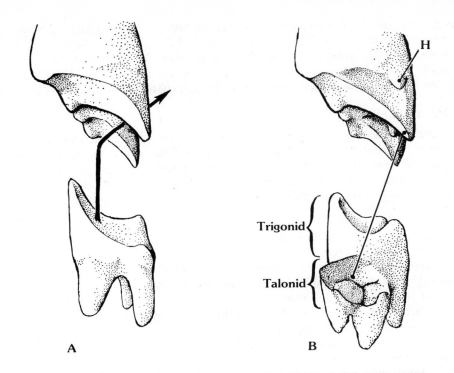

Figure 2-5. Left molar teeth of early mammals, seen from behind. (A) Early therian pattern; the arrow shows how the lower teeth move up between the uppers when the jaw closes. (B) Tribosphenic pattern; the straight line shows how the apex of the upper triangle (the protocone) fits into the talonid basin in occlusion. The drawing is oversimplified in several ways; for instance, the three cusps of the upper molars in A are not homologous with those in B. H—hypocone.

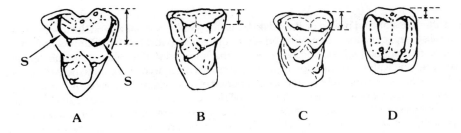

Figure 2-6. Upper molars of some early mammals. (A) A Cretaceous opossum, showing primitive shearing morphology. The transverse shearing edges (heavy lines marked S) are well developed, and so the stylar shelf (vertical arrow) is wide. (B) A *Purgatorius*-like early primate relative (*Palenochtha*). (C) A primitive ungulate. (D) An early rodent. The last three all have reduced shearing action.

The group of placentals of most evolutionary interest with respect to primates is the Order Insectivora, or insect eaters. This group currently includes such animals as the shrew and the mole. It was from this group that the early primates descended. Ancestral placental mammals were small, superficially mouselike representatives of the insectivores. The Order Primates was either a **Paleocene** or **Eocene** offshoot of an insectivorous stock (Chapter 14).

The Primates

Primate Traits. Primates form a mammalian order whose members typically exhibit a number of differentiating traits. It must be cautioned, however, that not all members of the order have all these traits. Furthermore, other mammalian orders possess some of these traits. For example, some marsupials possess nailed digits and prehensile (grasping) hands or feet, and a number of mammalian orders have clavicles, postorbital bars, and pectoral mammary glands.

Nails instead of claws on their digits
Prehensile hands and feet
Five fingers and five toes—a condition known as **pentadactyly**
Tendency toward complete bony enclosure of eye orbits
Forward placement of eye orbits
Opposability of the toe and/or thumb to the remaining digits
Enlarged cerebral hemispheres of the brain
One pair of mammary glands, thoracically placed
Well-developed clavicles
Reduced olfactory sense

In an evolutionary sense the primates are a good example of a diversified and successful group. Most common primate attributes stem from either of two factors: (1) retention of ancient or generalized vertebrate and mammalian traits and (2) development of an **arboreal** (tree-living) adaptation (see Chapter 11). Primates are generalized, arboreal, and intelligent animals broadly distributed throughout the Old and New World tropics. The order may be subdivided into four groups: **prosimians** (the most primitive and earliest of the group),[2] **ceboids** (New World monkeys), **cercopithecoids** (Old World monkeys), and **hominoids** (apes and humans).

And after passion and prejudice have died away, the same result will attend the teachings of the naturalist respecting that great Alps and Andes of the living world—Man. Our reverence for the nobility of manhood will not be lessened by the knowledge that Man is, in substance and structure, one with the brutes; for, he alone possesses the marvellous endowment of intelligible and rational speech, whereby, in the secular period of his existence, he slowly accumulated and organised the experience which is almost wholly lost with the cessation of every individual life in other animals; so that, now, he stands raised upon it as on a mountain top, far above the level of his humble fellows, and transfigured from his grosser nature by reflecting, here and there, a ray from the infinite source of the truth (Huxley, 1872:132).

---

[2]There is considerable discussion over the primate status of the prosimians. A number of paleontologists no longer refer to the prosimians as primates. For our purposes, it is best to know the possibility of the eventual removal of prosimians from the primate lineage.

Table 2-1. Vertebrate Evolution in Mesozoic and Cenozoic Eras

Era (and duration)	Period	Estimated time since beginning of each period (in millions of years—these times vary a few million years with different investigators)	Epoch	Life
		0.11	Holocene (recent)	Homo sapiens sapiens, the only species of hominids.
	Quaternary	1.8	Pleistocene	Modern species of mammals and their fore-runners; extinction of many species of large mammals; the great glaciations.
Cenozoic (age of mammals; about 65 million years)		5.5	Pliocene (the beginning of this epoch is debatable)	Appearance of many of today's genera of mammals.
		23.5 to 24	Miocene	Rise of modern subfamilies of mammals; spread of grassy plains; evolution of grazing animals.
	Tertiary	37 to 38	Oligocene	Rise of modern families of mammals.
		53 to 54	Eocene	Rise of modern orders and sub-orders of mammals.
		65	Paleocene	Dominance of archaic mammals.
	Cretaceous	145		Extinction of large reptiles and origin of Primates perhaps by end of period.

Table 2-1 continued.

Mesozoic (age of reptiles; lasted about 165 million years)	Jurassic	180	Reptiles dominant; first birds; archaic mammals.
	Triassic	230	First dinosaurs, turtles, ichthyosaurs, plesiosaurs.

The first occurence of microscopic marine invertebrates of a typically Pleistocene form was about either 0.8 million or 1.8 million years ago and this, according to some, is the technically correct date, but the Villafranchian land animals first appeared about 3.2 million years ago and many anthropologists include all of this interval in the Pleistocene. Recently Berggren and Van Couvering have given the date for the Miocene as 23.5 million to 5 million years ago.

The Human Primate

It is obvious that the criteria previously set forth place us in the mammalian subdivision known as the primates. Evidence for including us within the Order Primates is multifaceted, including data from such fields as comparative anatomy, behavioral observations (often called ethology), biochemistry, genetics, embryology, growth and development, and paleontology. Much of this evidence is discussed later in this book.

We Stand Alone. There are few who question our mammalian status or that we arose from an insectivorous stock through some small forms known as prosimians. What then makes us unique among the primates? Why are we included in a different taxonomic family than other members of the Order Primates? Evolutionarily the most significant of our uniquely human traits are: (1) a completely erect posture and habitual bipedal gait, (2) our abstract and symbolical communication known as language, (3) our capacity for abstract and symbolic thought, (4) our cultural way of life, providing as it does immense opportunities for learning and (5) our comparatively large brains.

We cannot deny that other animals, particularly other primates, learn by experience or observation. Some animals, including other primates, transmit learned behavior from one generation to another; this transgenerational passing of learned behavior is the basis for cultural behavior. Furthermore, some animals make and use tools—an activity once thought to be our preserve. Some animals also display behavioral patterns we readily understand. Yet, there are dramatic differences between ourselves and other members of the Order Primates. We can sit and speculate about this proposition—that is one of our unique traits.

While curiosity is a major trait of primates, we are perhaps the nosiest of the nosy. We climb a hill simply to see what lies beyond. Dostoevski once wrote, "Man needs the unfathomable and the infinite just as much as he does the small planet which he inhabits." As far as we now know, we alone among the primates have the capacity for self-reflection. The English author G. W. Corner writes, "After all, if he is an ape he is the only ape that is debating what kind of ape he is." We alone of all the primates have the ability to communicate about the past and plan for the future—our language allows us this unique trait. Probably we alone of all the animals have moral and philosophical ideas. The English writer Hazlitt notes, "Man is the only animal that laughs and weeps, for he is the only animal that is struck with the difference between what things are and what they ought to be."

We are undoubtedly mammals, and we are certainly primates. In contrast to many other primates, however, we are completely erect, we have a bipedal gait, we have an abstract means of communication called language, and we have an elaborate cultural way of life providing almost an endless means of elaborating on our genetic capabilities. We are the contemplative primate, the philosophical primate, the primate that ponders life and death. But we are still primates.

Bibliography

Berggren, W., and Van Couvering, J. 1974. The Late Neogene biostratigraphy, geochronology, and paleoclimatology of the last 15 million years in marine and continental sequences. *Paleography, Palaeoclimatology, Palaeoecology* 16 (1 and 2).

Clark, D. 1968. *Fossils, paleontology and evolution.* Dubuque, Ia.: Brown.

deRicqles, A. 1974. Evolution of endothermy: historical evidence. *Evolutionary Theory* 1:51.

Huxley, T. 1872. *Evidence as to man's place in nature.* New York: Appleton.

Kraus, B. 1964. *The basis of human evolution.* New York: Harper & Row.

Laporte, L. 1968. *Ancient environments.* Englewood Cliffs, N.J.: Prentice-Hall.

Lasker, G. 1973. *Physical anthropology.* New York: Holt, Rinehart and Winston.

Leakey, L., Prost, J., and Prost, S., eds. 1971. *Adam or ape.* Cambridge, Mass.: Schenkman.

McAlister, A. 1968. *The history of life.* Englewood Cliffs, N.J.: Prentice-Hall.

Racle, F. 1979. *Introduction to evolution.* Englewood Cliffs, N.J.: Prentice-Hall.

Romer, A. 1950. *Vertebrate paleontology.* Chicago: University of Chicago Press.

_____. 1970. *The vertebrate body.* Philadelphia: Saunders.

Savage, J. 1977. *Evolution.* New York: Holt, Rinehart and Winston.

Simpson, G. 1944. *The major features of evolution.* New York: Columbia University Press.

_____. 1958. *The meaning of evolution.* New York: Mentor Books.

Weller, J. 1969. *The course of evolution.* New York: McGraw-Hill.

Part Two

Evolutionary Theory

When I view all beings not as special creations, but as the lineal descendants of some few beings which lived long before the first bed of the Cambrian system was deposited, they seem to me to become ennobled.

From Charles Darwin, *The Origin of Species.*

Chapter 3

Light Thrown on Human Origins

As with most pioneers, Charles Darwin's intellectual journey was partially charted by those preceding him: some early Greek philosophers, Francis Bacon, Georges Buffon, his grandfather Erasmus Darwin, Jean Baptiste de Lamarck, and Thomas Malthus, and all had an impact on Darwin's work. The Church and its spokesmen were Darwin's major antagonists. The Biblical account stated the earth was of comparatively recent origin and that God created human life in His image. There was no time, no room in the Biblical scheme for evolutionary change. A prime requisite for Darwin's scheme was an extended time span over and above the Creation date established by Biblical scholars. This was provided in the works of such geologists as the Englishman Charles Lyell.

As is well known, Darwin's synthesis was not universally acclaimed as a scientific breakthrough. Darwin's work was not immediately accepted when it was finally published. Following is a discussion of this and other matters impinging upon Darwin's formulation of his theory.

Pre-Darwinian Views: Greek Philosophers through Lyell

The Opposition. Charles Darwin was a pioneer, exploring the realm of thought few before dared to explore. He did not pretend, though, that all his thoughts were original. In fact, Darwin often claimed no originality of his theory. His intellectual journey leading to the theory of evolution was not entirely unchartered. As is often true of most important generalizations, his central thesis of natural selection was not altogether new. As early as the fifth century B.C., Greek writers had hinted at the principle of natural selection.

Darwin planted his ideas in fertile intellectual soil and they grew. He marshaled overwhelming amounts of convincing evidence; his ideas ignited a fire utterly destroying or badly charring many intellectual edifices erected prior to 1859. The firemen who were rushed to extinguish Darwin's intellectual ideas (Creationists, for example), did not succeed. The fact of evolution is, however, still not universally accepted,[1] though Darwinism has become the central and fundamental component of scientific logic.

Greek Philosophies. Elements of the concept of gradual change, that is, that life is not fixed nor immutable, can be found in ancient Persian and Greek writings. The Greeks proceeded in their rationale from a priori grounds, from observation by unaided eye, logical arguments, and so-called common sense. Greek philosophical writings dating from the sixth century B.C. contain speculations about life originating in the sea. There are mythical ideas about the adaptive changes that occurred in the transition from an aquatic to a terrestrial existence. At least one Greek philosopher stated that fossils were animal remains. The Greek views of change, the crux of evolutionary theory, ranged from the idea that change is merely a sensory illusion to the notion that everything is always in a state of flux. Some fifth century B.C. writings contained a vague notion of organic evolution. These writings held that living things arose by fortuitous combinations of parts and that bad combinations did not survive. This is the germ of the principle of natural selection.

Aristotle (383-322 B.C.) probably provided the most important early scientific influence. Aristotle was a teleologist, a believer in intelligent design and in the idea that nature's processes are directed toward certain ends. Aristotle argued that there was a natural scale of organisms ascending to the development of humans; this concept was later labeled by such writers as Descartes as the "Great Chain of Being." Aristotle's views and his classification of plants and animals were, however, basically nonevolutionary, and in many ways his authority long inhibited development of evolutionary ideas. Little can be said of post-Aristotelian thought, for medieval scholastic philosophers contributed mostly to metaphysics and to moral philosophy. Some in this group established the notion that conditions of life were immutable, and the world was thought to be static from the moment of creation.

Lamarck. Although a number of early scientists implied evolution in their writings (Table 3-1), it was Jean Baptiste de Lamarck (1744-1829) who proposed a systematic theory for evolution as an explanation of life's diversity. Lamarck accepted the nonevolutionary idea that organisms could be ranked in a progressive series, with *Homo* at the apex. Lamarck considered evolution to be a constant striving, due to some inner drive for perfection, and considered change to be a constant striving, due to some inner drive for perfection, and environments.

Using a previously suggested idea, Lamarck argued that an organism acquired new traits by using or not using different parts of the body and that newly acquired behavioral or anatomical traits could be transmitted to the offspring. Lamarck believed that a trait, once acquired, could

[1]A recent example of this lack of complete acceptance is the refuting of Darwin's theory to one of two concepts of life's development in new science textbooks for 3.3 million elementary school children in California. This refutation is based on the argument that Christians (especially of the Creationist school) are deprived of "equal time" in the science textbooks. Recent litigation in Arkansas struck from that state's legal code an injunction against teaching evolution.

Times have changed these legal proceedings. There is nothing in the California situation that equals H. L. Mencken's record of the Scopes trial based on events recorded outside the courthouse in Dayton, Tennessee. Mencken wrote:

There was a friar wearing a sandwich sign announcing that he was the Bible champion of the world. There was a Seventh-day Adventist arguing that Clarence Darrow (Scopes's lawyer) was the beast with seven heads and ten horns described in Revelation XIII, and that the end of the world was at hand. There was an evangelist made up like Andy Gump, with the news that atheists in Cincinnati were preparing to descend upon Dayton, hang the eminent Judge Raulston, and burn the town.

Figure 3-1. Jean Baptiste de Lamarck.

be passed on to subsequent generations. His scheme is known as the theory of acquired characteristics.

Lamarck's importance lies in his proposal that life is dynamic and that there is a mechanism in nature that promotes ongoing change. His method of change is incorrect, however, for acquired traits are not passed to one's offspring. You can cut off the tails of rats for untold generations but still fail to produce a generation of rats born without tails. Although the details of Lamarck's schemes are incorrect, his emphasis on change gave impetus to the thoughts of others who would ultimately discover explanations for the change he proposed.

Lamarck's scheme is presented in Table 3-2.

The Geological Framework

A most important element for Darwin's scheme, an expanded time frame, was established by geologists. During the seventeenth century it was known that older rock layers were covered by younger rock layers. This orderly arrangement of layers, or strata, is called the law of superposition.

Around 1800, two French scientists were working in the fossil beds surrounding Paris. Both men, Georges Cuvier and Alexandre Brongniart, also discovered that certain fossils were restricted to a certain stratum. Additionally, they noticed that fossils changed in an orderly fashion from one stratum to the other. Comparing these fossils to then-living forms, they found that fossils from higher strata were more similar to modern forms than were fossils from lower strata.

With these facts, you might imagine that the geologists of the day would strike upon the idea of evolution. However, they were unable to explain why fossils in earlier and later strata differed. Their explanations usually bordered on the mysterious or cited divine intervention.

Table 3-1. Pre-Darwinian Thoughts

The following may be mentioned among pre-Darwinian students of natural science:

Francis Bacon (British, 1561-1626) was a firm Aristotelian and thought that species were incapable of change. He is generally credited with the revival of scientific inquiry.

Georges L. L. Buffon (French, 1707-1778) was, perhaps, the first true evolutionist, suggesting, with reservations, an evolutionary process based on the inheritance of acquired characters.

Erasmus Darwin (British, 1731-1802) was Charles Darwin's grandfather. His main theses were that earth's history was longer than specified by Archbishop James Ussher's chronology and that all life came from a common source.

At least three different men wrote of natural selection without, however, arriving at a firm statement of its evolutionary role. *Edward Blyth* (British) thought that natural selection, by discriminating against variation, would lead to immutability of species. *Patrick Mathew's* (British) discussion of natural selection was hidden in an appendix to a treatise dealing with naval timber and architecture. The third was *Charles Wells*, a South Carolina physician, who wrote of the idea as a commonplace fact in a paper on a white female, part of whose skin resembled that of an individual of African descent.

Jean Baptiste de Lamarck (French, 1744-1829) advanced the first comprehensive theory of evolution. He invoked the inheritance of acquired characters, now referred to as Lamarckism, although he was not the first believer in it. The usual example of Lamarckism is the giraffe, whose ancestor was assumed to have acquired its long neck by stretching to reach upper leaves on a tree and to have transmitted the acquired length to its progeny. It is more likely that giraffes with longer necks could obtain more food and thereby had an advantage over others, especially in times of drought, enabling them to leave more offspring. We know now that if their long necks were even in part hereditary, their offspring, more numerous than those of the others, would receive genetic instructions for the formation of longer necks. Thus, the average neck length of the next generation would be increased through a cumulative process we now label natural selection.

Thomas R. Malthus (British, 1766-1834) suggested in his "An Essay on the Principle of Population" that humans multiply geometrically while food supply increases arithmetically. Darwin credited reading of this essay with generating in his mind the notion that an average individual produces more offspring than can survive, thus permitting selection to occur.

Georges Cuvier (French, 1769-1832) was a defender of special creation and Lamarck's opponent in the evolutionary debate of the day. He recognized that fossils were extinct forms of life, following the discovery in 1790 by an English surveyor, William Smith, that different layers of rock contain different kinds of fossils. But his explanation was the theory of catastrophism, that is, that in the past, life on earth was destroyed several times, as in the Biblical account of the flood, and then created anew.

Charles Lyell (British, 1797-1875) countered catastrophism with the theory of *uniformitarianism*, which held that historical changes on earth were not due to a series of catastrophes but to the same gradual changes as may be observed today. This theory was an important cornerstone of evolutionary thought.

Adapted from I. M. Lerner, *Heredity, Evolution and Society,* 2nd edition, p. 34. W. H. Freeman and Company, San Francisco, © 1976.

Prior to the work of James Hutton and Charles Lyell, the world was considered to be approximately 4,000 years old. The Biblical scholar James Ussher, a Scottish archbishop, computed the age of each of the named generations recorded in the Bible and arrived at a date of 4004 B.C. for the creation. Reverend Dr. John Lightfoot, vice-chancellor of Cambridge University, later added that ". . . heaven and earth, centre and circumference, were created all together in the same instant, and clouds full of water. This work took place and man was created by the Trinity on October 23, 4004 B.C. at nine o'clock in the morning."

Figure 3-2. Georges Cuvier.

Table 3-2. Lamarckian Theory versus the Modern Theory of Adaptation

Lamarck
- Question: What causes adaptive variations to occur?
- Answer: Fullfillment of needs by action of inner feelings, inheritance of acquired characteristics, effects of environment.

Darwin:
- First question: What causes variation?
- Answer: I do not know.
- Second question: What causes any variation that happens to be adaptive to be preserved so that it can modify the descendants of its possessors?
- Answer: Natural selection.

Today:
- First question: What causes heritable variation?
- Answer: Random mutation and recombination of genes.
- Second question: What causes any heritable variation that may become adaptive under changed conditions to be preserved until those changed conditions arise?
- Answer: Preservation of genes until, under changed conditions and after reshuffling of the gene complex, their effects may become adaptive.

Adapted from G. de Beer, *Charles Darwin: A Scientific Bibliography*, p. 194. Natural History Library, New York, © 1965.

Long periods of time are often necessary for evolutionary change; the theological limit of 4,004 years was hardly enough time and was presented as strong contrary evidence to evolutionary change. The establishment of a suitable time frame was left to geologists, many of whom were strictly nonevolutionary. One of the best known geologists was the French scholar Cuvier, a young contemporary of Lamarck. Cuvier's scheme, known as **catastrophism,** claimed that various geological layers were deposited as a result of a series of cataclysms periodically overwhelming the earth and totally destroying life. After each cataclysm, new life appeared through a series of successive creations, each successive appearance of new life exhibiting an advance in complexity and superiority of organization over their extinct predecessors. Cuvier's belief that the last great cataclysm was the Biblical flood meant that human remains should not be discovered in previous layers. Cuvier is credited with saying, "Fossil man does not exist." Cuvier's scheme is important because it accounts for changes of form. Although Cuvier recognized that change occurred, he did not recognize that natural forces could account for differences in ancestral and descendant populations.

Cuvier's concept left little of substance for the budding group of scientists whose intent was to prove that life was much older than Biblical accounts and that recent forms of life result from millennia of previous change. The geologist Charles Lyell provided the necessary time frame with which Darwin and other evolutionists could work.[2]

Lyell rejected Cuvier's catastrophism, substituting in its place the principle of **uniformitarianism,** an idea first introduced by Hutton in 1785 and later independently developed by Lyell in his book *Principles of Geology,* published in 1830. The principle of uniformitarianism simply states that the same geological agents that operate in the present

[2]It is no exaggeration to say that Lyell's friendship was the most important influence in Darwin's career.

Figure 3-3. Charles Lyell.

could, given enough time, have caused changes in the past geological history of the earth. While Lyell's work provided the basis of a geological time span against which to construct an evolutionary scheme, Lyell seems to have been disturbed by the inclusion of humans in the evolutionary scheme. He accepted the fact that species became extinct and were replaced by others but was uncertain of the mechanisms. Since the uniformitarian view could not explain why new species developed, Lyell's critics adopted the only alternative view known to them—divine creation.

In the early decades of the eighteenth century, scientists felt obliged to resort to miracles, which they admitted being unable to comprehend, to account for natural phenomena. Unable to comprehend geological processes, many accepted Cuvier's explanation of catastrophism. Coupled with catastrophism was the belief in the divine creation of new species. How else, these scientists reasoned, could one account for the new life forms that followed the mass destruction espoused by Cuvier?

The idea of catastrophism and divine creation seemed to explain everything about the origin of new species and the neatly stratified rocks. The interrelationship of catastrophism and creationism was presented by the English clergyman William Paley in his 1802 book *Natural Theology.* Darwin read this book while he was at Cambridge. Paley argued that all living forms had a design; there was, therefore, a need for a great designer. Paley contended that God had designed all of life's magnificent adaptations.

Even Lyell, the geologist whose works had the most profound of effects on Darwin, turned to miracles or church doctrines to explain the appearance of new species. Lyell believed the earth always had living things on it, and he turned to the Bible to explain human origins and destinies.

The two leading tenets preceding Darwin's theory were: (1) life's inexorable ascent argues for a preordained directionality and (2) humans mark the ideal measure of perfection.

de Perthes. One of the first individuals to attempt to verify a prehistoric period in hominid history was Jacques Boucher de Perthes (1788-1868). Digging on the banks of the Somme River in northwestern France, he found many stones not indigenous to the walls of the pit in which they were recovered. Furthermore, the stones appeared to have been intentionally shaped into obvious forms. Other observers had also witnessed such rocks and termed them "figured stones" of unknown origin or "thunder stones" cast by God to earth during thunderstorms. De Perthes was convinced that these stones were made by prehistoric people, and he collected an immense amount of evidence in support of his theory. When he submitted his case in 1838 to various scientific groups, he was ridiculed. Not until after the publication of Darwin's work was de Perthes' theory considered possible by those daring to accept an evolutionary history.

Charles Darwin

Early Years. When a son was born to Robert and Emma Darwin on 12 February 1809 in Shrewsbury, England, few people except for close relatives and those present at the birth noticed the event. This is in sharp contrast to the mixed reaction greeting the birth of his book *On the Origin of Species by Means of Natural Selection or the Preservation of Favored Races in the Struggle for Life,* which first appeared in 1859. It is safe to say that his mother did not realize the amount of scorn that would subsequently be heaped on Charles, her second of two boys and fifth of six children.

Figure 3-4. Charles Darwin.

Even during his early years Charles Darwin seems to have been a naturalist. His father once commented, "You care for nothing but shooting, and rat-catching, and you will be a disgrace to yourself and all your family." Charles Darwin's school years were relatively uneventful. Not the best of students, he passed from subject to subject, from medicine to theology, depending upon his father's wishes. He was first and foremost a naturalist. Except for the value he found in some school acquaintances, Darwin considered much of his education a waste of time.

H.M.S. Beagle. On 29 August 1831 one of Darwin's friends wrote to tell him that Captain Fitzroy of the ship H.M.S. *Beagle* had invited a young man to sail around the world with him as a naturalist, without pay. Darwin's name was submitted to Fitzroy by a mutual friend. The files of the Admiralty contain the following letter referring to Darwin's nomination.

1 September 1831

Captain Fitzroy:
My dear Sir, I believe my friend Mr. Peacock of Trinity College Cambridge has succeeded in getting a "Savant" for you — a Mr. Darwin, grandson of the well known philosopher and poet — full of zeal and enterprise and having contemplated a voyage on his own account to S. America. Let me know how you like the idea that I may go or recede in time.

Francis Beaufort

Darwin's father was not keen on allowing his son to accept the invitation and at first Charles refused the offer. An uncle, Josiah Wedgewood (of dinnerware fame), convinced Charles's father that such a trip would be a perfectly suitable undertaking for a fledgling clergyman. The elder Darwin reconsidered and Charles Darwin joined the ship on 24 October 1831. Due to one mishap after another the departure was postponed until 27 December 1831.

Darwin's journey with Fitzroy covered 5 years and more than 40,000 miles. His observations were reinforced by the many important books that he read. One of these was Lyell's *Principles of Geology*. Darwin and Alfred R. Wallace, a codiscoverer of natural selection, had also read Malthus' (1776-1834) work, "An Essay on the Principles of Population."

Both Darwin and Wallace had traveled widely and observed in great detail the variation within plant and animal life. In contrast to Darwin, however, Wallace needed to work for a living and he did so by collecting rare tropical plants and animals for private collectors and

Figure 3-5. Alfred R. Wallace.

Figure 3-6. Thomas R. Malthus.

museums. As a result, he traveled more widely than did Darwin in both South America and Southeast Asia. Later in his life, Wallace wrote a number of books on evolution. These books, although of considerable interest, lacked the originality and intellectual character of Darwin's works.

Both Darwin and Wallace came on their understanding of the means by which selection works in nature from the same source—Thomas R. Malthus. Malthus showed how the reproductive capability of the human population far exceeds the natural resources available for sustenance. He argued that the size of human populations is limited by war, disease, famine, and that in the absence of "moral restraint" (Malthus was a clergyman), such factors would check what would otherwise be rapid population growth.

Darwin and Wallace read Malthus independently; both were struck with the possibility that Malthus' ideas held the key to understanding the evolutionary process. Malthus showed that what was true for populations of plants and nonhuman animals was also true for humans, that is, the reproductive potential vastly exceeds that necessary to maintain constant population sizes. Darwin and Wallace realized that those individuals who survived were somehow better adapted than those who did not. Variations that increased an organism's ability to produce fertile offspring would be retained, whereas variations decreasing fertility would be selected out.

Darwin and Wallace thus provided a rational and convincing explanation for population diversity and changes within populations over time. If humans are influenced by the same processes as other animals and plants, humans had to adopt a new attitude toward the rest of the natural world. They had to view themselves within the natural world and face a novel view of human origins.

Darwin's autobiography refers to events that most impressed him about his trip. The following passage enumerates four lines of evidence that led him to question and eventually reject the belief in the immutability of species with which he started his journey.

> During the voyage of the Beagle I had been deeply impressed by discovering in the Pampean formation great fossil animals covered with armor like that on the existing armadillos; secondly by the manner in which closely allied animals replace one another in proceeding southwards over the Continent; and thirdly by the South American character of most of the productions of the Galapagos archipelago, and more especially by the manner in which they differ slightly on each island of the group (quoted in de Beer, 1965:78).

The first line of evidence refers to the principle of "succession of types." In some areas species become extinct, as shown by their fossilized remains, while other similar species flourish. The second line of evidence refers to the principle of "representative species," that is, adjacent areas of a continent are inhabited by different but similar species that take each other's place. The third line of evidence concerns the resemblance of inhabitants of oceanic islands to those of the nearest mainland. For example, a few days after his initial arrival in the Galapagos Islands, Darwin's notebook records under the date 18 September 1835, "I certainly recognize South America in ornithology" (de Beer, 1965:81). Darwin recognized the similarity between the finches in the Galapagos and those on the mainland. The fourth line of evidence concerns differences between the island inhabitants in the Galapagos archipelago. The environmental conditions of the islands are quite similar and, if the character of the organisms inhabiting the islands was determined by these conditions, the species of each island should have been identical. Darwin was astonished to find otherwise.

Probably the best-known observations made by Darwin during the voyage of the *Beagle* were of the Galapagos finch population. These birds illustrate the effect of geographical isolation on the development of intraspecific variation (variation within a given species). Finches are common birds that have a wide geographic distribution. Basically, they are seed eaters whose short, stout beaks provide an efficient feeding mechanism. However, Darwin discovered that the Galapagos finches had a surprisingly wide variation of beak size and shape which was related to feeding on a wide variety of foods (Figure 3-7). Darwin reasoned that the first finches to inhabit the Galapagos rapidly increased in number due to the lack of competition for food and the lack of natural enemies. Increasing population size soon outstripped the main food supply, forcing individuals to seek alternative food sources (Figure 3-8). Finding less competition for alternative foods, subpopulations developed that continued to feed on less restricted sources. Modifications of beak size and shape that allowed maximum

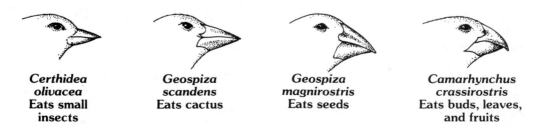

| Certhidea olivacea **Eats small insects** | Geospiza scandens **Eats cactus** | Geospiza magnirostris **Eats seeds** | Camarhynchus crassirostris **Eats buds, leaves, and fruits** |

Figure 3-7. Variation in finch beak as related to diet.

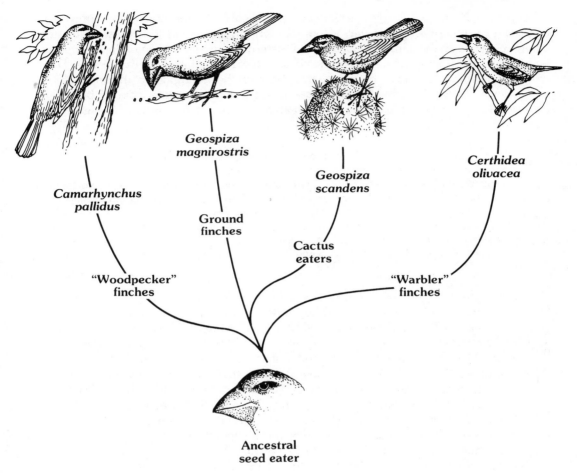

**Camarhynchus
pallidus**

**Geospiza
magnirostris**

**Geospiza
scandens**

**Certhidea
olivacea**

Ground
finches

Cactus
eaters

"Woodpecker"
finches

"Warbler"
finches

Ancestral
seed eater

Figure 3-8. Adaptive radiation of finches.

exploitation of a particular food niche appeared within each subpopulation. **Natural
selection** favored those finches that had the appropriately modified beaks, and these small
changes accumulated through the process of differential reproduction (individuals that have
adaptive traits are favored and succeed in reproduction. Less well-adapted individuals die off
or leave fewer progeny). This process ultimately led to the distinctive variation in beak types
noted by Darwin and still in existence today. This sequence of events is typical of adaptive
radiation, the phrase commonly applied to the evolutionary spread and differentiation of
descendants of one type of animal into progressively more dissimilar forms.

Flirting with Evolution. Darwin was confused about the creatures and plants he
observed; the finches and tortoises of the Galapagos archipelago led him to write toward the
end of his voyage, ". . . such facts would undermine the stability of species" (de Beer,
1965:82). Darwin returned to England with this heretical thought lurking in his mind. One of
the first writing adventures he undertook after returning was his *Journal of Researches*, a

descriptive narrative of his trip. The work contains slight hint of the intellectual turmoil he was beginning to experience; however, a footnote written in relation to his discussion of the difference between the flora and fauna on the eastern and western Andean slopes appears to be his first veiled public admission of the possibility of the mutability of the species. Darwin wrote, "The whole reasoning, of course, is founded on the assumption of the immutability of the species. Otherwise the changes might be considered as superinduced by different circumstances in the two regions during a length of time" (de Beer, 1965:85). As early as 1857, Darwin wrote:

> With belief of transmutation and geographical grouping we are led to endeavor to discover causes of changes, the manner of adaptation . . . instinct and structure becomes full of speculation and line of observation. . . . My theory would give zest to recent and fossil comparative anatomy; it would lead to closest examination of hybridity, to what circumstances favour crossing and what prevent it; and generation (sexual reproduction) causes of change in order to know what we have come from and to what we tend, this and direct examination of direct passages of structure in species might lead to laws of change, which would then be the main object of study, to guide our speculations with respect to past and future (quoted in de Beer, 1965:94).

Darwin wrote in his *Autobiography* that selection was the key to the mutability of species. "I soon perceived that selection was the keystone of man's success in making useful races of plants and animals. But how selection could be applied to organisms living in a state of nature remained for some time a mystery to me" (de Beer, 1965:97). Arriving at this momentous conclusion, Darwin refused to commit himself in print for some time. He wrote in his *Autobiography,* "In June, 1842, I first allowed myself the satisfaction of writing a very brief abstract of my theory in pencil in 35 pages; and this was enlarged during the summer of 1844 into 230 pages" (de Beer, 1965:119). This "abstract" was the first clear statement of Darwin's thoughts on evolution. A quote from Darwin's personal correspondence in 1844 notes, "If, as I believe, my theory in time be accepted even by one competent judge, it will be a considerable step in science" (de Beer, 1965:119). On 11 January 1844, Darwin wrote his friend and intellectual coconspirator J. D. Hooker, "At last the gleams of light have come, and I am almost convinced (quite contrary to the opinion I started with) that species are not (it is like confessing a murder) immutable" (de Beer, 1965:135).

Wallace Intrudes. Darwin's tranquility was shattered on 18 June 1858 when he received a short paper from Wallace containing a replica of his own theory of evolution by natural selection. Wallace asked Darwin to read his paper and if Darwin deemed it important, he was to send it to Lyell. Darwin was dumbstruck. Receiving Wallace's paper, coupled with such personal tragedies as the illness of his daughter and imminent death of his 18-month-old son, troubled Darwin deeply. He immediately read the paper and sent it on to Lyell with the accompanying note:

> Your words have come true with a vengeance that I should be forestalled. You said this, when I explained to you here very briefly my views of "Natural Selection" depending on the struggle for existence. I never saw a more striking coincidence; if Wallace had my MS sketch written out in 1842, he could not have made a better short abstract! Even his terms now stand as heads of my Chapters. So all my originality, whatever it may amount to, will be smashed though my book, if it will ever have any value, will not be deteriorated . . . (quoted in de Beer, 1965:149).

The Debut of Evolutionary Theory

After much consternation by Darwin himself, including veiled threats to burn his books lest others think him a plagiarizer,[3] Hooker and Lyell prevailed on Darwin to submit a joint paper to the Linnaean Society. A joint paper was presented before the Linnaean Society of London on 1 July 1858 and it was published in the Society's *Journal of Proceedings* on 20 August 1858 under the title, "On the tendency of species to form varieties, and on the perpetuation of varieties and species by natural means of selection."

What effect did that paper have on the world at that time? An idea that was later to set the intellectual world ablaze at first attracted little attention. Darwin writes, "Our joint productions excited very little attention, and the only published notice of them which I can remember was by Professor Haughton of Dublin, whose verdict was that all new that was in them was false, and what was true was old" (de Beer, 1965:150). The President of the Linnaean Society dismally concluded at the subsequent annual meeting that, "The year . . . had not, indeed, been marked by any of those striking discoveries which at once revolutionize, so to speak, the department of science on which they bear" (de Beer, 1965:150).

On the Origin of Species

The last chapter of Darwin's triumphant book *On the Origin of Species* was finished on 19 March 1859. Darwin spent more than 20 years with his labor of love; he wrote, "I am weary of my work. . . . facts compel me to conclude that my brain was never formed for much thinking" (de Beer 1965:151). The book was magnificently conceived and written, although Darwin doubted his own abilities to communicate via the written word. Darwin's publisher was John Murray. At Darwin's urging Murray reviewed several chapters, but Murray was bewildered and skeptical of the scientific validity of the book. After some delays, due to corrections and brief disagreements about the title, the book was finally published on 24

---

[3]"I would far rather burn my whole book, than that he [Wallace] or any other man should think that I had behaved in paltry spirit. . . ."

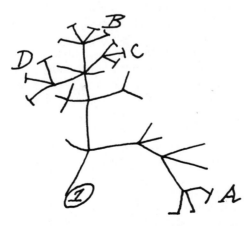

Figure 3-9. Darwin's first diagram of an evolutionary tree appeared in his "First Notebook on Transmutation of Species," 1837.

November 1859. The very day it appeared the total edition of 1,250 copies was sold to booksellers; a second edition was immediately scheduled and published on 7 January 1860. When the book was published, Darwin left his home to rest after writing his "accursed book."

Evolution

The accompanying papers, which we have the honour of communicating to the Linnean Society, and which all relate to the same subject, viz, the Laws which affect the reproduction of varieties, races, and species, contain the results of the investigations of two indefatigable naturalists, Mr. Charles Darwin and Mr. Alfred Wallace.

The gentlemen having, independently and unknown to one another, conceived the same very ingenious theory to account for the appearance and perpetuation of varieties and of specific forms on our planet, may both fairly claim the merit of being original thinkers in this important line of inquiry; but neither of them have published their views, though Mr. Darwin has for many years past been repeatedly urged by us to do so, and both authors having now unreservedly placed their papers in our hands, we think it would best promote the interests of science that a selection from them should be laid before the Linnean Society.

Partial contents of a letter written by Charles Lyell and Joseph D. Hooker to J. J. Bennett, Esq., Secretary of the Linnaean Society, addressed 30 June 1858. As a result of this letter, Darwin and Wallace's joint paper was presented to the world.

An insightful discussion of Darwin's book will be found in Kennedy's 1976 book *Human Variation in Space and Time.* Kennedy points out that *On the Origin of Species* is a composite of two complementary theories, only one of which was original to Darwin. The idea that each species was not independently created and had descended from other forms was not original to Darwin. During Darwin's time this idea was called the transmutation doctrine. Darwin built on this idea and insisted that the theory was incomplete until some mechanism was applied whereby this transmutation occurred. The delineation of this process, the mechanism of change, was Darwin's original contribution and came to be called natural selection.

The full title of Darwin's book reads *On the Origin of Species by Means of Natural Selection,* the subtitle being *The Preservation of Favoured Races in the Struggle for Life.* As Kennedy notes, the title manifests the major theme of the writer's thoughts. Darwin was discussing "species," not higher categories; he was not concerned with the origins and antiquity of life itself. The title makes it clear that Darwin saw a "selective" force working in the rise of new species and that this was a "natural" mechanism quite different from the artificial breeding practiced by horticulturists or in animal husbandry. The subtitle notes that during the "struggle" for life certain individuals are favored by their possession of adaptive traits and will succeed in reproducing themselves. Others less well adapted will die off or leave fewer progeny (differential reproduction), thus reducing their contribution to succeeding generations. Darwin's book is thus important in accounting for how the evolutionary process operates, as well as for its vast compilation of data documenting the fact of evolution.

Darwin's theory is based on two observations and two basic conclusions (Savage, 1969):

Facts

1. All organisms exhibit variability.
2. All organisms reproduce many more offspring than survive.

Conclusions

1. The environment selects those individuals best suited for survival, whereas individuals less suited fail to reproduce.
2. The traits favored by selection are passed to the next generation.

Interestingly, while Darwin's book received much scorn, Darwin made little mention of the possibilities of human evolution. Admittedly very little was known about fossil human remains at that time,[4] but Darwin avoided the subject of human evolution as ". . . so surrounded with prejudices." The subject of human evolution, however, received discreet recognition in the Conclusion: "When the views entertained in this volume on the origin of species, or when analogous views are generally admitted," among the accruing benefits will be that, "light will be thrown on the origin of man and his history." For some, the light subsequently thrown on the subject has tended to be blinding.

The Reactions. The publication of Darwin's work received mixed reaction (Figure 3-10 and 3-11). The biologist Huxley wrote, "How extremely stupid not to have thought of that" (de Beer, 1965: 156). Battles raged over Darwin's work and the famous Huxley (pro) and Bishop Wilberforce (con) debate typifies some of the scene. Especially poignant is Wilberforce's remark to Huxley as to whether he (Huxley) claimed his descent from a monkey through his grandmother or grandfather? Huxley's reply, recalled in a letter to a friend, included such remarks as ". . . would I rather have a miserable ape for a grandfather, or a man highly endowed by nature and possessed of great means and influence, and yet who employs these faculties and that influence for the mere purpose of introducing ridicule into a grave scientific discussion! I unhesitatingly affirmed my preference for the ape" (de Beer, 1965: 166). The Huxley versus Wilberforce debate was a microcosm of the debate pitting the nonevolutionists, who were backed by the Church, against the early evolutionists.

Darwin's reaction to the barrage was one of measured restraint. His feelings are perhaps best expressed in a letter that he wrote on 15 May 1860:

> They may all attack me to their hearts content. I am not case-hardened. As for the old fogies in Cambridge, it really signifies nothing. I look on their attacks as a proof that our work is worth the doing. It makes me resolve to buckle on my armour. I see plainly that it will be a long uphill fight. But think of Lyell's progress with Geology. One thing I see plainly, that without Lyell's years, Huxley's, and Carpenter's aid, my book would have been a mere flash in the pan. But if we all stick to it, we shall surely gain the day. And I now see that the battle is worth fighting (quoted in de Beer, 1965: 159).

Darwin's Death. Darwin died of a heart attack on 19 April 1882, at the age of 73. Darwin's family wished him buried in the village of Downe, but twenty members of Parliament, four of them fellows of the Royal Society, wrote the Dean of Westminster and suggested that Darwin be buried at Westminster Abbey. The funeral occurred on 26 April; the pallbearers included Darwin's intimate friends: Hooker, Huxley, Wallace, and other luminaries. Foreign diplomats were received from France, Germany, Italy, Spain, Russia, and America. An anthem was composed for the occasion and Beethoven's "Funeral's March" was played. Darwin lay near the graves of Newton, Faraday, and his old friend Lyell. Burial in Westminster was the only

---

[4]A brief note of what was known appeared in his subsequent book, *Descent of Man*.

Figure 3-10. In 1871, a cruel caricature in *The Hornet* labeled Darwin "a venerable orang-outang" and cited his contribution of "unnatural history."

Figure 3-11. An 1882 issue of the Viennese magazine *Kikeriki* published a cartoon of monkeys mourning the death of Charles Darwin. The monkeys moan, "Now that our benefactor has passed away, who will be our defender and champion our cause?"

national honor Britain bestowed upon one of her most illustrious native sons. Even the Beatles received higher acclaim in their heyday; John, Paul, Ringo, and George, M.B.E.

Although certain aspects of Darwin's scheme are found in the writings of scholars preceding him, his contribution reigns supreme. Darwin's principal contribution to modern evolutionary theory was his insistence that natural selection was the guiding force in evolutionary change. He insisted on natural selection as the mechanism that could account for diversity and change. Although other mechanisms were proposed, such as Lamarck's theory of acquired characteristics, these were of little scientific value. Darwin's principal failure, if he can be faulted for not having knowledge hardly available to him, was that he did not know the means whereby adaptive traits were generationally transmitted. Darwin did not know how variation itself was introduced into a population. He had no knowledge of the law of genetic inheritance. That contribution was made by Gregor Mendel.

This chapter outlines some of the early beliefs precedent to Charles Darwin's synthesis, the major opposition to which came from the theological order. Workers in other fields, especially geology, established an expanded time span, a most important element for Darwin's scheme. Darwin was greatly indebted to the geologist Charles Lyell. Darwin's principal contribution to modern evolutionary theory was his insistence that natural selection was the guiding force in evolutionary change. He insisted on natural selection as the mechanism which could account for diversity and change.

The missing link in Darwin's evolutionary scheme was his lack of knowledge of the means whereby traits are generationally transmitted. This was provided in the work of Gregor Mendel.

Bibliography

Appleman, P. 1970. *Darwin*. New York: Norton.

Barlow, N., ed. 1958. *The autobiography of Charles Darwin*. New York: Norton.

Darwin, C. 1958. *The origin of species*. New York: Mentor Books.

_____. 1965. *The expression of the emotions in man and animals*. Chicago: University of Chicago Press.

de Beer, G. 1965. *Charles Darwin: a scientific biography*. New York: Natural History Library.

Eiseley, L. 1961. *Darwin's century*. New York: Anchor Books.

_____. 1970. *The firmament of time*. New York: Atheneum.

_____. 1972. The intellectual antecedents of "The Descent of Man." In *Sexual selection and the descent of man, 1871-1971*, edited by B. Campbell, pp. 1-16. Chicago: Aldine.

Himmelfarb, G. 1959. *Darwin and the Darwinian revolution*. New York: Norton.

Kennedy, K. 1976. *Human variation in space and time*. Dubuque, Ia.: Brown.

Lerner, I. 1968. *Heredity, evolution and society*. San Francisco: Freeman.

Lovejoy, A. 1936. *The great chain of being: a study of the prehistory of an idea*. New York: Harper & Row.

Moore, R. 1961. *Man, time, and fossils*. New York: Knopf.

Peterson, W. 1979. *Malthus*. Cambridge: Harvard University Press.

Wilson, L. 1971. Sir Charles Lyell and the species question. *American Scientist* 59: 43-55.

Young, L., ed. 1970. *Evolution of man*. New York: Oxford University Press.

Chapter 4

Discovery of the Principles of Modern Genetics

The foundation of evolution, and of life itself, is the transmission of genetic material from one generation to the next. The recognition of the nature of genetic transmission came from the work of Gregor Mendel. Prior to the acceptance of Mendelian principles, the blending theory of inheritance and pangenesis were widely accepted. Mendel's contribution to modern genetics is commonly stated in the laws of segregation and independent assortment. It was not until after his death that Mendel's work was recognized as the breakthrough it constituted. The rediscovery, as it were, of Mendel's work came with the experiments of De Vries, Correns, and von Tschermak.

Genetics Before Mendel

Life begets life. This concept is essential to the theory of evolution. The foundation of evolution, and of life itself, is the transmission of genetic material—hereditary units called **genes**—from one generation to another. If life were continually created anew, as was thought in the nineteenth century, evolution would be a meaningless concept. Accepting the concept of life as a continuum raises two important questions: (1) how is life reproduced, and (2) how is the inherited information transmitted through the reproductive process?

Darwin's work made it clear that evolution functions through the selective preservation and elimination of inherited differences among individuals. There was, however, no clear understanding of how a given trait was passed from parent to offspring. It was believed that heredity was somehow transmitted with the blood, and that a child's blood is a blend of its parents' blood. One early explanation of family resemblances was the blending theory, which implied that offspring represented an intermediate blend of traits characterizing their parents. This idea of blending inheritance was prevalent in Darwin's time. The idea of blending inheritance presented a problem, however; if a child were the blend of its parents' traits, the succession of generations must result in loss of variation. The long-term effect of sexual reproduction would be reduction in variability, until all individuals were quite similar. In fact, variability is maintained.

Darwin believed, as did Lamarck, that acquired traits could be transmitted from parent to offspring. Darwin thought that particles in the body were influenced by the activities of the organism. These particles traveled to the reproductive system through the circulatory system and modified the sex cells in such a way that acquired traits could be passed to the next generation. This theory of heredity, known as pangenesis, has been discarded.

Mendel's Principles of Heredity

Genetics is the scientific study of heredity and variation. The field of genetics was given its name by William Bateson in 1906; however, its origins are traced chiefly to the discovery, about 40 years earlier, of the general laws of heredity by Gregor Mendel (Figure 4-1). Even before Mendel's time, however, experimental attempts to analyze the process of biological inheritance were made by studying the offspring of hybrids between plant varieties that differed in well-known traits. At this time, it was thought that certain parental traits, such as seed color, reappeared as separable traits in the descendents of hybrids. The crucial demonstration of the hereditary mechanism was the result of Mendel's carefully planned studies.

Mendel's Studies. Gregor Mendel (1822-1884) determined the fundamental principles of heredity while experimenting in a monastery garden in the 1850s and 1860s. In 1856 Mendel began the first of a series of experiments that eventually showed that inheritance, like evolution, is not chaotic or mere chance, but instead follows a set of rigid laws. The work of Darwin and Mendel is crucial for understanding evolutionary mechanisms.

Figure 4-1. Gregor Mendel.

From his youth, Mendel was interested in nature. In the monastic atmosphere where he spent much of his life, he was free to pursue his botanical experiments and spared the anxiety of the need to earn a livelihood. In a small garden Mendel experimented with crossbreeding of flowers and discovered that when he crossbred certain flower types, distinctive characteristics continually reappeared. These characteristics were thus said to breed true.

Mendel developed a systematic breeding procedure, realizing that his experiments needed to be done on a large scale to rule out chance (Table 4-1). To begin, Mendel needed plants that, when self-fertilized, showed no variability from generation to generation. He also needed a plant protected from foreign pollen. Legumes most nearly fulfilled his needs, and Mendel finally chose the garden pea for his experimental plant. The garden pea is ordinarily self-fertilizing and easily protected from outside pollen.

One of Mendel's assets was his ability to work systematically. He selected seven easily compared pairs of traits to study (Table 4-2).

Mendel began his hybridization experiments by crossing together each of the true breeding varieties that exhibited the alternative representation for a given trait, for example, wrinkled-seed plants with round-seed plants. Mendel made a number of fertilizations. When he opened the pods of his round-wrinkled hybrids, he found only round peas. Wrinkling, a trait of half the parents, was not evident. The same was true with the six other traits. When Mendel crossed tall and short plants, all the offspring were tall. When he crossed yellow peas with green peas, all the offspring were yellow. In each test plot only one trait prevailed in the first hybrid generation (Figure 4-2). Mendel called the trait that appeared the **dominant** trait, and the trait that did not appear the **recessive** trait.

Mendel sought to discover what happened to the recessive trait, which disappeared in the offspring of the so-called first filial (F_1) generation (Figure 4-3). Mendel noticed that when a tall

Table 4-1. Essential Steps of Mendel's Procedure

1. Locate two organisms of the same species that differ in a specific trait.
2. Mate those two organisms to produce a generation of offspring (called the first filial, or F_1, generation).
3. Inbreed the F_1 generation.
4. Classify the organisms produced by the F_1 generation with regard to the trait being studied.
5. Statistically analyze the results.
6. Once a trait has been studied intensively, the information obtained can be used to predict the results of subsequent matings of organisms that show this trait.

Table 4-2. Traits Chosen by Mendel for Study

Trait	Expression	
	Either	*Or*
1. Form of ripe seed	Round	Wrinkled
2. Color of pea	Yellow	Green
3. Color of seed coat	Gray	White
4. Form of ripe seed pod	Smooth	Constricted
5. Color of unripe seed pod	Green	Yellow
6. Position of flowers	Axial	Terminal
7. Stem length	Tall	Short (0.75 to 1.5 feet)

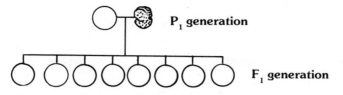

Figure 4-2. When Mendel crossed a plant produced by round seeds with a plant produced by wrinkled seeds, the hybrid seeds showed the trait of only one parent (round). Mendel termed this trait dominant.

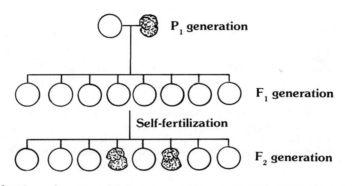

Figure 4-3. The production of a second hybrid generation by self-fertilization of the F_1 hybrids showed that the F_1 plants carried the characteristics of both original parents. The wrinkled trait, hidden in the F_1, reappeared in the F_2; the ratio in the F_2 was 3 round/ 1 wrinkled.

variety was crossed with a short variety, all F_1 plants were tall. What happens to the short variety; is the trait forever lost or only hidden temporarily? To solve this problem, Mendel self-fertilized the F_1 plants. He then made a careful statistical study of the resulting second filial (F_2) generation plants.

The recessive trait, the short variety, which had disappeared in the F_1 generation, was not permanently lost. Mendel observed that the trait reappeared in the next generation. Approximately one-fourth of the F_2 plants showed this formerly hidden trait. Furthermore, the trait reappeared unchanged in any respect. When F_2 plants showing recessive traits were permitted to self-fertilize, they continued to produce offspring showing only the recessive trait.

By contrast, the F_2 plants showing the dominant trait, tallness, seemed to be of two kinds when they were self-fertilized. Some plants gave rise only to plants showing the dominant trait for as many generations as they were studied. Some plants, however, acted the same way as had the original F_1 hybrids—they produced both tall and short offspring in the ratio of 3:1 (Figure 4-4). Evidently some F_2 tall plants were pure for this trait, whereas other F_2 tall plants carried the hidden recessive.

Mendel's Explanations. To explain his observations, Mendel proposed that the traits he studied were determined by separate hereditary factors (his name for genes) and that each individual possessed two representations of a given gene. Pure-breeding individuals have identical representations, for example, *AA* or *aa*, whereas hybrid individuals (individuals produced by pure-breeding parents of contrasting types) possess nonidentical

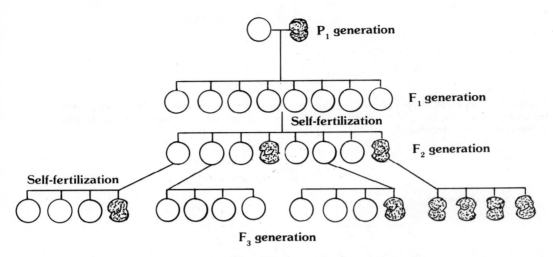

Figure 4-4. Mendel allowed plants produced by the second-generation seeds to self-fertilize. The third hybrid generation produced new combinations of characteristics. The wrinkled seeds produced only offspring having wrinkled seeds (and would always do so) as did some of the round seeds. Other round seeds repeated the 3:1 ratio.

representations, for example Aa. The different forms of the same gene, for example, A and a, are referred to as **alleles**.

The offspring from a given cross receive one gene from the male gamete and one gene from the female gamete. Hybrid individuals, then, produce two kinds of gametes. A and a, in equal numbers. The male and female gametes unite at random and, as a result, the cross $Aa \times Aa$ yields AA, Aa, and aa offspring in the ratio of 1:2:1, respectively (Figure 4-5). This ratio, based

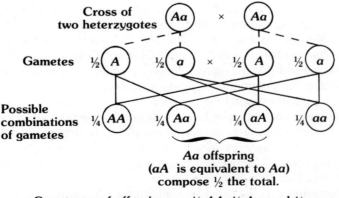

Genotypes of offspring are ¼ AA, ½ Aa, and ¼ aa, a ratio of 1:2:1.

Figure 4-5. The genotypes produced from a cross of two-heterozygous individuals $(Aa \times Aa)$.

on the *actual gene composition* (called the **genotype**) of each individual, is called the geno-typic ratio. Because *A* is dominant in its expression to *a*, the *external appearance* (called the **phenotype**)[1] of the hybrid is the same as that of the *AA* individual. Thus, the phenotypic ratio is 3:1, dominant to recessive.

The pure-breeding genotypes, *AA* and *aa*, are termed **homozygous** and the *Aa* condition is termed **heterozygous.** It follows, then, that individuals that exhibit the dominant phenotype can have either genotype *AA* or *Aa*. Both these genotypes are present in the F_2 generation and provide the results that Mendel observed when he allowed them to self-fertilize.

Mendel also studied the simultaneous inheritance of more than one trait. For example, Mendel studied the inheritance of a cross between round and yellow seeds and wrinkled and green seeds. Are these characteristics inherited independently, or are they inherited as a group? Figure 4-6 shows the results from such a cross. When a plant with two dominant characters, round seeds (*RR*) and yellow seeds (*YY*), is crossed with a plant having two recessive characteristics, wrinkled (*rr*) and green seeds (*yy*), Mendel found that the F_1 plants always showed both dominant traits. The F_2 generation derived from self-fertilizing F_1 plants produced all four phenotypic combinations: round-yellow, round-green, wrinkled-yellow, and wrinkled-green seeds.

The results suggested to Mendel that the two traits, seed shape and seed color, appeared to be inherited *independently* of each other. He reasoned that each trait was inherited independently when he noted that the phenotypic ratio for each was 3:1 (i.e., 3:1 green/yellow *and* 3:1 round seeds/wrinkled seeds). The representation of a combination of traits (e.g., round-yellow seeds) however, was equal to the product of their independent frequencies, or $9/16$ ($3/4 \times 3/4 = 9/16$). Likewise, round-green seeds composed 3/16 ($3/4 \times 1/4 = 3/16$) of the F_2, wrinkled-yellow seeds 3/16 ($1/4 \times 3/4 = 3/16$) of the F_2, and wrinkled-green seeds $1/16$ ($1/4 \times 1/4 = 1/16$). This result yields a 9:3:3:1 phenotypic ratio (Figure 4-6).

As a result of his quantitative approach, Mendel was able to interpret and understand the significance of the phenotypic ratios he observed in the F_2 generation. From a cross of one pair of hybrids (*Aa* × *Aa*), three genotypes (*AA, Aa,* and *aa*) are possible among the offspring (Figure 4-5). As the number of genes under consideration increases, the number of possible genotypes increases at an exponential rate. Thus, considerable variability is generated as a result of sexual reproduction.

It should be noted that traits result from processes of development initiated and modulated by the genotype. The genotype sets limits or ranges to the responses the individual makes to its environment. The diversity of phenotypes that arises from the interaction between a given genotype and the environment has been called the norm of reaction for that genotype. What is then inherited is the genotype with its norm of reaction, the capacity to respond during growth to a range of environmental conditions.

Mendel's work showed that hereditary traits are transmitted by a large number of independent, inheritable units today called genes. Each gene is now known to occupy a specific site (**locus,** plural **loci**) on a **chromosome** and genes occur in pairs in cells because chromosomes occur in pairs (Figure 4-7). The parents' traits are passed unchanged as units to the descendants. No blending of parental traits, as was long believed to occur, actually occurs.

---

[1]The genotype is determined by ancestry alone and is kept constant in different conditions and throughout life by the generally faithful reproduction of the genes in all cells of the individual. The phenotype is determined both by the intrinsic (genetic) factors received from the parents and by the continous response of the developing individual to the extrinsic (environmental) sources of food and energy.

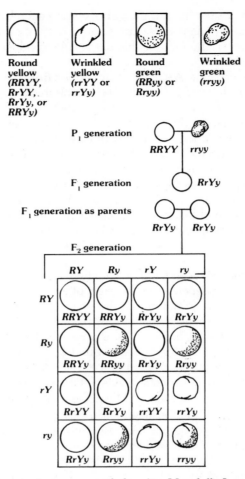

Figure 4-6. The Punnett Square is one way of showing Mendel's Law of Independent Assortment. A pea having two dominant traits (round and yellow, *RR* and *YY*) is crossed with a pea having two recessive traits (wrinkled and green, *rr* and *YY*). The gametes of the first plant (*RY*) combine with the gametes of the second (*ry*) to produce the hybrid (*RrYy*). When hybrids are crossed, their genes produce the combinations shown in the square, that is, four different-appearing kinds of peas in a ratio of 9:3:3:1.

Even recessive traits (such as wrinkled and green seeds), which do not appear in the F_1 of crosses between pure-bred lines, may appear unchanged in later generations.

Mendel's Laws

Mendel's main contributions to modern genetics are summarized as two so-called laws that can be stated as follows (exceptions to these "laws" are known):

Law of Segregation. The Law of Segregation states that *only one of a pair of genes is transmitted from parent to offspring. In the process of the segregation of genes, an individual receives equal amounts of genetic material contained in the sex cells from both parents.*

CHROMOSOME PAIR

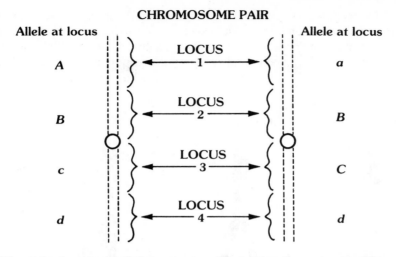

Figure 4-7. Diagram of one pair of chromosomes illustrating the concept of locus and allele. This pair has four loci, 1 through 4, with alleles *Aa* at locus 1, *BB* at locus 2, *Cc* at locus 3, and *dd* at locus 4. This individual is heterozygous at loci 1 and 3 and homozygous at loci 2 and 4.

Law of Independent Assortment. The Law of Independent Assortment states that every trait is inherited independently of every other trait. Different pairs of genes are passed independently to the offspring so that new genetic combinations not found in either parent can appear in the offspring (Figures 4-5 and 4-6).

Linkage

Mendel was aware that independent assortment did not always occur. For example, in his experiments with pea plants Mendel found that every plant having red flowers also had seeds with gray seed coats, whereas every plant having white flowers had seeds with white seed coats. If flower color and seed-coat color were inherited independently, some plants having red flowers should have had white seed coats and some plants having white flowers should have had gray seed coats. Yet, as Mendel noted (but was unable to explain), these combinations did not appear.

The major exception to independent assortment are genes linked together on the same chromosome. Although an organism may have hundreds of thousands of heritable traits, it has a limited, relatively small number of chromosomes, each of which carries many genes.[2] Because all the genes on a chromosome act as if they were strung together on a common strand, they are inherited together rather than independently. A group of traits carried on the same chromosome compose what is called a **linkage** group.

Linkage is complicated by the behavior of chromosomes. In cells preparing for sexual reproduction, chromosomes that bear genes that control the same traits pair and coil around

[2]The number of chromosomes in each cell ranges from 2 in the threadworm to 500 in the fern *Ophioglossum*. Humans have 46.

each other. This pairing and coiling is called **synapsis**. A mutual attraction seems to exist between two genes for the same trait. When synapsis occurs every gene on one chromosome is directly opposite its corresponding gene on the other chromosome. While the chromosomes are paired, they may break at a point and exchange corresponding segments. This exchange, called **crossing over**, results in pieces of chromosomes being exchanged between members of a pair (Figure 4-8).

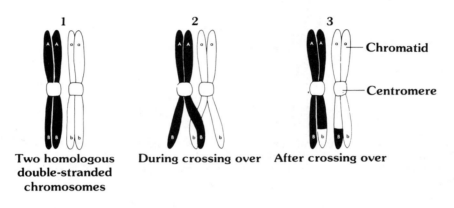

Figure 4-8. Crossing over between two homologous double stranded chromosomes.
(1) One chromosome bearing alleles *A* and *B* and another bearing alleles *a* and *b* lie side by side in synapsis during meiosis. (2) Breaks occur in a chromatid of each chromosome and fragments are exchanged. (3) After crossing over, one chromatid of the first chromosome has alleles *A* and *b*; one chromatid of the second chromosome has alleles *A* and *B*.

Mendel's combination of mathematics and botany was unheard of previously, and his ideas ran contrary to the belief that heredity was carried through the blood. Mendel wrote a report that he read in two sessions in early 1865 before the Brünn Society for the Study of Natural Science. The minutes of the meeting recorded no questions or comments. Mendel published his results in the Society's proceedings, which appeared in 1866. This report was met with silence and the implications of Mendel's work were unnoticed and ignored.

Summary of Mendel's Ideas

Mendel's major ideas can be summarized as follows.

1. Mendel noted that characteristics appeared in two contrasting forms, such as yellow or green seed color. Today these contrasting forms are called alleles. When organisms for opposite traits of a pair are crossed, only one trait of the pair appears in the F_1 generation.
2. Mendel believed that the traits he studied were each determined by a single pair of hereditary units today called genes. Mendel used letters such as *A, a, B,* and *b* to represent these traits. The trait not expressed in the F_1 generation was not lost; it reappeared in a definite percentage of the F_2 organisms.
3. Mendel demonstrated that one member (the dominant trait) of each contrasting pair could completely mask the appearance of the other member (the recessive trait) in a cross.

4. Mendel suggested that the pairs of traits found in hybrids separate from one another during the formation of the reproductive cells without being modified by their previous association with their opposites. This idea is the basis of Mendel's first law, the Law of Segregation. Today the term "segregation" is used to describe the separation of the genes of a pair.
5. Mendel suggested that every trait is inherited independently of every other trait. This idea is the basis of Mendel's second law, the Law of Independent Assortment.
6. Mendel believed that in each generation there occurred a recombination of genes carried by the reproductive cells. The recombination of genes from the parents depends on chance. Therefore, when there are many offspring, every possible combination of traits is produced.

Rediscovery of Mendel's Work

When he died in 1884, few scientists knew about the importance of Mendel's work. In the 1880s one of those asking how variations of life occurred was a botanist at the University of Amsterdam, Hugo De Vries. De Vries accepted Darwin's thesis that descent with modification is the main law in the organic world. If, however, natural selection has only small, individual variations to act on, how do wide interspecific differences occur?

De Vries (1900) was aware of the work of plant breeders whereby plants were selected to produce such desired traits as bright colors. He knew that if breeders wanted to produce a certain color tulip they could do so selectively. To obtain a completely different shade of color, however, they had to wait for nature to produce what De Vries called a mutation, that is, a distinct change from previously existing qualities. Darwin used the word "sport" for such suddenly appearing new traits and he emphasized their importance. However, in their dogged insistence on the role of natural selection, some of Darwin's followers tended to dismiss the effect of these sudden changes.

De Vries decided to watch for the occurrence of mutations. He reasoned that mutations were most likely in plants adapting to new living conditions. De Vries's discovery came with the evening primrose, *Oenothera lamarckiana*. He found ten specimens of a new type of primrose growing alone in a corner of a field that had not been invaded by other primroses. De Vries planted seeds from these plants and found that they bred true and produced petals unlike those of *O. lamarckiana*.[3] He named his new species *O. laevifolia*.

If living organisms change at one or a few points, the implication is that the traits must be produced by separate hereditary factors (genes). If each trait is indeed controlled by separate genes, each trait can vary independently of any other. Although he was working with segregated characteristics, not mutations, De Vries stated, "Attributes of organisms consist of distinct, separate, and independent units. These units can be associated in groups and we find, in allied species, the same units and groups of units. Transitions, such as we so frequently meet with in the external form both of animals and of plants, are as completely absent between these units as they are between the molecules of the chemist."

De Vries broke new ground and he introduced concepts at variance with most previously accepted beliefs. De Vries searched the literature for proof of his work that suggested that heredity is not a whole but a compound of separate units. He came to a reference to a hybridization experiment by Mendel noting that a ". . .constant numerical ratio among the types [is] produced by hybridization." Constant numerical ratios implied separate units.

---

[3]It should be noted that the mutation occurring in *Oenothera* is unusual.

De Vries tracked down Mendel's reference, and in 1900 he discovered Mendel's 1866 work. De Vries understood the importance of Mendel's work, and in a paper he read before the German Botanical Society in 1900, he gave full credit to Mendel's earlier discovery. A month after De Vries made his disclosure, a German scientist, Karl Correns (1900), told the German Botanical Society that he had also found Mendel's work. By further coincidence a third scientist, Erich von Tschermak (1900) of Vienna, made the same discovery at the same time. The remarkable triple discovery undid decades of neglect to Mendel's momentous work. Mendel posthumously received the recognition his work deserved, and at last the theory of evolution had verification.

The missing link in Darwin's evolutionary scheme was his lack of knowledge about the means whereby traits are transmitted generationally. This link was provided by Mendel's work. Mendel's work laid the basis for the science of genetics. His discovery of two basic principles, the Laws of Segregation and Independent Assortment, describe the manner in which genes are passed from one generation to another.

The chief principle that Mendel discovered has been found to be of general validity in all forms of life. The system of Mendelian heredity, primarily responsible for the continuity of living things through reproduction, is based on a multiplicity of genes, which separate and recombine as they pass from one generation to the next.

Bibliography

Beadle, G., and Beadle, M. 1966. *The language of life.* Garden City, N.J.: Doubleday.

Bennett, K. 1979. *Fundamentals of biological anthropology.* Dubuque, Ia.: Brown.

Correns, C. 1900. G. Mendel's law concerning the behavior of progeny of varietal hybrids. *Reports of the German Botanical Society* 18:158-68.

De Vries, H. 1900. Sur la roi de disjonction des hybrides. *Comptes-Rendus de l'Academie des Sciences* 130:845-47.

Goldstein, P. 1965. *Triumphs of biology.* Garden City, N.Y.: Doubleday.

_____. 1967. *Genetics is easy.* New York: Viking Press.

Iltis, H. 1932. *Life of Mendel.* New York: Norton.

Jolly, C., and Plog, F. 1976. *Physical anthropology and archeology.* New York: Knopf.

Kelso, A. J. 1974. *Physical anthropology.* Philadelphia: Lippincott.

Mendel, G. 1948. *Experiments in plant hybridization.* Cambridge: Harvard University Press.

Tjio, J., and Levan, A. 1956. The chromosome number of man. *Hereditas* 42:1-6.

von Tschermak, E. 1900. Concerning artificial crossing in *Pisum sativum. Reports of the German Botanical Society* 18:232-39.

Chapter 5

Cell Division and Gene Theory

The body is composed of many cells, and these cells are fundamentally similar in structure. Body cells multiply through a process called mitosis, and the potential sex cells undergo a special type of division called meiosis. Meiosis insures the reassortment of genes and thereby promotes genetic variability and the means whereby the chromosome number of a species is kept constant.

The gene theory of heredity, proposed by Thomas Hunt Morgan, suggests that traits are inherited with regularity because genes are transmitted according to a mechanical process.

Basic Components of Life

All substances are composed of atoms, which are the fundamental building blocks of all matter. Combinations of atoms are often joined to form molecules. Molecules vary greatly in size and shape according to the number and size of atoms they contain. Molecules found in living organisms tend to be large because carbon atoms, the basic constituent of such molecules, can bond easily with other atoms in a seemingly endless variety of possible combinations. The *arrangement* of atoms in a molecule in addition to the kind of atoms is important in determining what product will result from the configuration.

The molecules that are the major components of living organisms are water, salts, fats (lipids), carbohydrates, proteins, nucleic acids, and vitamins.

Each of these major components has one or more well-defined roles. Water is the solvent medium for all chemical reactions. Calcium sulfates and phosphates (examples of salts) are the framework materials of bone, teeth, and shells. Proteins and fats provide the framework for body structures such as muscles, tendons, and membranes. Proteins also act as **enzymes** (substances that speed chemical reactions), hormones, and antibodies, and fats also insulate the body and serve as a reservoir of energy. Carbohydrates are the structural materials and the only energy reservoirs in plants, and they are also the rapid-access energy-storage molecules in animals. Nucleic acids (DNA and RNA)[1] have the special role of transmitting hereditary information from generation to generation. Vitamins are necessary for many body functions.

Cell Structure

Cells are the basis of heredity and all structure and function in living things. All cells are structurally similar (Figure 5-1). A protective membrane surrounds a mass of living substance called protoplasm. The protoplasm is separated by the nuclear membrane into a dense part, the nucleus, and a less dense part, the cytoplasm. The nucleus is separated from the cytoplasm by a nuclear membrane. The cytoplasm consists of water, salts, carbohydrates, fats, proteins, and organelles (organized cellular subunits) concerned with cellular metabolism. The nucleus is the control center for the cell; it contains instructions for all the cell's functions. Each cell nucleus contains all the information needed to build the complete organism. The nucleus is directly associated with heredity.

The nucleus contains a dark-staining substance called **chromatin.** At certain stages in cell division the chromatin assumes the shape of separate, elongated bodies called **chromosomes.** In 1866 the biologist Ernst Haeckel proposed that the cell nucleus, containing the chromosomes, is the principal agent in inheritance. His idea proved a sound one.

---

[1]DNA is the abbreviation for deoxyribonucleic acid and RNA is the abbreviation for ribonucleic acid. The crucial role of these nucleic acids in heredity is the subject of Chapter 6.

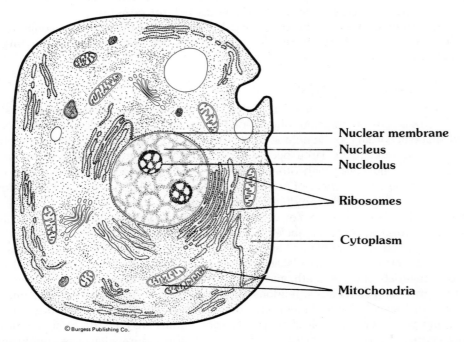

© Burgess Publishing Co.

Figure 5-1. Diagram of animal cell.

Cell Division

It was Rudolf Virchow who, in the mid-1850s, was the first to realize that cells arise only from preexisting cells by division. During division, the nucleus was found to consist of separate, small bodies, the chromosomes. It was not until Mendel's laws of heredity were rediscovered in 1900 and Walter Sutton's cytological studies of 1903 were done that the close parallel behavior of the chromosomes in meiosis and Mendelian laws was found. The mechanism of chromosomal division, the process whereby genetic continuity is maintained and variation is produced, is basic to the process of differentiation and evolutionary change within populations.

Mitosis

Mitosis is the mechanism whereby replicas of components of one cell's heredity (the chromosomes) are equally distributed into two daughter cells. This process endows them with the same basic hereditary information as the parent cells. The process of mitosis occurs in most cells of the body. It can be divided into five main stages, each of which has distinguishing features and merges gradually with the next (Figure 5-2).

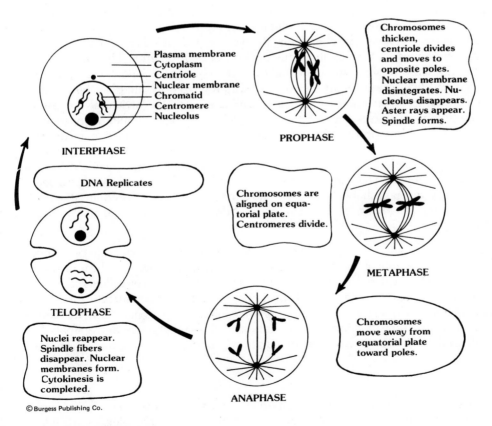

Figure 5-2. Animal mitosis.

1. Interphase. It was once thought that interphase was a "resting stage" because no visible cellular activity was discernible. It is now known, however, that intense metabolic activity occurs within the cell at this time. During interphase the chromosomes are quite long and slender and usually cannot be seen under a light microscope. The nucleus may contain one or more small bodies, the **nucleoli** (singular, **nucleolus**). The nucleoli are sites where nucleic acids and **ribosomes** (tiny structures in the cytoplasm that seem to be the centers for protein synthesis) are prepared for export to the cytoplasm.

2. Prophase. Prophase begins with the chromosomes becoming "fixed" as a ball of long threads. Chromosomes become thicker, shorter, and more tightly coiled as prophase proceeds, and each chromosome appears to be two closely related filaments termed the **chromatids.** The two chromatids are attached to each other at a point called the **centromere.** Nucleoli begin to disperse in early prophase. In late prophase the nuclear membrane begins to disintegrate and a spindle composed of protein fibers radiating out from the centrioles forms. The centriole is a small structure outside the cell nucleus that is associated with spindle formation. Chromosomes become attached to the spindle fibers by their centromeres and gradually move to the equator of the spindle.

3. Metaphase. Metaphase occurs when the chromosomes become oriented at the equatorial plate (the plane equidistant from the two spindle poles). At metaphase, each chromosome consists of a centromere holding two well-separated identical strands, the chromatids, with each chromatid oriented so as to be opposite a spindle pole.

4. Anaphase. Anaphase begins by completing the division of doubled chromosomes into two daughter chromosomes by the simultaneous division of centromeres. This process leaves each chromatid with a separate centromere. The chromatids, now called daughter chromosomes, gradually move apart as if being pulled toward opposite poles by the spindle fibers tugging at their centromere. Anaphase terminates with the arrival of the daughter chromosomes at opposite poles of the spindle. The groups of chromosomes at opposite poles are exact duplicates of the original chromosomal set. The cell begins to pinch inward late in anaphase.

5. Telophase. The chromosomes begin to reaggregate at telophase and the nucleoli become re-formed at the nucleolus. The chromosomes uncoil until they form fine threads that become progressively less distinguishable. The chromosomes become enclosed in the nuclear membrane to complete telophase, and cytoplasmic division separates the nuclei into two daughter cells.

Mitosis ensures the equitable distribution of the chromosomes. Most body cells undergo mitosis; the cellular material of one cell separates to form two cells. Because the total potential of the offspring is contained in the original parent, a single cell dividing by mitosis can produce no variation (assuming no change, or **mutation,** occurs in the hereditary information). The importance of mitosis is demonstrated by its widespread occurrence as a fundamental mechanism of cellular reproduction in the nonsexual cells of most plants and animals. Every typical multicellular organism develops by mitosis from a single cell, that is, the fertilized egg of its mother.

Meiosis

Whereas mitosis occurs in most body cells, **meiosis** occurs in the sex organs (testes in males, ovaries in females) that are found in all sexually reproducing creatures. Meiosis precedes the formation of mature sex cells called **gametes.** Male gametes are called spermatozoa and female gametes are called eggs, or ova (Figures 5-3 and 5-4).

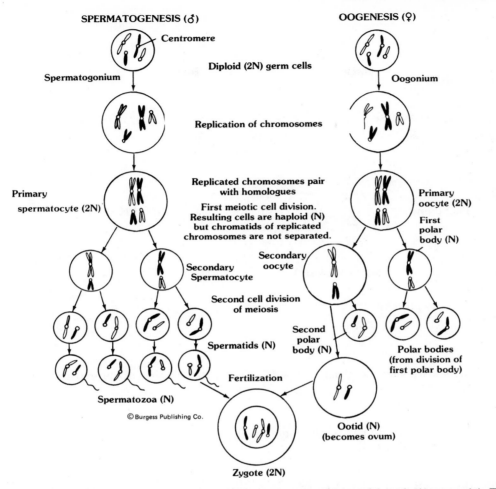

Figure 5-3. Comparison of meiosis in male (spermatogenesis) and female (oogenesis). The diploid number of chromosomes is 4, the haploid number, 2. Paternal chromosomes are arbitrarily denoted as the dark chromosomes and maternal chromosomes is the light ones.

The formation of precursor sex cells begins with a full complement of chromosomes, the specific number of which is characteristic for the species. Because these chromosomes occur in pairs, the cells are called **diploid** (2N) cells. The diploid number for humans is 46 chromosomes, and these 46 chromosomes occur in 23 pairs. One member of each pair of chromosomes is paternal (inherited from the father) and the other member is maternal (inherited from the mother). As a result of meiosis, the members of each pair of chromosomes separate from each other and each human gamete has a total of 23 chromosomes, the **haploid** (N) number.

Of the 23 pairs of chromosomes in the diploid human cell, 22 pairs are called **autosomes** and one pair, which works to determine the sex of the individual, is called **sex chromosomes**. Members of each pair of autosomes normally look identical and are called **homologous chromosomes**.

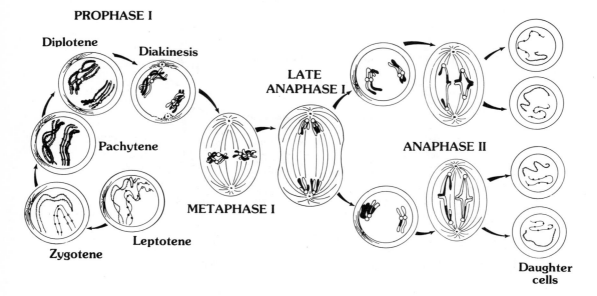

Figure 5-4. Meiosis, showing divisions I and II. The diploid number of chromosomes is 4, the haploid number, 2.

As can mitosis, meiosis can be divided into successive stages. In meiosis, however, *two* divisions of the nucleus (termed divisions I and II) occur (Figure 5-4). As a result of divisions I and II, four daughter cells are produced and each of these has only half the chromosome number of the original parent cell. Thus, in contrast to mitosis, the cells produced through meiosis are not identical with the parent cell.

Because it reduces the chromosome number from the diploid to the haploid state, meiosis is the process that underlies Mendel's principles. Meiosis is a reduction mechanism that balances the doubling in chromosome number that occurs when gametes of two parents fuse at fertilization in sexually reproducing organisms.

Following is a brief outline of the major features of meiosis following interphase in a diploid organism such as the human (Figure 5-4).

First division. The first division of meiosis consists of the following stages: (1) prophase I, which includes (a) leptotene, (b) zygotene, (c) pachytene, (d) diplotene, and (e) diakinesis, (2) metaphase I, (3) anaphase I, and (4) telophase I.

1. Prophase I. Prophase I lasts longer than prophase in mitosis and the volume of the nucleus is three to four times greater than that of the mitotic prophase nucleus. Synthesis of the heredity-carrying nucleic acids DNA and RNA occurs in interphase and prophase I. Prophase I is divided into the following stages.

a. Leptotene. Synthesis of DNA is completed in leptotene. Leptotene chromosomes differ from mitotic prophase chromosomes in that they appear longitudinally single rather than double.

b. Zygotene. Zygotene is characterized by active *pairing of homologous chromosomes.*[2] Pairing begins at one or more points along the chromosomes and proceeds in a zipperlike fashion. This pattern unites the chromosomes lengthwise. Pairing normally occurs between strictly homologous regions.

c. Pachytene. Pachytene occurs when pairing is completed. Each pair of chromosomes first appears to be one chromosome and in this state composes a bivalent. Halfway through the pachytene stage, the bivalents are visible as strands called chromatids, thus yielding four-stranded bivalents. Shortening and thickening of the bivalents render the chromosome pattern more distinct than it was in earlier stages.

d. Diplotene. Diplotene begins when the paternal and maternal chromosomes in a four-stranded bivalent start to separate and their centromeres move apart. The chromosomes do not completely separate but remain together at certain points where two of the four chromatids appear to form an X, crossing over one another (see Figure 4-8). These points of crossing are called chiasmata (singular, chiasma). The chiasma is the point of attachment between two nonsister chromatids during the first meiotic division. The two chromatids, at these points, break at the end of pachytene and are rejoined diagonally with the broken ends of chromatids from homologous chromosomes. The chiasma mechanism results from the exchange of parts between the paternal and maternal chromosomes in a homologous pair.

e. Diakineses. Diakinesis corresponds to the late prophase of an ordinary mitotic division. In diakinesis the bivalents appear much thicker and shorter and the chiasmata have slipped to the ends of the chromosomes because of further separation of homologous chromosomes.

2. Metaphase I. In metaphase I each bivalent becomes attached to the spindle by its two centromeres at the equatorial plate. The orientation of the bivalents on the spindle is determined by chance.

3. Anaphase I. In anaphase I the homologous centromeres segregate and apparently pull their attached chromatids to the spindle poles. Whole chromosomes, each one still in a duplicated state, become separated to the spindle poles resulting in two haploid groups of chromosomes. The actual reduction of chromosomal number per nucleus is completed by the end of the first meiotic division.

4. Telophase I. Telophase I resembles the telophase of mitosis in organisms that form interphase nuclei. The chromosomes may remain unchanged from the end of anaphase I until metaphase II.

Second Division. The second division of meiosis is superficially an ordinary mitosis in which the centromere again becomes functionally double at metaphase II and then splits so that paired chromatids separate from each other at anaphase II. The four haploid nuclei produced by meiosis become separated into daughter cells, all of which may differentiate into spermatozoa in the male and into one relatively large egg and three small cells (called polar bodies) that do not take part in reproduction in the female.

---

[2] The pairing of homologous chromosomes in meiosis is in contrast to mitosis, in which homologous chromosomes do not pair. This pairing creates an arrangement whereby one chromosome of each homologous pair can separate from the other, which does not occur in mitosis. Understanding this difference in the behavior of chromosomes in mitosis and meiosis is vital to your understanding of the significance of meiosis in reproduction and heredity.

Importance of Meiosis

The events of meiosis provide for keeping the chromosome number of a species constant from generation to generation. Body cells, including those that give rise to gametes, are diploid. In meiosis, the number of chromosomes in potential reproductive cells is halved from the diploid number (46 in the human) to the haploid number (23 in the human). Thus a human sperm or egg contains 23 chromosomes. When a sperm fertilizes an egg, the fertilized egg (**zygote**) that results contains 46 chromosomes, the diploid number again. The diploid zygote soon starts to divide, through mitosis, eventually to produce a multicellular organism. The zygote divides into two cells, these two divide into four, and so forth. As the new organism develops, groups of cells begin to differentiate, that is, to mass themselves into different tissues (aggregations of similar cells united to perform specific functions). Gradually, organs (combinations of tissues arranged in shapes that enable them to function together) develop.

The events of meiosis also insure the reassortment of genes located on different chromosomes. Meiosis can promote genetic variability through (1) random assortment of maternal and paternal chromosomes at anaphase in such a way that haploid cells contain a mixture of maternal and paternal chromosomes and (2) crossing over, which breaks apart linkage groups of genes by causing exchange of chromosome parts between homologous chromosomes, thus altering the set of genes that a chromosome possessed at the onset of meiosis. This reassortment of genes provides a vast amount of genetic novelty in each generation. Table 5-1 compares some important features of mitosis and meiosis.

Gene Theory of Heredity

Mendel had no way to inquire into what the hereditary units might be or where they were located. Mendel assumed that each hereditary determiner produced one character in the organism. Mendel believed there was a one-to-one relationship between the determiner and the trait. Modern geneticists have shown that many genes may interact to produce a given trait, and that many different traits may be affected by one gene.

Morgan's work on the fruit fly suggested the possibility of mapping the hereditary factors on each chromosome. It took Morgan 17 years and the breeding of millions of flies before he found that very precise locations (genes) on the chromosomes control specific traits in a fly. The Morgan group organized the then-known facts and from them proposed a theory that

---

Table 5-1. Comparisons of Mitosis and Meiosis

Mitosis	*Meiosis*
1. Occurs in most body cells.	1. Occurs in sex organs.
2. Produces more body cells.	2. Produces mature sex cells.
3. Maintains diploid chromosome number.	3. Reduces chromosomes to haploid number.
4. One cell division occurs to produce two cells.	4. Two cell divisions occur to produce four cells: (a) four sperm cells in males and (b) one egg and three polar bodies in females.
5. Results in replacement and repair of body cells and growth of body.	5. Results in haploid reproductive cells that can perpetuate the species.

attempts to explain the mechanism by which heredity operates. This theory, the gene theory of heredity, is summarized in Table 5-2.

Gene theory suggests that traits are inherited with regularity because genes are transferred according to a very mechanical pattern. Sudden appearance of strange and unexpected traits (mutations) results from sudden changes in specific genes.

Gene Expression

Because genes are inherited as discrete units, they are passed unchanged to the next generation. The effects of a gene may be masked by a dominant allele or altered by the influence of another gene or genes, but the gene remains ready to express itself in a new individual when conditions allow. This unaltered state ensures that variation is not lost but instead remains available as the raw material for the evolutionary progress. This demonstration in Mendel's experiments was crucial to the formulation of evolutionary biology.

Table 5-2. Gene Theory

1. Hereditary traits are determined by particles called genes.

2. Genes are transmitted from one generation to the next through the reproductive process.

3. Genes are strung in single file along the length of structures in the nucleus called chromosomes. Because chromosomes occur in pairs in diploid cells, genes also occur in pairs and a diploid cell has two complete sets of most genes.

4. Each gene has a definite locus on the chromosome.

5. The gene at a given locus on a chromosome may take one of several different (allelic) forms.

6. Each gamete has one complete set of genes carried in a single set of chromosomes (haploid state).

7. When two gametes unite, the resulting zygote receives two complete sets of chromosomes (one from each gamate) and thereby receives two complete sets of genes (diploid state).

8. When the zygote divides, initiating the process that results in an organism, each cell receives two complete sets of chromosomes carrying two complete sets of genes.

9. The interaction of the two complete sets of genes contained in each cell with each other and with the environment determines the traits that an organism shows.

10. When this new organism produces gametes, meiosis causes the paired chromosomes to separate. Only one member of each pair goes to any one gamete.

11. This separation of chromosomes provides the mechanism by which allelic genes are separated from one another.

12. Because each gene retains its own identity at all times, allelic genes separate in pure form.

13. Chance determines which gametes unite to produce the next generation. Chance determines the recombination of the segregated chromosomes.

14. The chance recombination of genes on these chromosomes results in various Mendelian ratios.

Adapted from P. Goldstein, *Genetics Is Easy*, p. 114. Viking Press, New York, © 1967.

In this chapter we have discussed the role of the basic components of life. The body is composed of many cells, the basis of heredity and all structure and function in living things. Body cells multiply through the process of mitosis, whereas potential sex cells undergo a division process called meiosis.

It was pointed out that there are a number of differences between mitosis and meiosis, in addition to the sites of occurrence. For example, whereas mitosis maintains the diploid chromosome number, meiosis, or reduction division, reduces chromosomes to the haploid number. Because it reduces the chromosome number from the diploid to the haploid state, meiosis is the process underlying Mendel's principles.

Gene theory suggests that traits are inherited with regularity because genes are transferred according to a mechanical pattern. The sudden appearance of unexpected traits (mutations) results from sudden changes in specific genes. Other than in the case of a mutation, genes are passed unchanged from generation to generation. This unaltered state ensures that variation is retained as the raw material for evolution.

Bibliography

Bennett, K. 1979. *Fundamentals of biological anthropology.* Dubuque, Ia.: Brown.

Goldstein, P. 1967. *Genetics is easy.* New York: Viking Press.

Morgan, T. 1932. *The scientific basis of evolution.* New York: Norton.

_____. 1935. The relation of genetics to physiology and medicine. *Annual Report of the Board of Regents of the Smithsonian Institution,* pp. 345-59.

Sciulli, P. 1978. *Introduction to Mendelian genetics and gene action.* Minneapolis: Burgess.

Williams, B. 1973. *Evolution and human origins: an introduction to physical anthropology.* New York: Harper & Row.

Chapter 6

Molecular Genetics

In this chapter the important role the DNA molecule plays in heredity is discussed. The chemical structure of the DNA molecule constitutes a coded message specifying the structure of all the proteins the body will manufacture during its lifetime. The function of DNA was realized through the work of many investigators, including Watson and Crick, whose double helix model showed the arrangement of the chains of DNA.

After outlining some of the important discoveries that led to a better understanding of DNA, we will also discuss the means of translation of the DNA and RNA codes into the making of the individual.

The Role of DNA

Chromosomes are composed chiefly of long strands of the nucleic acid called deoxyribonucleic acid (DNA) protected by proteins. The chemical structure of the DNA molecule constitutes a coded message specifying the structure of all the proteins the body will manufacture during its lifetime. The instruction for each protein has its own location (locus) on a particular chromosome. All life is assembled by one kind of genetic code carried on molecules of DNA. By all indications, the code is practically universal and is striking proof of the unity of *all* living things.

This chapter discusses the nature of DNA and gene action. As you will see, genes are segments of long molecules of DNA. Genes, in turn, produce substances that, as a result of their actions and interactions with other products of genes, act to determine inherited traits.

Genes: Protein or DNA?

As a result of the observations of several scientists (especially Walter Sutton and Theodor Boveri, who independently reported that the behavior of chromosomes in meiosis could account for Mendel's key observations) chromosomes were by the early 1900s thought to carry heredity. When cells divide by mitosis, however, the chromosomes double and are distributed to each new cell. A reduction to half the chromosome number must occur prior to reproduction if the offspring are to maintain the normal chromosomal complement of the species (meiosis accomplishes this needed reduction). Because only mature sex cells participate in reproduction, investigators interested in the nature of the gene had already turned their attention to the sex cells.

Besides studying the mechanism (meiosis) by which gametes are produced, scientists studied the chemical composition of the nuclei of gametes to determine whether the genetic material resided in the protein or the nucleic acids of the chromosome. Although it is clear today that nucleic acids are the genetic material, the first scientists who studied genes assumed that genes were proteins. To understand why, let us examine the structure of proteins.

Structure of Proteins. Proteins are large molecules formed of smaller molecules called amino acids that are linked together in chains of varying complexity. The simplest amino acid derived from protein is glycine (Figure 6-1). Only about 26 protein-forming amino acids are known (Table 6-1), but at least 10,000 different kinds of proteins occur in the human body. Differences among proteins result from variations in the presence and sequencing of the different amino acids. Several hundred amino acids compose a single protein and every amino acid must be in its proper place for proper functioning. Any change in the form or total number of amino acids may result in abnormal functioning or loss of functioning of the protein.

Every living cell contains many kinds of proteins, each of which is structurally adapted to carry out a specific function in development or maintenance. Some proteins serve as structural "building blocks" of cells and others function in the hormonal control of cellular processes. Proteins that control chemical reactions are called enzymes. Each enzyme has the ability to mediate at least one chemical reaction. All heritable traits are ultimately produced by chemical reactions controlled by one or more proteins plus the interaction of the genetic material with the environment. In development, proteins are the agents of the genes and control the many chemical actions that determine size, shape, and biological capabilities.

Scientists reasoned that the infinite number of different genes was explained by the fact that the arrangement of amino acids in the protein chain can vary in an infinite number of ways. Any slight change in the amino acid configuration might easily change the gene to produce a mutation.

Although the structure of proteins helped explain many of the observed facts, the questions remained as to how a chain of amino acids reproduces itself and how a protein can cause the synthesis of other proteins in the body.

Early twentieth-century scientists were so confident in the protein nature of genes that they practically ignored the possible role of the nucleic acids. These acids were discovered shortly after Mendel wrote his paper. Subsequent analyses of the nucleic acids, however, failed to show how the chemical nature of the nucleic acids allowed for the great variety required to

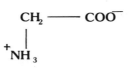

Figure 6-1. Structure of glycine, the simplest amino acid derived from protein. Abbreviations are: C—carbon; H—hydrogen; N—nitrogen; O—oxygen.

Table 6-1. Amino Acids that Occur Naturally in Proteins

Name	Abbreviation	Name	Abbreviation
1. Glycine	Gly	14. Cystine	Cys-SS-Cys
2. Alanine	Ala	15. Hydroxyproline	Hyp
3. Phenylalanine	Phe	16. Tyrosine	Tyr
4. Valine	Val	17. 3,5-Dibromotyrosine	—
5. Leucine	Leu	18. 3,5-Diiodotyrosine	—
6. Isoleucine	Ile	19. Thyroxine	—
7. Proline	Pro	20. Tryptophan	Try
8. Methionine	Met	21. Lysine	Lys
9. Serine	Ser	22. Hydroxylysine	Hyl
10. Threonine	Thr	23. Arginine	Arg
11. Asparagine	Asn	24. Histidine	His
12. Glutamine	Gln	25. Aspartic acid	Asp
13. Cysteine	Cys	26. Glutamic acid	Glu

account for so many genes. Without great variability the nucleic acids did not seem to qualify as the genetic material.

The search for genetic material continued into the second decade of the twentieth century, with some investigators favoring proteins and some favoring nucleic acids. As a result of some landmark studies, to be discussed in the pages that follow, nucleic acids gradually became accepted as the genetic material.

Studies and Structure of Nucleic Acids

Nucleotides. Between 1925 and 1930 P. Levene showed that nucleic acid, after separation from protein, could be divided into smaller fractions termed **nucleotides.** Nucleotides consist of three parts: a sugar, a phosphate (phosphorus-containing) group, and a nitrogen-containing portion called a base (Figure 6-2).

Sugars of Nucleic Acids. The sugar portion of nucleic acid can be of two types, although each contains five carbon atoms. The two sugar portions are termed ribose and deoxyribose, the latter differing from the former only by lacking one oxygen atom (Figure 6-3).

Although there are two types of sugars, specific nucleic acids contain only one type. Nucleic acids can be subdivided into two classes based on the sugar present: ribonucleic acid (RNA), with the sugar ribose, and deoxyribonucleic acid (DNA), with the sugar deoxyribose. RNA is commonly found outside the cell nucleus while DNA is almost exclusively found in the nucleus.

Levene also found that the four kinds of deoxyribonucleotides in DNA were present in equal amounts and joined in small chains of about four nucleotides each. Later it was found that DNA is actually present in very long chains composed of thousands of joined nucleotides. Levene's work indicated that DNA was a rather simple molecule and was not complex enough to explain the great diversity of life.

Bases of Nucleic Acids. DNA contains four kinds of nitrogen-containing molecules called bases: adenine, cytosine, guanine, and thymine. In RNA, another base, uracil, replaces thymine. These bases bond with each other in precisely determined pairs, with adenine always bonding to thymine in DNA and to uracil in RNA, and cytosine always bonding to guanine (Figure 6-4). As we will see (Chapter 7), the arrangement of these bases in nucleic acids is vital to the functioning of nucleic acids as the hereditary substance.

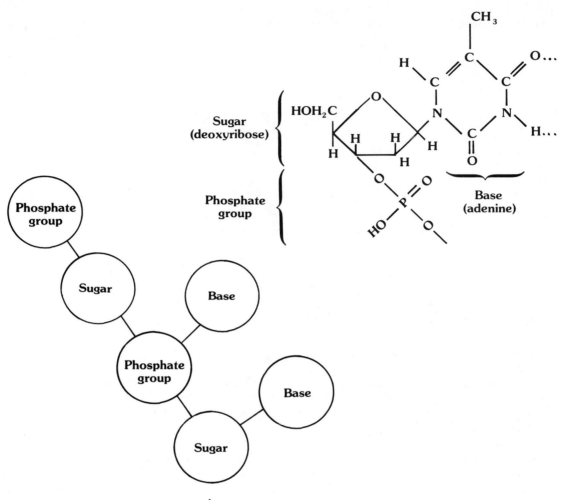

Sugar
(deoxyribose)

Phosphate
group

Base
(adenine)

Phosphate
group

Sugar

Base

Phosphate
group

Base

Sugar

A

Figure 6-2. A nucleotide. (A) Schematic view. (B) Detailed view.

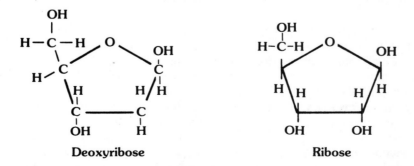

Deoxyribose

Ribose

Figure 6-3. Nucleotide sugars ribose and deoxyribose.

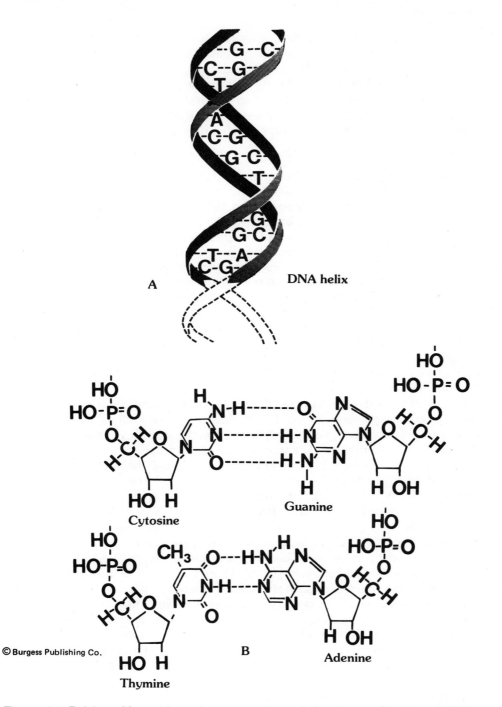

Figure 6-4. Pairing of bases (cytosine to guanine and thymine to adenine) in DNA. Thymine is replaced by a similar molecule, uracil, in RNA. (A) Schematic view. (B) Detailed view.

DNA is a long, chainlike molecule that provides sites of attachment for thousands of nucleotides. Because any of four different nucleotide bases can be at each position of the DNA chain, much variability or complexity can be attained simply by heterogeneous placement of bases along the chain. If each of the four DNA bases (thymine, guanine, cytosine, and adenine) composed a message, only four characters could be produced. If, however, two adjacent bases composed a message, 16 (that is, 4^2) messages could be contained in DNA. If three adjacent bases composed a message, 64 (that is, 4^3) messages could be contained.

Transformation

While Levene was investigating the DNA structure, F. Griffith, in 1923, conducted a series of experiments consisting of injecting nonvirulent and virulent pneumonia bacteria into mice. Mice injected with a nonvirulent bacterial strain lived. When the virulent strain was heated and killed and then injected into mice, the mice also lived.

After these experiments, Griffith injected another group of mice with two cultures simultaneously. This group of mice was injected with harmless living type II (R) cells, plus some harmless *heat-killed* type III (S) cells. Both injections were considered harmless; some of the mice, however, died of pneumonia. Although not a single living III (S) cell had been injected into the mice, living III (S) cells were recovered from the blood of sick mice. Because contamination with living III (S) cells was quickly deemed unlikely, this experiment suggested a transformation of some substance in the nonvirulent bacteria by virulent bacteria. The process of transformation of the bacteria raised a number of questions. For example, did the dead III (S) cells come back to life? Did something from the dead III (S) cells enter the living II (R) cells and change their harmless nature? Were harmless II (R) cells transformed into the virulent III (S) type?

It soon became obvious that the harmless II (R) cells could be transformed into the virulent bacteria merely by mixing them with the dead bodies of *heat-killed* III (S) cells. It was not known at this time how the process occurred, that is, how the dead III (S) cells could enter the living II (R) cells to transform them. The term "transforming principle" was assigned to this process, and it was left undefined. It was later recognized through the work of O. Avery, C. MacLeod, and M. McCarty that heating the III (S) culture killed the cells and caused them to release some of their DNA. The free DNA was then able to enter some of the living II (R) cells and transfer to them certain III (S) cell traits. Because DNA duplicates itself during cell division and passes along the traits it controls, more cells with III (S) traits gradually developed.

The transforming agent was unknown until the work by Avery and his colleagues in 1944. These investigators added nonvirulent bacteria to a culture medium and allowed it to reproduce; only nonvirulent bacteria were found. Then, DNA from virulent but heat-killed bacteria was added to a culture medium; no bacteria were found. Finally, nonvirulent bacteria and DNA from heat-killed, virulent bacteria were added to a culture medium that could keep virulent and nonvirulent bacteria separate. Nevertheless, even though the virulent and nonvirulent bacteria were separated, both virulent and nonvirulent bacteria were found on the medium, indicating very strongly that DNA is the transforming agent. Because the DNA of one organism can cause traits of another to be changed, DNA is further implicated as the genetic material.

Following the work of Avery, MacLeod, and McCarty, many additional transformation experiments were conducted successfully. Experiments were done using viruses as well as bacteria. In 1952 A. Hershey and M. Chase investigated the mechanism whereby a specific type of virus, a bacteriophage, infected and ultimately destroyed (lysed) bacteria. They showed that the virus infected the bacterial cell with DNA and not with protein to produce new viruses. Thus, DNA rather than protein must contain the hereditary information.

Shape of DNA

X-ray studies of crystallized DNA suggested a multiple-chain structure. Using X-ray diffraction to analyze DNA, Wilkins (1963) produced characteristic patterns that provided information about the arrangement of atoms in the DNA molecule. He made measurements on these patterns and estimated sizes, distances, and spaces in the molecule. The arrangement of spots on the patterns indicated to Wilkins that the DNA molecule had a spiral shape, rather than a flat, two-dimensional arrangement. Many scientists tried to build a three-dimensional model after Wilkins' discovery. The double helix model suggested by the team of Watson and Crick best fits the facts.

The Double Helix. In 1953 James Watson and Francis Crick synthesized the information concerning the structure of DNA, and, stressing the pairing of the nitrogen-containing base (i.e., adenine to thymine and cytosine to guanine), proposed a double-helix model. Watson and Crick showed that DNA is a double-stranded molecule, with each strand coiled around the other in a manner similar to a coiled rope. The structure of the coil is helical, as a spiral staircase, with the stairs always of the same length and the entire structure with the same diameter (Figure 6-4).

The Watson-Crick model shows a double spiral formed of intertwining DNA chains twisted about an imaginary cylinder. The long two spiral chains are composed of alternating sugar and phosphate groups. Nitrogenous bases attached to the sugars are arranged at right angles to the long axis of the spiral. Weak chemical forces (the hydrogen bonds) between matching bases of the two intertwining chains hold the molecule together (Figure 6-4).

An analogy can be made between the DNA molecule and a ladder. The uprights of the ladder correspond to the backbones of the two chains. Each ladder rung represents a base from one chain bonded to a **complementary base** from the second chain. The bonded bases (rungs) hold the uprights together. For a three-dimensional effect, you must imagine that the two uprights are twisted into intertwining spirals, with the rungs still holding them together.

Watson and Crick's model imposed physical limits on the dimension of the DNA structure. An important feature of this model is that it demonstrates that although the spirals are held together by bonding between the bases, only certain bases bond with one another. Because of size and chemical structure, only complementary bases can fit together. Only when each pair consisted of adenine (A) and thymine (T) or cytosine (C) and guanine (G) would the coils of the helix be equal in length and fit together. Therefore, only the combinations of A:T, T:A, C:G, G:C can form the ladder rungs, and other combinations are impossible.

The base pair arrangement means that the structure of one strand must be composed of bases that will bond with the other strand. If one strand has the bases ...ATGCA... the opposing strand must have the bases ...TACGT... at the same level. The 46 human chromosomes contain some 4 billion bases. The order of these bases is different for each living thing. The endless variety of this order of bases explains the limitless variety of the living world.

Duplication of DNA

A requisite characteristic of a substance that carries hereditary information from generation to generation is that it must be able to duplicate, and thereby create copies of, itself. The duplication of DNA is commonly called replication. The structure of DNA adapts it admirably to self-duplication. As Watson and Crick noted, each chain in the DNA helix is the

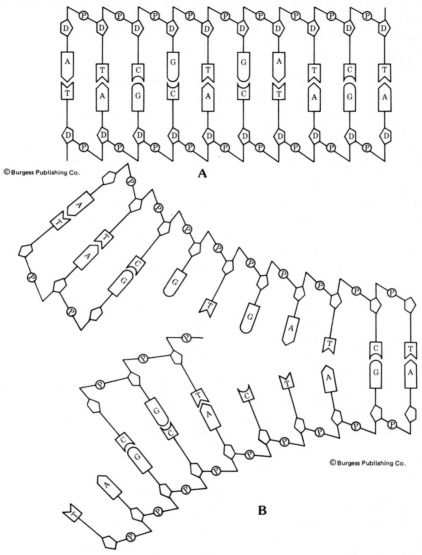

© Burgess Publishing Co.

A

© Burgess Publishing Co.

B

Figure 6-5. Replication of DNA. (A) Paired bases along segment of DNA. (B) Activated nucleotides attaching to sites on strands.

complement of the other. The sequence of bases on one chain is fixed by the sequence of bases on the other chain. Wherever one chain carries a thymine (T), the other must carry an adenine (A). Wherever there is a cytosine (C) on one chain, there must be a guanine (G) on the other.

During DNA replication, an enzyme temporarily separates the DNA strands. The cell contains a random collection of nucleotides that carry the bases adenine, thymine, cytosine, or guanine, and these nucleotides are enzymatically activated and ready to bond with complementary bases. Even as the double chain is separating, the free, active nucleotides are attached to spots where they fit—for example, every free thymine-nucleotide lines up opposite an adenine-nucleotide in the single chain and free guanine-nucleotides line up opposite cytosine-nucleotides (Figure 6-5).

When the process is completed, there must be two identical double-stranded molecules of DNA with exactly the same sequence of bases as the parent double strand. The DNA molecule replicates exactly. This theoretical description is supported by A. Kornberg's (1960) experimental demonstration that DNA can replicate itself in a test tube.

DNA as the Genetic Material

To serve effectively as a genetic material, a molecule must have the following capabilities.

1. It must be capable of enough variability to account for a wide variety of hereditary traits.
2. It must be able to reproduce itself so exactly that the same hereditary traits are transmitted each generation.
3. It must be capable of changing slightly over time and thus produce changes in hereditary traits.
4. It must be able to direct the synthesis of all the different kinds of molecules that participate in the development and functioning of an organism.

DNA, indeed, satisfies the requirements as the genetic material.

Chromosomes are composed chiefly of long strands of the nucleic acid called deoxyribonucleic acid (DNA). The chemical structure of the DNA molecules constitutes a coded message specifying the structure of all the proteins that the body will manufacture during its lifetime. The instruction for each protein has its own location (locus) on a particular chromosome. All life is assembled by one kind of genetic code carried on molecules of DNA and translated into action by ribonucleic acid (RNA). The first scientists who studied the nature of genes assumed that genes were proteins. However, as a result of some landmark research, nucleic acids gradually became accepted as the genetic material.

DNA contains four kinds of nitrogen-containing molecules called bases: adenine, cytosine, guanine, and thymine. In RNA, another base, uracil, replaces thymine. These bases bond with each other in precisely determined pairs. The arrangement of the bases in nucleic acids is vital to their functioning as the hereditary substance.

DNA is a long chainlike molecule with connecting links. The shape of DNA is best explained by the double helix model proposed by Watson and Crick. Watson and Crick's double helix model imposed physical limits on the dimension of the DNA structure. The double helix model demonstrates that only certain bases bond with each other. The sequence of bases on one chain is fixed by the sequence of bases on the other chain. DNA satisfies the requirements of the genetic material because (1) it is capable of variability while, at the same time, it reproduces itself so exactly that the same hereditary traits are transmitted each generation and (2) it is capable of directing the synthesis of all the different kinds of molecules that participate in the development and functioning of an organism.

Bibliography

Avery, O., MacLeod, C., and McCarty, M. 1944. Studies on the chemical nature of the substance inducing transformation of pneumococcal types. *Journal of Experimental Medicine* 79:137.

Crick, F., Barnett, L., Brenner, S., and Watts-Tobin, R. 1961. General nature of the genetic code for proteins. *Nature* 192:1227-32.

Griffith, F. 1923. The significance of pneumococcal types. *Journal of Hygiene* 27:113-59.

Goldstein, P. 1967. *Genetics is easy.* New York: Viking Press.

Hershey, A., and Chase, M. 1952. Independent functions of viral protein and nucleic acid in growth of bacteriophage. *Journal of General Physiology* 36:39-56.

Kornberg, A. 1960. Biological synthesis of deoxyribonucleic acid. *Science* 131:1503-8.

Levene, P., and Bass, L. 1931. *Nucleic acids.* New York: Chemical Catalog Co.

Sciulli, P. 1978. *Introduction to Mendelian genetics and gene action.* Minneapolis: Burgess.

Watson, J. 1968. *The double helix.* New York: Atheneum.

_____. 1970. *The molecular biology of the gene,* 2nd ed. Menlo Park, Calif.: Benjamin.

Wilkins, M. 1963. Molecular configuration of nucleic acids. *Science* 140:941-50.

Chapter 7

Gene Action

This chapter discusses the manner in which DNA controls the genetic code. Many genes are responsible for the production of enzymes, with one specific gene producing one specific enzyme. This concept is referred to as the one gene-one polypeptide concept. This general concept is true for all organisms, including humans.

Besides having the vital trait of being able to duplicate itself, DNA can also make another molecule, RNA (ribonucleic acid). RNA exists in three forms, each of which has its own function in hereditary transmission. The discovery of the ways in which DNA in the chromosome translates its hereditary messages into the structure of proteins is one of the outstanding achievements of molecular biology. This process is often called the transcription function of DNA. The nature of the transcription process and the genetic code are discussed.

Genes can undergo chemical changes, that is, they can mutate. The specific nature of gene mutations and chromosomal aberrations are discussed. As an example of a mutation we discuss sickle-cell anemia. We also discuss sex determination and the inheritance of X-linked traits, using color blindness as an example.

Genetic Information

DNA carries the genetic code, that is, messages controlling which traits will be expressed. The information in the genetic code must somehow be converted into action to produce a trait. Genetic material in interaction with the environment controls and produces traits (that is, controls the phenotype). A number of steps must take place for the genetic material to cause the expression of a trait.

Beadle and Tatum (1941), working with the mold *Neurospora*, concluded that many genes are primarily responsible for the production of enzymes, with one specific gene producing one specific enzyme. This concept is usually referred to as the one gene-one enzyme concept, or more recently the one gene-one polypeptide concept (a polypeptide is a simple nonprotein combination of several amino acids). This concept encompasses the following points: (1) biochemical pathways in organisms can be subdivided into separate steps, (2) each step is governed by the action of a specific enzyme, (3) each enzyme is controlled by a gene, and (4) the change in a gene may result in the change of an enzyme and thus change the way a single step of the pathway is carried out. The change in genes is a type of mutation. This general concept of one gene-one enzyme is true not only for the mold *Neurospora* but also for all other organisms, including humans. Genetic material thus seems to be intimately associated with protein production.

RNA

Besides being able to replicate itself, DNA can also make another nucleic acid, ribonucleic acid (RNA), which also has linearly arranged bases. DNA is found primarily in the cell nucleus—specifically the chromosomes. RNA, however, is produced in the nucleus and transplanted to the cytoplasm. In contrast to DNA, RNA forms a single rather than a double strand. One of the DNA bases, thymine (T), is replaced by uracil (U), in RNA (Figure 7-1). Other than these differences, RNA can be coded with a base sequence complementary to one of the pair of strands of a specific DNA molecule. All RNA is formed in the cell nucleus, with DNA serving as a pattern, or template. RNA exists in three forms: messenger RNA (mRNA), transfer RNA (tRNA), and ribosomal RNA (rRNA). The manufacture of mRNA by DNA is called **transcription**. Messenger RNA passes out of the nucleus to the **ribosomes** (granules in the cytoplasm, composed of rRNA and protein, where proteins are assembled) with the coded genetic message. The complex of several ribosomes plus attached mRNA is called a **polysome**. The segment of DNA coding the mRNA of a polysome constitutes a gene.

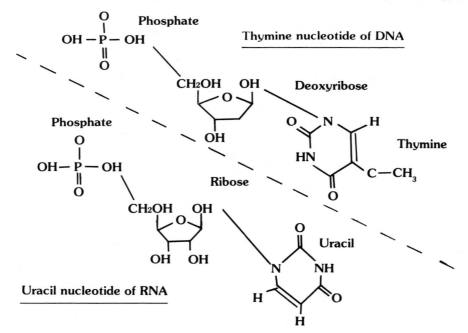

Figure 7-1. Thymine-containing nucleotide of DNA compared to uracil-containing nucleotide of RNA.

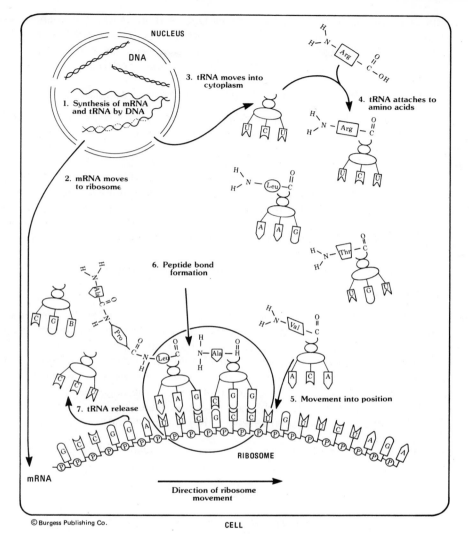

NUCLEUS

DNA

3. tRNA moves into
cytoplasm

1. Synthesis of mRNA
and tRNA by DNA

4. tRNA attaches to
amino acids

2. mRNA moves
to ribosome

6. Peptide bond
formation

5. Movement into position

7. tRNA release

RIBOSOME

mRNA

Direction of ribosome
movement

© Burgess Publishing Co.

CELL

Figure 7-2. Protein synthesis in the cell.

Messenger RNA enters the cytoplasm of the cell from the nucleus and attaches to the surface of a ribosome. The help of tRNA is now required (Figure 7-2). There are more than 26 different kinds of tRNA. Each tRNA has an attachment site specific for one of the 26 different amino acids. The tRNA is responsible for transporting amino acids to the ribosomes. Each mRNA has a series of **codons** (groups of three nucleotides) that can bond temporarily with the anticodon (the complement of an mRNA codon) of a tRNA molecule. The ribosomes travel along the coded mRNA, collecting charged tRNA and its attached amino acids. The anticodon of each tRNA is attracted to the corresponding codon of the mRNA so that each amino acid is brought to the proper position. The amino acids are thus fitted together in a sequence that was predetermined by the original DNA strand. When the amino acids are moved into their proper position, they are joined together by peptide bonds (Figure 7-2). The ribosomes discharge completed peptides, tRNA without amino acids, and mRNA. Through this activity, the coded message from the nuclear DNA is deciphered to produce proteins that compose the body.

The functions of the three kinds of RNA can be summarized as follows:

1. mRNA. Messenger RNA carries a message, that is, the code it has obtained from DNA for the structure of a protein. Proteins are assembled from amino acids through the process of translation of information coded in mRNA.

2. tRNA. Transfer RNA obtains amino acids and transfers them to the mRNA. Transfer RNA carries and transfers the proper amino acid (the one coded for by the DNA and whose message is carried by mRNA) because tRNA has a code complementary to the mRNA. Each tRNA carries one amino acid and is transferred to the site on mRNA for which it has the complementary code. The transfer process occurs on specific cellular structures, the ribosomes. Ribosomes hold the mRNA and the tRNA and allow the process of protein synthesis to occur.

3. rRNA. Ribosomal RNA is a constituent part of the ribosomes.

The Genetic Code

The discovery of the ways in which the nucleotide sequence in the DNA of the chromosome is translated into the sequence of amino acids in a protein is one of the outstanding achievements of molecular biology. The process is often called the transcription function of DNA to distinguish it from the duplication function in which DNA replicates itself (Figure 7-3).

A close correlation exists between the amount of protein synthesis that takes place and the amount of RNA present. It has been suggested that perhaps messages are transferred from DNA in the chromosomes to smaller RNA molecules that leave the nucleus and migrate into the cytoplasm. Perhaps RNA (that is, "messenger" RNA), carries the message from the DNA "blueprints" to the cell itself.

To function in heredity, the DNA molecule must have a way of storing information. The "blueprint" for a specific protein is a specific sequence of nucleotide bases in the DNA

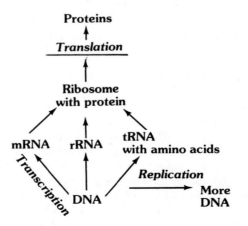

Figure 7-3. Relationship of nucleic acids to protein synthesis.

Table 7-1. The Genetic Code

First Letter	Second Letter				Third Letter
	U	C	A	G	
U[a]	phe[b]	ser	tyr	cys	U
	phe	ser	tyr	cys	C
	leu	ser	(1)*[c]	(3)*	A
	leu	ser	(2)*	trp	G
C	leu	pro	his	arg	U
	leu	pro	his	arg	C
	leu	pro	gln	arg	A
	leu	pro	gln	arg	G
A	ile	thr	asn	ser	U
	ile	thr	asn	ser	C
	ile	thr	lys	arg	A
	met	thr	lys	arg	G
G	val	ala	asp	gly	U
	val	ala	asp	gly	C
	val	ala	glu	gly	A
	val	ala	glu	gly	G

[a] The letters U, C, A, and G represent bases on mRNA. For example, the interaction of the codon UUU (first letter, second letter, third letter) of mRNA with the corresponding anticodon (AAA) of tRNA brings the amino acid called phenylalanine into position in a polypeptide chain because the tRNA that has the anticodon AAA carries phenylalanine.

[b] Phe is the abbreviation for the amino acid phenylalanine. For the names of other amino acids abbreviated here, see Table 6-1 (p. 63).

[c] (1)*, (2)*, and (3)* are stop codes, that is, they stop protein synthesis.

Adapted from P. Sciulli, *An Introduction to Mendelian Genetics and Gene Action*, p. 53. Burgess Publishing Company,© 1978.

molecule located in the cell nucleus. As has been stressed, however, actual protein synthesis in which specific amino acids become joined together in a specific sequence occurs outside the nucleus. DNA may be visualized as a set of coded instructions embodied in the sequence of its bases (adenine, cytosine, guanine, and thymine) that specifies the sequence of amino acids to be joined together to form a polypeptide chain. The question is, how does DNA with only these four bases code for a variety of proteins? Once the structure of the DNA molecule was known, it was suggested that what is called a "three-letter, nonoverlapping code" was sufficient as a genetic code. A "three-letter" code means that nucleotides, taken in groups of three called triplets or codons, can provide 64 (4 × 4 × 4) different combinations. A codon specifies one of 26 different amino acids, which in turn serve as the building blocks of proteins. For example, the DNA codon AAA specifies the amino acid phenylalanine through its mRNA codon UUU (Table 7-1). Because 64 specific triplet sites provide for more than the required 26 separate results, several codons must specify the same amino acid. More than one codon can carry the same message, that is, more than one codon may code for the same amino acid. Table 7-1 shows, for example, that both the codons UUU and UUC on mRNA code for phenylalanine. Codes in which different codons contain the same message are termed degenerate codes.

The arrangement for "reading" the code is important. For example, codons might or might not overlap each other in translating their message (Figure 7-4). A number of investigations have shown that a change in the nucleotides in a gene affects only one protein and only one amino acid in the protein, suggesting that the code is read in a nonoverlapping manner. That the code is nonoverlapping means that these codons have a beginning and an end. The RNA codons UAA, UAG, and UGA code for no amino acid, but function instead to terminate protein synthesis on the mRNA (Table 7-1).

Role of Gene Action in Protein Formation

The sequence of events by which the genetic code is translated into the formation of protein molecules (Figure 7-5) can be summarized in 14 steps (modified from Goldstein, 1967:228-30).

1. The nucleus directs all the manufacturing processes of the cell. The chromosomes contain many DNA "blueprints" giving coded instructions for the synthesis of a specific substance.
2. Certain DNA "blueprints" are copied when the chromosomes are actively dictating cell activities.
3. During the copying process, active DNA molecules serve as molds against which mRNA molecules are built. Information coded in the DNA "blueprint" is transferred to the mRNA.
4. The mRNA separates from the DNA model on which it was copied, migrates out of the nucleus, and attaches itself to a group of ribosomes somewhere in the cell.
5. The mRNA associated with rRNA is ready to serve as a template for protein synthesis.
6. The raw materials to be organized are the amino acids, which must be hooked together in the proper order to create a particular protein.
7. Amino acids must be activated before they can be joined together into the protein chains. Amino acids are activated in the cytoplasm under the influence of a special enzyme.
8. An activated amino acid can be picked up by a molecule of tRNA, thereby being attached to one end of the tRNA molecule. Each kind of tRNA has its own chemical shape and carries its own kind of amino acid. There must be at least 26 different kinds of tRNAs to transport the 26 kinds of amino acids.
9. The tRNAs act as vehicles that carry activated amino acids to places where they are needed.
10. All kinds of tRNAs approach the ribosomes to which a molecule of mRNA is fixed. They are attracted to empty sites on the mRNA, but they can only fit into those sites having the proper shape.

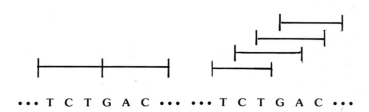

··· T C T G A C ··· ··· T C T G A C ···

Figure 7-4. Nonoverlapping and overlapping codons. Evidence suggests that messages are read as if the codons are nonoverlapping.

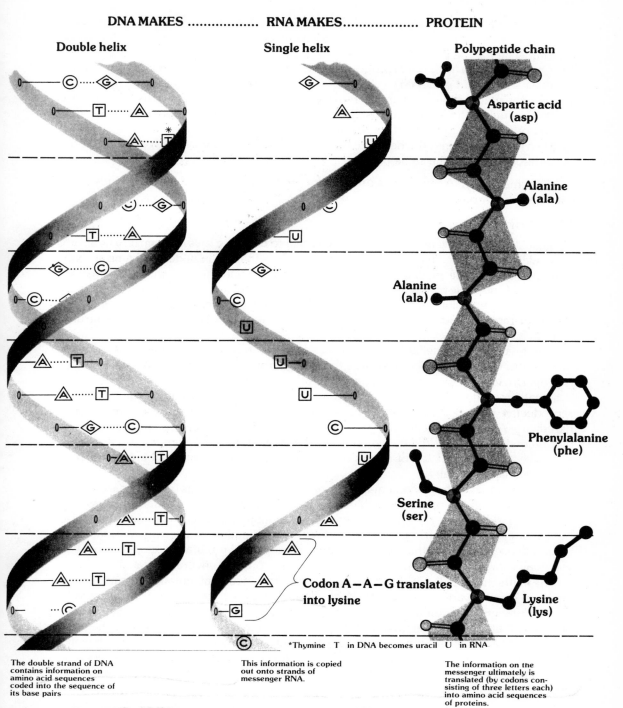

DNA MAKES .... RNA MAKES.................. PROTEIN

Double helix

Single helix

Polypeptide chain

Aspartic acid
(asp)

Alanine
(ala)

Alanine
(ala)

Phenylalanine
(phe)

Serine
(ser)

Codon A — A — G translates
into lysine

Lysine
(lys)

*Thymine T in DNA becomes uracil U in RNA

The double strand of DNA contains information on amino acid sequences coded into the sequence of its base pairs

This information is copied out onto strands of messenger RNA.

The information on the messenger ultimately is translated (by codons consisting of three letters each) into amino acid sequences of proteins.

Figure 7-5. Summary of protein synthesis.

11. The different tRNAs lining up along the mRNA chain must be in the order dictated by the instructions on the mRNA. This arrangement places the amino acids in the correct sequence for the particular protein being synthesized.
12. Once the amino acids are in proper sequence, they can bond together into long, complex chains that form proteins.
13. The completed protein separates from the ribosome complex and the tRNAs are released as they unload their amino acids. Each tRNA is now free to escort another amino acid of the proper kind to another appropriate site.
14. The mRNA remains attached to ribosomes. mRNA is repeatedly used to model molecule after molecule of the same protein.

In this manner DNA sets the basic pattern for protein synthesis, and the three kinds of RNA cooperate to carry out the pattern.

Mutation

Because it is an organic molecule, a gene is subject to the same laws of chemistry as all other molecules. One of the characteristics of a molecule is that it can undergo chemical change (mutation). The type of change depends on the conditions under which the change is occurring. A molecule may change in different directions at different times. Some changes that occur may be reversible, and because molecules differ in stability, some types change more readily or more frequently than others. These characteristics of molecules are also true for genes.

A mutation can be detected only if it causes a change from normal in an organism. The first mutation to receive intensive study was the change from red to white in the eye color of the fruit fly, *Drosophila*. Mutations may occur in body (somatic) cells or in the reproductive cells. A somatic mutation dies with the organism and does not affect heredity. A mutation in the reproductive cells, however, may be passed to the next generation, and the change may be hereditary. An inherited gene change may not be immediately evident, because it may be that of a recessive allele masked by the unchanged dominant allele. Most mutations are, in fact, recessive. However, a pair of recessive mutant genes may eventually be expressed in a homozygous individual.

With confirmation from mathematical testing, natural selection was unequivocally assigned the role of evolution's prime agent. Mutation was accorded a supplementary role. Although mutation could no longer be given full credit for adaptations witnessed in the natural world and hence for evolutionary change, research showed that mutation supplied the raw material for these changes. Without the new opportunities provided by mutation, populations would eventually stagnate and become unable to adapt to constant environmental change.

The mathematician R. Fisher stated in 1930 that the function of mutation is to maintain the stock of genetic variance at a high level. Nevertheless, laboratory work has shown that many mutations are detrimental and most drastic mutations are lethal. The fact remains, however, that although most big changes in an organism are often fatal, small changes or adjustments may be an improvement. A few mutations generally may prove beneficial. Mathematicians provided the answer to the next question to be resolved, that is, how can a rare, tiny, beneficial change spread through a population? Although harmful mutations may occur, vanish, and reappear in a species with predictable frequency, the mutations that ultimately spread throughout the species and become part of its normal genetic composition are beneficial. Mutations provide the population with the flexibility to adapt to altered conditions. It is this necessary flexibility that is the key to the evolutionary process—this slightly imperfect hereditary machinery that allows life to continue.

Some mutations are the result of mistakes at some point in the DNA molecule; these are the so-called point mutations. Point mutations may result from mistakes in the DNA replication process. Once alteration has occurred, it is the basis for the replication of further DNA with the same mistake.

Sickle-Cell Anemia. As an example of a mutation we discuss sickle-cell anemia, first discovered in 1910 by James B. Herrick (see Chapter 27 for a discussion of the etiology and adaptive nature of sickle-cell anemia). James Neel explained the mode of inheritance of sickle-cell anemia in 1949. Neel found that there were two allelic forms of the gene for hemoglobin production: gene A causes production of normal hemoglobin A; gene S causes production of sickle-cell hemoglobin S.

There are three possible genotypes:

1. *AA*—homozygous normal.
2. *AS*—heterozygous state, the normal gene is inherited from one parent, the sickle-cell gene from the other parent.
3. *SS*—the homozygous sickle-cell state in which the sickle-cell is inherited from both parents.

People with the genotype AA are normal; their red blood cells do not sickle. People of genotype SS suffer from sickle-cell anemia, their corpuscles sickle, and they may die early in life. The genotype AS carries the sickle-cell trait; individuals with this genotype can pass an S allele to their children.

In the same year that Neel demonstrated the mode of inheritance of sickle-cell anemia, Linus Pauling and a group of scientists demonstrated an electrical difference between the types of hemoglobin. Hemoglobin from a person with the sickle-cell trait (genotype AS) can be separated into two types by a method called electrophoresis. One type of the hemoglobin is identical with hemoglobin A and the other type is identical with hemoglobin S. This is to be expected if each gene synthesizes its own product. The normal allele produces hemoglobin A, the mutated allele synthesizes hemoglobin S.

The actual chemical difference between the two types of hemoglobin was demonstrated by Vernon M. Ingram (1956, 1958, 1961). Ingram showed that in the beta chain of 146 amino acids composing part of the protein of the hemoglobin molecule, the two hemoglobins differed in exactly one amino acid. In hemoglobin S, valine has replaced a glutamic acid in a fragment of the normal hemoglobin A (Figure 7-6). Mutation of allele A to allele S caused a change in the

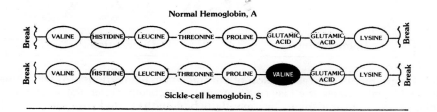

Figure 7-6. Normal and sickle-cell hemoglobins. The substitution of valine for glutamic acid at the place shown causes sickle-cell hemoglobin.

ability of a gene. The single altered amino acid makes a difference in the hemoglobin's functional ability and migration in an electrophoretic field.

Chromosomal Alterations. Chromosomal alterations include changes in chromosome number as well as in the structure of individual chromosomes. A chromosomal abnormality is a heritable change that may occur spontaneously or be induced artificially by exposure to mutagenic agents. Structural changes in chromosomes result from breakage and reunion in various ways that give new arrangements of genes outside the scope of recombination following crossing over at meiosis. The types of structural alterations include deletion, translocation, inversion, and duplication of a segment (Figure 7-7).

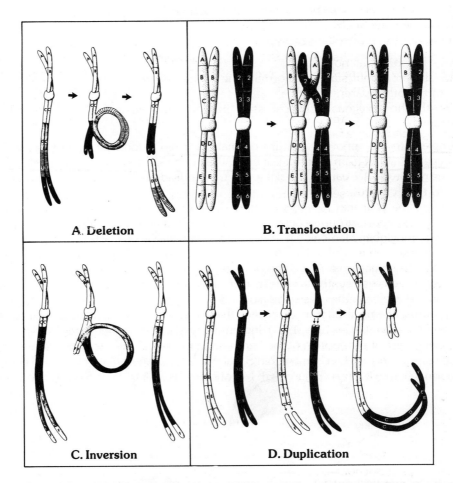

A. Deletion

B. Translocation

C. Inversion

D. Duplication

Figure 7-7. Diagrammatic representation of chromosomal aberrations. (A) Deletions occur when terminal breaks cause the loss of a segment of a chromosome. (B) Translocations occur when parts of chromosomes become detached and reunited with other non-homologous chromosomes. (C) Inversions occur when parts of chromosomes become detached and reinstated in such a way that the genes are in reverse order. (D) Duplications represent additions of chromosome parts arranged in such a way that segments are longitudinally repeated.

There are also changes in chromosomal number. The term **polyploidy** refers to a situation where the chromosomal number is greater than that in the diploid state (2N) but contains a complete haploid set (N). A polyploid with three sets (3N) of chromosomes is called a triploid, with four sets (4N) of chromosomes it is called a tetraploid. In humans, which have a diploid chromosomal number of 46, the 3N chromosomal number would be 69 and the 4N number would be 92. Although polyploidy is common and advantageous in some plants, it is highly detrimental in humans and other mammals.

Sex Determination

An individual's sex is determined by the combination of the so-called sex chromosomes. The total number of human chromosomes in a typical body cell is 46 (Figure 7-8), including 44 autosomes and two sex chromosomes. Sex chromosomes are of two identifiable types, the X chromosome and the Y chromosome. In the human, 44 autosomes plus an XX combination of sex chromosomes results in a normal female; 44 autosomes plus an XY combination results in a normal male (Figure 7-9). Eggs produced by the female have 22 autosomes plus an X chromosome. Sperm produced by the male have 22 autosomes plus either an X or Y chromosome. Eggs fertilized by sperm having Y chromosomes develop into males (22 + X from mother + 22 + Y from father = 44 + XY, a male), and eggs fertilized by sperm having X chromosomes become females (22 + X from mother + 22 + X from father = 44 + XX, a female).

Deviations from the normal number of chromosomes can lead to abnormalities in physiology, development, and behavior. About once in each 400 male births an additional X chromosome appears with the normal XY pattern (44 + XXY). This results in a male with altered and secondary sexual traits, a condition called Klinefelter syndrome (Table 7-2). If a female lacks an X chromosome, a situation occurring in about one in every 3,500 births, she manifests a pattern of abnormalities known as Turner syndrome (Table 7-3). The absence of one X chromosome produces a somatic cell chromosome number of 45 (44 + XO) instead of the normal 46.

Besides determining sex, the X and Y chromosomes differ in structure and in composition of genes. Genes on the X chromosome (traditionally called sex-linked genes, but more specifically called X-linked genes) are generally unmatched by corresponding alleles on the Y chromosome in humans. The tiny Y chromosome carries little known genetic information apart from gender determination, but the X chromosome carries perhaps 3,000 different loci. Because female mammals carry two X chromosomes, they may be homozygous or heterozygous for any one of these genes. Males, however, carry only one X chromosome, with no corresponding loci on the Y chromosome. In human males, therefore, genes on the X chromosome can express themselves without influence from alleles on the Y chromosome. Even recessive genes on the X chromosome are free to express themselves in the human male in the absence of any corresponding dominant alleles on the Y chromosome.

The well-known genes that have been identified as occurring on the X chromosome have nothing directly to do with sex determination. Examples are hemophilia (a condition in which the blood fails to clot normally), red and green color blindness, and G6PD deficiency (the latter provides protection from malaria and is discussed in Chapter 27). We know little about the Y chromosome's influence on inheritance in the male, but genes carried on the Y chromosome do in some way affect the development of male traits. All individuals without the Y chromosome (such as genotypes XX or XO) are female. Genes on the Y chromosome (Y-linked genes) determine traits that influence male growth and development to the extent that the sexes are demonstrably different (dimorphic). Traits determined by Y-linked genes are

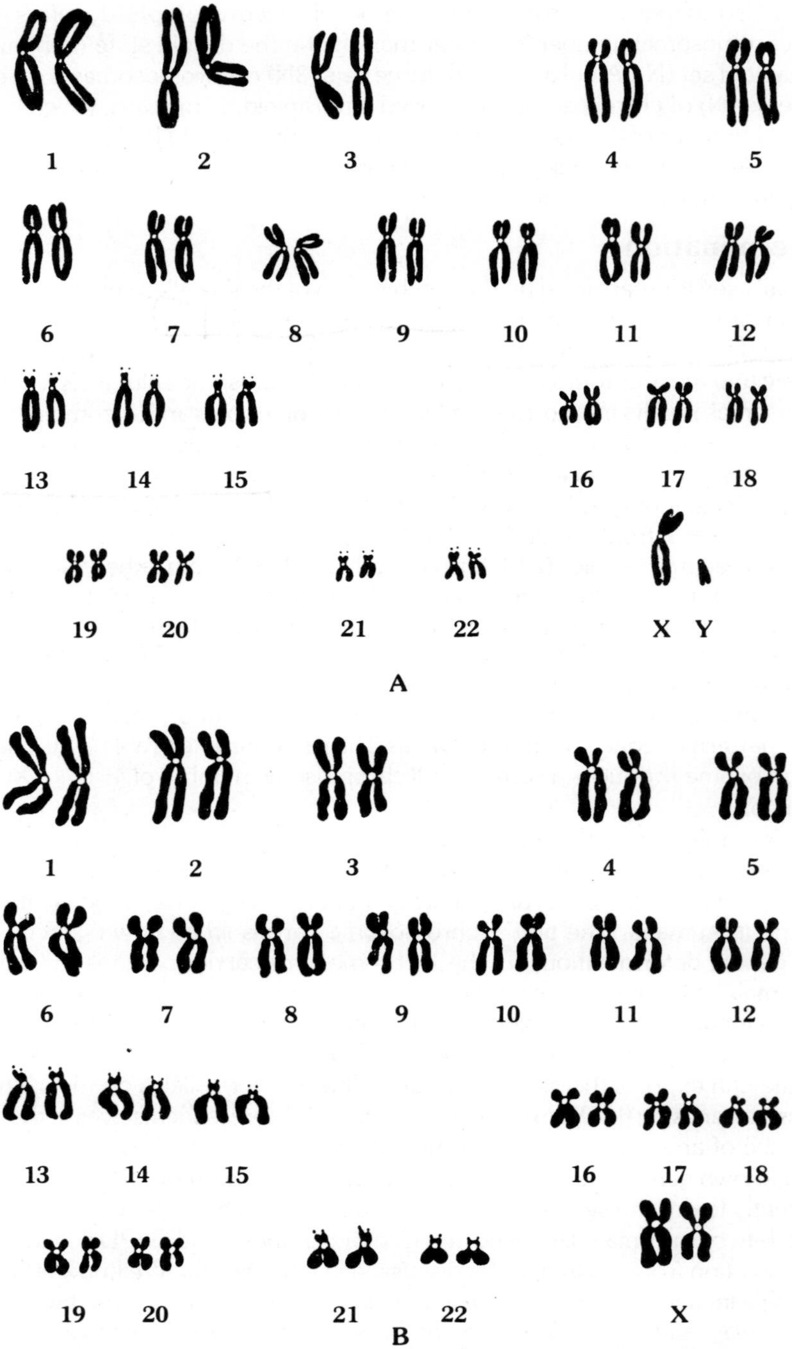

Figure 7-8. Autosomes and sex chromosomes in normal male and female. (A) Normal male: 44 autosomes (22 pairs) and *XY* sex chromosomes. (B) Normal female: 44 autosomes (22 pairs) and *XX* sex chromosomes.

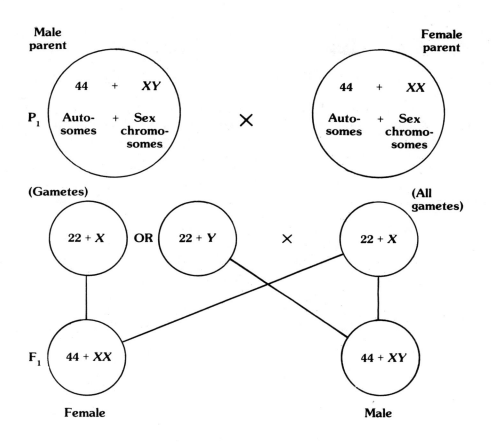

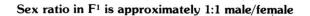

Sex ratio in F¹ is approximately 1:1 male/female

Figure 7-9. Sex determination by sex chromosomes in the human.

Table 7-2. Klinefelter Syndrome

Sex chromosomes	*XXY*
Phenotype	Male
Number of autosomes (haploid)	22
Somatic chromosome number	47
Fertility	Negative

Table 7-3. Turner Syndrome

Sex chromosomes	*X*
Phenotype	Female
Number of autosomes (haploid)	22
Somatic chromosome number	45
Fertility	Negative

called **holandric** traits. To date only one human trait seems definitely holandric. This trait is hairy pinnae, the tendency of fairly long hair to grow from the outer rim of the external ear (pinna).

X-linked genes become significant when harmful recessive alleles are in question. Heterozygosity in general provides a protection against such alleles. As long as the individual carries a normal allele in addition to the detrimental recessive one, that individual will be phenotypically normal. With regard to X-linked genes, female heterozygotes have this protection, but males do not, for they carry only one X chromosome; whatever genes are present on that X chromosome must be expressed.

Let us use red-green color blindness to illustrate the inheritance of a recessive, X-linked gene. If a woman carries the abnormal allele coding for red-green color blindness (X^c)[1] along with the normal allele (X^C) she will have normal color vision, because the normal allele is dominant. All her sons, however, have a 50-50 chance of inheriting from her the X chromosome with the abnormal allele. If they do inherit the abnormal allele, they will be color blind, because this recessive allele is the only allele at that locus. None of her daughters will show color blindness as long as their father has normal color vision (thus transmitting to them an X chromosome bearing the normal allele). Nevertheless, they still have a 50-50 chance of carrying the recessive allele and transmitting it to their offspring (Figure 7-10).

[1]The X denotes the X chromosome. The lowercase c denotes the allele for red-green color blindness. The allele for normal vision is denoted by X^C.

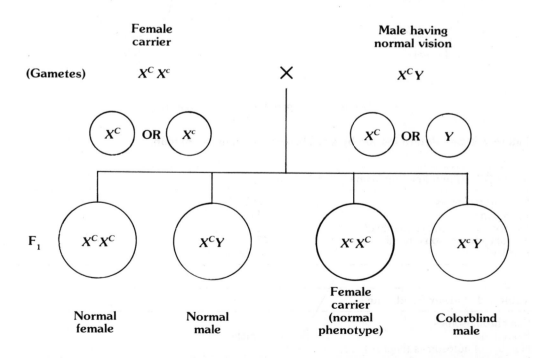

Figure 7-10. Inheritance of an X-linked trait, red-green color blindness, from a female carrier and a male who has normal color vision.

Anthropologists and Genetics

Genetic studies are of three main types: (1) Transmission genetics is the study of the mechanisms by which genes reproduce, segregate, and recombine, and of their spatial arrangement on the chromosomes. (2) Physiological genetics studies the causal relations between genes and the specific characters that arise in growth and development of the individual and how genes act as regulators of the life processes. (3) Population genetics studies how genes are distributed in populations, and is concerned with forces such as mutation and natural selection that tend to change the array of hereditary variety. Population genetics analyzes the process by which evolution occurs.

An important part of the study of human genetics is the understanding of genetic variability within human populations. The anthropologist studies the relationship of this variability to evolution. Anthropologists want to know why a certain allele has a high frequency in one population and a low frequency in another. Anthropologists are interested in the adaptive efficiency of a population to survive in its environment.

DNA is the genetic material that programs hereditary characteristics. DNA specifies the amino acid sequence in the biosynthesis of polypeptide chains that compose the primary constituents of proteins. This process is accomplished by DNA making mRNA. When mRNA passes into the cytoplasm, it directs the activity of tRNA at the cellular sites of protein synthesis, the ribosomes. A third RNA, rRNA, is a constituent part of the ribosomes. DNA specifications are coded in triplet sequences of nucleotides (called codons) that specify particular amino acids and form the genetic code.

Because it is an organic molecule, a gene is subjected to the same laws of chemistry as other molecules. One of the characteristics of a molecule is that it can undergo chemical change to become mutated. Most mutations are recessive. Although most major changes in an organism are often fatal, small changes or adjustments may be an improvement. A few mutations generally may prove beneficial.

A number of chromosomal aberrations may occur, including a change in chromosomal number as well as in the structure of the individual chromosome. Most such changes cause major alterations.

An individual's sex is determined by the combination of X and Y chromosomes. In the human, a chromosomal complement of 44 autosomes + XX is a female and a complement of 44 autosomes + XY is a male. Many traits are X-linked, that is, have a pattern of inheritance related to genes on the X chromosome.

Bibliography

Beadle, G. 1959. Genes and chemical reactions in *Neurospora. Science* 129:1711-15.

Beadle, G., and Tatum, E. 1941. Genetic control of biochemical reaction in *Neurospora. Proceedings of the National Academy of Sciences* 27:499-506.

Fisher, R. 1930. *The genetical theory of natural selection.* Oxford: Clarendon Press.

Goldstein, P. 1967. *Genetics is easy.* New York: Viking Press.

Ingram, V. 1956. A specific difference between the globins of normal human and sickle cell anemia haemoglobin. *Nature* 178:792.

_____. 1958. Abnormal human haemoglobins. I. The comparison of normal human and sickle-cell haemoglobins by "fingerprinting." *Biochimica et Biophysica Acta* 28:539.

_____. 1963. *The hemoglobins in genetics and evolution.* New York: Columbia University Press.

Markert, C., Shaklee, J., and Whitt, C. 1975. Evolution of a gene. *Science* 189:102-14.

Peters, J., ed. 1959. *Classic papers in genetics.* Englewood Cliffs, N.J.: Prentice-Hall.

Pauling, L., Itano, H., Singer, S., and Wells, I. 1949. Sickle cell anemia, a molecular disease. *Science* 110:543.

Sciulli, P. 1978. *An introduction to Mendelian genetics and gene action.* Minneapolis: Burgess.

Chapter 8

Evolutionary Theory: The Modern Synthesis

Population genetics is the focal point of the synthetic theory of evolution. The evolutionary process is the culmination of mutation, recombination and genetic drift, natural selection, and gene flow. This chapter discusses the mechanics of these four processes and the various levels of evolutionary change, that is, microevolution, macroevolution, megaevolution, and speciation.

Morphological Evidence

Evolution is defined as the change in gene frequency over time. It is, however, difficult to measure gene frequency changes directly between ancestral and descendant populations. This is particularly true when one studies the fossil record, whose story is written primarily in its skeletal remains. Evolution, as viewed in the fossil record, is primarily based on morphological changes through time. **Morphology** is the study of the form of the organism or of any of its parts. Analyses of morphological similarities and differences have been and always will be a basic part of evolutionary studies.

John Buettner-Janusch (1973) has noted that the amount of attention researchers gave to major problems in evolutionary biology changed as the theory of evolution became established. Once established that evolution occurred, the phylogenies of various plants and animals had to be determined. Today the process of speciation is the major concern.

If evolution has occurred, there must be observable proof of this process. There should be observable similarities among those species that have diverged from a common ancestor, for example. Nineteenth-century scientists sought proof of evolution in comparative anatomy, comparative embryology, paleontology, and biogeography. Twentieth-century scientists have added information from genetics, comparative biochemistry, molecular genetics, and ethology.

Comparative anatomy (the study of the organs, tissues, and systems of related groups) has revealed many fundamental structural similarities and traditionally presented some of the strongest evidence supporting organic evolution. Because the skeletal system, and especially the teeth, most commonly become fossilized, comparisons between living and extinct species are often based on the comparative anatomy of this system.

Figure 8-1 shows the skeletal system of five vertebrate animals. Although their posture and general appearance differ, all the skeletons are constructed along the same plan: skull, spinal column, shoulder girdle, hip girdle, and the limbs. The degree of similarity is striking when we note that *Seymouria* has been extinct for more than 230 million years.

Equivalent structures derived from a common genetic ancestor are called homologous structures. Each of the forelimbs in Figure 8-2 is adapted to a particular function, reflecting in terms of size and shape an adaptation to a particular life-style. Despite the wide range of functional adaptation, however, precisely the same bones occur in each forelimb.

All vertebrates begin life as a fertilized egg (zygote). Comparison of vertebrate embryos at equivalent stages of development reveals strong resemblances among the embryos during early formation. Using the human embryo as an example of comparative embryology, we note that at 8 weeks the human embryo has gill slits, a rudimentary tail, and circulatory system more similar to that of a fish than to the human adult. Such traits are lost or greatly modified during the later stages of development.

The presence of such sequences led to overgeneralizations such as the statement that ontogeny recapitulates phylogeny. The theory of recapitulation—the idea that the developmental stages of an organism repeat events of its evolutionary history—is an oversimplification. Strict application of the theory of recapitulation to all events of embryonic development is impossible. It seems likely, however, that similarities in vertebrate development reflect the retention of genetic material from an ancestral evolutionary line.

With the establishment of genetics and genetic concepts, research focused on evolutionary rates and the process of adaptation. Today the synthetic theory of evolution, as it is called, states that evolution acts on variable life forms through the process of adaptation and the action of natural selection. The synthetic theory of evolution draws its information from as many scientific branches of knowledge as are applicable.

Mechanisms of Evolution

The evolutionary process results from the action of **mutation, recombination, genetic drift, natural selection,** and **gene flow** (Figure 8-3). An essential feature of any "successful" population is population variability. Mutation is the exclusive supplier of new and different genetic material. Once mutation supplies the raw goods to the population, recombination distributes them. Recombination spreads mutant (new) genes throughout the population and develops new genetic combinations from old genotypes.

Recombination. New genetic combinations arise from an existing gene pool by the process of recombination. Recombination is the distribution vehicle for genes and gene combinations; it is the means whereby a population maintains genetic variability. One of the long-range advantages of sexual reproduction is that it produces genetic variability within a population by mixing genes of both parents. This process is accomplished through meiosis following fertilization.

Population variability (the infinite variety of possible genetic combinations) is the stuff of which evolution is made. Recombination enhances the effects of mutation by assembling a broad spectrum of gene combinations upon which natural selection acts. Recombination provides the genetic variability that is worked upon by the various forces producing evolutionary change.

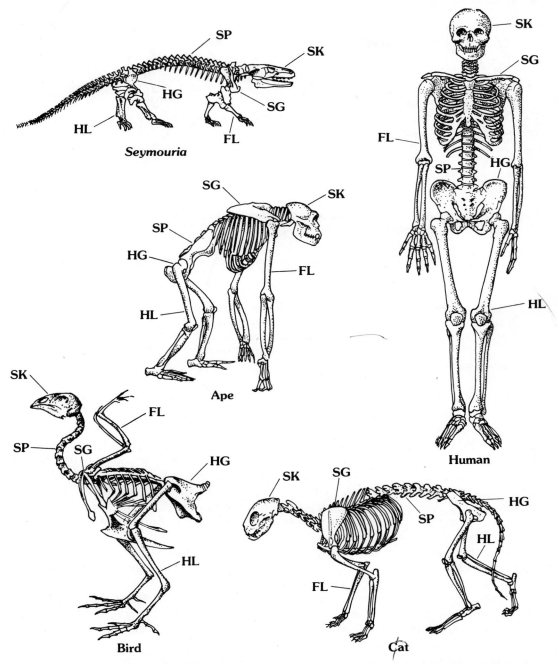

Figure 8-1. Comparative skeletal anatomy of vertebrates. SK—skull; SG—shoulder girdle; SP—spine; HG—hip girdle; FL—forelimb; HL—hind limb. The two girdles are composed of several bones and are important because they serve to connect the limbs to the axial skeleton and provide both support and freedom of movement for the appendages.

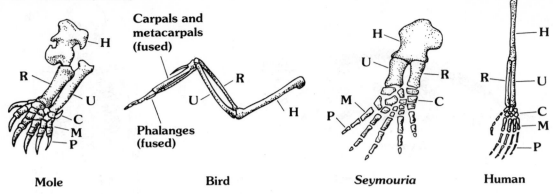

Figure 8-2. Homologous structures in vertebrate forelimbs. H—humerus; U—ulna; R—radius; C—carpals; MC—metacarpals; P—phalanges.

Savage (1969:45) describes the importance of recombination to the evolutionary process as follows:

> A single mutational change may be lost or passed on without great impact on a population, but if its effect is modified and enhanced by recombination an unending contribution to variation is begun. Variation is the raw material for evolutionary change; recombination is its principal source. Mutation alone has relatively little effect on variation without the pervasive impact of recombination.

What is the significance of the variability produced by recombination? Because most environments continually change (although at varying rates), the more variable the population, the greater its long-term chances for survival. The more closely the organism is adapted to the environment, the more specialized it is, the lesser its chances for survival if the environment changes. A good example is the koala bear, whose sole source of nutrition is eucalyptus leaves. These leaves are awful to the human taste. They are quite oily and tough. In connection with my research on Indian monkeys, I ate such leaves to see why the monkeys avoided them. If the leaves tasted as awful to the monkeys as they did to me, I understand. The eucalyptus connoisseur, the koala bear, definitely would disagree. Should something destroy the eucalyptus trees, koala bears would become extinct immediately. They are unable to digest another food source adequately. Under carefully controlled circumstances the koala bear is well adapted to its environment. No other animal is likely to outcompete the koala bear by making better use of its specialized food niche. In contrast to the koala bear *Homo sapiens* is a variable creature. This variability has enabled us to inhabit a great variety of climatic niches and to consume a great variety of foods. Theoretically at least, we are much better adapted to face some catastrophic event than the poor eucalyptus-leaf eater. Humans have an added advantage of being able to adapt with cultural means to changing environmental conditions.

Stini (1975) provides a clear discussion of the importance of population variability in terms of its evolutionary importance. Among humans, for example, there are estimates of upward of 50,000 to 60,000 loci, or gene pairs, per individual. Because these are reassorted independently of each other during sexual reproduction, the number of gene combinations, or genotypes, in our species is very large, especially if we assume that variability exists at a

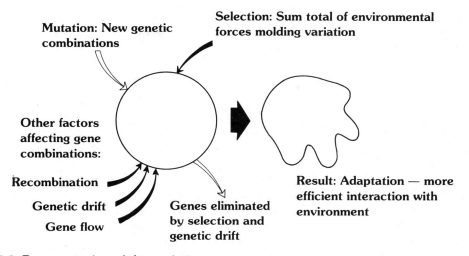

Figure 8-3. Representation of the evolutionary process.

number of these loci. "If we combine the observation of these mechanisms for the production of genotypic variability, mechanisms strongly dependent upon the process of sexual reproduction . . . we may reasonably infer that the maintenance of variability enhances the survivorship of the species" (Stini, 1975:2).

Some alleles are dominant over others, preventing the expression of recessive traits in the heterozygous state. This recessiveness allows some potentially harmful genetic traits to be carried from generation to generation and to be maintained within the gene pool. In this manner, new recessive mutations stand a better chance of remaining within the gene pool than if exposed to natural selection each time they appear.

Besides the fact that recessive mutations are retained within the population, other mechanisms, such as segregation and recombination, preserve genetic variability within the species. Added to this is the possibility of **pleiotropy,** whereby a gene at one locus influences more than one phenotypic trait, and contemporary sexually reproducing populations possess a number of mechanisms, for example, social regulations governing marital or breeding combinations, for generating infinite variety. Thus, even though mutations are rare, numbering from one out of every 100,000 to one out of every million gametes, species are capable of meeting environmental changes with at least some individuals genetically capable of coping.

Natural Selection. Charles Darwin's prime contribution to evolutionary theory was the idea of natural selection as the guiding force of evolution. Darwin's original ideas were interpreted by others who saw the evolutionary process as the struggle for existence between individual organisms. This generated the now famous phrase, "Survival of the fittest," which was not Darwin's phrase but that of the English social philosopher Herbert Spencer. The phrase stuck, and the outlook engendered a "survival of the fittest" ideology. Some have used this ideology to justify social inequities, unethical mercantile practices, aggression, colonialism, racism, and overzealous missionization. This is a gross misuse of Darwinian theory. Obviously, evolutionary theory did not always work on the side of the angels, nor are all its believers angels.

Darwin's concept of natural selection may be paraphrased as follows:

1. Individuals differ among themselves.
2. Individual differences are partially determined by hereditarily transmissible factors. (Darwin was ignorant of the means whereby this was accomplished.)
3. Whenever these differences impart greater or lesser fitness, the traits of the more fit individuals will be increasingly represented in succeeding generations.

Genetic fitness refers to an organism's ability to adapt to the environment and subsequent success in leaving fertile surviving offspring. The more genetically fit, the better an organism's ability to transmit its genes. A trait which does not affect one's reproductive success is not considered evolutionarily significant.

In evolutionary terms it is significant that trait frequencies change over time. As they change, the observable traits (the phenotypes) change with them. The forces of evolution act on these phenotypes to hinder reproduction of nonadaptive traits. In genetic or population studies, fitness is determined by the criterion as to whether a trait that is expressed does or does not contribute to differential reproduction.

Once change has occurred, natural selection acts to encourage some genes and gene combinations over others through reproductive advantage. As we will see in Chapter 26, natural selection has acted to preserve certain body traits in one environment and other traits in other environments. Natural selection encourages those genes or gene combinations that assure the highest level of adaptive efficiency between the population and the environment. For example, natural selection favors those koala bears whose genes and gene combinations allow for the most efficient chewing and digestion of eucalyptus leaves. Individuals who get the most food and leave the most offspring with the least amount of energy expenditure are selected for. The less well-adapted organisms normally have less chance to leave a substantial number of offspring, or, under severe limitations, the organism dies.

Because it favors and encourages gene combinations, natural selection is the artist, the creative force, in evolution. Selection has been the principal force operating over millions of years to enable the development of new adaptations to the world's diverse environments. Natural selection is responsible for the evolution of the present diversity of life. Because the environment changes, the nature of selection also fluctuates and what may be adaptive today may be maladaptive tomorrow. This, again, points out the importance of maintaining population variability. Selection can have several effects: for example, directional selection does not usually act to reduce genetic variability; stabilizing selection, however (e.g., the favoring of the heterozygotic condition), can conserve or even increase genetic variability. It could be said that evolutionarily successful species consist of forms that have been selected for as a result of their capacity for variability. Evolution is a meaningless concept unless one views the process in the environmental context (including the cultural milieu of humans). The forces of selection channel variation along particular lines of environmental stability.

The major features of natural selection can be summarized as follows:

1. Selection is the sum total of environmental factors favoring differential reproduction within a population.
2. The environment operates as the selective force in this process, favoring variants best adapted to meet a set of environmental particulars and removing those less well adapted.
3. Natural selection favors traits bringing an organism into an effective adaptive relationship with the environment.

4. Natural selection usually results in a reduction of variation because it "weeds out" less well-adapted forms. As discussed in Chapter 27, however, some forms of natural selection such as balanced polymorphisms result in selection for increased variability.

Natural selection is comparable to a good stockbroker, selecting from among the many stocks those likely to yield the highest return. Traits that are selected for or against are neither good nor bad; they are merely adaptive or nonadaptive. There is increasing evidence, however, that this is not an all-or-none proposition, for some traits may be of neutral value.

Natural selection is not just a process that eliminates traits, genes, or individuals from a population. Natural selection is positive differential reproduction. The reproductive capacity of certain genotypes is higher than the capacity of others. Individuals whose genotypes allow them to produce more viable offspring are said to enjoy the advantages of positive differential reproduction. Natural selection operates on the individual, but it is the population that adapts through variation.

Adaptation. Adaptation is the end result of natural selection acting on a variable gene pool to produce a population that interacts efficiently with its environment. The end product of evolutionary change is the establishment of organisms that function more efficiently in certain environmental situations than their predecessors. Any characteristic (behavioral or morphological) advantageous to an organism's coping with its environment is said to be adaptive.

Biological adaptations can occur in various ways; some are permanent, that is, they represent changes in the genetic structure of the population. According to scientists favoring this definition, adaptation has not occurred unless a population has experienced some alteration of gene frequencies. By contrast, adjustments that occur within an individual's lifetime (acclimatizations) and that are not acquired specifically through inheritance or transmitted to succeeding generations fail to qualify as evolutionary adaptations. By excluding adjustments not directly reflecting an altered genetic constitution, a rigidly genetic definition of adaptation places the term within an evolutionary perspective. Wallace and Srb (1964) have said that "adaptation is evolution."

The process of adaptation includes movement into an econiche, or adaptive zone. This adaptive zone is comprised of the physical and biotic environment. The physical environment is composed of physical and chemical factors (i.e., the air that is breathed, water, and soil). The biotic environment includes faunal and floral components. Habitation of an econiche is not a haphazard process because organisms must adapt to their total surroundings, including all existing foods, competitors and enemies, and all forms of life affecting the given organism in any way. Furthermore, the adaptive zones change; the course of the adaptive history of any group may be seen as a shifting series of adaptive zones. The order in which organisms move into a niche influences their use of that niche. The first organisms moving into a new niche theoretically have that whole niche open to them because of lack of competition. To reduce competition, subsequent inhabitants usually occupy successively narrower portions and they tend to be more specialized than previous inhabitants. The narrower the niche, the less variable the population and the greater the chances of extinction.

Levels of Evolutionary Change

Evolutionary rates are dissimilar and depend on many factors, for example, type of habitat, generation time, and number of offspring. Furthermore, as George Gaylord Simpson (1951, 1953) has often noted, a group of organisms can go through stages of differing evolutionary speed. One type of evolutionary change, referred to as **microevolution,** occurs through those small changes within a potentially continuous population that are responsible for differences arising between related populations. An example is the great array of domestic breeds of dog. In contrast to microevolutionary changes, which do not isolate breeding populations from one another, **macroevolutionary** changes usually encompass the rise and divergence of discontinuous groups (Figure 8-4). The large-scale evolution studied by the paleontologist in the fossil record is due to macroevolutionary processes. The major differentiation between macroevolutionary and **megaevolutionary** change is that the latter normally occurs in small, rapidly evolving populations moving into new habitats. Megaevolution (or quantum evolution) is a temporary phenomenon characteristic of populations in temporary states of disequilibrium. Both macroevolution and megaevolution result in genetic discontinuity, speciation, and the production of new forms. The concept of speciation is discussed in the next chapter.

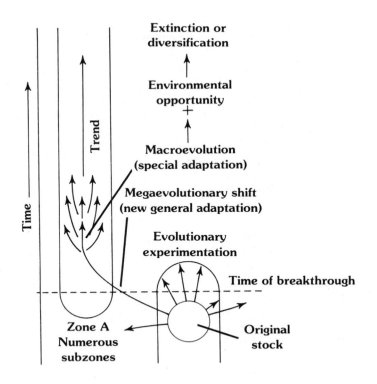

Figure 8-4. The process of evolution above the species level.

New genetic combinations are introduced into populations through random mutations. The useful, that is, adaptive, mutations increase an organism's chance of survival. They are then distributed throughout the population. Evolution, through

natural selection, leads to an improvement of the adaptive relations between organisms and their environment. Evolutionary rates are dissimilar and a population may pass through stages of differing evolutionary rates.

Bibliography

Bodmer, W., and Cavalli-Sforza, L. 1976. *Genetics, evolution and man.* San Francisco: Freeman.

Buettner-Janusch, J. 1973. *Physical anthropology: a perspective.* New York: Wiley.

Cavalli-Sforza, L., and Bodmer, W. 1971. *The genetics of human populations.* San Francisco: Freeman.

Grant, V. 1963. *The origin of adaptations.* New York: Columbia University Press.

King, J., and Jukes, T. 1969. Non-Darwinian evolution. *Science* 164:788-97.

Lerner, I. 1968. *Heredity, evolution and society.* San Francisco: Freeman.

Mayr, E. 1974. Behavior programs and evolutionary strategies. *American Scientist* 62:650-59.

Racle, F. 1979. *Introduction to evolution.* Englewood Cliffs, N.J.: Prentice-Hall.

Rensch, B. 1959. *Evolution above the species level.* Englewood Cliffs, N.J.: Prentice-Hall.

Ross, H. 1966. *Understanding evolution.* Englewood Cliffs, N.J.: Prentice-Hall.

Salthe, S. 1972. *Evolutionary biology.* New York: Holt, Rinehart and Winston.

Savage, J. 1969. *Evolution.* New York: Holt, Rinehart and Winston.

Simpson, G. 1951. *The meaning of evolution.* New York: Mentor Books.

_____. 1953. *The major features of evolution.* New York: Columbia University Press.

Smith, J. 1966. *The theory of evolution.* Baltimore: Penguin Books.

Solbrig, O. 1966. *Evolution and systematics.* New York: Macmillan.

Stini, W. 1975. *Ecology and human adaptation.* Dubuque, Ia.: Brown.

Volpe, E. 1967. *Understanding evolution.* Dubuque, Ia.: Brown.

Wallace, B., and Srb, A. 1964. *Adaptation.* Englewood Cliffs, N.J.: Prentice-Hall.

Williams, B. 1973. *Evolution and human origins: an introduction to physical anthropology.* New York: Harper & Row.

Chapter 9

Evolutionary Systematics

Some basic concepts of modern evolutionary systematics are considered in this chapter. Here we are concerned with some principles of modern taxonomy and classification; we shall also briefly discuss some rules of nomenclature. In Chapter 13 we discuss some of the problems of classification with reference to the primate fossil record. Understanding the world of living organisms requires ordering this multiplicity of plants and animals into some sort of rational, manageable system. Consequently, systematics is as old as our desire to understand life, and the effort to understand and order the variability of life has led to the development of all branches of biology. The field of taxonomy, once concerned only with an effort to classify, has been transformed into a method of discovering and understanding nature's order.

Described Species

Solbrig (1966) has estimated that 1,500,000 species have been described and classified. Of all the major plant and animal groups, however, only the birds with 8,650 species and perhaps the gymnosperms among the plants with about 650 species have been more or less completely surveyed. Our knowledge of the kinds and numbers of all other groups is incomplete, and it has been estimated that there are more than 100,000 undescribed species of flowering plants, 20,000 species of fishes, and more than 1,000,000 species of insects. Against this background, the primate fossil record, indeed the human fossil record with all its entanglements and taxonomic arguments, seems to be relatively complete and well understood. We shall soon see, however, that as we study the Order Primates and especially the Family Hominidae (of which we are part) taxonomic methodology becomes blurred and nomenclature somewhat misused.

Terminology

It is essential that we first establish definitions for a number of terms that are often misused and misunderstood. Systematics, according to Simpson (1961), is the scientific study of the types and diversity of living organisms and of the interrelationships among them. Systematics studies the ordering of life; it is a very general and inclusive activity accepting data from any and all of the sciences. Once comparative studies have provided data concerning traits by which interrelationships may be established, a formal system of relating organisms to one another and placing them into groups, that is, classification, is then used.

Systematics (the study of the diversity of animals and their interrelationships) and **taxonomy** (the theoretical study of how classifications are made) are two terms that are often used interchangeably although their meanings do differ. Placing living organisms into groups based on relationships between them is the act of classification. Buettner-Janusch (1973:28) states: "The subjects of classification are organisms; the subjects of taxonomies are classifications; and the subjects of systematics are everything that is relevant to the study of organisms." The assignment of names to groups of plants or animals is nomenclature.

Several Principles of Classification

The principal reason for constructing a classification is to provide a simple reference system. The present hierarchical system of classification is based on the original eighteenth-century work of the Swedish naturalist Carolus Linnaeus. It is important to note that the Linnaean system is hierarchical, that is, categories are based on inclusive traits. Groups at the top (i.e., kingdoms) are most inclusive and groups at the bottom (i.e., species) are least inclusive. Each category within the classification includes a group or groups of related organisms, the members of which are classified together because they share many of the same traits. There are three basic steps in classification: (1) the delineation of the categories, (2) the establishment of relationships within and between categories, and (3) the formation of a hierarchy. These relationships are established in two ways: first, by overlapping or coincidence of dissimilar categories and, second, by subordination of some classes to others or by inclusion of one class within another (Solbrig, 1966).

The act of classifying is hampered by many problems, not the least of which is that the Linnaean system was not designed to convey evolutionary information. When established the Linnaean system was thought to represent the "real world" as ordained by the Supreme Being. All forms represented in the Linnaean system were thought to be permanent and immutable results of a special creation. The nonevolutionary orientation of the Linnaean system has resulted in a number of consequences; the Linnaean system is so devised that the categories and taxa[1] are unable to reflect the true nature of evolutionary change; it is able only to represent discontinuous relationships; it is a static two-dimensional framework, whereas evolution is dynamic and multidimensional and is the result of change through time. Although the Linnaean system was devised within a nonevolutionary framework, since the work of Darwin the zoological classificatory system has been slowly overhauled to incorporate the viewpoint that the living world is constantly changing, evolving new forms from old. With some success we have borrowed the form of the Linnaean system while changing its function.

Although various rules are used to establish categories within the classification, it must be remembered that the system is arbitrary and that the taxonomist imposes names on the natural order for convenience. Disregarding the philosophical viewpoint with which one approaches the classificatory scheme, classification is not a real biological phenomenon; rather it is a set of analytical categories used to order data. The procedures employed in

[1]A taxon (plural taxa) is a group of creatures within the classificatory scheme related to one another by descent from a common ancestor; this group is distinctive enough to be given a name to differentiate it from other groups.

Figure 9-1. Carolus Linnaeus.

determining the taxon to which an organism belongs include a subjective element, that of weighting characters. This subjective element produces many of the problems noted throughout this book.

Rules of Nomenclature

The establishment of a name to identify a form is based on a number of rules and is not, or should not be, a haphazard affair. A set of arbitrarily agreed-on rules, embodied in the "codes"

MAMMALIA.

ORDER I. PRIMATES.

Fore-teeth cutting; upper 4, parallel; teats 2 pectoral.

1. HOMO.

Sapiens. Diurnal; varying by education and fituation.

  2. Four-footed, mute, hairy.   *Wild Man.*

  3. Copper-coloured, choleric, erect.   *American.*
      Hair black, ftraight, thick; *noftrils* wide, *face* harfh; *beard* fcanty; *obftinate*, content free. *Paints* himfelf with fine red lines. *Regulated* by cuftoms.

  4. Fair, fanguine, brawny.   *European.*
      Hair yellow, brown, flowing; *eyes* blue; *gentle*, acute, inventive. *Covered* with clofe veftments. *Governed* by laws.

  5. Sooty, melancholy, rigid.   *Afiatic.*
      Hair black; *eyes* dark; *fevere*, haughty, covetous. *Covered* with loofe garments. *Governed* by opinions.

  6. Black; phlegmatic, relaxed.   *African.*
      Hair black, frizzled; *fkin* filky; *nofe* flat; *lips* tumid; *crafty*, indolent, negligent. *Anoints* himfelf with greafe. *Governed* by caprice.

Monftrofus Varying by climate or art.
  1. Small, active, timid.   *Mountaineer.*
  2. Large, indolent.   *Patagonian.*
  3. Lefs fertile.   *Hottentot.*
  4. Beardlefs.   *American.*
  5. Head conic.   *Chinefe.*
  6. Head flattened.   *Canadian.*

    The anatomical, phyfiological, natural, moral, civil and focial hiftories of man, are beft defcribed by their refpective writers.

Vol. I.—C   2. SIMIA.

Figure 9-2. Linnaeus' classification of the genus *Homo*.

of nomenclature, governs the application of names. These rules have been established over a number of generations and include a combination of historical elements with practical rulings to ensure clarity and usefulness. Nomenclature is the device used to eliminate confusion and ensure one common language in biological classification.

    The Law of Priority. The rules of nomenclature follow a number of precedents. The law of priority applies to all names used as of 1 January 1758. The first name (taxon) validly used after this date has priority if used correctly and proposed and published according to the rules established in the International Code of Zoological Nomenclature. Later forms given the same name are referred to as synonyms. The law of priority may be ignored in certain instances, for example, if dropping a commonly held taxon in favor of a prior, but obscure, taxon will cause unnecessary confusion. In matters such as this, or in other instances of dispute about nomenclature, the decision is made by the International Commission on Zoological Nomenclature.

Certain conventions are followed in forming the names of some of the higher categories. These conventions are illustrated in Table 9-1.

Table 9-1. Names of Higher Categories

Category	Suffix	Stem	Name of Higher Category
Superfamily	-oidea	Homin	Hominoidea
Family	-idae	Homin	Hominidae
Subfamily	-inae	Homin	Homininae

Occasionally, names are applied that later must be dropped, or "sunk." The "sinking" of a taxonomic category may result from a number of factors, for example, analysis of data may eventually reveal that the form actually does not differ significantly from specimens already described. In this event the form takes the name of the original specimen. To take an example from the human fossil record, when Middle Pleistocene hominid material was first uncovered in China it was given the name "Sinanthropus"; later analysis proved that "Sinanthropus" was similar to hominid material uncovered earlier in Java, that is, *Homo erectus*. The genus "Sinanthropus" was thus "sunk" in favor of the earlier proposed genus *Homo*.

The official name of an organism contains a number of parts, its **genus** (e.g., *Homo*) and **species** (e.g., *sapiens*) and **subspecies** (e.g., *sapiens*) if such is determined and applicable. Assignment of generic and specific names follows the Linnaean system of establishing a binomial (i.e., a two-term) name. It is obligatory to apply the binomial to each newly described species. Taking as an example modern hominids, the binomial reference is *Homo* (the genus) and *sapiens* (the species), that is *Homo sapiens*. To differentiate modern hominids from ancestral forms we add a third modifier, the subspecific designation; thus we establish the taxon of *Homo sapiens sapiens*. The genus designation always begins with a capital letter, the species and subspecies designation with a small letter. Each binomial is unique and is not applied to another. The binomial always appears in italics; the names of taxa higher than a genus, for example, family, are not italicized but they too begin with capital letters.

We mentioned that the assignment of names follows a number of rules set forth in the *International Code of Zoological Nomenclature*. Besides the law of priority, there is also a rule called the *designation of types*. Whenever a new species is described a *type specimen* must be designated. The type is a particular specimen—a skull, for example—that establishes the criteria for a certain classification, and the type is the form to which all subsequent forms are compared. Types are established at the species, genus, and family levels. The type of a species is an individual specimen, for a genus the type is a species, and for a family the type is established on a genus. The type specimen, being only one specimen, may unfortunately not be typical of the group it represents. It must be remembered that type specimens of species, for example, are the real entities to which the species name is attached, but they do not and cannot represent or even typify the range of variation within the group for which they stand. When other finds of the same species are made at the same time, they are listed as referred specimens within the species "hypodigm." The hypodigm is a list of all known similar individuals.

The word "type" as used in "type specimen" does not apply to, and must not be confused with, the typological concept of species favored by eighteenth- and nineteenth-century nonevolutionists. A characteristic of the Linnaean system is that it adhered to the Platonic concept of *eidos* (idea, type, essence). This principle was embodied in the concept of the type, the idealization of an individual as a representative of all other individuals of the species. This concept of type grew out of the belief in the immutability, or fixity, of the species and led to the false acceptance of the premise that a single specimen—the type—would be a sufficient sample of the species. Although Darwin recognized the importance of population variability, typological thinking did not cease until the dynamics of population genetics became known and accepted. Continued acceptance of the nonevolutionary concept of type dominated early hominid classification, however, and unfortunately still appears today. Only with the development of population genetics and the realization that populations and not individuals are the evolutionary units did systematics shift from considering individual specimens to studying series and mass samples.

The net effect of the taxonomic system is often one whereby species, once they have become established, appear almost to be fixed in their classification. It must be borne in mind, however, that a biological entity, represented by a title such as *Homo erectus,* is (or was) a dynamic, living creature; it was not a fixed type. Eventually *Homo erectus* changed to the extent that scientists who discovered the subsequent remains (i.e., the remains of descendents of *H. erectus)* called them something else, that is, *Homo sapiens.* Because *H. erectus,* at this point in our knowledge, appears to have been our antecedent, there was a biological continuum between ourselves and them. Therefore, although scientific convention draws discrete boundaries between *H. sapiens* and *H. erectus,* these boundaries did not and could not have existed in biological reality.

Speciation

The species concept is the key in modern evolutionary biology. Most paleontologists prefer to characterize the species as an objective, nonarbitrary grouping. This is a group of actually or potentially interbreeding animals reproductively isolated from other such groups.

Various kinds of species are recognized: species living in areas with overlapping home ranges are **sympatric. Allopatric** populations occupy separate nonoverlapping geographical areas. Some fossil populations are in the same species as living animals; however, groups whose ranges do not overlap in time are called allochronic species or paleospecies.

Most material discussed in this book is fossil material, so we are usually referring to evolutionary species. An evolutionary species is an ancestral-descendant sequence of populations separately evolving from others (Buettner-Janusch, 1973; Simpson, 1961). Allochronic species, or paleospecies, are difficult to distinguish because of the incompleteness of the fossil record. Because species often change very slowly, the evidence would show slight gradual changes in the organisms, so that determining just when one species evolved into another is impossible.

Although it is commonly stated that one of the characteristics of evolution is slow, gradual change, there is another possibility. Sometimes during the process of speciation one recognizes spurts of adaptive evolutionary change. This pattern of evolution, in which long periods of stasis (relative stability) are broken by short bursts of evolutionary change stimulated by speciation, is called **punctuated equilibrium.** It is possible that such a spurt was responsible for the divergence of the hominids and pongids, especially if the biochemical evidence for a late divergence of hominids and pongids is correct. This possibility is discussed more fully in Chapter 22.

Any new species must originate from another species. This process of speciation can occur in two ways. The evolution of one species from another of the same lineage is called **anagenesis (phyletic evolution).** Although phyletic evolution is a real phenomenon, the division of a lineage into temporal species is somewhat arbitrary. Phyletic evolution is the main form of hominid speciation.

Cladogenesis is the splitting of one lineage into two. In this process, one ancestral species becomes two or more descendant species. This splitting takes time to occur and only happens when populations are geographically, or spatially, isolated from one another. Cladogenesis is most likely to occur in narrowly ranging populations. Because humans are a widely ranging species, many authors feel that cladogenesis has rarely characterized human evolution.

Reproductive isolation is the principal criterion for defining genetic species. Reproductive isolation is often synonymous with geographical isolation, which is one of the most important ways in which speciation occurs. A population that radiates into a number of different habitats, each with its own peculiarities, tends to adapt to these local conditions. Such adaptation, molded by natural selection, may eventually result in genetic differences in various local areas. Eventually the differences will magnify into **speciation** with its concomitant reproductive isolation.

Although geographical isolation is a major source of speciation, other factors also need to be considered. Among other important isolating mechanisms are behavioral patterns. Although behavioral isolating mechanisms (such as mating patterns) are not well studied, they undoubtedly play a role in speciation. In effect, any mechanisms leading to isolation and impeding gene flow between segments of a population could eventually lead to reproductive isolation and speciation; this is, however, not always true. In addition to geographical and ethological isolation, there is temporal and seasonal isolation in which mating occurs at different seasons in different populations, and mechanical isolation, for example, when, as among some insects, the morphology of the genitalia prevents copulation. Most likely, speciation within the Order Primates resulted from geographical isolation.

The biological species concept (BSC)[2] has been recently subjected to heavy criticism from certain evolutionary theorists (e.g., Ehrlich, Holm, and Parnell, 1974; Sokal and Sneath, 1963, 1973; Sokal and Crovella, 1970; Sokal, 1973). Some of the criticisms are as follows: (1) The BSC applies only to sexually reproducing organisms—hence biologists who study nonsexual organisms must use different species criteria. This means biology has different types of "species" and this can be confusing. (2) The BSC can really only be applied to neontology because the criterion of interbreedability can never be adequately tested paleontologically. (3) Actual testing of interbreedability under *natural* conditions occurs only when populations are sympatric. If they are allopatric—if they never meet—biologists can only assume species or subspecies status. (4) Arbitrary decisions on species status must frequently be made because biologists find a continuum, or smooth, unbroken gradient, between completely intersterile populations and those that are completely infertile. It is a matter of choice as to how to classify those in the middle—those with incomplete gene pool protection. (5) Much stress has been placed on the contention that the BSC is defined on one level (genetic: whether or not organisms have the ability to interbreed) but is usually actually distinguished by phenetic (morphological) criteria. Sokal and Crovella go into elaborate detail on this point, and they note that the ability to interbreed has never *really* been tested for any two species. If several

[2]Simpson does not like the term biological species concept. He notes that the species concept is a genetically based concept. To him, all species concepts are inherently biological.

individuals or small populations can interbreed, decisions are then made (it is assumed that other individuals or populations that *look similar to these* follow the same rule). Strictly speaking, the ability to interbreed should be checked for all individuals of both groups to really test the BSC. Further, they note that phenetics is used even at the preliminary stages of deciding which groups to study. Point 5, the critics say, indicates that the BSC is really based on morphology (phenetics) regardless of what the ideal definition says.

Most of this criticism is associated with the school of numerical taxonomy, adherents of which feel that the BSC is implicitly phenetic anyway—so why not make it explicitly phenetic? If the BCS were explicitly phenetic, all biologists could use the same species and more objectivity would be injected into the species-naming process. The subjectivity of the BSC bothers these critics. (Shaw [1969] has attacked the use of the species concept in paleontology. Ehrlich and Raven [1969] and Ender [1973] attack the notion that gene flow is the principal force binding a species.)

Higher Categories

A higher category includes taxa from lower levels in the Linnaean hierarchy, for example, a genus contains various species. The human and nonhuman primate fossil record primarily reveals materials referred to the genus and species categories.

The genus is a different type of category from the species; it typically contains several related species.[3] Paleontologists generally refer to the genus as a stage arbitrarily separated from other stages in an evolving sequence. The genus is often characterized as a definite evolutionary unit, and is considered hardly more arbitrary than the species.

Extinction

The term extinction is applied to describe the disappearance of an animal group, such as a species, from the evolutionary record. A species may become extinct in two ways: First, the species may develop a lifeway such that climatic change would prevent its continued existence. For example, the koala bear's dependence on eucalyptus leaves would doom the koala bear if such trees should no longer exist. This is an example of a negative role played by environmental selection in evolution. Second, a species may become extinct when it is consumed or destroyed by another species.

While taxonomy is a useful tool in understanding the vast array of life, it has its limitations. One of the major stumbling blocks is the limited amount of evidence concerning fossil forms and the ignorance about the direction of evolutionary trends and rates of evolution. This lack of data creates a serious problem, because without data, weighting of characters in classification is largely subjective, and a truly evolutionary classification will never be a reality.

Because of problems mentioned here and in Chapter 13 the reader may question the validity and wisdom of attempting to classify organisms so that the classification will reflect their evolutionary relationships. However, the careful study of genetics, function, morphology, behavior, and ecological relationships, among others, can provide many clues. Even so, as the next chapters will indicate, different scientists

[3]Some genera are monotypic, that is, they contain only one species.

read the available information differently. Granted, there are problems; however, as Solbrig (1966:120) states, "It should be remembered that science can at best present a statistical approximation to reality, and the best we can hope for is relative truth."

The species concept is one of the most important in modern evolutionary biology, and is essential for any discussion of systematics and taxonomy. Most paleontologists refer to the species as an objective, nonarbitrary grouping. Species living in areas with overlapping home ranges are referred to as sympatric species. Allopatric populations of a species occupy separate, nonoverlapping home ranges. Groups whose ranges in time do not overlap are called allochronic species. Species differentiation is due to reproductive isolation, which primarily results from geographical or behavioral isolating mechanisms.

A genus is a taxon containing various species. The genus is often considered to be a natural unit of species closely related by descent.

Bibliography

Buettner-Janusch, J. 1973. *Physical anthropology: a perspective*. New York: Wiley.

Cain, A., and Harrison, G. 1960. Phyletic weighting. *Proceedings of the Zoological Society of London* 135:1.

Ehrlich, P., and Raven, P. 1969. Differentiation of populations. *Science* 165:1229-32.

Ehrlich, P., Holm, R., and Parnell, D. 1974. *The process of evolution,* 2nd ed. New York: McGraw-Hill.

Ender, J. 1973. Gene flow and population differentiation. *Science* 179:243-50.

Garn, S. 1971. The improper use of fossil nomenclature. *American Journal of Physical Anthropology* 35:217.

Huxley, J., ed. 1940. *The new systematics*. Oxford: Oxford University Press.

Mayr, E. 1969. *Principles of systematic zoology*. New York: McGraw-Hill.

Shaw, A. 1969. Adam and Eve, paleontology, and the non-objective arts. *Journal of Paleontology* 43:1085-98.

Simons, E. 1972. *Primate evolution*. New York: Macmillan.

Simpson, G. 1945. The principles of classification and a classification of mammals. *Bulletin of American Museum of Natural History* 85.

_____. 1951. *The meaning of evolution*. New York: New York American Library.

_____. 1961. *Principles of animal taxonomy*. New York: Columbia University Press.

Sneath, P., and Sokal, R. 1973. *Numerical taxonomy*. San Francisco: Freeman.

Sokal, R. 1973. The species problem reconsidered. *Systematic Zoology* 22:360-74.

Sokal, R., and Crovella, T. 1970. The biological species concept: a critical evaluation. *American Naturalist* 104:127-53.

Sokal, R., and Sneath, P. 1963. *Principles of numerical taxonomy*. San Francisco: Freeman.

Solbrig, O. 1966. *Evolution and systematics*. New York: Macmillan.

Part Three

Reconstructing the Past: Behavioral Studies

Many "human" interludes, flashes or episodes of behavior reminiscent of human behavior, occur in the daily lives of monkeys and apes. . . . Such similarities reflect the fact of continuity in human evolution. . . .

A great deal more could be learned from in-the-wild observations of species even more closely related to man. If ancestral hominids still roamed river valleys and savannas and coastal plains, say, bands like those whose traces are found in Bed I at the Olduvai Gorge or at Torralba-Ambrona, investigators could obtain firsthand records of early hunting methods and social organizations. In the absence of such bands, however, we ourselves can serve as subjects for research in living prehistory. We are all relics to some extent and, as such, provide a legitimate source of clues to the nature of prehistoric man.

From J. Pfeiffer. 1972. *The Emergence of Man*, 2nd ed. New York: Harper & Row.

Chapter 10

Reconstructing the Past

This chapter would probably have seemed to be a fictionalized tale to early twentieth-century anthropologists. Here and in the following chapters we review techniques and the subjects on which much of the data presented in section II are based. We can tell much about our past from studying nonhuman primates, social carnivores, and elephants. There exist, in a greatly decimated state, populations living in much the same way that our ancestors lived when they passed through the hunting-gathering stage on their way toward industrialization. We can use these sources to reconstruct our past.

Rationale for Use of a Comparative Approach

Lancaster (1975) notes two lines of evidence that can be employed to reconstruct our evolutionary history. First, we have the fossil and archaeological record itself, that is, any traces of past behavior and bones that have fortunately become preserved. All such artifacts are important clues in understanding and reconstructing how a species looked and how it lived. This record, however, is always incomplete because it is based on relative degrees of preservation (Table 10-1). More importantly, many aspects of behavior simply do not fossilize—and we are left to make inferences. Vital questions about our behavior and social organization can, at best, only partially be solved by the fossil and cultural record. That we should seek this kind of information indicates that behavioral changes, as well as anatomical changes, were important factors in our divergence from our pongid relatives.

The fossil record raises many questions and the modern world is full of potential comparisons yielding answers to some of these questions. The problem is to find the source or sources most likely to yield the most appropriate answer(s). In terms of understanding not only human evolution, but modern human behavior, there are three major sources whose behavior can yield useful comparisons. The first is various contemporary groups of the human species. Today we find many different human groups living in different habitats to which they have adapted with varied cultural traditions. We can study particular human groups living

Table 10-1. Major Behavioral, Anatomical, and Physiological Changes in Hominids Since Hominids and Pongids Diverged

Trait[a]	Visible in the Fossil and Archaeological Record	Inferred
Anatomical and Physiological Traits		
Postcranial modification for bipedalism	X	
Modification of hands for effective tool use and manufacture	X	
Reorganization and enlargement of brain	X	
Reduction of face and jaws, remodeling of cranium, face, and jaws	X	
Reduction of body hair and changes in glands of the skin		X
Modified estrous cycle		X
Modification of vocal tract for speech	X?	X
Changes relating to birth processes, for example, lengthening of gestation, delayed maturation	X	X
Behavioral and Social Changes		
Development of and consistent use of tools	X	
Inclusion of meat protein in diet, hunting behavior	X	
Temporarily defined home base	X	
Food sharing and gender division of labor	X?	X
Controls on emotional displays		X
Larger social groups	X	
Dwelling structures of a permanent nature	X	
In much later periods we have evidence of art, symbolism, and spiritualism	X	
Extension of social bonding mechanisms	X?	X

[a]These categories of traits should not be considered absolute differentiators of hominids and nonhuman primates. For example, data exists regarding (1) irregular manufacture and use of tools among some of the modern apes, (2) consumption of animal protein, hunting, and scavenging among some monkeys and apes, and (3) psychological attachment to a home area. It is more likely that the combination of these and other factors, rather than the presence of any one of them, resulted in the differentiation of human and nonhuman primates. More items will be added as the fossils and archaeological record increase in composition.

today in ways or habitats similar to those of early hominids. The few surviving groups of hunter-gatherers live a way of life that may help us understand the quality of social and emotional life of times past. Certainly crowded conditions such as present in many of today's large cities are not comparable to the life style of our ancestors.

No modern hunter-gatherer population provides a perfect model for Pliocene-Pleistocene hominids, nor for hominids subsequent to this period. They do, however, offer us patterned regularities that provide guidance in matters of interpretation. For example, early hominids existed and modern hunter-gatherers exist in relatively low-density populations because of their position on the food-getting pyramid. The low population density among hunter-gatherers was maintained by widely spaced births, frequent infanticides, and occasional episodes of locally intensified death rates during droughts, food shortages, and other conditions of stress.

Gifford (1980) has recently discussed the contributions of ethnoarchaeology, that is, the use of living populations for reconstructing the past. As she notes, there has been considerable debate among archaeologists concerning the nature and limits of ethnographic analogy for analyzing prehistoric human behavior. Modern observable cultural systems do not necessarily reflect the total range of prehistoric systems. Being bound by strict analogy severely limits the range of possible interpretations. Freeman (1968) argues that direct analogies between modern hunter-gatherers and earlier hominid species may be misleading, because in such cases we may be studying the material effects of cultural behavior in adaptive systems vastly different from those of modern hominids. Nevertheless, Gifford (1980:105) states, "The key to elucidation of the past by studies of the present lies in assuming a comprehensive approach to the study of process and effect. By closely defining site formation processes, one can frame and test hypotheses concerning areas of knowledge which at present remain hazy."

The extant nonhuman primates provide a second source of information for reconstructing our past because of our shared phylogenetic relationship and because many of them, such as savannah baboons, live in a habitat similar to that which we assume was inhabited by our ancestors.

Some of the kinds of questions we can answer from observing nonhuman primates follow. We can draw inferences about social organization and certain aspects of our predecessors' social behavior by watching nonhuman primates now living in these areas. Their mode of adaptation to habitat pressures, such as food-getting, predator avoidance, and aspects of their social structure, are all important clues to our mode of adaptation in similar circumstances. We know that tool use and manufacture were important features of hominid evolution, and until recently most thought that these were uniquely human traits. However, chimpanzees make and use tools in a wide variety of circumstances. Since the chimpanzee is our closest nonhuman primate relative, it is relevant to understanding our evolutionary history to know in what situations and how the chimpanzee uses tools. Furthermore, we should learn why the chimpanzee makes tools and many other nonhuman primates do not. Answers to these questions can help reconstruct the adaptive situation leading to our ancestors' commitment to tool use and manufacture.

Social carnivores have provided many useful clues to our evolutionary past (see, for example, van Lawick and van Lawick-Goodall, 1970). In contrast to nonhuman primates, who are basically vegetarians with an occasional addition of meat to the diet, such animals as hunting wild dogs, lions, and hyenas provide clues as to the earliest hunting methods, the adaptiveness of food sharing, and the use of communicative signals during hunting. The

Figure 10-1. A young male bonnet macaque (*Macaca radiata*) from India.

Figure 10-2. A lioness.

archaeological record suggests that meat eating and tool using were important at an early stage in hominid evolution. When considering factors such as the size of the home range, hunting techniques, and the kinds and sizes of animals available to a non–tool-using hunter, the social carnivores provide many useful insights.

We are not going to argue that we are, or ever were, nothing more than social carnivores, or that modern nonhuman primates are a total reflection of our evolutionary past. It must be remembered that modern social carnivores and nonhuman primates have evolved, as have we, and that they can serve only as models. Furthermore, we have just as much to learn when they provide negative answers clarifying our uniqueness as when they provide answers highlighting our commonalities. If we find a behavioral characteristic differentiating us from these models, we may be finding a behavior unique to hominid evolution. The more we know about the evolutionary history and adaptations of our phylogenetically related primate relatives and the ecologically related social carnivores, the more we learn about processes which shaped our evolutionary past. Nonhuman primates, social carnivores, and extant hunting-gathering populations present us with an array of natural experiments in their various adaptations to multiple habitat demands. Their way of coping helps us better understand our way of coping. Quoting Lancaster (1975:5): "We can understand the whole of human nature if we appreciate both the ways in which we are like other forms of life and the ways in which we are unique."

Modern Hunter-Gatherers

Research Outlook. Studies of the rapidly disappearing modern hunter-gatherers are important. A 1966 estimate notes 30,000 hunter-gatherers in a world population of 4 billion persons; since then the number has been further reduced. The distribution of hunter-gatherers is shown in Figure 10-3.

Past treatment of the hunter-gatherers has been deplorable. They were considered to be subhuman breeds with a lower mentality and they were missionized, dispossessed, hunted, slaughteréd, fed poisoned food, and further exploited. Today we recognize such groups as remnants of what was once a vast population who by their remarkable adaptations to various environments offer many insights into certain ecological adaptations.

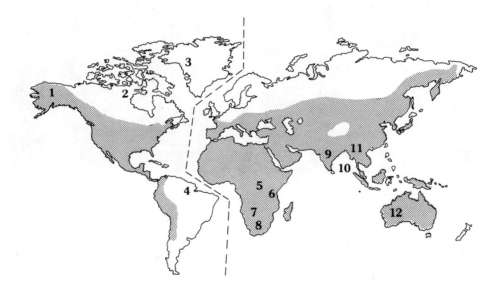

Some known living sites of contemporary hunter-gatherers.

1 Eskimos, Alaska
2 Eskimos, Northwest Territory
3 Eskimos, Greenland
4 Akuri, Surinam
5 Pygmies, Congo
6 Ariangulo, Tanzania
  Boni, Tanzania
  Sanye, Tanzania
7 Koroka, Angola
  Bantu, Angola
8 Kalahari !Kung San Bushmen, South Africa, Botswana
9 Birhar, Central India
10 Andaman Islanders, Andaman Island
11 Rue, Thailand
12 Australian Aborigines, Australia

Figure 10-3. The world distribution of hunter-gatherers in 10,000 B.C. compared with the known living sites of contemporary hunter-gatherers. In 10,000 B.C. hunter-gatherers composed 100 percent of the world population of 10 million. Contemporary hunter-gatherers compose less than 0.001 percent of the world population of 4 billion. Darkened areas = world distribution in 10,000 B.C. Numbers = present distribution.

Figure 10-4. Australian aborigines.

Besides the ever-present problem of funding anthropological research, anthropologists meet other difficulties in studying hunter-gatherers in their natural way of life. Many governments make the hunter-gatherers' life unbearable. In 1960 visiting pediatricians from Makerere University proclaimed Hadza children among the healthiest in East Africa. However, most Hadza were then forced to settle on a reservation where they lived in much closer contact with one another; within a year about one-fourth of the children died from an epidemic.

Australian Aborigines. One of the first to attempt to study hunter-gatherer peoples with this new perspective was Richard Gould (1968a, 1969), an archeologist. Gould worked in the Gibson Desert in western Australia with a two-family group of 13 aborigines (3 women, 2 men, and 8 children). These were among the very few people in the world still making and using stone tools regularly. Gould and his wife lived with this group and others for extended lengths of time over a 15-month period during which they learned their language, slept by their campsites, and walked with them in search of food.

Gould's investigation was the first of its kind, the first time a professional archaeologist had used his training in a systematic and intensive study of a hunting-gathering group. The Goulds observed and noted how aboriginal groups lived, collecting information that might bear on the interpretation of prehistoric sites and reconstruction of prehistoric social behavior. The information included observations on the details of tool making, hunting, camping, composition of living floors, and the very elaborate system of social behaviors, including religious practices.[1]

Gould's approach to aboriginal life has yielded vast quantities of important data. Above all it has yielded a new perspective. According to Gould, such work ". . .suggests new possibilities and analogies to us, and helps us to get unstuck for a limited range of ideas" (Pfeiffer, 1969:329).

During the height of the Australian summer (in December and January) a day begins just before sunup. Work (obtaining the daily sustenance) begins around 6 or 7 A.M., before it becomes unbearably hot. The group divides into two parties in search of food; everyone leaves camp. The women gather plant foods and may walk 4 or 5 miles with long wooden water bowls on their heads and nursing children on their hips or on their backs.

When the women are out collecting, men are hunting, generally a less dependable way of obtaining food in the desert. Hunting generally occurs from ambush; when possible, hunters take advantage of a water hole, hoping to ambush a thirsty emu, kangaroo, or wallaby. Women are more apt to provide the daily food (perhaps ngaru fruits, a pale green fruit the size of a small tomato) than the men. On most occasions all the men show for their efforts is a lizard or two. Roughly 60 to 70 percent of the aborigines' diet is plant food. Meat consists chiefly of lizards, rabbits, snakes, birds, and other small game.

The basis for the Australian aborigines' remarkable adaptation to their rather harsh desert environment includes a technology similar to that found 30,000 years ago. A common aboriginal tool is the so-called "adz-flake," a thick tool with a fairly steep edge. This tool closely resembles the sort of scrapers common to many prehistoric sites, for example, the ground stone axes common to the Mesolithic about 10,000 years ago. The aborigines use their teeth either as tools or for making some kinds of tools. The premolar teeth nibble flakes from stone; the teeth and supporting jaw structure are so strong that the aborigine can remove the top of a tin can by making successive bites along the rim. There are reasons to believe that Upper Paleolithic tool makers similarly used their dental structure for tool manufacture.

The study of aborigine tooth use is an example of how a study of modern hunter-gatherers can also help us understand some of the morphological traits found in the fossil record. Since dental remains compose a large proportion of the fossil record and since a number of inferences are based on dental wear patterns, it is helpful to note how modern populations use their teeth. For example, if teeth are used as tools, what types of wear patterns result? What types of wear patterns result from various types of diets? Can gritty diets affect the crown surfaces as is claimed for the robust variety of australopithecines? A study of dental use can also be helpful in understanding cranial morphology; for example, does the use of the teeth as tools affect the chewing musculature and surface features of the cranium or mandible? These questions can be raised from the fossil record and partly answered from the modern ethnographic record.

A basic implement of the Australian aboriginal hunting kit is the spear thrower, a tool also serving as a crude kind of archive, the closest thing to a written record among people who do not write. Decorations carved on wood have practical as well as religious and aesthetic meanings. Wavy and zigzag lines and a variety of geometric and irregular forms represent symbols of religious belief—a belief in what the aborigines call "dreamtime" when their

---

[1]Australian aborigines possess a complex set of religious beliefs and one of the most complex kinship systems known to modern scholars.

ancestors, supernatural beings in the guise of humans and animals, rose and roamed the earth's surface and created the world.

The symbols decorating the spear throwers are personal symbols, meaning different things to different hunters. They may assist the hunter in firmly establishing in his mind locations of sacred places and water holes on which survival may depend. Perhaps the decorated spear throwers dating from the Magdalenian period of the Upper Paleolithic depicted similar things.

Ainu. Another greatly reduced population is the Ainu (Figure 10-5), inhabiting Hokkaido island, Japan. Although some Ainu were still engaged in hunting-gathering until about 1950, the Japanese government has been encouraging them to change their way of life since the 1880s. The government has been rather successful in forcing the Ainu to become farmers. Fortunately, a study by the Japanese anthropologist Hitoshi Watanabe (1972) and his associates has reconstructed their former way of life.

Basically, the Ainu live as did prehistoric populations in western Europe some 15,000 years ago. They settled in river valleys and geared their existence to nature's cycles, to the seasons and wanderings of migratory herds. The Ainu's habitat is cold and rather inhospitable at various times during the year. The manner in which the Ainu cope with the essential task of surviving in this habitat, particularly storing food for lean times and getting about in the snow, are useful examples for reconstructing the life of the European Neanderthals. For example,

Figure 10-5. Ainu family and two-room hut.

based on his Ainu studies, Watanabe suggests that the Neanderthals may have only been able to follow their game across open tundra country where winds freeze and harden the snow cover. However, snowshoes, or some similar adaptation, are needed to move through the forests. That invention may not have come until the Magdalenian.

Kalahari !Kung San Bushmen. A concentrated long-term effort is being expended to gather information on the Bushmen living in the Kalahari desert of Botswana. A group of Harvard scientists began the study in 1967, working under a grant from the National Institutes of Health. Approximately one-third of all existing hunter-gatherers (some 9,000 persons) inhabit the Kalahari desert. The study group concentrated on the inhabitants of one small area of this 350,000-square-mile expanse. The study area has a radius of less than 20 miles and is surrounded by vast stretches of waterless expanse. It includes 11 permanent water holes and wells, between 400 and 500 plant and animal species, and about 450 Bushmen.

The Harvard project investigated such topics as health, nutrition, family and group structure, child rearing, personal relationships, rituals, technology, and general ways of coping with the environment. Archaeologists with the project studied Bushmen living floors, excavating them and asking explanations of what they uncovered, hoping to generate alternative interpretations for prehistoric living sites. Bushman garbage dumps were analyzed to see what kinds and amounts of accumulations were left. From this we hope to gather a clearer understanding of the many seemingly prehistoric "garbage dumps," for example, how many people it took to accumulate the debris, how much, and what items are most likely to be preserved.

Much time was spent watching what Bushmen eat and their manner of obtaining food. Before the study it was assumed that the hunter-gatherer's life bordered on starvation and that the task of finding food was an all-consuming activity; for the Bushman, food gathering requires only a bare minimum of equipment; the basic tools include a pair of unworked hammerstones for cracking nuts and a digging stick. The most important item is the "kaross," a combination garment and receptacle made of antelope hide draped over the woman's shoulder. Into the pocket formed by draping they stuff food, such as nuts, berries, and roots, and their children.[2] Obtaining meat protein is a much harder task requiring a more complicated tool assemblage; however, the !Kung San Bushman is an excellent hunter and trapper (Lee, 1978).

A study was made of Bushman productivity in relation to the food resources available to them. With their present tools and knowledge, and at their present population level, Bushmen could not exceed a daily fuel supply of 3,200 calories—no matter how hard they worked. The Bushman has achieved 60 percent of a theoretical maximum production level with few technological advantages. The Bushman model may be a reflection of basic forces and relationships found in the study of all communities, at all technological levels. An analysis of Bushman economics is being attempted in the hope of generating a broad mathematically based theory that can be applied to world problems far more complex than those of the Kalahari. Such a theory may permit planners to predict more precisely the impact of new programs in industry, public health, and education on the course of social development.

Studies of Bushman social behavior and organization are also being undertaken. A study is being made of the choice of living sites; we hope to get a clearer idea of living-floor patterns found at long-deserted sites. Lee studied the factors that force people to move from one camp

---

[2]One of the first tools which prehistoric populations developed may have been some sort of carrying device.

Figure 10-6. A Kalahari !Kung San Bushman husband and wife. The wife is 9 years old; the marriage was prearranged.

to another and found that Bushman groups typically occupy a camp for weeks and months before they literally eat their way out of it. Such very basic data may help explain some of the migrations of prehistoric populations.

Summary. Because events in the prehistoric past cannot be observed directly, the anthropologist can only reconstruct them from material evidence. Such reconstruction is based on analogy, whereby the identity of unknown forms or relations may be inferred from those already known. One of the problems with this approach is immediately evident. For example, living societies whose technology is similar to that inferred from the archaeological record are sometimes viewed as exact analogs for the reconstruction of the entire prehistoric culture. Living societies still using stone-tool technologies, such as the Australian aborigine, have been used as analogs to prehistoric Paleolithic European hunting societies of tens of thousands of years ago.

Obviously, this kind of analogy is suspect. It is founded on one criterion, technology, and ignores other variables in time and space. In linking the Australian aborigine with the Paleolithic of Europe, the analogy disregards a temporal separation of more than 10,000 years and a spatial distance of more than 10,000 miles (Sharer and Ashmore, 1979). Nevertheless, modern hunter-gatherers may provide a clue to the dynamics of the band existence of prehistoric peoples (Howell, 1979). Studies of hunter-gatherers may provide clues to why our complicated lives sometimes produce excessive stress; from the so-called primitive societies we may learn lessons that better enable us to cope with our technological societies.

One result of studies of hunting-gathering societies is the establishment of the so-called "magic numbers" idea proposed about 15 years ago by a University of California at Los Angeles anthropologist Joseph Birdsell (1972). The "magic numbers" of 25 and 500 refer to sizes of hunter-gatherer bands and tribes, respectively. Investigators regard these numbers as hints to the existence of social regularities that we do not yet understand. Birdsell, studying rates of population growth among Australian aborigines, noted that band size ranged from 20 to 50 persons. He selected 25 as a representative size. Since, studies of Kalahari !Kung San Bushmen and the Birhar of northern India have provided data to support the number 25 as being an average group size. From these figures we postulate that prehistoric populations probably averaged close to 25 members per band; supporting evidence comes from some prehistoric living-floors. Although there is nothing absolute about this number, it may represent an equilibrium number. The number 25 may have something to do with the most efficient working groups of adult males and is consistent with the range of primate groups generally.

The second "magic number," 500, is placed as an average for a "dialect" tribe of hunter-gatherers, that is, a group all speaking the same dialect. This is a purely human phenomenon and holds not only for aborigines but for the Shoshoni of the Great Plains and the Andaman Islanders in the Bay of Bengal. The number 500 is an equilibrium value and not an absolute figure. Birdsell has noted that the sizes of individual tribes may range from extremes of about 200 to more than 800 persons. The 500 number becomes clear and meaningful only after taking into consideration the census figures for a large number of tribes.

The number 500 apparently reflects certain features of the human communication system. Furthermore, groups of 500 members may breed more effectively than smaller or larger groups. The unity of hunting-gathering societies depends on face-to-face contact, on close intimacy among members of its component bands. This unity creates the impression of belonging to an extended community, even though various bands may live miles apart and come together only at certain times of the year. The intimacy is based on not only the same language, but a store of shared knowledge.

There are apparently "laws" governing the extent of sharing. There seems to be a basic limit to the number of persons who are capable of knowing one another well enough to maintain a tribal identity at the hunter-gatherer level, who communicate by direct confrontation, and who live under a diffuse and informal influence, perhaps a council of elders. Morris (1967) has discussed this phenomenon in his book *The Naked Ape*. Furthermore, Murdock (noted in Pfieffer, 1969) has demonstrated the validity of the number 500 in technologically advanced societies. For example, an architect's rule of thumb states that the enrollment of an elementary school should not exceed 500 pupils if the principal expects to know them all by name.

The underlying mechanism accounting for the "magic numbers" is yet to be resolved. The memory capacity of the human brain must be relevant. Additionally, we have mentioned the factors of an effective gene pool, the establishment of feelings of intimacy, and perhaps the effective functioning of "loose," or informal, social control mechanisms.

Nonhuman Primates

As creatures most closely related to us, nonhuman primates have been studied from various perspectives (Figure 10-7). Most early work was biomedical and only comparatively recently has behavioral research become a major component of nonhuman primate studies. The study of primate social behavior is one of the most rapidly growing and exciting fields in the behavioral sciences. The growth of and fascination in such studies owes much to the fact that

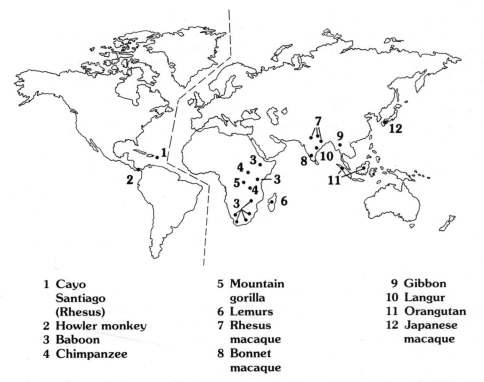

1 Cayo
  Santiago
  (Rhesus)
2 Howler monkey
3 Baboon
4 Chimpanzee

5 Mountain
  gorilla
6 Lemurs
7 Rhesus
  macaque
8 Bonnet
  macaque

9 Gibbon
10 Langur
11 Orangutan
12 Japanese
   macaque

Figure 10-7. Survey of some studies of nonhuman primates. (All but #2 are Old World forms, and #1 is an introduced and artificially fed population.)

nonhuman primates, because of their special relationship to us, have attracted the attention of many disciplines, for example, anthropology, psychiatry, psychology, biomedical fields, and zoology. Each discipline varies in the extent and vigor to which it studies primate social behavior and each offers something different in terms of perspective, theory, content, and method. No single discipline dominates the field. This is a mixed blessing. Primate studies provide a new approach to comparative animal behavior that cuts across traditional boundaries and itself accommodates many disciplines.

It is difficult to conduct a study of nonhuman primates in the natural setting. The investigator must be many things at once: psychologist, anthropologist, zoologist, botanist, geneticist, animal lover, and above all, a very patient individual. It was originally assumed that if you have seen one monkey, you have seen them all, but now we know this is a very inaccurate assumption. Our research has centered on a few primates in various parts of the world. We know something about the prosimians on the island of Madagascar, a fair amount about some South American monkeys, a good bit about such Old World monkeys as baboons, macaques, and some colobines (leaf eaters), and a fair share about apes. We hope that the information we now have is fairly representative of some aspects of primate behavior and social organization.

The study of primate behavior is still in the gathering stage; premature theories were proposed, only to be retracted when more data accumulated or when research showed that primates differ from one another. We still propose theories, only now they are less sweeping, based on more data, and, we hope, tested by field and laboratory study. Primate research follows various strategies; the least complicated treats the nonhuman primate as a human model as in biomedical research. Another approach, one with which anthropologists are more familiar, is the evolutionary-comparative perspective, which uses living nonhuman primates as a means of looking into our past to decipher evolutionary trends in human behavior.

Observers of behavior record what their subjects do—when, where, and for how long. Field observers restrict descriptions to behavior because of the difficulty of taking complex laboratory equipment into the field and because they wish to minimize disruption. The most common tools of the trade include paper and pen for taking notes (a small tape recorder or stenorette is sometimes substituted), a good pair of binoculars, and a good camera equipped with a telephoto lens. These basics, plus a good pair of legs for hiking, perseverance to sit long hours awaiting the arrival of your subjects, an open, inquisitive mind, and 18 eyes appropriately scattered about your head for looking in all directions at once are the essentials. Under natural conditions field workers observe how animals react to changing social and environmental conditions, how they interact with each other, and how they obtain food. If the society observed is social by nature (almost all primate societies are), the observers attempt to describe its structure.

Behavioral observation of the sort normally conducted by anthropologists, psychologists, and zoologists in the field is called ethology. The observer, the ethologist, searches for the functions of the observed behavior patterns, trying to understand what selection pressures have shaped their evolution. The ethological approach attempts to reconstruct the phylogeny of motor patterns and to explore the processes underlying ontogeny by investigating the releasing stimuli and the underlying physiological processes. Ethological studies begin with a description of the behavioral repertoire of a species, the ethogram. The ethogram should be a complete description of an animal's behavioral patterns as well as a discussion of the form and function of such behaviors.

One of the goals of the ethologist is to record directly the behavior of individuals as it occurs. Using various analytic techniques, ethologists seek to find recurring "constellations" of behavioral patterns. Such behaviors are considered to be more closely related to one another than to other behavior patterns outside the constellation. Behavioral constellations are the bases for more general behavior categories, for example, maternal behavior, hunting, and aggression, which can be defined in terms of their consequences.

A key element of the ethological approach is an emphasis on the evolutionary significance of behavior. For example, to appreciate the development of human behavioral patterns such as facial expressions, gestures, and body postures, we must compare these with the behavioral patterns of those animals with whom we most recently shared an ancestry, the nonhuman primates. McGrew (1972) notes that such comparisons exist on several levels; for example, on the morphological level similar muscles produce similar behavioral patterns. Many patterns show operational similarities between different structures acting together. Functional similarities also exist whereby interpersonal sequences of behavioral patterns may result in similar social consequences. Finally, situational similarities occur; for example, pushing and pulling commonly occur in aggressive situations. One could list a host of human and nonhuman primate behavioral patterns that are comparable.

Ethologists are also concerned with comparing the behavior of different populations of the same species. This intraspecific comparison provides an indication of the species' adaptability to different habitat requirements; phylogenetically advanced animals generally show relatively complex adaptive behavior.

Why Observe? The purpose of naturalistic primate studies has been consistent—to collect meaningful and accurate data that will advance our knowledge and understanding of the complex behavior of primates, including ourselves. There has been a continuity of effort to observe and describe both similarities and differences characteristic of nonhuman primates. Attempts have been made to conduct systematic studies of all observable modalities of behavior at the same time we seek plausible explanations or descriptions of behavioral determinants.

Field studies of the last few years have provided a new appreciation of the variety and complexity of primate social behavior. These investigations demonstrate the remarkable variability of social behavior. Primate studies have made major contributions to behavioral science and it is significant that the potential of scientific knowledge about primate behavior remaining to be tapped greatly exceeds that already achieved.

Field studies of monkeys and apes have added considerably to our understanding of hominid evolution. For example, Jay (1968:487-88) has noted:

> A great deal can be learned from the bones that comprise our fossil records, but the life of ancient primates comprised much more than the obvious function of these bony parts. For example, a certain kind of roughened surface on a fossilized ischium (the seat) merely indicates that the primate has ischial callosities. But by looking at how living primates with these callosities behave it is possible to infer that in all likelihood the ancient animal slept sitting up rather than on its side in a nest. This may seem trivial, but when many such clues are gathered and collated, the total picture of an animal's way of life fills in to a closer approximation of what it must have been.
>
> Our ancestors were not the same as the living primates, but the rich variability of behavior of modern monkeys and apes makes it possible to reconstruct the most probable pattern of related forms in the past.

Studies of nonhuman primates in their habitats already have resulted in the following suggestions about how life probably was for our ancestors (Washburn and Moore, 1974):

1. Our life was probably always social, for almost all monkeys and apes live in social groups. Social behavior seems to be deeply rooted in our evolutionary past.
2. Our daily life was restricted to a certain area. Today, primates live in limited ranges that are determined by food, water, and safe sleeping areas and escape routes. The size of the range varies greatly according to the amount and distribution of resources, among other variables. As long as our ancestors were primates, they were restricted to narrow ranges. By the time they became hunters, they roamed over wider areas. This assumption is supported by data on such social carnivores as hyenas, wild hunting dogs, and lions.
3. In many species of monkeys and apes the female is sexually receptive only during relatively short time periods. Loss of the estrous cycle, the time of sexual receptivity, may have provided an evolutionary advantage by reducing the fighting and tension that the sexual cycle often produces in nonhuman primates. Humans are the only primates that are conceivably sexually receptive 24 hours a day, 365 days a year.
4. In the wild monkeys rarely are observed using tools or, better stated, manipulating objects. When they do so, it is usually done to exhibit antagonism.

In primatology, early insights on animal ethology were vitalized and expanded by empirically based analyses of how, when, and with what force natural selection acts within a particular social group. New sets of questions are being asked that are not included in early primate studies, especially the relationship between ecology, group demography, and major events of the life cycle. New data on the cost and efficiency of, for example, reproduction, differences in dispersion, mortality, and energy requirements are being sought.

Characteristics of Nonhuman Primate Societies

Jolly and Plog (1976) note five basic types of nonhuman primate social organizations: (1) noyau, (2) territorial pair, (3) one-male group, (4) multi-male troop, and (5) one-male groups within a multi-male troop. We shall briefly discuss the characteristics of these various social groupings.

Noyau. The noyau may be the most primitive primate social organization. In this group, males and females defend territories, males are solitary, and females are often accompanied solely by their immature offspring. Each male has a territory overlapping that of several females, with whom he mates. This organization typifies some nocturnal prosimians, such as pottos and bush babies.

Territorial Pair. This social organization, typical of gibbons, was seen by some early investigators as the basis of the human family. In the territorial pair a male and a female are paired in a territory that they defend against other such pairs. The male and female of the gibbon territorial pair drive out other members of the same sex, including their maturing offspring. This behavior minimizes population concentrations in small areas. There is minimal sexual dimorphism in pair-organized species.

The One-Male Group. This social organization is found in many nonhuman primates such as some members of the genus *Cercopithecus,* some colobines, and the savannah-dwelling patas. All members of the social unit forage and move together. Nonattached males either live alone or in all-male groups. As is the case among south Indian common langurs, the entrance of such males to a bisexual group may precipitate considerable aggression and infanticide.

Multi-Male Troop. The multi-male troop characterizes many nonhuman primates and its appearance was once considered universal due to the findings made in early studies of savannah-dwelling baboons. Multi-male troops, especially those living on the savannah, are large social organizations. Patterns of social organizations are often characterized by a dominance structure in which members are ranked among themselves. Priority in mating is often, but not exclusively, determined according to the dominance structure, with dominant males perhaps contributing a larger proportion of the genes to the gene pool.

One-Male "Harem" Group. This group, in which a male lives with a "harem" of females, lives within a larger multi-male structure. Among hamadryas baboons, for example, the leader male is the focus of the group, receiving the most **grooming** (picking through one's own hair or the hair of another animal with fingers or teeth) and controlling the behavior of the harem. Mating with females is the sole prerogative of this male.

Most monkeys and apes live well-organized lives in social groups organized according to rules established on the basis of age, sex, and relative dominance. These groups are characterized by group cooperation, status differentiation, a rather complex communication system, and social traditions. Some nonhuman primates are **territorial,** that is, they defend the area in which they live, and some exhibit the rudiments of tool using and tool making. Against this background, culture (the human social milieu) is clearly a greatly elaborated expression of the primate way of life. Its distinctly human hallmark is language.

Monkey and ape societies have certain unique traits differentiating them from other animal societies. For the most part, they are permanent, year-round bisexual organizations as opposed to the seasonal, sometimes unisexual groupings of many other social animals. In contrast to many other mammalian groups wherein the mother rears her young exclusively, the primate infant is raised and socialized within the stable social group (although socialization is still primarily left to the females). Social behavior is the key to understanding primate life. Because of the highly social nature of nonhuman primates we must view natural groups, as well as individuals, as the adaptive units of the species (Figure 10-8).

Social living places a premium on learning. Many less intelligent animals, such as birds and fish, have social behaviors, but these are largely dependent on fixed and innate cues. Primates, by contrast, respond not only to fixed cues, but to subtle variances. Since there is great individual and behavioral variability, a nonhuman primate must be flexible and discriminating in its response. One highly important adaptive trait common to nonhuman primates is their degree of flexibility and adaptability.

In a previous paper (Poirier, 1969:130-31), I noted:

> Because much of primate behavior results from a sizeable learning component, and learning may not be transferable to all segments of the population, we must be prepared to find and report intertroop behavioral variability. For this reason intraspecific comparative studies are imperative before it can be stated with any degree of confidence whether a particular behavioral pattern or mode of social organization characteristic of one particular social group also typifies the genus or even the species.

And,

> To understand the habitat shift which occurred in Pliocene times, we must be cognizant of the behavioral background of the higher primates. This successful habitat shift obviously involved behavioral plasticity, e.g., the ability to adapt to new surroundings, and a constant curiosity leading to the acquisition of new traits meeting the challenge of the habitat. Non-human primates are endowed with the ability to meet such a challenge. Behavioral flexibility . . . was probably the essential trait allowing these qualities to develop.

The importance of the fact that most primates are social animals residing in highly complex, year-around social groups of varying size and composition is crucial. The social group has long been the primate niche; indeed, the social group has long been the mammalian niche. Group characteristics vary, and the degree of sociality, dominance, sexuality, and interanimal relationships varies; however, most primates spend part of their life in close association with conspecifics. Within the social group an animal learns to adapt to its surroundings. Differences among primate societies depend on the species' biology, and to a great extent on the circumstances in which animals live and learn. The composition of the social group, the particular balance of interanimal relationships, constitutes the character of the social environment within which youngsters learn and mature. Because of the highly social nature of nonhuman primates we must view groups, as well as individuals, as the adaptive units of the species.

Since most primates live a rather complex social life, they must learn to adjust to one another, they must learn to get along; compared to most of the rest of the animal world primate societies may have the greatest differentiation of *learned* social roles. The primate brain is a complex and efficient learning mechanism, and Diamond and Hall (1969) specify the mammalian association cortex as the neocortex subdivision where prime evolutionary advancements have occurred. Some (e.g., Radinsky, 1975) disagree, however. Although

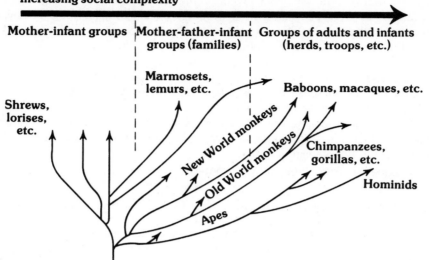

Figure 10-8. Trends in primate social evolution. (This chart lists representative species.)

primate learning skills are not solely accountable by the volume of the neocortex relative to total brain volume, it is significant that the primate neocortex is proportionally larger than that of carnivores and rodents (Harman, 1957). The complex cognitive processes and advanced learning skills are accommodated by increased cortical fissuration, increased numbers of cortical units in the cortex fine structure, and the refinement of the subcortical structure interrelating the thalamus and cortex (Norback and Moskowitz, 1963; Rumbaugh, 1970).

Social living is requisite for the young primate to perform effectively as an adult of its species. Animals with restricted social experiences, for example those raised in isolation or in unnatural conditions, exhibit some degree of social maladjustment, most especially in mothering, sexual, grooming, and aggressive behavioral patterns (Mason, 1960, 1961a,b, 1963). Laboratory studies suggest that the full development of an animal's biological potentialities requires stimulus and direction from social forces such as are usually supplied from the social group (Harlow, 1963, 1965; Mason, 1963, 1965).

While troop, or social, life is important, it must be cautioned that not all primates have the same degree of social life. Among Nilgiri langurs, for example, social relations are not oriented toward individual protection by cooperative group action, but instead by an individual's dashing through the nearest trees (Poirier, 1969a, 1977).[3] Why, then, does the Nilgiri langur still live in a social group if the animals do not take full advantage of the opportunities of group life in the form of protection, grooming, and play? Washburn and Hamburg (1965) suggest that a primary reason for group existence is learning, the group being the center of knowledge and experience far exceeding that of its individual constituents. Within the group experience is pooled and generations linked; troop traditions (the sum total of individual learning

---

[3]An analogous situation is found among patas (Hall, 1968) and their social structure shows many similarities to that of the Nilgiri langur.

experiences) are more advantageous than individual learning in many situations (Kummer, 1971; Poirier, 1972, 1977). Tradition pools individual experiences and is superior to individual learning if the new behavior is difficult to acquire individually in direct interaction with the environment. Troop tradition is based on a long life expectancy (a primate biological trait) and a leading role for older animals (in fact, primate societies may be viewed as gerontocracies).

Within the social context the animal is socialized and learns what foods to eat, who existing predators are, and the correct mode of behavioral interaction. Primates learn their mode of survival by living in a troop where they benefit from the shared knowledge and experience of the species (Poirier, 1970a, 1971). The primary reinforcement for all normal primate learning is the social context, the group in which the infant is born and nurtured. Even sensorimotor activities such as observing, manipulating, and exploring that indicates individual independence receive some facilitation, or inhibition, from the group setting. Contrasting group social structures impose differences in learning patterns leading to individual behavior formation and imply that group modification will alter the socialization process, yielding individuals with different behaviors (Poirier, 1972; 1973b, 1977; Sugiyama, 1972).

Learning to be flexible and adaptable, learning to exist and coexist within the social context, learning one's role in the social order, is at an optimum for primates. Primates inherit an ease of learning, rather than fixed instinctive patterns; they easily, almost inevitably, learn behaviors essential for survival. Primates learn to be social, but they are so constructed that under normal circumstances learning almost always occurs (Washburn and Hamburg, 1965). Presumably in most higher mammalian systems, and particularly in primate social systems, individual behaviors are controlled by a continuous process of social learning arising from group interactional patterns. Learning to act according to social modes is extremely important, for animals whose behavioral traits do not conform sufficiently to group norms are less likely to reproduce and may be ejected. Social selection of this type apparently has a strong stabilizing influence on the genetic basis of temperamental traits and motivational thresholds, for Crook (1970) suggests that primate societies might shape the genetic basis of individual social responses.

Learning during socialization and the emergence of one's social role has a preponderant influence in shaping individual behavior. Social conformity and the maintenance of a group structure result from the adoption of traditional behaviors characteristic of the total social system, and are primarily accomplished by three interacting groups of factors (Crook, 1970): (1) the species repertoire of biologically programmed neonate reflexes and social signals, plus innate factors affecting temperament and tendencies to learn some responses more readily than others, (2) the behavior of individuals composing the social milieu, which partly controls the emergence of individual role playing, and (3) direct environmental effects, that is, availability of need-reducing commodities and consequent behavioral learning that exploits the world in the manner ensuring greatest individual survival.

Brief History of Primate Studies

Early 1900s. Perusal of the nonhuman primate behavior literature written over the last 60 years clearly indicates major research trends. In the late 1920s and 1930s a 3-month observation period was considered sufficient; now anything less than one calendar year is inadequate and even this is the minimum. During the early years, pre- and immediately post-Darwin, anecdotal accounts were given great credit. Many accepted the following account as truth. As soon as a howler monkey (a South American monkey) is wounded, so this story goes, its fellows gather round, and place their fingers in the wound,

> as if they were desirous of sounding its depth. If the blood then flows in any quantity, they keep it shut up, while others get leaves, which they chew and thrust into the orifice. I can affirm having seen this circumstance several times with admiration (Zuckerman, 1963:10).

A very readable account of the early fascination, and disgust, which humans felt towards their nonhuman primate relatives is given in the book *Men and Apes* by Morris and Morris.

Prior to the twentieth century, our knowledge of nonhuman primate behavior was anecdotal and consisted mainly of travelers' tales and miscellaneous reports. Sometimes the further from the truth, the more absurd the report, the greater credibility it seemed to have. Apart from the mythological literature surrounding some of the primates, volumes of pseudo-scientific information existed.

Yerkes. Due to the efforts of the late psychologist Robert M. Yerkes of Yale University, the 1920s witnessed the beginning of scientific research into nonhuman primate behavior. Yerkes never entered the jungle to study primates; he watched his chimpanzees climb trees in his backyard in New Hampshire. In 1929 the Yerkeses published their important book entitled *The Great Apes: A Study of Anthropoid Life,* compiling all then-known facts about the great apes. Yerkes was amazed how little factual information existed, so in 1929 and 1930 he sent two students to Africa—Harold Bingham to study the gorilla and Henry Nissen to study the chimpanzee. In 1930 Yerkes opened the famed Laboratories of Primate Biology at Orange Park, Florida, which has been moved to Emory University in Atlanta and has been renamed the Yerkes Regional Primate Research Center.

Carpenter. The first major breakthrough in primate field studies came in 1934 when the late C. R. Carpenter spent two years studying Central American howler monkeys on Barro Colorado Island. This island is situated in the midst of Gatun Lake and was formed with the building of the Panama Canal. Carpenter's work on Barro Colorado Island stands as an early monument of scientific methodology. From here Carpenter went on to study other primates and eventually established the rhesus monkey colony at Cayo Santiago (Santiago Island) off the eastern coast of Puerto Rico. Carpenter and Yerkes were interested in primate studies for their own sake; they studied animals in their natural settings to know something about the animals. They were also interested in relating their work to humans.

Zuckerman. The English zoologist Sir Solly Zuckerman founded a second tradition, that of studying nonhuman primates because they can tell us something about ourselves. In 1933 Zuckerman traveled to South Africa to study chacma baboons inhabiting the cliffs near Capetown. He also studied the hamadryas baboons held captive in the London Zoo. His studies led him to postulate a sweeping theory of the beginning of human social behavior. Zuckerman argued that sexual behavior (the prolonged willingness on the part of the female to mate) was the original social force binding the primate social group. This theory was revised in the late 1950s and early 1960s when it was discovered, on the basis of other baboon studies, that nonhuman primates actually partake in little sexual behavior. Furthermore, sexual behavior can actually be a disruptive force rather than a cohesive bond and in many species is seasonal and all troop members may not show it. Saayman (1975), however, has recently resurrected Zuckerman's hypothesis. Saayman does argue for the binding force of sexual behavior. The best position presently is to recognize that there are pros and cons on both sides of the argument.

Köhler. In the early 1900s, Wolfgang Köhler researched "insight learning" among chimpanzees; his are the famous experiments of chimpanzees stacking boxes to obtain bananas. Köhler began a third tradition in primate research, modern primate psychology, which studied the abilities and limitations of reasoning by higher primates. As an outgrowth of this tradition, chimpanzees and gorillas were brought into one's home where their development was compared to the human child's. Such studies are recalled in Hayes's book *The Ape in Our House*, Hoyt's highly readable book *Toto and I: A Gorilla in the Family*, the Kellogg's book *The Ape and the Child*, and Temerlin's *Lucy: Growing Up Human*.

Japanese Colonies. Immediately following World War II Japanese primatologists developed a tradition of primate studies that changed many of our concepts about primate social organization and behavior. The Japanese established **provisioned colonies** of the indigenous Japanese macaque. Free-ranging colonies were artificially supplied food and these provisioned troops in various parts of Japan have been studied over the past 20 years.

Washburn and DeVore. In the late 1950s S. L. Washburn and I. DeVore traveled to eastern Africa to conduct a study of savanna-dwelling baboons. This study led the way in questioning Zuckerman's "sexual bond" hypothesis. Washburn and DeVore hoped they would discover something about our savanna-dwelling ancestors of the Lower Pleistocene; baboons were used as models for deciphering early hominid social behavior and organization.

Centers for Primate Research. Primate behavior is generally studied under the following conditions: in any of the seven National Primate Research Centers, in seminatural provisioned colonies established at Cayo Santiago, Puerto Rico, or Barro Colorado, Canal Zone, in the provisioned colonies at the Japan Monkey Centre, or under strictly natural field conditions where the scientist gets whatever information can be collected. The research is determined by the type of information one wishes to gather and by one's training. Historically, psychologists have worked in laboratory conditions that allow testing of specific hypotheses in a strictly controlled environment and long-term observation of individual animals and/or problems. Work with the introduced provisioned colonies and at the Japan Monkey Centre provides access to genealogically known animals. Investigators at such centers have kept meticulous records that supply the much needed depth perspective sorely missing from studies in the wild. Field-oriented scientists, anthropologists and zoologists, are most apt to work in the natural settings.

The natural setting is the appropriate situation in which to investigate such problems as the relationship of behavior to population pressure, predator pressure, and social structure. The laboratory is the place for answering specific questions often raised in the field, which need a controlled testing situation. Space is a major problem in the artificial colonies; crowding leads to an exaggeration of such patterns as aggression and sexual behavior—perhaps for lack of something better to do. Because of an artificial food supply relatively unrestricted population growth occurs and unusually large troop sizes result. The provisioned colonies at Cayo Santiago and the Japan Monkey Centre have reacted to overcrowding by group fission, that is, the monkeys divide into smaller groups, usually along kinship lines. This in itself is an interesting social phenomenon.

Future Primate Studies. Future primate studies (and many now under way) will be long-range, topic-oriented research projects. The 1-calendar-year study will give way (if money becomes available) to 2- or 3-year studies by a multidisciplinary team. These studies will be more problem oriented and will study specific topics such as socialization, adaptation to the habitat, and predator avoidance. Since it is now clear that there is much variability among free-ranging, undisturbed primate populations, and since we know there are substantial differences between and within species, we can expect that more species from a wider ecological range will be studied. There will also be more studies of the same species in different habitats to see what influence habitat has on social organization and behavior. Past studies have offered leads about the future; the future will tell how true these leads have been.

Caution. Modern primates are not exact representatives of our way of life millions of years ago. Nonhuman primates have evolved. They are the end product, as are we, of millions of years of evolution. However, although there are problems with reconstructing hominid behavior patterns from nonhuman primates, the method is still very valuable. An analysis of modern monkey and ape behavior has made it possible to reconstruct some of the early stages of human development; later phases may require a different approach.

Social Carnivores

Have you ever thought that we might learn a good deal about ourselves, about our evolutionary past, from watching the lion, tiger, hyena, or wild dog? Until recently only a few anthropologists and others who reconstruct human evolution did. A study by G. Schaller and G. Lowther of some of Africa's social carnivores changed that notion. In 1969 they published a joint article entitled "The Relevance of Carnivore Behavior to the Study of Early Hominids." While the search for clues about our past among nonhuman primates is reasonable on phylogenetic grounds, it is less so on ecological grounds. Social systems are strongly influenced by the habitat. Monkeys and apes are essentially vegetarians, living in groups confined to small home ranges; we assume, however, that our ancestors were widely roaming hunters and gatherers for perhaps two million years of our evolutionary history. This way of life is in strong contrast to that of modern nonhuman primates. Schaller and Lowther concluded that more could be learned about the genesis of our social systems by studying phylogenetically unrelated but ecologically similar forms than by studying nonhuman primates. Social carnivores were the obvious choice. Some selective pressures influencing the social existence of social carnivores also had an effect on human societies. In Chapter 17 we follow the Schaller and Lowther approach.

Social carnivores and such gnawing rodents as the porcupine are being studied from another perspective. Some investigators are watching what animals such as leopards eat, and are especially interested in the remains of a meal. Which bones are eaten, which are left behind, and the state of the leftovers are all important clues that allow us to decide whether bone accumulations are those of an ancient hominid or of an ancient carnivore. Porcupine burrows are being excavated in an attempt to see which bones such rodents store and how they eat these bones. The reasoning is the same—a scientific approach to determine which bone accumulations were left by humans and which by nonhumans. This approach provides a practical analysis of Raymond Dart's proposed australopithecine osteodontokeratic culture. One of the questions that arises is: Were the South African accumulations left by australopithecines, were they remains of a social carnivore's meal, or were they just some hungry porcupine's debris? This problem is discussed in Chapter 17.

Other Clues: Elephants

John Eisenberg studied the Ceylon elephant hoping to learn more about ourselves. We share with the elephant a similar life span and a record of having been able to coexist rather peacefully, at least until recently. Elephants have a basic social unit centered around a pregnant female associated with other females (often including the pregnant female's mother and sisters) and their offspring. Bulls (males) of 20 to 30 years live in less cohesive groups that

Table 10-2. The Comparative Method: Some Traits of Modern Baboons, Chimpanzees, Pliocene-Pleistocene Hominids, and Modern *Homo*

Baboons	*Chimpanzees*	*Pliocene-Pleistocene Hominids*	*Modern* Homo
		Habitat	
Varies, open-country savanna and forest. Stay close to trees for rest and refuge. In some areas use cliffs and rocks.	Savanna and forest, spend time in trees for feeding and sleeping.	Terrestrial, perhaps slept in trees, savanna dweller.	Terrestrial, wide variety of habitats.
		Diet	
Primarily vegetarian. Some groups opportunistically eat and hunt meat.	Mostly vegetarian, occasionally hunts small animals.	Omnivorous, small seeds and grains, meat scavenged and hunted.	Omnivorous.
		Subsistence Pattern	
Foraging and occasional hunting and sharing of meat in some groups.	Foraging, some hunting and meat sharing.	Foraging, hunting and gathering, probably food sharing.	Wide variety of subsistence patterns.
		Social Organization	
Varies with habitat. Strict dominance, sexual dimorphism, tight groups in savanna. In forest, slight dominance and looser groups. Multimale and harems among hamadryas.	Varies with habitat, more tightly knit in savanna, relaxed dominance, group structure varies and many subgroups visible, prolonged mother-infant contact.	Based on comparative primate and social carnivore evidence, there may have been some kind of dominance structure, the mother-infant pair strong, sexual division of labor.	Wide variety of social organizations and ideologies.
		Tool Use and Manufacture	
Does not make and use tools.	Makes and uses tools, but not dependent on tools.	Many tools made of stone, Oldowan tradition.	Dependent on tools.
		Locomotion	
Quadrupedal.	Brachiation and quadrupedal in trees, knuckle-walk and bent-knee bipedalism on the ground.	Bipedal.	Bipedal.

Adapted from B. G. Campbell, *Humankind Emerging*, p. 197. Little, Brown and Company, Boston © 1976.

are occasionally accompanied by one to three "satellite" males, 11 to 14 years old. The oldest bulls, males aged 40 or more, often travel alone.

During dry periods large elephant herds, some containing more than 300 animals, may form loosely organized groups. Eisenberg has used this situation to test the idea that "when an animal like man or the elephant attains a certain body size and brain size, it is capable of unique memory feats" (quoted in Pfeiffer, 1972:336). Migration may mean moving over any one of a number of complicated routes, traveling long distances, and avoiding villages. This ability requires a considerable grasp of knowledge, of intelligence.

The elephant's environment also has a 10-year drought cycle that requires memorization of additional data that must be retained for a decade or more and then be recalled during a crisis situation. The elephant's size apparently not only provides it with predator protection; it also pays off in terms of proportionate brain size and memory capacity that permits shaping long-term survival strategies. Research on elephants may be expected to increase the understanding of the role of memory in human evolution.

What traditionalist would have suspected that in order to learn about our past we would be studying nonhuman primates, feeding leopards, crawling into hyena dens, excavating porcupine burrows, and watching elephants? It is happening and there is no telling what we may study tomorrow. We are at the point where we are open-minded enough to try anything that may provide clues to our past. We are finally reaching the ultimate in evolutionary theory; we are using all the information at hand to reconstruct and form a theory of primate evolution.

Bibliography

Ardrey, R. 1966. *The territorial imperative*. New York: Dell.

_____. 1968. *African genesis*. New York: Dell.

_____. 1970. *The social contract*. New York: Atheneum.

Beck, B. 1975. Primate tool behavior. In *Socioecology and psychology of primates*, edited by R. Tuttle, pp. 413-47. The Hague: Mouton.

Birdsell, J. 1972. *Human evolution*. Chicago: Rand McNally.

Campbell, B. 1976. *Humankind emerging*. Boston: Little, Brown.

Carpenter, C. 1964. *Naturalistic behavior of nonhuman primates*. University Park: Pennsylvania State University Press.

Carthy, J., and Ebling, F., eds. 1964. *The natural history of aggression*. New York: Academic Press.

Chance, M., and Jolly, C. 1970. *Social groups of monkeys, apes and men*. London: Cape.

Chapple, E. 1970. *Culture and biological man*. New York: Holt, Rinehart and Winston.

Cohen, Y., ed. 1968. *Man in adaptation—the biosocial background*. Chicago: Aldine.

Crook, J., ed. 1970. *Social behavior in birds and mammals*. New York: Academic Press.

Darling, F. 1964. *A herd of red deer*. New York: Doubleday.

Diamond, S., and Hall, W. 1969. Evolution of the neocortex. *Science* 164:251-62.

Eibl-Eibesfeldt, I. 1970. *Ethology—the biology of behavior*. New York: Holt, Rinehart and Winston.

Eisenberg, J., and Dillon, W., eds. 1971. *Man and beast: comparative social behavior*. Washington, D.C.: Smithsonian Institution Press.

Freeman, L. 1968. A theoretical framework for interpreting archaeological materials. In *Man the hunter*, edited by R. Lee and I. DeVore, pp. 262-67. Chicago: Aldine.

Gifford, D. 1980. Ethnoarchaeological contributions to the taphonomy of human sites. In *Fossils in the making: vertebrate taphonomy and paleoecology*, edited by A. Behrensmeyer and A. Hill, pp. 94-107. Chicago: University of Chicago Press.

Gould, R. 1968a. *Chipping stone in the outback*. Garden City, N.Y.: Natural History Press.

_____. 1968b. Living archaeology: the Ngatatjara of Western Australia. *Southwestern Journal of Anthropology* 24:101-22.

_____. 1969. *Yiwara: foragers of the Australian desert*. New York: Scribner.

Hahn, E. 1971. *On the side of the apes*. New York: Crowell.

Hall, K. 1968. The behavior and ecology of the wild patas monkey, *Erythrocebus patas,* in Uganda. In *Primates: studies in adaptation and variability,* edited by P. Jay, pp. 32-119. New York: Holt, Rinehart and Winston.

Harlow, H. 1963. Basic social capacity of primates. In *Primate social behavior,* edited by C. Southwick, pp. 153-61. Princeton, N.J.: Van Nostrand.

_____. 1966. The primate socialization motives. *Transactions and Studies of the College of Physicians of Philadelphia* 33:224-37.

Harman, P. 1957. *Paleoneurologic, neoneurologic and ontogenetic aspects of brain phylogeny.* James Arthur lecture on the evolution of the human brain. New York: American Museum of Natural History.

Howell, N. 1979. *Demography of the Dobe !Kung.* New York: Academic Press.

Jay, P., ed. 1968. *Primates: studies in adaptation and variability.* New York: Holt, Rinehart and Winston.

Jolly, A. 1972. *The evolution of primate behavior.* New York: Macmillan.

Jolly, C., and Plog, F. 1976. *Physical anthropology and archaeology.* New York: Knopf.

Knapp, P. 1964. *Expression of the emotions in man.* New York: International University Press.

Köhler. W. 1956. *The mentality of apes.* New York: Humanities Press.

Kruuk, H. 1972. *The spotted hyena.* Chicago: University of Chicago Press.

Kummer, H. 1971. *Primate societies.* Chicago: Aldine-Atherton.

Lancaster, J. 1975. *Primate behavior and the emergence of human culture.* New York: Holt, Rinehart and Winston.

Lee, R. 1978. The !Kung San. New York: Cambridge University Press.

Lewis, J., and Towers, B. 1969. *Naked ape or* Homo sapiens? New York: Humanities Press.

Lorenz, K. 1961. *King Solomon's ring.* New York: Crowell.

_____. 1967. *On aggression.* New York: Harcourt, Brace & World.

McGrew, W. 1972. *An ethological study of children's behavior.* New York: Academic Press.

Mason, W. 1960. The effects of social restriction on the behavior of rhesus monkeys. I. Free social behavior. *Journal of Comparative and Physiological Psychology* 53:582-89.

_____. 1961a. The effects of social restriction on the behavior of rhesus monkeys. II. Tests of gregariousness. *Journal of Comparative and Physiological Psychology* 54:287-96.

_____. 1961b. The effects of social restriction on the behavior of rhesus monkeys. III. Dominance tests. *Journal of Comparative and Physiological Psychology* 54:694-99.

_____. 1963. The effects of environmental restriction on the social development of rhesus monkeys. In *Primate social behavior,* edited by C. Southwick, pp. 161-74. Princeton, N.J.: Van Nostrand.

_____. 1965. The social development of monkeys and apes. In *Primate behavior,* edited by I. DeVore, pp. 514-44. New York: Holt, Rinehart and Winston.

Mech, D. 1966. *The wolves of Isle Royale.* Washington, D.C.: U.S. Government Printing Office.

Montagu, A., ed. 1968. *Man and aggression.* New York: Oxford University Press.

Morris, D., ed. 1967. *Primate ethology.* Chicago: University of Chicago Press.

Morris, D. 1967. *The naked ape.* New York: McGraw-Hill.

_____. 1969. *The human zoo.* New York: McGraw-Hill.

Morris, D., and Morris, R. 1966. *Men and apes.* New York: McGraw-Hill.

Napier, J., and Napier, P. 1967. *A handbook of living primates.* New York: Academic Press.

Norback, C., and Moskowitz, N. 1963. The primate nervous system: functional and structural aspects of phylogeny. In *Evolutionary and genetic biology of primates,* Vol. I, edited by J. Buettner-Janusch, pp. 131-75. New York: Academic Press.

Pfeiffer, J. 1969. *The emergence of man.* New York: Harper & Row.

_____. 1972. *The emergence of man,* 2nd ed. New York: Harper & Row.

Poirier, F. 1968a. Analysis of a Nilgiri langur (*Presbytis johnii*) home range change. *Primates* 9:29-44.

_____. 1968b. The Nilgiri langur (*Presbytis johnii*) mother-infant dyad. *Primates* 9:45.

_____. 1969a. The Nilgiri langur troop: its composition, structure, function and change. *Folia Primatologica* 19:20.

_____. 1969b. Behavioral flexibility and intertroop variability among Nilgiri langurs of South India. *Folia Primatologica* 11:119-33.

_____. 1970a. Nilgiri langur ecology and social behavior. In *Primate behavior: developments in field and laboratory research,* Vol. 1, edited by L. Rosenblum, pp. 251-383. New York: Academic Press.

_____. 1970b. The Nilgiri langur communication matrix. *Folia Primatologica* 13:92-137.

_____. 1971. Socialization variables. Paper presented to 70th American Anthropological Association, New York.

_____. 1972. Introduction. In *Primate socialization,* edited by F. Poirier, pp. 3-29. New York: Random House.

_____. 1973a. Nilgiri langur behavior and social organization. In *Essays to the chief,* edited by F. Voget and R. Stephenson, pp. 119-34. Eugene: University of Oregon Press.

_____. 1973b. Primate socialization and learning. In *Learning and culture,* edited by S. Kimball and J. Burnett, pp. 3-41. Seattle: University of Washington Press.

_____. 1981. *Fossil evidence: the human evolutionary journey.* St. Louis: Mosby.

Radinsky, L. 1975. Primate brain evolution. *American Scientist* 63:656-63.

Reynolds, P. 1977. The emergence of early hominid social organization. I. The attachment systems. *Yearbook of Physical Anthropology* 20:73-95.

Reynolds, V. 1967. *The apes.* New York: Dutton.

Rumbaugh, D. 1970. Learning skills of anthropoids. In *Primate behavior: developments in field and laboratory research,* Vol. I, edited by L. Rosenblum, pp. 2-70. New York: Academic Press.

Saayman, G. 1975. The influence of hormonal and ecological factors upon sexual behavior and social organization in Old World primates. In *Socioecology and psychology of primates,* edited by R. Tuttle, pp. 181-204. The Hague: Mouton.

Schaller, G. 1972. *The Serengeti lion.* Chicago: University of Chicago Press.

Schaller, G., and Lowther, G. 1969. The relevance of carnivore behavior to the study of early hominids. *Southwestern Journal of Anthropology* 25:307.

Schultz, A. 1969. *The life of primates.* New York: Universe Books.

Service, E. 1966. *The hunters.* New York: Prentice-Hall.

Sharer, R., and Ashmore, W. 1979. *Fundamentals of archaeology.* Menlo Park, Calif.: Benjamin/Cummings.

Sugiyama, Y. 1972. Social characteristics and socialization among wild chimpanzees. In *Primate socialization,* edited by F. Poirier, pp. 145-63. New York: Random House.

Temerlin, M. 1975. *Lucy: growing up human.* Palo Alto, Calif.: Science and Behavior Books.

Thompson, J. 1975. A cross-species analysis of carnivore, primate and hominid behavior. *Journal of Human Evolution* 4:113-24.

Tiger, L. 1969. *Men in groups.* New York: Vintage.

Tiger, L., and Fox, R. 1971. *The imperial animal.* New York: Holt, Rinehart and Winston.

Tuttle, R., ed. 1972. *The functional and evolutionary biology of primates.* Chicago: Aldine-Atherton.

van Lawick, H., and van Lawick-Goodall, J. 1970. *Innocent killers.* New York: Ballantine Books.

Washburn, S., ed. 1961. *Social life of early man.* Chicago: Aldine.

Washburn, S., and DeVore, I. 1961. The social life of baboons. *Scientific American* 204:62-71.

Washburn, S., and Hamburg, D. 1965. Implications of primate research. In *Primate behavior,* edited by I. DeVore, pp. 607-22. New York: Holt, Rinehart and Winston.

Washburn, S., and Moore, R. 1974. *Ape into man: a study of human evolution.* Boston: Little, Brown.

Watanabe, H. 1971. *The Ainu ecosystem.* Seattle: University of Washington Press.

Yerkes, R. 1943. *Chimpanzees—a laboratory colony.* New Haven: Yale University Press.

Zuckerman, S. 1963. Human sociology and the sub-human primates. In *Primate social behavior,* edited by C. Southwick, pp. 7-16. Princeton: Van Nostrand.

Chapter 11

Primate Behavior: The Monkeys and Prosimians

The subject of primate behavior can be presented in many ways, including the following: (1) with highlights of studies of various groups, for example, baboon studies, macaque studies, or langur studies, (2) in terms of behavioral patterns or social structures, for example, one-male groups, large versus small groups, or territorial versus nonterritorial animals, or (3) in terms of habitat, for example, arboreal versus terrestrial, savanna versus forest dwellers, or diurnal versus nocturnal animals. This chapter highlights various studies of monkeys and prosimians.

Pliny's Reports

The Roman historian Pliny the Elder provided one of the first written reports about monkeys. His description of what was known about the common monkeys of his day, which he mistakenly called apes, follows. From his reference to the "dog's headed ape," it is clear that he is referring to the baboon.

> The different kinds of apes, which approach the nearest to the human figure, are distinguished from each other by the tail. Their shrewdness is quite wonderful. It is said that, imitating the hunters, they will besmear themselves with bird-lime, and put their feet into the shoes, which, as so many snares, have been prepared for them. Mucianus says, that they have even played at chess, having, by practice, learned to distinguish the different pieces, which are made of wax. He says that the species which have tails become quite melancholy when the moon is on the wane, and that they leap for joy at the time of the new moon, and adore it. . . . All the species of apes manifest remarkable affection for their offspring. Females, which have been domesticated, and have had young ones, carry them about and shew them to all comers, shew great delight when they are caressed, and appear to understand the kindness thus shewn them. Hence it is, they very often stifle their young with their embraces. The dog's headed ape is of a much fiercer nature, as is the case with the satyr.

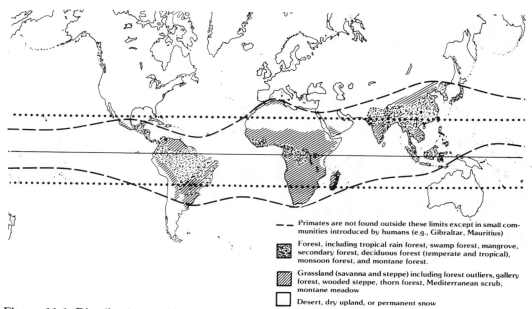

- - - Primates are not found outside these limits except in small communities introduced by humans (e.g., Gibraltar, Mauritius)

Forest, including tropical rain forest, swamp forest, mangrove, secondary forest, deciduous forest (temperate and tropical), monsoon forest, and montane forest.

Grassland (savanna and steppe) including forest outliers, gallery forest, wooded steppe, thorn forest, Mediterranean scrub, montane meadow

Desert, dry upland, or permanent snow

Figure 11-1. Distribution and habitats of living nonhuman primates.

Some of what Pliny records is true. Monkeys do show emotion and females (in most species) take close care of their young, carrying, grooming, and embracing them. Conversely, monkeys do not wear shoes, disguise themselves with bird-lime, or play chess! Some monkeys have, however, been trained to work: in Australia a baboon drives a tractor; in South Africa a baboon helps throw the switch at a rail junction; and in southeastern Asia macaques help harvest coconuts.

Prosimians

The Prosimii is the primate group least closely related to the human and constitutes a suborder apart from the monkeys, apes, and humans. Anatomically, some of the Prosimii have changed little from the earliest primates. Therefore, they offer some useful insights into early stages of primate evolution. Some Prosimii forms, such as some of the Lemuriformes, show close parallelisms with the monkeys and apes.

Most prosimians have smaller, flatter braincases than other primates. A pointed muzzle is often tipped by a naked rhinarium. In these and some other features, prosimians more closely resemble the ancestral nonprimate mammal than do the monkeys and apes. However, prosimians clearly show their primate affinities with hands and feet adapted for climbing by grasping.

The living prosimians fall into two infraorders, Tarsiiformes and Lemuriformes. Members of the family Tarsiidae belong to a group known as tarsiers (Figure 11-2). These are small, nocturnal animals with long tails, greatly elongated hindlimbs, and big, bulging eyes. The enormously enlarged eyes are used for locating insect prey at night and the elongation of the hindlimbs is an adaptation to hopping and leaping from branch to branch. Tarsiers are native to Southeast Asia; they are strictly arboreal, usually found in small groups or in pairs, and feed on insects, lizards, and fruits. There are some data on naturalistic behavior; however, tarsiers fare poorly in captivity.

The Lemuriformes is composed of two groups, the lorises and the lemurs, that have two different evolutionary histories. The lorises, members of the family Lorisidae, have representatives living in both Africa and Asia. Lorises are nocturnal animals and live either solitary or pair existences. Their diet is varied and includes insects, lizards, fruits, seeds, and leaves. The Asian members of the subfamily Lorisidae include the slender and slow loris; the African members are the potto and angwantibo.

The other subfamily of Lorisidae is Galaginae. This subfamily includes the galagos, some of which are called bush babies. These are social primates, apparently territorial, and insectivorous in diet. The galagos' principal locomotor mode is labeled vertical clinging and leaping. As a point of interest, it has been suggested by some (e.g., Napier and Walker, 1967) that this mode of locomotion was important in the evolution of bipedalism.

As already mentioned, there is a concentration of prosimians, members of the families of Lemuridae, Indriidae, and Daubentoniidae, on the island of Madagascar (Malagasy Republic). It is believed that the early ancestors of these animals are long removed from the monkey stock and have undergone their own independent adaptive radiation into a variety of forms.

Figure 11-2. Adult Philippine tarsier.

Lemurs belong to the family Lemuridae. While some members of the family are nocturnal and solitary, the ring-tailed lemur (Figure 11-3) is diurnal and lives in social groups. The family Indriidae includes forms known as the indri, avahi, and sifaka. These are the most monkeylike of the prosimians. Little is known about the social behavior of the indri. Avahi are reputed to live in family units composed of two to four individuals. The family Daubentoniidae contains the aye-aye. Aye-ayes are distinctive in the development of two large, chisellike teeth in the front of the jaw and an elongated nail on a long, thin, middle finger. The aye-aye is nocturnal and uses its teeth to tear open tree barks to get at grubs, which it then "spears" with its modified nail.

The social organization of the Malagasy lemurs provides some clues as to the nature of the earliest primate social organizations. One of the Malagasy forms, *Lepilemur*, lives in individual territories (Charles-Dominique and Hladik, 1971; Hladik, 1975). This type of social organization is characteristic of that described for many other so-called solitary primitive mammals. Hladik (1975) notes that females defend these territories against other females of the species. However, a female may share her territory with one or several of her daughters for a year or two. Males have territories that extend over one or several of the female territories, and these are defended against incursion from other males. As a result some extra males, those without these territories, live outside the nucleus of the population as peripheral males. Such males are common in most primate species.

A major component of the nocturnal activity of the *Lepilemur* is a motionless watching at the border of the territory. At nightfall, *Lepilemur* makes certain specific calls that function to locate each animal, and its territory, to its neighbors. Such calls, known as territorial calls[1], are common to territorial nonhuman primates such as langurs, colobines, and gibbons. Hladik notes that nearby animals can probably identify one another by their calls, for there are slight differences in the calls of each animal. (I was able to notice the same thing in my field study of South Indian Nilgiri langurs. Animals had distinctive vocal patterns distinguishing them from one another.)

The food of this prosimian, consisting mainly of foliage and flowers, is very abundant in all parts of its territory. This may explain why the animals do not move much and why they spend most of their time on watch for competitors at the territorial boundaries.

Prosimian ancestry diverged from ours in the Paleocene or early Eocene, long before the evolution of higher primates. Anatomically, and in some respects behaviorally, these animals are probably closer to the common ancestor of the primate stock than they are to more highly evolved primates. In 1863, T. H. Huxley noted, "Perhaps no order of mammals presents us with so extraordinary a series of gradations as this—leading us insensibly from the crown and summit of the animal creation down to creatures from which there is but a step, as it seems, to the lowest, smallest, and least intelligent of the placental mammals" (Jolly, 1966:8). Interestingly, although their anatomy is primitive for a primate, their social structures resemble those of monkeys. Many lemur species have multiple-male groups, and infants of either sex remain lifelong members of the bisexual social group. The bisexual, year-round social organization appears to be an ancient primate pattern. Lemurs provide a third, independent evolutionary line to compare with New and Old World primates.

Alison Jolly conducted a major study of lemur behavior that was subsequently published in her 1966 book entitled *Lemur Behavior: A Madagascar Field Study*. Among the most

---

[1]Such calls are also known as "loud calls" or "spacing calls" and are common not only to territorial primates. These calls serve to space neighboring groups.

Figure 11-3. A ring-tailed lemur, a Malagasy prosimian.

important aspects to emerge from Jolly's study are observations of the elements of lemur behavior common to other primate societies and of traits on which primate sociality may ultimately be based. Because they breed seasonally, the social Lemuroidea offer one final objection to the hypothesis that sex may be the major bonding force in primate societies. Presumably they have always bred seasonally, for they never developed a monthly cycle. Yet they share the basic primate social order of a bisexual, year-round, lifelong social organization that must be based on cohesive forces other than permanent sexual attraction.

Jolly also suggests that the ultimate derivation of adult social behaviors may stem directly from the infant's grooming and play behavior. The mother is the infant's first, and ultimate, social mate; the mother-infant dyad (group of two) may be the basis for establishing relationships vital to adult social ties.[2] If friendly social relations are derived from the mother-infant interaction, it suggests that mature social primates retain many infantile characters. This retention of infantile traits into adulthood is known as **neotony.** The original cohesive force in primate social evolution might be an infantile or juvenile attraction to others that was retained in adulthood.

Jolly's research also points to the relationship between the development of higher levels of intelligence and social living. Primate social behavior demands learning; it also makes learning possible. There seems to be a close relationship, a continual interaction, between intelligence and social dependence. Intelligence integrates an animal into a group (in which different animals play different roles, or the same animal plays many roles) and makes the individual more dependent on the group. This dependence, in its turn, allows and encourages increasing social intelligence. Social life may be a primate trait; but, intelligence and group dependence interrelate and reinforce each other as a normal adjunct of natural selection.

New World Monkeys

New World monkeys are aboreal animals ranging from southern Mexico to further south. New World monkeys are only found in tropical rain forests, but inhabit a wide variety of econiches within the rain forests. The evolutionary radiation of New World monkeys never developed a terrestrial, savanna-dwelling species comparable to, for example, the baboon.

Some New World monkeys of the Family Cebidae closely resemble the Old World monkeys, and it is difficult to believe that they are only distant relations. There are, however, important cranial and dental differences. South American monkeys have three premolars whereas Old World monkeys have two. Another major difference is nasal shape (Figure 11-4); the nostrils of New World monkeys are more widely spaced than those of Old World monkeys. Furthermore, the nostrils of New World monkeys face sideways rather than forward or down. Some New World monkeys also have prehensile tails, allowing them to use their tail as a fifth hand for grasping.

New World monkeys provide an evolutionary radiation that has in some respects paralleled that of the **catarrhines,** the Old World monkeys. For example, the spider monkey, as does the gibbon, has long, slender arms, from which it frequently swings beneath branches. Furthermore, as is the gibbon, it is mainly a **frugivorous** (fruit-eating) form and hangs from a branch while eating. Because of such parallelisms, the behavior of New World monkeys can often help reconstruct, through analogy, stages through which fossil catarrhines passed in their evolutionary history

[2] I have argued this point in a number of previous publications (see Poirier, 1968b, 1969a, 1970a, 1972, 1973b).

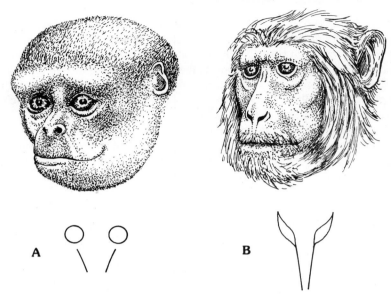

Figure 11-4. A comparison of the nose shapes of (A) New World and (B) Old World monkeys.

New World monkeys fall into two groups: the Callithricidae and the Cebidae. Marmosets and tamarinds are included in the Callithricidae. These are miniature monkeys, small enough to be held in one hand. Many are decorated with pompously colored patches or hair tufts. Marmosets have the generalized primate diet including insects, small vertebrates, and forest fruits. They seem to live in family groups of three to eight members; however, larger groups have been observed.

Titi Monkeys. The Cebidae is a large, diverse group. The most primitive member of the group is the titi (*Callicebus*) monkey, a small, thickly haired animal that runs quadrupedally and leaps through the trees. These monkeys live in pairs or small family groups averaging three to five animals. Each family recognizes a small forest area as its own domain that may be defended with vocalizations and certain threatening postural cues. Loud vocalizations emitted early in the morning seem to be spacing mechanisms signaling a group's location. The vocalizations serve to maintain group separateness. Titis form strong, long-lasting monogamous sexual bonds.

Squirrel Monkeys. The familiar Central and South American squirrel monkey is a small, arboreal quadruped, with a long and thickly haired tail. Because of its size and docility, it is a popular pet and is often used in brain research. A number of transplanted colonies such as Florida's Monkey Jungle have been established for tourists. This colony has been studied by John and Janice Baldwin (1971) who then undertook a comparative study of squirrel monkeys in their native habitat. Such studies provide an insight into an animal's means of coping with environmental change.

Howler Monkeys. Howler and spider monkeys are the best-known South American primates. The howler monkey (Figure 11-5) is aptly named; it possesses a deep, booming vocalization that once heard is not soon forgotten. Howlers come in different sizes and colors; however, most are large and robust prehensile-tailed monkeys with long black, brown, or copper-red hair, depending on the species. Beneath the chin a vocal apparatus, the larynx, is specialized for producing loud vocalizations. Howlers often hang or swing by their arms, somewhat reminiscent of the best Old World brachiators, the gibbons.

Howler monkeys live in groups averaging about 18 animals; however, group sizes range from 2 to 45 animals. Females usually outnumber the males, a common feature of most primate societies. The number of females to males is often expressed as the **socionomic sex ratio**. For example, 2:1 means two females for every male. Although most howler groups are bisexual, males occasionally live alone. Each howler group moves within a fairly well-defined home range defended against intrusion by other groups. Territory is maintained by howling and shaking and breaking branches, acts that substitute for physical aggression. Howling occurs early in the morning and is a means of locating and spacing groups. There is no clear pattern of male dominance and both males and females care for the young.

Spider Monkeys. Spider monkeys (Figure 11-6) are the nearest New World equivalents of the Old World gibbons. Their long arms, hooklike hands, and prehensile tail make them supreme acrobats. They are particularly prized as zoo animals because of their range of acrobatic wizardry. As an animal that often sits and climbs trees in an erect position, and that often walks bipedally semierect, the spider monkey is getting a close look as a possible model for the development of hominid bipedalism. A number of anatomical and locomotor studies of the spider monkey promise to provide some interesting insights for reconstructing hominid locomotor patterns.

Spider monkeys live in groups varying in size according to the type of habitat. Group sizes range from a small family group to large aggregations of 100 or more animals. Females outnumber males. Females with their offspring seem to form a cohesive subgroup within the larger social grouping. Male dominance behavior is evident.

Old World Monkeys

Because they are phylogenetically closer to humans than New World monkeys are, Old World monkeys are a source of continuing interest even though few of the many different Old World monkeys have been studied. Major studies have been conducted on macaques, baboons, langurs, and some African cercopithecines such as the vervets and patas (Figure 11-7 and 11-8).

Old World monkeys belong to the Superfamily Cercopithecoidea. This superfamily has been very successful; it numbers 12 genera and 61 species and exploits a wide variety of habitats.

Old World monkeys share a number of anatomical features distinguishing them from the apes. In contrast to the apes, monkeys have a tail. The trunk of the Old World monkey resembles that of a dog's in shape; it is long and narrow from side to side and deep from front to back. When moving quadrupedally, monkeys rest on their palms or on their finger pads, and not on their knuckles or fists, as do chimpanzees, gorillas, and orangutans. Old World monkeys move through the trees quadrupedally and span distances by jumping—they are not brachiators. All Old World monkeys have molars with pairs of cusps connected by crests. This configuration is termed a bilophodont molar.

Within the Old World monkey group we can distinguish between two distinct subfamilies:

Colobinae. The Colobinae is a subfamily composed mainly of arboreal monkeys whose stomachs are specialized for digesting leafy matter. The Asian langurs and the African colobus belong to this group.

Figure 11-5. A mantled howling monkey (*Alouatta palliata*).

Figure 11-6. A spider monkey (*Ateles*). Note the relatively long arms and prehensile tail.

**Figure 11-7. Adult female vervet
(*Cercopithecus aethiops*) with young
infant at her breast.**

**Figure 11-8. Adult male patas monkey
(*Erythrocebus patas*) with food in mouth.**

Cercopithecinae. The Cercopithecinae is a diverse subfamily containing many different forms. Lacking the stomach specializations of the colobines, the cercopithecines possess cheek pouches than can be filled with food that can be eaten at leisure. A wide variety of cercopithecines inhabits Asia and Africa. The Asian cercopithecines are commonly called macaques. The African cercopithecines form a more diverse group that includes the baboon, among other kinds.

Macaques. These ubiquitous laboratory primates were known for their use in biomedical and psychological testing long before anything was known about their naturalistic behavior. Macaques are especially interesting because of their wide geographical and ecological habitation. They inhabit tropical rain forests, monsoon forests, mangrove swamps, Himalayan montane forests, and temperate forests of China and Japan. They are also found in the grasslands and dry scrub areas in India and Ceylon (now called Sri Lanka). Additionally, they have been transplanted to a number of zoo colonies. Carpenter established a rhesus colony on the tiny island of Cayo Santiago, off the east coast of Puerto Rico. Macaques range from being almost completely arboreal to being almost completely terrestrial, depending on the habitat. Besides trees, they inhabit cliffs and rocky places, and in India they live in cities, temples, and railroad stations. The major macaque groups on which we have naturalistic behavioral data are the Indian rhesus and bonnet macaques, the Japanese macaque, the "Barbary ape" or Gibraltar macaque, on the island of Gibraltar[3] and in Morocco, and the pig-tail macaque in Malaysia.

[3]These monkeys are the charge of the British Gibraltar regiment who feed and care for them. The legend is that the British will remain on the island as long as the monkeys, and vice versa.

Primate Behavior

Ootacamund, South India, January 1966

For the first time in what seems to be ages, I am again well and ready to watch monkeys. The morning is quite chilly, it rained heavily last evening. The dew hangs heavy. The clouds roll across the sky in multiple patterns. At this altitude of 7800 feet you can almost touch and walk upon them.

I arrive at Governors Shola Forest Reserve, exhilarated to be back on my feet and hopeful that the females have not yet had the babies their stomachs seemed no longer able to hold six weeks ago. I waited impatiently to see the infants, for I badly want to study the mother-infant relationship. How will the troop's male react to the infants? Did the lowest ranking female in the dominance hierarchy give birth? What would the infants look like? What is their future as people destroy the niche? I badly wanted answers.

06:00   Clouds have settled in the valley leaving the impression of cotton snow. The bluish tint to the hills (from which they are named, the Nilgiris—the Blue Hills) is a sight through a dreamlike vapor. The scene is beyond description. I photograph this loveliness with my Nikon, but I know the pictures will not reflect what I see in my mind's eye.

I parked my jeep by a stream, which was now running rather fast. The winter monsoons (though slight this year) have been good the last few days. I walked along the stream, hoping to see, or smell, if the monkeys were recently here. I found many tracks in the mud, recognizing those of the sambar (a large deerlike creature), deer, wild boar, and leopard. Nocturnal creatures retreated for their sleep, leaving this scene to we diurnal creatures.

I walked upstream collecting new plant samples for later identification. I also collected soil samples from areas where I previously witnessed monkeys eating dirt. This earth-eating may be a response to the gastric upset common to these monkeys—so fond of lousy tasting leaves. I photographed some plants, made some new rough maps, and continued to look for the animals. I focused on the tree tops, hoping the monkeys would be sunning themselves in the few rays the sun struggled to provide. I banked on finding them in one of their favorite groups of sleeping trees within the home range. However, since I had not joined them in a while, I was unsure which one of the three areas Group A now fed and slept in. Because of the rather large size of the home range (compounded by the height dimension) I arbitrarily chose the sleeping site which seemed to be the favorite of A group, composed of 1 male and 5 females. (I assumed this to be a rather new group since infants were absent and all the females and the male were of reproductive age.) I was sorely disappointed. I sat to rest, brood, and collect some thoughts to write in my damp notebook, thankful that I long since switched to ball pen and carried spare pencils. Damp paper is a bear to write on.

At 07:15, I spotted monkeys high in an *Acacia* tree voraciously eating seeds long dismissed as inedible for my tastes. The male was absent. I waited. Then I heard his loud, booming, echoing call—his morning location to adjacent troops (in this case being three). The sound thrilled me, as usual. He leaped through the trees, crashing dead branches to the ground. He made magnificent 30 foot leaps. I knew males of adjacent troops watched as intently as I. Then silence. I approached to about 20 yards, he was nervously grinding his canines producing a squeaking noise. He defecated and urinated, as is also usual (I was glad I was not beneath him!) An erect penis indicated his tense state. I left, knowing he would soon join the females. Males of the adjacent troops then responded. The calls echoed through the forest's stillness for distances up to a mile away.

Females fed unconcerned with the male's show. Their disinterest often surprised me. Even when males of adjacent troops occasionally rushed through their troop, they fed unconcernedly. They would not be harmed, but it took me months to learn that. Then, I saw a reddish-brown bloob, two bloobs, then three. Damned, the infants were born when I was sick. The hassle with customs to get my film to record the first few days was wasted. My trip to Madras, my annoyance, a waste. I quickly put that aside when I noticed that the females left their infants. The infants screamed loudly, but their mothers were off feeding in adjacent trees. The subordinate female (she at least still looked pregnant) moved among the babies. They quieted some and briefly grappled with one another. (I later learned that Nilgiri langur females "baby sit" for one another. Surprisingly, especially in light of other primate studies, these mothers were rather lackadaisical in their maternal care.)

Excerpt from my notes during my study of Nilgiri langurs.

The rhesus is the best-known macaque (Figures 11-9 and 11-10). One of the first rhesus macaque studies was undertaken in the temples of North India. Indians tolerate and feed the monkeys; the monkeys are protected in the temple habitat, and many rhesus troops live permanently in various temples in North India. To a lesser degree, the same is true of the South Indian bonnet macaque (Figure 11-11).

Provisioned Colonies: Cayo Santiago and Japan Monkey Centre. The transplanted Cayo Santiago rhesus colony is a source of longitudinal (long-term) data. Carpenter made the first studies of these animals in the 1940s; they have been studied since that time. The other well-known macaque group is the Japanese macaque (Figure 11-12). Some provisioned colonies have been the object of intensive study for the past 30 years, principally by workers from Kyoto University and the Japan Monkey Centre. The Cayo Santiago and Japanese macaque colonies have yielded very useful information, some of which has altered earlier conceptions of hominid evolution.

Data derived from the provisioned macaque colonies have been especially eye-opening. During the long period of observation individual animals, their genealogies (traced through the female, because paternity in natural conditions is almost impossible to determine), and their individual dominance positions became known. These conditions led to such information as the fact that one's position in the social order is a reflection of the mother's position within that order,[4] that there is relatively little sexual behavior between a mother and her offspring (the biological basis of the incest taboo may be older than human cultural behavior),[5] that there are many behavioral differences between groups, that new behaviors can be learned and transmitted, that there are optimum group sizes (growth beyond which leads to group disintegration and increased aggression), and that there are group traditions (such as specific foods and travel routes). The complexity of primate society as revealed by these studies was quite unexpected by the many scientists who believed in the very uniqueness of our cultural and social traditions. We seem to be finding the roots of many of our cultural manifestations among the behaviors and social organizations of some of the better-known and understood nonhuman primates.

[4]The argument here is that a dominant mother supports her infant in any altercations, so the infant has fewer subordinate sessions. Furthermore, the infant learns dominance from watching its mother's behavior. Infants of dominant mothers also have more opportunity to interact with animals of high status. Finally, dominant mothers are less possessive of their infants, so the infants have an opportunity for more social interaction and at earlier ages than is generally true of infants of subordinate animals (Poirier, 1970c, 1972, 1973a, 1974 discusses this at length).

[5]Some information, however, suggests that mother-offspring matings among macaques occur more frequently than originally supposed.

Figure 11-9. Young adult male rhesus macaque (*Macaca mulatta*) threatens with open mouth.

Figure 11-10. Rhesus macaques (*Mucaca mulatta*) feeding. Female in center has cheek pouches full of food.

Figure 11-11. Juvenile bonnet macaque (*Macaca radiata*).

Figure 11-12. Japanese macaques (*Macaca fuscata*). Two adult females in a grooming bout. The youngster is a yearling.

The following description summarizes the major characteristics of macaque society. Macaques are social animals; their societies are characterized by clear-cut **dominance hierarchies,** especially among males. Their societies are male dominated, but they may be female-focal. Researchers can trace kin relationships through the mother, and most of the job of socializing the infant falls on the female. The female provides group continuity. Males police the group; they minimize disruption and impose discipline on the group. Relationships between animals vary and interanimal relationships such as grooming seem to be especially based on kinship and individual personality.

The rhesus and Japanese macaque group structure is composed of a number of subgroupings. The central part of a Japanese macaque troop contains dominant males, dominant females, and their offspring. Subordinate Japanese macaque infants have little to do with the dominant males; it is likely they will eventually leave the group. Solitary or peripheral males (animals living on the edge of the troop) are common. Subadults and young adults often spend some part of their lives outside the group either living alone or in all-male groups.

Consistent with their complex social groups, macaques have a rich communicatory network. Their gestural and vocal communicative matrix is varied and expressive. Grooming is very common and many hours are spent in mutual grooming bouts. Grooming behavior serves two functions; it helps keep the hair or any wounds free of debris, and it helps cement social relationships. It might also be noted that the animals simply find grooming "pleasurable," as is judged by their behavior during grooming episodes.

Macaque infants and juveniles spend a good part of each day in social play, most of which occurs in subgroups composed of animals of the same age and sex. Young infant play groups are sexually integrated; however, females leave the play groups by 1.5 years, at which time play is quite rough. By 1.5 years males and females begin to assume different social roles. This early differentiation of social roles is in training for adult life. Young females begin to show intense interest in newborn siblings. Females spend considerable time together; within this context young females learn the mothering role. Much of this learning is observational; however, a young female may hold, handle, and carry her siblings or other infants. She thus practices her mothering role. This is very strong contradictory evidence to the proposition that mothering is instinctive behavior (Poirier, 1972, 1973b).[6] (Contrary to what is commonly thought, social roles based on gender are not the sole property of the human primate.)

Baboons. Relatively speaking, baboons (Figure 11-13) are the African counterpart of the Asian and North African macaques. Baboons have been the subject of numerous behavioral studies since Washburn and DeVore's (1961) work in the late 1950s. Much has been written about baboon social life and until recently baboons were the model of what many knew of primate behavior. Unfortunately that clouded the picture. Original studies of savanna baboons emphasized their strong male dominance, tight troop structure, and relatively high level of aggression. More recent studies of forest-living baboons give a different perspective (Rowell, 1972). Forest-living baboons have smaller groups, less male aggression, and less tightly knit groups.

Baboons are a diverse group inhabiting such vegetational zones as subdeserts, savannas, acacia thornveld, and rain forests. Minor baboon habitats include rocky cliffs and gorges (the hamadryas baboon in Ethiopia) and seaside cliffs (the chacma baboon in South Africa). All

---

[6]While mothering may not be "instinctive" in the classical sense of the word, many would argue that there is a genetic base or "biological tendency," making it easier for females to learn.

baboons sleep in trees, excepting the hamadryas, which often converge a few hundred strong to sleep on isolated rock outcrops. Their diet is varied—baboons are omnivorous, and their diet includes fruits, grasses, seeds, roots, lizards, and occasionally other meat. There are troops in South Africa that regularly kill domestic sheep and there are reports of predatory behavior by some East African baboon troops.

Savanna Baboons. Savanna baboons have been studied in both East and South Africa. Some of the most comprehensive studies have been made in East Africa, where baboons have been studied by various investigators. These baboons live in closed male-dominated groups. The males play the major role in protecting the group from outside predation (e.g., by cheetahs and lions); they also police the troop by mediating dominance encounters. Grooming is a prime ameliorant of aggression and is a frequent social behavior. Sexual behavior is limited; during breeding, consort pairs (a male and female mating pair) are common on the troop's periphery. When a female enters estrus (i.e., when she is sexually receptive) she mates with many males, subordinates first. The most dominant males may mate last, when the female is at the height of estrus and is most likely to ovulate. Clues as to the state of estrus seem to be olfactory and visual; the male sniffs and visually and orally inspects the vaginal area.

Gelada Baboons. The gelada, *Theropithecus gelada* is a terrestrial vegetarian. The gelada mainly inhabits the Ethiopian highlands, living in troops of up to 400 animals.[7] Geladas are beautifully adapted to their cliff habitat. During movement females and young move closest to the cliff edges where the males protect them from predatory attack. Whenever danger threatens, the whole troop moves to the cliff edge. The females and young first descend the cliff face to the ledges; the males act as a shield above them. The troop sleeps on the cliff edges.

What seems to be one large gelada troop is actually a combination of smaller one-male units. The existence of the one-male units is particularly evident during the dry season when food is scattered. At this time male bands, varying in size from 4 to 12, separate from one another and forage independently. When these one-male groups rejoin they become intermixed into the larger troop; this is typical when food is plentiful. Females tend to remain closely associated with one male only and restrict their sexual activity to him.

[7]The behavior of the gelada is reported by Crook, 1966, among others.

Figure 11-13. Subadult olive baboons (*Papio anubis*).

Hamadryas Baboons. The hamadryas daytime foraging unit consists of one adult male and multiple females. At night many one-adult male groups congregate at one sleeping cliff, an adaptation to the lack of places to sleep. The major hamadryas study was undertaken in Ethiopia by Hans Kummer (1968).

The one-adult-male, multiple-female hamadryas organization is vigorously preserved. The leader male of the "harem" group prevents mating between younger males in his groups and the females. Younger males must wait until the older male gives way, or they may form their own group by "adopting" young juvenile females. These juvenile females are a few years from sexual maturity and male sexual gratification is delayed until later in life. The male has a specialized behavior called the neck bite, which is used to retrieve any female who strays from his group. The male approaches the female and mouths or gums her neck. The skin is not broken. A female whose neck is bitten immediately follows a male back to her group. The male hamadryas' neck bite and the female's following response are very important communicative mechanisms, functioning to maintain the hamadryas one-adult-male, multiple-female social unit.

Characteristics of Baboon Social Organization. Baboons, and to a lesser extent macaques and langurs, clearly demonstrate that social behavior and organization are influenced by the habitat. Savanna-dwelling baboons live in larger, more tightly knit groups than forest baboons. Hamadryas baboons, and to a lesser extent geladas, show a completely different social organization.

Baboon troop sizes usually vary from 8 to 200; 40 to 80 animals is a common average. Females usually outnumber males by a ratio of from 4:1 to 14:1. Group dominance hierarchies are stable; the male plays a major role in maintaining group calm. Intertroop relationships are usually nonaggressive; in fact, they may be amicable. Groups are largely stable and grooming seems to be an important behavior helping to maintain group stability. Play behavior is a very important element of a young baboon's life. The communication repertoire is rich in gestural and vocal patterns.

Langurs and Colobines (Leaf Eaters). Increasingly we learn more about this widespread Asian and African group. In Asia these monkeys are referred to as langurs, in Africa as colobus monkeys (Figures 11-14 and 11-15). They are primarily arboreal rain-forest dwellers and have in common their specialized stomachs, which are elaborately sacculated organs. This is their adaptation to a bulky, fibrous, hard-to-digest leafy diet. Fruits, small insects, and tree bark augment this diet.

North Indian Langurs. Major studies of Asian leaf-eating monkeys have occurred in India and Ceylon. Some work has also been conducted in Malaysia. The Hanuman monkey or common langur inhabiting both North and South India is the best-known Asian leaf eater. The North Indian common langur was one of the first nonhuman primates to be studied. This study emphasized certain characteristics of North Indian langurs that were then assumed common to all leaf eaters. For example, North Indian langurs live a very peaceful life; feeding is a major and a time-consuming activity. Most North Indian langurs live in bisexual groups in which females outnumber males by as much as five to one. There are multiple-male groups, but there are also all-male groups and solitary males. North Indian langur groups live in home ranges that are not defended and therefore are not called territories. Altercations between animals of different groups are few.

Variations on a Theme. Subsequent studies by a number of individuals, including myself, of langur populations in South India and other parts of Asia disagreed in substantial measure with some of the conclusions made from earlier studies. This disagreement taught us a most

Figure 11-14. Adult male Nilgiri langur (*Presbytis johnii*) feeding. Note the leaves in mouth.

Figure 11-15. Mother and infant African black and white Colobus monkey (*Colobus guereza*).

important lesson, which is also applicable in reconstructing hominid evolution. One primate is not typical of all the primates; there are substantial differences, even among members of the same species. These differences are in large measure habitat-dependent. Natural selection operates on behavior and social organization to select for the "tolerable," not always the optimal, solution to ecological problems.

Studies subsequent to that in North India raised a number of doubts as to the commonality of many behavioral traits. All langurs are peaceful, at least most of the time, and in comparison to more terrestrial species. However, it was discovered that in some areas these animals are also quite territorial. The same is true of the now-studied African leaf eaters. Males, especially, guard their territories against intrusion by males of adjacent troops. Territories are maintained with loud, booming vocalizations, jumping through trees, and shaking branches. Physical contact is rare, however.

Infanticide Among Langurs. Infanticide is a very interesting behavioral pattern found among some langurs, as well as some other nonhuman primates and lions. Many langur groups are one-adult-male, multiple-female groups. Excess males live either alone or more often in all-male (sometimes called bachelor) groups. Aggression is quite common when males of an all-male group approach and attempt to join a bisexual group. One outcome of this aggression is that all the infants of the bisexual group are killed by the new males and all resident males are then driven from the group. This harsh action seems to bring the females to sexual readiness. The new male copulates with the females, ensuring that all the subsequent infants are his own. What makes this behavior so very interesting is that it appears only in some North and South Indian common langur groups and perhaps in Ceylon. These are mostly the one-adult-male and multiple-adult-female social groups. The behavior is also periodic and happens about once every 4 years. Although we are unable to adequately interpret this phenomenon, it has been suggested that high population densities may be one cause of the aggression or that killing the infants may be a form of incest avoidance. Since the changeover occurs about once each 4 years and since one result of the change is that young males are driven from the troop at about sexual maturity, it is an ultimate means of avoiding mother-son, father-daughter, and brother-sister mating. This explanation is as controversial as it is intriguing. Hardy (1977) discusses infanticide as a reproductive strategy in detail.

Instances of Primate Adaptability. Rowell (1972, 1979) differentiates between social structure (meaning such measures as population density, group size, and demographic features) and social organization, which she limits to the pattern of interactions between individuals. We must expect social structure to vary over time in primate groups, and to the extent that social structure limits and influences social organization, we may find different social patterns described not only for different troops of the same species, but also for the same troop at different times (Bernstein and Smith, 1979). One result of the many baboon studies has been the documentation of a number of instances of troop-specific social traditions. Two of the most interesting examples are documentation of hunting and meat eating in an East African troop and crop raiding in another East African troop. The hunting tradition occurs among a troop of olive baboons (*Papio anubis*) living on a farm near Gilgil, Kenya. In 1970 and 1971, R. Harding witnessed 47 cases of predation during 1,032 hours of observation; this was the highest rate of predation reported for any nonhuman primate. During this period the baboons in this troop preyed on cape hares, birds, and young gazelles. All but three cases of predation witnessed resulted from adult male activity, and in all but one instance the adult male ate the meat.

In 1972 through 1974 Strum (1975) witnessed 100 cases of predation during 1,200 hours of observation. In 1970 and 1971 males did 94 percent of the killing and 98 percent of the eating of prey; adult females did 6 percent of the killing and 2 percent of the eating. During 1972 through 1974 Strum noted that males did 61 percent of the killing, females 14 percent, juveniles 16 percent, and an unidentified age group 9 percent. Hence, a 4-year period witnessed the spread of a troop tradition virtually throughout the age classes in this troop.

The change in participation of predatory activities altered the profile of the prey. Although the tradition had spread to new troop members, adult males were still present during 93 percent of the predatory episodes and one male ate meat in 91 percent of the recorded instances. Meat-eating and predatory activities were individual matters, and some males were more active than others. The same holds true for the females; some females were interested in the kill and others were not. Furthermore, those females who participated in the capture of prey were not always the same females who consumed the meat. Nevertheless, the interest of some females in the capture and consumption of prey equaled that of some of the males.

During Harding's study, juvenile interest in consumption was slight; by 1974, however, juvenile interest heightened. Strum suggests that once a juvenile was successful in obtaining meat its interest in meat and participation in consumption heightened. The kill sites soon became a gathering place for youngsters and one can suggest that during this time youngsters learned to eat meat by watching the adults. Juveniles were observed to prey on birds, hares, and even one gazelle. Infants did eat some meat; they did not, however, capture their prey. A successful relay system of capturing the prey soon became the rule.

Meat was passed among individuals. When one animal was displaced or lost interest in the prey, meat was shared by various group members. Females were observed to share meat with youngsters and some males and females shared meat with one another. This sharing of food was observed *only* during meat eating, and sharing of food between a female and a youngster was only observed in this circumstance.

One of the most important implications derived from these observations is that nonhuman primates can successfully hunt without even the rudiments of language. This is borne out by observations of predation by social carnivores and chimpanzees. Obviously hunting behavior alone was not the impetus for human language.

A further instance of the development of a troop tradition is noted in studies by Maples (1969) and Maples et al. (1976) of crop-raiding baboons in southeastern Kenya. In contrast to savanna-living baboons, these animals have a dispersed troop structure and are quiet compared to savanna troops. Confirmatory evidence for Maples' suggestion come from my own studies in South India (Poirier, 1969b, 1970a, 1977b) and on St. Kitts, West Indies (Poirier, 1972b, 1977b). In both India and on St. Kitts the animals not only adapted to new food sources, but to the continual harassment of local farmers and their dogs. The potato and cauliflower were introduced to the Nilgiris in India 80 to 100 years ago and are now the main agricultural crops. The home range of one of the Nilgiri langur groups studied included large cultivated tracts of potato and cauliflower. Local informants related that the farms ringing the area were at most 25 to 30 years old. Considering that these are the sole farms in this area, this local langur population only recently adapted to this new food source.

The behavior of farm-raiding groups, both in India and on St. Kitts, as among the baboons studied by Maples, was different from that of forest groups. Because raiding usually occurs when humans are absent, these animals have marked activity peaks in the early morning and afternoon before and after the farmers have left the fields. In both the cases that I witnessed, the proximity and threat of humans has altered the animal's reactions to them. This is particularly noticeable when comparing the interest and/or fright commonly shown humans in the forests.

The St. Kitts green monkeys raid cultivated farm plots and sugar cane plantations. Crop raiding yields fascinating information concerning adaptive processes, for raiding consists of a number of behavioral adaptations that may have appeared in connection with the competition between human and monkey. While crop raiding is of recent origin in India, it has been established for 300 years on St. Kitts. In India, as well as on St. Kitts and in Kenya, adult males play a particular role as lookouts, as sentinel animals. Adult males in India and on St. Kitts position themselves in clear view high in trees; while farmers focus on them, other animals enter the plots and take the crops. This sentinel pattern seems to be an elaboration of the male's role.

Clearly certain behavioral and dietary patterns change in the presence of human intervention. Groups that live in areas where they are forced into continual interaction with human populations and that exploit this situation to their benefit (i.e., by crop raiding) differ behaviorally and in terms of their social organization from other members of their species.

The acceptance of the new dietary items just discussed has correlates in information published by Japanese investigators subsumed under the title "subcultural propagation." Kawamura (1959) discusses the "sweet-potato-washing sub-culture" among members of the Koshima mocaque troop, Itani (1958) reports how the candy-eating habit spread among members of the Takasakiyama troop, and Yamada (1963) discusses the propagation of wheat-eating among the membership of the Minoo-B troop. Tsumori (1967) discusses the transmission of these feeding behaviors and notes that the acquisition of these new behaviors is largely determined by age and/or sex differences. The dominance and kinship relationship between the animals involved also affected the rapidity of the acceptance or rejection of a new behavioral trait.

There are five major themes in primate social organization: (1) dominance and dominance hierarchies, (2) the mother-infant bond and the social unit focused around the females, (3) the sexual bond between males and females, (4) the separation of roles between adult and young, and (5) the separation of roles according to gender (Lancaster, 1975). Each species, and perhaps each group within a species, has its own combination of these factors; each places different emphasis on these factors according to habitat and evolutionary-historical factors, which weave a collection of individuals into a social system. However, we must bear in mind that in primates it is the social system which enables group members to meet the demands of everyday life.

Many of the themes binding human society are shared by our nonhuman primate relatives and many existed long before hominids appeared. Nonhuman primate social organization and behavior set the stage for the evolution of the human way of life. "By understanding the social behavior and adaptations of our closest relatives we can far better understand how and why human beings are both like and different from other primates" (Lancaster, 1975:41)

Our knowledge of the behavior and social organization of prosimians and monkeys is limited to a number of studies on a few species. Few species have been the subject of longitudinal studies or studied in varying habitats. The major prosimian habitat is the island of Madagascar, the Malagasy Republic. Lemurs offer a number of insights into the behavioral patterns of the most primitive, the first evolved, nonhuman primates. Many lemurs share the year-round permanent social organizations of their more highly evolved monkey and ape relatives.

New World primates are almost strictly arboreal. Anatomically and in some respects behaviorally distinct from Old World primates, New World primates have not been intensely studied. Although there is increasing interest in these animals, much work remains to be done.

The best-known Old World monkeys are some species of baboons, langurs, and macaques. Because of the establishment of such research facilities as Cayo Santiago and the Japan Monkey Centre, we have access to many longitudinal data on both rhesus and Japanese macaques, and these data are having a marked influence on the formulation of theories of primate behavior and human evolution. Since the early work of Sir Solly Zuckerman, baboons have been the focus of a number of studies. Baboons provide very interesting data as to the adaptations needed for coping with a savanna environment (probably the environment of ancestral hominids). They also tell us how a species adapts to various habitats; similar data on habitat adaptation comes from studies of Asian and African leaf-eating monkeys.

There is still much work to be done. The major limitations now seem to be financial—there is a lack of funding. Future studies will be long term and problem oriented in contrast to the shorter studies of recent years.

Bibliography

Altmann, S., and Altmann, J. 1970. *Baboon ecology.* Chicago: University of Chicago Press.

Baldwin, J. 1971. The social organization of a semi-free-ranging troop of squirrel monkeys (*Saimiri sciureus*). *Folia Primatologica* 14.23.

Bernstein, I., and Smith, E. 1979. In summary. In *Primate ecology and human origins,* edited by I. Bernstein and E. Smith, pp. 341-51. New York: Garland.

Bertrand, M. 1969. *The behavioral repertoire of the stumptail macaque.* Basel: Karger.

Buettner-Janusch. J., ed. 1962. *The relatives of man: modern studies of the relation of the evolution of nonhuman primates to human evolution.* New York: New York Academy of Sciences.

Carpenter, C. 1964. *Naturalistic behavior of nonhuman primates.* University Park: Pennsylvania State University Press.

Charles-Dominique, P., and Hladik, C. 1971. Le Lepilemur du sud de Madagascar: écologie, alimentation et vie sociale. *La Terre et la Vie* 25:3-66.

Chevalier-Skolnikoff, S., and Poirier, F., eds. 1977. *Primate bio-social development.* New York: Garland.

Crook, J. 1966. Gelada baboon herd structure and movement. *Symposium of the Zoological Society of London* 18:237.

DeVore, I., ed. 1965. *Primate behavior.* New York: Holt, Rinehart and Winston.

Dolhinow, P., ed. 1972. *Primate patterns.* New York: Holt, Rinehart and Winston.

Eimerl, S., and DeVore, I. 1965. *The primates.* New York: Time-Life Books.

Etkin, W., ed. 1967. *Social behavior from fish to man.* Chicago: Phoenix Science Series.

Hladik, C. 1975. Ecology, diet and social patterning in Old and New World primates. In *Sociobiology and psychology of primates,* edited by R. Tuttle, pp. 3-37. The Hague: Mouton.

Hrdy, S. 1977. *The langurs of Abu.* Cambridge: Harvard University Press.

Itani, J. 1958. On the acquisition and propagation of a new food habit in the natural groups of the wild Japanese monkey at Takasakiyama. *Primates* 1:84-98.

Jay, P., ed. 1968. *Primates—studies in adaptation and variability.* New York: Holt, Rinehart and Winston.

Jolly, A. 1967. *Lemur behavior—a Madagascan field study.* Chicago: University of Chicago Press.

Kawamura, S. 1959. The process of subcultural propagation among Japanese macaques. *Primates* 2:43-60.

Kummer, H. 1968. *Social organization of hamadryas baboons—a field study.* Chicago: University of Chicago Press.

Lancaster, J. 1975. *Primate behavior and the emergence of human culture.* New York: Holt, Rinehart and Winston.

Maples, W. 1969. Adaptive behavior of baboons. *American Journal of Physical Anthropology* 31:107-11.

Maples, W., Maples, S. M., Greenhood, W., and Walek, W. 1976. Adaptations of crop-rading baboons in Kenya. *American Journal of Physical Anthropology* 45:309-18.

Mason, W. 1971. Field and laboratory studies of social organization in *Saimiri* and *Callicebus.* In *Primate behavior: developments in field and laboratory research,* Vol. 2, edited by L. Rosenblum, pp. 107-38. New York: Academic Press.

Napier, J., and Napier, P., eds. 1970. *Old World monkeys.* New York: Academic Press.

Napier, J., and Walker, A. 1967. Vertical clinging and leaping, a newly recognized category of locomotor behaviour among primates. *Folia Primatologica* 6:180-203.

Poirier, F. 1968a. Analysis of a Nilgiri langur (*Presbytis johnii*) home range change. *Primates* 9:29-44.

_____. 1968b. The Nilgiri langur (*Presbytis johnii*) mother-infant dyad. *Primates* 9:45-68.

_____.1969a. The Nilgiri langur troop: its composition, structure, function and change. *Folia Primatologica* 19:20-47.

_____.1969b. Behavioral flexibility and intertroop variability among Nilgiri langurs of South India. *Folia Primatologica* 11:119-33.

_____. 1970a. Nilgiri langur ecology and social behavior. In *Primate behavior: developments in field and laboratory research,* Vol. I, edited by L. Rosenblum, pp. 251-383. New York: Academic Press.

_____. 1970b. The Nilgiri langur communication matrix. *Folia Primatologica* 13:92-137.

_____. 1970c. Characteristics of the Nilgiri langur dominance structure. *Folia Primatologica* 12:161-87.

_____. 1972a. Introduction. In *Primate socialization,* edited by F. Poirier, pp. 3-29. New York: Random House.

_____. 1972b. The St. Kitts green monkey (*Cercopithecus aethiops sabaeus*): ecology, population dynamics, and selected behavioral traits. *Folia Primatologica* 17:20-25.

_____. 1973a. Nilgiri langur behavior and social organization. In *Essays to the chief,* edited by F. Voget and R. Stephensen, pp. 119-34. Eugene: University of Oregon Press.

_____. 1973b. Socialization and learning among nonhuman primates. In *Learning and culture,* edited by S. Kimball and J. Burnett, pp. 3-41. Seattle: University of Washington Press.

_____. 1974. Colobine aggression: a review. In *Primate aggression, territoriality and zenophobia,* edited by R. Holloway, pp. 123-58. New York: Academic Press.

_____. 1977b. The human influence on subspeciation and behavior differentiation among three non-human primate populations. *Yearbook of Physical Anthropology* 20:234-41.

_____. 1981. *Fossil evidence: the human evolutionary journey.* St. Louis: Mosby. 1972.

Quiatt, D., ed. 1972. *Primates on primates.* Minneapolis: Burgess.

Reynolds, V. 1967. *The apes.* New York: Harper & Row.

Rowell, T., 1972. *Social behaviour of monkeys.* New York: Penguin Books.

_____. 1979. How would we know if social organization were *not* adaptive? In *Primate ecology and human origins,* edited by I. Bernstein and E. Smith, pp. 1-22. New York: Garland.

Sauer, F., and Sauer, E. 1963. The South-west African bush-baby of the *Galago senegalensis* group. *Journal of Southwest Africa Scientific Society* 16:5-35.

Southwick, C., ed. 1963. *Primate social behavior.* Princeton, N.J.: Van Nostrand.

Strum, S. 1975. Primate predation: interim report on the development of a tradition in a troop of olive baboons. *Science* 187:755-57.

Tsumori, A. 1967. New acquired behavioral social interactions of Japanese monkeys. In *Social Communication among primates,* edited by S. Altmann, pp. 207-21. Chicago: University of Chicago Press.

Washburn, S., and DeVore, I. 1961. The social life of baboons. *Scientific American* 204:62-71.

Washburn, S., and Moore, R. 1974. *Ape into man—a study of human evolution.* Boston: Little, Brown.

Yamada, M. 1963. A study of blood relationships in the natural society of the Japanese macaque. *Primates* 4:43-67.

Chapter 12

Primate Behavior: The Apes

This chapter discusses various aspects of the behavior and econiche of the apes—the chimpanzee, gorilla, orangutan, and gibbon. The historical background for studies of each of these apes is discussed. Modern studies of apes have helped alter our conceptions of early phases of human evolution. For example, studies of modern chimpanzees in their present-day environment have helped redefine some of our conceptions of what it means to be human.

This chapter also discusses the fascinating and sometimes controversial studies of linguistic training among the chimpanzees and gorillas. The various language projects among the apes, such as teaching chimpanzees and gorillas to communicate using American Sign Language, and teaching chimpanzees to communicate using colored plastic discs and a computer, are reviewed.

Early Association and Amazement

In the jungles of Africa and Asia, hidden among cool leaves live the apes. Hard to find, harder still to observe, they lead their independent, foraging lives. Man's wars do not concern them. Each day gibbons leap among the trees, solitary orangs climb from branch to branch, groups of chimpanzees gather, and gorillas peer over giant lobelias. Theirs is a world of greens and browns, a friendly world where only Cousin Man is to be feared (Reynolds, 1967: unnumbered).

Europeans have known some apes, such as the gorilla, for slightly more than a hundred years. Our early conceptions of the African apes (gorillas and chimpanzees) range from their being regarded as subhuman animals to ferocious man-killing, man-eating, human female-ravishing beasts. These assumptions are far from true. Our association with one of the Asian apes, the gibbon, has been less dramatic and less emotional. The gibbon has always evoked amazement at its arboreal skills. The English naturalist William Charles Martin wrote the following about a female gibbon. "It is almost impossible to convey in words an idea of the quickness and graceful address of her movements; they may indeed be termed aerial as she seems merely to touch in her progress the branches among which she exhibits her evolutions." As with other apes, stories were woven around the orangutan. In seventeenth-century Europe tales were told of male orangutans lustfully and shamelessly carrying women and girls into the woods to ravish them. The Bornean translation for orangutan, "man of the woods," tells us something about native feelings toward the animal. A Dutch physician noted from Java in the 1640s that "the Javanese maintain these animals can speak but refuse to do so for fear of being made to work" (Mydans, 1973:30).

The earliest descriptions of African apes were derived from exaggerated tales and native folklore reported by travelers. Many explorers looked down on the natives and used native tales or actual sightings of apes as ways to demean the natives. Two major themes emerge in the early writings: (1) that apes could walk bipedally erect (in fact they were often illustrated holding a walking stick) and (2) that apes could speak if they wished.

The Chimpanzee

Early Association. Some of the first reports on chimpanzees come from anatomical treatises. The Dutch physician Tulp published an anatomical description of the chimpanzee as early as 1641 (Figure 12-1), an excerpt of which follows.

> It was in body neither fat nor graceful, but robust; yet very nimble and very active. The joints are in truth so tight: and with vast muscles attached to them: so that he dares anything; and can accomplish it. In front it is everywhere smooth; but hairy behind, and covered with black hairs. The face counterfeits man; but the nostrils are flat and bent inward, like a wrinkled, and toothless old woman (quoted in Reynolds 1967:44).

A most fascinating report of one of the first chimpanzees to be seen by continental Europeans was published in the September 1738 edition of *The London Magazine.*

> A most surprising Creature is brought over in the Speaker, just arrived from Carolina, that was taken in a Wood at Guinea: it is a female about four foot high, shaped in every part like a Woman excepting its head, which nearly resembles the Ape: She walks upright naturally, sits down to her food, which is chiefly Greens, and feeds herself with her Hands as a human Creature. She is very fond of a Boy on board, and is observed always sorrowful at his Absence. She is cloathed with a thin Silk Vestment, and shows a great Discontent at the opening of her Gown to discover her Sex. She is the Female of the Creature, which the Angolans call Chimpanzee, or the Mockman (quoted in Reynolds, 1967:51).

The name "chimpanzee" is about the only part of this highly fanciful tale which modern scientific studies have not dispelled.

Studies of wild chimpanzees actually began with the nineteenth-century work of the zoologist R. L. Garner, who chose the jungles of Gabon, West Africa, as his study area. He built a cage in the jungle from where he attempted to observe the chimpanzees. (Unfortunately, he almost drowned as the cage was placed in a dry riverbed, which just happened to flood!) Garner was the first European to report what has been called the chimpanzee carnival, or "kanjo." The following quotation of his is an exquisite example of the mix between fact and fancy characterizing much of the early literature.

One of the most remarkable of all the social habits of the chimpanzee, is the *Kanjo,* as it is called in the native tongue. The word does not mean "dance" in the sense of saltatory gyrations, but implies more the idea of "carnival." It is believed that more than one family takes part in these festivities.

Here and there in the jungle is found a small spot of sonorous earth. It is irregular in shape, but is about two feet across. The surface is of clay, and is artificial. It is superimposed upon a kind of peat bed, which, being very porous, acts as a resonance cavity, and intensifies the sound. This constitutes a kind of drum. It yields rather a dead sound, but of considerable volume.

This queer drum is made by chimpanzees, who secure the clay along the bank of some stream in the vicinity. They carry it by hand, and deposit it while in a plastic state, spread it over the place selected, and let it dry. I have, in my possession, a part of one that I brought home with me from the Nkhami forest. It shows the fingerprints of the apes, which were impressed in it while the mud was yet soft.

After the drum is quite dry, the chimpanzees assemble by night in great numbers, and the carnival begins. One or two will beat violently on this dry clay, while others jump up and down in a wild and grotesque manner. Some of them utter long, rolling sounds, as if trying to sing. When one tires of beating the drum, another relieves him, and the festivities continue in this fashion for hours (quoted in Reynolds, 1967: 114-15).

Garner's work supplied little factual knowledge, but it set the tone by insisting on an observational approach. After Robert Yerkes established his chimpanzee colony in Florida, he sent one of his students, Henry Nissen, to West Africa to study wild chimpanzees. During the early part of 1930 Nissen collected 49 observation days with wild chimpanzees during which he learned many hitherto unknown facts. His study led him to question the idea that chimpanzees lived in "families" and that there was much hostility between animals of different "families." Furthermore, Nissen noted the large terrestrial component of chimpanzee locomotion.

Modern Studies. The next study of chimpanzees was carried out in East Africa by Adrian Kortlandt, a zoologist from Amsterdam, in 1960. His study group included animals that regularly raided a paw-paw plantation. Kortlandt spent several seasons at this plantation, observing from blinds (one of which was 80 feet high in a tree), watching chimpanzees come and go carrying their bananas and paw-paws. He notes: "On windy days the trees swayed so much that I could not use my field glasses. When a tropical thunderstorm came up unexpectedly, I could only pray that I would not be electrocuted."

Kortlandt's study dispelled the notion that chimpanzees lived in "family groups" or "harems." Instead, he found that they tended to keep together in "nursery groups" composed of mothers with their offspring. Kortlandt also distinguished sexual groups and groups consisting of adult males and childless females.

In experiments in the natural setting and in a zoo colony, Kortlandt collected instances of chimpanzees brandishing weapons. He witnessed them aiming and throwing sticks at snakes and at pictures of carnivores projected on zoo walls. Based on these observations, Kortlandt suggested that chimpanzees are not originally rain-forest inhabitants. (See Horn, 1977, 1979 for a rebuttal of this position.) Instead, he labels them "eurytropic" animals, that is, they live in a wide variety of habitats, including dry woodland and savanna zones. These are the areas where we believe ancestral hominids first diverged from an apelike ancestor.

Kortlandt continues that in this habitat, with its tall, isolated trees, ancestral chimpanzees developed their long arms as a climbing adaptation. What caused the chimpanzees to leave the plains and go into the forests? Kortlandt says our ancestors were to blame; by setting fires

Figure 12-1. Tulp's (1641) "orang-utang" is known to have been a chimpanzee.

humans eliminated the chimpanzees' food supply and drove them into the forests. Additionally, early humans hunted the chimpanzees and drove them to the forest. According to Kortlandt, his argument explains why chimpanzees still brandish sticks above their heads in fright or during displays. Such displays, of little use in the jungle because the sticks get caught in the low-lying limbs, were once useful in the savanna. Kortlandt suggests that the reason chimpanzees are so frightened of us is because our ancestors once hunted them (and very unfortunately we still do). Kortlandt explains chimpanzees' eating meat by suggesting that ancestors of chimpanzees ate meat. According to Kortlandt, modern chimpanzees have a latent carnivorous habit.

Kortlandt's theory seemingly explains why chimpanzees are so adaptive and intelligent. There is, however, no sure way to relate tool using, meat eating, or weapon using to a remote way of life. More likely, such patterns simply reflect the wide range of chimpanzee adaptability. Some chimpanzees and some other nonhuman primates such as baboons do eat more meat than was previously suspected. However, most chimpanzees do not habitually eat meat or hunt and it seems highly unlikely that chimpanzees are latent carnivores, as Kortlandt suggests.

In the last 20 years or so, different investigators have studied the chimpanzee. The best examples of the various studies are those by Vernon and Frances Reynolds, Jane Goodall and subsequently studies by both her and Hugo van Lawick, and members of the Japan Monkey Centre's Kyoto University African project. The Reynolds' study was conducted in the Budongo Forest of Uganda, Goodall's study in the Gombe Stream Reserve of Tanzania.

Goodall's African story began when she was a young secretary, fresh out of high school, to the late Louis Leakey, who observed that she showed real promise as a field researcher and offered her an opportunity to study chimpanzees if she would obtain university training. After training at Cambridge, Goodall returned to conduct her research, armed with an intense determination and affection for these animals.

Goodall's task was not an easy one. When she began her studies in the Gombe Stream Reserve, in 1960, she arose at dawn and spent the day atop a rocky hill overlooking the forests and Lake Tanganyika, where she could observe and be observed as a harmless, unassuming member of the forest community. Social acceptance by her fellow primates was long coming. Some days she spent 12 hours in the field, climbing up and down slopes and forcing her way through dense vegetation to view the chimpanzees. She often heard calls in the distance, but when she arrived at the spot the animals were long gone. During the first few months chimpanzees would run from her as soon as she approached to within 500 yards. After much persistence, she began to be accepted as an unobtrusive stranger, first merely avoided but later actually ignored by the chimpanzees.

Goodall's study is unique not only because of the chimpanzee's special place in terms of its relationship to us, but also because Goodall learned to know the individual animals (and affectionately gave them such names as "Fifi," "Figan," "Flo," and "David Graybeard"), their personalities, and their "families" over the long period of observation. Furthermore, much of what she witnessed was documented by photographs by Hugo van Lawick. Goodall's study has documented changes within the chimpanzee's life cycle (the individual growing up), she has studied individual animals in the context of their natural environment and provisioned at her camp, and she conducted her study with meticulous care and affectionate concern for the animals. This is documented in her two popular books *My Friends the Wild Chimpanzees* and *In the Shadow of Man*.

The results of Goodall's study can be summarized as follows, using Hamburg's (1978: xxvii) words.

> The picture of chimpanzee life that emerges is fascinating. Here is a highly intelligent, intensely social creature capable of close and enduring attachments, yet nothing that looks quite like human love, capable of rich communication through gestures, postures, facial expressions, and sounds, yet nothing quite like human language. This is a creature who not only uses tools effectively but also *makes* tools with considerable foresight; a creature who does a little sharing of food, though much less than man; a creature gifted in the arts of bluff and intimidation, highly excitable and aggressive, capable of using weapons, yet engaging in no activity comparable to human warfare; a creature who frequently hunts and kills small animals of other species in an organized, cooperative way, and seems to have some zest for the process of hunting, killing, and eating the prey; a creature whose repertoire of acts in aggression, deference, reassurance, and greeting bear uncanny similarities to human acts in similar situations.

Chimpanzees and Tools. So much has come from the Goodall studies, and from others working out of her field station, that we can only touch on the highlights. Prior to Goodall's observations, one of the major definitions of humans was that we are tool makers. We made tools—that separated us from the rest of the primates; this was an absolute. Then, Goodall not only saw, and photographed, chimpanzees *using* tools, she also witnessed them *making* tools. Chimpanzees use the objects of their environment as tools to a greater extent than any other living animal excepting ourselves. Numerous times chimpanzees were seen to break off grass stems or thin branches that they carried with them for short distances. These implements are poked into termite mounds to get at the termites. After termites bite the probe, the chimpanzee runs the probe across its front teeth and eats the termites. Fascinating as this may be, the chimpanzee adds more; if the probe does not fit the hole, the chimpanzee shapes it until it does; leaves are stripped from a stem to make the tool suitable for "termite fishing." The edges of wide blades of grass may be stripped to make the appropriate tool. Not only is a tool used, a tool is made. To quote Goodall:

> Ardent angler, Fifi seeks an opening in a termite mound by bending low for a close look and a quick sniff. After breaking into a narrow tunnel sealed by clay, she inserts a blade of grass. Her average catch: half a dozen of the forest delicacies. Patient chimpanzees capture scores of insects at a single setting (van Lawick-Goodall, 1967).

Chimpanzees have also been observed to use leaves as tools; they have been seen to chew wads of leaves to make them more absorbent. This wad is then used as a sponge to sop rainwater that can't be reached with the lips. The initial modification of a handful of leaves is another example of tool use.

> Ingenuity provides a drink for a thirsty ape. Finding rainwater cupped in a fallen tree, but out of reach of his lips, Figan manufactures a "sponge." First he briefly chews a few leaves to increase their absorbency, then dips the crumpled greenery into the natural bowl and sucks out the liquid. By fashioning a simple tool he saves himself the bother of walking to a stream for a drink (van Lawick-Goodall, 1967).

Figure 12-2. Chimpanzee cleaning termites off a twig.

Figure 12-3. Chimpanzee about to raise twig to lips to feed.

Figure 12-4. Inserting a tool.

Chimpanzees have been seen to use leaves to wipe the remnants of a brain from the inside of a baboon skull and to dab at a bleeding wound on the rump. They also used leaves as toilet paper in the case of diarrhea. Some chimpanzees have used leaves to wipe themselves clean of mud and sticky foods. Chimpanzees have been seen to use stout sticks as levers to enlarge the opening of an underground bees' nest. They have used sticks to pry open banana boxes stored at the observation camp, much to the chagrin of the Goodall staff.

What differentiates chimpanzee tool use and manufacture from ours? Basically, three important things: (1) We use tools to make other tools—chimpanzees apparently do not; at least, they have not been seen doing so. (2) We use tools much more frequently, and in more circumstances, than do chimpanzees. (3) We depend on tools for our survival whereas the chimpanzee does not. It has been argued that we make tools for future use whereas other tool-making animals drop the tool immediately after use. This is an interesting point, but chimpanzees have been seen to carry "termiting" sticks for rather long distances and, at times, from mound to mound, looking for a meal. We make tools for later contingencies, and we save them for long periods. The chimpanzee does not, but why should the chimpanzee store tools when sticks and grass are so prevalent? Perhaps when we began to use scarcer materials, we then began to save them for future use. If we must keep such "loaded" phrases as "man the tool maker," it might more correctly read "man the consistent tool maker," or "man the tool maker, who makes tools from other tools," or "man—who saves tools for future use."

Predatory Behavior. Until rather recently it was assumed that hominids were the only predatory, carnivorous, food-sharing primates. We now know that chimpanzees not only eat meat, and much more frequently than originally assumed, but they also hunt meat in small, organized male groups. Chimpanzees also share their kill. "The Gombe Stream chimpanzees are efficient hunters; a group of about forty individuals may catch over twenty different prey animals during one year" (van Lawick-Goodall, 1971:282). The most common prey include young bush pigs, baboons, and young or adult colobus monkeys.

A concentrated 12-month study of chimpanzee hunting behavior has been undertaken by Geza Teleki at the Gombe Reserve. During his year's stay at Gombe, Teleki witnessed 30 episodes of predation, 12 of them successful. Interestingly, the animal most often preyed on is another primate: leaf-eating monkey, baboon, or other forest-dwelling primate. There is no evidence that chimpanzees take or even pursue animals weighing more than 20 pounds.

Teleki isolated three major components of chimpanzee predatory behavior. The first he calls the "pursuit." The second event, the "capture," is a brief period ending with the initial dismemberment of the prey. The third and longest event, "consumption," consists of highly structured activities. Once, Teleki observed a consumption period lasting 9 hours in which 15 chimpanzees took part.

The pursuit phase of the hunt takes various forms, one being simple seizure of the prey. The chimpanzees takes advantage of a fortuitous situation by lunging at and grabbing the prey. Other forms of pursuit are chasing the prey, which may require a dash of 100 yards or more, and stalking, which can last more than an hour. Both chasing and stalking seem to be premeditated. On occasion both clearly use a strategy and maneuvers aimed at isolating or cornering the prey.

One of the major problems in interpreting these predatory episodes was to discern how they were coordinated. Gombe chimpanzees are usually very vociferous, especially during the morning and evening. That, however, is not the case when they are pursuing prey.

Figure 12-5. Chimpanzee cleaning the flesh from a skull of a red colobus monkey.

Regardless of the time of day or the number of chimpanzees involved in the chase, all remain silent until the prey is captured or the attempt is broken off. This means, of course, that the hunters do not coordinate their efforts by means of vocal signals. Neither did I observe any obvious signaling gestures, although cooperation in movement and positioning was evident (Teleki, 1973:37).

It is still not known how chimpanzees coordinate their hunts; perhaps some as yet imperceptible body signals are used.

In contrast to the quiet characterizing a hunt, "The instant of acquisition is usually signaled by a sudden outburst of vocalization; the cries not only end the silence of the hunt but their volume and pitch serve to draw other chimpanzees from distances of a mile or more" (Teleki, 1973:37). Chimpanzees quickly kill their prey; if the prey is in the hunter's grasp, the chimpanzee may simply twist or bite the back of its neck. Or the chimpanzee may bang the prey's head on the ground. If more than one animal captures the prey, the prey may be literally torn apart as each captor tugs on a different limb.

Chimpanzee predatory behavior is of marked interest to anthropologists, who are used to considering humans as the sole predatory primate. Of equal interest is the fact that the prey is shared among fellow chimpanzees. In Teleki's (1973:40) words:

Considering the length of time devoted to consumption, the small size of the prey animals, and the number of chimpanzees that congregate in sharing clusters, the conclusion is almost inescapable that social considerations and not merely nutritional ones underlie the Gombe apes' predatory behavior.

Chimpanzees share their meat by responding to another animal's "request" (Figure 12-6). Meat can be requested in various ways; the requester can approach the possessor closely, face to face, and peer intently at the possessor of the meat. Alternatively the requester can extend a hand, open and palm up (in a begging position), holding it under the possessor's chin.

Chimpanzee predatory behavior is of importance in understanding certain behavioral traits. First, predatory behavior requires group cooperation for a common cause, obtaining meat. A second important trait is sharing the meat among one's social fellows, essentially just for the act of sharing. Information from Japanese chimpanzee studies (Toshiada et al., 1979) reveals that meat is not shared among these groups. Thus, sharing may be a local social tradition. A third point of significance is the questions that chimpanzee predatory behavior and food sharing raise for interpreting hominid evolution. For example, could predation have developed among primates before the advent of the early hominids? If predation, cooperative hunting, and socially structured food sharing were prehominid traits, this would cast one more element of doubt on some current evolutionary hypotheses, that is, the complex of erect posture, free hands, and tool use as prerequisites to the emergence of hunting behavior would be called into question. Similarly, the hypothesis that the open savanna is the habitat where hunting most likely developed must also be questioned. Actually, it is in the woodland-savanna where today one finds the highest density of mammals. One cherished belief must surely be abandoned—that is, that socially organized hunting among primates is solely a human property.

Figure 12-6. Chimpanzee sharing food. Note hand under chin as a begging gesture.

McGrew (1978) distinguishes sex differences in mode of food acquisition among chimpanzees. There is a significant difference in the animal-prey intake of male and female chimpanzees at Gombe. Males consume more meat from birds and mammals and females consume more insects. This differentiation in dietary intake may be related to the female's more frequent ant and termite fishing and dipping. McGrew (1978:449-50) states:

> Male chimpanzees obtain meat by stalking, pursuing, capturing, killing, dividing, and distributing a single mammalian prey. This behavior often involves primarily male groups roaming relatively great distances and acting cooperatively when the appropriate situation fortuitously arises—in short *hunting*.

Conversely,

> Female chimpanzees . . . obtain ants and termites by prolonged, systematic, and repetitive manipulative sequences. Several chimpanzees may work side by side, but basically the activity consists of an individual accumulating a meal of many small units that are usually concentrated at a few known permanent sources—in short *gathering*.

McGrew's deliberate choice of the words "hunting" and "gathering" suggests that he feels there is some continuity between chimpanzee feeding and the possible feeding behaviors of the early hominids. The possibility of deliberate differentiation of feeding behaviors by male and female chimpanzees might suggest a reevaluation of the hominid fossil record (Chapter 17).

Social Organization. Through the efforts of dedicated observers, we are getting a clearer impression of chimpanzee social life and social organization. One of the most striking facts originally offered about chimpanzee social organization was the presumed flexibility of the social structure. Forest-living chimpanzees are often found in any one of four types of bands: (1) adult males only, (2) mother and offspring and occasionally a few other females, (3) adults and adolescents of both sexes, but no mothers with young, and (4) representatives of all categories mixed together. The composition and size of these bands may change as individuals wander off and groups split or combine with other groups in the vicinity.

Sugiyama (1972) has discussed the role of flexibility within chimpanzee society. In his study, conducted in the Budongo Forest of Uganda, Sugiyama located 50 to 60 animals organized into what he called a regional population. Occasionally most of the chimpanzees of this population formed a party that moved together; usually, however, they formed parties of less than 10 or moved alone. They also gathered into one party that subsequently divided into two or more groups. The home range of this population was surrounded by the ranges of other regional populations. These home ranges frequently overlapped and sometimes members of one regional population joined members of another. When large groups divide, they often maintain associative and friendly contact with their rich vocal and behavioral communication. Quoting Sugiyama (1972:159-60): "Chimpanzee society ensures the free and independent movement of each individual based on highly developed individuality without the restriction of either territoriality or hierarchy. On the other hand, a chimpanzee enjoys the benefits of group life in that it can avoid the enemy and find fruits with less effort."

Although there is a loose dominant and subordinate relationship among individuals within most primate groups, chimpanzee social life is not rigidly organized into a dominance hierarchy. A major element in rigidly hierarchial primate societies is that each animal must adjust its movements and behaviors to others in the troop. Sugiyama argues that a rigidly organized social order cannot be maintained when individuals do not subordinate their personal desires for the good of troop unity or solidarity. Some argue that Sugiyama's statement implies too much motivation. The flexible nature of the chimpanzee social order may be one resolution of the problem of maintaining order while allowing individual freedom. "This kind of social organization may be one of the original factors raising individuality to the level of personality. Chimpanzees have not rejected group life, but they have rejected individual uniformity and the pressure of a dominance hierarchy" (Sugiyama, 1972:160).

Chimpanzee social organization is flexible and adaptable. Budongo chimpanzees, for example, change their behavior markedly when they approach open terrain. In the forest they are relaxed and their social organization is loose; they become tense and vigilant in open spaces, such as when crossing a road or moving into the savanna-grassland. Some of Sugiyama's coworkers, for example Itani and Suzuki (1967) and Nishida (1968), note that chimpanzees in the savanna move in structured groups similar to those of savanna-dwelling baboons. Interestingly, the effect may also work the other way. Studies of forest-dwelling baboons (Rowell, 1966, 1972) suggest that they do not have hierarchies and generally live relaxed lives, more comparable to the forest-dwelling chimpanzees with looser social structures. Forest-living baboons are also freer to move from troop to troop, and adult males do not defend the troop during emergencies, as is so true on the savanna.

Figure 12-7. A young chimpanzee nurses.

Figure 12-8. Chimpanzees engaging in grooming behavior.

Similar changes may have occurred among ancestral hominids. As these animals left the relative safety of the forest and trees, they may have adapted by modifying their social organizations. The once rather carefree, relatively peaceful life in the forest, with its flexible social organizations, was presented with new pressures, new dangers. The loosely knit social organizations became, in time, tightly and rigidly organized social structures.

The most recent information suggests that chimpanzees live in permanent communities. The usual view of chimpanzee social units has been that they are bisexual with both males and females associating more with each other than with members of other social groups. Wrangham (1978) proposes a model to account for what has previously seemed to be a completely fluid social structure. He suggests that although males are grouped into separate social groups (or communities), lactating females may be spread geographically in relation to other females and independently of the males. Females may range at the edges of two male communities and associate with males of both communities and females with ranges within either of the two male group ranges. As are female orangutans, female chimpanzees are distributed individually according to foraging needs. The social system is adapted to female distribution.

In most group-living primates outbreeding is promoted by males moving out of their natal groups. The opposite situation is true for chimpanzees, however. Pusey (1978) describes temporary and permanent transfers between communities by young females. While temporary transfer may be accomplished by both young nulliparous females (those without infants) and some older females, only young nulliparous females, usually those in estrus, have been observed to transfer permanently to a new community. Community boundaries are determined by activities of bands of males, who may be closely related, who patrol the boundaries of the group.

Goodall (1979) notes that Gombe has been roughly divided by two separate groups that were once part of a single group. There is a very fluid, overlapping area between the two new groups (Bygott, 1972, 1974). During 1974 and 1975 four chimpanzees were attacked and killed for no apparent reason by "northerners" deep in the southern area. Goodall speculates that the northern chimpanzees were on "patrol" at the time of the killing. She suggests that a sense of territoriality and overcrowding produced by human destruction of the habitat may be related to the killings.

Borders between the two groups at Gombe are amorphous, and Goodall suggests that the relative strength of neighboring groups defines the territorial boundary at any given time. Once in a new terrain, adult males start sniffing leaves, walking stealthily, maintaining silence and climbing trees to search the area for hours at a time. If neighboring chimpanzees are seen, the "patrol" often makes a rapid group attack. Goodall relates that "The sheer savagery of the attacks was very hard for us to believe." Attacks lasted 15 to 20 minutes and observers " . . . had the impression that killing was intended." Goodall adds that the violent behavior " . . . seems to be attractive, especially to young adults." When the patrol returned to its own area, members of the patrol seemed highly agitated and often proceeded to hunt.

Goodall's (1979) studies have also increasingly reported the incidence of infanticide by mothers. Goodall suggests (personal communication) that infanticide may be more frequent than originally assumed. As with Dian Fossey's gorillas and the previously noted case of the langurs, the exact causes of this behavior are not known. In all three instances, however, over-crowding looms large as a suspected cause.

The Gorilla

> Few animals have stirred public and scientific interest as the gorilla has done. Discovered over a hundred years ago, it remained a creature of mystery. The gorilla has been shot, captured, and photographed, but its reputed belligerence and remote habitat discouraged firsthand scientific study (Schaller, 1963:cover).

This was the dominant attitude until George Schaller made public the results of 466 hours of direct contact with mountain gorillas in the Virunga Volcanoes region of the eastern Congo, western Uganda, and western Ruanda. The most recent studies of the gorillas are being undertaken by Dian Fossey, who has been working with gorillas for more than 12 years.

Earliest Reports. The earliest report of the gorilla came in the eighteenth century. The name then given the gorilla was "Impungu," apparently a native term. The report follows:

> Of this animal there are three classes or species . . . This wonderful and frightful projection of nature walks upright like man; is from 7 to 9 feet high, when at maturity, thick in proportion, and amazingly strong; covered with longish hair, jet black over the body, but longer on the head; the face more like the human than the Chimpenza, but the complexion is black; and has no tail (quoted in Reynolds, 1967:53).

Figure 12-9. The face and head of an adult male gorilla.

Figure 12-10. The face and head of a young adult female gorilla.

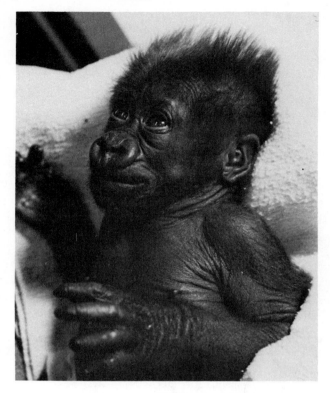

Figure 12-11. A baby gorilla, approximately 2 months of age.

By the end of the eighteenth century, when the chimpanzee, orangutan, and gibbon were comparatively well known, the gorilla was still an anecdotal nightmare. A typical report, printed in an 1847 publication, follows.

> . . . the *ingena,* an animal like the orangutan, but much exceeding it in size, being five feet high and four across the shoulders. Its paw was said to be even more disproportioned than its breadth, and one blow of it to be fatal. It is seen commonly by them when they travel to Kaybe, lurking in the bush to destroy passengers, and feeding principally on wild honey, which abounds. Among other of their actions . . . is that of building a house in rude imitation of the natives, and sleeping outside on the roof of it (quoted in Reynolds, 1967:54).

The gorilla was scientifically unknown until 1847, when it was first described on the basis of skeletal materials, primarily a skull. Gorillas were known from West Africa in the nineteenth century; gorillas in East Africa were first discovered by Europeans as late as 1902. The first European to report seeing an East African gorilla was a German army officer, Captain Oskar von Beringe, after whom a gorilla subspecies, *Gorilla gorilla beringei* was named. (Many now include the gorilla in the same genus, *Pan,* as the chimpanzee.)

The American missionary T. Savage, in the original scientific description of the gorilla, wrote the following account in the *Boston Journal of Natural History,* 1844:

The *enge-enas* (gorillas) are exceedingly ferocious, and always offensive in their habits, never running from man as does the chimpanzee. They are objects of terror to the natives, and are never encountered by them except on the defensive. . . . When the male is first seen he gives a terrific yell, that resounds far and wide through the forest. His underlip hangs over the chin, and his hairy ridge and scalp are contracted upon the brow, presenting an aspect of indescribable ferocity. He then approaches the hunter in great fury, pouring out his horrid cries in quick succession. The hunter waits until the animal grasps the barrel of his gun, and as he carries it to his mouth, he fires. Should the gun fail to go off, the barrel is crushed between the teeth, and the encounter soon proves fatal to the hunter (quoted in Reynolds, 1967:135-36).

After gorillas were discovered, one of the best-known big-game hunters, P. der Chaillu (an American trader on the West African coast who turned zoologist-explorer), set out for Africa to hunt them. He claimed to have been the first European to have hunted and killed a full-grown male gorilla.

Previous to Schaller's attempts at naturalistic studies, Garner, Akeley, and Bingham attempted to study gorillas. Their great contribution was an insistence that the gorillas were not ferocious beasts; unfortunately this message was lost. The early 1950s witnessed renewed attempts to study gorillas.

Schaller. The transformation of ideas about gorillas and their acceptance as nonviolent creatures is the result of Schaller's study (1963, 1964), begun when Schaller and John Emlen surveyed the gorilla population at Virunga. When Emlen left, Schaller and his wife, Kay, remained behind for 10 months of extensive study of 10 separate gorilla groups. These 10 groups included 200-odd animals that lived in the Hagenia woodland zone at about 10,000 feet. This thick mountain forest is the home of the mountain gorilla. Today some 5,000 to 15,000 gorillas live here in danger of extinction. They are forced to retreat further up the mountainside as humans occupy the lower slopes and turn them over to their cattle.

Schaller habituated gorillas to his presence by slowly approaching them, alone and in full view. After a number of approaches he was accepted as an innocuous addition to the scenery. Schaller became familiar with his animals in much the same way each of us monkey and ape watchers become familiar with our subjects. Physical defects, behavioral quirks, locomotor patterns, and voice patterns are used to identify individual animals.

Schaller did not find a savage beast; he discovered a big, nonaggressive vegetarian. Because they have enormous appetites, gorillas spend 6 to 8 hours a day eating; there is little time for anything else. Gorilla aggressive behavior is very rare, and usually consists of an irritable slap or threatening stare. No fights were witnessed. Once the gorillas discovered Schaller was not dangerous, their curiosity replaced fear—they observed Schaller observing them. Even if he blundered on the gorillas feeding, Schaller was not attacked. In contrast to his predecessors, Schaller learned gorilla communicative gestures; if he frightened an animal, Schaller merely shook his head, as subordinate gorillas do, and he was ignored.

Schaller's study uncovered a host of previously unknown facts about gorillas and his work disproved many fables. Schaller found that gorillas live in fairly stable social groups, 17 members being an average. Gorilla groups range from solitary males to groups of 30 or more animals, each containing at least one dominant silver-backed (so-called because of graying of the hair about the rump and up the back) male and a few younger and less dominant adult black-backed males. A group also contains a number of females and their offspring. Contacts between members of different groups are nonaggressive; animals may leave one group and simply join another.

The silver-backed male leads and controls the group; he determines when and where it should travel, and how fast. He stays behind and intimidates intruders with the famous chest-beating display: he rises on his hind feet, soundly beats his resonating chest, and throws sticks or other nearby objects into the air. The act is an intimidating display and seldom leads to attack.

Each gorilla group wanders over its own range, which is usually 10 to 12 square miles. Most of the time gorillas are quiet. They are normally quadrupedal, terrestrial, knuckle-walking animals. They usually sleep in a crudely constructed ground nest rather than in tree nests common to other apes. Schaller's study portrays the gorilla as a lazy wanderer, one who likes to doze or sunbathe in the midmorning. As Reynolds (1967:149) notes, "Perhaps the worst that can be said about the temperament of the wild gorilla is that it is morose and sullen; at best it is amiable, lovable, shy and gentle."

Fossey. Dian Fossey has spent more than 12 years studying gorillas in Ruanda. Many of her findings reflect those of Schaller's, but she did find some interesting differences. Some of the most outstanding differences between her study and that of Schaller's are as follows: Schaller found group sizes to average 16.9 animals (a range of 3 to 20 animals per group), whereas Fossey found sizes to vary from 9 to 14 (with a range of 9 to 30) animals. Both studies found that a gorilla group contains at least one silver-backed male and one or more females, and maintains relative stability over time. Schaller's study showed that females first gave birth at about age 6, whereas Fossey suggests that the mean age of parturition is much older. Fossey also feels that wild gorillas live longer than the 15 to 30 years suggested by Schaller. Schaller noted only 1 of 12 interactions to be antagonistic, whereas Fossey noted 15 percent of all physical interactions as violent. Fossey attributes the main cause of interactions as attempts to solicit females (Fossey, 1979).

One of the most interesting outcomes of Fossey's study is the discovery of infanticide practiced by the silver-backed males. Schaller never noted this. Fossey reports three known cases of infanticide and three suspected cases. She feels that this phenomenon, which she labels as rare, may be more frequent than she can currently document. Fossey has documented one case of cannibalism in which an infant was eaten. The infant's remains were found in the dung of its mother and its brother. The details of the cannibalism and the motives are still unknown to Fossey and she warns against an overemphasis on this incident. Rather, she says, "I want you to think of the mountain gorillas as a harmonious group."

One of the groups with which Fossey is most familiar is Group Four. This group has changed its composition a number of times since first being found: animals have died and wandered off and new infants were born. However, Group Four, like most gorilla groups, is fairly stable. Gorillas travel together in small groups and do not mingle in larger units such as the chimpanzee regional populations. These groups are apparently held together by the leadership of the silver-backed male.

Gorilla groups have imprecise home ranges that vary as the silver-backed male explores and extends the range. Home ranges frequently overlap, causing intermittent clashes. However, gorillas are not territorial. One way of avoiding contact within a home range is to overgraze the border area, making it seem as if all the food is gone. Gorillas may also build their ground nests close together, giving an impression of numerous animals in a tightly knit group. The vast wanderings about the home range may be one way of ensuring the food supply.

Gorillas in the wild have never been observed to drink; they seem to obtain their water directly from the lush vegetation. Gorillas are primarily herbivorous in nature, but they consume meat in captivity. Gorillas consume small gray snails found beneath the leaves of the nettle and they eat slugs found inside rotting trees. They have a zest for sweet foods, and their favorite foods are vines and fungus.

By the time gorillas are 6, they are young adults. The female gorilla gives birth at about age 7 and she is a solicitous mother. Males are gentle with infants and do not avoid them. Males and females have their own dominance hierarchies.

Gorilla social behavior is less frequent than that witnessed among chimpanzees. Fossey has seen considerable play behavior, contrasting with Schaller's reports. Gorillas do little social grooming, and most often an animal grooms itself. Females show no signs of estrus; they are, however, ready to mate once a month for several days. Males are not sexually jealous and mating does not lead to aggression, but there is some competition for females. Males forming their own groups may obtain females by a show of force and "kidnapping" females from another group.

Communicating with Chimpanzees and Gorillas. Because of the excitement generated by news releases in recent years concerning human-chimpanzee attempts to communicate, there will be few readers who are not aware of the efforts being made to test the language abilities of nonhuman primates (see Mounin, 1976, and Desmond, 1979, for reviews). The first rearing experiment with a chimpanzee was made by a Soviet scientist, N. Kohts. In 1913 she acquired a young chimpanzee, Joni, approximately 2 years old. She raised this animal until it was about 4 years 6 months old, during which time she conducted comparable observations on her son.

Kohts's study was followed by that of the Kelloggs (Kellogg and Kellogg, 1933), who acquired a 7-month-old chimpanzee named Gua. They used their son Donald as a control to compare the abilities and intellectual and motor development of both infants. During early development the chimpanzee, Gua, performed better than her human male counterpart, Donald. Gua learned to react to certain words and phrases of her "parents." During the first part of the study Gua surpassed or equaled Donald in a number of test situations. During the last part of the study, however, Donald's linguistic competence overtook Gua's and he surpassed the chimpanzee in comprehension. The study ended when Gua was 16 months old, at which time she had learned to use certain gestures consistently as communicatory signals. Although Gua did respond to human verbal communicatory signals, she was unable to duplicate them.

The next major experiment in which a chimpanzee was reared in a home was made by the Hayeses (Hayes, 1952; Hayes and Nissen, 1971). The chimpanzee was named Vicki, a 3-day-old female acquired from the nursery at the Yerkes Regional Primate Center. Vicki was raised as a human child until her death at age 6½. The Hayeses' study was unique in that they attempted to teach this chimpanzee to speak. The results of the Hayeses' labors were not particularly noteworthy—the chimpanzee was taught to produce some hoarse sounds that the Hayeses interpreted as "momma," "cup," "pappa," and possibly the word "up." Although the Hayeses concluded that it was difficult, perhaps impossible, to teach a chimpanzee to speak, they did establish that one could communicate with the chimpanzee using gestural cues.

In addition to attempting to teach Vicki to speak English, the Hayeses conducted extensive teaching and observation of their "daughter." Vicki's early development maintained the pace of a normal human child, and in some cases surpassed it—especially in terms of motor development and manipulative activities. There is some interesting evidence in the Hayeses' work that Vicki recognized objects, including other chimpanzees, but she seemed to place herself in the same group as her "parents," that is, among humans!

The Hayeses' work had a strong impact and was a catalyst to a later study by two psychologists, Beatrice and Alan Gardner, at the University of Nevada. The Gardners' subject was a young female chimpanzee named Washoe. The Gardners' project called for raising their chimpanzee in a communicative environment that was amenable to the chimpanzee's natural manipulative talents. They chose American Sign Language (ASL) as their medium of communication (Gardner and Gardner, 1969, 1971).

Washoe was wild-born and acquired by the Gardners at the age of 11 months. She was housed in a trailer in the Gardners' yard and provided with a stimulating environment that included human companions, who worked in shifts during the day. The sole means of communication between Washoe and her human companions was ASL, which was taught to Washoe by members of the research team proficient in the medium. Washoe's acquisition of ASL was evaluated either live by the staff or from film played to native "speakers" of ASL, for example, deaf observers. The deaf observers soon were able to comprehend 90 percent of Washoe's signs.

After 7 months of training Washoe acquired signs rapidly; she reliably used nouns, verbs, and other words and began to transfer sign meanings to appropriate contexts. With an increase in her vocabulary she began to put words together and form rough sentences. After 36 months Washoe had learned 85 signs; after 51 months her vocabulary increased to 132 signs that were consistently and correctly used. (See, however, Rumbaugh et al. [1980] for a rebuttal of this claim of correct and consistent usage.) Her sentence structure resembled the first sentences of young children.

Soon Washoe was using signs to communicate her desires and also in "conversations" with herself. Washoe would sign when she wished to play, when she wished more food, when she wished to go into the yard, and to convey other messages.

The Gardners' experiments showed that some form of two-way communication could be established between a human and a chimpanzee if the appropriate medium was used. The Gardners' study was extended by one of their ex-students, Roger Fouts, who took Washoe to the Institute of Primate Studies in Norman, Oklahoma. Fouts continued to work with Washoe and he soon began to teach ASL to other chimpanzees, including two males and two females. Fouts's continuing work shows that Washoe is not a unique example of chimpanzee intelligence or adaptability (Fouts, 1973, 1975).

Fouts reports that as of 1975 Washoe had 160 signs in her vocabulary. While the size of the vocabulary is interesting, Fouts feels it is also interesting to note the manner in which she combines the signs. Washoe combines signs and she shows a preference in her sign order that Fouts feels may be interpreted as the rudiments of syntax. She prefers the use of the pronoun sign for "you" preceding the sequence of a verb and the pronoun sign for "me."

Fouts was interested in knowing if Washoe would use her language of ASL when communicating with other chimpanzees. Washoe has used signs with other chimpanzees; unfortunately, however, the other chimpanzees at Oklahoma are either lacking training in ASL or are deficient in their ASL sign vocabulary. Even so, the investigators have noted that the chimpanzees will sign to one another in situations such as mutal comforting, eating, and general play activities such as tickling games. For example, one of the male chimpanzees, Booee, was observed to approach another male, Bruno, and, using ASL, ask Bruno to "tickle Booee."

The Gardners (1971) noted that Washoe not only produced those signs that they had taught her, but she also produced her own signs. For example, Washoe invented her own sign for the word "bib." One of the chimpanzees at Oklahoma, a female named Lucy, has also invented her own signs. Lucy, who is being reared in a human home, enjoys going for a walk. When she is out walking she is taken on a leash. When Lucy wishes to go out she signs "leash," which she does with a sign she invented herself—a hooking action with her extended index finger on her neck. Some of the chimpanzees at Oklahoma may have also changed the grammatical function of a word; that is, a noun was changed to an adjective. Lucy has used the sign for "dirty" in instances other than that in which she was taught. Fouts (1975) notes that she once signed "dirty cat" to a strange cat with which she had been aggressively interacting. Although Lucy needs to be leashed for her enjoyable walks, she dislikes being tethered. Therefore, the leash is often signed as "dirty leash."

Two other studies were conducted on communication between humans and chimpanzees. One study was conducted by Ann and David Premack, two psychologists at the University of California, Santa Barbara. The communication medium in this experiment was plastic symbols of different shapes and colors (Premack, 1971a,b; Premack and Premack, 1972). These symbols were stuck to a magnetic board. The subject in this experiment was a 5-year-old female named Sarah.

Sarah was taught that to receive a piece of banana, she had to place a plastic symbol onto the magnetic board. She learned this rapidly, and her vocabulary was expanded to include different color symbols for different fruits. After obtaining a competence in this series of tests, Sarah was introduced to the verb "give." After mastering the use of the verb, she was required to end a "sentence" with her name, Sarah, to receive her reward. Sarah was also required to master the interrogative "?", and "yes," and "no." Furthermore, Sarah mastered color names, position words such as "in," and quantifiers such as "one," "none," "all," and "several."

After 18 months of training, the Premacks felt that Sarah had achieved a language that compared in many ways to that of a 2½-year-old child. Sarah acquired a vocabulary of 130 terms which were used correctly 75 to 80 percent of the time.

Another study is being conducted at Yerkes Regional Primate Center, Atlanta, by Duane Rumbaugh and colleagues (Rumbaugh et al., 1973; Rumbaugh, 1977). The communication medium is a computer and the subject a female chimpanzee named Lana. Lana has been taught to work a console with 25 keys bearing color-coded symbols that represent vocabulary terms. Lana's language has been called "Yerkish" after the name of the primate center. After 6 months of training Lana learned to use the computer console with ease and she now effectively communicates with her human friends. She can communicate her wishes by pressing the correct keys. Unless the keys are pressed in the correct order to produce a coherent sentence, Lana's request is ignored. Should she wish to request an M and M candy, she would press the keys to read "Please machine give me M and M period." Should Lana's human companions wish to communicate with Lana, they also do so through the medium of the computer console. The Rumbaugh experiment holds the promise of devising a language training program for helping mentally retarded human children.

Studies in communication similar to those done with chimpanzees have been undertaken on other great apes. Fouts (1975) did a short exploratory study with one infant male orangutan to determine if he could acquire some signs. The orangutan was able to learn a few signs (such as for drink, food, and tickle) and he combined them into two-sign combinations. One experimentor (Furness, 1916) was able to teach an orangutan two vocal words, similar to the Hayeses' result with Vicki.

Koko is a 7-year-old "talking" gorilla with whom F. Patterson (1978a,b) began communicating with sign language in July, 1972. Patterson (1978a:449) notes:

My colleagues were not very sanguine about teaching Koko sign language. Some questioned the gorilla's dexterity as compared with the chimpanzee's. Others were skeptical about the animal's intellect.

One of the best indicators of human intelligence is that of vocabulary development. Over the first 1.5 years, Koko acquired about one new sign each month. After 36 months she reliably learned to use 184 signs and by age 6 years, 6 months she used 645 different signs. Patterson estimates that Koko used regularly and appropriately about 375 of these signs.

Koko's performance on intelligence tests was closely monitored. In 1975 her intelligence quotient (IQ) measured 84 on the Stanford-Binet Intelligence Scale. Five months later, at 4 years, 6 months, the IQ had risen to 95, only slightly below the average for a human child of the same age. Her IQ has consistently ranged between 85 and 95.

Koko exhibits some interesting behavioral patterns. For example, Patterson is convinced that sometimes Koko deliberately disobeys—her punishment is banishment to a corner of the room. A prime trait of human language is that of displacement, the ability to refer to events removed in time and space from the communicative act. This is considered a major test for determining the presence or absence of language. Various traits in Koko's communication seem to indicate that she has the ability for displacement. For example, three days after Koko bit Patterson, Patterson (1978a:449) recorded the following "conversation":

Patterson: "What did you do to Penny?"
Koko: "Bite." (When the incident originally occurred, Koko referred to it as a scratch.)
Patterson: "You admit it?"
Koko: "Wrong bite."
Patterson: "Why bite?"
Koko: "Because mad."
Patterson: "Why mad?"
Koko: "Don't know."

The entire conversation concerns recollection of a past emotional event and is not the type of discussion ". . . one would expect to have with an animal whose memories were dim, unsorted recollections of pain and pleasure. . ." (Patterson, 1978a:459).

Further suggestion that Koko may be able to displace events comes with her predilection to lie. Once, while Patterson was writing, Koko took a red crayon and began to chew it. Patterson asked Koko, "You're not eating that crayon, are you?" To this question Koko signed "Lip," and began moving the crayon across her upper and then her lower lips as if applying lipstick.

Koko also seems to have the ability to distinguish between past and future events. For example, she has begun to use the sign "later" to delay discussion of possibly unpleasant subjects.

Previous studies with chimpanzees showed that some seem to have the capacity to draw on different gestures to describe a new object or event. Washoe, for example, once described swans as "water birds." Koko also seems to have generated compound names to describe novelties in her environment. For example, she referred to a zebra as a "white tiger," to a Pinocchio doll as an "elephant baby" (an interesting association between a long nose on the doll and an elephant's trunk), and to a mask as an "eye hat."

These experiments have generated a good deal of scientific interest and excitement. They have enabled us to communicate more than ever before with our closest relatives in the animal kingdom. Although there has been a failure to teach the chimpanzees or other great apes to speak a language, as could possibly have been predicted, these experiments do show us something of the range of ape intelligence and adaptability. It is important, however, to bear in mind that the results of all these experiments are due to humans teaching animals new techniques. The abilities witnessed in the various experiments may not indicate the range of abilities among wild animals. These experiments are also forcing us to rethink our definitions of what is human, as is also true of studies of chimpanzees in the wild. The gap between what it means to be human and what it means to be ape is closing. We are definitely different; that difference, however, is not so much quantitative as it seems to be qualitative.

Rumbaugh et al. (1975:400) best sum the philosophy of this work in a discussion of Lana's abilities.

> At present, however, in the interests of remaining objective rather than fanciful, a very real temptation in this area of research, we stop well short of concluding or even suggesting that Lana has demonstrated productive language capabilities. She has, nonetheless, impressed us with her achievements, and, at times, we believe that the greatest barrier to even more rapid progress on her part is our limited understanding as to how to best convey to her what it is that we are trying to reach. She remains highly motivated and gives us reason to believe that she "enjoys" the challenge of new tasks and disdains the routine.

Rumbaugh et al. (1978) have questioned the recent studies suggesting linguistic abilities in chimpanzees. They are particularly reluctant to accept some of the evidence coming from studies of Washoe (using ASL) and Sarah (who uses colored plastic discs). They do feel, however, that their chimpanzees at the Yerkes Regional Primate Center have met the criteria for linguistically mediated behavior. Two of their chimpanzees have demonstrated the ability to learn to use graphic symbols to ask one another for tools needed to obtain food, showing that they comprehend the symbolic and communicative function of the symbols they use.

Based on this work, Rumbaugh et al. feel that their results raise questions concerning chimpanzee research employing other forms of symbolic communication systems. They feel that there is little evidence to demonstrate that either Washoe or Sarah has fully comprehended the symbolic nature and communicative potential of their respective gestural (Washoe) and graphic token (Sarah) symbol systems.

The following criticisms of the work on Washoe and Sarah are from Rumbaugh et al. (1978) and serve to illustrate the type of criticisms being raised about "talking apes." Work with the apes has, for the most part, used a highly sophisticated and competent language-using human in the role of either recipient or transmitter in every linguistic situation. This essentially allows the ape to "fill in the blanks" while the basic interchange is controlled by the human. Rumbaugh et al. (1978) feel that the work with Washoe, for instance, has not demonstrated (1) that the chimpanzees are gesturing to one another and not humans nearby, (2) whether the signals used in ASL gestures were essentially different from those nonverbal signals reported for wild chimpanzees, (3) whether the recipient of the signal altered his or her behavior in response to the signal, and (4) whether the animals were able to shift from transmitter to receiver role. They feel that these criteria were met in their study where the two chimpanzees communicated only to one another, reversed roles, and reacted to one another's communication.

The questions at Rumbaugh et al. raise can be summed as follows (1978:522): "Thus, while there are abundant descriptions of very interesting and suggestive phenomena, there are few firm data, collected in controlled, blind-test situations, to support the contention that either Washoe or Sarah are employing symbolically-mediated abstract communication similar to that involved in human language." Although it can be assumed that not all investigators will agree with this conclusion, it must be realized that the work with "talking apes" is being widely followed and the conclusions to be drawn from this research are still to come.

Others besides Rumbaugh et al. have raised serious questions about the linguistic skills of chimpanzees and gorillas. Terrace (1979) and Terrace et al. (1979), for example, have noted that although projects teaching chimpanzees and gorillas to use language have shown that these apes can learn vocabularies of visual symbols, ". . . there is no evidence . . . that apes can combine such symbols in order to create new meanings" (Terrace et al., 1979:900). They further note that evidence showing that apes can create sentences can be explained by reference to simpler nonlinguistic processes. Terrace et al. suggest that an ape's language learning abilities are severely restricted. Although "apes can learn many isolated symbols, . . . they show no unequivocal evidence of mastering the conversational, semantic, or syntactic organization of language" (Terrace et al., 1979:901).

Terrace's opinions are best summed in his 1979 book, in which he notes several ways in which the chimpanzee's utterances differ from the developing language of human children. For example, his chimpanzee, Nim, rarely signed spontaneously and usually signed only in response to a trainer's promptings. Forty percent of the time Nim repeated the signs made by the trainer without adding any new signs of his own. Terrace argues that Nim was not actually creating his own sentences, but was instead acting more or less similar to a trained dog. On occasions when Nim did expand on his trainer's utterances, he tended to use signs, such as "Nim," "me," "you," and "eat," that did not add any new information.

Terrace's criticisms of the ape language research have not been met with gratitude, to say the least, from those researchers whose work Terrace questions. Particularly distressed by Terrace's criticisms are the Gardners, Fouts, and Patterson.

The current controversy surrounding the ape language research has three major points (Marx, 1980): (1) The philosophical part of the debate revolves around the issue of whether humans are unique in their ability to use language. (2) The debate is also linguistic, and the issue revolves around the nature of language. There is no general agreement about what is or is not language. (3) Finally, there is the issue of methodology. Is there any way in which a human investigator can assess the language capacities of an ape? There is no means to know what an ape is thinking when it uses a sign or other symbol to act as a word.

The Orangutan

Although orangutans share many traits with the other pongids, they are unique in several respects. They live in Southeast Asia, as do the gibbons; however, they are closer in size and temperament to their African relatives, the gorilla and chimpanzee. In contrast to chimpanzees, orangutans seem to be shy and retiring. Although they are arboreal, they move with quiet deliberation. Orangutans have always raised the primatologists' curiosity, their "odd" looks being one of the reasons. The cheeks of male orangutans bulge out in fleshy pads, unique among primates. Below this is a large air sac connected to the larynx that can be blown up to resemble an enormous goiter. This sac acts as a resonator or helps produce sustained sounds. The old idea that this sac was filled with air to keep an orang afloat in water is fanciful at best. Orangutans in the jungle have been heard to give loud burps that may function as warning signals. The evolutionary history of the male cheek pouches is unclear; however, they

Figure 12-12. An adult female orangutan.

Figure 12-13. A young orangutan.

may be a reflection of sexual dimorphism and a function of sexual selection (Horr, personal communication).

Once there may have been at least 500,000 orangutans inhabiting the vast jungles from the Celebes to North China. Harrisson (1962) has suggested that in the early Christian era there were probably more orangutans than people in Borneo. A recent estimate places the current Borneo orangutan population at 9,000 animals, and this low level cannot be maintained for long. It should be noted, however, that Rijsken (1978) feels that their numbers may be higher than previously estimated.

The orangutan faces extinction due to a number of circumstances, primarily human encroachment on its habitat. Humans have hunted orangs for food (cooked bones believed to belong to the orangutan have been found in Niah Cave in West Borneo from a site that dates to 35,000 years ago) and for display in zoos. More ominous, however, is the human destruction of the habitat by cutting down the primary forests for timber and clearing the land for farms and factories.

Preserving the Orangutan. The first major conservation effort was undertaken by Barbara and Tom Harrisson, who reared baby orangutans in their Sarawak home. These animals were confiscated before they were to be exported. The Harrissons established a program in which they tried to rehabilitate young orangutans, eventually to be set free in their jungle habitat. The program had some success.

An effort was made in Sabah to rehabilitate orangutans and return them to their natural habitat. The experiment was conducted under the direction of a Ceylonese zoologist, Stanley de Silva, in the Sepilok Forest Reserve, 10,000 acres of virgin jungle located about 15 miles inland from the port of Sandakan in northern Borneo (Mydans, 1973). The program began in 1964; as of 1973, 51 animals had been taken into the project, all reclaimed from the native population. Some of these animals died; however, all but eight disappeared into the forest to join their wild relatives.

Naturalistic Studies. A major problem with studying orangutans is that they live in inaccessible swampy tropical jungles; hours or days of searching may reveal nothing. Furthermore, orangutans are primarily wandering, solitary animals and it is difficult to find them; once located they are difficult to follow. However, both Schaller and Davenport, who spent short periods of time observing them, note that they can be followed without too much trouble. Their slow, precise movements make them easy targets; they seem to be too big to flee nimbly in the trees and do not run rapidly quadrupedally on the ground. Orangutans are the slowest of the apes and they seem to be too big for the trees and too arboreal for their size.

Davenport (1967) conducted a study of orangutans in the state of Sabah, Borneo. He studied animals for a total of 192 animal-hours of day observation and observed the following groupings: one family group composed of two adults and a dependent infant; three of mother-child pairs, one with an independent infant and two with dependent infants; and seven of lone animals (four adults and three subadults). All these were located in primary forest; the heaviest concentration was in the Sepilok Forest Reserve, where de Silva established the rehabilitation project.

Some of Davenport's observations follow: The type of locomotion the orangutan uses depends to a great degree on the type and structure of the vegetation. Orangutans manifest a diversity of locomotor patterns: quadrupedal on the tops of branches, suspended by all fours from a branch, bipedal locomotion atop a branch, and **brachiation** (that is, arm-swinging beneath branches). Regardless of the locomotor pattern, the animals were always cautious and deliberate.

In a number of instances in which Davenport observed the animals, resting or sleeping nests were used or made. Usually a new nest is built for nighttime sleeping. The time needed to construct a nest and the method employed depended to some extent on the site and materials available. Characteristically, all animals selected a firm branch on which smaller branches grew. Three times Davenport observed the animals building an overhead shelter to protect them from a heavy rain.

Although Davenport witnessed minimal manipulation of the environment other than nest building, interesting examples of tool use have been reported from the de Silva project. One of the animals in the project, a female named Joan, was observed to use a dead branch as a club, as though to pound a pole into the ground. Captive orangutans have been seen using tools. Orangutans at the Harrissons' rehabilation center have been seen poking into termite mounds and ant nests, sometimes with sticks.

Continuing studies by Birute Galdikas-Brindamour (1975), among others, add considerably to our knowledge about orangutans. The orangutan social group, if it can be called that, is a mother and her infant. The orangutan generally avoids contact with others of its species and has no social life as is typical of the other great apes. A mother and her infant may meet another mother and infant and spend a day or two foraging next to them. However, there is minimal social interaction. After weaning, a female youngster will probably travel close to her mother for several more years, and may spend most of her life in the same few square miles as her mother.

Galdikas-Brindamour found as many as nine animals together. However, when more than five animals are together, tensions rise and the unstable group divides into smaller units. The first social unit is the mother-infant dyad. When the orangutan becomes a subadult at age 4 or 5, it joins its peers and forms a social unit. Mixed male and female pairs are common; however, these are not sexual partnerships and the partners avoid mating. Adult males are loners who avoid interanimal contact and who are only social during mating. Males do not move together, and the only social meetings with each other are most often of an aggressive nature. These meetings were rare among Horr's (1977) subjects but occurred more often among animals observed by Galdikas-Brindamour. Males contend aggressively for females and Galdikas-Brindamour found many animals with scratches, broken fingers, and gouges.

Adult males are intolerant of infants, and young mothers avoid males until their offspring are large enough to move and survive independently. Mothers have no predators to fear and thus have no need for male protection.

The only "social" behavior in which adult males indulge is mating. Males battle for females, and Galdikas-Brindamour suggests that a number of males may be killed in the process of trying to acquire a female for mating. Female orangutans show no external signs of estrus such as the swelling found in chimpanzees and many monkeys. A female reveals her hormonal state by certain "flirting behaviors." When a transient adult male finds an estrous female he follows her about for days. Resident males in an area may stay in one place for several years and choose a female with whom they spend several days each month. Some male consorts stay with the females when they are pregnant. Young males may force females to mate with them. However, females seldom, if ever, become pregnant as a result of these forced matings with the young males. This process seems to assure that only larger males will father the next generation.

Galdikas-Brindamour found that orangutans are much more terrestrial than previously thought. In fact, adult males may spend considerable time on the ground. They have also been seen to wade in water, in contrast to gorillas and chimpanzees. Some orangutans have been observed to enter flooded plots to obtain desired foods. They will eat flowers, leaves, eggs, and insects. Some orangutans have been seen to raid beehives for honey.

Horr (1977:293) has described orangutan maturation and socialization:

> Unlike most other higher primates, young orangs do not mature in the context of a group or troop of several individuals of all ages and sexes in which long term relationships are developed on the basis of daily, face-to-face contact. Not only is there no cohesive, geographically bounded "troop" such as one might expect for baboons or macaques, but there are apparently no instances in which a large number of orangutans come together for coordinated movement from place to place or for feeding.

Among orangutans the only face-to-face social unit of any longevity is the adult female and her dependent offspring. This unit is usually composed of a female and one offspring; however, two or three infants may be in reasonably close association. The mother-offspring unit sleeps, moves, and feeds together. Maturing offspring ultimately separate from the maternal unit.

Among Borneo orangutans, the mother-offspring units range habitually over small jungle areas, perhaps one-fourth of a square mile in size, that are conservative over time and space. Although home ranges are small, and a female could cross the range within a day, movement is generally restricted to a small area. Mother and offspring home ranges are not exclusive, and adjacent units overlap to varying degrees. Such overlaps do not, however, result in large aggregations of animals.

Adult males range over larger areas than adult females. Male ranges are 2 or more square miles in area and overlap the ranges of several adult females. As males move over their range they emit loud trumpeting vocalizations carrying for long distances in the jungle. Such calls serve to announce the male's presence, give females a chance to localize the male and either choose to meet him or move away, and, finally, allow males to avoid or challenge one another. There is no evidence that males are territorial in the classic sense.

Juveniles form the final category of members in orangutan "society." At a certain point in development, juveniles leave the maternal unit and establish their own adult ranging patterns. Juvenile females leave their mothers somewhat later than juvenile males. Females may establish overlapping home ranges with their mothers. Juvenile males move farther from the mother (thus helping to prevent incest between males and their mothers and sisters) and are often located alone in the forest. Young males may form brief "social" associations with other juvenile males, but there are no juvenile male peer groups. There is no evidence for independent juvenile females.

> Summarized briefly, orangutan social organization is based on mother-offspring units moving in conservative, partly overlapping home ranges, with adult males ranging over much wider areas to cover more than one female range. Juveniles transit from moving with their maternal unit to assuming adult ranging patterns, with an intermediate semi-solitary phase in between (Horr, 1977:295).

Horr (1977) suggests that the orangutan social structure is an adaptation to the environment. Critical food items are thinly distributed throughout the forest, and large concentrations of apes would rapidly exhaust the food supplies in any given area. Female-offspring ranges are the minimal area of support. Males are unimportant in defense of the young against predators. Thus a system of ranging males ensures an adequate conception

Figure 12-14. A brachiating gibbon. Note hand positions and how long the arms are compared to the legs.

rate. Permanent male-female bonds would further deplete the home range of food supplies and force females to move over larger ranges, risking their lives and those of their infants. Females are sexually receptive only on an average of once each 2.5 to 3.5 years, and males further maximize their reproductive success by ranging over wide jungle areas.

The Gibbon

Reports of the gibbon, the smallest of the apes, are scattered throughout the early primate literature. Early reporters were enamored with the gibbon's abilities to walk bipedally on the ground and its loud, sonorous, booming vocalizations impressed many observers. Early naturalists were also quite impressed by the fact that gibbons live in monogamous groups containing a male, female, and their nonadult offspring. The Yerkeses book *The Great Apes* contains the following passage from the early field work of R. A. Spaeth on the Thailand gibbons.

> . . . gibbons were for the most part in family groups . . . they have their young in the early summer and spring. . . . The gibbon has only one young a year and it takes three or four years for them to mature, so a family frequently consisted of two or more young ones in various stages of growth beside the father and mother. They hang onto the mother with an extraordinary strong grip as she swings through the trees. She appears to be not the least incommoded by the baby hanging to her and swings along as unconcernedly as though she were alone (quoted in Yerkes, 1929:59).

The locomotor pattern of the gibbons is interesting. Gibbons move from tree to tree by brachiation (figure 12-14). However, because they are small, and mostly upright in the trees, they tend to be bipedal when coming to the ground. When locomoting bipedally, gibbons use their long arms for balance by keeping them above their head or at their sides, or they may place their hands on the ground and swing through their arms. Siamangs are closely related arboreal primates. They are twice as big as gibbons, but they are quite similar in locomotion and behavior.

The first full-scale investigation of wild gibbons was launched jointly by Harvard and Columbia Universities in 1937. Among its members was C. R. Carpenter. Carpenter found that, when youngsters reached sexual maturity, males excluded their sons and females their daughters from the family group. Sexually mature males and females forced from the family may then form their own mated pairs with others in a similar situation.

Carpenter also found that gibbons were territorial, that is, they defended the area in which they lived. Territorial defense does not take the form of physical altercations; it is instead a battle of loud vocalizations and vigorous chases. Each group knows its territorial boundaries; if this area seems in danger of encroachment by an adjacent group, the group rushes to the spot and calls and shakes branches until the trespassers retreat. Similar observations of territorial defense have been made for some other arboreal primates.

During the 1960s Carpenter's ideas were reexamined by John Ellefson. Ellefson worked in Malaysia where he studied the same species of gibbon as did Carpenter. Ellefson's reports confirm Carpenter's observations of family groups, territorial behavior, and minimal aggression and sexual behavior. Subsequent studies by members of the Japan Monkey Centre lend further support to Carpenter's observations.

Table 12-1. Comparison of the Great Apes

	Chimpanzee	Gorilla	Orangutan
Group Traits			
Size and composition	Subgroups of 2 to 15, number of different kinds of groups.	Five to 17, average size 12; each group with dominant silver-backed male.	Mother-infant dyad most stable; adolescents may move in groups of two or three.
Dominance	Males dominant over females; one dominant leader male may be present.	Males dominant; silver-backed male is dominant.	No hierarchy, male seems to preside in a home range.
Aggressive interactions	Frequent peaceful mixing with community; aggression against strangers.	Peaceful within group.	Rare intimate communication between groups; adult males may fight over estrous females.
Adult grooming	Considerable heterosexual and homosexual grooming.	Occasional female-male grooming; little male-male grooming.	Slight, except estrous female grooming male; no male-male grooming.
Communication			
Vocalizations	Wide variety of different sounds.	Wide variety of sounds; silver-backed male vocalizes most, females least; silver-backed males may vocalize to space groups.	Few vocalizations; males have locating calls and calls to attract females.

Table 12-1. Comparison of the Great Apes.

	Chimpanzee	Gorilla	Orangutan
Facial expressions	Many facial expressions.	Less varied than chimpanzee.	Few seen in wild, but many seen in captivity.
Postures	Several cues.	Several cues.	Few observed.
Displays	Ritualized outbursts.	Chestbeating.	When courting or to frighten intruders.
Habitat			
Arboreal or terrestrial	Both, nest in trees.	Mostly terrestrial.	Mostly arboreal; males travel on ground and will come down to feed.
Water	Avoids, but will drink.	Avoids, obtains most from foods.	Wades through and will drink.
Diet	Mostly frugivorous; will prey on other primates.	Mostly herbivorous; insects and snails.	Frugivorous; insects and bark.
Other Traits			
Sexual dimorphism	Males slightly larger than females.	Males much larger than females; develop white hair on back with age.	Males twice as large as females; develop cheek pads, throat pouches, and sometimes beards.
Movement	Knuckle-walk; brachiate in trees; bipedal for short distances.	Knuckle-walk; bipedal for short distances.	Fist-walk; rarely bipedal.
Nest building	Tree nests for sleeping.	Tree and ground nests.	Tree nests.
Tool use	Makes various kinds of tools.	No tools.	Tools made in captivity.

Adapted from B. Kevles, *Watching the Wild Apes*, p. 154, E. P. Dutton & Company, New York, © 1976.

Our associations with our pongid relatives vary from one of amazement and amusement at the brachiating gibbon to one of fear of the gorilla. Of all the apes, perhaps the chimpanzee holds the greatest fascination for anthropologists. Jane Goodall's detailed chimpanzee study has revealed a number of fascinating observations. We now know that chimpanzees use and make tools. Another study by Geza Teleki has shown that chimpanzees eat meat which they hunt in small organized groups.

George Schaller's study of the mountain gorilla has shown that instead of being brutal, ferocious animals, gorillas are gentle, giant vegetarians. Dian Fossey's current study of lowland gorillas should add fascinating comparative data. Data on the orangutan are rapidly filling the gap on comparative pongid behavior and social organization.

Bibliography

Bygott, J. 1972. Cannibalism among wild chimpanzees. *Nature* 238:410-11.

_____. 1974. Agonistic behavior and dominance in wild chimpanzees. Ph.D. dissertation. Cambridge University.

Carpenter, C. 1940. A field study in Siam of the behaviors and social relations of the gibbon (*Hylobates lar*). *Comparative Psychological Monographs* 615.

Davenport, R. 1967. The orang-utan in Sabah. *Folia Primatologica* 5:247-63.

Desmond, A. 1979. *The ape's reflexion*. New York: Dial Press.

Ellefson, J. 1968. Territorial behavior in the common white-handed gibbon, *Hylobates lar* Linn. In *Primates: studies in adaptation and variability*, edited by P. Jay, pp. 180-200. New York: Holt, Rinehart and Winston.

Fossey, D. 1970. Making friends with mountain gorillas. *National Geographic* 137:285.

_____. 1978. Development of the mountain gorilla (*Gorilla gorilla beringei*): the first thirty-six months. In *The great apes*, edited by D. Hamburg and E. McCown, pp. 139-87. Menlo Park, Calif.: Benjamin/Cummings.

Fouts, R. 1973. Acquistion and testing of gestural signs in four young chimpanzees. *Science* 180:978-80.

_____. 1975. Capacities for language in great apes. In *Sociology and psychology of primates*, edited by R. Tuttle, pp. 371-91. The Hague: Mouton.

Furness, W. 1916. Observations on the mentality of chimpanzees and orangutans. *Proceedings of the American Philosophical Society* 45:281-90.

Galdikas-Brindamour, B., and Brindamour, R. 1975. Orangutans, Indonesia's "people of the forest." *National Geographic* 148:444-74.

Gardner, B., and Gardner, R. 1971. Two-way communication with an infant chimpanzee. In *Behavior of nonhuman primates*, edited by A. Schrier and F. Stollnitz, pp. 117-84. New York: Academic Press.

_____. 1974. Comparing the early utterances of child and chimpanzee. In *Minnesota Symposium on Child Psychology*, No. 8, edited by A. Puck, pp. 3-23.

_____. 1978. Comparative psychology and language acquisition. In *Psychology: the state of the art*, edited by K. Salzinger and F. Denmark, pp. 37-76. *Annals of the New York Academy of Sciences* 309.

Gardner, R., and Gardner, B. 1969. Teaching sign language to a chimpanzee. *Science* 165:664-72.

Goodall, J. 1979. Life and death at Gombe. *National Geographic* 155:592-620.

Harrisson, B. 1962. *The orangutan*. London: Collins.

Hayes, C. 1952. *The ape in our house*. New York: Harper and Brothers.

Hayes, K., and Nissen, C. 1971. Higher mental functions of a home-raised chimpanzee. In *Behavior of nonhuman primates*, edited by A. Schrier and F. Stollnitz, pp. 60-116. New York: Academic Press.

Horn, A. 1977. A preliminary report on the ecology and behavior of the Bonobo chimpanzee (*Pan paniscus*, Schwarz 1929) and a reconsideration of the evolution of the chimpanzee. Ph.D. dissertation. Yale University.

_____. 1979. The taxonomic status of the Bonobo chimpanzee. *American Journal of Physical Anthropology* 2:273-82.

Horr, D. 1975. The Borneo orang-utan: population structure and dynamics in relationship to ecology and reproductive strategy. In *Primate behavior: developments in field and laboratory research*, Vol. 4, edited by L. Rosenblum, pp. 307-23. New York: Academic Press.

_____. 1977. Orang-utan maturation: growing up in a female world. In *Primate bio-social development*, edited by S. Chevalier-Skolnikoff and F. Poirier, pp. 289-321. New York: Garland.

Itani, J., and Suzuki, A. 1967. The social unit of chimpanzees. *Primates* 8:355.

Kellogg, W., and Kellogg, L. 1933. *The ape and the child*. New York: McGraw-Hill.

Kortlandt, A., and Kooji, M. 1963. Protohominid behavior in primates. *Symposium of the Zoological Society of London* 10:61.

Marx, J. 1980. Ape-language controversy flares up. *Science* 207:1330-33.

McGrew, W. 1978. Evolutionary implications of sex differences in chimpanzee predation and tool use. In *The great apes*, edited by D. Hamburg and E. McCown, pp. 441-64. Menlo Park, Calif.: Benjamin/Cummings.

McGrew, W., Tutin, C., and Baldwin, P. 1979. New data on meat-eating by wild chimpanzees. *Current Anthropology* 20:238-40.

Mounin, G. 1976. Language, communication, chimpanzees. *Current Anthropology* 17:1-22.

Mydans, C. 1973. Orangutans can return to the wild with some help. *Smithsonian* 4:26-33.

Nishida, T. 1968. The social group of wild chimpanzees in the Mahali Mountains. *Primates* 9:167-224.

Patterson, F. 1978a. Conversations with a gorilla. *National Geographic* 154:438-65.

_____. 1978b. The gestures of a gorilla. Sign language acquisition in another pongid species. *Brain and Language* 5:72-79.

Premack, A., and Premack, D. 1972. Teaching language to an ape. *Scientific American* 227:92-99.

Premack, D. 1971a. Language in chimpanzee? *Science* 172:808-22.

_____. 1971b. On the assessment of language competence in the chimpanzee. In *Behavior of nonhuman primates,* edited by A. Schrier and F. Stollnitz, pp. 186-228. New York: Academic Press.

Pusey, A. 1978. Intercommunity transfer of chimpanzees in Gombe National Park. In *The great apes,* edited by D. Hamburg and E. McCown, pp. 465-80. Menlo Park, Calif.: Benjamin/Cummings.

Ransom, T., and Rowell, T. 1972. Early social development of feral baboons. In *Primate socialization,* edited by F. Poirier, pp. 105-45. New York: Random House.

Reynolds, V. 1965. *Budongo: a forest and its chimpanzees.* New York: Natural History Press.

_____. 1967. *The apes.* New York: Harper & Row.

Rijksen, H. 1978. A field study on Sumatran orangutans (*Pongo pygmaeus*). Ecology, behavior and conservation. Wageningen, Netherlands: Veenman and Zonen.

Rowell, T. 1966. Forest living baboons in Uganda. *Journal of Zoological Society of London* 149:344.

_____. 1972. *Social behavior of monkeys.* New York: Penguin Books.

Rumbaugh, D., ed. 1977. *Language learning by a chimpanzee: the Lana project.* New York: Academic Press.

Rumbaugh, D., Gill, T., and von Glasensfeld, E. 1973. Reading and sentence completion by a chimpanzee (*Pan*). *Science* 182:731-33.

Rumbaugh, D., von Glasenfeld, E., Gill, T., Warner, H. Pisani, P., Brown, J., and Bell, C. 1975. The language skills of a young chimpanzee in a computer-controlled training situation. In *Socioecology and psychology of primates,* edited by R. Tuttle, pp. 391-403. Chicago: Aldine (Mouton World Anthropology Series).

Rumbaugh, D., Savage, S., and Boysen, S. 1978. Linguistically mediated tool use and exchange by chimpanzees (*Pan troglodytes*). *The Behavioral and Brain Sciences* 4:539-54.

_____. 1980. Do apes use language? *American Scientist* 68:49-61.

Schaller, G. 1963. *The mountain gorilla.* Chicago: University of Chicago Press.

_____. 1964. *The year of the gorilla.* Chicago: University of Chicago Press.

Sebeok, T., and Umiker-Sebeok, U., eds. 1980. *Speaking of apes: a critical anthology of two-way communication with man.* New York: Plenum.

Sugiyama, Y. 1969. Social behavior of chimpanzees in the Budongo Forest, Uganda. *Primates* 10:197.

_____. 1972. Social characteristics and socialization of wild chimpanzees. In *Primate Socialization,* edited by F. Poirier, pp. 145-64. New York: Random House.

Teleki, G. 1973. The omnivorous chimpanzee. *Scientific American* 228:33.

Terrace, H. 1979. Is problem-solving language? *Journal of Experimental Analysis of Behavior* 31:161-75.

_____. 1979. *Nim: a chimpanzee who learned sign language.* New York: Knopf.

Terrace, H., Petitto, L., Sanders, R., and Bever, T. 1979. Can an ape create a sentence? *Science* 206:891-902.

Toshiada, N., Yehara, S., and Ramadhani, N. 1979. Predatory behavior among wild chimpanzees of the Mahale Mountains. *Primates* 20:1-21.

van Lawick-Goodall, J. 1967. *My friends the wild chimpanzees.* Washington, D.C.: National Geographic Society.

_____. 1971. *In the shadow of man.* Boston: Houghton Mifflin.

Wrangham, R. 1978. Sex differences in chimpanzee dispersion. In *The great apes,* edited by D. Hamburg and E. McCown, pp. 481-90. Menlo Park, Calif.: Benjamin/Cummings.

Yerkes, R., and Yerkes, A. 1929. *The great apes.* New Haven: Yale University Press.

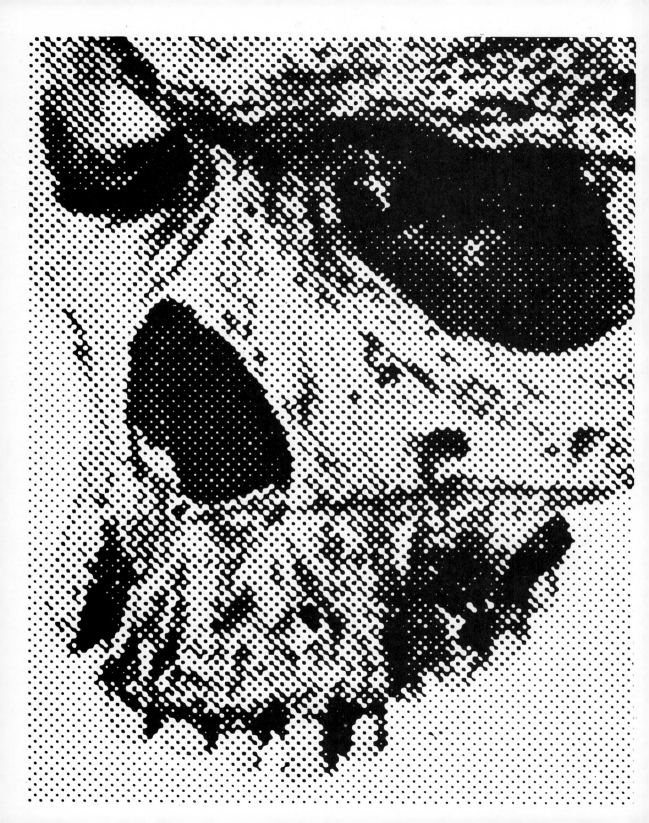

Part Four

The Fossil Record: Recovering the Past

In anticipating the discovery of the true links between the apes and man in tropical countries, there has been a tendency to overlook the fact that, in luxuriant forests of the tropical belts, Nature was supplying . . . an easy and sluggish solution, by adaptive specialisation, of the problem of existence in creatures so well equipped mentally as living anthropoids are. For the production of man a different apprenticeship was needed to sharpen the wits and quicken the higher manifestations of intellect . . . in my opinion, Southern Africa, by providing a vast open country with occasional wooded belts and a relative scarcity of water, together with a fierce and bitter mammalian competition, furnished a laboratory such as was essential to this penultimate phase of human evolution.

From Raymond Dart, *"Australopithecus africanus:* The Man-Ape of South Africa." *Nature*, Vol. 115, February 1925.

Chapter 13

Dating Methods and the Paleontological Approach

The basic problem confronting the paleontologist is that of evaluating evolutionary changes. The paleontologist tries to establish which of a host of possible and possibly conflicting relationships is most consistent with the pattern of hominid evolution. There are a number of alternative possibilities for reconstructiong hominid evolution; the choice of which is most likely governed, among others, by the propositions discussed in this chapter.

Establishment of Taxonomic Relationships

The various activities of paleontological research are interdependent and interrelated, yet time and human limitations make its practice multiphased and time consuming. The recovery and collection of fossils is preceded by such activities as extensive planning, geological surveys, and solutions to problems specific to the locale. Because modern excavation techniques require patient work, a relatively complete account of any fossil group must await the collection and analysis of a fairly large sample. Then follows the long and tedious task of comparing the material to other possibly related forms to establish its taxonomic affinities. The establishment of affinity must solve problems of the geographical and temporal variation of related samples from other localities of known stratigraphic relationship, as well as problems of sample variation.

Pitfalls and Problems. Physical anthropologists have been notorious for misclassifying the Hominidae (the family of fossil and living hominids). There is, however, a growing tendency to pay closer attention to principles of modern classification. Two events had special impetus in fostering this more critical attitude. One was the early dispute over the status of the Lower Pleistocene australopithecines; were they hominids (humans) or pongids (apes)? The second was exposure of the fraudulent nature of the Piltdown remains.[1] The Piltdown controversy

[1]For more than 40 years, this odd assemblage of remains, consisting of fossilized hominid cranial fragments and an ape's mandible and canine, was the subject of controversy and speculation. The solution to the problem came when, in November 1953, it was announced that the mandible and canine were both those of a large modern ape which were remarkably faked to simulate fossils.

forced many human evolutionists to take a more cautious view of the weight of interpretation and speculation based on fragmentary fossil remains. Piltdown's unmasking forced anthropologists to the realization that hominid evolution occurred through relatively small and perhaps subtle morphological changes and required a more rigorous, less impressionistic approach to interpretation.

What are some of the guidelines that the scientist must follow in evaluating the fossil material? First, there should always be economy of hypotheses; all available, reliable material and its affinities should be embraced by a single coherent scheme. The simplest is often the correct explanation. The fraudulent nature of Piltdown was first suggested by the fact that the remains could not fit into any unitary evolutionary scheme encompassing the rest of the then known hominid remains.

Sample Size and Composition. Taxonomic relationships must be based on well-authenticated, reliably dated, and fairly complete fossil assemblages. This criterion is often most difficult to meet. We are extremely fortunate when we find a fairly complete assemblage capable of being dated. If a new specimen is uncovered, and if the interpretation of the form is inconsistent with present taxonomic schemes, it may be best to defer judgment until further material is uncovered. This caveat based on sample size could well be applied toward withholding judgment on such controversial forms as *Ramapithecus*. Age changes can lead to considerable modification in the structural details and proportions of the skeleton. Age changes are so marked that it would be grossly improper to compare a few measurements of the adult skull of an ancestral hominid with those of a juvenile pongid and to infer from such comparison that the former is not markedly different from the apes in general.

Primates generally exhibit considerable **sexual dimorphism,** that is, physical differentiation between male and female forms, which is an important consideration in interpreting fossil materials. Although there is continuing argument, some investigators have suggested that differences between the australopithecine forms, which are often used to establish separate species, may not be taxonomically relevant but may be reflections of australopithecine sexual dimorphism (Wolpoff, 1976).

Relevant Traits. Two of the most common errors committed in assessing taxonomic affinities stem from the failure to recognize that some traits have more taxonomic relevance than others. Some traits are better differentiators of generic or family status and others may be better for specific differentiation. In assessing the earlier representatives of the family Hominidae, skeletal characters of the pelvis and hind limbs are more important than those of the forelimbs. Unfortunately, we can't always find the most relevant morphological remains; in fact, we are lucky to find any remains whatsoever.

Mosaic Evolution. Different parts of the body evolve at different rates, and at each stage (grade) in the evolutionary scheme, different morphological traits will be of different taxonomic value. Different parts of the body evolve at different rates because at different points in its evolutionary history a group faces different problems of adaptation. One of the first adaptive changes made by early hominids is bipedalism. Therefore, we should expect to find that features differentiating early hominids and pongids are to be found primarily in their locomotor apparatus. A case in point is the original refusal to accept the Javan form, "Pithecanthropus," as a member of the genus *Homo*. When "Pithecanthropus" was first uncovered, paleontologists refused to accept the contemporaneity of the femur (upper leg bone) with the skull and face, for the skull was still relatively primitive while the femur was relatively modern. A further example is provided by the brain of *Australopithecus;* fossilized cranial bones indicate that *Australopithecus* lacked space for either a large **cerebrum** (the

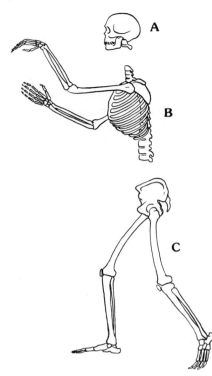

Figure 13-1. The three major body complexes. (A) Head and face. (B) Thorax and upper limbs. (C) Pelvis and lower limbs.

part of the brain that controls reasoning and learned hand movements) or for a large motor cortex. The archaeological, comparative anatomical, and fossil records all indicate that a brain of modern size and form evolved long after our ancestors were ground-living, stone-tool-making gatherers and hunters.

    Clades, Derived Traits, and Ancestral Traits. To depict evolutionary history and to establish clades (groups of species related through a common ancestry), scientists construct **phyletic trees.** A phyletic tree is a branching diagram representing the evolutionary relationships of a group of species. Relationships within and between groups are based on a number of criteria, some of which were previously discussed (Chapter 9). The following principles are basic to the establishment of a phyletic relationship: (1) forms sharing detailed resemblances are usually closely related, (2) clades are recognized by shared **derived traits,** and (3) shared derived characteristics related to function may be the result of parallelism or convergence (discussed in the next section) and are weak indicators of cladistic relationships.

    In their anatomical structure, all life forms exhibit derived traits and **ancestral traits.** Derived traits are the result of recent adaptations and ancestral traits are inherited adaptations from a form's ancestors. Because of the persistence of ancestral traits, different species never come to resemble one another in all respects. This holds true even when such species follow a very similar life style. Living forms may evolve similar derived traits, but ancestral traits that are preserved usually betray their differing evolutionary histories.

Although ancestral traits are our clues to evolutionary history, derived characteristics can be equally revealing. Whenever two evolving species develop a trait independently, they do so because they have a behavior for which the structure in question is adapted. Because species that have similar behavior develop similar structures, it is often possible to deduce the behavior of extinct fossilized forms by studying the behavior of living animals with similar anatomical adaptations. This approach was discussed more fully in Chapter 10.

Parallelism and Convergence

Similar structures, adaptive relationships, or behaviors can occur in different groups as a result of similar evolutionary opportunities. A fundamental principle of evolutionary biology is that if two organisms are similar in appearance, they are related to each other. It is on this basis that relationships are deduced from the fossil record. There is a problem, however, because the phenomenon of similarity may be due to parallelism or convergence. Parallelism and convergence do not necessarily imply a close phylogenetic relationship. Parallelisms are structural developments within a group that occur independently in more than one segment of that group and that are probably due to similar evolutionary conditions. For instance, Simons (1972) notes that among the primates, which are basically arboreal, long forearms have evolved a number of times as adaptations for hanging and feeding, from ancestors with shorter forearms. Convergence occurs when remotely related forms come to resemble each other, for example, flipperlike fins in whales, seals, and sea cows. When two animal species or major groups that are not closely related develop similarities in adaptive relationships or structures, the two groups are said to have converged.

Clark (1967) and Simpson (1951, 1953) caution against overreliance on parallelism to explain similarities in the fossil record. If we constantly refer similarities to parallelism, we render the concept of evolution meaningless. The term parallelism is usually restricted to development of similar adaptive features in animals that are related, for example, animals belonging to the same order. Thus, parallel resemblances are probably the realization of a genetic potential present in the entire group. Certain New and Old World members of the Order Primates, for example, show parallel adaptations to an arboreal environment.

Pleistocene Paleoclimatology and Climatic Indicators

Past climates fluctuated, their cycles directly and indirectly affecting hominid evolution. For example, the huge intermittent northern hemispheric Pleistocene ice sheets affected the migration patterns and subsequently the gene pools of both migratory animal populations and of populations dependent on migratory animals as food sources. Past climatic fluctuations directly affected the abundance and distribution of flora and fauna. Various means have been devised to determine paleoclimates. Among these are deep sea core analysis and study of changing land and sea levels, river terraces, and African **pluvials.** All these indicators appear to be linked to the ebb and flow of the Eurasian glaciations.

Glaciations. To the average reader the Pleistocene epoch is commonly known as the "Ice Age." Newer evidence, however, suggests the existence of pre-Pleistocene glaciations. Glacial fluctuations were a most dramatic event of the Pleistocene epoch, influencing land and sea levels and floral and faunal distributions and leaving conspicuous remains of their past extent. Even at their maximum, the ice sheets never covered more than one-third of the earth's surface and occurred only during one-eighth of the Pleistocene time span. However, because of their impact, glacial periods are convenient boundary markers of the Pleistocene Epoch.

Table 13-1. Nomenclature of European and North American Pleistocene Glaciers

Pleistocene		European	North American
Late	Würm Glaciation	Würm	Wisconsinian
	Riss-Würm interglacial		
	Riss Glaciation	Riss	Illinoian
	Mindel-Riss interglacial		
Middle	Mindel Glaciation	Mindel	Kansan
	Günz-Mindel interglacial		
Early	Günz Glaciation	Günz	Nebraskan
	Villafranchian		

Major theories of glaciation say that glaciers were caused by some unusual movement or change in the earth's orbit or axis.

Glacial periods were originally defined in the Alps. Four periods were originally named and subdivided into two or more cold phases, or stadials, that were separated by interstadials. Glacial periods alternated with warm periods known as interglacials, three of which are major. Pleistocene chronology and climatic history is complicated. There is growing recognition of as many as eight glaciations in the past 700,000 years. The first glacial period, the Günz, seems to have been a largely local phenomenon whereas in the remaining three glacial periods extensive ice sheets occurred in Europe. It is difficult to correlate European glacial periods with those occurring elsewhere, but there is general consensus (which is speedily weakening) that glaciation is roughly synchronous throughout the northern hemisphere (Table 13-1).

Glaciations periodically removed large areas of northern Eurasia and North America from habitation and intermittently restricted faunal movement in some areas while encouraging it in others. Local glacial manifestations periodically created barriers to movement and channeled activity along new routes or completely prevented it. This indirectly led to establishing new life patterns that affected subsequent evolutionary history. Our knowledge of hominid evolutionary history is also affected by the fact that preexisting cultural and **osteological** (bone) remains in glacial areas were lost to us, as were remains deposited during glacial times. The latter were subsequently submerged during interglacial times.

Pluvials. While glacials prove to be convenient, albeit sometimes confusing, markers of the European, North American, and Eurasian Pleistocene, pluvials, or periods of higher rainfall and lake levels, can serve to demarcate local sequences in the African Pleistocene. Since glaciers form and grow with increased precipitation, it seems reasonable to correlate high latitude glaciers with low latitude pluvials. Despite the original enthusiasm, it has been difficult to correlate glaciations and pluvials, even though there is little doubt that climatic conditions favoring glaciations were directly or indirectly responsible for the pluvials. Although referring to increased precipitation, pluvials are not necessarily synonymous with the Biblical Noachian flood. Older notions of major changes accompanying the pluvials, for example, of deserts rapidly changing to forest due to increased rainfall, are unfounded.

Floral and Faunal Indications of Pleistocene Paleoclimates

The previous information is part of a scientific armory used to provide climatic data. Floral and faunal remains provide climatic data; furthermore, they help place a site within a chronological sequence. Analysis of fossilized pollen, **palynology,** is one of the most valuable aids for determining past climatic conditions. When the nearly indestructible pollen granules settle to the ground they become incorporated into the deposits and are almost indefinitely preserved in the absence of lime. Since pollens of various floral species are rather individualistic and in many cases can be readily identified as to genus, pollen analysis can be applied to solving problems relating to the paleoenvironment. While pollen analysis is useful for historically reconstructing local vegetation, a major drawback is the local nature of much flora which negates cross-analysis of grains from different sites. Pollen analysis has been employed in dating and determining the environment of *Homo erectus* in China and has suggested the possibility that one of the Shanidar skeletons (designated number IV) from Iraq was buried on a bed of wild flowers.

Faunal Markers. Through faunal analysis, one can reconstruct paleoenvironmental conditions, since fauna changes in response to climatic oscillations. There is a continual emergence and spreading of new forms and extinction of old faunal types. The most useful mammalian groups for correlating Pleistocene deposits include the elephant, rhinoceros, bear, hyena, deer, and antelope.

Elephants are important demarcators of Pleistocene subdivisions (Table 13-2). The dating of virtually all European hominid fossiliferous sites relies on the contiguous evidence of associated fossil elephant remains. Fossil hyenas, especially *Crocuta crocuta*, have proved useful for the purposes of relative dating. The absence of the species *C. crocuta* from such European sites as the Mauer sands (yielding a Middle Pleistocene *H. erectus* mandible) indicates a pre-Mindel time position.

Mammalian remains also aid the dating of deposits by indicating a climatic stage. For example, in Britain it may be inferred that a hippopotamus-bearing deposit is of a different period than one containing musk ox. African fossil mammalia have proven especially useful for inferring Pleistocene climatic stages. Fossil invertebrates, freshwater and land mollusca (e.g., snails), as well as insects, are all valuable climatic indicators.

Dating Fossil Materials

Fossil remains are placed within a recognized time frame so that the osteological evidence can be interpreted and placed within a taxonomic scheme and so that the environmental information for a site can be correlated with the fossil remains. Rigorous dating techniques also eliminate questionable materials such as Piltdown. When considering the age of a fossil specimen answers to two important questions are sought: (1) What is the relationship of the fossil material to the geological, floral, faunal, and archaeological sequence? and (2) What is the chronological age of the specimen in years? The first query asks if the remains are contemporaneous within their context, and therefore whether the site's faunal, climatic, and

Table 13-2. Correlation of Elephant and Hominid Remains in Europe

Fossil Hominid	Fossil Elephant	Glacial Period
Homo sapiens (Classic Neanderthals)	Elephas primigenius	Würm Glaciation
H. sapiens (Ehringsdorf, Germany)	late E. antiquus	Riss-Würm interglacial
H. sapiens (Steinheim, Germany)	E. antiquus	Mindel-Riss interglacial
H. erectus (Heidelberg or Mauer mandible (Germany)	E. antiquus	Günz-Mindel interglacial

archaeological information can be properly associated with the find. The answer to the second query provides a figure—the chronometric age of the find.

Chronologically ordering fossil remains is fundamental to understanding their evolutionary relationships and significance. To establish the contemporaneity of fossil or archaeological material with the deposit in which it lies, it must first be demonstrated that the deposit has not been disturbed. It must be shown that there is no possibility of an intrusive burial or derivation from younger or older deposits. Unless these conditions are met, all dates must be viewed as suspect. One of the excavator's major tasks is to fully document the site's condition at the time the excavated deposit was formed; photographs, maps, and charts are absolutely necessary. This phase, as much as the actual excavation, requires much time and expertise. A poorly excavated site is largely devoid of scientific value and an undated site is of questionable value and continually open to speculation.

There are basically two types of dating methods, **relative dating** and **chronometric dating,** and both are useful to the paleoanthropologist. Relative dating establishes that one thing—a bone, tool, or other remains—is older or younger than something else. Relative dating arranges things in chronological order, although the total time span and interval between the things so ordered is unknown. Relative dating establishes a chronological sequence; absolute dating determines age in terms of years. Chronometric dating provides the ultimate evolutionary framework; it determines the age of a specimen or source deposit and yields a numerical, chronological figure. An important element in any dating scheme is cross-dating, which establishes relationships between assemblages, or significant elements therein, from various geographic locales. Cross-dating ties sites into a preexisting scheme; sites must be cross-dated with other sites to establish temporal relationships.

Relative Dating

Typological and Morphological Dating. One of the first excavation procedures is to determine whether archaeological and/or osteological materials are contemporaneous with the deposit in which they lie. One must also determine the site's stratigraphy, that is, the relative vertical placement of objects in the soil. Given an undisturbed site, materials at the lowest levels must be the oldest. In the absence of an undisturbed stratified site, other methods—typological and morphological dating—that yield far less conclusive evidence may be employed. Typological dating is based on the fact that over time manufactured objects undergo stylistic changes. On this basis it is often possible to arrange objects in a relative time sequence.

When material is found unaccompanied by organic material useful in age determinations, or when a fossil is found lying above ground out of context, it can sometimes be dated according to its form, or morphology. Morphological dating should only be attempted when a large, well-known fossil series with a well-documented evolutionary history is available.

Fluorine, Nitrogen, and Uranium Dating. A major mode of relative dating is dating of bone either to establish the contemporaneity of various osteological remains in a deposit or of bone to the soil deposit itself. Buried bone witnesses chemical compositional changes of varying rates. The three major analytical methods of measuring this chemical change are fluorine, nitrogen, and uranium dating (Oakley, 1970). These dating methods are especially important in disturbed sites where it is necessary to establish contemporaneity. The relative age of bone can be determined by comparing its chemical composition with fossil bone of known ages either from the same site or same age if they are preserved under comparable conditions.

Fluorine dating depends on ground water seepage through bone; fluorine in the water combines with the bone's calcium to form a compound, fluorapatite. The amount of fluorapatite in various bones in a site determines their contemporaneity or lack thereof. Fluorine dating allows bones of an assemblage to be tested for stratigraphic equivalence, for contemporaneous bones should contain roughly equal amounts of fluorapatite. The most famous case of fluorine dating is the uncovering of the Piltdown hoax.

Nitrogen dating is often coupled with fluorine dating; the results complement one another. Bones accumulating little fluorine retain much nitrogen, and vice versa. Nitrogen tests are used to determine whether enough collagen (protein) degradation has occurred to attempt to radiocarbon date the bone directly. The Galley Hill material and the Piltdown fraud were fluorine and nitrogen tested before the bones themselves were finally radiocarbon dated.

The possibility of uranium dating was noted as early as 1908 when it was established that mineral phosphates, including fossil bones, contained uranium. Uranium circulating in the blood stream is fixed in the mineral matter of bone, probably through calcium replacement. The same replacement process occurs in buried bone through percolation of ground water containing traces of uranium. The longer a bone is buried, the more uranium it absorbs. Since uranium is radioactive, its content within bone can be determined by measuring radioactive deterioration. Radioactivity varies in bones from different sites, but its progressive accumulation with increasing age has been established. Uranium analysis serves, as does fluorine analysis, to distinguish between specimens that may be younger or older than the source deposit. Uranium analysis is superior to fluorine dating because it is not necessary to destroy the bone to do the analysis.

These three dating techniques do not permit cross-dating; their prime value lies in determining the relative ages of bone or bone objects from the same deposit. Because of the many variables, it is usually impossible to use fluorine, nitrogen, or uranium as more than a rough guide to the geological age of an isolated specimen. Ground soils vary, allowing differing amounts of percolating water through. Fluorine cross-dating is especially hampered by the fact that the amount of fluorine permeating a bone depends on how much is present in the ground water, and this varies with the locale.

A final note on relative dating is that stratigraphy can be used to establish a chronological scheme. Simply, those materials found in the deepest soil layers are usually, but not always, the oldest. Those materials found closer to the surface are not as old. This, of course, is true only for undisturbed sites. This method is useful if no dates have been, or can be, established geologically.

Chronometric Dating

Chronometric dating techniques yield chronological figures and paleontologists rely heavily on **radiocarbon** (C[14]) **potassium-argon** (K-Ar), and **fission-track** (uranium) **dating** (Table 13-3). The C[14] technique, devised by the physicist W. F. Libby, has been in use since 1949. Although any organic material is theoretically capable of C[14] dating, the best substance is charcoal; fortunately charcoal is a common organic remainder in archaeological sites, and 1 gram of charcoal is an adequate sample. Radiocarbon dating is fairly sound, provided proper precautions are taken in selecting samples and ensuring that they are not contaminated by additional radiocarbon from more recent material or contaminated in the laboratory.

Table 13-4 lists the half life (the time required for half of the atoms in a sample of a radioactive substance to disintegrate) of some of the elements used in radioactive dating. It

Table 13-3. Some Major Methods for Determining Chronometric Ages

Time Period	Dating Method
Modern period to 4,500 years ago.	Historical documents, tree-ring (dendrochronology). glacial varve bristlecone pine.
Recent times to about 50,000 years ago.	Radiocarbon, amino acid racemization, bristlecone pine.
400,000 to 500,000 years ago.	Various means used but there is no good accuracy here. Many of these dates are placed according to relative dating.
500,000 years ago to age of earth.	Potassium-argon, fission-track.

Adapted from B. G. Campbell, *Humankind Emerging*, p. 77. Little, Brown and Company, Boston, © 1976.

also lists some dating methods not found in Table 13-3, which primarily lists dating methods of use in studying the primate fossil record.

Radiocarbon (C¹⁴) Dating. Wood charcoal is best for C^{14} dating; burned bone is often dated but unburned bone is seldom submitted for dating although it can be dated. A fairly large sample of unburned bone is needed because it does not contain much carbon. However, unburned bone contains a substance called collagen that is rich in carbon and can be extracted and dated. A few finds have been directly C^{14} dated but, because most skeletal materials are incomplete, researchers are hesitant to destroy the amount necessary for the procedure. They rely then on C^{14} dates of associated but more expendable materials.

Radiocarbon is present in the cellular structure of all plants and animals. Organisms lose C^{14} at a steady rate, but they also consume it. Plants maintain their C^{14} level through the process of oxygen exchange with the atmosphere, animals through eating plants or other animals that have eaten plants. Radiocarbon is maintained as long as the organism is alive; intake promptly ceases at death, and C^{14} levels begin to disintegrate radioactively. Disintegration proceeds at a known rate, based on the C^{14} half life of 5,730 years. By measuring the amount of C^{14} in a dead organism, it is possible to calculate the length of time in "radiocarbon years" that has elapsed since the organism died.

Radiocarbon dates are expressed in terms of a date midway between two points, representing a margin of error of one standard deviation. The limits are indicated by plus and minus signs. A typical date reads 40,000 plus or minus (+) 1,000 years. Radiocarbon dating is generally limited to a range of approximately 50,000 to 70,000 years. However, with new enrichment methods C^{14} dates can be extended to as much as 100,000 years.

Three types of C^{14} dating errors reduce the efficiency of the technique (Butzer, 1964): (1) statistical-mechanical errors, as are indicated by the plus or minus dates, (2) errors related to the C^{14} level of the sample itself, and (3) errors related to "contamination," that is, laboratory storage, preparation, and management. Errors relating to the C^{14} level in the sample are due to past fluctuations of C^{14} intake, and unequal C^{14} concentration in different materials, as well as to contamination. At certain times in the past some dates diverge from the true age of the sample more than at other times. When reading a C^{14} date it must be asked what is being dated, for various dates are of different reliability and not strictly comparable owing to differences in techniques and basic assumptions on the part of the laboratory doing the

Table 13-4. Radioactive Elements Useful in Establishing Mineral Ages

Parent Element	Decay Product	Half Life	Remarks
Uranium 238	Lead 206	4.51 billion years	These three parent-decay product sets occur together and serve as checks on one another. Especially useful in rocks older than 60 million years. Unfortunately rather rare.
Uranium 235	Lead 207	710 million years	
Thorium 232	Lead 208	13.9 billion years	
Rubidium 87	Strontium 87	50 billion years	These three sets, but particularly potassium-argon, are proving of great value because they are widespread in occurrence. Used in dating rocks older than 1 million years.
Potassium 40	Argon 40	1.33 billion years	
Potassium 40	Calcium 40	1.33 billion years	
Carbon 14	Nitrogen 14	5,730 years; some argue a half life of 5,568 years.	Useful in dating rocks and events between 50,000 and 70,000 years in the past.

Adapted from L. Dillon, *Evolution: Concepts and Consequences*, p. 171. The C. V. Mosby Company, St. Louis, © 1973.

testing. It is thus most important to have a series of dates from any one laboratory to test for reliability. One date from one sample from one laboratory compared to one date from one sample from another laboratory is of limited value.

Bristlecone Pine Dating. A number of factors have upset the C^{14} chronology. For example, at times the rate of C^{14} production fluctuated so rapidly that samples of different ages show an identical concentration of C^{14} decay even though the older sample allowed for more radioactive decay. There is also a strong indication that fluctuations in C^{14} concentrations are correlated with the level of solar activity. Furthermore, climatic change may have influenced the concentration of C^{14} in the atmosphere.

Radiocarbon dates are being revised, or supplanted in some cases, by what is known as the bristlecone pine chronology. The California bristlecone pine (*Pinus aristata*) lives a long life. Bristlecone pines as old as 4,600 years have been authenticated. The major research is being done by Charles Wesley Ferguson of the Tree-Ring Research Laboratory at the University of Arizona. Using bristlecone tree-ring sequences, Ferguson established a continuous chronology reaching back nearly 8,200 years. The divergence between the C^{14} and tree-ring dates is not serious after 3,500 years ago. Before that time, however, the difference becomes progressively larger and amounts to as much as 700 years by 4,500 years ago.

Potassium-Argon (K-Ar) Dating. Radiocarbon dating encompasses the last stage of hominid evolutionary history, leaving approximately 95 percent of evolutionary history beyond our grasp. This gap is now being dated with other techniques; one such technique— K-Ar dating—was devised by J. Evernden and G. Curtis. This technique ascertains the age of volcanic materials and other igneous rocks (rocks of volcanic origin), as well as tektites (glasslike objects probably formed during the impact of large meteorites on the earth's surface). The K-Ar technique dates the source deposits and *not* the fossil or cultural remains themselves. Potassium-argon dating ascertains the rate of potassium and argon decay; K-Ar dates a time span from 500,000+ years ago to 3 billion years ago.

Potassium-argon has been particularly useful for dating volcanically derived East African deposits. Bed I Olduvai Gorge, Tanzania, which contains some of the early East African hominid remains, was dated by K-Ar determination. This method has also been used to help determine the age of *H. erectus* from the Trinil faunal beds in central Java.

The major drawback of K-Ar dating is the difficulty of collecting datable material; K-Ar determinations are of use primarily in volcanic areas. The scattered nature of volcanic deposits becomes extremely distressing when some areas, such as the South African australopithecine deposits, go undated because of lack of volcanic soils. Another source of concern is statistical error. So, as with C^{14} dates, K-Ar dates are often given within plus or minus ranges.

Fission-Track Dating. A newer dating technique, fission-track dating, originally developed to date manufactured glass, has recently been applied to Olduvai Bed I. The technique is fairly simple; the procedure calls for counting the number of tracks caused by spontaneous fission of uranium^{238} during the lifetime of the sample. Dating depends on the density of such tracks and the number of uranium atoms, which is found from the increase in track density produced by neutron irradiation and induced fission of uranium^{235}. The material used to fission-track date Olduvai Bed I consisted of specimens from the volcanic deposit used for the K-Ar date. The fission-track date was 2.0 million years ±25 percent, which compares well with the average K-Ar date of 1.8 million years. Fission-track dating is important because the possible sources of error differ from those of K-Ar. If the dates from the two different methods agree, then a fairly accurate age determination is assured.

Amino Acid Racemization. This chronometric dating technique was recently applied to proposed early hominid materials. Technically, the process of racemization is the conversion of an optically active substance into a racemic or optically inactive substance. All amino acids do not racemize at the same rate and when considering skeletal material in the age range of 5,000 to 100,000 years aspartic acid provides the best results. This method has some advantages over radiocarbon dating in that smaller quantities are needed. Second, the practical dating range of 100,000 years is appreciably longer than the 50,000-year range of radiocarbon dating (Bada et al., 1974). Some note caution regarding the effects of heat, soil pH, and climate on amino acid dating.

Paleomagnetism, one other dating method, deserves mentioning because it is becoming of increasing importance in cross-checking K-Ar dates. Paleomagnetic dating is based on the fact that the earth's magnetic field is continually changing, both in direction and intensity, and these changes can leave natural records. Such changes are essentially instantaneous, taking only 5,000 years to occur. Geomagnetic polarity epochs have been established that last between 0.5 million and 1.0 million years. Polarity was reversed between 0.5 million and 2.5 million years ago and before 3.4 million years ago. It has been possible to determine the history of polarity changes over the past 4 million years or so with some precision and to construct what is now called "reversal chronology." Throughout the late Cenozoic magnetic polarity has changed at fairly irregular but frequent intervals (Cox et al., 1967). Throughout this time, there has been no period longer than about 600,000 years that has not witnessed a paleomagnetic change. The duration and frequency of events is unique for each major segment of the late Cenozoic.

Reversal chronology was first applied to East African lava; subsequently it was established that polarity stratigraphy can sometimes be determined in sediments also (Grommé and Hay, 1963; Isaac, 1967; Musset et al., 1965). Paleomagnetic dating has been applied at Olduvai (Leakey, 1975), Lake Turkana (Brock and Isaac, 1974), and Omo (Shuey et al., 1974).

At Omo, the unusually thick, essentially continuous deposition record provides an opportuniy to examine the sequence of polarity changes over several million years. This record has then been checked against the epochs and events defined in the Magnetic Polarity Time Scale. The results have agreed in large part with those produced by the K-Ar range (Howell, 1975). On the basis of both K-Ar and paleomagnetic reversal data the Shungura Formation at Omo, the source of 9 out of 12 hominid remains, has been given a date of 2.9 million to 1 million years ago.

At Lake Turkana paleomagnetic dates at first seemed to be helpful in establishing a geophysical chronology (Brock and Isaac, 1974). However, Richard Leakey (1975) reports that paleomagnetic dates are less reliable at Lake Turkana than previously thought, and feels it best to withhold judgment on these dates for the time being.

Mary Leakey (1975) reports that a series of paleomagnetic dates is available for Olduvai Bed IV. These dates have forced a revision of the dating of that bed. Based on paleomagnetic reversal, Bed IV is now considered to be not less than 700,000 years old, instead of the 500,000-year-old date first given.

Other Techniques. Other nonradioactive chronometric dating techniques include glacial-varve counting (i.e., counting layers of soil deposition in glacier-fed lakes), tree-ring dating (or dendrochronology, counting of growth rings in trees), and thermoluminescent dating, which dates anything exposed to heat.

This chapter reviews some of the criteria and methods for interpreting and dating the fossil record. Without reference to a documented time span and interpretive framework, fossil remains are of limited value. As more criteria are established and as dating and interpretive techniques are further refined, we lessen the possibility of fraudulent finds such as Piltdown. New methods may eventually date currently undatable sites, for example, the South African australopithecine remains.

The major hindrance in interpreting fossil materials is a lack of large samples wherein age and sexual differences are recognized. Until we can estimate ranges of population variability, we are faced with continual taxonomic arguments. Sites providing the most useful data are usually chronometrically dated, either by potassium-argon dating for early human sites or radiocarbon dating for later dating.

Until rather recently, the discovery of new evidence on primate evolution and the early stages of human cultural development was largely the result of accident. Now, however, sufficient material has been uncovered for planned research to proceed. Within the past decade or so, the outlook in fossil studies has changed. We have witnessed changes such as the following: (1) paleoanthropology is more concerned with framing questions than with simply collecting more tools and fossils, (2) the successful application of newer dating techniques has allowed the establishment of a better time scale, and (3) the understanding of human evolution has expanded as the study of human evolution became more interdisciplinary.

Bibliography

Aitken, M. 1961. *Physics and archaeology.* New York: Interscience.

Bada, J., Schroeder, R., and Carter, G. 1974. New evidence for the antiquity of man in North America deduced from aspartic acid racemization. *Science* 184:791-93.

Brill, R., Fleischer, R., Price, R., and Walker, R. 1964. The fission-track dating of man-made glasses. *Journal of Glass Studies* VI:151.

Brock, A., and Isaac, G. 1974. Paleomagnetic stratigraphy and chronology of hominid-bearing sediments east of Lake Rudolf, Kenya. *Nature* 247:344-48.

Bronowski, J., and Long, W. 1951. Statistical methods in anthropology. *Nature* 168:794.

Butzer, K. 1964. *Environment and archaeology, an introduction to Pleistocene geography.* Chicago: Aldine.

Cain, A., and Harrison, G. 1960. Phyletic weighting. *Proceedings of the Zoological Society of London* 135:1.

Campbell, B. 1976. *Humankind emerging.* Boston: Little, Brown.

Clark, W. Le Gros, 1964. *The fossil evidence for human evolution: an introduction to the study of paleoanthropology.* Chicago: University of Chicago Press.

Colbert, E. 1949. Some paleontological principles significant in human evolution. In *Early man in the Far East,* edited by W. Howells, pp. 103-47. Philadelphia: American Association of Physical Anthropologists.

Coon, C. 1962. *The origin of races.* New York: Knopf.

Cox, A., Dalrymple, G., and Doell, R. 1967. Reversals of the earth's magnetic field. *Scientific American* 216:44-54.

Damon, P., Ferguson, C., Long, A., and Wallick, E. 1974. Dendrochronologic calibration of the radiocarbon time scale. *American Antiquity* 39:350-66.

Davis, M. 1969. Palynology and environmental history during the Quaternary period. *American Scientist* 57:317.

Day, M. 1971. Postcranial remains of *Homo erectus* from Bed IV, Olduvai Gorge, Tanzania. *Nature* 232:383.

Dillon, L. 1973. *Evolution: concepts and consequences.* St. Louis: Mosby.

Dimbleby, G. 1970. Pollen analysis. In *Science in archaeology,* edited by D. Brothwell and E. Higgs, pp. 139-49. New York: Praeger.

Eckhardt, R. 1972. Population genetics and human origins. *Scientific American* 226:94-103.

Emiliani, C. 1970. The significance of deep-sea cores. In *Science in archaeology,* edited by D. Brothwell and E. Higgs, pp. 99-107. New York: Praeger.

Fleisher, R., Leakey, L., Price P., and Walker, R. 1965. Fission-track dating of Bed I, Olduvai Gorge. *Science* 148:72-74.

Garn, S. 1971. The improper use of fossil nomenclature. *American Journal of Physical Anthropology* 35:217.

Grommé, C., and Hay, R. 1963. Magnetization of basalt, Bed I, Olduvai Gorge, Tanganyika. *Nature* 200:560-61.

Harrison, G., and Weiner, J. 1963. Some considerations in the formulation of theories of human phylogeny. In *Classification and human evolution,* edited by S.L. Washburn, pp. 75-84. New York: Viking Fund Publications.

Higgs, E. 1970. Fauna. In *Science in archaeology,* edited by D. Brothwell and E. Higgs, pp. 195-96. New York: Praeger.

Holloway, R. 1972. Australopithecine endocasts, brain evolution in the Hominoidea, and a model of hominid evolution. In *The functional and evolutionary biology of primates,* edited by R. Tuttle, pp. 123-52. Chicago: University of Chicago Press.

Howell, F. 1975. An overview of the Pliocene and Earlier Pleistocene of the Lower Omo basin, Southern Ethiopia. In *Human origins: Louis Leakey and the East African evidence,* edited by G. Isaac and E. McCown, pp. 227-68. Menlo Park, Calif.: Benjamin.

Huxley, J., ed. 1940. *The new systematics.* Oxford: Oxford University Press.

Isaac, G. 1967. The stratigraphy of the Peninj Group—Early Middle Pleistocene formation west of Lake Natron, Tanzania. In *Background to evolution in Africa,* edited by W. Bishop and J. Clark, pp. 229-57. Chicago: University of Chicago Press.

Jolly, C., and Plog, F. 1979. *Physical anthropology and archaeology*, 2nd ed. New York: Knopf.

Leakey, M. 1975. A summary and discussion of the archaeological evidence from Bed I and Bed II, Olduvai Gorge, Tanzania. In *Human origins: Louis Leakey and the East African evidence*, edited by G. Isaac and E. McCown, pp. 431-60. Menlo Park, Calif.: Benjamin.

Leakey, R. 1975. Evidence for an advanced Plio-Pleistocene hominid from East Rudolf. In *Human origins: Louis Leakey and the East African evidence*, edited by G. Isaac and E. McCown, pp. 343-52. Menlo Park, Calif.: Benjamin.

Libby, W. 1955. *Radiocarbon dating*. Chicago: University of Chicago Press.

Mayr, E. 1963. The taxonomic evaluation of fossil hominids. In *Classification and human evolution*, edited by S.L. Washburn, pp. 332-47. New York: Viking Fund Publications.

Musset, A., Reilly, T., and Raja, P. 1965. Palaeomagnetism in East Africa. In *East African Rift System: report of the Upper Mantle Committee*—UNESCO seminar, Nairobi 1965, Part II, pp. 83-94. Nairobi: University College.

Oakley, K. 1953. Dating fossil human remains. In *Anthropology today*, edited by A. Kroeber, pp. 43-56. Chicago: Aldine.

—————. 1966. *Frameworks for dating fossil man*. Chicago: Aldine.

—————. 1970. Analytical methods of dating bones. In *Science in archaeology*, edited by D. Brothwell and E. Higgs, pp. 23-34. New York: Praeger.

Oakley, K., and Groves, C. 1970. Piltdown man: the realization of fraudulence. *Science* 169:789.

Oakley, K., and Montagu, A. 1949. A reconsideration of the Galley Hill skeleton. *Bulletin of British Museum* 1:25.

Pilbeam, D. 1972. *The ascent of man*. New York: Macmillan.

Pilbeam, D., and Simons, E. 1965. Some problems of hominid classification. *American Scientist* 53:327.

Poirier, F. 1981. *Fossil evidence: the human evolutionary journey*. St. Louis: Mosby.

Price, P., and Walker, R. 1963. A simple method of measuring low uranium concentrations in natural crystals. *Applied Physics Letters* 2:32.

Renfrew, C. 1971. Carbon 14 and the prehistory of Europe. In *Avenues to prehistory*, edited by B. Fagan, pp. 239-49. San Francisco: Freeman.

Schultz, A. 1963. Age changes, sex differences, and variability as factors in the classification of primates. In *Classification and human evolution,*edited by S. Washburn, pp. 85-115. New York: Viking Fund Publications.

Shuey, R., Brown, F., and Cross, M. 1974. Magneto-stratigraphy of the Shungura formation, southwestern Ethiopia; fine structure of the lower Matuyama polarity epoch. *Earth and Planetary Science Letters* 23:249-60.

Simons, E. 1968a. Some fallacies in the study of hominid phylogeny. In *Perspectives on human evolution*, edited by S. Washburn and P. Jay, pp. 18-40. New York: Holt, Rinehart and Winston.

—————. 1968b. Assessment of fossil hominids. *Science*160:672.

—————. 1972. *Primate evolution: an introduction to man's place in nature*. New York: Macmillan.

Simpson, G. 1945. The principles of classification and a classification of mammals. *Bulletin of American Museum of Natural History* 85.

—————.1951. *Horses*. London: Oxford University Press.

—————. 1953. *The major features of evolution*. New York: Columbia University Press.

—————. 1961. *Principles of animal taxonomy*. New York: Columbia University Press.

Sokol, R., and Sneath, P. 1963. *Principles of numerical taxonomy*. San Francisco: Freeman.

Washburn, S. 1967. The analysis of primate evolution, with particular reference to the origin of man. In *Ideas on human evolution*, edited by W. Howells, pp. 154-71. New York: Atheneum.

Weiner, J., Oakley, K., and Clark, W. Le Gros. 1953. The solution of the Piltdown problem. *Bulletin of British Museum* 2:139.

Wolpoff, M. 1976. Some aspect of the evolution of early hominid sexual dimorphism. *Current Anthropology* 17:599-606.

Chapter 14

Early Primate Evolution

Most paleontologists are of the opinion that early primates, called prosimians, evolved from an insectivorous stock sometime during the Paleocene or the Eocene geological epoch. One viewpoint holds that early primate evolution basically occurred within an arboreal (tree living) niche as a refuge zone free from competition from insectivores generally. Major early changes noted in primate evolution (i.e., dental and facial changes) were primarily associated with diet and later skeletal modifications with locomotor changes possibly associated with getting around the arboreal habitat.

Eocene prosimians show a number of features suggesting adjustments to getting around the arboreal habitat; some of the major changes appeared in the facial and limb skeleton. During the Eocene there was the widespread extinction of many primates and replacement by their advanced relatives, the monkeys.

Early Primates

Our remote prosimian ancestors were probably beady-eyed, bewhiskered, long-snouted animals looking and perhaps behaving similar to small rodents. One view suggests that before becoming arboreal they scurried through the fallen leaves and undergrowth of the tropical forests searching for food, probably insects. Early primate evolution coincided with a time when the earth was geologically restless; the reigning reptiles, not adapted to the rapidly changing ecological conditions, became obsolete. There were violent earthquakes and volcanic eruptions, and mountains were rising; retreating waters exposed larger and larger land masses. There seems to have been an enormous expansion of the number and variety of ivy, shrubs, and trees.

According to one viewpoint the early primates and rodents competed intensively on the ground and in the trees. Until recently rodents had the best of the struggle, and even today rodents are represented by 3,000 species and primates by only about 200 species. Some early primates were terrestrially oriented and became extinct after about 10 million years; those who were arboreal fared better. Many paleontologists feel that the prosimians entered the trees as a refuge zone where competition was less intense and living more complicated. The prosimians were forced to adapt to a strange new world, a new dimension of life among the dense foliage, branches, and forest canopies. (An alternate to this arboreal hypothesis of early primate evolution was suggested by Cartmill [1975] and will be discussed later in this chapter.)

The time of appearance, deployment, and extinction of the early primates indicates competitive relationships within the group. Rodents first appeared in the late Paleocene (60 million years ago), after which no new primate group showed clear rodentlike adaptations. The main period of rodent radiation occurred during the Eocene and coincided with the decline and extinction of primitive primates in North America and Europe. The rodent-primate competition must have been close and crucial to their mutual evolutionary histories.

Continental Drift

Within the past 20 years the concept of continental drift became firmly established (Wilson, 1972). It has now been shown that the crust of the earth is a shifting, erupting force. The continental mass sits atop a denser mantle in the earth, the so-called plates. These plates may thrust on one another causing great uplifting. The earth's supercontinent, called Pangea, had been gradually breaking apart throughout the Mesozoic Era and by the end of the era the pieces had become the separated land masses shown on today's maps. If seas expanded and contracted and mountain barriers rose and eroded, migration routes and contact were open and restricted. Thus, the moving continents affected the movements and lifeways of living things. In all the changing environments some species survived and others perished. During this time, for example, dinosaurs and many other reptiles disappeared and a host of new mammals appeared.

In the 1950s and 1960s the answer to how the continents moved was finally revealed: vast volcanic intrusions along midocean ridges were continually shoving the sea floors and continents away from the ridges. The motions of the continents have now been described. The relation of the African plate to the Euroasiatic plate and the relations of Africa to South America are important to understanding early phases of primate evolution.

It was traditionally thought that monkeys in the New and Old Worlds were similar because of parallel evolution, that is, that they both arose from the same stock and evolved in similar directions. It was believed that New World monkeys arose from an ancestral North American early primate stock. Newer data, for example, biochemical evidence of close similarity between New and Old World primates (Chapter 22), have shown, however, that they both shared a very long period of common ancestry. Because South America and Africa were once much closer together about 35 million to 40 million years ago than they are in modern times, New World monkey ancestors may have drifted from Africa to South America on some sort of natural raft. Continental drift and the biochemical evidence suggest a different version of much of primate evolution than originally thought.

It has been suggested that not only the Platyrrhini (New World monkeys) but the caviomorph rodents as well (found now only in South America) had their origins in Africa. The suggestion is that during the late Eocene monkeys rafted across the narrow South Atlantic. Because this idea requires crossing water, it is in this respect similar to a North American origin of South American primates. The idea of an African origin, however, is advantageous in that it accounts not only for the platyrrhines but also for the South American rodents, both of which resemble early African fauna.

Food Habits: You Are What You Eat

Primate Diets. Major stages in primate evolution occurred within the arboreal habitat; two of the major adustments required for arboreal life are a shift in dietary preference and habitat exploration, the latter accompanied by structural changes in the limbs as noted during the Eocene. Most available foods within the arboreal habitat are vegetal and most primates are essentially vegetarians. However, many modern primates may best be described as opportunistic **omnivores,** that is, they feed on insects and other food sources when available. Some primates have become "secondarily" carnivorous.

Dental Traits. Teeth form a major portion of the early primate remains. The major features distinguishing early primate dentitions reflect an important dietary shift. The change was not an absolute total shift away from an older diet; rather, it took place through a relative increase in the importance of fruit, leaves, and herbaceous matter (**herbivorous** diet), and a decrease in feeding on insects. Dietary changes characterizing the earliest stages of primate evolution may actually have occurred as a series of overlapping shifts. First, a large, sparsely inhabited frugivorous-herbivorous (fruit, bud, and leaf) niche must have been available. The changes necessary to adapt to these new foods were largely behavioral, for example, there was a slow shift in food preference. Once a preference for, or sustained interest in, small fruits, berries, and leaves became established at the expense of a more **insectivorous** diet, selection favored populations that could most efficiently use these foods. Once this process was operative, a second stage was entered necessitating changes in dentition and the digestive tract.

The diet of the insectivorous stock from which the earliest primates evolved included soft-bodied invertebrates (animals lacking backbones), animals that are easily sliced and swallowed. The teeth of insectivores are characteristically tall and sharp with acute **cusps** (elevations of the tooth crown surface). Such teeth are poorly suited for chewing the rough, tough-shelled seeds or fibrous fruits found within the arboreal habitat. Early in primate evolution there was selection pressure for shorter and more bulbous (rounded) cusps and for grinding of foods.

Facial and Cranial Changes. Subsequent modifications followed the basic dietary change and modification of the chewing apparatus. A major change was reduction of the

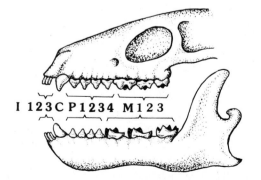

Figure 14-1. The dentition of an assumed early placental mammal that gave rise to the primates. I—incisors, C—canines, P—premolars, and M—molars.

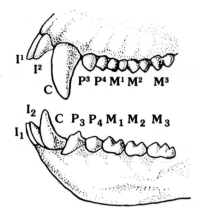

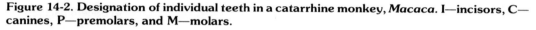

Figure 14-2. Designation of individual teeth in a catarrhine monkey, *Macaca*. I—incisors, C—canines, P—premolars, and M—molars.

snout, probably related to a reduction in size and/or crowding of the incisors, canines, and premolars, and to an increasing reliance on the hands for picking up objects such as foodstuffs that were conveyed from hand to mouth. The configuration of the **zygomatic arches** (cheekbones) also changed, becoming broad and strong. This was presumably related to the increasing bulk of a stronger **masseter muscle** complex; these muscles are chiefly concerned with a grinding mode of mastication.[1] Major craniofacial changes are noted during the Eocene with the onset of *stereoscopic vision,* that is, the convergence of the two visual fields on one object, and an increasing reliance on the visual sense.

Paleocene Primates

Some argue that the earliest evidence of this prosimian stock derives from the Middle Paleocene epoch, approximately 55 million to 60 million years ago, in North America from fossiliferous sites in Colorado, Montana, New Mexico, Wyoming, and Texas. These remains are assigned to the Superfamily Plesiadapoidea (Table 14-1). One of the four possible Paleocene prosimian families, the Carpolestidae, exhibits the dental changes mentioned already. The family Carpolestidae (the name means fruit stealers) is based on fossilized jaws and teeth. The teeth were presumably adapted to splitting open seeds and hard, woody stems; the second premolar is greatly enlarged and serrated (sawlike) to form a longitudinal cutting edge (Figure 14-3).

Dental patterns of these Paleocene forms suggest that many were adapting in new ways to a new diet characteristic of a group during the invasion of a new habitat. The variety of molar patterns exhibited by the Paleocene fossils suggests that they were not adapted to chewing the fibrous outer body cover of animal bodies. Subsequent specializations of the incisors and canines may be related to diversified specializations of a herbivorous or frugivorous diet.

If some of the Paleocene forms are primates they are unique in the development of their incisors. The loss of piercing canines and nipping incisors indicates invasion into a broad herbivorous-frugivorous niche. The emphasis on the incisors and deemphasis on canines indicates a general lack of predatory behavior.

[1]If you touch your cheeks and grit your teeth, you can feel these muscles.

Table 14-1. Some Members of the First Possible Primate Superfamily, the Plesiadapoidea[a]

Family	Epoch	Distribution	Traits
Plesiadapidae	Paleocene, Eocene	Europe, North America	Medium-sized, vegetarian, had large chiseling incisors.
Carpolestidae	Paleocene	North America	Rodent-sized, omnivorous, had enlarged incisors and premolars.
Paromomyidae	Late Cretaceous, Paleocene, Eocene	Europe, North America	Diverse group, rodent-sized, had very long incisors.
Picrodontidae	Paleocene	North America	Two tiny mouselike animals, had specialized teeth. Nectar and insect eaters?

[a]Some authorities do not accept this superfamily as primates.

Adapted from C. Jolly and F. Plog, *Physical Anthropology and Archeology*, p. 116. Alfred A. Knopf, Incorporated. New York, © 1976.

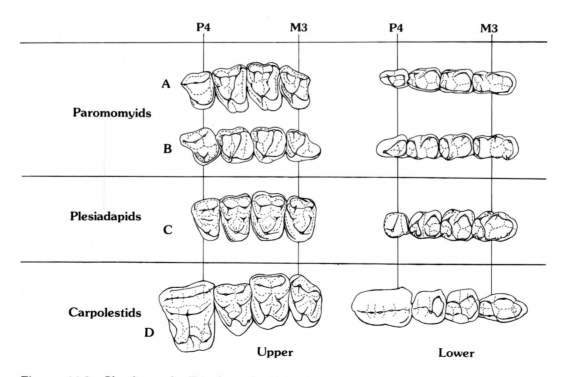

Figure 14-3. Cheek teeth (P4 through M3) of plesiadapoids (semidiagrammatic). (A) *Paramomys maturus* (mid-Paleocene). (B) *Phenacolemur jepseni* (early Eocene). (C) *Pronothodectes matthewi* (mid-Paleocene). (D) *Carpodaptes hazelae* (late Paleocene). Not to same scale.

Purgatorius is one of the earliest forms designated as a possible primate (Van Valen and Sloan, 1965). A later species of *Purgatorius* is based on a sample of approximately 50 isolated teeth from a single Paleocene quarry site in Eastern Montana. While there are primate characteristics in the molar teeth, we must withhold judgment of the primate status of this form until further information is available.[2]

Trends in Eocene Primate Evolution

The Arboreal Habitat. A second major adaptation to arboreal life was an adjustment to getting around in the trees, to exploiting this three-dimensional world. Major trends appear in the hands, feet, skull, and face of Eocene fossils, dating from 36 million to 50 million years ago. The Eocene Epoch witnesses the maximal radiation (divergent development) of the prosimii; as many as 43 genera and three families, Adapidae (Figure 14-4), Tarsiidae, and Anaptomorphidae have been recognized (Table 14-2). This number will likely be reduced when we learn more about population variability within the group.

Limb Structure. Included within the general structural limb adaptations to arboreal life are grasping hands and feet equipped with nails instead of claws. There are exceptions to this pattern among modern primates, for example, the Southeast Asian tree shrew (Figure 14-5), which many reject as a primate, possesses claws on all its digits. The loris, a small Southeast Asian nocturnal form, uses so-called claws on its third and fourth digits for cleansing its hair of debris. The hands and feet are characterized by pentadactyly (the presence of five fingers and toes) and by a grasping thumb and big toe. Using modern primates as a comparative source, it can be suggested that these contained ridged and slightly oily tactile pads on their tips.[3] Another important characteristic of the primate limb structure is retention of two separate forearm bones, the **ulna** (on the little-finger side of the arm) and the **radius** (on the thumb side). This allows for forearm rotation and greater mobility, a useful adaptation for jumping and grasping necessitated by an arboreal life.

---

[2]Some scholars feel that the Paleocene forms cannot be classified as primates. If not primates, these forms may suggest the direction primate evolution was taking.

[3]Our fingerprints are derived from these ridged pads.

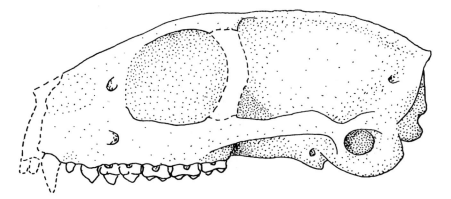

Figure 14-4. Reconstructed skull of the Eocene adapid *Pronycticebus gaudryi*.

Table 14-2. Some Members of the "Second Wave" of Primate Evolution

Taxon	Epoch	Distribution	Traits
Lemur forms			
Family Adapidae	Eocene, Oligocene	Europe, North America, Asia, Africa	Diverse group of medium-sized lemurs.
Subfamily Adapinae	Eocene, Oligocene	Europe, Asia, Africa, North America (?)	Herbivores, some small, large-eyed lemurs.
Subfamily Notharctinae	Eocene	North America	
Tarsier forms			
Family Tarsiidae	Eocene to Recent	Europe, Asia, North America	Includes living *Tarsius,* a small animal.
Family Anaptomorphidae	Eocene to Miocene	Europe, Asia, North America	Tarsierlike primates.
Subfamily Anaptomorphinae	Eocene	North America	Small, had large eyes; dentition suggests mixed diet.
Subfamily Omomyinae	Eocene to Miocene	Asia, Europe, North America	Widespread group, had generalized diet.

Adapted from C. Jolly and F. Plog, *Physical Anthropology and Archeology,* p. 120. Alfred A. Knopf, Incorporated. New York, © 1976.

Figure 14-5. Southeast Asian tree shrew.

Changes in Skull. The Eocene witnessed major changes in the primate skull that seem adaptive for arboreal life. A major change is the reduction of the snout or nasal area and the forward rotation of the eye orbits, both of which suggest a reduction of reliance on the **olfactory** sense. This is emphasized by the lack of a naked rhinarium (e.g., the wet nose of a dog) among most modern members. A shift in the senses meant a reorganization of the brain, for example, a reduction of the olfactory and an enlargement of the visual brain center.

Fossil evidence indicates the increasing importance of the visual sense. The suggestive evidence appears as the shifting of the orbits from a lateral to frontal position and enclosure of the eyes with a protective bone casing. Forward orbital rotation resulted in stereoscopic vision. This is an adaptation to spatial orientation and may perhaps be associated with jumping from one tree limb to another. Leaping from branch to branch in search of food requires that the tree-dweller continually make distance judgments and, to the degree that visual fields overlap, image fusion and improvements of depth perception are necessary.[4]

As a result of the shift in position, the primate eye is more vulnerable than that of most terrestrial mammals, whose line of sight is laterally directed. The eye of most prosimians is protected only by a slender bar of bone, but among the suborder Anthropoidea (Old and New World monkeys, apes, and humans), the entire orbit is surrounded by a ring of bone resulting in a distinct eye socket.

Other morphological changes related to behavior appear early in primate evolution. Although there is minimal suggestive evidence, early prosimians may have possessed **ischial callosities** (a specialized skin structure present even in the fetus) that allow primates to sit on hard branches for endless time periods.[5,6] Upright sitting freed the hands for other activities, such as pulling food to the mouth; such behaviors coincidentally improved hand-eye coordination. This is a **preadaptation** (a behavior or structure of value in later evolutionary stages) for tool use and bipedalism.

Evidence for these trends can be found among some Eocene prosimians. The family Adapidae, including the genera *Notharctus* from North America (Figure 14-6) and *Adapis* from France, exhibits these trends. The limb structure of Eocene forms is characterized by an opposable big toe and thumb. The snout was still quite long (resulting in a **prognathic** face), but the orbits have rotated forward indicating stereoscopic vision. Other Eocene forms show a general shortening of the snout and a forward shifting of the **foramen magnum** (the hole through which the spinal cord passes). These changes, coupled with forelimb shortening, indicate that these animals kept an erect posture while hopping and sitting.

Changes in Ear. It has been suggested that a major trend in early primate evolution was a reorganization of the structure and function of the middle ear (Figure 14-7). This restructuring

[4]Misjudged leaps can result in fatal falls. Even the most accomplished arboreal primate acrobat, the gibbon, often falls from misjudged leaps or broken branches.

[5]That the lack of such structures is definitely disadvantageous is attested to by primatologists who sometimes sit on the same limbs watching the monkeys. For us, the usual result is that our legs "fall asleep." Some modern nonhuman primates lack ischial callosities.

[6]Nonhuman primates possess other adaptations for sleeping; for example, many species of monkeys sleep out on small, slender limbs where they are relatively safe from predators. Should a large-size predator attempt to climb out on the limb, the limb would shake and the monkeys would be aroused to the potential danger. Another of the adaptations for sleeping safely is found among the apes; both chimpanzees and orangutans build nests in the trees in which they sleep. The gorilla also builds a nest; however, it is placed on the ground. Few trees have branches strong enough to hold a large adult gorilla for the night.

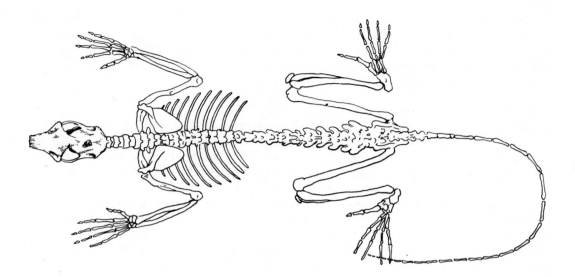

Figure 14-6. Reconstructed skeleton of the Middle Eocene primate *Notharctus*. Scale is × 0.20.

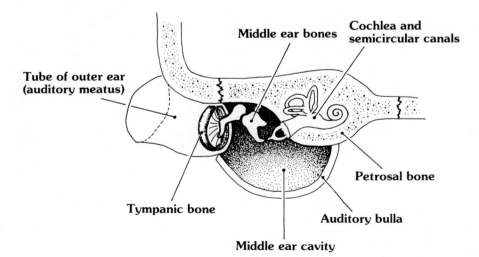

Figure 14-7. Diagrammatic section through the right ear region of a therian mammal, seen from the front. In primates, the bulla is an extension of the petrosal bone; in most nonprimates, it is either cartilaginous or formed by a separate entotympanic bone.

is believed to have allowed for better balance while leaping and may have enhanced the ability to make constant adjustments in body position. The argument is that the ability to determine position is important to an animal that habitually glides, leaps, or relies occasionally, but crucially, on exacting balance. The highly advanced middle ear cavity of the Paleocene form *Plesiadapis,* especially in comparison with its relatively primitive **postcranial** (below the head) skeleton (Figure 14-8) suggests that its locomotor pattern, possibly in combination with its feeding adaptations required a highly developed sense of balance and suggests an arboreal life style. Despite its advanced ear cavity, controversy exists as to whether *Plesiadapis* was arboreal; some interpret it to have been terrestrial.

Alternative Interpretations

Arboreal Hypothesis. The orthodox theory of early primate evolution ties our evolutionary heritage to the arboreal habitat and has been appropriately labeled the arboreal hypothesis. This hypothesis was originally propounded by the British anatomists G. Elliot Smith and F. Wood Jones. It is this arboreal hypothesis to which many refer when attempting to explain the early primate fossil record. The major new challenge to this hypothesis is made by Cartmill (1975), whose views follow this summary.

The arboreal hypothesis of primate origins ties the major adaptations of early primates to the tree-dwelling habitat. For example, the grasping hands and feet are supposedly related to grasping and hanging to thin branches. Jones felt that the fore and hind limbs of the early primates had different functions and that these were of potential evolutionary significance. Jones argued that the hands were the grasping and exploratory organs while the hind limbs supported and propelled the body. These adaptations led to further anatomical and behavioral changes.

Jones argues that early in primate evolution the body posture becomes upright and the grasping hands gradually replace the jaws in obtaining food. The jaws gradually reduce in size,

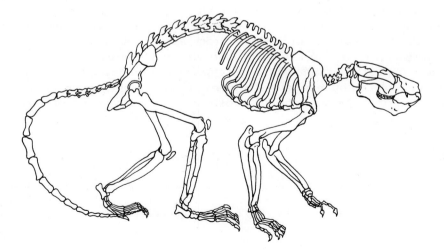

Figure 14-8. Skeletal reconstruction of *Plesiadapis* based on cranial and postcranial remains found in France and Colorado. Scale is × 0.25. *Plesiadapis* is one of the oldest possible primate fossils.

the face becomes smaller, and the eye orbits shift to a more forward position. These changes are accompanied by alterations in the nervous system, that is, the olfactory sense becomes reduced in importance and the visual sense becomes elaborated. This leads to a restructuring of the brain and further anatomical changes in the facial and jaw regions.

Cartmill's (1975:15) impression of this process is as follows:

> The result of all these trends is a lemurlike primate. To make a monkey out of a lemur, all that is needed is to carry these trends a bit further, resulting in a larger brain, a shorter face, defter hands, more closely set eyes and so on. All these things are prerequisites for the evolution of humans. . . . The theory is persuasive, neat and fairly comprehensive. It does provide an explanation for most of the peculiarities of primates. I am going to argue, however, that it is not adequate.

Visual Predation Hypothesis. Cartmill (1972, 1975) offers an alternate interpretation of the processes of early primate evolution that he labels the visual predation hypothesis. Cartmill feels that Beecher's (1969) hypothesis concerning the construction of the ear and its implication that early primates were arboreal is of no help in discerning how early primates lived. Cartmill argues that the arboreal hypothesis of primate evolution which states that the early primates lost their sense of smell, developed stereoscopic vision, and replaced claws with nails because of the demands of an arboreal existence is erroneous and incomplete. He suggests instead that the grasping hind feet and close-set eyes characteristic of primates originated as part of an adaptation to visually directed predation on insects that live among the slender branches in the undergrowth and lower canopies of tropical forests. "Clawless digits, grasping feet and close-set eyes; these and other features common to most living primates all suggest that the last common ancestor of the living primates was a small visual predator inhabiting the lower strata of tropical forests" (Cartmill, 1975:20-21).

The drastic reduction of Late Eocene primates and their virtual disappearance from Europe and North America by the middle Oligocene (25 million to 35 million years ago) was due to many causes. Rodent competition greatly restricted the primate zone and drove primates into the trees. Progressive cooling and a reduction of the tropical forests may have driven the primates from the more temperate zone. Forms unable to compete in a fauna with a full representation of modern mammals were presumably replaced by monkeys. More progressive monkey groups were probably a decisive factor in the extinction of prosimians over large areas of Europe.

Bibliography

Bamlach, R., Scotese, C., and Ziegler, A. 1980. Before Pangea: the geographics of the Paleozoic world. *American Scientist* 68:26-38.

Barth, F. 1950. On the relationships of early primates. *American Journal of Physical Anthropology* 8:139.

Beecher, W. 1969. Possible motion detection in the vertebrate middle ear. *Bulletin of the Chicago Academy of Science* II:155.

Campbell, B. 1966. *Human evolution.* Chicago: Aldine.

Cartmill, M. 1972. Arboreal adaptations and the origin of the order primates. In *The functional and evolutionary biology of primates,* edited by R. Tuttle, pp. 97-122. Chicago: Aldine-Atherton.

_____. 1975. *Primate origins.* Minneapolis: Burgess.

Clark, W. Le Gros. 1969. *History of the primates.* Chicago: Phoenix Books.

_____. 1971. *The antecedents of man.* Chicago: Quadrangle Books.

Haines, R. 1958. Arboreal or terrestrial ancestry of placental mammals? *Quarterly Review of Biology* 33:1.

Jolly, C., and Plog, F. 1976. *Physical anthropology and archeology.* New York: Knopf.

Marshall, L., Butler, R., Drake, R., Curtis, G., and Tedford, R. 1979. Calibration of the great American interchange. *Science* 204:272-79.

Pfeiffer, J. 1969. *The emergence of man.* New York: Harper & Row.

Schwartz, J., Tattersall, I., and Eldredge, N. 1978. Phylogeny and classification of primates revisited. *Yearbook of Physical Anthropology* 21:92-133.

Simons, E. 1972. *Primate evolution: an introduction to man's place in nature.* New York: Macmillan.

Simpson, G. 1955. The Phenacolemuridae, new family of early primates. *Bulletin of American Museum of Natural History* 105:411.

Szalay, F. 1968. The beginnings of primates. *Evolution* 22:19.

_____. 1972. Paleobiology of the earliest primates. In *The functional and evolutionary biology of primates,* edited by R. Tuttle, pp. 3-36. Chicago: Aldine-Atherton.

Szalay, F., and Delson, E. 1978. *Evolutionary history of the primates.* New York: Academic Press.

Van Valen, L., and Sloan, R. 1965. The earliest primates. *Science* 150:743-45.

Wilson, J., ed. 1972. *Continents adrift.* San Francisco: Freeman.

Chapter 15

Pongid Evolution

Pongid evolution commenced during the Oligocene epoch, about 35 million years ago, and reached its height during the Miocene epoch beginning about 25 million years ago. In neither geological epoch did the ancestral forms markedly resemble modern pongids other than in certain dental traits.

One Miocene hominoid group, the dryopithecines, has had a particularly important impact in reconstructing primate evolutionary history. This group was strongly touted as the last common stock of pongids and hominids. It was argued that modern pongids and hominids can trace their ancestry back to some dryopithecine ancestry. The discovery of new fossil materials, however, has cast doubt on this scenario and there are now doubts as to the possible role of the dryopithecines in the immediate hominid lineage.

Oligocene Evolution—The Higher Primates of the Fayum, Egypt

An incomplete picture of Oligocene primate evolution comes largely from the Fayum (Arabic, El Faiyum) region south of Cairo, Egypt, which has been excavated periodically since the early 1960s by a team led by Elwyn Simons.[1] Fayum deposits yield the oldest undoubted ape skeletal materials, along with fossils of long-extinct monkeys. In terms of the fossil record, monkeys and apes are distinguished by anatomical traits and/or complexes. Much that distinguishes them is related to differences in locomotor adaptations. For example, modern monkeys have tails and are generally quadrupedal. Modern apes lack tails and tend toward brachiation in the trees and knuckle- or fist-walking on the ground. The cranial capacities of apes are generally larger than those of monkeys. As we go back in time, however, the distinguishing traits become blurred. Fayum apes, for example, had relatively small brains, were arboreal quadrupeds, and some evidently still possessed tails. The dental structure of Oligocene apes, especially molar cusp patterns, is unique to pongids, however.

---

[1] However, some of the Fayum material has been available since the early 1900s.

Table 15-1. The Major Fayum Primates

Oligopithecus (oligo = few, pithecus = ape).[a] This is the oldest Fayum primate, dating to 32 million years ago.

Parapithecus (para = near, pithecus = ape, i.e., near ape, about 30 million years ago).

Apidium (named after Apis, the sacred bull of Egypt, about 30 million years ago).

Parapithecus and *Apidium* are related. Both were squirrel-sized and both left numerous fossils.

Propliopithecus (pro = before, plio = more, pithecus = ape). A form dating to about 30 million years ago. Medium-sized. About size of small monkey. Perhaps ancestral to *Aegyptopithecus.*

Aegyptopithecus. A form that dates to about 28 million years ago. *Aegyptopithecus* is related to the dryopithecines. Largest of Fayum forms. Size of medium-sized monkey.

Aeolopithecus (named after Aeolus, god of winds). This form dates to about 28 to 30 million years ago. Small ape with large canines.

[a]Although these names are descriptive, not all generic names are descriptive in nature.

Figure 15-1. More than 30 million years ago, *Propliopithecus* may have lived in trees lining the banks of the primitive Nile River. The primitive proboscidean *Moeritherium* approaches the water from the left. The long-nose crocodile *Tomistoma* frightens a giant dassie, *Megalphyrax.* In the background stand the great horned creatures, *Arsinoitherium.*

Three genera compose the major Fayum remains. The oldest of the materials is a form known as *Oligopithecus.* There are also the forms *Propliopithecus,* dating back 30 million years, and *Aegyptopithecus,* dating back 28 million years, sometimes referred to as the "first true ape"[2] (Table 15-1).

[2]There are also two other forms, *Parapithecus* and *Apidium,* which may be related to *Oreopithecus* found in Miocene-Pliocene deposits in Italy.

Habitat Reconstruction. The excellent reconstruction of the Fayum habitat provides a rather vivid picture of the area approximately 30 million to 35 million years ago. Although the Fayum is today desert, during the Oligocene it was a lush tropical area (Figure 15-1). Studies of fossilized seed pods, pollens, and wood have helped determine the forest's character. It was most probably a tropical gallery forest, and it is also likely that there were areas of open savanna or coastal plains.

The recovery of large quantities of fish and land vertebrates immensely helped the reconstruction of the habitat. In addition to the fish bones, skeletal remains of large amphibious mammals resembling sea cows were uncovered. Reptiles were represented by tortoises similar to those existing today in the Galapagos Islands. There is no evidence of animals related to the antelope, water buffalo, giraffe, or leopard, or any animals characteristic of modern Africa. The total Fayum assemblage indicates a warm, well-watered lowland, with vegetation-clogged rivers grading into sluggish deltaic streams and brackish estuaries that provided grazing land. The forest canopy was the environment of the Oligocene Fayum primates.

The Fossil Evidence

A large portion of the Fayum primate material consists of young animals that may have met their death due to misjudged leaps between branches overhanging the streams. Their inexperience and age is evidenced by the incomplete tooth eruption on many of the jaw fragments.

Oligopithecus. The oldest of the Fayum materials is *Oligopithecus,* an unknown form until the first excavation season in 1964. It has been dated to approximately 32 million years ago. The material classified as *Oligopithecus* consists of a left mandibular half from which the incisors and last molar are missing. However, the **dental formula** has been reconstructed as 2, 1, 2, 3, (that is, 2 incisors, 1 canine, 2 premolars, and 3 molars in each half of each jaw), that of all modern Old World higher primates—monkeys, apes, and humans. We are not certain to what forms *Oligopithecus* was ancestral, although some suggest that it may be related to Old World monkeys. According to another viewpoint the extreme primitiveness of molar crown patterns in *Oligopithecus* suggests that the find cannot be classed either as an ancestral cercopithecoid or an ancestral hominoid. Thus, its ancestral position to later Fayum forms is questionable.

Propliopithecus. One of the best-known and most controversial Oligocene primates is *Propliopithecus haeckeli,* which is represented by two nearly complete mandibular halves and about a dozen teeth. The dental formula of *Propliopithecus* is 2, 1, 2, 3. The teeth are simple in pattern; the canines are fairly short and light, and the premolars are unspecialized and lack the **sectorial** (unicuspid) pongid characteristic. Judging from the tooth sockets and adjacent bone, the incisors appear to have been vertically implanted rather than angling forward as is the case with monkeys and apes.

Propliopithecus may represent a small-faced arboreal ape stock, lacking large canines and slicing incisors. *Propliopithecus* is representative of an early pongid stock. Some members of this group gave rise to *Aegyptopithecus,* which is probably ancestral to the dryopithecines.

Aegyptopithecus. *Aegyptopithecus* is dated to approximately 28 million years ago, that is, 8 million to 10 million years earlier than previously known fossil ape skulls, the dryopithecines. Although incomplete, *Aegyptopithecus* is one of the best-preserved pongid fossil skulls. Numerous dental similarities between *Aegyptopithecus* and East African dryopithecines, of approximately 16 million to 20 million years ago, suggest that *Aegyptopithecus* was in or near their ancestry. *Aegyptopithecus* is almost twice as large as the other Oligocene primates. It may have weighed 9 to 16.5 pounds (Gingerich, 1977).

Besides the skull, *Aegyptopithecus* is known from four incomplete lower jaws and six isolated upper teeth. Several dental features suggest that *Aegyptopithecus* could have evolved from the earlier *Propliopithecus*.

Because postcranial material from Oligocene forms has been virtually unknown, a limb bone recently described from the Fayum Oligocene is particularly important (Fleagle et al., 1975). The material is a nearly complete right ulna. The fossil ulna is attributed to *A. zeuxis*, a skull of which was found near it at the same quarry and level. Many features of the ulna contrast rather strongly with terrestrial Old World forms and compare favorably with arboreal primates. It has been suggested that *Aegyptopithecus* was an arboreal quadruped. Morphological traits, especially characteristics of the elbow area, indicate that *Aegyptopithecus* was well adapted to climbing and possibly to hanging by the forelimbs. The morphological traits of the ulna support a reconstruction of locomotor behavior that could give rise to both brachiation and arboreal and terrestrial quadrupedal locomotion.

Morphologically and chronologically *Aegyptopithecus* could be ancestral to the Miocene dryopithecines and may be the direct forebear of such apes as the modern chimpanzee; thus, the line leading to modern apes and humans perhaps first evolved from *Aegyptopithecus* in the Oligocene. Another form, *Aeolopithecus*, is perhaps a branch leading to the gibbon and closely related siamangs. (Although their ancestry may thus be traced to Africa, modern gibbons and siamangs can only be found in Asia.) The stock from which this group evolved could be the earlier *Propliopithecus*, itself evolved from an earlier connecting link such as *Oligopithecus*.

Summary. The selective pressures of the arboreal life characteristic of millions of years ago forced a comparatively primitive primate stock in the direction of pongid evolution. For example, near the end of the Oligocene, evolutionary pressures produced a form possessing a monkey's skull and ape's teeth. This was *Aegyptopithecus*. The Fayum primates provide fossil evidence of the process of primate evolution from approximately 28 million to 32 million years ago. In the Fayum, in one area of forest where many rivers once entered the sea, early primate populations flourished.

Ciochon and Savage have argued that Burma may be the point of origin of the anthropoids. They base their argument on finds dated to 40 million years ago, that is, approximately 10 million years before the Fayum finds.

The new materials, placed in the genera *Pondaungia* and *Amphipithecus*, come from the Pondaung Hills in Upper Burma. To date, the fossil material consists of four mandibular fragments. Ciochon noted that the dental remains belonged to a form approximately the size of modern gibbons. He noted further that the new discoveries are substantially more complete than earlier finds and are believed to have come from primates that attained a size equal to that of living Burmese gibbons. Ciochon feels that this relatively large body size, coupled with advanced features of the dental crown morphology, extreme depth of the jaw below the molar teeth, and the presence of a well-buttressed, fused lower jawbone all support the hypothesis that the Burmese primates from the late Eocene period (40 million years ago) are the earliest known anthropoids. However, until maxillae and crania are uncovered, the significance of these new materials is debatable.

Miocene Evolution: The Dryopithecines

The Miocene witnessed the flowering of pongid evolution. In the Miocene, spanning an age from 25 million to 18 million years ago, ancestral forms of modern pongids are represented in the fossil specimens known as the dryopithecines. The term "dryopithecine" means oak-ape; the first East African remains occur with fossilized oak wood. The name "dryopithecine" is a generalized term for the Miocene pongid forms. Although many different generic names have been applied to these forms, three separate genera are now recognized among the dryopithecines: the genus *Dryopithecus* found in Europe, the genus *Sivapithecus* found in Asia and perhaps in Africa, and the genus *Proconsul* found in Africa. It should be noted that some authorities prefer to recognize these forms at the subgenus, rather than the genus level. It is felt here, however, that there is enough diversity among the forms to warrant a generic designation. That designation is followed in this chapter. Some authorities refer to the members of the genus *Dryopithecus* as dryopithecids and to members of the genus *Sivapithecus* as the sivapithecids.

During the Miocene the earth experienced extensive tectonic movements, great mountain ranges arose, and continents drifted apart. Volcanoes actively changed the face of the African continent and a series of geological disturbances created the Great Rift Valley. Climatic shifts occurred—as the climate continued to cool great forests began to shrink and temperate conditions began to spread southward over Europe.

Geographical Distribution. Dryopithecine material is spread throughout the Old World: Europe, Asia, and Africa (Table 15-2). The first dryopithecine mandible was found in France in 1856. Most Asian dryopithecine material is from India, primarily from the Siwalik Hills of North India. In the early 1900s, G. Pilgrim and G. Lewis uncovered and described many new dryopithecine forms, most of Miocene age. Although Asian dryopithecines are poorly represented outside India, the known scattered remains in the Soviet Union and China suggest that further work will reveal a wider distribution. The most extensive series of dryopithecine fossils comes from Miocene deposits in and around the Kavirondo Gulf of Lake Victoria in Kenya, East Africa. In 1931 a paleontological expedition to Kenya uncovered considerable dryopithecine material, which by 1933 was organized into three genera and species. This material includes forms considered ancestral to modern gorillas and chimpanzees. From 1939 to 1949 much additional primate material was recovered from East African Miocene deposits. These collections were reviewed in 1950 and 1951, by W. E. Le Gros Clark and Louis Leakey, who proposed three species of *Proconsul*[3] from the Rusinga site: *P. africanus, P. major,* and *P. nyanzae.* In 1963 and 1970 new material was described from Uganda and Kenya.

The East African material is definitely of Miocene age because K-Ar dating reveals that the main fossiliferous zones at Rusinga are some 18 million years old. Although some specimens may date to 20 milliion to 22 million years ago, most of the pongid material is probably dated to between 17.5 million and 18.5 million years ago. Dating of the Indian dryopithecines is based on faunal associations. The Nagri faunal zone in North India is generally accepted as later Miocene or early Pliocene. Since the Nagri overlies the Chinji, the latter is considered to be older, perhaps of Middle Miocene dating.

---

[3]The name *Proconsul* was taken from a zoo chimpanzee named "Consul." "Proconsul" was considered its ancestor.

Table 15-2. Some Major Dryopithecine Sites

Europe		
Site	Remains	Age
St. Gaudens, France	*Dryopithecus fontani*	Mid-Miocene
Eppelsheim, Germany	*D. fontani*	to Mid-Pliocene
Vienna Basin, Austria	*D. fontani*	
Georgia, USSR	*D. fontani*	

Asia[a]		
Siwalik Hills, India	*Sivapithecus indicus,* *S. sivalensis*	Early Miocene
Yunan, China	*S. indicus*	
Pasalar, Turkey	*S. indicus*	
Candir, Turkey	*S. indicus*	
Saudi Arabia (Dam formation)	*Sivapithecus sp.?*	

Africa[b]		
Maboko Island, Kenya	*Proconsul sivalensis, P. africanus*	Late Miocene
Rusinga Island, Kenya	*P. nyanzae, P. africanus,* *P. sivalensis*	to Early Pliocene
Songhor, Kenya	*P. major, P. nyanzae*	
Koru, Kenya	*P. major, P. africanus*	
Napak, Uganda	*Micropithecus clarki*	
Moroto, Uganda	*P. major, S. africanus*	

[a]There appears to be a growing acceptance to placing the Asian dryopithecines in the genus *Sivapithecus*.

[b]There appears to be a growing acceptance to placing the African dryopithecines in the genus *Proconsul*.

The known range of dryopithecine habitation has increased with the announcement of remains in Saudi Arabia dated to 14 million to 15 million years ago (Andrews et al., 1978). The faunal assemblage suggests linkage with Africa and not with the Chinji association of India. This is not surprising, because there was free migration between Arabia and both North and East Africa during this time (Hamilton et al., 1978). Five specimens have been recovered (from calcareous pebbly grit) in the Dam formation. These specimens, consisting of a maxilla and four isolated teeth, have their closest affinity to the Miocene dryopithecines of East Africa.

These materials are important because of their age and geographical location. The closest East African equivalent to the Saudi Arabian finds is probably Maboko Island, from where *Sivapithecus africanus* remains have been uncovered. This is the only recognized *Sivapithecus* in Africa. The Saudi and African *Sivapithecus* share what is probably a derived characteristic in the enlarged premolars compared to the molars. There are also differences, and in these the Saudi finds retain, with *Proconsul* species, what is probably a primitive condition for Hominoidea. The Saudi finds cannot, however, be grouped with *Proconsul* (Andrews et al., 1978).

Because Saudi Arabia must have been close to the migration routes between Africa and Eurasia, it is interesting that these specimens are not linked with contemporaneous species of *Sivapithecus* in Turkey (Andrews and Tobien, 1977). The Turkish deposits at Pasalar are similar in age to the Saudi deposit, but the *Sivapithecus* species share traits with later Miocene species of the genus from India and Pakistan not present in the Saudi specimens. This is an indication that the new specimens from Saudi Arabia represent a primitive branch of dryopithecines not directly related to later pongid lines.

Morphological Characteristics. How did the dryopithecines look and how did they live? Much of the reconstruction is based on the East African material from around Lake Victoria. The presence of so many animal remains in shallow-water lake deposits suggests that they were vulnerable when they came to the water to drink and that they were killed there. The relative absence of limb bones may be due to the fact that, because of their high marrow content, the majority of the bones were broken and eaten by large hyenas or other carnivores. The same factors would account for the almost complete absence of skulls that, due to their brain content, would be liable to be eaten by large carnivores

The most complete cranial material belongs to *Proconsul africanus* from East Africa. The skull is lightly built and rather small, suggesting an animal more the size of an Old World monkey than a modern ape. Gingerich (1977) suggests an average body weight of about 50 pounds. In contrast to modern apes, the skull lacks the heavy bone structures characteristic of the sagittal and nuchal regions. There are no heavy ridges (the **supraorbital torus**) above the eye sockets, so characteristic of modern apes and larger Old World monkeys. As evidenced by features of an **endocranial cast** (fossilized cast of the brain), *Proconsul*'s brain was smaller and less complex than that characteristic of most modern primates. The muzzle is rather small and narrowed in front, and the nasal aperture is monkeylike. This particular skull is from one of the small species, and a newer find, named *Micropithecus clarki*, is reconstructed to belong to a tiny ape (Fleagle et. al., 1978).

The limb bones are crucial for resolving the Hominidae and Pongidae relationship. The limbs of Miocene apes lacked many structural specializations associated with brachiation, the mode of locomotion associated with some modern pongids.[4] The limb bones strongly suggest that the ancestral apes led a different mode of life than modern apes. Apart from the incomplete **humerus** (the arm bone) from France and from two other partial pieces, the only knowledge we have of dryopithecine forelimbs is from *Proconsul* remains in Kenya.

The humerus from Saint Gaudens, France, has been potassium-argon dated to approximately 12.5 million to 14 million years ago. In size and morphology it most closely resembles a chimpanzee humerus. Upper-limb skeletal remains from Kenya combine features typical of tree-living quadrupedal monkeys with characteristics no less distinctive of brachiating apes. However, the upper-limb structure also manifests features later seen in modern apes. Dryopithecines form an important link between quadrupedal monkeys and modern apes, because their generalized upper-limb structure could have provided the basis for the evolutionary development of the hominid upper-limb structure.

The fragmentary hind limb and foot bones are of the greatest importance in reconstructing dryopithecine locomotor patterns. The hind limbs and forelimbs suggest that the dryopithecines were active running and leaping creatures not particularly specialized for an arboreal life. Certain aspects of the heel suggest that the dryopithecines were capable of

---

[4]It is important to note that even though some of the modern apes, for example, the gorilla, chimpanzee, and orangutan, spend time on the ground in various locomotor patterns, it is assumed they passed through a prior brachiating stage in their evolutionary history.

Proconsul

Songhor, 19 May 1975

We drive to Songhor, a *Proconsul* site of immense importance. The drive from Fort Ternan takes approximately 40 minutes. The security guard at the site allows us to make camp—again thanks to Richard Leakey. The Songhor site sits on the Kano Plain which itself dates to the Miocene geological epoch. The oldest date on the Kano Plain is approximately 23 million years old according to potassium-argon dates on volcanically derived material. Much of the area now surrounding Songhor is largely planted over in sugar cane. In fact, another near-by site, Koru, is all but erased because of cultivation.

The Songhor sites are actually a small number of hills eroded out from the action of rain. In fact, the rain-caused erosion is used to locate fossils which appear on the surface. Although no excavations are actually now in progress the guard searches for fossils twice a week. These remains are then shipped to Nairobi for scrutiny. The earth at Songhor is red, although gray ash is in evidence.

We visually search the Songhor area and see some faunal remains which have been eroded free. During our search we find (actually a better term is "see" for Kenya's excellent tough antiquity laws forbid disturbing fossiliferous or artifactual remains at any of the national monuments. The penalty for ignoring this procedure is justifiably harsh) what appears to be a monkey molar, which I tentatively identify as a possible second mandibular molar. We also see a rodent skull and some rodent teeth. An undescribed *Proconsul* canine, broken in half, has recently been uncovered and awaits its delivery to Nairobi. In 1973 Peter Andrews worked at Songhor and uncovered some new dryopithecine remains.

On 20 May we get mired in thick mud as we attempt to break camp and leave Songhor for Rusinga Island. During our vigil to be "rescued" we search the areas and locate what may be another monkey tooth which was apparently dislodged during the night's heavy rain.

Rusinga Island, 20 May 1975

After a few hours we are freed from the Songhor mud and proceed to drive to Rusinga. On the way we stop at Kisumu to pick up Mr. Erastro Ndere who has worked on Rusinga. We locate Ndere because of his Yale University jacket which he tells us was presented to him by Dr. David Pilbeam. Because of the late hour we spend the night in Kisumu.

On 21 May we proceed to Mbita Point where we camp and make arrangements to hire a lorry to take us across the ferry to Rusinga. On 22 May we cross the ferry, about a five minute ride, to Rusinga. Rusinga is a rather large island which rises out of Lake Victoria. The ride from the ferry landing to our first stop, the Kiahera Formation, is about 45 minutes. On the way to Kiahera we pass the memorial to the late Luo leader Mr. Tom Mboya. The Kiahera Formation contains considerable fossilized plant materials and seeds which proved most useful for determining the Miocene habitat of *Proconsul*.

From Kiahera we proceed to Kaswanga (also spelled Kathwanga) where the mandible of "*Kenyapithecus africanus*" was found washed out in 1967. At Kaswanga we find (= see) the remains of what may be monkey teeth, ungulate teeth (perhaps from a buffalo), and some fresh water snails—all useful for determining the habitat.

As at Songhor the sites at Rusinga are usually water eroded. The beds at Rusinga are lowish hills of lava flows and some sediments. The geology of the island is now readily deciphered—at least by a trained geologist. There are plentiful supplies of mica (a member of the group of mineral silicates which crystallize in monoclinic forms that separate into very thin leaves) which have caused some problem in terms of dating the deposits.

Excerpt from my notes during a tour of Songhor and Rusinga Island.

RUSINGA ISLAND AND SONGHOR

A. Crocodile plates.

B. A rodent cranium.

C. A fragmented ungulate rib, Rusinga Island.

D. A tooth lying in situ. Adjacent to the tooth is a fragmented piece of limb bone, possibly from an ungulate.

standing erect on the hind feet. The hind limbs provide a suitable antecedent for subsequent evolutionary developments along the divergent lines of the brachiating specialization of later modern large apes and the limb structure of erect, bipedal hominids.

Much has been written about dryopithecine dentition, not only because teeth compose much of the skeletal asemblage but also because of their characteristic molar crown pattern. The dryopithecine Y-5 molar cusp pattern has been a hominoid trait that has persisted (with variations) for at least 20 million years.[5] Dryopithecine dentition, although typically pongidlike, shows some differences from that of modern apes (Figure 15-2). The incisors are relatively small, the tooth row tends to converge anteriorly (is wider at the back), and the upper molars show pongid traits. The canine and premolar teeth are typically apelike. When the teeth are occluded (when the upper and lower teeth contact), the canines overlap and are strongly projecting. The first lower premolar is sectorial (the medial surface is sheared away and thus accommodates the upper overlapping canine). The sectorial premolar may be a mechanism whereby canines maintain their sharpness and is not necesarily a response to large, overlapping canines.

Because of the pongid characteristics of the canines and premolars, some have questioned the validity of postulating a hominid derivation from a dryopithecine ancestry. The question arises: Are the dryopithecines the last common ancestor of humans and apes? Even though dryopithecine canines are rather large and the first premolar sectorial, subsequent evolutionary pressures could have reduced the canines and transformed the unicuspid, sectorial premolar to the hominid **bicuspid** (two-cusped) premolar. This viewpoint argues for a secondary reduction in canine size. As evidence, adherents of this viewpoint cite the fact that the newly erupted human canine may be quite sharply pointed and project beyond the level of adjacent teeth, and that the human canine has an unusually large root indicating some special function during its evolutionary history. They also cite fossil evidence showing a reduction in canine size between the Middle Pleistocene form *Homo erectus* and modern *Homo*.

Dryopithecine Phylogeny

Although dryopithecines were probably related to later apes, their locomotor patterns and habitat differed. Postcranial evidence suggests that *P. major* was more active and less terrestrial than living gorillas. There is nothing suggestive of a brachiating locomotor adaptation. *Proconsul africanus* appears ancestral to modern chimpanzees. According to Corruccini and Henderson (1978) palatofacial measurements of the Rusinga (*P. africanus*) and Moroto (*P. major*) specimens in comparison with monkeys and apes fail to support a special relationship between dryopithecines and extant pongids. This view is part of the growing skepticism (expressed by a number of paleontologists) concerning the relationship between dryopithecines and modern pongids. Dentally and cranially it is possible that changes in this lineage were connected with dietary changes and related to increasing body size. Postcranial remains indicate that *P. africanus* was a small, lightly built, arboreal quadruped, yet a quadruped in which arm-swinging was becoming a major component of its locomotor

[5]The Y-5 pattern is so designated because the molar surface sports five cusps separated by grooves in the form of a Y. This pattern is common to the lower molar teeth of fossil hominids. In modern hominids, however, there is frequently a reduction or absence of the fifth cusp (called the hypoconulid) and the formation of a + fissure pattern, that is, a +4 or +5 pattern. This is especially true of the second and third molars. Morris (1970) raises some doubts as to the efficiency of using the Y-5 as a diagnostic taxonomic character.

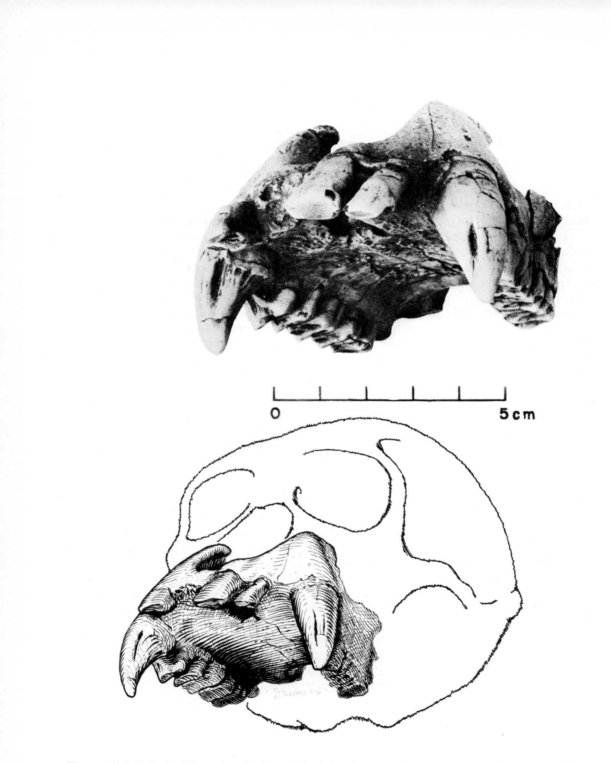

Figure 15-2. Palate of *Proconsul major*, called the Moroto palate after Moroto, Uganda, where it was found.

capacities. In the Miocene, gorilla and chimpanzee ancestors were probably small, lightly built and mainly arboreal creatures.

In size *P. nyanzae* is midway between *P. major* and *P. africanus*. The smallest *P. nyanzae* specimens overlap those of *P. africanus*, and the largest, those of *P. major*. In overall morphology *P. nyanzae* is closest to *P. major*, although there are some dental differences. *P. nyanzae* is abundant at Rusinga, but missing from other East African sites containing *P. major*. This may be a sampling error, or it may reflect a major habitat difference between the two.

The postcranial remains, if they belong to *P. nyanzae*, indicate that, as were other dryopithecines, they were relatively lightly built, actively arboreal, and quadrupedal. In 1967 Louis Leakey suggested that some postcranial remains associated with *P. nyanzae* should be attributed to *Kenyapithecus africanus*—which he considered an ancestral hominid. Many however, disagree with his assessment. At any rate, there have been numerous suggestions that *P. nyanzae* might be close to the hominid ancestral line.

The evolutionary relationship of the dryopithecines to subsequent hominoids is open to much controversy. For quite some time, the dryopithecines were considered to be the last common stock of the pongids and hominids. It was argued that various dryopithecine forms gave rise to modern pongids. It was also suggested that because of the shared Y-5 molar cusp pattern, combined with the suggestion that *Ramapithecus* was possibly a hominid, that one member of the dryopithecine lineage also led to the hominids via *Ramapithecus*. This view is now under severe attack, drawing its support from the questioning of the hominid status of *Ramapithecus* and from the evidence as presented by the immunological record (see Chapters 16 and 22). The original scheme, that is, that the dryopithecines gave rise to the hominids, will now be discussed; following this discussion is a newer, more acceptable scenario that suggests that the dryopithecines had little to do directly with the hominid lineage.

Dryopithecines as Hominid Ancestors

Presumably dryopithecines arose in Africa and then spread throughout the tropical rain forest then covering most of Europe and Central Asia. Paleontological evidence suggests that the radiation of the living hominids had already occurred in the Miocene. The morphological variation characteristic of the dryopithecines is important; because of the variation and because of minor living habits, the genus differentiated. Some dryopithecines adapted to a life in or near the trees. These may have led to the modern chimpanzee and gorilla. Some suggest that others went a different path and became hominids. The ape group eventually died out in Europe, presumably unable to adapt to shifting habitat conditions caused by slight cooling of the earth and perhaps being outcompeted for a dwindling food supply. Those in Africa survived.

The arugment for a dryopithecine ancestry of hominids suggests that the line leading to hominids forever left the trees and moved into the savanna-grasslands fringing the forests. They were preadapted for terrestrial life; they had good hand-eye coordination. When they became bipedal or semierect, their hands were freed to manipulate the environment and this eventually led to tool use. Their eyes were attuned to distinguishing things from the environment and for aiming weapons. The brain and nervous system were attuned to exploration. The new habitat bombarded them with new and exciting stimuli, forcing them to adapt to new conditions.

There are other suggestions as to how dryopithecine evolution proceeded. One viewpoint follows. Based on finds made in 1977 in Turkey, western China, and Pakistan, it has been suggested that the dryopithecine species from eastern Europe and Asia all share with *Ramapithecus* (the first form recognized as a hominid by some) such derived humanlike features as thick molar enamel, large molars in relation to body size, and heavily buttressed jaws as an adaptation to heavy chewing stresses.

Early African dryopithecines appear to have been forest dwellers. By approximately 17 million years ago at least one dryopithecine group entered Eurasia over a forest "corridor" where it adapted to a life in more open habitats. This environment required feeding on harsher food plants, leading to faster tooth wear. These early "ground apes," using Simons' terminology, developed thicker enamel and larger molars while retaining large front teeth. Members of this genus are known as *Sivapithecus* and they are found from Hungary to China.

In Eurasia, as well as in East Africa, one finds *Ramapithecus*. This form differs from *Sivapithecus* in having low-crowned canines, a trait shared with later hominids. *Gigantopithecus* occurs in Pakistani locales yielding remains of *Ramapithecus* and *Sivapithecus,* and differs from *Ramapithecus* in its huge jaws and canines.

One result of recent Miocene hominoid finds is the realization that they were a far more diverse group than originally assumed. Pilbeam et al. (1977) have recently uncovered three species of hominoids from the Potwar Plateau, Pakistan. These forms, known as *Sivapithecus, Gigantopithecus,* and *Ramapithecus,* are referred to as sivapithecids by Pilbeam. He argues that it is impossible to show that any of these is a hominid ancestor.

Pilbeam's analysis of these forms differs from previous interpretations. Previously, these forms were divided into two distinct groups, the hominids (e.g., *Ramapithecus*) and pongids (e.g., *Sivapithecus* and *Gigantopithecus*). (Not all agree that *Ramapithecus* is a hominid, however, and some, such as L. Leakey, argue that *Sivapithecus* might be a hominid. Others argue that *Gigantopithecus* is close to the hominid line). Many investigators also argue that once the pongid and hominid lines arose from a common ancestor they gradually evolved toward their present-day representatives.

The assumption that Miocene hominoids could be divided into two groups led to the assumption that simple markers, such as tooth-enamel thickness, could be used to classify the species. These markers now appear to be uninformative and possibly misleading. According to Pilbeam, Miocene hominoids shared features with both hominids and pongids and cannot be accommodated by a dichotomous classification scheme.

The sivapithecids appeared during the Miocene when some heavily forested areas gave way to mixed environments of dense forest, savanna woodlands, and open areas. Pilbeam argues that the sivapithecids differed from the earlier dryopithecids. Dryopithecids lived both before and during the Miocene in heavily forested regions of Africa and Europe. They may never have left these areas for the more open environments. The sivapithecids, by contrast, may have lived on the boundary between the forests and open areas and may have exploited both for their foodstuffs.

If this interpretation is correct, if it is true that sivapithecids appeared during the Miocene when forests gave way to mixed environments, what does this indicate about evolutionary relationships? Pilbeam argues that changes in feeding behavior, which are related to habitat changes, may be a key to understanding later stages of hominoid evolution. Miocene hominoids dwelling in mixed environments could have evolved from isolated populations of forest-dwelling dryopithecids in response to the changing environment in certain areas of Africa and Eurasia.

Pilbeam stresses that none of the three species of Miocene hominoids found in Pakistan resembles either pongids or modern hominids. The sivapithecids all have jaws and teeth similar to those of East African hominids living about 4 million years ago. The sivapithecids and later hominids have large jaws and cheek teeth that are large relative to the body size. In contrast, apes and forest-dwelling monkeys have small jaws and cheek teeth. The dryopithecids, which Pilbeam argues are ancestral to both the sivapithecids and modern pongids, have small cheek teeth and jaws.

How did the dryopithecids and sivapithecids become differentiated? Lovejoy (personal communication) suggests a birth-spacing mechanism as an explanation. He suggests that the sivapithecids were successful (e.g., they occupied more area and existed in greater numbers than other species) because they overcame the birth-spacing problem. Living nonhuman primate females rarely become pregnant while carrying dependent young. Those with long-term dependent young have a long period between births. This long period causes a problem for modern pongids. For example, modern chimpanzees give birth on the average of once every 5.6 years. Old World monkeys have lifespans comparable to that of apes, but they bear offspring every 2 or 3 years. Thus, monkeys are more prevalent than apes.

Lovejoy suggests that early hominoids gained a competitive advantage over other nonhuman primates because they overcame this birth-spacing problem. More than the demography of the early hominoids was affected by this development. Hominoids may have become bipedal partly as a response to carrying several dependent young, and having several dependent offspring may also have influenced hominoids to band together and develop a social organization for mutual support and protection.

Given these problems, one can speculate about the long-term consequences for this evolving lineage. For example, females might have been under more intense selection because of their mothering and care-taking roles. Perhaps females evolved the first bipedal mechanisms to accommodate this carrying of dependent young. Furthermore, using the sociobiologist's suggestion of kin selection, males may have been drawn more tightly into the social group to protect their genetic investment in their offspring. Other possible side-effects, such as the organization of tight female subgroups and the female's role as the bearer of cultural knowledge, are discussed in Chapter 21.

Aberrant Apes?

To complete this review of pongid evolution we turn to two forms whose ancestry is unclear. At one time or another both have been considered ancestral to modern hominids, a likelihood most now reject. One of the forms, *Oreopithecus bambolii,* or the "abominable coal man," derives from coal beds of Tuscany, Italy. The other form, *Gigantopithecus,* is considered by some to be a gigantic ape from China and North India.

Oreopithecus. *Oreopithecus* (ore = mountain) remains come from beds in Italy dated to about 10 million to 12 million years ago. Since its description in 1872, it has been labeled a hominid, pongid, or cercopithecoid. In 1954 it was labeled a hominid, and a search was conducted for more remains. In 1958 J. Hürzeler uncovered most of an intact skeleton of a young adult. *Oreopithecus* has always been a taxonomic problem because it has characteristics intermediate between monkeys, apes, and humans. *Oreopithecus* was approximately 4 feet tall and weighed about 88 pounds. Judging from the 1958 skeleton, it was probably the size of a medium-sized chimpanzee. The face is strikingly short (a hominid trait), resulting in projecting nasal bones, the latter of which is perhaps due to crushing. Above the eyes there is a thick bony ridge and the tooth row is parallel. Both are nonhuman traits. The upper canine is short and the premolars bicuspid—hominid traits.

The postcranial remains reflect monkey and ape characteristics, but the latter predominate. The arms were longer than the legs, a condition peculiar to habitual brachiators. The relative length of the arms compared to the legs (the intermembral index) is closest to that of the knuckle-walking gorilla.

There has been continual argument about the cranial capacity of *Oreopithecus*. The cranial capacity of the 1958 form has been estimated at between 276 and 529 cubic centimeters (cc). W. Straus, who studied the material in detail, feels an average of about 400 cc is most appropriate. Newer estimates place a figure of 200 cc as generous but even this would be a relatively large-sized brain for a relatively short, light animal.

Although its taxonomic position is conjectural, *Oreopithecus* has been described as a somewhat aberrant brachiating ape or an aberrant monkey. There is some controversial evidence in the foot and pelvis suggesting that the direct ancestors of *Oreopithecus* possessed some adaptations to erect bipedalism before adapting to an arboreal existence.

Gigantopithecus—A Gargantuan Hominid Ancestor? Of all fossil pongids, *Gigantopithecus* has had perhaps one of the most colorful histories; it has been called everything from an ape to a giant hominid. It has also been labeled the ancestor to the modern elusive "yeti," the abominable snowman. Early mention was made of *Gigantopithecus* by G. R. von Koenigswald in 1935 on the basis of some teeth found in a Chinese drugstore. (The Chinese collected fossilized teeth and bones, referred to as "dragon bones," which they ground and mixed into aphrodisiacs and other herbal medicines.) Since, other *Gigantopithecus* remains have come from India and Kwangsi Province, China. A number of lower jaw fragments and well over 1,000 isolated teeth now exist; no other skeletal parts are available. On the basis of the size of its teeth and jaws, some have judged that *Gigantopithecus* weighed more than 600 pounds and stood at least 6 feet tall. These figures are almost certainly inflated, however. It may have ranged in time from about 5 million to 9 million years ago in India to approximately 500,000 years ago in China.

The Chinese variety of *Gigantopithecus* received attention in 1955 when the Chinese paleontologist Pei found 47 teeth among a shipment of dragon bones. Tracing the teeth to their source, a cave in the face of a limestone cliff, three additional teeth were uncovered. A large mandible and teeth were found in an adjacent farmer's field.

In 1968 a *Gigantopithecus* mandible was uncovered in the Siwalik Hills about 200 miles from New Dehli from deposits dating to 5 million to 9 million years ago. The form was considered to be a young animal, judging from the amount of enamel wear on the teeth. The molar teeth of *Gigantopithecus* contrast with those of modern apes; the molars of the former are composed mostly of enamel. The characteristic *Gigantopithecus* molar teeth are considered to be an adaptation to heavy chewing of abrasive foodstuffs. Mandibular shape and incisor size also support the view that *Gigantopithecus* was a heavy chewer.

Jolly (1970) attempted to explain *Gigantopithecus* dental characteristics by comparing its teeth with those of the gelada, *Theropithecus gelada*. Jolly calls his explanation the "T-complex" or seed-eating hypothesis and feels that "T-complex" traits are functionally related to and are an evolutionary product of a specialized diet. In this diet large quantities of comparatively small, tough morsels such as grass, seeds, stems, and rhizomes are ingested and prepared by powerful and continuous chewing with the molar teeth. "T-complex" dental characteristics include the following: the molar teeth are high-crowned and largely composed of dentine. As the animal grows older the teeth become packed together in the jaws in a process called **mesial drift,** which is associated with strenuous chewing. Other characteristics include changes in jaw structure, vertical implantation of incisors, and reduced canines.

In formulating the seed-eating hypothesis, Jolly (1970) noted the existence of a number of morphological and functional parallels between early hominids and the gelada. These parallels include the following:

1. Both occupied a grass land—open country habitat.
2. Both possess reduced incisors and canines relative to the premolars and molars.
3. Both show crowding of the molars and the presence of interproximal wear.
4. In both forms the anterior of the temporalis muscle is forward on the frontal bone, maximizing the power and efficiency of the muscle.
5. Both forms have a robust and thick mandible under the molar teeth.

Gigantopithecus probably originated in India and spread north and east. If the dating is correct, the Indian predates the Chinese variety by millions of years. The best candidate for an ancestral position to *Gigantopithecus* is the Indian dryopithecine, *S. indicus*. To what forms was *Gigantopithecus* ancestral? Most argue that *Gigantopithecus* represents a side branch in pongid evolution, a pongid line adapted to a special mode of feeding. If Jolly is right, the lineage leading to hominids independently adapted a similar mode of feeding during the first 10 million years of its evolutionary history. Dental resemblances between the two are accounted for by independent similar adaptations to similar habitats and not by a phylogenetic relationship. In the end differences rather than similarities between the forms became significant.

The interpretation of pongid evolution is not without controversy. Most paleontologists are unwilling to admit pongid ancestors very much prior to the early Oligocene geological epoch. Our major Oligocene evidence comes from the Egyptian Fayum as *Oligopithecus,* the oldest remains; *Aeolopithecus,* considered ancestral to Asian gibbons, and *Aegyptopithecus,* ancestral perhaps to chimpanzees. Another form, *Propliopithecus,* is probably an ancestral pongid; in fact it may be ancestral to *Aegyptopithecus.*

Oligocene pongids are generally regarded as ancestral to Miocene dryopithecines, among which we may find ancestors of modern chimpanzees, gorillas, and possibly orangutans. The dryopithecines were a widespread group inhabiting the then tropical forests (and possibly savanna woodlands) of Europe, Africa, and Asia. It was once widely accepted that one of the dryopithecines, perhaps *Proconsul nyanzae,* was an ancestral candidate to subsequent hominids. However, this is questionable.

Paleoenvironmental data suggest that many of the most important stages of primate evolution occurred within a mixed, or mosaic, environmental context. The first appearance of the primates occurred within a subtropical or semitropical environment in the middle latitudes. The warm climate prevailing in the middle latitudes during much of the Tertiary favored primate dispersal at comparatively high latitudes. Oligocene Fayum primates probably lived in a mosaic of forest and parklands, seasonally flooded by a large river and its delta. East African early Miocene hominoid remains came from humid drainage basins including tropical forests and mosaics of forest and savanna.

Two controversial primates appear during the Pliocene epoch, *Gigantopithecus* in India (and later in Pleistocene China) and *Oreopithecus* in Italy. Both have at one time or another been considered hominids. *Gigantopithecus* has had a particularly colorful history as a gigantic hominid ancestor, ape ancestor, or ancestor of the abominable snowman. While most consider both forms aberrant apes, some refer *Gigantopithecus* close to the hominid ancestry.

Bibliography

Andrews, P., and Tobien, H. 1977. New Miocene locality in Turkey with evidence on the origin of *Ramapithecus* and *Sivapithecus*. *Nature* 268:699-702.

Ankel, F. 1972. Vertebrate morphology of fossil and extant primates. In *The functional and evolutionary biology of primates,* edited by R. Tuttle, pp. 223-40. Chicago: Aldine-Atherton.

Beadnell, H. 1905. *The topology and geology of the Fayum province of Egypt.* Cairo: Survey Department.

Bishop, W., Miller, J., and Fitch, F. 1969. New potassium-argon determination relevant to the Miocene fossil mammal sequence in East Africa. *American Journal of Science* 267:669.

Butzer, K. 1977. Environment, culture and human evolution. *American Scientist* 65:572-84.

Cachel, S. 1976. The beginnings of the Catarrhinae. In *Primate functional morphology and evolution,* edited by R. Tuttle, pp. 23-26. The Hague: Mouton.

Campbell, B., and Bernor, R. 1976. The origin of the Hominidae—Africa or Asia? *Journal of Human Evolution* 5:441-54.

Chesters, K. 1957. The Miocene flora of Rusinga Island, Lake Victoria, Kenya. *Paleontographica* 101:30.

Clark, W. Le Gros, and Leakey, L. 1951. *The Miocene Hominidae of East Africa.* London: British Museum (Natural History).

Corruccini, R., and Henderson, A. 1978. Palato-facial comparison of *Dryopithecus (Proconsul)* with extant catarrhines. *Primates* 19:35-44.

Evernden, J., Savage, D., Curtis, G., and James, G. 1964. Potassium-argon dates and the Cenozoic mammalian chronology of North America. *American Journal of Science* 262:145.

Fleagle, J., and Simons, E. 1978. *Micropithecus clarki,* a small ape from the Miocene of Uganda. *American Journal of Physical Anthropology* 49:427-40.

Fleagle, J., Simons, E., and Conroy, G. 1975. Ape limb bone from the Oligocene of Egypt. *Science* 189:135-36.

Gingerich, P. 1977. Correlation of tooth size and body size in living hominoid primates, with a note on the relative brain size of *Aegyptopithecus* and *Proconsul*. *American Journal of Physical Anthropology* 47:395-98.

Gingerich, P., and Schoeninger, M. 1977. The fossil record and primate phylogeny. *Journal of Human Evolution* 6:483-505.

Gregory, W., Hellman, M., and Lewis, G. 1938. *Fossil anthropoids of the Yale-Cambridge Indian Expedition of 1935.* Carnegie Institute of Washington Publication 495.

Groves, C. 1967. Ecology and taxonomy of the gorilla. *Nature* 213:890.

—————. 1970. *Gigantopithecus* and the mountain gorilla. *Nature* 226:973.

Hamilton, W., Whybrow, P., and McClure, H. 1978. Fauna of fossil mammals from the Miocene of Saudi Arabia. *Nature* 274:248-49.

Jolly, C. 1970. The seed-eaters: a new model of hominid differentiation based on a baboon analogy. *Man* 5:1.

Kinzey, W. 1970. Rates of evolutionary change in the hominid canine teeth. *Nature* 225:296.

—————. 1971. Evolution of the human canine tooth. *American Anthropology* 73:680.

Kolata, G. 1977. Human evolution: hominoids of the Miocene. *Science* 197:244-46.

Kurtén, B. 1972. *Not from the apes.* New York: Pantheon.

Leakey, L. 1967. An early Miocene member of the Hominidae. *Nature* 213:155.

Morris, D. 1970. On deflecting wrinkles and the *Dryopithecus* pattern in human mandibular molars. *American Journal of Physical Anthropology* 32:97.

Napier, J., and Davis, P. 1959. *The forelimb skeleton and associated remains of Proconsul africanus.* London: British Museum (Natural History).

Osborn, H. 1907. The Fayum expedition of the American Museum. *Science* 25:513.

Oxnard, C. 1967. The functional anatomy of the primate shoulder as revealed by comparative anatomical, osteometric and discriminant function techniques. *American Journal of Physical Anthropology* 26:219.

Pilbeam, D. 1967. Man's earliest ancestors. *Science Journal* 3:47.

_____. 1968. *Tertiary Pongidae of East Africa: evolutionary relationships and taxonomy.* Bulletin 31, Peabody Museum of Natural History. New Haven: Yale University.

_____. 1970. *Gigantopithecus* and the origins of the Hominidae. *Nature* 225:516.

_____. 1972. *The ascent of man.* New York: Macmillan.

Pilbeam, D., Barry, J., Meyer, G., Ibrahim Shah, S., Pickford, M., Bishop, W., Thomas, H., and Jacobs, I. 1977. Geology and paleontology of Neogene strata of Pakistan. *Nature* 270:684-89.

Pilbeam, D., Meyer, G., Badgley, C., Rose, M., Pickford, M., Behrensmeyer, A., and Ibrahim Shah. I. 1977. New hominoid primates from the Siwaliks of Pakistan and their bearing on hominoid evolution. *Nature* 27:689-95.

Pilbeam, D., and Simons, E. 1971. Humerus of *Dryopithecus* from Saint Gaudens, France. *Nature* 229:406.

_____. 1971. A gorilla-sized ape from the Miocene of India. *Science* 173:23.

Robinson, J. 1972. *Early hominid posture and locomotion.* Chicago: University of Chicago Press.

St. Hoyme, L., and Koritzer, R. 1971. Significance of canine wear in pongid evolution. *American Journal of Physical Anthropology* 35:145.

Simons, E. 1959. An anthropoid frontal bone from the Fayum Oligocene of Egypt: the oldest skull fragment of a higher primate. *American Museum of Natural History Novitiates* 1976:1.

_____. 1962. Two new primate species from the African Oligocene. *Postilla* 64:1-12.

_____. 1965a. The hunt for Darwin's third ape. *Medical Opinion and Review,* November, p. 74.

_____. 1965b. New fossil apes from Egypt and the initial differentiation of the Hominoidea. *Nature* 205:135.

_____. 1967. The earliest apes. *Scientific American* 216:28-35.

_____. 1968. Hunting the "dawn apes" of Africa. *Discovery* 4:19.

_____. 1972. *Primate evolution: an introduction to man's place in nature.* New York: Macmillan.

Simons, E., and Chopra, S. 1969. A new species of *Gigantopithecus* (Hominoidea, Primates) from North India with some comments on its relationship to earliest hominids. *Postilla* 138:1-18.

Simons, E., and Pilbeam, D. 1965. Preliminary revision of the Dryopithecinae (Pongidae, Anthropoidea). *Folia Primatologica* 3:81.

Smith, E. and Pirie, P. 1973. Tooth size and body size—Is there a correlation? Paper presented to 72nd American Anthropological Association, New Orleans.

Szalay, F. 1972. Paleobiology of the earliest primates. In *The functional and evolutionary biology of primates,* edited by R. Tuttle, pp. 3-35. Chicago: Aldine-Atherton.

Tattersall, I. 1970. *Man's ancestors: An introduction to primate and human evolution.* London: Murray.

van Couvering, J., and Miller, J. 1969. Miocene stratigraphy and age determinations, Rusinga Island, Kenya. *Nature* 221:628-32.

von Koenigswald, G. 1967. Miocene Cercopithecoidae and Oreopithecoidae from the Miocene of East Africa. In *Fossil vertebrates of Africa,* Vol. 2, edited by L. Leakey, pp. 39-51. London: Academic Press.

Weidenreich, F. 1945. Giant early man from Java and south China. *Anthropological Papers of the American Museum of Natural History* 40:1-134.

Wolpoff, M. 1971. Interstitial wear. *American Journal of Physical Anthropology* 34:205.

Chapter 16

Ramapithecus: An Early Hominid or a Pongid?

This chapter reviews the evidence about a fossil named *Ramapithecus*. Although known largely from a few jaw fragments and teeth, *Ramapithecus* was, and still is (by a few paleontologists) considered to be the first evidence of a hominid in the fossil record. That view, however, is widely challenged.

Ramapithecus remains have been found in a variety of sites dating between 8 and 14 million years ago. Most *Ramapithecus* remains come from Europe, Turkey, northern India, Pakistan, and from Kenya. The remains indicate a small creature weighing about 31 pounds.

We will discuss the geographical distribution and habitat of *Ramaithecus*. The conclusion to be drawn in the chapter is that *Ramapithecus* is not the ancestral hominid as was once widely accepted. This conclusion is drawn from the morphological evidence as well as from new viewpoints suggested by the biochemical evidence of similarities in blood proteins and of DNA in modern humans and chimpanzees. The close similarity between these forms suggests a later divergence of humans from apes than is now possible if *Ramapithecus* is an ancestral hominid.

Original Discovery and Description

In 1934 G. Edward Lewis described a fossil primate found in northern India. Although Lewis classified this fossil as a pongid, he emphasized that it displayed human traits. Little attention was paid to Lewis' original description. Later, Lewis wrote (1937:145), "While the Siwalik genus *Ramapithecus* and the South African *Australopithecus* (which was described 13 years earlier, and dismissed by most as a pongid) are still apes, by definition, they are almost on the human threshold in their human known anatomical characters." It was not until the 1960s, primarily through the work of Elwyn Simons, that *Ramapithecus* began to receive serious consideration as a possible hominid. Simons was supported by Louis Leakey, who offered his opinions on the basis of his new finds in Kenya, East Africa.

Geographical Distribution and Econiche

For a while it looked as though *Ramapithecus* was a primate genus geographically restricted to India and Pakistan. In 1960, however, Louis Leakey reported the discovery of fossil maxillae, parts of which contained teeth, from the Fort Ternan site in Kenya, about 40 miles east of Lake Victoria. This is the best-dated *Ramapithecus* site. Biotite (a common constituent of crystalline rock) collected from above the site is dated at 14 million years ago (Evernden and Curtis, 1965).

African *Ramapithecus* = *Kenyapithecus* of Louis Leakey

Fort Ternan, 18 May 1975

The drive to Fort Ternan from Baringo took approximately six hours over some rather rough dirt roads. In order to locate the site we stop at Fort Ternan Station, a town along the rail line. Fort Ternan Station is primarily a row of wooden frame stores. At the site we meet with the security guard, Mr. Thuo, who, because of Richard Leakey's kind letter of introduction, allows us to camp.

Fort Ternan site sits on a hill overlooking extensively cultivated fields of cane and corn. The original owner, Mr. Wicker, left a few years ago. It was Mr. Wicker who contacted Louis Leakey and first reported the existence of fossiliferous remains. The site is an excavation in the side of the hill surrounded by a number of test pits which cut across and run up and down the hill. A fair amount of largely fragmented bone still exists in the "garbage" silt taken from the main site and the test pits.

The main site is a horseshoe-shaped area approximately 40 feet wide at the mouth and 15 feet wide at the back. Since the hill slopes, there is no average depth from the top of the hill to the floor of the excavation; however, the highest point is approximately 18 feet. Leakey's original site is now the bottom floor. The site recently dug by Peter Andrews is still covered because of the dirt falls from the hill. The *Ramapithecus* bed stands out as a clearly visible whitish-gray lens. The *Ramapithecus* bed contains considerable amounts of animal bones including elephant, lion, and antelope. This fauna is useful in reconstructing the habitat. There is a considerable amount of fossilized faunal remains scattered about the site.

At the top of the hill one can recognize a second bed. This postdates the *Ramapithecus* bed and contains considerable faunal remains. To the right of the main excavation area is another smaller excavation, in which nothing has been found.

Excerpt from my notes during my visit to Fort Ternan.

Fossil materials referred to the genus *Ramapithecus* have also been recovered from southern Germany and in north-central Spain. More recently *Ramapithecus* mandibular remains have been described from Greece and date from 8 million to 12 million years ago, or even a little earlier. The discovery of *Ramapithecus* material from Hungary (Figure 16-1) was announced by Kretzoi (1975). In 1973 a mandible of *Ramapithecus* was unearthed near Candir, some 40 miles northeast of Ankara, Turkey. *Ramapithecus* material is also known from China on the basis of five fossilized teeth dating to 10 million years ago. *Ramapithecus* seems to have had a rather widespread geographical distribution (Table 16-1). Although the exact nature of its habitat is still unclear, there are indications that *Ramapithecus* moved in both the savannas and the forest.

Ramapithecus material from India comes from the Chinji and Nagri formations which, according to faunal analysis, date from 10 to 12 million or 12 to 14 million years ago. The habitat of the Indian *Ramapithecus* has been the subject of debate. Tattersall (1969a, 1975) sug-

FORT TERNAN

A. The landscape surrounding the Fort Ternan site.

B. Looking into the Fort Ternan excavation pit.

C. The Fort Ternan excavation pit. Note the stratigraphy which is clearly visible on the wall.

D. A wall near the "Kenyapithecus" locality.

E. Fossilized faunal remains lying at the "Kenyapithecus" locality.

F. Fossilized bone at Fort Ternan. The bones are probably from the limb of an ungulate.

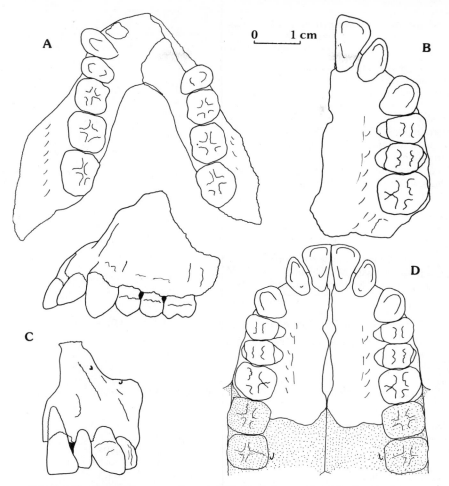

Figure 16-1. (A) *Sivapithecus alpani (Ramapithecus?).* **(B)** *Rudapithecus hungaricus (Ramapithecus?).* **(C)** *Rudapithecus hungaricus (Ramapithecus?).* **(D)** Occlusal view of reconstructed palate (stippled area is reconstructed). *Rudapithecus hungaris (Ramapithecus?).* All are from Hungary.

gests that the habitat may have consisted of tropical forests interspersed with broad rivers and trees. Tattersall's reconstruction is based on the faunal assemblage supposedly associated with *Ramapithecus,* very little of which he feels belong to savanna-adapted forms. Tattersall also notes that soil sediments indicate a humid, tropical climate with heavy seasonal rainfall, resulting in short, destructive floods and wide, shifting rivers flowing through heavily forested flat country with numerous water bodies and a relatively small number of open clearings. Although there were forests during the Chinji, Tattersall feels they were more broken by the succeeding Dhok Pathan period. Simons and Tattersall suggest that *Ramapithecus* lived in a predominantly forested habitat. They argue (1971:54) that early hominids " . . . were first tempted to the forest floor by food items of high nutritive content which occurred there. Primary among these would have been grains, tubers, roots, and possibly meat."

Table 16-1. Some Major *Ramapithecus* Materials

India and Pakistan

Right maxillary fragment with premaxillae and dentition.
Mandibular portions with molars intact.
Right and left mandibular rami.
Right maxillae.
Upper first molar.
Maxillary fragment with three molars.
Left mandibular ramus with P_3^a through M_3.
Mandibular fragment.
Left mandibular fragment with P_4 through M^3.
Partial mandible with roots of P^3 through M_3.

China

Five lower teeth.

Africa (All from Fort Ternan, Kenya)

Left maxillary fragment with canine roots, P^3 and crowns of P^4 through M^2.
Right maxillary fragment with M^1, M^2, and roots of M^2.
Mandibular fragment—left body of horizontal ramus.

Europe

Right mandibular fragment with M_2 (Greece).   Upper molar (Germany).

Kretzoi (1975) reports the following material from Hungary:
a. 1967—mandibular ramus
b. 1968—mandible
c. 1972—M1
d. 1974—left maxilla and palate, M^2, left maxilla, M^3, and corpus and fragments of the left mandible
e. 1975—M3.

He further lists the following postcranial materials:

a. distal fragment of left humerus
b. caput of left femur
c. distal end of left tibia
d. proximal end of left tibia
e. left astragalus
f. distal part of phalanx I
g. medial fragments of phalanx I
h. distal parts of phalanx II

Mandible (Candir, Turkey)

^{a}P = premolar, M = molar. Subscript number denotes tooth in mandible (lower jaw); superscript number denotes tooth in maxilla (upper jaw); number neither subscripted nor superscripted denotes tooth for which jaw is undetermined. For example, P_3 = a third premolar from mandible; M^2 = a second molar from maxilla; M1 = a first molar, jaw undetermined.

According to Butzer (1977), the late Miocene Nagri beds yield evidence of marked seasonal waterflow. Associated floral and faunal remains belong to fringing forests and mosaics of open woodlands and savanna. Butzer argues that the evidence shows that early and mid-Miocene hominids were found in complex mosaic environments. This situation should have favored ecological diversity and adaptive radiation among the rapidly evolving forms sharing overlapping geographical ranges.

Simons (1977) suggests that much of Eurasia 10 to 12 million years ago was covered with forest. Since this forest cover was not tropical, there was no yearlong fruit production and continuous vegetative renewal common to the forests where modern pongids dwell. In this environment large Miocene pongids might have experienced food shortages. Perhaps there was a tendency to pursue an alternate food strategy—foraging on the ground and along the edges of the forest for small, tough foods such as nuts or roots. This diet would have provided pressures for the survival of individuals with robust jaws and thickened tooth enamel (such as is postulated in Jolly's "T'complex").

Faunal remains associated with *Ramapithecus* from Turkey include forms at home in both the forest and savanna. The faunal assemblage from Greece indicates a savanna-and-steppe habitat; here too one finds *Ramapithecus* but no pongids. The situation is different in Hungary, India, and Pakistan, where the fauna and flora show elements of a subtropical and warm temperature niche. In these areas *Ramapithecus* and the pongids *Gigantopithecus* and *Sivapithecus* appear together.

Some of the best ecological information comes from East Africa. During the Early Miocene, tropical rain forests extended far eastward into Kenya. Toward the end of this period, volcanos formed in Kenya, particularly in the area of Fort Ternan from where we have the oldest *Ramapithecus* remains. The slopes remained forested, but the base of the mountains had a savanna environment.

Faunal remains at Fort Ternan belong to four major environmental groups: (1) a savanna group, including elephants and giraffes, (2) an aquatic group, which probably lived in a nearby stream, (3) a forest group, including squirrels and pongids of the dryopithecine group, and (4) a group that seems to have lived in the area between the forest and the savanna. *Ramapithecus* is included in this last group of animals from a mixed environment.

Morphological Considerations

There has been a considerable amount of analysis of the *Ramapithecus* remains, the vast majority of which consists of jaws and teeth (Figure 16-2). Many of the earlier taxonomic positions were flawed because interpretations were made in the absence of any consideration of the fossil or modern hominid condition, as well as little consideration of the pongid condition.

At least 13 specimens of *Ramapithecus* are recognized; 11 belong to *R. punjabicus* and 2 to *R. wickeri* (Conroy and Pilbeam, 1975; Khatri, 1975). *Ramapithecus* resembles *Sivapithecus* in many ways. Indeed, some paleontologists place the ramapithecines within the genus *Sivapithecus* (Chapter 15). The taxonomic position of *Ramapithecus* and indications of its lifestyle are based on the analysis and interpretation of its dental mechanics. It was Simons (1961, 1964, 1968, 1977) and Louis Leakey (1968, 1970) who noted a number of *Ramapithecus* dental traits that they felt indicated to its hominid status. For example, Simons (1964:530) argued as follows:

> These hominids were not feeding and fighting the way apes feed and fight . . . They certainly could not have used their small teeth as effectively as apes in shredding up plants and in aggressive displays against predators. Instead it seems likely that their hands were playing a major role in food-getting and defense. Furthermore, the extensive use of the hands implies that they walked upright, although we need a great deal more evidence before we can prove that beyond doubt.

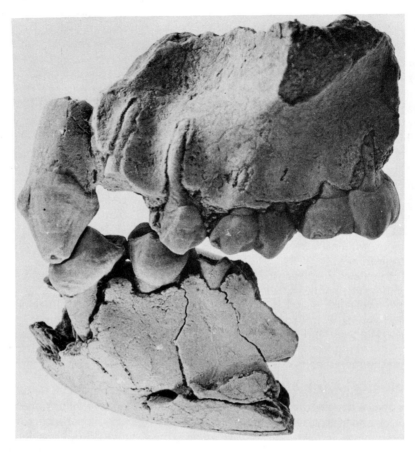

Figure 16-2. *Ramapithecus* mandible and maxilla.

Tattersall (1975:28) argued as follows:

> . . . the dental mechanisms quite evidently played a crucial role in the hominid/pongid divergence, and *Ramapithecus* falls quite unequivocally on the hominid side of the divide. Irrespective of what its mode of locomotion or other unknown characteristics may have been, *Ramapithecus* as known, had crossed the hominid threshold in the critical area of dental adaptation. . .

A number of characteristics led many to conclude that *Ramapithecus* had a short, flat, and deep face. The upper and lower jaws were heavy, the anterior dentition (incisors and canines) was reduced, and the size of the molar occlusal areas was increased. These features, in conjunction with advanced occlusal and interproximal wear, led to the conclusion that the dental apparatus of *Ramapithecus* was that of a powerful chewer.

One characteristic diagnostic of hominids is that the canine teeth in both sexes are low-crowned and shaped similar to incisors. The evidence as to the size and shape of the

Ramapithecus canines is ambiguous for the major materials consist only of a visible socket in some of the Asian and European jaws and one preserved canine from Fort Ternan. Compared with the molars, the Fort Ternan canine looks small, perhaps merely because the molars are large. Furthermore, since we have no idea whether the specimen belonged to a male or female, it tells us little about whether the canine was sexually dimorphic.

A possible explanation for the chewing apparatus of *Ramapithecus* is that *Ramapithecus* occupied an econiche outside the forest where it foraged on the tough foods of the savanna. Other than clues based on its dental apparatus, however, nothing definitive can be said about its status or lifeways. This is a problem because in addition to dental features, other derived features characterize the later hominids—in particular a pelvis and hind limb adapted to bipedalism. There is no evidence to argue conclusively for the locomotor adaptation of *Ramapithecus*.

Louis Leakey (1968) argued that he had recovered the postcranial remains of a form he called *Kenyapithecus africanus* from Rusinga Island and Songhor, Kenya. Leakey claimed that this form was a representative of the earliest ancestral hominid group. However, since most paleontologists argue that *K. africanus* is nothing more than one of the dryopithecines, these postcranial remains are little help in reconstructing *Ramapithecus'* locomotor patterns.

Tattersall (1975) has argued that *Ramapithecus* was primarily arboreal in its morphology and behavior, and perhaps moved through the trees in much the same way as modern orangutans. As noted earlier, however, both he and Simons argue that most, if not all, of its food was obtained at ground level. Perhaps *Ramapithecus* is a transitional form from an arboreal to a terrestrial habitat.

Statements about *Ramapithecus* based on the present material are further complicated by the fact that *Ramapithecus* was not the only Miocene primate to show superficial hominidlike traits in its jaws and teeth. The chimpanzee-sized form *Sivapithecus* and the much larger *Gigantopithecus* (Chapter 15) are found with *Ramapithecus* in both Asia and Europe. Remains of both *Sivapithecus* and *Gigantopithecus* clearly suggest that these forms, as well as *Ramapithecus,* may have had a similar adaptation to open country life.

Taxonomic Status

Because of the scanty remains, there is a vigorous controversy as to the taxonomic status of *Ramapithecus*. For a while, many argued that *Ramapithecus* was the first example of the hominid lineage in the fossil record and that it was derived from some member of the dryopithecines. Not everyone agreed with this position, however, and reservations were expressed throughout the 1970s. For example, Robinson (1972:255) stated:

> . . . examination of the *Ramapithecus* material . . . has convinced me that there is not one specifically hominid feature known in this form and that in all respects it is more pongid than hominid. I do not believe that it is a hominid or that it was ancestral to hominids . . . let it suffice here to say that the canine, upper incisor, P^3, the upper precanine diastema, and the nature of the wear on the upper and lower teeth all indicate closer resemblance to pongids than to hominids.

With the growing acceptance of the time scale presented by the immunological evidence (Chapter 22), a more complete fossil record, and further analysis of the remains, there has been a continual review of the taxonomic status of *Ramapithecus*. A consensus is emerging that stresses the nonhominid features of *Ramapithecus*. Following are the major points on both sides of the controversy.

Ramapithecus *as a Hominid*. Simons (1977) published a review of the *Ramapithecus* material in which he argued that *Ramapithecus* evolved from an earlier dryopithecine lineage. Dryopithecines also gave rise to two other genera: *Sivapithecus* and *Gigantopithecus*. These three genera differed from one another largely in facial size. *Sivapithecus* and *Gigantopithecus* both have large faces whereas *Ramapithecus* has a small face. However, there are resemblances between the three; for example, all have cheek teeth with thick enamel. While such commonality may indicate the relatedness of the three genera, it may also reflect similar responses to similar environmental conditions.

The dryopithecine group with the closest ties to *Ramapithecus* seems to be *Sivapithecus*. Louis Leakey recognized this similarity as early as 1968, when he suggested that the Indian and African *Sivapithecus* stood in a close phylogenetic relationship to *Ramapithecus*.

Simons (1977) discusses the morphological links between *Ramapithecus* and the later hominids. It was once thought that hominids did not possess a simian shelf (a torus or horizontal ridge of bone projecting inward from the inside of the mandible). Whenever a form was found possessing a shelf it was placed among the nonhuman primates. However, it was later realized that shelflike ridges are present in the mandibles of both *Ramapithecus* and especially the robust form of *Australopithecus* (see also Frayer, 1974) as well as in gorillas and chimpanzees. Furthermore, the mandibles of both *Ramapithecus* and *Australopithecus* are buttressed against heavy chewing stresses by not one shelf but two. The presence or absence of a shelflike ridge as a diagnostic characteristic for differentiating hominids from pongids is apparently useless.

The dental arcade of extant pongids is generally U-shaped and the two sides of the jaw are parallel. In Miocene apes, however, the arcade is V-shaped and the two sides of the jaw diverge in the rear. The dental arcade of most *australopithecus* specimens is also recognized as being V-shaped. The dental arcade of modern hominids is neither U- nor V-shaped but more semicircular in outline. Therefore, both the semicircular arcade of modern *Homo* and the U-shaped arcade of modern pongids presumably arose from a V-shaped form (Frayer, 1974).

The mandibles of *Australopithecus* and *Ramapithecus* are about as thick, from the cheek to the tongue side, in the molar region as they are deep from top to bottom. This robusticity contrasts with the modern pongid mandible. The molar teeth of both *Ramapithecus* and *Australopithecus* convey the same impression of robusticity. The molars are large and flat, and when viewed from above they possess a rounded outline. In contrast to dryopithecines (excluding *Sivapithecus*) and modern chimpanzees and gorillas, they have thick enamel.

The first and second molars of *Ramapithecus* and *Australopithecus* show differential wear, indicating that the eruption of these permanent teeth was separated by a considerable length of time. Simons suggests that this may be related to a slowing of the maturation rate, which would have allowed more time for learning. Frayer (1974) and Greenfield (1979) have doubts.

Simons states that *Ramapithecus* and *Australopithecus* also shared characteristics of the ascending ramus of the mandible. (However, so do a number of other forms.) The rami of both forms are typically aligned more at a right angle than those found in modern hominids and pongids. The rami also seem to have been proportionately higher. The front of the ramus, the coronoid process, is shifted slightly forward with respect to the cheek teeth. This shift is probably correlated with changes in the maxillae and lower face. Simons argues that the similarity of traits in *Ramapithecus* and *Australopithecus* must have some meaning.

There are resemblances between *Ramapithecus* and the first members of the genus *Homo*. Some members of *H. erectus*, for example, "Pithecanthropus" IV and Sangiran II from Java, show some similarities to *Ramapithecus.* The maxillary canines of Sangiran II are comparatively large. Moreover, whereas many *Australopithecus* premolars are "molarized," those of Sangiran II are not. The maxillary teeth of Sangiran II overlapped the teeth of the lower jaw to such an extent that they caused wear facets to appear on the opposing canine and the mandibular first premolar (P$_3$). There is also evidence of a small diastema.

For many years the diastema in "Pithecanthropus" IV and Sangiran II was viewed as an anomaly. However, one of the best new Lower Pleistocene finds from Ethiopia shows a diastema and the fit of the upper teeth closely resembles that of *Ramapithecus.*

Simons suggests that the simplest way to resolve the complex relationships that the dental adaptations suggest is to postulate that the hominid stock ancestral both to primitive *Homo* and *Australopithecus* resembled *Ramapithecus* more closely than did later *Australopithecus* representatives. The resemblance centers on the possession of large canines. Louis Leakey suggested an alternative, postulating that *Homo* and *Australopithecus* branched independently and directly from *Ramapithecus.* A third suggestion, incompatible with the evidence Simons reviews, is that *Ramapithecus* and other hominids emerged independently from the parental stock of Miocene apes.

Wolpoff (1980) has summarized the argument for *Ramapithecus* as a hominid as follows. He notes that the ramapithecines are at the right place and time to be hominid ancestors. Their morphological distinctions from the earlier dryopithecines either parallel the later hominids if they are not ancestral to hominids, or foreshadow them if they are ancestral to later hominids. Wolpoff notes that this provides circumstantial evidence that the later hominids originated among the ramapithecines and states (1980:123), "The fact is that if the hominids did not originate among the ramapithecines, no other potential ancestral form is known after the middle Pliocene."

Ramapithecus *as a Nonhominid*. Simons' arguments nowithstanding, the number of paleontologists questioning the supposed hominid status of *Ramapithecus* continues to increase. Simons (1968) notes that there are two major alternatives. First, *Ramapithecus* may be some sort of relatively small-faced ape that is only coincidently morphologically similar to the hominids. In this regard, Frayer (1974) and Greenfield (1979) both argue that the total morphological pattern of *Ramapithecus* is quite similar to fossil and some extant pongids. They add that very few morphological and metrical details of *Ramapithecus* closely align this genus with the hominids. Table 16-2 compares various traits of *Ramapithecus* used to argue for hominid status along with Frayer's own reappraisal of these traits.

Simons also notes that there is not now enough material to judge conclusively whether or not *Ramapithecus* is a hominid. This problem was met by referring to *Ramapithecus* as a "dental hominid," taking into consideration that the majority of the material is dental evidence. Pilbeam (1972) noted that the question of whether or not *Ramapithecus* is a hominid depends on where one chooses to recognize the split of the hominids from the hominid-pongid stock. This boundary is likely to be arbitrary, and of the three sets of criteria used to differentiate hominids from pongids, cranial features, dentition, and postcranial materials, primarily dental remains of *Ramapithecus* are known.

As noted, some of the dental traits of *Ramapithecus* can be related to dietary patterns. Jolly's "T-complex" (described in Chapter 15) might help explain the tooth pattern of *Ramapithecus.* If so, *Ramapithecus* might simply be considered a savanna-adapted, small-object feeder. *Ramapithecus'* dental structure might not reflect a phylogenetic relationship to hominids, but perhaps is simply a parallel development. However, both Wolpoff (1971) and Groves (1970) raise questions about the heuristic value of the "T-complex." Wolpoff, for

Table 16-2. Frayer's (1974) Reappraisal of *Ramapithecus*

Trait	Argument for Hominid Status	Frayer's Reappraisal
Dental arcade	Parabolic	Can no longer be considered a reasonable reconstruction. Indian specimens show U-shaped arch; African specimens show V-shaped arch.
Palate depth	Deep, well arched	Palate depth does not discriminate *Ramapithecus* from *Dryopithecus* but rather underscores interrelationships between African and Indian *Dryopithecus* and *Ramapithecus*.
Incisor angle	Vertically implanted	Roots not vertically implanted; whether crowns are vertical or not is difficult to determine.
Canine diastema	None present	Recent reconstruction indicates its presence.
Lower premolars	Homomorphic	Lower P_3 is sectorial.
Simian shelf	Absent	Present.
Premaxillary area	Relatively short compared to extinct and extant pongids	Lies within the range of the dryopithecines.
Relative incisor size	Reduced	Uncritical when only comparing with male dryopithecines. Generally, *Ramapithecus* canine is morphologically like pongid or dryopithecine canine.
Mandibular corpus	Short and thick	No significant variation from contemporaneous dryopithecines.
Dental wear	Heavy, occlusal and interstitial wear, differential wear	Neither consistent nor conclusive.

Adapted from D. Frayer, "A Reappraisal of *Ramapithecus*," pp. 19-30. *Yearbook of Physical Anthropology 19,* © 1974.

example, feels that the existence of the "T-complex" and its value for interpreting the habitat of *Ramapithecus* is subject to question.

One of the most recent attempts to reject *Ramapithecus* as a hominid comes from Greenfield (1979). He feels that *Rampithecus* and *Sivapithecus* are almost indistinguishable and, since *Sivapithecus* has priority, he refers *Ramapithecus* there. According to Greenfield, *Sivapithecus* is a dryopithecine genus that apparently radiated throughout Eurasia and Africa during the Middle Miocene. Greenfield also feels that the Middle Miocene *Sivapithecus* shows more similarities to the hominids from Hadar and Laetoli (Chapter 17) than *Sivapithecus* shows to extant pongids.

In Greenfield's reclassification, the genus *Sivapithecus* contains four species, including two species, *S. africanus* and *S. brevirostris*, formerly classified as *R. wickeri* and *R. punjabicus*, respectively. In Greenfield's view, the contemporary species of *Sivapithecus* are characterized by a similar set of traits and could, on morphological grounds, be in the ancestry of *Australopithecus*. In fact, he argues (1979:544), "The Hadar, Laetoli and Lothagam *Australopithecus* materials . . . exhibit far more features reminiscent of a *Sivapithecus*-like ancestor than later *Australopithecus*."

The evolutionary time frame of hominid-pongid evolution based on immunological evidence of similarities has been presented as some of the strongest evidence against the *Ramapithecus*-as-hominid viewpoint. Comparison of blood proteins (e.g., albumins, transferrins, hemoglobins) and of DNA has shown a sequence similarity of more than 99 percent between humans, chimpanzees, and gorillas. This remarkable similarity makes them as similar as such closely related species as the horse and zebra or the grizzly and polar bear. At least 40 different proteins have been independently tested by dozens of investigators and they confirm the close relationship between humans, gorillas, and chimpanzees. Those arguing for the nonhominid status of *Ramapithecus* feel that such close similarity supports the conclusion that these three hominoids diverged from a common ancestor between 4 million and 6 million years ago. That common ancestor was most certainly some kind of ape, and perhaps *Ramapithecus* was the common ancestor of later pongids and hominids.

The biochemical adherents argue that to consider *Ramapithecus* a hominid requires that primate proteins have evolved at half the rate of shark, fish, frog, snake, kangaroo, mouse, and elephant proteins. They suggest that such would constitute a "special creation." Adherents of *Ramapithecus* as a hominid have argued that proteins evolve more slowly in animals with longer generation times (Chapter 22). This would refute the evidence that mouse and elephant proteins have evolved at the same rate, as have lemur and human proteins. The external check on the constancy of the molecular clock is supported by evidence from numerous proteins that have different rates of change. For example, evidence of rates of change in cytochrome c, albumin, transferrin, and hemoglobin all indicate the same divergence times. Zihlman and Lowenstein (1979:91) conclude their discussion of *Ramapithecus* as follows: "The case for *Ramapithecus* as an ancestral human has been weak from the start and has not strengthened with the passage of time."

Ramapithecus is an enigmatic fossil form. Once touted as the first hominid form, its hominid status is now much in doubt. The final taxonomic designation of Ramapithecus depends on the discovery of more materials, particularly the face, head, and postcranial remains.

The many arguments revolving around the taxonomy of Miocene hominoids are clarified somewhat by the ecological information. Many propose a general arboreal primate adaptation, with a progressive trend toward terrestrial living. Others prefer to seek hominid origins among brachiating or knuckle-walking predecessors. The paleoenvironmental evidence does not support any one theory. Rather, this evidence shows that early and mid-Miocene hominoids were found in complex mosaic environments. This situation would have favored ecological diversification and adaptive radiation among the rapidly evolving forms sharing overlapping geographical ranges (Butzer, 1977). Evidence from Pakistan strongly suggests such with its assemblage of Sivapithecus, Gigantopithecus, and Ramapithecus remains.

Bibliography

Andrews, P. 1971. *Rampithecus wickeri* mandible from Fort Ternan, Kenya. *Nature* 231:192.

Andrews, P., and Tobien, H. 1977. New Miocene locality in Turkey with evidence on the origin of *Ramapithecus* and *Sivapithecus. Nature* 268:699-701.

Ayala, F. 1970. Competition, coexistence and evolution. In *Essays in evolution and genetics in honor of Thedosius Dobzhansky,* edited by M. Hecht and W. Steere, pp. 121-58. New York: Appleton-Century-Crofts.

———————. 1971. Competition between species: frequency dependence. *Science* 171:820-24.

———————. 1972. Competition between species. *American Scientist* 60:348-57.

Behrensmeyer, A. 1978. The habitat of Plio-Pleistocene hominids in East Africa: taphonomic and micro-stratigraphic evidence. In *Early hominids of Africa,* edited by C. Jolly, pp. 165-91. London: Duckworth.

Butzer, K. 1977. Human evolution: hominoids of the Miocene. *Science* 197:224-46.

———————. 1978. Geoecological perspectives on early hominid evolution. In *Early hominids of Africa,* edited by C. Jolly, pp. 191-213. London: Duckworth.

Conroy, G. 1972. Problems in the interpretation of *Ramapithecus:* with special reference to anterior tooth reduction. *American Journal of Physical Anthropology* 37:41.

Conroy, G., and Pilbeam, D. 1975. *Ramapithecus:* a review of its hominid status. In *Palaeanthropology, morphology, and paleoecology,* edited by R. Tuttle, pp. 59-86. The Hague: Mouton.

Delson, E. 1978. Models of early hominid phylogeny. In *Early hominids of Africa,* edited by C. Jolly, pp. 517-40. London: Duckworth.

Frayer, D. 1974. A reappraisal of *Ramapithecus. Yearbook of Physical Anthropology* 18:19-30.

Gelvin, B. 1976. Odontometric affinities of *Ramapithecus* to extinct and extant hominoids. *American Journal of Anthropology* 44:217.

Greenfield, L. 1974. Taxonomic reassessment of two *Ramapithecus* specimens. *Folia primatologica* 22:97-115.

———————. 1979. On the adaptive pattern of *Ramapithecus. American Journal of Physical Anthropology* 50:527-48.

Groves, C. 1970. *Gigantopithecus* and the mountain gorilla. *Nature* 226:974.

Hrdlička, A. 1935. The Yale fossils of anthropoid apes. *American Journal of Science* 229:533-38.

Kennedy, G. 1978. Hominoid habitat shifts in the Miocene. *Nature* 271:11-12.

Khatri, J. 1975. The early fossil hominids and related apes of the Siwalik foothills of the Himalayas; recent discoveries and new interpretations. In *Paleoanthropology, morphology and paleoecology,* edited by R. Tuttle, pp. 31-58. The Hague: Mouton.

Kolata, G. 1977. Human evolution: hominoids of the Miocene. *Science* 197:244-45, 294.

Kretzoi, M. 1975. New ramapithecines and *Pliopithecus* from the Lower Pliocene of Rudábanya in northeastern Hungary. *Nature* 257:578-81.

Leakey, L. 1968. An early Miocene member of Hominidae. In *Perspectives on human evolution,* edited S. Washburn and P. Jay, pp. 61-85. New York: Holt, Rinehart and Winston.

———————. 1969. Ecology of North Indian *Ramapithecus. Nature* 223:1075.

———————. 1970. Newly recognized mandible of *Ramapithecus. Nature* 225:199.

———————. 1971. Bone smashing by late Miocene Hominidae. In *Adam or ape,* edited by L. Leakey, J. Prost, and S. Prost, pp. 443-47. Cambridge, Mass.: Schenkman.

Lewis, G. 1934. Preliminary notice of the new man-like apes from India. *American Journal of Science* 27-161.

———————. 1937. Taxonomic syllabus of Siwalik fossil anthropoids. *American Journal of Science* Series 34:139-47.

Pilbeam, D. 1972. *The ascent of man.* New York: Macmillan.

Pilgrim, G. 1910. Notices of new mammalian genera and species from the tertiaries of India. *Geological Survey of India Records* 40:63-71.

———————. 1915. New Siwalik primates and their bearing on the question of the evolution of man and the Anthropoidea. *Geological Survey of India Records* 45:1.

Piveteau, J. 1957. *Traite de paleontologie,* Tome VII. *Primates.* Paris: Masson & Cie.

Prasad, K. 1964. Upper Miocene anthropoids from the Siwalik beds of Haritalyangar, Himachal Pradesh, India. *Paleontology* 7:124.

———————. 1969. Observations of mid-Tertiary hominids *Sivapithecus* and *Ramapithecus. American Journal of Physical Anthropology* 31:11.

Robinson, J. 1972. *Early hominid posture and locomotion.* Chicago: University of Chicago Press.

Simons, E. 1961. The phyletic position of *Ramapithecus. Postilla* 57:1-5.

——————. 1964. On the mandible of *Ramapithecus. Proceedings of the National Academy of Sciences* 51:528-35.

——————. 1968. A source for dental comparison of *Ramapithecus* and *Australopithecus* and *Homo. South African Journal of Science* 64:92.

——————. 1969. Late Miocene hominid from Fort Ternan, Kenya. *Nature* 221:448.

——————. 1976. The nature of the transition in the dental mechanism from pongids to hominids. *Journal of Human Evolution* 5:511-28.

——————. 1977. *Ramapithecus. Scientific American* 236:28-35.

Simons, E., and Pilbeam, D. 1972. Hominoid paleoprimatology. In *The functional and evolutionary biology of primates,* edited by R. Tuttle, pp. 36-62. Chicago: Aldine-Atherton.

Simons, E., and Tattersall, I. 1971. Origins of the family of man. *Ventures,* Spring, p. 47.

Tattersall, I. 1969a. Ecology of North Indian *Ramapithecus. Nature* 224:451-52.

——————. 1969b. More on the ecology of North Indian *Ramapithecus. Nature* 224:821-22.

——————. 1972. Of lemurs and men. *Natural History* 81:32.

——————. 1975. The evolutionary significance of *Ramapithecus.* Minneapolis: Burgess.

von Koenigswald, G. 1973. *Australopithecus, Meganthropus,* and *Ramapithecus. Journal of Human Evolution* 2:487.

Wolpoff, M. 1971. Interstitial wear. *American Journal of Physical Anthropology* 34:205.

——————. 1980. *Paleoanthropology.* New York: Knopf.

Zihlman, A., and Lowenstein, J. 1979. False start of the human parade. *Natural History* 88:86-91.

Chapter 17

Pliocene–Early Pleistocene Hominids

The early history of paleoanthropology is a record of frustrated, disappointed scientists speaking to a world of skeptics. In the last chapter we noted the case of G. Edward Lewis and *Ramapithecus*. In this chapter and the next we will have further evidence in the cases of Raymond Dart and *Australopithecus* and then Eugene Dubois and "Pithecanthropus."

Because of the wide range of conflicting opinions, it is difficult to resolve the conflicting viewpoints at present. Most assuredly, some of the interpretations will be rejected with the finding of more materials and a reanalysis of the data. Today the main alternatives championed by various schools of thought are the one-genus hypothesis, the dietary hypothesis, the third hominid model proposed by R. Leakey, the pronouncement of a new taxon (*Australopithecus afarensis*) by Johanson, White, and Coppens (1978), and the sexual dimorphism hypothesis. Each hypothesis is discussed in its own right.

A Brief History: First Disbelief

Dart. In 1925 Raymond Dart, then professor of anatomy in Witwatersrand University in Johannesburg, South Africa, first announced the discovery of the early australopithecine material. (A number of writers colloquially refer to this group as "Dartians.") A description of Dart's findings first appeared on 7 February 1925 in the British science journal *Nature*. Dart's findings and preliminary description were based on a skull and an associated natural endocranial cast uncovered in limestone deposits in 1924 (Figure 17-1).[1] The skull originated

---

[1] An endocranial cast is the mold of the interior of the braincase. An endocranial cast can sometimes provide valuable evidence as to the general form and proportions of the brain, for the latter fits quite closely within the braincase. Some have tried to read too much from such casts, for example, whether the brain is sufficiently developed to allow for speech. Such an interpretation is difficult at best, and the results are almost always greeted dubiously.

from a limestone cliff formation at a site variously called Taung or Taungs (Ta-ung = place of the lion).

Dart recalls the long, tedious process of separating the fossil from its sand and limestone imprisonment as follows. "No diamond cutter ever worked more lovingly or with such care on a priceless jewel—nor, I am sure, with such inadequate tools. But on the seventy-third day, December 23, the rock parted. I could view the face from the front, although the right side was still imbedded. [The complete extraction process took 4 long years.] The creature which had contained this massive brain was no giant anthropoid such as a gorilla. What emerged was a baby's face, an infant with a full set of milk teeth and its permanent molars just in the process of erupting. I doubht if there was any parent prouder of his offspring than I was of my Taungs baby on that Christmas" (quoted in Pfeiffer, 1969:63).

Dart was convinced this skull belonged to some "manlike ape," for certain facial and dental traits, as well as traits of the endocranial cast, suggested that the skull more closely resembled hominids than pongids. The paleoclimatic data suggested that the specimen lived not in the tropical forest habitats typical of pongids but in relatively dry conditions. This is now in doubt (Butzer, 1974). Dart dubbed his fossil *Australopithecus africanus* and stated, "The specimen is important because it exhibits an extinct race of apes intermediate between living anthropoids and man."

Raymond Dart's Initial Discovery of the Taungs Baby
(Australopithecus africanus)

Toward the close of 1924, Miss Josephine Salmons, student demonstrator of anatomy in the University of Witwatersrand, brought to me the fossilized skull of a cercopithecoid monkey which, through her instrumentality, was very generously loaned to the Department for description . . . this valuable fossil had been blasted out of the limestone cliff formation . . . at Taungs. . . . Important stratigraphical evidence has been forthcoming recently from this district concerning the succession of Stone Ages in South Africa . . . and the feeling was entertained that this lime deposit, like that of Broken Hill in Rhodesia, might contain fossil remains of primitive man.

I immediately consulted Dr. R. B. Young, professor of geology about the discovery, and he, by a fortunate coincidence, was called down to Taungs almost synchronously to investigate geologically the lime deposits of an adjacent farm. Professor Young was enabled to inspect the site of the discovery and select further samples of fossil material for me . . . These included a natural cercopithecoid endocranial cast, a second and larger cast, and some rock fragments disclosing portions of bone.

In manipulating the pieces of rock brought back by Professor Young, I found that the larger natural endocranial cast articulated exactly . . . with another piece of rock in which the broken lower and posterior margin of the left side mandible was visible. After cleaning the rock mass, the outline of the hinder and lower part of the facial skeleton came into view.

Apart from this evidential completeness the specimen is of importance because it exhibits an extinct race of apes *intermediate between living anthropoids and man.*

. . . I propose tentatively, then, that a new family of Homo-simiadae be created for the reception of the group of individuals which it represents, and that the first known species of the group be designated *Australopithecus africanus,* in commemoration, first of the extreme southern and unexpected horizon of its discovery, and secondly, of the continent in which so many new and important discoveries connected with the early history of man have recently been made, thus vindicating the Darwinian claim that Africa would prove to be the cradle of mankind.

Excerpts from Dart's original report in *Nature,* 1925, 115:195.

Broom. While Dart's interpretations were being bantered about, the late Robert Broom, who was an extremely competent and well known paleontologist, entered the scene. He traveled to Johannesburg and soon became convinced that Dart's interpretations were correct. From deposits at Sterkfontein and Kromdraai, South Africa, he uncovered a remarkable series of australopithecine fossils, including portions of skulls, jaws, many teeth, and limb bone fragments.

Broom was into his eightieth year when he published his findings in a 1946 monograph; however, despite additional proof of Dart's suggestions and Broom's scientific caution, others remained unconvinced that Dart's fossils represented a form intermediate between apes and human. Broom's illustrations, freehand drawings by himself, seemed rather crude and unfinished; however, they later proved quite accurate. As has too often been true, Broom indulged himself in naming his fossils, establishing a number of taxa without genetic reality. The Sterkfontein material was allocated to the genus "Plesianthropus," although it was quite similar to *Australopithecus,* and the Kromdraai material was assigned to a new genus, "Paranthropus."

The debate over the australopithecines' hominid status continued into the early 1950s. As more material was uncovered, including material from new East African sites, and as scientists reviewed the material, the position of *Australopithecus* as a hominid group became recognized.

First Appearance and Geographical Distribution

Geological Disturbances, Environmental Changes. The australopithecines (defined in the widest sense) first appeared between 4 million and 5 million years ago, when the earth was geologically restless. The subsequent geological epoch, the Pleistocene, was marked by periods of warm and cold weather, distinguished at the end by major swings between glaciations and interglaciations. About 2 million to 3 million years ago there were tectonic earth

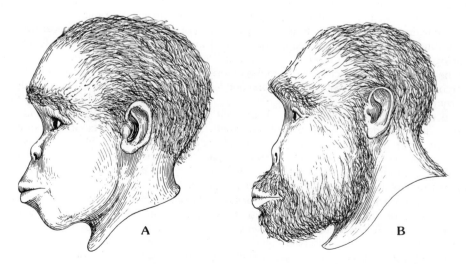

Figure 17-1. Broom's conception of the Taungs baby. A. Australopithecus africanus. B. A reconstruction of "Paranthropus robustus" from Kromdraii.

movements and cooling of the climate. **The Villafranchian fauna,** an important new mammalian group, first appeared in Europe, Asia, and Africa at this time.

The African Pleistocene was marked by continued shrinking of the forests and expansion of savanna grasslands. In some areas wet periods, the pluvials, alternated with the drier interpluvials. Giant earthquakes opened the cavernous Great Rift Valley in East Africa and lowered or emptied many lake beds. The southernmost part of the African continent remained stable, but the northern areas experienced convulsive changes.

South Africa. Australopithecines were first uncovered in South Africa, primarily as a result of extensive limestone quarrying. The material comes largely from three sources: limestone quarry sites, rock pile dumps resulting from the limestone quarry operations, and fissure and cave deposits filled with breccia. The five major South African australopithecine sites are located in three widely separated regions (Figure 17-2). It was originally assumed that Taung was in dry country, whereas the other four sites were well watered. These habitat differences may have existed during australopithecine times, but this is a matter of dispute.

Taung is a limestone plateau cut by deep cracks; animal bones have fallen into these crevices along with sand. Sterkfontein is a cave site that had a hole in the roof during australopithecine times. The three remaining sites are ordinary caves. In contrast to Bed I, Olduvai, South African sites cannot certainly be designated habitation or occupation areas. For example, both Taung and Sterkfontein seem to be refuse pits.

Because all five sites were originally uncovered by quarrying operations, the remains are out of stratigraphic context, making dating a nightmare. Attempts have been made to stratify the South African sites chronologically using soil analysis and faunal and tool associations — relative dating techniques. Although there are various age estimations for the South African sites, an oldest-youngest sequence of Makapan-Sterkfontein-Swartkrans-Kromdraai is generally agreed on. The temporal placement of Taung continues to be problematical.

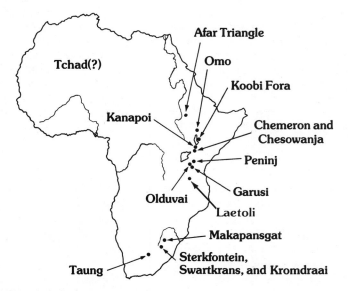

Figure 17-2. Distribution of African Lower Pleistocene sites.

Australopithecus, "Zinjanthropus," Homo habilis, Homo erectus
Olduvai Gorge, 28 May 1975

We drove down to Olduvai from our camp at Ngorongoro Crater. The drive is dusty over dirt roads and takes about 1½ hours. The drive from the cool, cloudy, and rainy Ngorongoro Crater to the dry, dusty Olduvai Gorge is quite a change. Olduvai Gorge itself is a flat table with many side faults. The first introduction to Olduvai is the visitors gate where one contacts a guide to take you through the Gorge. We first go to the small educational building for a brief lecture and then a visit to the small museum before proceeding into the Gorge itself.

The stratigraphy at Olduvai is quite clear. Much of the area is eroded and quite water-worn. The gorge still must contain many undiscovered sites, but there are so many side faults that some of the sites will probably never be discovered. However, Dr. Mary Leakey still surveys the Gorge regularly.

The first site which we visit is the "Zinjanthropus" locality situated in a small gully. This site is identified by a stone marker, as are the other major sites at Olduvai. There are still some faunal remains scattered about the area. From here we move on to the *Homo habilis* locales, OH 7 and OH 8, found about 500 yards from the "Zinjanthropus" locale. OH 7 and 8 locales sit side-by-side in a cut. The only material left here are the markers to distinguish the sites.

From here we go on to the Stone Circle site which is now covered by a stone house to protect the site. The stone circle is laid out in a partial semi-circle with some stones from the circle piled in a corner—the remnants of the dig before it was realized what was being excavated. Approximately 15-20 feet from the stone circle is the so-called garbage pit which contains some spheroids and choppers scattered about. Many of the tools are marked with signs. Much of the bone in the garbage pit is cracked. From the highest point to the bottom of the excavation is approximately ten feet. Outside the house there is considerable quartz material, some of which looks as if it could have been fabricated.

From the Stone Circle we go on to visit some of the other sites in the Gorge. We finally move on to the JK site which is where Mary Leakey excavated footprints and finger marks amidst some holes dug in the ground. Because the site has not yet been fully published, photographs are forbidden. The site is covered by a large tarpaulin, the covered area measures approximately 100 × 100 feet. We are able to see many of the footprints and the hand scrapings on the ground. There are quite a few holes dug in the ground (some of which are about 1-2 feet deep). The area at the time that *Homo erectus* visited the locale was quite muddy. The locale has good stratigraphy, and sits on a slight slope. Outside the covered area there is considerable quartz on the ground and some still in situ. Much of this material looks worked and could have been utilized as scrapers and cutting implements.

Excerpts from my notes during my visit to Olduvai Gorge.

East Africa: Olduvai Gorge. Olduvai Gorge, one of the major East African early hominid locales, is a well-stratified, steep-sided gorge stretching for about 25 miles across the Serengeti Plain in northern Tanzania not far from the Ngorongoro Crater. Olduvai Gorge is about 300 feet deep and is geologically stratified into five beds; the oldest and lowest bed, Bed I, dates from the Early Pleistocene (Figure 17-5). The earliest site in Bed I has been K-Ar dated to approximately 1.8 million years ago.

Olduvai was discovered in the early 1900s, but its fossilized hominid treasures remained unknown for many years. Through the dedicated efforts of the Leakeys, Olduvai Gorge has

Figure 17-3. A view of the stone circle. The rock pile at the rear is made of stones originally taken from the circle wall.

Figure 17-4. The remnants of part of the "garbage dump" at the stone circle (DK) site. The small horizontal markers indicate stone tools and fractured bone.

unfolded its secrets to the scientific world (Table 17-1).[2] The first important australopithecine discovery was made in July, 1959 when Mary Leakey found a bit of skull and, stuck firmly in the face of a nearby cliff, two very large premolars. It took 19 days to free the teeth and part of the palate from the rocks. Leakey originally assigned this skull and these teeth to the taxon "Zinjanthropus." "Zinjanthropus" has since been classified as one of the robust australopithecines.

The following quotation from Tobias (1978) recounts Leakey's unveiling of "Zinjanthropus" in South Africa.

"I shall never forget that exciting morning in the Witwatersrand University's Anatomy Department. . . . One by one, Louis and Mary drew forth the parts of Dear Boy's skull from the flory box in which these had been packed. Unveiled before us was the superbly-preserved and

---

[2]For a most insightful view of the Leakeys and their research, refer to Cole, 1975.

massive-toothed hominid cranium that was soon to become the first fossil skull ever dated by the newly introduced potassium-argon technique. . . . Professor Dart, one or two others and I, who were privileged to be present at that instant, were nearly overcome by the high emotion of our first sight of the Crown Jewel of East African fossils. I remember Raymond Dart, dewy-eyed, saying, 'After your thirty years' struggle, I am so happy, Louis, that this has happened to you of all people'."

The following from Louis Leakey's letter to P. Tobias recounts the recovery of what appears to be the type specimen of *H. habilis,* OH 7, a child's skull.

[13 December, 1961] Confidentially, we have what I am nearly sure is part of a right temple of the "child."

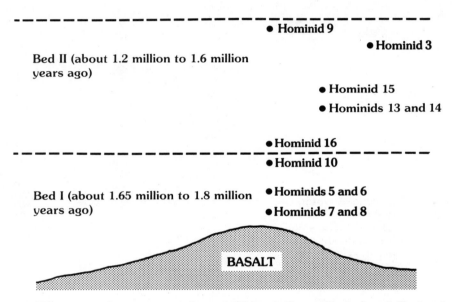

Figure 17-5. Diagrammatic representation of Olduvai Gorge Beds I and II showing the approximate placement of some of the hominids.

Table 17-1. Nature of Sites in Beds I and II, Olduvai

Living floors—occupation debris found on old land surfaces, paleosoils, with vertical dimension of only a few inches (0.3 feet).

Butchering or kill sites—artifacts associated with skeleton of large mammal or group of smaller animals.

Sites with diffused material—artifacts and faunal remains found throughout site with considerable thickness of clay or fine-grained tuff.

River or stream channel sites—occupation debris incorporated in filling of former river or stream.

Adapted from M. Leakey, "A Summary and Discussion of the Archaeological Evidence from Bed I and Bed II, Olduvai Gorge, Tanzania," p. 432. In G. Isaac and E. McCown, eds. *Human Origins: Louis Leakey and the East African Evidence,* W.A. Benjamin, Incorporated, Menlo Park, California © 1976.

OLDUVAI GORGE

A. Looking into Olduvai Gorge from the Education Centre. Note the different layers of stratigraphy in the center of the picture.

B. Looking across Olduvai Gorge. Note the road in the center of the picture.

C. Area around "Zinjanthropus" discovery. (It would be to your right if you were looking at the "Zinjanthropus" marker.)

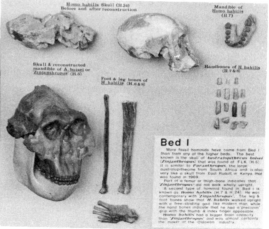

D. A display of Olduvai fossils.

The Omo Valley. Another very important East African site is the Omo Valley of Ethiopia. The fossil potential of the Omo Valley was first recognized in 1891, but the region is so remote that when work began in the valley supplies and personnel had to be flown in by light planes and helicopters. The first major paleontological work occurred in 1933. A detailed examination in 1966 paved the way for a systematic multidisciplinary study by the International Omo Research Expedition in 1967 and 1968, which included participants from Kenya, France, and the United States.

The Omo Valley is one of the most significant hominid fossiliferous locales yet discovered (Tables 17-2 and 17-3). Mammalian faunal assemblages from Omo indicate that the past climate was very different from today's parched conditions. The oldest hominid remains date to approximately 4 million years ago by K-Ar determination. As of 1976, 17 locales yielding hominid remains of varying ages had been uncovered.

Omo appears to hold (1) the presence of *A. africanus* or a smaller allied species between less than 3 million and 2.5 million years ago, (2) the persistence of this form or a derivative species until less than 1.9 million years ago, (3) the presence of a robust australopithecine, *A. boisei*(?), between less than 2.1 million and 1 million years ago, (4) a hominid dentally similar to *Homo habilis* that appeared by less than 1.85 million years ago, and (5) *H. erectus,* which appeared by 1.1 million years ago.

Table 17-2. Hominid Materials from Omo Valley

Usno Formation and Members B through F and Lower Units of G from the Shungura Formation

This material is referred to *Australopithecus* with affinities to *A. africanus.* The oldest specimens are generally small, have simple dental morphology, and might represent a distinctive but related lower taxonomic category.

Shungura Formation

Members E, F, G, and perhaps L: hominids attributed to robust australopithecine, *A. boisei* (?).

Members from G, H, and Mb: a partial cranium with maxillary dentition comes from Mb. Material G-28 is quite similar to that of *Homo habilis* (OH 7, 13) from Olduvai. Also some teeth from these members.

Uppermost Member K; cranial fragments with features diagnostic of *H. erectus.*

Table 17-3. Inventory of Hominid Skeletal Parts from the Omo Succession as of 1976

Formation	Crania	Mandibles	Teeth	Postcranials
Shungura	3 incomplete 2 fragments	9	187	8
Usno			21	
Totals	3 incomplete 2 fragments	9	208	8

Adapted from F. Howell and Y. Coppens, "An Overview of Hominidae from the Omo Succession, Ethiopia," p. 523. *In* Y. Coppens, F. Howell, G. Isaac, and R. Leakey, *Earliest Man and Environments in the Lake Rudolf Basin,* University of Chicago Press, Chicago © 1976.

Lake Turkana. Since 1968 a very important East African site has been located at Lake Rudolf, since renamed Lake Turkana by the Kenya government. This site is the largest source of Late Pliocene to Early Pleistocene sites known to paleontologists. The locale is an area of approximately 400 square miles. Although this site is still in the early stages of excavation, numerous hominid fossils have been uncovered there (Table 17-4). A number of very early archaeological sites, with accepted stone tools and broken bones, have been located. The fossiliferous beds yielded a series of comparatively well-preserved hominid crania and postcranial bones. The hominid materials show a remarkable amount of variability in size and morphology. The limb bones show contrasting robust or massive specimens and more slender ones.

The oldest fossil materials from Lake Turkana are pig bones dated to approximately 4 million years ago. Stone tools were found in association with one of the cranial remains. The Lake Turkana area appears to have been an occupation site, that is, an area where hominids made tools, hunted, or scavenged. Elements of the Turkana stratigraphy overlap the upper part of the Omo sequence; faunal remains indicate an age equivalence with the lower part of the Olduvai formation.

Hadar, Afar Triangle. Recent finds in the Afar Triangle of northeastern Ethiopia are the result of an international expedition led by D. Johanson (United States), M. Taieb (France), and A. Asfew (Ethiopia). This expedition unearthed a number of materials including half a maxilla with its teeth intact and a complete mandible. The scientists first suggested that some of these materials belonged to the genus *Homo* and may date to 3 million or 4 million years ago. The revised taxonomic status of this material is discussed later. In addition to this material, the group found a skull fragment and leg bones of a form they consider to be *Australopithecus* dating to 3 million years ago.

In late December 1974 Johanson announced the discovery of "Lucy" (named after the Beatles' tune "Lucy in the Sky with Diamonds"), a female hominid, whose bones constitute the ". . . most complete early man discovery ever made in Africa." Lucy's pelvis marks her as a female, an individual about 3 feet, 6 inches tall. She had her third molars and was considered to be an adult. Approximately 40 percent of Lucy's skeleton was uncovered.

Stratigraphic evidence suggests that Lucy died near a lake margin. Faunal remains suggest that she lived in a lush grassland environment, perhaps with open savanna woodlands.

Table 17.4. Lake Turkana Remains

Relative Numbers of Specimens of Hominidae from Lake Turkana as of 1976

Genus	Number of Specimens	Percentage
Australopithecus	49	55
Homo	29	32.6
Indeterminate	11	12.4

Portions of Hominid Specimens from Lake Turkana as of 1976

Postcranial	50
Crania, maxillae, and mandibles	59
Isolated teeth	16

Adapted from R. Leakey, "An Overview of the Hominidae from East Rudolf, Kenya," p. 483, and W. Bishop, "Thoughts on the Workshop," p. 588. *In* Y. Coppens, F. Howell, G. Isaac, and R. Leakey, eds., *Earliest Man and Environments in the Lake Rudolf Basin,* University of Chicago Press, Chicago © 1976.

Fossilized turtle and crocodile eggs were found, along with fossilized crab claws. Is it possible that Lucy ate such foods?

Johanson relates his discovery of Lucy as follows:

> . . . Suddenly, I found myself saying, "It's hominid!"
>
> Something else caught my eye. "Do you suppose it belongs with those skull fragments next to your hand?" Startled, Tom sent his glance after mine. It was high noon that memorable day when the realization struck us both that we might have found a skeleton. An extraordinary skeleton.
>
> We looked up the slope. There, incredibly, lay a multitude of bone fragments—a nearly complete lower jaw, a thigh bone, arm bones, ribs, vertebrae, and more! Tom and I yelled, hugged each other, and danced, mad as any Englishman in the midday sun.

During 1975 the success at Hadar continued, the expedition finding the remains of a cluster of hominids. The finding of these five to seven individuals, the so-called "first family," resting in proximity raised a number of questions such as: Are they related? Were they a family or did they all die at the same time? How did they die? Johanson feels it is possible that all the individuals died at the same time. His coworker, Taieb, notes that the geology of the site, lakeshore and riverine deposits, suggests that the group died together, perhaps in a flash flood. The materials from Afar Locality 333 (Al 333) consist of jaws, teeth, leg bones, hand and foot bones, a fossilized footprint, ribs, and a partial adult skull. Additionally, there is an infant's nearly complete lower jaw. In all, there is evidence of old and young adults and children. The mandibles had the V-shape common to many australopithecines.

Johanson's first finds were located 26 meters below volcanic deposits dated to 3.1 million to 3.25 million years ago. Since geologists are not sure how long it took these 26 meters of sediments to accumulate, the current estimate of 3.5 million to 4 million years for the new finds is based partly on comparisons of animal fossils with similar faunal remains in other parts of Africa.

Johanson's finds have raised speculation as to the place of origin of early hominids. The Afar finds are from the northeastern edge of Africa. At one time (about 3 million years ago) Africa and Arabia were joined. The finding of hominids at the edge of Africa raised the possibility that their origins may lie elsewhere, or, perhaps, an early migration of hominids from Africa is possible.

Johanson relates the discovery of the "first family" as follows:

Discovery of Afar Remains

The going-away party of the night before still rich in my memory, I watched with some wistfulness as the camp we called home began to disappear. Tents were folded unceremoniously; crates of scientific instruments and precious specimens had already been loaded into waiting Land-Rovers.

Three times before in as many years, I had said goodbye to this sunparched piece of Ethiopia, and I marveled again that such a time-ravaged, barren place could have such a hold on my emotions. Yet here had come discoveries to set any anthropologist's heart soaring, discoveries that are writing new chapters in the annuals of early man research.

In our luggage, packed as gingerly as if it had been nitroglycerin, lay the oldest remains of the genus *Homo*. . . ever unearthed. And not just a few fragments, but pieces enough to identify men, women, and children—perhaps a family—who died together three million years ago. The find was unprecedented—the earliest group of associated individuals ever found (Johanson, 1976:791).

HADAR REGION

A. View of the Hadar region, Ethiopia. It was in this area that Dr. Don Johanson and his coworkers found the remains of "Lucy" and other hominids, some of which they claim belong to the genus *Homo*.

B. Don Johanson excavating a 3-million-year-old mandible.

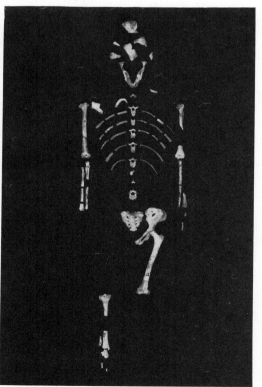

C. The skeletal remains of "Lucy" from Ethiopia.

Corvinus (1976) discusses some of the tools found at Hadar. Excavations parallel to those that uncovered "Lucy" revealed two Early Stone Age industries. One composes an Acheulian workshop. The other, a stratigraphically younger industry, constitutes a degenerate biface-flake industry. The oldest known artifacts from Hadar are a few basalt flakes (from the Afaredo site). The silt yielding these tools is stratigraphically younger than the hominid levels and older than the Acheulian horizon. The time span separating the hominids from the flake-bearing silts seems to be rather short.

Gray (1978) discusses the Hadar paleoenvironment. Approximately 3 million years ago there was a lake in the area. Erosion of the ancient lake shores has exposed vast numbers of animal fossils. These animals were apparently sustained by substantial tracts of lush vegetation. More than 70 species of animals, ranging from crabs to crocodiles to birds to large mammals, have been identified at Hadar. The mammals, such as various antelope, rhinoceros, hippopotamus, and pig, are most useful because much is known about the behavior and habitat of their modern descendants.

Taieb has divided the ancient Hadar deposits into four major subdivisions. The lowermost and uppermost members yielded no hominid remains and very few other fossil materials. The middle two layers, however, are most important. The lower of the two, the Sidi Hakoma Member, gives evidence of a rather small lake, surrounded by swamps except for locations where small rivers were flowing into the lake. The mud deposits yielded a high proportion of a small antelope called the dik-dik, as well as fossils of the living bush pig. Both animals today inhabit bushy areas, where there is some vegetation cover. Remains of impala, baboon, rhinoceros, and hippopotamus were found in the sandy levels. The hippopotamus indicated the presence of water, while the other forms are today predominantly open-country dwellers, preferring grassy areas. There seems to be some environmental contrast within one major unit, indicating the presence of an environmental mosaic.

In later Sidi Hakoma times there is evidence of expansion of the lake. Shortly thereafter there is evidence of fully aquatic conditions, and the number of fossils is substantially reduced.

The lower portions of the Denen Dora Member show the effect of the lake expansion. This expansion is accompanied by a dramatic shift in the nature of the fossil animals found, with relatives of living waterbuck and reedbuck becoming most dominant. These animals tend to prefer wooded regions to help avoid predators, but spend considerable time grazing in open grass. They are always found near water.

Shortly thereafter, the lake level is temporarily lowered. Here again the impala is abundant, but the common baboon, rhinoceros, and hippopotamus are uncommon. Instead, along with impala, there are remains of numerous relatives of living kudu, which tend to inhabit somewhat heavier cover. Perhaps this is a situation where environmental zones are in close proximity to one another, perhaps even varying seasonally.

Other Remains. Other East African australopithecine material is largely fragmentary. The Peninj mandible with all its teeth, found in the Peninj River beds near Lake Natron in Tanzania, has been dated to about 1.5 million years ago. Some regard it as a robust australopithecine with affiliations to the Olduvai "Zinjanthropus" or South African *A. robustus* group.

In 1939 fragmentary hominid remains were uncovered at Garusi, northwest of Lake Eyasi, Tanzania, from deposits dating to the lower Omo beds. Kanapoi in northwest Kenya had yielded the distal end (elbow segment) of a humerus. Enclosing geological deposits are 2.5 million to 3 million years old. Another discovery at Lothagam including a piece of mandible, first molar crown, and preserved roots of the other molars has been dated to about 5 million years ago. Extensive fossiliferous beds have been uncovered at Baringo Basin in the northern

BARINGO BASIN

A. The dry Kapthurin River bed.

B. One of the walls lining the Kapthurin River in the area of the Chemeron Beds.

C. The area of the Chemeron Beds (which are approximately halfway up the wall). The walls are more than 100 feet high.

Rift Valley in Kenya where excavators recognize beds spanning from the Late Miocene to Late Pliocene, from the time of *Ramapithecus* to the earlier *Australopithecus*. Fragments of two fossil hominids from the Chemeron and Ngorora Beds have been recovered. The Chemeron material dates from 3 million to 3.5 million years ago, the Ngorora material to around 9 million years ago. Because of the time span, the Ngorora material is exciting, for it fills the gap between *Ramapithecus* and *Australopithecus*.

Hominids Outside Africa. The early hominids may have extended beyond Africa, a possibility based on dental comparisons and jaw fragments attributed to the Javan form "Meganthropus paleojavanicus." Besides anatomical similarities, further suggestive evidence comes with redating. "Meganthropus" was originally assumed to be from the Lower Middle Pleistocene. Recently, however, the layer underlying the "Meganthropus" deposit has been dated to about 1.9 million years ago, placing it within the australopithecine time span. First considered a robust form, many now refer to this as *H. erectus*.

Although not widely reported, early Pleistocene forms occur in China. Lan-Po (1975) reports the discovery of two fossil incisors dating to about a million years ago from Yuanmou County, Yunnan Province, which were recovered in 1965. In 1961, 1,962 artifacts dating to approximately a million years were uncovered in Hsihoutu Village, Shansi Province. These stone implements include cores, flakes, scrapers, and choppers. Although no hominid remains were uncovered, a large number of fossil vertebrates were found along with the stone tools.

Tools dating to the Pliocene-Pleistocene have also been uncovered from India. No hominid fossils dating to that time period have been uncovered, however.

Lifeways

Tool Use: First Disagreement. Until recently (and there are still some lingering disbelievers) there was considerable disagreement over whether early hominids made and used tools. On the pro side are stone objects found in deposits yielding australopithecine remains. Opponents argued according to anatomical considerations; it was held that the early hominid brain was too small for the necessary intellectual activity allowing the fashioning of tools from local objects. This notion was so solidified that when tools were recovered from Sterkfontein in 1956, they were immediately and widely attributed to more advanced hominids.

Comparative Data. The brain-size limitations argument has now been largely dismissed, directly by associated tool and early hominid remains from the same deposits and indirectly by the fact that our nearest primate relative, the chimpanzee, makes tools (Chapter 12). Chimpanzees make twig tools for probing into termite mounds to get the termites. They break twigs into suitable lengths and even remove side branches obstructing their probing. Some diehards refer to this as "tool modifying" and not "tool making," a distinction hardly warranted. Chimpanzees have been seen to wander from the immediate proximity of the termite mound to collect appropriate stalks, which they carry back with them; this indicates some premeditation. Tool making for the purposes of termiting is not an instinctual pattern; it is observationally learned behavior or trial-and-error behavior. Tool using and termiting represent the emergence of a primitive culture, if one element of culture can be defined as "behavioral patterns transmitted by imitation or intuition." However, there is a gap between the mental ability allowing one to undertake such simple tasks that fulfill the need for some immediately visualized requirement and the conceptual capacity of the human mind allowing fabrication of implements for future contingencies.

Anatomical Considerations. Stone implements are now recognized with hominid remains at the South African sites of Swartkrans and Sterkfontein and in East Africa at Olduvai, Omo, Lake Turkana, and Afar. The evidence suggests that the early hominid brain was capable of the intellectual activity needed for tool making and tool using. Anatomical evidence arguing for the ability of tool making also lies in the hand bones. John Napier (1962a, b) concluded from his study of hand bones from Bed I Olduvai that they had a **"power grip,"** that is, the sort of grip used when wielding a hammer. They may also have had some **"precision grip,"** that is, the grip used in holding small objects by opposing the thumb and fingers to one another (Figure 17-6). (This is the grip you use when holding a pen or pencil). By practical experimentation, Napier demonstrated that the power grip was sufficient for making not only the crude tools called **"pebble tools"** but even for making the more advanced types of **"hand axes"** similar to one of the tools recovered at Sterkfontein. However, only the precision grip could have been used on the small flakes found at Olduvai.

Interpreting Tool Usage. Once it was realized that ancestral humans made and used tools, such handiworks were assigned names based on their probable function(s). The first such tool accordingly named was the coup-de-poing, a French term that translates as "hand axe." Other functional names have been applied to tools such as "blade," "point," and "scraper." Although such names have wide usage, there is little verifying experimental work. A recently developed set of methods named microwear analysis can reveal the functions of early flint tools based on studies of the form of microscopic traces of wear on the working edges.

One of the first attempts at microwear analysis was done by the Russian prehistorian S. A. Semenov (1964). When published in English, Semenov's work raised the curiosity of many scholars in Britain and the United States. However, because of many problems, European and American scholars concentrated on studies of edge damage that could be observed with low-powered stereomicroscopes.

A leading proponent of microwear analysis is R. Keeley, who designed a set of experiments to analyze the functions of a series of nearly 200 tools, processing a wide variety of foodstuffs

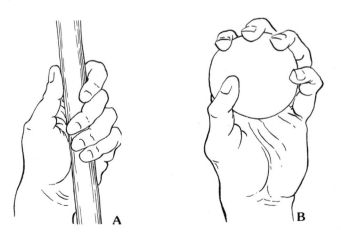

Figure 17-6. Hand grips. (A) Power grip. (B) Precision grip.

Table 17-5. Scheme of Temporal Relationships of Late Pliocene-Pleistocene Fossiliferous Localities Yielding Hominidae in Eastern Africa

Age (Millions of Years)	SERENGETI (Tanzania)	OMO BASIN (Ethiopia)	LAKE TURKANA (Kenya)	TURKANA DISTRICT (Kenya)	BARINGO BASIN (Kenya)	KAVIRONDO GULF (Kenya)	AFAR (Ethiopia)
0—	MASEK BEDS IV III						
1—	II	SHUNGURA FORM.	KOOBI FORA		CHESOWANJA		
2—	I	USNO FORM.					
3—			Kubi Algi Mb			KANAM	
4—	LAETOLI	MURSI FORM.		KANAPOI upper fossil beds LOTHAGAM HILL	CHEMERON	KANAM	
5—				lower fossil beds			
6—							
7—							
8—							

AFAR: The remains at Afar date to between 3.5 million and 4 million years ago. The stratigraphy has not been defined.

Adapted from F. Howell, "Pliocene/Pleistocene Hominidae in Eastern Africa: Absolute and Relative Dates," In Bishop and J. Miller, eds., *Calibration of Hominid Evolution*, Scottish Academic Press, Edinburgh, © 1972.

and other items in many ways. Keeley found that different activities produced a characteristic kind of work polish on the tool being used. Keeley (1979:105) states, "This being the case, it should be possible to infer from the traces of microwear observable on a Paleolithic tool just what use that particular tool had served."

Keeley established six broad categories of polishes: (1) Wood polish. The tool edge shows a polish consistent in appearance regardless of the type and state of the wood being worked. The polish is also consistent regardless of the manner of tool use; (2) Bone polish. In this instance, the edge of the tool is bright, but the polish has a rough, uneven texture lacking the smoothness characteristic of wood polish. Furthermore, there are numerous pits on an otherwise bright surface; (3) Hide polishes. In this instance, the tool edges do not develop a single distinctive kind of polish. Hides polishes differed in appearance depending on the kind of material being worked; (4) Meat polish. The tool edge used to slice meat and other soft animal tissue develops a microwear quite similar to that produced by working fresh hide. The polish is, however, easily distinguished from that created by working dry hide, bone, antler, wood, and nonwoody plant materials; (5) Antler polish. Tool edges used to work antlers exhibit one or another of two distinctive polishes depending on how the tool was used. Scraping, planing, or graving antlers leaves a polish that resembles bone polish—bright but pitted; (6) Nonwoody plant polish. Tool edges used to cut nonwoody plant stems, such as grasses or bracken, acquire what Keeley labels a "corn gloss." This produces a very smooth, highly reflective surface with a "fluid" appearance.

While it is clear that work polishes alone enable one to infer the purpose for which materials were processed, one must rely on several other kinds of microwear evidence if one wants to determine how implements were used. Most important are the distribution and orientation of such linear wear features as striations. Other evidence includes the location and nature of edge damage and the location and extent of the polished working portions. This evidence is considered in relation to the general size and shape of the tool.

Keeley analyzed the Acheulian tool assemblage from the English site of Hoxne to produce the following picture of implemental activities. Hoxne tool manufacturers used their tools for butchering, wood working, and hide working, and for boring wood and bone. Some tools were also used to slice or cut plant material other than wood. The hunters at Hoxne may have gathered reeds or bracken for bedding. Butchering was done by flake tools, as well as by the so-called hand axes.

Among the Upper Industry tools at Hoxne there were small numbers of flake implements that are traditionally called "side scrapers" and may have played a role in dressing hides.

Finally, one bifacial tool from Clacton, a 250,000-year-old English site, evidenced wood polish on its working surface. The damage on the working surface was due to a rotary motion such as boring. The tool was turned in a clockwise direction while downward pressure was being applied. Keeley suggests that the pattern was consistent with right-handed tool users.

Given the kind of analysis performed by Keeley, it is now possible, assuming suitable preservation, to determine not only how tools were used but also what they were used on. Information derived from future microwear studies should enable prehistorians to discuss the technology and economy of early hominids on a more solid basis.

The Evidence. A major impediment to fully understanding the technological abilities of early hominids stems from the fact that it is hard to recognize early tools. Undoubtedly, much of the earliest use of tools consisted of simply picking some object, a stone, bone, or stick, from the environment, using it once or twice, and discarding it. Many of the earliest examples of tools are lost to us because the materials used (such as wood or bone) have decayed or are indistinguishable.

The first stone tools are referred to the Oldowan tradition. The chopper is a tool typically found in Lower Pleistocene sites (Figure 17-7). This is often a smooth, rounded cobblestone or oblong block given a rough cutting edge by knocking flakes from both sides (bifacially flaked). Most of the earliest choppers found at Olduvai are about the size of a tennis ball or slightly smaller; some tools must have been held between the thumb, ring, and index fingers and used for such purposes as preparing small pieces of plant or animal food. The Olduvai sites also contain possible bone tools; a flattened and highly polished rib from a zebra or some other horselike species may have been used to rub hides or make them smooth and pliable. A similar tool comes from Sterkfontein.

Jones (1979) has recently provided some experimental data concerning the manufacture and use of the Olduvai bifaces. Jones found that quartzite bifaces are efficient tools because the tool edges remain sharp during use and can be easily resharpened by secondary flaking. Such bifaces were very efficient for skinning and cutting. Basalt bifaces were also efficient when used for skinning and cutting meat. In contrast to quartzite bifaces, however, primary flake edges of basalt bifaces cannot be effectively resharpened following blunting.

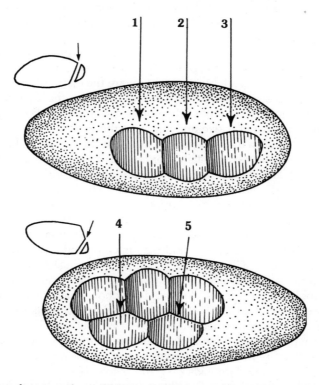

Figure 17-7. Manufacture of a pebble tool. Flakes are removed by striking a series of sharp blows (1 through 3) near the natural edge of a pebble. The pebble is turned over and blows 4 and 5 are struck on the ridges formed by the initial flaking. The resulting tool has a wavy but strong edge.

As Jones notes, the mechanical properties of the materials used to make the bifaces at Olduvai vary, leading to differences in work capabilities and their apparent effectiveness as tools, Jones notes that it is necessary to consider the size, shape, and flaking properties of the raw materials when assessing the technological sophistication of the manufacturers. Some of the bifaces now termed to be crude or primitive are, according to Jones's data, the products of sophisticated and efficient techniques of stone tool manufacture.

Dart made a painstaking analysis of several thousand South African bone fragments; skulls and neck vertebrae from large animals predominate, and Dart concluded that the heads of these animals were severed before being carried off into the South African caves or rock shelters. Dart suggests that the australopithecines possessed an osteodontokeratic tool assemblage, that is, they made tools from bone, teeth, and antlers, and not only from stone (Figure 17-8). Dart suggested that many of the bone fragments served as weapons: the long bones of the arms and legs as clubs; splintered and sharply pointed bones, antelope horns, and canines as daggers; shoulder bones and jaws of larger animals as scrapers and sawlike blades. Dart further argues that some long bones show definite evidence of deliberate shaping for tools by flaking and of having been used in scraping and rubbing (dressing) animal hides. He argues that bone implements preceded those of stone; and where Dart has demonstrated that bones could be used as tools, not everyone agrees they were.

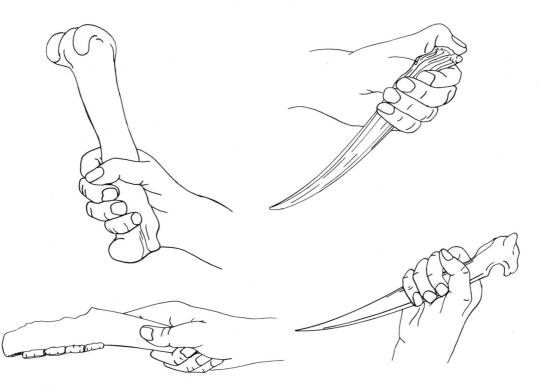

Figure 17-8. Uses of animal remains as tools and weapons by early hominids based on Dart's ideas.

An alternative explanation to Dart's osteodontokeratic culture is provided by Brain (1967a, b, 1968). After studying Hottentot goat remains he concluded that the Makapansgat assemblage may result from hominid and carnivore hunting activities in association with scavenging behavior, perhaps by hyenas. This conclusion is based on bone assemblages seen in Hottentot villages where goats are eaten and the remains then scavenged by dogs. In this case there is a high proportion of half mandibles and distal humeri. Brain's data raise serious questions about Dart's osteodontokeratic culture because these data maintain that early hominids selectively collected particular skeletal parts for tools.

It has also been argued that the Transvaal sites were not actual hominid occupations, but that the bone accumulations reflect passive collections by natural agencies. Hyenas have been suggested as the possible collectors of the bones in the South African caves. However, Hughes's (1954, 1958) work on hyena lairs reveals that some localities lack bone, while others containing bone exhibited evidence of porcupine activity. Hughes suggested that porcupines played a role in the South African bone accumulations. However, the Swartkrans remains revealed less than 5 percent of the bones exhibiting porcupine gnawing.

Brain's (1968, 1970) study of hyena scavenging of carnivore kills notes that only minor portions of bone remained following intensive scavenging. Work in East Africa suggests that young hyenas collect bones. It is therefore possible that some of the South African bone deposits are due to hyena activities. Leopards also seem to have played some role in the bone accumulations (Brain, 1968, 1970). Leopards carry their prey into trees to avoid scavenging and to consume their food leisurely. Today trees in the high veld of the Transvaal are frequently found situated near openings of dolomitic caves. If this was true in the past, some leopard prey remains may have fallen into the cave site. In fact, Brain (1970) has shown that the two puncture marks on the occipital of a partial cranium from Swartkrans (SK 54) match nicely with the mandibular canines of a fossil leopard.

The Oldowan Tradition

The name for the Oldowan tradition comes from the tools found at Olduvai Gorge dated to 1.8 million years ago. However, the tools from Olduvai were preceded by others, such as those found at Afar. Oldowan tools are slightly modified stone pieces, often hard to distinguish from rocks naturally flaked by the wear and tear of millions of years of lying above ground or being buried deep below the surface. Butzer (1971) estimated that using the Oldowan tool maker's techniques, a pound of rock would produce a cutting edge of only about 2 inches (5 centimeters). The resulting edge, however, was sharper than teeth for cutting skins. Oldowan tool makers were selective in their choice of raw materials; many stones from which tools were made are exotic and brought from some distance.

We are yet unable to understand fully the range of use of the Oldowan tools. Many have suggested that they were used for meat-processing activities, but it is also possible they were used to prepare vegetable foods. Most likely their major value was as an all-purpose tool. Oldowan tools may have been used for working wood and making other tools and shelters, such as the postulated windbreak at the Olduvai stone circle site.

Other Cultural Remains. Other evidences of cultural remains have been recovered. Volcanic dust, an excellent preservative, covers most of the **living floors** (places where objects remained in their original context) at Olduvai. A living floor is meticulously excavated so that each item remains in place, for the position of each item is as important as the item itself. Once cleared, the floor is mapped and measured to ensure the location of each artifact.

Mary Leakey has drawn a large map of the 2,400-square-foot living floor where she and her husband Louis uncovered the *Australopithecus* skull. The map illustrates the precise location of more than 4,000 artifacts and fossils. The core area where the artifacts are concentrated is bordered on one side by a pile of larger bone fragments and unshattered bone. Leakey sees this area as a "dining room" complex, the bordering area as a garbage dump. An almost bare arc-shaped area lying between the two may have been a windbreak of branches; or, it may have served as a protective fence to keep out predators. The living floor is probably a home base; the accumulated remains suggest that hominids lived there at least seasonally over the years. Based on the accumulated remains, it is suggested that the inhabitants may have achieved a new type of social stability and possessed a sense of group belonging.

Site Location. We will briefly discuss possible factors influencing site selection by the early hominids (Table 17-6). It is no mere coincidence that many early sites are located along freshwater courses. Besides the fact that water moves artifacts, bones and other debris, thus affecting their distribution on the landscape, early hominids and their descendants apparently chose to live alongside or near water sources. Of necessity, the early hominids stayed close to water sources until they had some means of carrying water. Furthermore, sites located near water offered the best locales for collecting certain kinds of plants and for seizing some unsuspecting prey when it came to drink. Later big-game hunters and sedentary farmers also used land close to stable water sources. These water sources offered big-game hunters a plentiful supply of big game. As suggested by the remains at Torralba and Ambrona, Spain, and possibly at Olorgesailie, Kenya, animals may have been killed once they became entrapped in mud.

East Turkana hominid and archaeological sites lie in delta and stream deposits, mainly short-lived silty or sandy channels, as well as in extensive delta-mouth marshes, mudflats, and shore zones that were probably seasonally dry (Butzer, 1977). Gracile and robust forms are not restricted to distinct microsedimentary environments. This is probably significant.

There appear to be more robust australopithecine than gracile remains in stream deposits, while remains of both types occur in equal proportions in lake-margin deposits. This suggests that robust forms may have preferentially exploited food sources in the fringing forests of stream valleys. Both gracile and robust forms, however, favored the more open vegetation of the shore and delta plains, suggesting a microenvironmental difference between the forms.

Along the Omo River, robust and gracile australopithecines temporally overlap and are occasionally found in the same sites. Most fossil sites are related to stream channels or delta distributaries of the ancient Omo River. The preponderance of robust forms seems to correspond with the comparable situation at Lake Turkana. Afar remains come from lakeshore and stream deposits, similar to deposits at Lake Turkana. The Bed I hominid site at Olduvai Gorge is associated with interdigitated stream and lake deposits. Robust australopithecine remains and an early form of *Homo* were found near the fluctuating shoreline of a large alkaline lake or along the intermittent streams that emptied into the margins of the lake basin.

In the Great Rift Valley, australopithecines are associated with compartmentalized tectonic lowlands, but South African remains come largely from ancient caverns and fissures. Neither the Swartkrans, Sterkfontein, nor Kromdraai sites were typical caves and none was used as a hominid shelter. A study of sediments washed into these caves indicates ongoing environmental change, but it is likely that open grasslands were prevalent. Generally, it can be

Table 17-6. Ecological Features of Potential Importance to Hominid Habitat Preferences in Four Types of Environments Typical of Pliocene-Pleistocene and Recent East Africa

	Saline Lake Margin	Fresh Lake Margin	Ephemeral Fluvial	Perennial Fluvial
Water available	Permanent	Permanent	Seasonal, waterholes	Permanent
Salt available	Permanent	Absent	Seasonal	Absent or rare
Predictability of food sources	Moderate	High	Low to moderate	High
Large trees	Absent	Present	Restricted, present	Present
Shade	Restricted	Abundant	Restricted, ample	Abundant
Edible plants (diversity)	Low diversity	Moderate diversity	Seasonal to moderate	High
Visibility	High	Moderate to restricted	High to moderate	Low to moderate
Water dependent herbivores	Permanent, seasonal highs	Permanent, seasonal highs	Dispersed	Permanent, seasonal highs
Water independent herbivores	Occasional	Occasional to rare	Present, dispersed	Occasional to rare
Mammalian carnivores	Present, seasonal highs	Present	Seasonal highs	Present
Crocodile	Permanent	Permanent	Seasonal	permanent
Fish, turtle	Permanent, seasonal high	Permanent, seasonal high	Seasonal, vary	Permanent, seasonal high
Small mammals, reptiles	Rare	Present	Present	Present

Adapted from A. Behrensmeyer, "Taphonomy and Paleoecology in the Hominid Fossil Record," p. 48. *Yearbook of Physical Anthropology,* © 1975.

inferred that South African australopithecine sites were related to open, grassy environments with local or scattered tree growth and uniform precipitation in the range of 600 to 800 millimeters per year.

The earliest African hominids lived in a wide variety of environments. East African sites are primarily found in rift valleys. South African sites are most plentiful in upland plains of a rolling plateau landscape. However, African sites shared a number of common features:

1. all shared a single macroenvironment—a semiarid or subhumid climate, characterized by alternating wet and dry seasons and savanna vegetation.

2. all sites were at mesoenvironmental interfaces or in ectones between open and closed vegetation.
3. the sites were all located in mixed environments.

The location of all early hominid sites in mixed environments in the seasonally dry African savanna is important. Pliocene-Pleistocene hominids were largely sympatric, and a sympatric distribution characterized the higher primates as early as 14 million years ago in the Miocene. Pliocene-Pleistocene hominid evolution occurred within similar overall environments.

Butzer feels there is no environmental evidence to support the argument for a shift from a herbivorous to an omnivorous diet in the wake of increasing aridity and reduced arboreal vegetation during the critical period between the late Miocene and early Pleistocene. Butzer feels that the evidence points instead to mosaic evolution and ecological separation of the hominids. Although the information is inconclusive regarding the ecological differentiation of Pliocene-Pleistocene hominid lineages, the East Turkana information suggests that gracile forms may have preferred more open habitats than robust forms. Dental evidence may not be of much help in resolving this problem or in resolving phylogenetic relations. The dental evidence may only imply that early hominids ate a variety of foods, making any interpretation of dental wear difficult and obscuring any significant differences in overall dietary preferences. Despite some ecological variation, Butzer (1977:576) feels that there is ". . .no correlation between different types of australopithecines and drier or wetter settings. Neither is there any external evidence to support the notion that gracile and robust lineages had different diets."

Associated Fauna. In times past, the African plains sustained an incredible fauna (Figure 17-9), surpassing modern-day game preserves. There is evidence of much large game; the

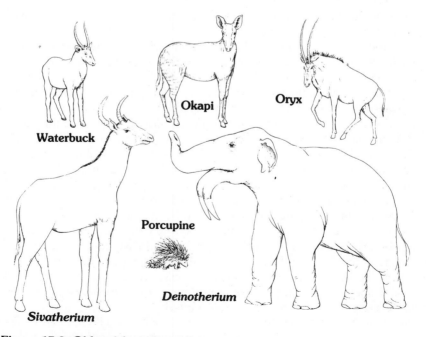

Figure 17-9. Olduvai faunal remains.

largest creatures were the elephants and their relatives. Although resembling modern elephants, they were generally shorter legged, and their teeth were more primitive. One of the most remarkable forms was the deinotherium, or hoetusker, an elephantlike form lacking large upper tusks typical of modern elephants. Instead, its lower jaw carried two great down-curving tusks that resembled an enormous hoe; these must have been impressive creatures.

Rhinoceroses were known to the australopithecines as were horses, which included both zebralike forms and the now extinct three-toed hipparions roaming in enormous herds over the Pliocene Old World. A related extinct group was the chalicotheres—great horselike creatures with enormous claws rather than hoofs. These claws may have been fatal to many early hunters.

Giraffes, looking much the same as modern forms, were present, as was the enormous antlered giraffe, or sivatherium. Despite their massive size, there is evidence that sivatheriums were attacked and killed by early hunters. Hippopotamuses abounded by the lakes and rivers; in the plains, bush, and forest there were various pig forms. Some of the pigs were gigantic and might have been dangerous adversaries to an unwary hominid.

Early Hominids as Prey. The early hominids possibly faced an array of carnivorous predators, the most formidable of which belonged to the cats. There is no evidence of the presence of hunting dogs which, working in large packs, can overcome most wild animals. Representatives of the great cats included the leopard and lion or animals immediately ancestral to them. Among the now-extinct forms were saber-toothed cats and the dirk-tooth (the dirk-tooth was the size of a leopard but heavier)—an agile hominid could have avoided them. Most dangerous perhaps were the lion-sized *Dinofelis* cats possessing moderately enlarged upper canines. These were probably more agile than the dirk-tooths and may have ambushed more than one hapless hominid.

If early hominids kept to open country away from thickets and if they traveled in groups, they would probably have been molested only rarely. Even when encountering a predator at close range, they might have put it to flight by using such typical primate intimidating behaviors as vocalizing, throwing objects, and shaking branches. Hominids would be most vulnerable when they came to water to drink, and present fossil accumulations suggest that our ancestors were most vulnerable exactly in such situations. Despite their potential disadvantages in this faunal array, early hominids survived. Therefore, they must have had some selective advantage(s), either biological or cultural, permitting their survival.

Food Sources. How did the early hominids support themselves? What did they do for food? How did they get it? The early hominids were probably hunters, foragers, and scavengers; there is direct evidence for this lifeway in the form of large bone accumulations at some sites. Some contend that such accumulations are the work of carnivores, such as hyenas, porcupines, and leopards. In an effort to determine whether the accumulations were left by hominids or carnivores, carnivore food remains were studied and we can now distinguish fairly accurately between remains left by carnivore and hominid predators.

Broken bones found in such profusion in Lower Pleistocene deposits are mostly from various kinds of antelope, both large and small. They also include bones of horses, giraffes, rhinoceroses, warthogs, baboons, and small reptilian remains and some bird skulls and egg shells. Most bones were split, perhaps to get the marrow. Evidence from Olduvai indicates that adult animals in their prime were also hunted.

It is difficult to assess the nature of food sources. Robinson (1952, 1954, 1963a, b) maintains that the robust form, the species *A. robustus,* was mainly a vegetarian. Robinson's dietary hypothesis is discussed later in this chapter. Most observers feel that the australopithecines were to some degree carnivorous; however, vegetable foods were surely incorporated in the diet.

Clark (1976) notes that 60 to 80 percent of the food of most modern hunters and gatherers consists of vegetable matter (Lee and DeVore, 1968; Woodburn, 1968) and suggests that the food of early hominids was predominantly vegetable (i.e., consisted primarily of herbaceous plants). Unfortunately, such food leaves little fossilized remains. Clark (1976:23) suggests that numerous polyhedral and other heavier stones found in the early sites could have been used for ". . . preparing the otherwise unpalatable parts of plants by breaking down of fibrous portions." The so-called choppers could be effective for pointing a stick to be used as a digging tool. Two broken bones from Olduvai collections show striations and polishing claimed to be similar to that produced by rubbing or digging in the ground.

Clark (1976:42) states, ". . .unfortunately, we have as yet no direct means of knowing for what purposes many of these tools were used." There may be a relationship between light-duty tools such as flake knives, small scrapers, and chopping tools and butchering. However, large cutting tools appear to be only incidentally associated with meat eating and other hunting pursuits (Clark and Haynes, 1970). Clark (1976) suggests that since cutting tools are often found at waterside sites they were general-purpose tools that could be related to vegetable collecting and preparation rather than solely meat preparation. At Kalambo Falls, Zambia, various edible fruits, seeds, and nuts are found associated with later Paleolithic living sites (Clark, 1969, 1974).

If early hominid radiation was partially based on newly emergent fruit-and-seed-eating strategies (Jolly's seed-eating hypothesis), certain segments of the woodland-bushland successions probably played unique roles in those adaptations. One question yet to be answered is: What effect, if any, did the early hominid communities have on the structure and dynamics of the floral community (Peters, 1979)?

In the dry season, planting and harvesting from various woodland/bushland tree legumes and from a variety of bush tree and liana species in thickets and groves could have regionally supported relatively large numbers of hominids (Peters, 1979; Stebbins, personal communication). Dry-season hominid scavenging and hunting would be likely where game was concentrated near water holes in rivers, and at springs and drips.

Comparative Data: Hunting Carnivores. The manner in which early hominids obtained meat protein has received wide attention. The easiest means of acquisition are hunting and scavenging. In a recent study, Schaller and Lowther (1969) undertook to determine early hominid hunting methods by studying the behavior of African social carnivores. The social systems of the wolf, wild dog, spotted hyena, and lion resemble those of early hominids; the social carnivores hunt over large areas in search of prey. Schaller and Lowther attempted to describe some aspects of carnivore behavior bearing special relevance to the study of hominids when the latter were at a stage of cultural development lacking fire and sophisticated projectile weapons.

Social Organization: Hunting. Hunting in the open savanna implies a rather cohesive social organization; coordination and cohesion of group activities depends on the establishment of some subtle communication system. This is not to imply that these hunters were capable of articulate speech, for there can be no anatomical evidence to support this or refute it. Furthermore, social carnivores manifest various forms of cooperation, especially during hunting, without articulate speech. Even without an elaborate communicatory network and with their small brains, social carnivores use a variety of cooperative hunting techniques. The social carnivore evidence indicates that a carnivorous hominid could have used cooperative hunting techiques, such as relay races to wear down the prey, driving it to members lying in ambush, and encircling and attacking it from many directions to obtain their meat. Lacking technologically advanced implements, early hominids must have hunted from ambush or by such means as driving the prey into rivers, over cliffs, or into deep mud. Most likely they used methods less dependent on speed and physical prowess than on group cooperative behavior.

Mary Leakey (1976) provides evidence concerning the hunting methods of the Olduvai hominids. The discovery of an extinct elephant, *Deinotherium*, embedded in clay deposits and associated with a number of stone tools suggests that it may have been driven into swamps to be killed. The repeated discovery of animals that seem to have died in a similar circumstances lends support to this assumption. Remains of two antelope heads similarly embedded in clay, one in Bed II and another in Bed IV, further support this suggestion. Depressed fractures of the frontlets of three skulls from site FLK North indicate that the animals were killed by a blow from close quarters. The fractures are all above the eye orbits, the most vulnerable part of the skull. Spheroids (rounded stones) found at Olduvai may have been used as bola stones that were thrown at animals to bring them down.

Food Sharing. Food sharing, atypical of our nonhuman primate relatives, is typical of social carnivores.[3] Some food sharing probably characterized the early hominids; males probably hunted, obtained the choice pieces, and divided the remainder among the old, infirm, females, and young. Those remaining behind probably collected roots, tubers, and berries. If data from modern hunter-gatherers are indicative these gathered food sources, usually obtained by females, were the dietary mainstay.

Once food sharing began, it is likely that rules governing the priority of shares appeared. The more complicated the rules and the more members with whom food had to be shared, the greater the pressures for increasing the complexity of the communicatory network. Perhaps some of the first social rules regulating human behavior stemmed from the hunting situation. While the hunting activity itself may not have required complex communicatory behavior, the rules of sharing may have and this may be one basis selecting for symbolic communication, language.[4]

How To Get by: Prey Selection. Schaller and Lowther's study suggests that the ease with which meat can be obtained varies seasonally. The four major methods for obtaining meat probably included scavenging for meat among migratory animals, driving other predators from their kills, capturing sick animals or the newborn of large mammals, and by hunting itself. Evidence from the social carnivores suggests that most prey are vulnerable animals; given a choice, weak, young, and old animals are most often taken. The hunts of early hominids must have had a relatively high rate of failure, and, as is consistent with the Olduvai and Taung remains, much of the prey must have been weak, young, or old.

Group Size. Given that there are advantages and disadvantages to group hunting, there must have been an optimum group size. Most nonhuman primates live in groups of 5 to 100 animals;[5] group sizes vary according to the habitat, among other factors. Terrestrial species almost always live in larger groups and groups of forest species are generally smaller than those of open-country forms. Social carnivore group sizes vary with the species and habitat.

[3]It is important to note, however, that hunting chimpanzees do share their kill. They have a specialized begging gesture, palm up, hand outstretched, when wanting to share. See Chapter 12.

[4]However, group-hunting carnivores also share food with youngsters and others left behind, and there is no use of language.

[5]Larger groups are known. For example, artifically fed Japanese macaque troops are recorded to be as large as 750 animals.

The group sizes of contemporary hunting and gathering groups vary; the most effective social group among the African Bushmen is from three to four families to upwards of 100 people. The size and structure is flexible and the group reaches its maximum size when food is plentiful. The same is noted for the African Hadza and Mbuti Pygmy. The hunting and gathering group ranges within the confines of a circumscribed unit of relatively small size. Group size fluctuates in proportion to the amount and distribution of resources, although the average size tends toward 25 members. Sugiyama (1972) notes a similar pattern of group flux among chimpanzees. When food is plentiful a number of groups gather in an area to feed; when food is scarce separate foraging groups go their own way. It is quite likely that social groups of ancestral hominids behaved accordingly.[6]

Infanticide. Joseph Birdsell suggests that early hunters were dependent on a generalized and localized fauna and flora. Modal group size probably approached 25, matings were exogamous (outside the immediate group), and the groups were male dominated. When large food sources were regionally or seasonally concentrated, local groups would become larger, and the social rules would be more complex. Birdsell feels that family size was maintained with systematic female infanticide and suggests that infanticide claimed between 15 and 50 percent of the live births.

Lifespan. Australopithecine lifespans were short; of the gracile forms (here designated *A. africanus*) from the Transvaal caves, more than one-third (35 percent) died prior to adulthood. The robust form *(A. robustus)* from Swartkrans and Kromdraai was worse off, for well over 75 percent of the remains are of children and youngsters. Survivorship rates of the two species may have differed: *A. africanus* succumbed at an average of 22.9 years and *A. robustus* at an average of 18.0 years. Although *A. africanus* may have lived somewhat longer than *A. robustus* on the the average, the maximum age reached by each was similar. Perhaps the robust forms at Swartkrans and Kromdraai belong to the last of their stock; their high mortality may indicate mounting environmental pressures. However, because of the small sample size, Mann (1975) feels that this type of exercise is fruitless.

A Look in the Mirror

One very important fact often overlooked when discussing the Lower Pleistocene hominid morphology is the scattered nature of the remains (Table 17-7). Our interpretations are often skewed by the nature of the materials; some sites yield disproportionate remains. A statistical analysis of almost any anatomical part over the entire African sample is likely to be heavily biased by characteristics and samples from such South African sites as Swartkrans and Sterkfontein. One well-preserved skeleton could make a major difference to the composition of any of the samples. Although early hominid remains are numerous, some parts are poorly represented. The remains of a small number of well-preserved specimens often predominate; as with an iceberg, there is still so much below the surface.

As Behrensmeyer (1975) notes, the preburial survival potential of bones relates to the great variability of their size, shape, and density. Relatively light bones, such as vertebrae or bones with a high surface-to-volume ratio, such as ribs, tend to be more easily transported and weathered than limb parts and teeth. Considering the survival potential of parts such as the cranium and teeth, it is obvious that teeth are more likely to survive stream transport than the

---

[6]For a fuller discussion of group sizes refer to Lee and DeVore, 1968, especially pp. 245-48.

Table 17-7. Percentages of Hominid Skeletal Remains from Three East African Locales

Items	Olduvai Beds I through IV	Shungura, Omo	Koobi Fora, Lake Turkana
Isolated teeth	33%	90%	11%
Associated teeth (number of occurrences)	16%	0%	3%
Mandibles	2%	4%	34%
Cranial parts	23%	2%	19%
Associated cranial and mandibular parts	7%	1%	3%
Postcranial (isolated)	5%	5%	24%
Postcranial (associated)	12%	0%	5%
Associated cranial and postcranial parts	2%	0%	2%
Total number of specimens represented in this table for each locale	43	167	106

Adapted from A. Behrensmeyer, "Taphonomy and Paleoecology in the Hominid Fossil Record," p. 41. *Yearbook of Physical Anthropology,* © 1975.

larger and more fragile cranium. However, in weathering conditions with temperature extremes and moist soil, as is typical of East African savannas, teeth may crack and disintegrate long before the skull.

Carnivore and scavenger activity causes initial alteration of the number of different bones available for fossilization. Most early hominid fossil remains were likely scavenged before burial. Lighter elements would be less susceptible to burial and more likely destroyed by abrasion and weathering than denser bone elements. This study of the processes of burial and fossilization, **taphonomy,** can help answer how bones relate to the environment where the hominids lived.

As an example of the survival potential of bones, Behrensmeyer cites the Lake Turkana sample. As of 1973, this sample contained 120 hominids, representing a time span of 1.5 million years. Assuming an average lifespan of 25 years (Mann, 1975) and a stable average population of 50 individuals, the sample of 120 specimens may come from an actual total of 3 million individuals. In other words, only four hundred thousandths (0.00004) of the original number of hominids are represented by this fossil sample. It must also be remembered that Lake Turkana is one of the best-known fossil hominid collections.

Jaws and Teeth. Dental traits have received more attention than any other skeletal remains; a major reason for this is that so many teeth have been preserved. Australopithecine teeth (permanent and deciduous) are essentially hominid; the total dental pattern conforms with the Family Hominidae. There is no canine diastema or only a small diastema. The upper incisors are small. The canines are larger than commonly true in modern populations, but are reduced compared with pongids. The canines are not pointed; early they wear flat at the tip and do not project beyond the level of adjacent teeth (Figure 17-10). The first premolars are bicuspid. The detailed pattern of the molar cusps resembles that of subsequent hominids, *H. erectus* and *H. sapiens.*

Dentally, the early hominids are clearly distinct from pongids, but, although essentially hominid, there are some differences from the teeth of *H. sapiens*. The premolar and molar teeth are large; the third lower molar commonly exceeds the length of the second. There are some other distinguishing traits, but these are evidently primitive hominid characters, for they also appear among Middle Pleistocene *H. erectus*.

Dentally, the early hominids were characterized by rather short canines, relatively vertically implanted incisors, relatively large premolars, and molars possessing thick enamel. Dental variability increased over time and hominids that had hyperrobust cheek teeth and large chewing musculature developed. Other hominids had teeth and musculature more comparable to those of the Middle Pleistocene *Homo* (Peters, 1979).

Cranium and Face. The morphology and dimension of the skull first inclined anatomists and anthropologists to suggest that *Australopithecus* was an ape allied to the gorilla or chimpanzee rather than a primitive member of the Hominidae. The small brain case and massive, projecting jaws give a superficial pongid look (Figure 17-11). However, as more crania were uncovered and critically examined, this resemblance was found to be superficial.

Brain Size. At first many felt that the australopithecine cranial capacity was too small to include them within the Hominidae. The **range of variation** in australopithecine cranial capacity is from approximately 400 to 600 + cc; this compares with a range of 1000 to 2000 cc for modern *Homo*.[7] Modern chimpanzees, approximately the same size as the early australopithecines, yield a range of 320 to 485 cc, with a mean of 394 cc for a sample of 144 individuals.

Compared with modern hominids, Pliocene-Early Pleistocene hominids had relatively small cranial capacities (even when adjusted for the brain size/body size ratio). However, even the smaller-brained hominids had relatively larger cranial capacities than contemporaneous pongids. It is assumed that the functional significance of larger later hominid cranial capacities reflects increasing capabilities for technology and complex social behavior. Long-term memory may also have been facilitated by the increasing cranial capacities. As Peters (1979:263) notes, "This becomes environmentally significant, for example, when coupled with the use of fire, because short-term successional patterns could then be modified, and results monitored in quasi-experimental fashion by the earliest 'fire ecologists'."

Evolutionary changes in cranial capacity are often correlated with overall change, for example, increasing complexity, in hominid technological capability. However, technological increases in complexity lag behind evolutionary changes in cranial capacities. This is most apparent from the last 100,000 years in prehistory. The earliest examples of stone artifacts do not appear to display evidence that their makers had any more neurological capacity for technology than that possessed by the living chimpanzee (Peters, 1979).

Holloway (1974, 1975) has studied the internal casts of australopithecine brain cases. Holloway has been able to show three important ways in which the australopithecine brains differed from those of pongids.

1. There is an expansion of the posterior parietal association areas.

---

[7]There are a number of problems associated with obtaining brain size estimates. Cranial capacity, for example, is only an approximation of the size of the brain. All three methods of obtaining brain size estimates, the determination of volume of a natural and an artifical brain case, and the determination of the capacity of the brain case, only provide an estimate of the volume of the space of the cranium. They do not provide an estimate of the volume of the brain itself, for the cranial cavity accommodates much more than simply brain (Tobias, 1971).

2. There is greater complexity of the frontal lobes, especially in some of the speech areas.
3. There is an expansion of the temporal lobes.

These three features correspond to some of the unique developments of the human brain. "The expansion in the frontal and parietal regions seems to underly the complex neural models whose behavioral manifestations are regarded as culture" (Wolpoff, 1980:143). Holloway argues that the australopithecine brains differ from ours in size more than in organization.

Skull of **Australopithecus robustus.** Reference should be made to the skulls of the robust variety of australopithecine. A major characteristic of *A. robustus* skulls is the presence of a **sagittal crest,** a bony ridge dissecting the midline of the top of the skull. A well-

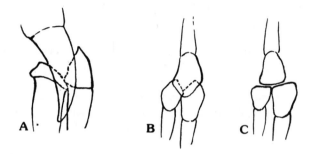

Figure 17-10. Occlusion of canines in apes and hominids. (A) An ape's upper canine overlaps and touches the lower first premolar and lower canine; in biting and chewing, it grinds a shearing edge against these teeth. (B) Initially the unworn canine in hominids (*Australopithecus* and *Homo*) overlaps the same two lower teeth, but (C) a rotary chewing motion wears the teeth down to a certain extent. Eventually, the points of all three teeth wear, and all of them acquire smooth occlusal surfaces. Modern *Homo sapiens* generally does not chew enough to arrive at stage C, and the teeth may remain at stage B.

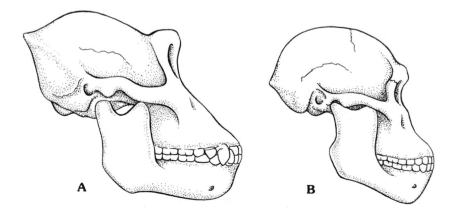

Figure 17-11. Skull of (A) a female gorilla compared with (B) a late australopithecine (*Australopithecus africanus*).

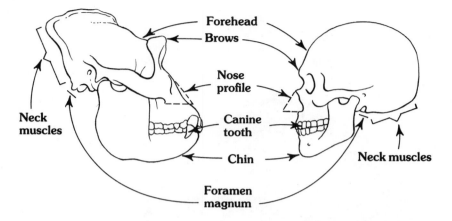

Figure 17-12. The skull of a gorilla compared with that of modern *Homo*.

developed sagittal crest is typical of large pongids (Figure 17-12), and when a crest appeared on an australopithecine skull, some assumed it was strictly comparable with the crest of pongids. However, while the robust australopithecines possess a crest, they share many cranial characteristics with the gracile australopithecines.

Hints at Posture. One of the features of the well-preserved Sterkfontein skull number 5 is the height of the cranial vault over the eyes (Figure 17-14). The relative height of the australopithecine skull exceeds the range of variation in pongid skulls and comes within the hominid range. The back of the skull (the nuchal area) suggests the hominid type of head balance on the neck, a reduction of the neck muscles, and a slight facial reduction. These reflect the assumption of an erect or semierect posture.

Two features of the australopithecine skull—cranial height and level of the **nuchal crest**—are directly or indirectly related to the pose of the head upon the vertebral column. Australopithecine neck musculature was not extensively developed to support the head in relation to a forward-sloping cervical spine, as is typical of modern large pongids. This, in conjunction with pelvic and limb morphology, indicates a shift toward an upright posture.

Pelvis and Limb Bones. No part of the postcranial anatomy shows more marked contrasts between modern anthropoid apes and humans than the pelvis (Figure 17-15). A primary factor determining the evolutionary separation of the Hominidae and Pongidae was the divergent modification of the locomotor skeletons for different life styles. The pelvis of *H. sapiens* and its ancestors became modified to accept an upright bipedal posture. If, as we suggest, these early forms are representatives of a hominid stock, their limb and pelvic structure is relevant to the determination of their taxonomic status. Several australopithecine pelvic remains come from South Africa. All exhibit hominid traits although there are some differences from the modern hominid pelvises (Figure 17-16). The same is true of the "Lucy" pelvic material recently excavated from Ethiopia.

Functional Implications. There are two major questions we can ask: Are these characteristics meaningful in terms of the functional anatomy of the limb skeleton, and can we make inferences from these characteristics as to the manner of posture and locomotion? The

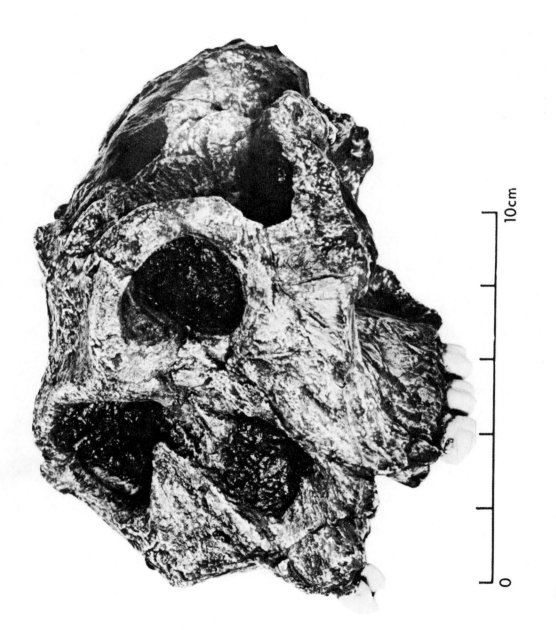

Figure 17-13. Swartkrans cranium.

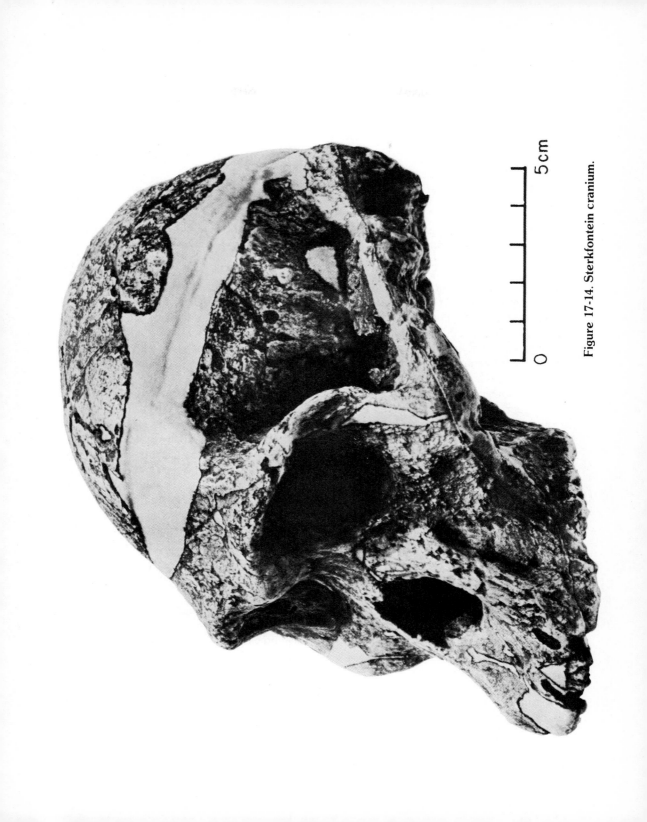

Figure 17-14. Sterkfontein cranium.

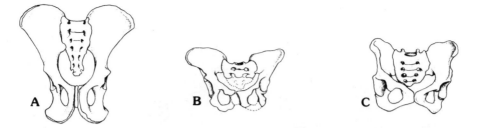

Figure 17-15. The pelvis of (A) chimpanzee, (B) *Australopithecus,* and (C) *Homo sapiens.* All are drawn to the same scale.

answers are: yes, the morphological traits reveal much about the functional anatomy of the limb skeleton, and yes, we can make inferences as to posture and locomotion. For example, the broadening of the ilium (the uppermost part of the pelvis) extends the area for attachment of the gluteal muscles used for balancing the trunk on the lower limbs. Other changes realigned the pelvis and corresponding muscular structure, allowing bipedal locomotion. The configuration of the australopithecine pelvis suggests they were capable of an erect posture and bipedal locomotion.

In a number of recent publications (i.e., Lovejoy, 1973, 1975; Lovejoy et al., 1973) and in personal communications C. Owen Lovejoy has argued that the pelvic structure of the early hominids was better adapted to bipedalism than is the modern *H. sapiens* pelvic structure. According to Lovejoy this is particularly true of females. Given the small cranial capacities of the early hominids there would have been less conflicting pressure selecting for effective bipedalism on the one hand and a large birth canal on the other. In modern females, however, the pelvic structure is the result of adaptive pressures both for effective bipedalism and for a birth canal that can accommodate a large-brain infant. Lovejoy is of the opinion that in modern *Homo* the pressures are stronger for giving birth to large-brained infants and that the pelvic girdle adaptations for bipedalism are therefore compromised. In light of this argument the modern human male pelvis more accurately mirrors the ancestral condition than does the modern female pelvis. Lovejoy et al. (1973:778) state:

> Those morphological differences between *Australopithecus* and modern man which are of mechanical significance appear to be related to the combination of a fully bipedal striding gait with different degrees of encephalization, rather than to differences in the gait pattern itself.

Not everyone agrees on the extent or capacity for bipedalism among the early hominids. For example, Oxnard and Lisowski (1980) argue that the Olduvai foot specimen numbered OH (Olduvai hominid) 8 is not adapted for bipedality in the same manner as among hominids and that the OH 8 foot displays features that resemble those found in the feet of arboreal creatures. Oxnard and Lisowski suggest that the foot of OH 8 belongs to an animal that, whatever else it was capable of doing, might have also been capable of climbing and other arboreal activities (Oxnard, 1975). Oxnard and Lisowski suggest that the foot of OH 8 may

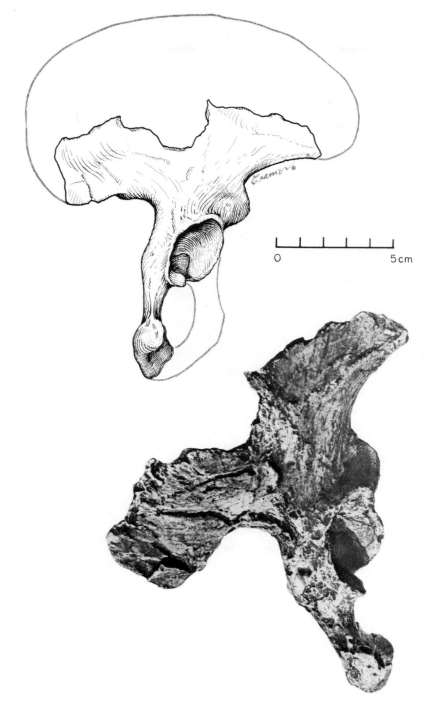

Figure 17-16. Swartkrans innominate bone.

have been that of an animal capable of some type of bipedal walking, but it is likely that the form placed its feet on the ground more in the manner of the chimpanzee or gorilla. These authors suggest, however, the possibility that the foot was still well adapted for arboreal activities in a manner similar to that of modern hominids. Oxnard and Lisowski visualize a creature capable of both arboreal and terrestrial activities, but they reject the position that the foot is from a creature with strictly human bipedality.

After analyzing the locomotor behaviors of modern chimpanzees and humans, Prost (1980) concludes that the australopithecines possessed anatomical traits that were adapted to arboreal quadrupedal vertical climbing, while at the same time having the capacity to perform terrestrial bipedalism virtually identical to that of humans. Prost suggests that certain "brachiating" traits in the human were at the same time reflections of an adaptation to vertical climbing, for example, those traits that the human pectoral limb shares in common with the ape, or brachiating, pectoral limb. If we evolved from climbers, we need never have had a brachiating ancestry. The brachiating theory of human origins would be superfluous.

Prost states that the australopithecines look about 80 percent "bipedal" in their morphology. Their "bipedal" traits, he argues, are probably climbing traits, and the predominance of "bipedal" traits does not guarantee bipedalism. Prost suggests that the australopithecines were preeminent climbers and facultative bipeds, adapted to life in the trees by climbing, but moving on the ground as humans do. Hominids became consistent bipeds coincident with their becoming terrestrial exploiters of the food niche. With a shift to consistent bipedalism, climbing adaptations were lost and bipedal refinements were acquired.

Leg Bones. Leg bones, the **tibia** and **fibula** (Figure 17-17), uncovered at Olduvai indicate that the bipedal adaptation was well advanced in the ankle. The South African site at Kromdraai yielded one of the ankle bones, the talus, evidencing an intermediate condition

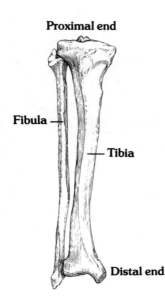

Figure 17-17. Landmarks on a modern tibia and fibula.

between that of *H. sapiens* and the pongids. The hominid conditions of the bone would have permitted enough stability at the ankle joint for weight-bearing in the erect posture.

   Foot. An almost complete foot skeleton, missing the toes and part of the heel, has been found at Olduvai (Figure 17-18). The foot is small and shows a remarkable anatomical resemblance to the foot of *Homo.* There is no divergence between the first and second toes typical of the pongid grasping feet. The foot does, however, differ somewhat from that of modern *Homo,* for the transmission of weight and propulsive effort through the forepart of the foot was not as fully evolved as in modern hominids. The foot bones suggest that the striding gait typical of *H. sapiens* had not evolved.

   Upper Limbs. The scanty evidence indicates that the hand and upper-limb bones were not specialized for arboreal activities, as they are in modern pongids. Nevertheless, in a recent study, R. Susman and J. Stern argue that the hand of OH 7 had the functional capacity to partake in suspensory locomotion. They suggest (1979:572) that ". . . early hominids may have retained a capacity for climbing even past the point at which the foot became adapted for bipedalism." Although little is known of the upper extremities, evidence suggests that the australopithecines possessed mobile arms and a hand with an opposable thumb capable of the fine manipulative movements needed for holding and grasping small objects. The hands could use tools, and there is no anatomical reason why they were incapable of fabricating them.

   Cranial and postcranial features demonstrate that early hominids relied on terrestrial bipedality. Additional pelvic and femoral changes in early Pleistocene *Homo* may be related to increasing brain size, as suggested by Lovejoy. Since hominid bipedality does not promote speed, nor does it necessarily promote endurance compared with a variety of quadrupedal animals, the hominids were perhaps bipedally specialized for effective transport (e.g., water and food) and weapons use.

   Early hominids, especially those of the genus *Australopithecus,* also appear to have possessed an upper limb and shoulder morphology more adapted to arboreal modes than subsequent middle Pleistocene hominids and modern *Homo.* An arboreal-terrestrial and bipedal-terrestrial habitat and postural capabilities was presumably the hallmark of the early hominids (Peters, 1979).

Taxonomy

   The Roots of Discord. The early hominids were a morphologically diverse group, a fact indicated by the various schemes devised to accommodate them (Table 17-8). Some authorities recognize one genus *Australopithecus* containing various species. Others recognize two genera, *Australopithecus* and *Homo,* with a number of species. For some the only differences within the group are between robust and gracile forms, known respectively as *A. africanus* and *A. robustus.* Some argue that all the forms from the Lower Pleistocene should simply be placed in the genus *Homo.* Others argue that size differences within the grade do not reflect taxonomic differences but only extremes of sexual dimorphism.

   One Lower Pleistocene Hominid Genus? Many feel that Lower Pleistocene hominids can be accommodated within the one genus *Australopithecus,* or even *Homo,* with a number of specific designations. Scientists of this persuasion feel that the anatomical differences are not of the same degree as those usually regarded as adequate for generic distinctions. There are differences, but such is to be expected, given the accepted time span of the group—from about 5 million or more years to perhaps 750,000 years ago—and their geographical range from Ethiopia to South Africa. Such differences may only permit a broad subdivision within the two main groups. Hominids from Kromdraai, Swartkrans, Olduvai (i.e., "Zinjanthropus") and

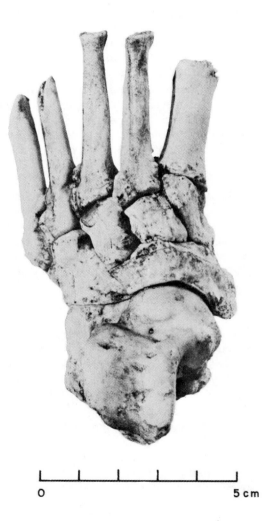

Figure 17-18. Olduvai articulated foot.

Table 17-8. Pliocene-Pleistocene African Hominids

South Africa		
Form		*Age (Millions of Years)*
	Gracile group	
Australopithecus africanus	Taung (Dart, 1924)[a]	
	Sterkfontein (Broom, 1936, 1947)	
	Makapansgat (1948)	
	Robust group	
A. robustus	Kromdraai (Broom, 1938)	2.0-1.5
	Swartkrans (Broom, 1949)	2.0-1.5

East Africa		
	Gracile group	
Homo habilis	Olduvai (L. and M. Leakey, 1960)	1.8
	Lake Turkana (R. Leakey, 1969	
	through 1974)	1.8
	Omo (Howell, 1967 through 1974)	3.0
	Hadar (Taieb and Johanson,	
	1973 through 1975)	3.0
A. africanus	Kanapoi (Patterson, 1965)	4.0
	Lothagam (Patterson, 1967)	5.5
	Hadar (Taieb and Johanson,	
	1973 through 1974)	2.9
	Lake Turkana (R. Leakey, 1969	
	through 1974)	1.8
	Robust group	
A. boisei	Olduvai (L. and M. Leakey, 1959)	1.75
	Lake Turkana (R. Leakey, 1969	
	through 1974)	1.8
	Omo (Howell, 1967 through 1974)	3.0

[a]Dates following individual names refer to year or years when reports of these finds were published.

Adapted from B. G. Campbell, *Humankind Emerging,* 2nd ed., p. 148. Little, Brown and Company, Boston, © 1979.

some remains from Omo and Lake Turkana appear to be larger, with more massively constructed skulls, larger jaws and teeth, and a somewhat larger cranial capacity than those from Taung, Sterkfontein, Makapansgat, Olduvai ("pre-Zinj"), and some materials from Omo and Turkana. The typical australopithecine traits are less extreme in this latter group.

One-genus adherents recognize two major species; the gracile forms are maintained in the species *A. africanus,* the robust forms in the species *A. robustus.* Of the two, *A. africanus* is smaller, lighter built, and more slender in skeletal morphology. The robust form is larger and exhibits pronounced bony ridges and crests on the skull. *A. africanus* is considered to have occurred earlier in time and to be more "advanced" than *A. robustus.* However, *A. robustus* is considered to be more specialized and somewhat divergent from the main line of hominid evolution.

Dietary Hypothesis. This view was first expounded by John Robinson, who originally maintained that differences within the australopithecine groups warrant recognizing two genera, *Australopithecus* and *Paranthropus*. However, Robinson (1972) has now suggested that *Australopithecus* should be included in the genus *Homo* and that *Paranthropus* is a parahominid group distinct from fully bipedal, erect, culture-bearing animals. Robinson feels that the robust variety was a vegetarian and that *Homo*, the gracile form, was a carnivore. The dietary habits are based on postulated habitat differences and are reflected in dental and cranial traits. Robinson feels that the cranial architecture of the robust form is related to its dental specialization.

Robinson's argument rests on the size disparity between anterior and posterior teeth in the robust form. Although many question the supposed disparity, Robinson feels the variance reflects dietary specializations. The larger canine and incisor size of the gracile form supposedly reflects its carnivorous nature, and the large molars and reduced canines and incisors of the robust form indicate its vegetarian nature. Robinson argues that the teeth of the robust form are specialized for crushing and grinding food, supporting his contention by noting that enamel flakes were detached from the molar grinding surfaces. The enamel chipping is supposedly caused by grit adhering to the roots and tubers that supposedly formed a large portion of its diet.

Robinson has unrelentingly argued that something similar to the gracile form is the basis of later hominids. The robust form is a specialized offshoot that changed relatively little during its evolutionary career and eventually became extinct. The evolutionary inertia witnessed in the robust form is related to its supposedly not being a tool maker and probably only a nominal tool user. The gracile form, by contrast, made and used tools and most likely hunted.

DuBrul (1977) attempted to define the diets of the gracile and robust australopithecine forms by investigating jaw mechanics and by comparing these forms with bears eating comparable foods. The grizzly bear (of the Genus *Ursus*) is at an extreme of carnivorous adaptation whereas the giant panda (of the Genus *Ailuropoda*) is at an extreme of herbivorous adaptation. Using these bears as extant models, DuBrul suggests that the australopithecine forms represent two distinctly different forms based on different feeding behaviors. He disagrees with the suggestion made by Pilbeam (1972) and others that all the differences between the two forms are subservient to simple increases in cheek-tooth size. Instead, he argues that selection acted on the integrated oral complex as a total feeding device, of which the dentition was but one component.

DuBrul suggests that *A. africanus* was probably omnivorous and would eat anything, including some meat. *A. boisei* (a robust form) exhibits all the features of extreme herbivory.

Contrasting with Robinson's position that the robust and gracile australopithecines represent two separate evolutionary lines is the the interpretation of Brace (1972), McHenry (1975), Pilbeam and Gould (1974), and Wolpoff (1974); all of whom argue that differences between the two groups of australopithecines are simply due to the large body size of the robust forms. The robust form has been estimated to be between 10 and 25 percent bigger than the gracile australopithecines (Lovejoy and Heiple, 1970; McHenry, 1974, 1975). These authors argue that australopithecines are examples of allometry (differential growth of parts of the body in relation to growth of the entire organism). In allometric growth, the shape of an animal can change as a result of changes in overall size, and such shape changes do not necessarily denote any adaptive shift. If allometry is working among the australopithecines, the large molar teeth of the robust forms only represent the needed tooth area to provide for a larger animal, and do not represent evidence for any dietary differences (Wood and Stack, 1980).

The major proponents of the allometric viewpoint are Pilbeam and Gould (1974). Recently, however, Wood and Stack (1980) have argued that the important differences in dental proportions between the gracile *A. africanus* and the robust *A. robustus* and *A. boisei*, do not correspond with allometric trends noted among modern primates. They suggest that the differences in dental proportions between the gracile and robust australopithecines may be significant morphological adaptations, perhaps indicating dietary modification or social behavior.

Homo habilis. The argument that *H. habilis* is a valid taxon is most closely associated with its original proponent, Louis Leakey. In 1961 Leakey announced recovery of material from Bed I, Olduvai, from a new site slightly lower than the one where the discovery of the hominid, "Zinjanthropus," had previously been announced. Leakey named his new form *Homo habilis*. Assignment of this form to the genus *Homo,* that genus to which we belong, reflects Leakey's feeling that *Homo habilis* was a precursor of modern hominids. Leakey subsequently made other finds at Olduvai that he assigned to *H. habilis*.

Homo habilis has a larger brain than some of its contemporaries; its brain size has been estimated at 680 cc. It is said to have had a smoother skull, especially in comparison to robust australopithecines. The teeth are supposedly more humanlike. The modern-looking foot from Bed I is attributed to *H. habilis,* and Leakey and some others place the Bed I hand bones with the *H. habilis* type. Some material from the Omo excavations has provisionally been assigned to *H. habilis*.

According to the supporters of *H. habilis* this form lived side-by-side with the robust australopithecines in East Africa between 1 million and 2 million years ago. Leakey argues that its head shape resembled ours, that their hands allowed manufacture of precision tools, that they walked erect, and that they built shelters. Leakey feels they represent a separate line of hominid evolution; members of this group manufactured the tools found throughout East and South African Lower Pleistocene depositions. Leakey is convinced that *H. habilis* is on the direct line to modern *Homo* and that other claimants to that position should be ignored.

Those arguing counter to Leakey and his supporters call *H. habilis* another gracile australopithecine. Some view *H. habilis* as merely an advanced member of the gracile group, a form on its way toward the next hominid evolutionary stage. A meeting of the minds is not in sight, and we must simply await further developments.

Third Hominid Model. The possibility that a third hominid line existed in the Lower Pleistocene was proposed by Richard Leakey and his coworkers and was first announced in 1972 at a meeting of the Zoological Society of London. Leakey stated, ". . . preliminary comparisons with other evidence indicate the new material will take a central place in re-thinking and re-evaluation of the evidence for the origin of *Homo sapiens,* modern man's species." Leakey's 1972 remarks were based on materials derived from Lake Turkana deposits now dated to approximately 1.8 million years ago.

Leakey's original proposal for a third hominid line is primarily based on his wife's painstaking reconstruction of hundreds of skull fragments. This material is referred to as KNM (Kenya National Museum)-ER (East Rudolf)[8] 1470 (Figure 17-19). The fragments were found protruding from a steep slope at a level below a stratum of volcanic tuff first dated to 2.6 million years ago. Casts of the reconstructed skull yield estimates of a cranial capacity slightly more

[8]Although the Kenya government renamed Lake Rudolf as Lake Turkana, Ethiopia still refers to the area as Lake Rudolf.

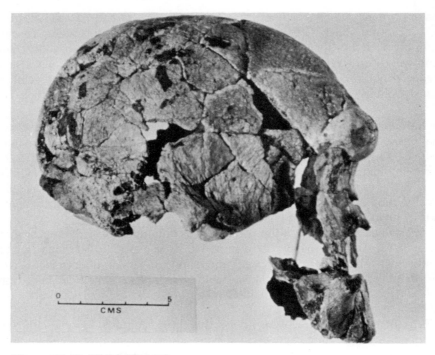

Figure 17-19. KNM-ER 1470.

than 775 cc, more than the previously known australopithecine range based on a small sample. Furthermore, the brow ridges are less prominent than in *H. erectus.* The smaller brow ridges, plus a cranial capacity overlapping the range of early *H. erectus,* coupled with a pre-*H. erectus* date, raises questions on the actual place of *H. erectus* in subsequent hominid evolution. The cranial capacity of KNM-ER 1470 is larger than *Australopithecus,* the skull is more rounded, postorbital constriction less evident, and there is no sagittal cresting. The face and palate are robust, however, and the teeth were undoubtedly large.

Pebble tools and stone chips have been recovered from the same site. Four limb bones come from the site where the skull was uncovered, in a deposit of the same age. The limb bones are morphologically consistent with an erect, bipedal stance, as one would infer from the limb material discovered by Johanson from deposits 4 million years old and from the Laetoli footprints, both of which indicate habitual bipedalism.

Further discoveries from Pliocene-Pleistocene sediments of East Turkana include more cranial material, upper and lower limb bones, several toe bones, two teeth, some vertebrae, and hand bones (Table 17-9). These materials have been described by Leakey and his coworkers.

When Leakey first announced the discovery of KNM-ER 1470 he stated that the material provides "clear evidence" that, rather than evolving from *Australopithecus,* a "large brained, truly upright and two-legged form of the genus *Homo* existed contemporaneously with *Australopithecus* more than 2.5 million years ago." He further stated, "The skull is different from other known forms of early man and thus does not fit into any of the presently held theories of human evolution."

Table 17-9. Remains Attributable to *Homo* in the East Turkana Succession

Museum Number	Possible Date
Cranial Evidence	
KNM-ER 1470[a]	35 meters below KBS tuff dated to 1.8 million years ago.
KNM-ER 1590	Below KBS tuff.

Mandibles and isolated teeth

At the close of the 1972 season, 28 mandibles were collected; 13 have one or more preserved tooth crowns. Fifteen individuals are repesented by isolated teeth only; all but one are specimens of permanent teeth.

KNM-ER 730	Just below Koobi Fora tuff dated to 1.57 million years ago.
KNM-ER 992	1.3 million years ago.
KNM-ER 820 (juvenile mandible)	1.6 million to 2.6 million years ago.

Postcranial Evidence

At the close of the 1972 season, 24 postcranial bones and four sets of associated limb bones were collected.

KNM-ER 737 (left femoral shaft)	1.6 million to 1.8 million years ago.
KNM-ER 164 (two proximal hand phalanges, one cervical and one thoracic vertebra)	1.6 million to 1.8 million years ago.
KNM-ER 803 (partial skeleton)	1.6 million years ago.
KNM-ER 813 (right talus and tibial fragment)	Broadly contemporaneous with 730.
KNM-ER 1472 (right femur—complete)	More than 2.6 million years ago.
KNM-ER 1475 (right femur—proximal end)	2.7 million years ago.
KNM-ER 1481 (lower limb—partial skeleton)	More than 2.6 million years ago.
KNM-ER 1591 (humerus—lacking head)	1.6 million to 1.8 million years ago.

[a] The forms listed separately in this table are those materials receiving some detailed study to date.

Adapted from B. Wood, "Remains Attributable to *Homo* in the East Rudolf Succession," p. 502, and M. Day, "Hominid Postcranial Remains from the East Rudolf Succession: A Review," pp. 508-9. *In* Y. Coppens, F. Howell, G. Isaac, and R. Leakey, eds. *Earliest Man and Environments in the Lake Rudolf Basin,* University of Chicago Press, Chicago © 1976.

Are any of the anatomical features of KNM-ER 1470 so different from corresponding parts of previously known forms that they fall outside the range of the population variability of these forms? Whether or not KNM-ER 1470 represents a previously undescribed form, Leakey's new materials add more fuel to the fires of controversy, and it is becoming increasingly apparent that the picture of hominid evolution is more complicated than once thought.

Richard Leakey announced (1976 and personal communication) the discovery of other remains from Lake Turkana. This material includes an upper part of a skull (KNM-ER 1590) and a hipbone. Leakey feels that this skull looks just the same as KNM-ER 1470.

It is crucial to the maintenance of Leakey's scheme that there be no doubt as to the dating of KNM-ER 1470. If the material should postdate the australopithecines, this could help explain its "advanced" traits, for example, large cranial capacity and lack of brow ridges. It is important, therefore, that recent dating of the Koobi Fora formation at East Turkana conflicts with the originally published date given as 2.6 million years ago for KNM-ER 1470 (Curtis et al., 1975). Some of the first to raise questions about the 2.6 million-year-old-date for the KBS tuff were paleontologists, for faunal remains from the tuff did not compare favorably with remains from other, supposedly well-calibrated localities.

Curtis et al. redated the KBS tuff using the conventional K-Ar dating method. Using pumice, they calculated an age of 1.60 ± 0.04 million years on six other analyses. Although this new dating is inconclusive, as was perhaps the original date, there now seems to be further question concerning the appropriate time span, and therefore the ultimate importance, of KNM-ER 1470. The newest date for the Lake Turkana tuff is 1.8 million years ago (Drake and Curtis, 1979) and this date appears to be the date gaining the widest acceptance.

According to Leakey's third hominid model, some of the East Turkana remains fall within the genus *Australopithecus,* including large and small members as well as an intermediate form. These specimens may represent a single species of A. *boisei* recorded at Olduvai and may be best represented by OH 5 ("Zinjanthropus"). The large amount of variation in size, demonstrated by crania, mandibles, and and some postcranial evidence, may be attributed to sexual dimorphism. Three crania, KNM-ER 406, 407, and 732, demonstrate the apparent sexual dimorphism. KNM-ER 406 is a large robust cranium with sagittal and nuchal crests, and KNM-ER 407 and 732 are more gracile specimens lacking cresting. Postcranial remains seem to support the single species contention.

The sample of specimens that Leakey attributes to *Homo* is small compared to that of *Australopithecus.* Certain species show traits contrasting markedly with those of *Australopithecus* from the same East Turkana locales. A number of mandibles from the upper members of Koobi Fora and Ileret have been assigned to *Homo.* The best examples are KNM-ER 992 and 820, which have been compared to *H. erectus.*

The alleged "small" form of the genus *Homo* derives from the Lower Member of Koobi Fora. This "small" form is best represented by the mandibles KNM-ER 1501 and 1503. The mandibles are small and lightly built and have small dentition. There are no known crania.

The alleged "large" form of the genus *Homo* is represented by crania KNM-ER 1470 and 1590 and by some mandibular material such as 1802. KNM-ER 1470 has a cranial capacity of 775 cc while that of 1590 may be larger. This material contrasts with other examples of the genus *Homo* except with certain Olduvai specimens assigned to *H. habilis,* for example, the skulls OH 7, OH 13, and OH 16.

There are also a number of forms that are too fragmentary for definite classification. These fall into the indeterminate category. Several other specimens in this group do not show traits entirely consistent with either *Homo* or *Australopithecus.* The skull of KNM-ER 1805, for example, has both sagittal and nuchal crests, but a relatively small mandible. This contrasts with the expected situation in which cresting is associated with large teeth. It also appears to have a relatively large cranial capacity compared with East Turkana remains of *Australopithecus.* Do the small teeth and large cranial capacity separate this form from *Australopithecus,* or are they acceptable traits within a range of variation? Are they perhaps representative of another species of *Australopithecus?*

A second cranium, 1813, also found in situ, but from deposits close to the age of the KBS tuff, has a cranial morphology similar to that of KNM-ER 407 and 732. It is considered to be a female representative of *Australopithecus.* However, it has relatively small maxillary dentition. The cranial capacity is probably less than 500 cc, quite below that of the *Homo* forms KNM-ER 1470 and 1802. The maxillary dentition suggests attribution to the "small" form of the genus *Homo* while the cranial capacity argues for the genus *Australopithecus.* Should the dental characeristics outweigh the other traits? What was the pace and form of mosaic evolution at this time period and among this group?

Finally, a well-preserved, relatively large mandibular specimen, KMN-ER 1482, from below the KBS tuff, suggests evidence, according to Richard Leakey, for a third hominid genus in the Lower Member of East Turkana. This mandible shows significant differences from either *Australopithecus* or *Homo*. The importance of this limited sample is unknown.

The large robust *Australopithecus* is well represented. This species may be sexually dimorphic and seems to change little over time. Dental, cranial, and postcranial evidence all bear witness to the existence of the genus *Homo*. There is little or no evidence for the gracile form of *Australopithecus* at Lake Turkana, although KNM-ER 1813 may fit in this taxon. Perhaps there is evidence at Lake Turkana of a small-brained *Homo*. Leakey argues that it is clear that a "large" form of *Homo* was contemporary with both the "small" hominid and the robust *Australopithecus*. Further analysis will prove or disprove this idea.

Pliocene-Pleistocene evolution from Lake Turkana appears to be very complex. There is confusion not only on generic affinities, but on ranges of variation, sexual dimorphism, and individual variability.

Homo or Australopithecus afarensis? In October, 1975 (Leakey et al., 1976) Mary Leakey announced recovery of new fossils dated between 3.5 million and 3.77 million years old. Samples of tuff stratigraphically identical with those containing the specimens are more than 3.5 million years old. The geographical and stratigraphic locations of the individuals' remains do not, however, suggest that they once formed a social group, as is the case for Johanson's Ethiopian materials. This site, Laetoli, yielding the material (see Howell, 1972, for a discussion of the biostratigraphy) is approximately 30 miles south of Olduvai Gorge and has been known for some time. However, these materials are the first important hominid fossils to be recovered at this site.

Laetoli has provided a rich collection of teeth and jaw fragments, and most of them are surface finds. The fossils evidently represent at least 13 individuals. Three finds, a mandible with deciduous and permanent teeth intact and two isolated groups of deciduous and permanent teeth, are embedded in volcanic tuffs. The two most complete remains consist of a child's mandible and the mandible of an approximately 15-year-old individual.

The Laetoli fossil material, including the original Garusi maxillary fragment, seems to represent one phylogenetic entity or lineage. Mary Leakey feels that the variations in the material are related to size and stem from individual and sexual factors. She feels that there is strong resemblance between the materials from Laetoli and later specimens assigned to the genus *Homo* in East Africa.

> Such assessment suggests placement of the Laetoli specimens among the earliest firmly dated members of this genus. It should come as no surprise that the earlier members of the genus *Homo* display an increasing frequency of features generally interpreted as 'primitive' or 'pongid like', which indicate derivation from as yet largely hypothetical ancestors (Leakey et al., 1976:466).

Mary Leakey feels there is strong resemblance between her material and that of Johanson's from Afar, but strongly disagrees as to its taxonomic ascription. Johanson and White (1979) include the material in their new taxon *A. afarensis* while Leakey refers it to *Homo*.

From the Laetoli beds at Laetoli, Mary Leakey (1979) has discovered hominid footprints dated to 3.5 million years ago. These footprints provide the oldest evidence of hominid bipedalism. Furthermore, the prints suggest a foot of modern construction. The prints belong to two or three individuals, one larger than the others. Based on the length of the imprints and the stride length, two individuals were less than 5 feet tall. The larger individual may have been 4 feet, 8 inches tall and the smaller individual about 4 feet tall. So far, the footprint trail is about 23 meters in length.

The disagreement between Johanson and Leakey has recently received wide press and scientific coverage (i.e., Johanson et al., 1978; Johanson and White, 1979). Johanson argues that the materials from Ethiopia and Laetoli share an array of distinctive morphological characters, suggesting that they belong to a single species of *Australopithecus* that differs considerably from previously described species. Johanson and White name this new species *A. afarensis* and suggest that it constitutes that oldest indisputable evidence of the Family Hominidae. This fossil assemblage is characterized by substantial size variation, which is interpreted as reflecting sexual dimorphism. They feel the new taxon displays a complex of primitive dental, cranial, and possibly postcranial characteristics.

Dental remains compose the largest portion of the Pliocene hominid sample from Hadar and Laetoli. Johanson and White (1979) argue that the adult and deciduous dentitions are intermediate between Hominidae and Pongidae in most of their features. They suggest that the materials from Hadar and Laetoli are one evolving lineage. Postcranial materials from both sites clearly indicate that the hominids were adapted to bipedalism; thus this is the earliest osteological evidence of bipedalism in the hominid fossil record.

According to Johanson and White (1978:325):

> . . .these forms represent the most primitive group of demonstrable hominids yet recovered from the fossil record. Although clearly hominid in their dentition, mandible, cranium, and postcranium, these forms retain hints of still poorly known Miocene ancestry.
>
> Bipedalism appears to have been the dominant form of terrestrial locomotion employed by the Hadar and Laetoli hominids.

Johanson and White suggest that dental measurements provide a link between the South African forms from the Sterkfontein type site and Makapansgat gracile australopithecines and the material from Hadar and Laetoli. They suggest that *A. afarensis* is the basal australopithecine stock from which *A. africanus* and *A. robustus* diverged in one direction to eventually become extinct, and *H. habilis* diverged in another direction to give rise to subsequent hominids.

Johanson and White suggest an apparent standstill in hominid evolution between the Hadar and Laetoli fossils separated by 0.5 million years. They feel the first evidence for the genus *Homo* in the fossil record appears with *H. habilis,* a form characterized by progressive brain enlargement associated with increasing cranial elaboration.

Johanson and White's claims conflict with those of Mary and Richard Leakey. Johanson and White now drop the claim that *Homo* coexisted with *Australopithecus* at Afar. They conclude that the remains represent only one species. Even though a fair amount of variation exists in certain fossils, they attribute the difference to sexual dimorphism.

Richard Leakey rejects the suggestion that differences between the fossils can be attributed to sexual dimorphism and argues that they reflect generic differences. This would, of course, lend support to his ideas that at least two genera of hominids, *Homo* and *Australopithecus,* coexisted at Lake Turkana. Leakey also suggests that *Homo* and *Australopithecus* coexisted as far back as 3 million to 4 million years ago. Johanson and White see only one lineage, *A. afarensis*, at that time.

Sexual Dimorphism. Wolpoff (1976a) suggests that the pattern of australopithecine sexual dimorphism differs from that of other higher primates: posterior-teeth dimorphism, mandibular-corpus dimorphism, and probably body-size dimorphism are at the extreme of higher-primate range. Canine dimorphism is, however, considerably less than in most living primates, excluding modern *Homo*. Wolpoff feels that the primary cause of the difference between hominid and pongid trends in the evolution of sexual dimorphism is the increasing importance of tools as a supplement and replacement for the canines in hominid evolution.

In Wolpoff's opinion the data suggest that the australopithecines were both polytypic and significantly sexually dimorphic. "In all, the australopithecines were unlike any living primate, combining the polytypism of living humans with the sexual dimorphism of baboons. Only the most variable of the higher primates can be used as an analog for australopithecine variation" (1976b:596). He asserts that the marked sexual dimorphism in Lower Pleistocene hominids as represented by the South African and Lake Turkana assemblages occurred independently in both gracile and robust forms and therefore does not offer a point of contrast between them.

Brace has commented rather widely (and has been widely misquoted) on the possible extent of the sexual dimorphism in the hominid fossil record. Until rather recently there has been an attempt to minimize the importance of sexual dimorphism in assessing early hominid remains. Because we have judged variation in the hominid fossil record from that exhibited among modern *Homo*, we may have seriously underestimated its importance in earlier hominid populations. Many investigators have not been alert to the possibility of greater contrasts between males and females than those that characterize modern populations. As Brace (1972) notes, the earliest terrestrial hominids should be expected to have the least effective cultural means of self-protection. Consequently, they may display a degree of sexual dimorphism approaching and perhaps equaling that exhibited in modern terrestrial nonhuman primates.

Many authors suspect that sexual dimorphism among the Pliocene-Pleistocene hominids was considerably greater than that within modern *Homo*. The conception of the robust Swartkrans form versus the gracile Sterkfontein form may be due to contrasts between males and females. While Brace has been falsely accused of suggesting that all males lived at one site and all females at another, it is seemingly possible that male specimens have been used to characterize one site and female specimens another site. Brace (1972) suggests that if a range of variation for males and females were constructed for each site, the average differences between the sites would be less than now held possible. If the Pliocene-Pleistocene hominids exhibited a dimorphism similar to that of baboons or gorillas (the latter of which is unlikely because none of the early forms were as large as gorillas), we should expect that cranial form differed in similar proportion between males and females. The persistence of large and small forms at Omo and Lake Turkana suggests that sexual dimorphism characterized the Pliocene-Pleistocene forms for a long time.

Perhaps the extremes of variation in early hominid populations can be accounted for by sexual dimorphism, perhaps not. However, this possibility has not yet been put to a systematic test. Whether sexual dimorphism accounts for all, or most, of the variation among the Pliocene-Pleistocene hominids is still a matter of debate.

The early hominids existed from perhaps as far back as 6 million or 7 million years ago, primarily in Africa. The East African forms seem to predate those in South Africa. The early hominids are a morphologically diverse group and, depending on whose interpretation one follows, some members of the group gave rise to the next hominid, *Homo erectus*. Some members of the group made and used tools, and some hunted. They lived in relatively small, bisexual, male-dominated groups, probably averaging 25 members.

The remarkable quantity of Lower Pleistocene materials conforms with a taxonomic position within the Hominidae and some members of the group appear to be the immediate evolutionary precursors of *H. erectus*.

Bibliography

Ayala, F. 1970. Competition, coexistence and evolution. In *Essays in evolution and genetics in honor of Theodosius Dobzhansky,* edited by M. Hecht and W. Steere, pp. 121-58. New York: Appleton-Century-Crofts.

_____. 1971. Competition between species: frequency dependence. *Science* 171:820-24.

_____. 1972. Competition between species. *American Scientist* 60:348-57.

Behrensmeyer, A. 1975. Taphonomy and paleoecology in the hominid fossil record. *Yearbook of Physical Anthropology* 19:36-50.

_____. 1977. The habitat of Plio-Pleistocene hominids in East Africa: taphonomic and micro-stratigraphic evidence. In *Early hominids of Africa,* edited by C. Jolly, pp. 165-91. London: Duckworth.

Behrensmeyer, A., and Hill, A., eds. 1980. *Fossils in the making: vertebrate taphonomy and paleoecology.* Chicago: University of Chicago Press.

Birdsell, J. 1968. Some predictions for the Pleistocene based on equilibrium systems among recent hunter-gatherers. In *Man the hunter,* edited by R. Lee and I. DeVore, pp. 229-49. Chicago: Aldine.

Bishop, W. 1976. Pliocene problems relating to human evolution. In *Human origins: Louis Leakey and the East African evidence,* edited by G. Isaac and E. McCown, pp. 139-54. Menlo Park, Calif.: Benjamin.

Brace, C. 1972. Sexual dimorphism in human evolution. *Yearbook of Physical Anthropology* 16:31-49.

Brain, C. 1967a. Bone weathering and the problem of bone pseudo-tools. *South African Journal of Science* 63:97.

_____. 1967b. Hottentot food remains and their bearing on the interpretation of fossil bone assemblages. *Scientific Papers of the Namib Desert Reserve Station* 32:1.

_____. 1968. Who killed the Swartkrans ape-man? *South African Museums Association Bulletin* 9:127.

_____. 1970. The South African australopithecine bone accumulation. *Transvaal Museum Memoir* 18.

Broom, R. 1925a. Some notes on the Taungs skull. *Nature* 115:569.

_____. 1925b. On the newly discovered South African man-ape. *Natural History* 25:409-18.

Broom, R., and Robinson, J. 1949. A new type of fossil man. *Nature* 164:322.

_____. 1952. Swartkrans ape-man. *Transvaal Museum Memoir* 6.

Broom, R., and Schepers, F. 1946. The South African fossil ape-men, the Australopithecinae. *Transvaal Museum Memoir* 2.

Butzer, K. 1971. Another look at the australopithecine cave breccias of the Transvaal. *American Anthropologist* 73:1197.

_____. 1974. Paleoecology of South African australopithecines: Taungs revisited. *Current Anthropology* 15:367.

_____. 1977. Environment, culture and human evolution. *American Scientist* 65:572-84.

————————. 1978. Geoecological perspectives on early hominid evolution. In *Early hominids of Africa,* edited by C. Jolly, pp. 191-213. London: Duckworth.

Campbell, B.1968. The evolution of the human hand. In *Man in adaptation: the biosocial background,* edited by Y. Cohen, pp. 128-30. Chicago: Aldine.

————————. 1979. *Humankind emerging,* 2nd ed. Boston: Little, Brown.

Carney, J., Hill, A., Miller, J., and Walker, A. 1971. Late australopithecine from Baringo District, Kenya. *Nature* 230:509.

Clark, J. 1969. *Kalambo Falls prehistoric site,* Vol. II.Cambridge: Cambridge University Press.

————————. 1976. African origins of man the toolmaker. In *Human origins,* edited by G. Issac and E. McCown, pp.-1-54. Menlo Park, Calif.: Benjamin.

Clark, J., and Haynes, V. 1970. An elephant butchery site at Mwagnadas village, Koranga, Malawi, and its relevance for paleolithic archaeology. *World Archaeology* I:390-411.

Clark, W. Le Gros. 1967. *Man-apes or ape-men?* New York: Holt, Rinehart and Winston.

————————. 1964. *The fossil evidence for human evolution.* Chicago: University of Chicago Press.

Cole, S. 1975. *Leakey's luck.* London: Collins.

Coon, C. 1962. *The origin of races.* New York: Knopf.

Curtis, G., Drake, R., Cerling, T., and Hampel, A. 1975. Age of KBS tuff in Koobi Fora Formation, East Rudolf, Kenya. *Nature* 258:395-98.

Dart, R. 1925a. *Australopithecus africanus:* the man-ape of South Africa. *Nature* 115:195.

————————. 1925b. The word "Australopithecus" and others. *Nature* 115:875.

————————. 1925c. The Taungs skull. *Nature* 116:462.

————————. 1926. Taungs and its significance. *Natural History* 26:315-27.

————————. 1949. The predatory implemental technique of *Australopithecus. American Journal of Physical Anthropology* 7:1.

————————. 1956. Myth of the bone-accumulating hyena. *American Anthropologist* 58:40.

————————. 1957. The osteodontokeratic culture of "*Australopithecus prometheus.*" *Transvaal Museum Memoir* 10.

————————. 1960. The bone tool manufacturing ability of "*Australopithecus prometheus.*" *American Anthropologist* 62:134.

————————. 1971. On the osteodontokeratic culture of the Australopithecinae. *Current Anthropology* 12:233.

Day, M. 1976. Hominid postcranial remains from the East Rudolf succession : a review. In *Earliest Man and environments in the Lake Rudolf basin,* edited by Y. Coppens, F. Howell, G. Isaac, and R. Leakey, pp. 507-21. Chicago: University of Chicago Press.

Day, M., Leakey, M., and Olson, T. 1980. On the status of *Australopithecus afarensis. Science* 207: 1102-3.

Day, M., and Napier, J. 1964. Hominid fossils from Bed I, Olduvai Gorge, Tanganyika: fossil foot bones. *Nature* 201:967.

Day, M., and Wood, B. 1968. Functional affinities of the Olduvai hominid 8 talus. *Man* 3:440.

Drake, R., and Curtis, G. 1979. Radioisotope dating of the Laetoli beds, the Hadar formation and the Koobi Fora-Shungura formations. Paper presented to 48th Annual Meeting of American Association of Physical Anthropologists. San Francisco.

DuBrul, E. 1977. Early hominid feeding mechanisms. *American Journal of Physical Anthropology* 47:305-21.

Falk, D. 1979. On a new australopithecine partial endocast. *American Journal of Physical Anthropology* 50:611-14.

Frisch, J. 1965. *Trends in the evolution of the hominid dentition.* Basel: Karger.

Goodall, J. 1965. Chimpanzees of the Gombe Stream Reserve. In *Primate behavior,* edited by I. DeVore, pp. 425-73. New York: Holt, Rinehart and Winston.

Gray, T. 1979. Environmental and chronological implications from the Hadar formation fauna. *American Journal of Physical Anthropology* 50:444-45.

Hay, R. 1963. Stratigraphy of Beds I through IV, Olduvai Gorge, Tanganyika. *Science* 139:829.

_____. 1976. *Geology of Olduvai Gorge.* Los Angeles: University of California Press.

Heiple, K., and Lovejoy, C. 1971. The distal femoral anatomy of *Australopithecus. American Journal of Physical Anthropology* 10:179.

Holloway, R. 1972. Australopithecine endocasts, brain evolution in the Hominoidea, and a model of hominid evolution. In *The functional and evolutionary biology of primates,* edited by R. Tuttle, pp. 185-203. Chicago: Aldine-Atherton.

_____. 1974. The casts of fossil hominid brains. *Scientific American* 231:106-15.

_____. 1975. *The role of human social behavior in the evolution of the brain.* James Arthur lecture on the evolution of the human brain. New York: American Museum of Natural History.

Howell, F. 1968. Omo research expedition. *Nature* 219:567.

_____. 1969. Remains of hominidae from Pliocene/Pleistocene formations in the lower Omo basin, Ethiopia. *Nature* 223:1234.

_____. 1972. Pliocene/Pleistocene hominidae in eastern Africa: absolute and relative dates. In *Calibration of hominoid evolution,* edited by W. Bishop and J. Miller, pp. 331-68. Edinburgh: Scottish University Press.

Hughes, A. 1954. Hyenas versus australopithecines as agents of bone accumulation. *American Journal of Physical Anthropology* 12:467.

_____. 1958. Some ancient and modern observations on hyenas. *Koedoe* 1:105.

Isaac, G. 1978a. The food-sharing behavior of protohuman hominids. *Scientific American* 238:90-109.

_____. 1978b. Food sharing and human evolution: archeological evidence from the Plio-Pleistocene of East Africa. *Journal of Anthropological Research* 34:311-25.

Isaac, G., Leakey, R., and Behrensmeyer, A. 1971. Archeological traces of early hominid activities east of Lake Rudolf, Kenya. *Science* 173:1129.

Johanson, D. 1976. Ethiopia yields first "family" of early man. *National Geographic* 150:790-811.

Johanson, D., and Taieb, M. 1976. Plio-Pleistocene hominid discoveries in Hadar, Ethiopia. *Nature* 260:293-97.

Johanson, D., and White, T. 1980. On the status of *Australopithecus afarensis. Science* 207:1104-5.

Johanson, D., White, T., and Coppens, Y. 1978. A new species of the genus *Australopithecus* (Primates: Hominidae) from the Pliocene of eastern Africa. *Kirtlandia* 28:1-14.

Jones, P. 1979. Effects of raw materials on biface manufacture. *Science* 204:835-36.

Keeley, L. 1979. The functions of Paleolithic flint tools. Reprinted in *Human Ancestors,* edited by G. Isaac and R. Leakey, pp. 102-9. San Francisco: Freeman.

Lancaster, J. 1978. Carrying and sharing in human evolution. *Human Nature* 1:82-89.

Lan-Po, C. 1975. *The cave home of Peking man.* Peking: Foreign Language Press.

Leakey, L. 1958. Recent discoveries at Olduvai Gorge, Tanganyika. *Nature* 181:1099.

_____. 1959. A new fossil skull from Olduvai. *Nature* 184:491.

_____. 1960a. The affinities of the new Olduvai australopithecine. *Nature* 186:458.

_____. 1960b. Recent discoveries at Olduvai Gorge. *Nature* 188:1050.

_____. 1963. Very early East African hominidae and their ecological setting. In *African ecology and human evolution,* edited by F. Howell and F. Bourliere, pp. 448-57. Chicago: Aldine.

_____. 1966. Homo habilis, Homo erectus and the australopithecines. *Nature* 209:1279.

_____. 1967. *Olduvai Gorge,* Vol. 1. *A preliminary report on the geology and fauna, 1951-61.* Cambridge: Cambridge University Press.

Leakey, L., Evernden, J., and Curtis, G. 1961. Age of Bed I, Olduvai Gorge, Tanganyika. *Nature* 191:478.

Leakey, L., Tobias, P., and Napier, J. 1964. A new species of the genus *Homo* from Olduvai Gorge. *Nature* 202:5.

Leakey, M. 1971. *Olduvai Gorge,* Vol. 3. *Excavations in Beds I and II, 1960-63.* Cambridge: Cambridge University Press.

_____. 1976. A summary and discussion of the archaeological evidence from Bed I and Bed II, Olduvai Gorge, Tanzania. In *Human origins: Louis Leakey and the East African evidence,* edited by G. Isaac and E. McCown, pp. 431-60. Menlo Park, Calif.: Benjamin.

Leakey, M. 1979. Footprints frozen in time. *National Geographic* 155:446-57.

Leakey, M., Clarke, R., and Leakey, L. 1971. A new hominid skull from Bed I, Olduvai Gorge, Tanzania. *Nature* 232:308.

Leakey, M., Hay, R., Curtis, G., Drake, R., Jackes, M., and White, T. 1976. Fossil hominids from the Laetoli beds. *Nature* 262:460-66.

Leakey, R. 1970. In search of man's past at Lake Rudolf in Kenya. *National Geographic* 137:712.

——————. 1971. Further evidence of Lower Pleistocene hominids from East Rudolf, North Kenya. *Nature* 231:241.

Leakey, R., and Isaac, G. 1972. Hominid fossils from the area east of Lake Rudolf, Kenya: photographs and a commentary on context. In *Perspectives on human evolution,* edited by S. Washburn and P. Dolhinow, pp. 129-41. New York: Holt, Rinehart and Winston.

——————. 1976. East Rudolf: an introduction to the abundance of new evidence. In *Human origins: Louis Leakey and the East African evidence,* edited by G. Isaac and E. McCown, pp. 307-32. Menlo Park, Calif.: Benjamin.

Leakey, R., and Walker, A. 1980. On the status of *Australopithecus afarensis. Science* 207:1103.

Lovejoy, C. 1973. The gait of australopithecines. *Yearbook of Physical Anthropology* 17:147-61.

——————. 1975. Biomechanical perspectives on the lower limb of early hominids. In *Primate functional morphology and evolution,* edited by R. Tuttle, pp. 291-327. The Hague: Mouton.

——————. 1978. A biomechanical review of the locomotor diversity of early hominids. In *African Hominidae of the Plio-Pleistocene,* edited by C. Jolly, pp. 240-56. London: Duckworth.

Lovejoy, C., and Heiple, K. 1970. A reconstruction of the femur of *A. africanus. American Journal of Physical Anthropology* 32:33-40.

Lovejoy, C., Heiple, K., and Burstein, A. 1973. The gait of *Australopithecus. American Journal of Physical Anthropology* 38:757-80.

McHenry, H. 1974. How large were the australopithecines? *American Journal of Physical Anthropology* 40:329-40.

——————. 1975. Fossil hominid body weight and brain size. *Nature* 254:686-88.

McHenry, H., and Corruccini, R. 1978. The femur in early human evolution. *American Journal of Physical Anthropology* 49:473-87.

——————. 1980. On the status of *Australopithecus afarensis. Science* 207:1103-4.

McKinley, K. 1971. Survivorship in gracile and robust australopithecines: a demographic comparison and a proposed birth model. *American Journal of Physical Anthropology* 34:417.

Mann, A. 1975. *Paleodemographic aspects of the South African australopithecines.* Philadelphia: University of Pennsylvania Press.

Morse, D. 1974. Niche breadth as a function of social dominance. *American Naturalist* 108:818-30.

Napier, J. 1962a. Fossil hand bones from Olduvai Gorge. *Nature* 196:409.

——————. 1962b. The evolution of the human hand. *Scientific American* 207:56-62.

Oxnard, C. 1975. *Uniqueness and diversity in human evolution: morphometric studies of australopithecines.* Chicago: University of Chicago Press.

Oxnard, C., and Lisowski, P. 1980. Functional articulation of some hominoid foot bones: implications for the Olduvai (hominid 8) foot. *American Journal of Physical Anthropology* 52:107-17.

Patterson, D., Behrensmeyer, A., and Sill, W. 1970. Geology and fauna of a new Pliocene locality in Northwestern Kenya. *Nature* 226:918.

Patterson, D., and Howells, W. 1967. Hominid humeral fragment from the early Pleistocene of Northwestern Kenya. *Science* 156:64.

Peters, C. 1979. Toward an ecological model of African Plio-Pleistocene hominid adaptations. *American Anthropologist* 81:261-78.

Pfeiffer, J. 1969. *The emergence of man.* New York: Harper & Row.

Pilbeam, D. 1972. *The ascent of man.* New York: Macmillan.

Pilbeam, D., and Gould, S. 1974. Size and scaling in human evolution. *Science* 186:892-901.

Poirier, F. 1981. *Fossil evidence: the human evolutionary journey.* St. Louis: Mosby.

Prost, J. 1980. Origin of bipedalism. *American Journal of Physical Anthropology* 52:175-89.

Robinson, J. 1952. The australopithecines and their evolutionary significance. *Proceedings of the Linnean Society of London* 3:196.

_____. 1954. The genera and species of the Australopithecinae. *American Journal of Physical Anthropology* 12:181.

_____. 1963a. Australopithecines, culture and phylogeny. *American Journal of Physical Anthropology* 21:595.

_____. 1963b. Adaptive radiation in the australopithecines and the origin of man. In *African ecology and human evolution,* edited by F. Howell and F. Bourliere, pp. 385-416. Chicago: Aldine.

_____. 1966. The distinctiveness of *Homo habilis. Nature* 209:953-60.

_____. 1972. *Early hominid posture and locomotion.* Chicago: University of Chicago Press.

Schaller, G., and Lowther, G. 1969. The relevance of carnivore behavior to the study of the early hominids. *Southwestern Journal of Anthropology* 25:307.

Semenov, S. 1964. *Prehistoric technology: an experimental study of the oldest tools and artifacts from traces of manufacture and wear,* translated by M. Thompson. New York: Barnes and Noble.

Simons, E. 1978. Diversity among the early hominids: a vertebrate paleontologist's viewpoint. In *African hominidae of the Plio-Pleistocene,* edited by C. Jolly, pp. 543-66. London: Duckworth.

Steudel, K. 1980. New estimates of early hominid body size. *American Journal of Physical Anthropology* 52:63-70.

Sugiyama, Y. 1972. Social characteristics and socialization of wild chimpanzees. In *Primate socialization,* edited by F. Poirier, pp. 145-63. New York: Random House.

Susman, R., and Stern, J. 1979. Telemetered electromyography of flexor digitorum profundus and flexor digitorum superficiales in *Pan troglodytes* and implications for interpretation of the O.H.7. hand. *American Journal of Physical Anthropology* 50:565-74.

Taieb, M., Johanson, D., and Coppens, Y. 1975. Expédition internationale de l'Afar, Ethiopie (3e campagne, 1974); découverte d'hominides Plio-Pléistocènes à Hadar. *Comptes rendus des séances de l'Academie des Sciences* 1297-1300.

Tobias, P. 1967. *Olduvai Gorge,* Vol. 2. Cambridge: Cambridge University Press.

_____. 1971. *The brain in hominid evolution.* New York: Columbia University Press.

_____. 1972. Progress and problems in the study of early man in sub-Saharan Africa. In *The functional and evolutionary biology of primates,* edited by R. Tuttle, pp. 63-94. Chicago: Aldine-Atherton.

Walker, A., and Leakey, R. 1978. The hominids of East Turkana. *Scientific American* 239:54-66.

White, T. 1980. Evolutionary implications of Pliocene hominid footprints. *Science* 208:175-76.

Wolpoff, M. 1970. The evidence for multiple hominid taxa at Swartkrans. *American Anthropologist* 72:576.

_____. 1976a. Primate models for australopithecine sexual dimorphism. *American Journal of Physical Anthropology* 45:497-510.

_____. 1976b. Some aspects of the evolution of early hominid sexual dimorphism. *Current Anthropology* 17:579-606.

_____. 1980. *Paleoanthropology.* New York: Knopf.

Wood, B. 1976. Remains attributable to *Homo* in the East Rudolph succession. In *Earliest man and environments in the Lake Rudolph basin,* edited by Y. Coppens, F. Howell, G. Isaac, and R. Leakey, pp. 490-506. Chicago: University of Chicago Press.

Wood, B., and Stack, C. 1980. Does allometry explain the differences between "gracile" and "robust" australopithecines? *American Journal of Physical Anthropology* 52:55-62.

Woodburn, J. 1968. An introduction to Hadza ecology. In *Man the hunter,* edited by R. Lee and I. De Vore, pp. 49-55. Chicago: Aldine.

Chapter 18

Homo erectus

Homo erectus lived from approximately 250,000 or 300,000 to more than 1 million years ago. A major feature of Middle Pleistocene hominid evolution is an elaboration of cultural adaptations. By the time of *H. erectus* the story of hominid evolution is increasingly that of culture. Middle Pleistocene hominids led a hunting and gathering life. Because of similarities to modern populations, they are included in the genus *Homo*.

Discovery of *Homo erectus* Remains

Dubois. The first Middle Pleistocene fossil hominids appeared in 1891 when a Dutch physician, Eugene Dubois, reported the discovery of a skull, thigh bones, and several bone fragments from Trinil, a site on the Solo River in Central Java. Early in his career Dubois joined the Dutch Colonial Service and traveled to Indonesia hoping to uncover the "missing link." Several years before, the German biologist Ernst Haeckel had postulated a theoretical ancestral hominid line. Haeckel had only fragmentary information with which to work; the only well-known remains were discovered 20 years previously in the Neander valley of Germany. Haeckel suggested that the hominid line began among some extinct Miocene apes and reached *Homo sapiens* by way of an imagined group of speechless "ape-man."

Applying Haeckel's terminology to the bones he uncovered, Dubois established the Genus "Pithecanthropus." Since the thigh bones resembled those of modern *Homo,* Dubois concluded that his "ape-man" walked erect in the fashion of *H. sapiens.* He named his genus and species "Pithecanthropus erectus," or "erect ape-man." The generic name was eventually dropped and the form renamed *H. erectus.* Dubois' contention that he had recovered an ancestral hominid had a poor reception at first because scientists hesitated to accept the association of an archaic skullcap with a relatively modern femur.

Morphology

Dental and Cranial Traits. The morphological characters of *H. erectus* are sufficiently consistent and distinctive to justify their inclusion in the genus *Homo;* however, they differ

301

from modern *Homo* in a number of details. The species *H. erectus* is characterized by a cranial capacity of between 750 and 1200 cc. The mean capacity for all 12 Asian skulls is 929 cc. Javan forms average 70 cc less, that is, 859 cc, and the Chinese forms 114 cc more, that is, 1043 cc. There is marked flattening, or **platycephaly,** of the *H. erectus* skull vault and the *H. erectus* face is characterized by large brow ridges above the eye orbits. Behind the brow ridges the skull is marked by postorbital constriction that in modern populations is elevated because of an increasing brain size. A sagittal ridge highlights the skull's midline; the cranial bones are thick; the nasal bones are flat and the face more prognathic than in modern populations (Figure 18-1).

What proportion of the increasing cranial capacities of *H. erectus* can be attributed to body size is unknown because there are too few postcranial remains to determine if *H. erectus* was larger than the australopithecines. However, Wolpoff (1980) notes that, considering the *H.*

Figure 18-1. Skull and restored head of "Java man" (*Homo erectus*).

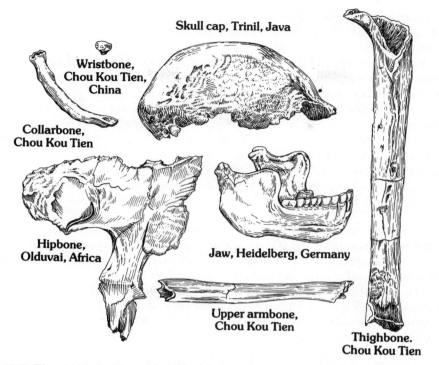

Skull cap, Trinil, Java

Wristbone, Chou Kou Tien, China

Collarbone, Chou Kou Tien

Hipbone, Olduvai, Africa

Jaw, Heidelberg, Germany

Upper armbone, Chou Kou Tien

Thighbone. Chou Kou Tien

Figure 18-2. The seven fossils represented here include virtually every kind of *Homo erectus* material found.

erectus sample as a whole, a substantial amount of the cranial capacity increase over the australopithecines may be the result of an increase in body size.

The heavily built *H. erectus* mandible lacks a chin. The teeth are larger than those of modern populations. The canines are sometimes slightly projecting and the dental arcade is modern. Posterior tooth (premolars and molars, especially) size reduction is one of the most dramatic changes that occurs between the australopithecines and *H. erectus,* and an equally great reduction occurs over the time span of the *H. erectus* lineage. The structure supporting the posterior teeth, that is, the mandible, also reduces in size. The limb bones are essentially modern (Figure 18-2).

The assumption that *H. erectus* is ancestral to *H. sapiens* is based on the following criteria: (1) Morphologically *H. erectus* conforms very well with the theoretical postulates for an intermediate stage in the evolution of later hominids. (2) The existence of *H. erectus* in the early part of the Pleistocene, antedating any well-authenticated *H. sapiens,* provides it with an antiquity conforming well with its supposed phylogenetic relations. (3) Some *H. erectus* materials illustrate a satisfactorily graded series of morphological changes from one type to another.

Review of Sites

Java. Asian Middle Pleistocene sites are found primarily in China and Java with the oldest known remains coming from Java. Java, among other islands of western and northern

Indonesia, received invasions of Pleistocene animals from both India and China. The Djetis faunal beds are the oldest Javan beds. Besides the "Meganthropus" remains,[1] there is one specimen consisting of the occipital of a skull plus the palate and teeth (except the incisors) known as "Pithecanthropus IV" (or P-IV); two fragmentary mandibles; and the skullcap of an infant, called *H. modjokertensis.* All these fossils are probably *H. erectus.* The overlying Trinil faunal beds (the source of the original "Pithecanthropus"), contain fauna largely of South Chinese origin. As might be expected because the Trinil beds are younger than the Djetis beds, there are morphological differences between forms from the two beds. Because the Trinil beds may preserve fossils of widely varying age, there is some doubt about the relationship of the Trinil skullcap of *H. erectus* and the postcranial bones.

The Trinil faunal beds contain examples of the earliest Javan tools, named the Patjitanian, which are crude but clearly worked flake materials. These are technically advanced over earlier tools found in Malaysia, called Anyathian, which are not associated with hominid remains.

Jacob et al. (1978) announced the discovery of two stone tools from the Sambungmachan deposits that may range from 900,000 to 700,000 years old. Both implements are made of basaltic andesite and are large cobbles. The first tool is an alternately retouched end and side chopper and the second is a retouched flake.

Other Javanese sites have yielded Middle Pleistocene fossil materials; between 1936 and 1939 workers identified a fossil deposit at Sangiran very similar to the fossiliferous beds at Trinil. Material from an older layer, the Djetis faunal beds, originally called "P. erectus II" was remarkedly similar to Dubois' original find. The material from the Djetis beds, "Meganthropus paleojavanicus," was discussed in Chapter 17. Dating for the Trinil and Djetis faunal beds has been nettlesome. The Trinil beds are K-Ar dated to about 710,000 years ago and the Djetis beds are provisionally dated to about 2 million years ago.

The Solo remains from the Ngandong beds are morphologically similar to material from Africa, such as the material from Broken Hill, Zambia. The Solo remains consist of 11 skulls that were recovered between 1931 and 1941. The skulls lack a face. There are also two incomplete lower leg bones, the tibiae. The skulls have marked cranial flattening (platycephaly), powerful development of the supraorbital tori, and thick cranial walls. The cranial capacity ranges between 1150 and 1300 cc. Tentatively, these remains are attributed to *H. erectus.*

China. China has yielded fossils comparable to those from Java. In the 1920s and 1930s an international team digging at Chou Kou Tien about 25 miles from Peking uncovered the remains of approximately 40 individuals associated with tools, evidence of fire, thousands of animal bones, and much fossilized pollen. The hominid remains were first put into the taxon "Sinathropus pekinensis"; however, their similarity to the Javan hominids led to abandonment of the taxon. The material is now considered a subspecies of the Javanese *H. erectus* and is classified *H. erectus pekinensis,* although Chinese paleontologists still refer to them as the genus "Sinanthropus." The Chou Kou Tien remains consist of skullcaps, teeth, jaws, and some postcranial material; however, they lack faces, as does most of the Javan material. In line with their supposed date of 350,000 to 400,000 years ago, remains from the lower cave at Chou Kou Tien are more modern looking than their Javanese cousins.

---

[1]The size of the "Meganthropus" molar teeth led F. Weidenreich to postulate that a giant race of hominids once roamed about Asia. He considered *Gigantopithecus* a member of this group.

Figure 18-3. Chou Kou Tien.

Chou Kou Tien. Until recently most Chinese representatives of *H. erectus* came from Chou Kou Tien (Figure 18-3), which has long been the haunt of "dragon bone" collectors whose finds supplied many Chinese drugstores. In the early 1900s a German paleontologist, K. A. Herberer, found a human tooth in a Chinese drugstore and for the next 24 years various scientists, having traced the tooth back to Chou Kou Tien, worked or watched the site. In 1921 they found bits of quartz. Since animals neither eat nor use quartz, and since quartz has no business in a limestone cave, it was recognized as a tool. More quartz tools were subsequently recovered.

Human teeth were sifted from the Chou Kou Tien debris in 1923 and 1926; in 1927 the Swedish paleontologist B. Böhlin produced one more tooth. This was given to D. Black, professor of anatomy at Peking University, who allocated the tooth to a new hominid taxon "Sinanthropus pekinensis."

From 1927 to 1937 the site was worked under the direction of W. C. Pei and the French theologian, philosopher, and paleontologist Père Teilhard de Chardin. Before excavations were completed this team was joined by Franz Weidenreich, who subsequently described all but one of the original skulls. The Chinese government resumed work in the 1950s, recovering an additional skull in 1959.

The Chou Kou Tien *H. erectus* deposits (known as Locality 1) yielded the remains of about 40 individuals, including 14 skulls, 12 mandibles, 147 teeth, and some cranial remains. The material was mostly fragmented; however, there was enough to allow for rather complete reconstruction. Early in World War II, at the commencement of the Japanese occupation, all the skulls were mysteriously lost; nothing remains of the original material but a fine set of casts made in the basement of the University Museum in Philadelphia, a lone tooth in Sweden, and a new Chinese mandible and skull. Weidenreich also wrote a complete and fine set of detailed monographs. Recent attempts have been made to locate the "Sinanthropus" material and perhaps some of the originals will yet be found. (Shapiro [1971] recounts attempts to relocate the material.)

Much faunal material was associated with the *H. erectus* remains; deer bones were most numerous, an indication that venison formed a substantial part of the *H. erectus* diet. Also found among the debris were numerous elephant, rhinoceros, and giant beaver remains. Quantities of broken and splintered bones indicate that they had been split for their marrow. High and low in the deposit were layers of ash and burnt bone; perhaps these were hearths where hunters sat and cooked their meat.

Discovery of *Homo erectus pekinensis* (Peking Man)

At the laboratory we [Teilhard de Chardin and P. Leroy] met Pei Wen-chung with whom we had a long discussion. We were on the point of leaving, when Teilhard asked him pointblank, "Hasn't anything really new been found at Choukoutien?" "No," replied Pei, "we are still turning up lots of remains of stag, tiger, hyena and all kinds of small mammals." Then, as an afterthought he added, "Oh yes, I found this." From the drawer of his desk he took out a few fragments of quartz which he handed to Teilhard. Teilhard did not hesitate for an instant. At first glance he had seen that these quartz fragments bore signs of deliberate shaping. "The quartz has been worked," he said. Pei's delight knew no bounds. "So these stone fragments found near skulls must therefore be Sinanthropus' tools?" "There is no doubt about it," replied Teilhard. "So Sinanthropus was a man?" "That is my opinion," answered Teilhard.

From the UNESCO Courier, August-September, 1972, pp. 55-56.

The floral and faunal evidence at Chou Kou Tien suggests a northern temperate zone. Mammalian remains associated with a tropical or polar climate are rare. Evidence from different cave layers suggests climatic shifts during the long history of occupation at Chou Kou Tien, first by *H. erectus* and later by *H. sapiens*.

The mountainous areas to the north and west of Chou Kou Tien were typified by mixed forests of pine, cedar, elm, hackberries, and Chinese redbud. Various animal forms inhabited this region, such as bison, saber-tooth tigers, tigers, leopards, cheetah, horses, wooly rhinoceros, striped hyena, sika deer, and elephant, among others. There was a big river and possibly a lake to the east. These contained various water species and along the shore-lines grew reeds and plants that were home for buffalo, deer, otter, beaver, and other animals.

Some of these species formed the diet for *H. erectus*. Undoubtedly, they were big-game hunters. However, there is strong evidence that the daily meal consisted more often of small animals such as hedgehogs, frogs, and hare. Ash layers in the cave abounded with the bones of these animals and of others such as hamsters, mice, black rats, and harvest mice. There is also evidence of ostrich eggs.

The inhabitants of Chou Kou Tien also must have exploited vegetable foods; these foods, however, fossilize poorly. Charred hackberry seeds are found, these being the only evidence to date of plant food.

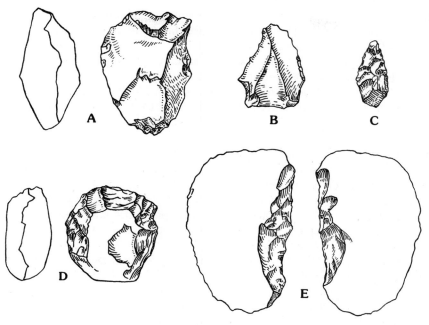

Figure 18-4. Tools from "Sinanthropus" beds at Chou Kou Tien. (A) Small chopping tool. (B) Flake. (C) Point. (D) Chopper. (E) Cleaverlike tool.

Scattered among the bones were evidences of a few hominid trunk and limb bones and cranial pieces. Many facial and jaw fragments were present, but these were separated from the braincase. The case has been made that "Peking man" was a cannibal. If so, cannibalism then, as today, was probably ritualistic[2]; human meat was probably never an important element of the human diet.[3]

Numerous stone tools were uncovered from Locality 1 (Figure 18-4). Since there are no nearby quartz hills, the tools were either carried or traded into the cave. The characteristic tool is a pebble trimmed to make an edged blade. Many of the stone tools are large and crudely worked; few display an even, uniform edge. Some tools may have been used to work animal skins which might have been worn or used as enclosure walls to keep out the cold. *H. erectus* at Chou Kou Tien also made bone tools.

The raw materials used by the inhabitants at Chou Kou Tien for making tools were hard minerals and rocks derived from outside the cave. These included rock crystal, vein quartz, flint, opal, sandstone, and quartzite. Rock crystal probably came from nearby granite hills and the other raw materials from a nearby river bed.

The tool manufacturers often selected oval-shaped pebbles to make single- or double-edged axes called choppers or chopping tools. These are found in most layers in the cave

[2]Among modern groups, cannibalism is usually practiced in burial rites (Chapter 27), consuming the brain of a vanquished foe, and when food is short, such as the cases reported recently in Alaskan and South American plane crashes.

[3]Evidence supporting this is discussed by Garn and Block, 1970.

deposit. Most chopping tools are made from sandstone and vary in shape from round discs to irregular triangles and long slabs. These tools are easily blunted and there is bountiful evidence of blunt and resharpened choppers in the cave.

Scrapers were made from vein quartz flakes of various sizes and shapes. Most scrapers are unifacially flaked. The most finely made stone tools were pointed stone tools. Approximately 100 such tools have been discovered to date, 73 percent of which are made from quartz. The tool makers were quite proficient in producing these tools. Manufacture required the splitting off of a flake from a larger stone and then trimming it all the way around to produce a slender point.

Bone tools were also found at Chou Kou Tien. Fragments indicate that antlers were broken into short pieces. Antler roots may have served as hammers and the tines could have been used for digging, as suggested by the deep criss-crossed scratches on them. Many antler pieces seem to have been scorched, perhaps to develop weak spots and allow easier working.

A number of sika and thick-jawed deer skulls were found, but few were complete. Some skulls show the results of repeated whittling. More than 100 such specimens have been recovered and perhaps the skulls served as "bowls."

A review of *H. erectus* culture at Chou Kou Tien suggests the following: (1) Fire was a basic item, for there are substantial amounts of charcoal and burned bone. (2) The favorite food seems to have been venison; some 70 percent of the animal bones belong to deer. (3) Fruits such as the hackberry (a relative of the wild cherry) were consumed.

Lan T'ien. A second important Chinese site is at Chenchiawo in Lan T'ien District, Shensi Province, where a mandible was recovered in 1963. In 1964 at Kung-wang-ling Hill (12.5 miles away) facial fragments, a tooth, and a good skullcap were recovered; the material apparently came from the same individual. Both sites predate Chou Kou Tien and may be contemporaneous with the Javan Djetis faunal beds. The older date of the Lan T'ien materials is consistent with their more primitive morphology; the jaw is more robust than Chou Kou Tien. In many respects the skull recalls the Djetis material—it is low and thick with massive brow ridges. The cranial capacity is approximately 780 cc, close to that of the Djetis skull. Lan T'ien is the first fossil evidence congenitally lacking the third molar, a condition known as dental agenesis.

The Chinese paleontologist Woo feels that the Lan T'ien material is of a female and is morphologically closely allied with Chou Kou Tien. However, he notes some differences, which he feels call for a new specific designation. He classifies the material "Sinanthropus lantianensis"; most other paleontologists prefer the designation *H. erectus lantianensis*.

The close phylogenetic relationship between the Javan and Chinese material is expressed by retaining all the material in the same genus and species, *H. erectus*. The most recent Asian material is from Locality 1 at Chou Kou Tien. The major differentiating features are in the skull and teeth; the cranial capacity of "Peking man" is larger and its teeth smaller than preceding *H. erectus* forms. Asian *H. erectus* populations did not differ postcranially, approaching modern populations in their postcranial anatomy.

All the Asian forms had equally thick skulls and all had large brow ridges. There are, however, major differences in cranial capacity. The mean capacity of the Javan material is estimated at 975 cc or slightly less; the Lan T'ien material at 780 cc; and the Locality 1 material at 1075 cc. Because of sexual dimorphism, values for males are higher than those of females.

Europe. Until recently, European *H. erectus* populations were scarcely known, and even now we have more cultural than osteological remains. The northwest quadrant of the Old World yields most of the skeletal remains; however, there are still large, serious gaps.

The *H. erectus* sample of Europe appears rather late compared to the long evolutionary sequence of this species in Asia and Africa. The European specimens appear to be roughly contemporaneous with *H. erectus* from Chou Kou Tien. As Wolpoff (1980) notes, including these specimens within the *H. erectus* taxon is more a matter of tradition than the result of any distinctive morphological complex. Because they are among the latter specimens in the *H. erectus* time span, they resemble early *H. sapiens* in a number of ways. Conversely, slightly later European forms (which Wolpoff designates as *H. sapiens)* such as Petralona, Steinheim, and Bilzingsleben show a number of *H. erectus* features and a good case can be made for including them within this taxon. Europe provides a good example of how arbitrary the division of a lineage can be when the sample is large.

Mauer Mandible. The first *H. erectus* osteological material recovered from Middle Pleistocene Europe is the Heidelberg or Mauer mandible from the Mauer sands in Germany. After a 20-year vigil, it was uncovered in 1907 from a sandpit in the village of Mauer 6 miles southwest of Heidelberg. It lay 78 feet below the surface in deposits dated to about 360,000 years ago. The Mauer mandible is approximately the same age as *H.erectus* from Locality 1 at Chou Kou Tien and the *H. erectus* finds from Ternifine in North Africa.

The chinless mandible is well preserved; most of the teeth are moderately worn. The mandible is large and massive, one of the largest yet found; its most striking characteristic is the great breadth of the ascending ramus, the vertical strut of bone underlying the back of your cheekbone that carries at its posterior corner the condyle articulating the jaw with the skull. The width of the ascending ramus is undoubtedly related to mandibular length and suggests powerful, efficient jaw muscles. Because of the large mandibular size, one might expect to find large teeth. However, their size is proportionately small.

Beyond guessing that it possessed a wide, not strongly projecting face, we cannot reconstruct the Heidelberg skull. Despite its large size, the jaw and teeth reflect Heidelberg's inclusion in the genus *Homo.* The Heidelberg material is most often assigned to the taxon *H. erectus heidelbergensis.* However, some refer it to a primitive species of *H. sapiens.*

Vértesszöllös. Other possible European *H. erectus* populations have come to light. Sixty years after the Mauer discovery, an **occipital** bone and some deciduous teeth were uncovered from Vértesszöllös, a site dating to 400,000 years ago located west of Budapest, Hungary. Vértesszöllös appears to have been a campsite in a small saucerlike depression that seems to have been inhabited during the cool seasons of the year, perhaps because of its proximity to a hot spring. Many pebble tools were collected in and around the site; these pebble tools are the first undisputed early European tools. The occipital bone was recovered during dynamiting at the site, but no other skull parts were recovered. Charred bone indicates use of fire.

This material represents the oldest cranial evidence from Europe. The bone is rather thick and possesses a well-marked nuchal ridge for neck muscle insertion; nevertheless, some investigators feel that the bone represents a more advanced population than *H. erectus.* One of the cranial capacity estimates is 1400 cc, well above *H. erectus* and within the range of modern populations. Some classify the occipital bone within the species *H. sapiens,* distinguishing it as a subspecies *palaeohungaricus,* that is, *H. sapiens palaeohungaricus.* This would place a progressive *H. sapiens* contemporaneously with the *H. erectus* populations of about 400,000 years ago. The potential importance of the specimen lies in the knowledge it provides concerning evolutionary changes at the very end of the *H. erectus* lineage or the very beginning of the *H. sapiens* lineage.

Přezletice. Another European hominid fossiliferous site is Přezletice near Prague, Czechoslovakia. The site was first recognized in 1938 as a result of quarrying operations; it was excavated in the early 1960s and has yielded a tiny molar fragment and approximately 50 stone implements. On faunal comparisons, Přezletice may turn out to be one of the oldest European hominid sites. On the basis of the time period, the scanty remains are referred to the *H. erectus* populations; but much more information is badly needed. It has recently been argued that the Přezletice molar is not from a human but from a bear.

Petralona. The petralona skull was discovered from a Greek cave (Petralona) in 1959. This skull is the first of its kind found in the Balkan peninsula. The skull, encrusted with limestone, is in an excellent state of preservation. First reports confused the skull with Neanderthal materials and it was assigned a late Pleistocene date. However, recent work on the cave's fauna indicates that it is not later than the Riss Glacial, and, in fact, may date to Pre-Mindel. If this earlier dating stands, the skull may be contemporaneous with the Heidelberg mandible (Howells, 1973).

Morphologically the skull is large; however, cranial capacity estimates are disputed. Although estimates of 1440 cc and 1384 cc have been proposed, Howells (1973) feels an estimate of 1220 cc is more proper. Hemmer (1972) feels that in skull shape and brain size Petralona conforms with *H. erectus.* Howells (1973:78) feels that ". . . from its size and form it appears to rate as a moderately advanced specimen in the whole *H. erectus* spectrum, and one differing from the Olduvai and Far Eastern examples. . . ." The Petralona skull might prove to be a most interesting specimen when fully described, for its possible early date and "advanced" features might fit well with the supposed "advanced" traits of Vértesszöllös.

Other material has been announced in Greece. An elephant and stone weapons dated to 700,000 years ago come from the sandhill plains of Kozani-Ptolemaida in northern Greece. According to the Greek anthropologist Poulianos, the elephant remains were evidence of a kill. The elephant was cut in half and one half was dragged off. This is similar to the pattern to be discussed at the Torralba-Ambrona site in Spain.

In addition to various primitive stone implements, two so-called stone weapons described as resembling something between a sledge hammer and a human fist were recovered. Poulianos said there were clear signs of deliberately made hand-grips on them. The weapons were apparently used in killing animals in the hunt.

Bilzingsleben. Hominid remains were found in 1972 at Bilzingsleben, Germany. Since the original find, four hominid skull fragments and a single molar tooth were recovered (Vlček, 1978). The morphology of the skull fragments closely approaches that of OH 9.[4] The brow ridges are well developed, the skull bones thick, and the occipital is marked by a strong horizontal torus. The bones were associated with a Clactonian flake industry and numerous butchered animal bones.

Arago Cave, Tautavel, France. Arago Cave is located north of the Roussillon plain, at the southern tip of the Corbieres mountains, near the village of Tautavel in the Pyrenees. An examination of materials from Arago occurred as early as 1963; however, it was in 1967 that undisturbed archaeological levels were reached and excavations began. The Arago material dates to approximately 200,000 years ago. The presence of a large archaic horse, small wolf, large panther, and fragments of extinct rodents relatively date the site to the very beginning of the Riss Glaciation (de Lumley and de Lumley, 1973). The human material from Arago consists of many isolated teeth, phalanges, parietal fragments, a mandible with six teeth

---

[4]OH 9 is a specimen from Olduvai Gorge that is discussed later in this chapter.

(Arago II), a half-mandible with five teeth (Arago XIII), and the anterior portion of an adult cranium found in 1971.

Arago is a large cave, 15 feet deep and 33 feet wide at its maximum. As early as 1838, "antediluvian" (a term used to refer to forms that preceded the presumed Biblical flood of Genesis 7) animal bones were reported from the cave. Excavation occurred in a series of layers, each defined by a set of faunal remains, tools, pollen grains, and other climatic and cultural indicators. The level most recently excavated was laid down during a dry, cold period when the cave was intermittently occupied. When it was abandoned sand blew in, covering the human relics and providing a clean floor for subsequent inhabitants. More than 20 habitation levels were laid down in the period represented by the newly discovered skull.

The de Lumleys feel that the cave was inhabited by groups of prehistoric hunters who regularly returned to establish camp. According to the de Lumleys the prehistoric hunters lived in a dimly lit area, some distance from the cave's entrance in a sandpit between a dune accumulating in the entry and another dune being formed at the rear of the cave. The habitation soils are littered with bone fragments and flint or quartz tools. In some areas the abundance and disposition of the remains suggests a tool-making work area. In other areas piles of bones more than 50 centimeters deep represent accumulating food debris. There are also large stone slabs that the de Lumleys state were brought into the cave and were perhaps used to avoid sinking into the sand.

More than 100,000 artifacts have been uncovered at Arago. Most of the materials are attributed to the early Tayacian assemblage, with the exception of upper levels containing middle Acheulian tool types. Most of the Tayacian materials were made of quartz; some were made of flint and quartzite. Arago Cave has yielded many pebble tools, including choppers and chopping tools. Hand axes are rare—there is less than one hand axe per 1,000 retouched artifacts. Some of the small stone materials are comparable to specimens from Vértesszöllös.

The Arago skull has massive brow ridges, a markedly flat forehead more horizontal than vertical (opposite the case in modern *H. sapiens*), and a narrow elongated brain case. The skull possesses some characteristics reminiscent of the preceding Far Eastern *H. erectus*. Because of the absence of maxillary tooth wear the skull is thought to be that of a youth aged approximately 20 years.

The first skeletal evidence to appear was two massive teeth found protruding above the sand. Further excavation during the summers of 1969 and 1970 revealed two mandibles at approximately the same level. Neither of these apparently belongs with the skull, which lacks a mandible. The mandibles are chinless and seem to have been prognathic. The primitiveness of the mandibles is evidenced by midsection thickening (25 millimeters, almost 1 inch). They are considerably thicker than the older Heidelberg mandible. The heavier of the two mandibles is thought to belong to a male, the other to a female.

Torralba and Ambrona: Big-Game Hunters. European *H. erectus* left substantial evidence of its cultural way of life. Major cultural remains have been uncovered from France and Spain; neither area, however, yields hominid skeletal remains. That *H. erectus* was pursuing a hunting way of life is evident at the Spanish sites of Torralba and Ambrona, originally uncovered in the late 1800s during laying of a pipeline. They were dug by an amateur archaeologist who published a preliminary paper on the findings. Many years later F. C. Howell discovered the paper and began digging in 1961.

Ambrona Valley was part of a major animal migration route for large herds of deer, horses, and elephants. Torralba and Ambrona are open-air sites (that is, they are out in the open) that

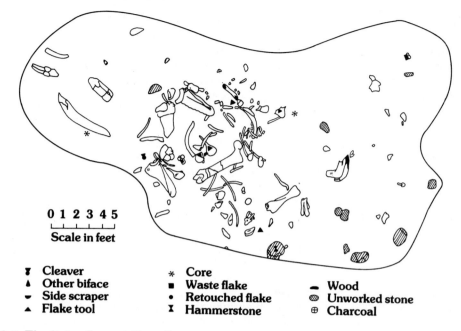

| 0 1 2 3 4 5 |
| Scale in feet |

⌇	Cleaver	*	Core		
▲	Other biface	■	Waste flake	━	Wood
⌄	Side scraper	•	Retouched flake	⬯	Unworked stone
▲	Flake tool	Ⅰ	Hammerstone	⊕	Charcoal

Figure 18-5. The living floor at Torralba.

served primarily as butchering and killing stations. Detailed stratigraphic and pollen analysis yields a date of 300,000 years ago. The chronological and tool record indicates that a *H. erectus* population visited this area, perhaps seasonally, to hunt game and gather plant foods (Figure 18-5).

The enormous quantity of elephant bones at Torralba and Ambrona is intriguing and suggests that these elephants were hunted and butchered at the site. The remains belong to a now extinct straight-tusked form that is somewhat larger than modern African elephants. Remains of about 30 elephants, 25 horses, 25 deer, 10 wild oxen, and 6 rhinoceroses are concentrated in a relatively small area. One 270-square-foot area contained the left side of a large adult elephant with tusks and bones in place; the head and pelvis are missing. There are also four flake tools, indicating that the elephant was butchered at the site.

Why was the elephant cut in such fashion; why was half the body missing? Perhaps the elephant was caught in a muddy swamp, struggled to get free, and when it finally fell exhausted on its side it was killed and butchered. How did the elephant get into the swamp—did it blunder in or was it herded in? Torralba lies in a steep-sided valley where the water level rises to within a few inches from the surface and where animals would be mired in mud. The terrain 300,000 years ago was even wetter than it is now. Perhaps hunting bands stood on the high ledges overlooking the valley, following the herd movements. Perhaps a young and unwary animal wandered from the herd and found itself caught in the mud; it would be relatively easy to run down the hill and make the kill.

Possibly the hunters played an active role by driving the animals into the swamp. Howell has collected much material showing evidence of burning. Charred materials are scattered about the site and not distributed in a manner suggestive of a hearth; whoever was lighting the fires

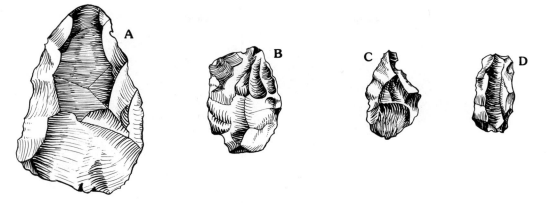

Figure 18-6. An Acheulian tool kit from Torralba, Spain, includes (A) a 10-inch quartzite cleaver, (B) a small flint cleaver, (C) a screwdriver-ended piece of chalcedony, and (D) a double-edged sidescraper made of jasper.

was apparently burning grass and brush over an extensive area. This evidence, plus the elephant remains in the swamps, suggests that fires were deliberately set to drive animals into the swamps. Once mired in mud they were relatively defenseless. At Ambrona, Howell uncovered a killing and butchering site where elephant remains abound. One area included most of the skeleton of an enormous bull elephant; judging by wear on the molar teeth the animal was undoubtedly old.

There were indications of living structures at Ambrona. Workers found what may be a hearth and nearby were three grapefruit-sized stones resembling parts of a circle or stone ring. Similar stone rings come from Torralba; these might be part of a conical, tepeelike structure. Modern Eskimos build similar shelters by hanging hides from a central pole and arranging stones in a circle to hold the hides in place.

Torralba and Ambrona yielded a rich and varied tool collection indicating a wide range of daily subsistence activities (Figure 18-6). Some stone tools probably served for heavy-duty chopping and hacking, others for skinning, slicing meat, and perhaps woodworking. There is also a large collection of other tools. These tools appear at an earlier time in the archaeological record than many previously expected, and they signify the early appearance of a relatively advanced technology.

There are a number of bone tools at Torralba, making it one of the very few sites where undoubted bone tools have come from a living floor. Some tools appear to be duplicates of more familiar stone implements; the function of some of these is unknown. There are also wooden tools, waterlogged implements showing marks of use, that somehow survived in the clayey, boggy deposits. A few pieces might have served as spears; these are the oldest known weapons, invented early in the history of hunting.

Terra Amata. Henry de Lumley (1973) uncovered a Middle Pleistocene site in southern France, located on a hillside on the French Riviera on a dead-end street called Terra Amata (Figure 18-7). The site was uncovered during clearing for a shipyard and the construction of luxury apartments. Beginning 28 January 1966 and continuing until 5 July of the same year, 300 workers spent 40,000 man-hours excavating the site. The excavated area encompasses

Figure 18-7. Structure at Terra Amata. Oval huts, ranging from 26 to 49 feet in length and from 13 to 20 feet in width, were built at Terra Amata by visiting hunters. A reconstruction shows that the walls were made of stakes, about 3 inches (8 centimeters) in diameter, set as a palisade in the sand and braced on the outside by a ring of stones. Some larger posts were set up along the axes of the huts, but how these and the walls were joined in unknown; the form shown is conjectural. Hearths were protected from drafts by a small pebble windscreen.

144 square yards and includes 21 separate living floors. Excavation proceeded using only trowels and brushes; the digging uncovered 35,000 objects, the location of each of which was plotted on 1,200 charts. Casts were made of 108 square yards of living floor and the progress documented by 9,000 photographs.

Superimposed living floors were uncovered in three separate locales; 4 are on a beach section formed by a sandbar, 6 on the beach, and 11 on a dune island. On the slopes of an ancient sand dune, de Lumley uncovered remains of a number of oval huts ranging from 26 to 49 feet long and 13 to 20 feet wide. They may have housed 10 to 20 people. Perhaps the huts were made of sturdy branches, bent to interlock at the top, with an entrance at one end and a hole in the top for ventilation. Presumably the branches were supported by posts and rocks placed against them.

A hearth located at the center was a basic feature of each hut. These hearths are either pebble-paved or shallow pits, a foot or two in diameter, scooped from the sand. A little stone wall standing at one end of the hearth may have served as a wind screen. Areas closest to the hearths are cleared of debris, perhaps indicating that persons slept there. This practice is common among Australian aborigines and other modern hunting groups.

Terra Amata yielded no hominid skeletal remains; however, there are two indirect clues of the inhabitants. An imprint of a right foot, 9.5 inches long, is preserved in the sand. The person making the imprint is estimated to have been 5 feet, 1 inch tall. Another source of evidence for human habitation is fossilized feces (**coprolites**), analysis of which indicates that the sites were seasonally occupied in early summer and spring. These were seasonal camping sites, as were Torralba and Ambrona.

Animal bones uncovered at Terra Amata include bird, turtle, and eight species of mammalian skeletal remains. There is abundant evidence that the inhabitants were big-game hunters; in order of their abundance, the inhabitants preferred stag, extinct elephant, wild boar, ibex, and Merck's rhinoceros. Most remains are those of young animals that were undoubtedly easiest to bring down. There are also indications that the inhabitants ate oysters, mussels, and limpets and the presence of fish bones and vertebrae indicates that they also fished.

The Terra Amata inhabitants left many traces of their tools; most stone tools are referred to as early Acheulian. Some tools were locally manufactured, the hut floors evidencing tool-making activity. The tool-maker's place within the hut is indicated by a patch of living floor surrounded by a litter of tool-manufacturing debris. Ground impressions may have been places where they sat, sometimes perhaps on skins. At another French site, Lazaret cave, dated to approximately 130,000 years ago, there is an indication that the inhabitants slept on seaweed beds. There are a few bone tools; one elephant leg bone was hammered to a point. A pointed bone fragment was probably fire hardened; one end of a third fragment was smoothed by wear, while still another may have served as an awl and some fragments may have been scrapers.

Some domestic furnishings have been uncovered. Flattened limestone blocks may have provided convenient surfaces on which to sit or break bone. A semispherical imprint in the sand might be an impression of a wooden bowl; if it is, it constitutes the earliest trace of a container yet uncovered. This imprint is filled with a whitish substance. In a corner, near the "bowl," excavators found lumps of the natural pigment red ocher. Some of these lumps were worn smooth and pointed like pencils at the end, indicating that they may have been used to color the body in preparation for some ceremony. Similar red ocher lumps derive from later Upper Pleistocene sites.

Africa. *Homo erectus* remains have been uncovered from North, East, and South Africa. The North African material is limited to Morocco and Algeria. There are four Moroccan sites: Sidi Abd er-Rahman[5], Temara (or Smuggler's Cave), Rabat, and Tangiers. The oldest site, Sidi Abd er-Rahman, was excavated in 1953 and yielded a mandible associated with an evolved Acheulian industry.

Smuggler's Cave, near Temara, is about 33 miles northeast of Casablanca. Among some undescribed hominid remains, there was a nearly complete mandible associated with artifacts of the final Acheulian industry. The material resembles other North African remains. The Rabat remains were blasted out in 1933; portions of the lower and upper jaws and braincase are all that remain of what was once probably a complete skull. The remains date to the end of the last European interglacial. The Tangiers material consists of a child's upper jaw.

The Ternifine remains were recovered in 1954 and 1955, from a rich site in a sandpit southeast of Oran, Algeria. Faunal evidence indicates that this is the oldest northwest African site. The material consists of a right parietal and three lower jaws resembling those of Asian *H. erectus*.

[5]The word "Sidi" indicates a Muslim holy man; the site was a cemetery for Muslim holy men.

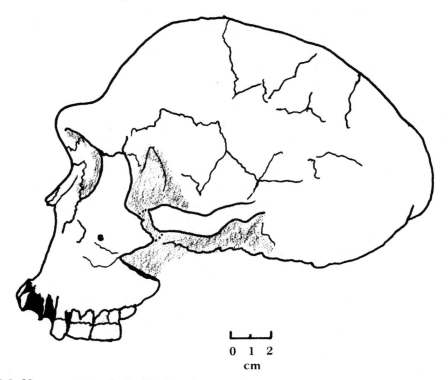

Figure 18-8. *Homo erectus* **(Lake Turkana).**

East Africa. East African *H. erectus* remains consist of material from Olduvai, Lake Turkana, Ethiopia (Figure 18-8), and cultural associations from Olorgesailie. Approximately 15 to 20 feet below the surface of Bed II of Olduvai, near the margin of an ancient lake, Louis Leakey recovered the skullcap of a hominid labeled Olduvai hominid 9, or "Chellean Man." Some 100 yards away lay numerous hand axes and abundant mammalian remains; the long bones were apparently split for their marrow. The remains are dated to the Middle Pleistocene. The skull resembles those from the Far East; unfortunately there is no face.

According to Rightmire (1979), the Bed II OH 9 material is dated to approximately 1.2 million years and shows similarities to the material from Koobi Fora, Lake Turkana, known as 3733. OH 9 suggests a long presence of *H. erectus* in East Africa beginning at least 1.2 million years ago. The smaller but more complete cranium from Koobi Fora established the presence of *H. erectus* in East Africa even earlier, that is, about 1.5 million years ago. The OH 9 and the 3733 materials resemble each other in many respects, and Rightmire suggests the possibility that the Turkana population could be ancestral to that at Olduvai. The current evidence suggests that *H. erectus* in Africa predated the onset of the Middle Pleistocene by 0.7 million to 0.8 million years. Therefore, they might more properly be assigned to the Lower Pleistocene.

Artifactual and skeletal remains have been recovered from Bed IV, Olduvai. A left femoral shaft and hip bone of *H. erectus* have been found in association with an Acheulian industry. This is the first direct association at Olduvai of a well-defined tool assemblage with *H. erectus* remains. Most tools are hand axes resembling those of the Early Acheulian series of Middle Bed II.

Femoral and pelvic remains were found during the 1970 excavations. This discovery (christened Olduvai hominid 28) is of the greatest importance because it sheds light on the structure and function of *H. erectus* hominid lower limbs. Functionally, the alternating pelvic tilt mechanism of striding bipeds was well established. The center of gravity was approximately as in modern bipeds; the weight of the upper body was transferred to the pelvis in a manner consistent with upright bipedalism. There are also indications that powerful knee extension was possible. OH 28 was an habitual biped.

Louis Leakey and the Discovery of *Homo erectus* at Olduvai

Another accidental discovery of the greatest importance took place in 1961—the find of remains of the same type of man as in China and Java, but twice as old in East Africa as in the Far East. This time the accident was due to an error on the part of one of my staff. The geologist working with me returned to camp one day with a draft plane table map of a certain part of the Gorge. I looked at it and said, "But you have left out one long narrow side gully." He replied, "I have not," and I said, "I am sorry, but you have; come over with me tomorrow morning and I will show you."

When we got to the long and rather grass and bush filled gully, and he had to admit that he was in error, I looked back towards our camp site and suddenly on the far side of the Gorge I saw a very small area of exposed fossil beds. . . .

Although I had explored Olduvai on foot since 1931 I knew, at once, that I had never set foot in that tiny exposure. But for the error on the part of my student which had taken me back to the point from which I saw it, I might still never have seen it. . . . As soon as we got back to camp, I went off again to locate this hidden patch of exposures, and as I walked on to it I almost trod on a half exposed fossil human skull. That was the first *Homo erectus* skull from Olduvai.

From The UNESCO Courier, August-September, 1972, p. 29.

Olorgesailie Occupation Remains. From Olorgesailie, in the Rift Valley about an hour's drive from Nairobi, Leakey and Isaac discovered an extensive *H. erectus* living site. Isaac's 1977 monograph on Olorgesailie provides considerable information. Today, Olorgesailie is in a semiarid environment. However, geological and paleobotanical evidence from Pleistocene sediments at Olorgesailie clearly indicate that for prolonged periods there was a stable freshwater lake in the area. The nearest equivalent today is Lake Naivasha. Whether the former lake at Olorgesailie was made possible by a different climatic regime or by different drainage conditions has yet to be determined. The freshwater conditions of the former lake at Olorgesailie contrast markedly with the highly saline water conditions of neighboring Lakes Natron and Magadi. It seems that former climatic conditions were wetter than today.

Isaac states that the two lowest date values of 0.425 million and 0.486 million years (K-Ar dates) are valid estimates. No specific dating evidence in East Africa or elsewhere precludes an age of 400,000 years for the fossil and artifact assemblage at Olorgesailie. Paleomagnetic determinations showed weak polarity that is consistent with an age of less than 700,000 years.

The Olorgesailie occupation areas appear to have been discrete patches of stone and bone accumulations that may have coincided with natural boundaries such as the bank of a sandy runnel or the limit of shade provided by a larger tree. The inhabitants could have built shelters, for example, hedges, that disappeared over time. Smaller occupation areas may have held 4 or 5 adults in a group; larger areas may have accommodated more than 20 adults. Based on the accumulation of a ton or more of stone artifacts and **manuports** (materials carried into the site, but which do not necessarily show use), it is estimated that the sites were continuously occupied for 2 to 3 months.

Archeological assemblages at Olorgesailie are later in the East African technological and typological sequence than the lower Acheulian assemblages from Olduvai Bed II. All the assemblages from Olorgesailie seem less refined than the Acheulian tools from Kalambo Falls, for which there is a minimum C^{14} determination of $61,700 \pm 1,300$ years. Some of the artifact concentrations seem to be remnants of shifting home bases of itinerant bands.

The abundance and appearance of faunal remains make it obvious that the inhabitants were hunters and scavengers. Large mammalian remains predominate and there is a superabundance of a large, extinct baboon at one site. Rodent, bird, and reptilian bones are relatively scarce. Most bone material is splintered; either the inhabitants pulverized the bone or scavengers moved in after they left camp. One area appears to be a hippopotamus butchery site.

Within one oval-shaped occupation area, 19 by 13 meters, the excavators found 1000 kilograms (2,200 pounds) of stone artifacts, rubble, and unmodified cobbles. The abundance of bones of an extinct baboon attests either to continued extremely successful hunting or to a massacre of a single troop. (The present-day Hadza of Tanzania surprise a troop of sleeping baboons and club the baboons to death.) There is scant evidence as to the hunting methods of the Olorgesailie inhabitants; however, hunters lacking such weapons as bows may have killed a large number of baboons by drugging them at a water hole.

Olorgesailie provides little evidence for the use of fire. At site I-3 there is a hearthlike depression filled with stone and bone, but there is no trace of charcoal. However, negative evidence from very old sites or unprotected sites is of little significance.

At all the sites except three, the preservation of bone is too fragmentary to allow anything other than broad considerations. The most consistent remains are from game animals such as bovids, hippopotamus, and equids. The persistent presence of hippopotamus tusk fragments and some elephant tooth lamellae without associated skeletal parts requires some explanation. The tusks may have been used as tools, for some show damaged tips. Thus, their presence may have nothing to do with the diet of the Olorgesailie human inhabitants. Meat from the pachyderm carcasses may have been introduced as "fillets" to the home base. The fragments of hippopotamus bones may thus represent otherwise undocumented meat sources. The fact that the sites yield little bone suggests that very large quantities of bone were never present and dependence on meat for food was not necessarily a feature of life in all Acheulian groups (Isaac, 1977).

Olorgesailie provides the following insights into Middle Pleistocene hominid social life. The inhabitants lived in groups of 4 to 30 adults; the smaller number probably results from temporary splitting of a relatively stable band of 20 to 30 members. The sites are either seasonal occupation grounds, or they suggest a sectional differentiation of labor. The inhabitants subsisted on hunted or scavenged food, or they partook in the systematic killing of baboons.

Lake Turkana. Richard Leakey (1970 a,b) has announced the recovery of *H. erectus* from Lake Turkana. The remains, the most complete *H. erectus* skull yet discovered, were reconstructed by A. Walker of Harvard. The skull called 3733 looks almost identical to *H. erectus* from Chou Kou Tien. Quite unpredictably, however, the Lake Turkana material dates to 1.5 million years ago.

It has been recently announced that seven footprints dating to 1.5 million years ago have been uncovered at Lake Turkana. It has been estimated that the individual making the prints was 5 feet to 5 feet, 6 inches tall and weighed about 120 pounds. Although both *Australopithecus* and *H. erectus* fossils have been found at the site, Behrensmeyer suggests that the prints were left by *H. erectus* because its fossilized remains are preserved in nearby strata, but the bones of *Australopithecus* are not. Tools made of pebbles and cobbles have also been recovered from the same strata. It is no surprise that the prints indicate an erect, bipedal gait.

Other African Remains. In October 1976 new materials were found in Ethiopia showing that *H. erectus* was also inhabiting this region of East Africa. This material comes from the Afar region, which has also yielded "Lucy" and other remains found by D. Johanson. "Bodo man" (so named because it was found in Ethiopia's Bodo region) consists of approximately 53 percent of the cranium and face. Pictures show the form possessed large brow ridges and a prognathic face. Preliminary reports indicate that this skull was found in association with an abundance of stone tools. Preliminary indications reveal a date of at least 500,000 years ago.

In addition to the hominid materials and volcanic stone tools there is an abundance of faunal remains including elephants, hippos, horses, rhinos, giraffes, pigs, rodents, reptiles, and fish. These remains will be most useful in reconstructing the habitat. According to John Kalb, a geologist on the research team, "Bodo man" made camp near the edge of a lake.

A number of African remains have recently been transferred (some more tentatively than others) to the taxon *H. erectus*. For quite some time this material was associated with the Neanderthals; recent reanalysis, however, seems to have confirmed the link with *H. erectus*.

The Broken Hill (Rhodesian) skull (Figure 18-9) was found in 1921 during opencast mining of lead and zinc ores at Broken Hill in what is today Zambia. Recent studies have attempted to provide a date for the Broken Hill material. Faunal studies and amino acid racemization determinations suggest an age of about 130,000 years. The Omo II fossil (Day, 1971) from the Kibish Formation is similar to Broken Hill and has a similar tentative date. Both Rightmire (1979) and Bilsborough (1979) agree that Broken Hill has many of the same traits as the Middle Pleistocene *H. erectus* materials.

Another skull, the Saldanha skull, is almost identical in contour and morphological details to Broken Hill. The Saldanha skull was found in 1953 at Hopefield near Saldanha Bay, 90 miles north of Capetown, South Africa. Hand axes and flake-tool implements were recovered along with the skull. Although the date has not been firmly established, it could be as old as 100,000 years. Both Rightmire (1979) and Bilsborough (1979) place this skull with *H. erectus*.

Site Distribution

The distribution of Middle Pleistocene cultural evidence suggests that major tropical African settlements were in open or lightly wooded country in proximity to water. Asian and European sites are often in caves, suggesting a cooling of the climate and the appearance of cultural adaptations facilitating life under such conditions.

Middle Pleistocene sites take the appearance of areal tool and bone concentrations; some parts of such "cultural floors" were primarily used for tool making, others for butchering. Various site patterns indicate they were seasonally occupied or that several groups temporarily and contemporaneously occupied the site. The lack of appreciable thickness to the "floors" indicates their temporary nature.

Acheulian Tradition

About 1.5 million years ago a new cultural phase appeared. Archaeologically, this stage is characterized by the appearance of new and different kinds of tools in Africa. This new stone-

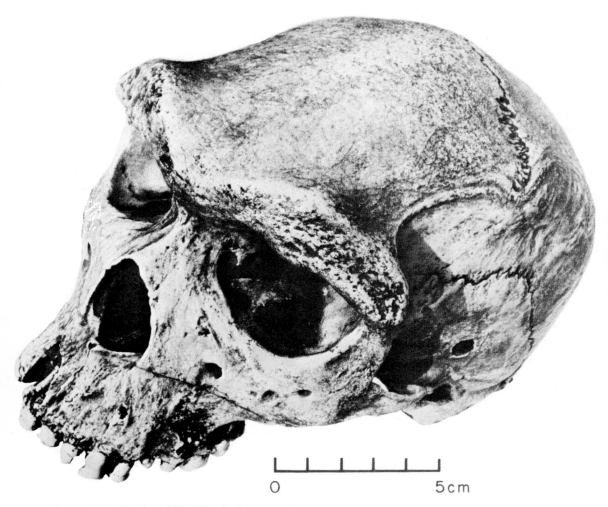

Figure 18-9. Broken Hill (Rhodesian) cranium.

working technique, called the Acheulian, allowed greater precision in the shaping of stone. Furthermore, tools of the **Acheulian tradition** are more standardized and specialized.

The Acheulian tradition is the most widespread and, aside from the Oldowan, the longest-lasting cultural tradition in the fossil record. The tradition first appears at Olduvai above volcanic tuffs separating the upper from the lower members of Bed II and is believed to date to about 1.5 million years ago. A possibly related industry of picks and steep scraping tools comes from the Karari Plateau, Lake Turkana, and dates between 1.3 million and 1.5 million years ago. At Lake Natron, to the north of Lake Turkana, two other Acheulian occupation floors date to about 1.3 million years ago. There is evidence of an East African Acheulian tradition lasting until about 190,000 years ago. Elsewhere, evidence of an evolved Acheulian continues until 115,000 to 125,000 years ago, although by that time it acquired a more specialized and regional character (Clark, 1976).

The Acheulian represents a mode of life that appears to have persisted for a relatively long time and allowed adaptation to a variety of tropical, temperate, and even cold environments. The basic Acheulian tool kit includes a simple, versatile range of cutting, scraping, piercing, chopping, and pounding tools used to prepare animal and plant materials. Additionally, bones were broken and trimmed to use as tools and wood was worked into spears. Site remains indicate a heavy reliance on animal food sources; however, plant remains are less likely to fossilize. The overall range of bone remains indicates both opportunistic hunting and specialized techniques, for example, the fire drives at Ambrona and Torralba.

In contrast to the earlier record, dietary preferences focused attention on a generally limited range of food sources. As a result, relatively large territories may have been required to obtain food, so fewer members of a population could be supported in any one area than was true with earlier hominids. A survey of known *H. erectus* remains indicates an underlying preference for open, grassy habitats possessing large herds of gregarious herbivores, an abundant food source. Butzer (1977) suggests that this argues for a self-regulating mechanism akin to a biological homeostatic equilibrium. It also implies to Butzer a low level of manipulatory, cognitive, and organizational skills, perhaps due to biological and intellectual limitations as well as to a limited amount of cumulative experience.

The Acheulian stone tool culture does not exhibit a unilinear progression to a more varied, sophisticated form through time. Overall, Acheulian tool kits include some items refined over preceding forms. However, at any one site one can find "deterioration" rather than improvement in artifactual skills. Such "deterioration" may simply be due to specialized site functions and impermanence. Butzer (1977) feels this can be best explained by small widely dispersed hunting-gathering populations numbering 20 to 50 individuals per group and including one or two competent tool makers. A single group might not meet another for a long time.

Butzer (1977) paints a picture of small bands of technologically simple hunter-gatherers spread over wide intervals across the open areas of Africa and Eurasia. This is compatible with the osteological evidence for considerable morphological variability. "Eventually, it should be expected that if sufficiently numerous populations were isolated in a peripheral continental area or by surrounding unattractive biomes, spurts of biological evolution or cultural innovation (or both) would be increasingly likely" (Butzer, 1977:50). As increasingly large and differentiated populations migrated from their original centers, major discontinuities appeared in the cultural context of surrounding areas.

Site Characteristics. The distribution of Acheulian cultural remains suggests that major tropical African settlements were in open or lightly wooded country in close proximity to water sources. The lack of evidence for hominid activity in tropical rain forests may be due to, among other factors, poor preservation conditions. Furthermore, if herd hunting were a major economic strategy that employed group or multigroup cooperation, optimal habitats would not have included tropical rain forest environments.

Middle Pleistocene sites appear as tool and bone concentrations; some parts of such living floors were primarily used for tool making, others for butchering. Five major types of sites were associated with *H. erectus* material (Clark, 1976):

1. Sites where several different kinds of activities occurred. Tool kits at these sites are mixed Oldowan and Acheulian types, along with unmodified waste from the process of tool manufacture.
2. Butchering sites. Such sites are found at Isimilia, Tanzania, and at one of the lower levels at Olorgesailie, Kenya, where some disarticulated and incomplete hippopotamus carcasses

are associated with heavy-duty or occasional large cutting tools and small flake concentrations. Similar materials are found with elephant remains and other game at Torralba and Ambrona, Spain.

3. Sites with concentrations of large cutting tools and varying amounts of light-duty equipment, and having little or no associated bone. Examples of these are the partly excavated surface at Melka Kontoure, Ethiopa, and the waterside site of Latamme, northern Syria. At the latter, large cutting and light-duty tools are associated with large limestone blocks suggesting some type of shelter.

4. Sites yielding many light-duty small tools but few and poorly made large cutting tools. Such sites are found at Bed II, Olduvai, a site in Bed II, Olorgesailie, and at Broken Hill, Zambia.

5. Workshop sites. Such sites are found from the Vaal River (Canteen Kopje), from the Transvaal, South Africa, and from the Sahara. These sites have small concentrations or huge spreads of debris lying adjacent to sources of raw material such as river boulders.

The Acheulian Tradition

The characteristic Acheulian tool was the hand axe, a pear-shaped tool about 6 inches (15 centimeters) long with a cutting edge and a somewhat pointed end. The hand axe was manufactured by taking a number of flakes from a core. The hand axe was a versatile tool. Another characteristic Acheulian tool was the cleaver, which had a straight sharp edge in contrast to the pointed hand axe. Flake tools are also found at some Acheulian sites.

The Acheulian tool tradition appears to be an advance over the preceeding Oldowan tool tradition. It has been suggested that the manufacturers of the Acheulian tools had greater manual dexterity. If this is true, it indicates some changes in neural structure, changes allowing or making easier more forethought in the manufacturing process. Acheulian tools also show a wider sampling of raw materials, perhaps indicating a greater awareness of the environment.

The precision evident in the manufacture of Acheulian tools was apparently due to a new flaking method, the soft percussion (soft hammer) technique. In this technique, a stone flake was detached from the core using a wooden, bone, or antler hammer. The use of these materials, which are softer than stone, allowed more control of the final product in terms of flake length, width, and thickness.

In contrast to the all-purpose Oldowan tools, Acheulian tool assemblages regularly yield tools apparently tailored for different purposes. This is perhaps a reflection of increasing complexity of the social organization and of the wider range of habitats in which the manufacturers lived.

"When *Homo erectus* Tamed Fire, He Tamed Himself"

This subtitle is from an article by Pfeiffer (1971) that first appeared in the *New York Times Magazine* in 1966. Fire has always had a place in our lives; as the first natural "domesticated" force, it represented a kind of biological declaration of independence. Outside Africa, fire and *H. erectus* are synonymous. With purposeful use of fire, early hominids began to shape the world according to their design; by bringing fire into its living space, *H. erectus* carved, out of darkness, zones of light and warmth that provided relative freedom from predation. Fire opened new living areas, lighting and warming damp, dark caves where many *H. erectus* remains occur. Fire, by changing living habits, may have indirectly altered the brain's structure and enhanced our ability to learn and communicate. The oldest hearth remains come from the 750,000-year-old Escale cave in southern France. At a depth of 45 feet excavators uncovered proof of deliberately made fires—traces of charcoal, ash, fire-cracked stone, and five reddened hearth areas up to a yard in diameter.

Why was fire used? Fire was of minimal value while humans remained in our tropical African homeland; however, as it grew colder, as they migrated north, fire may have provided warmth. Fire was probably originally obtained from such ready-made sources as volcanic eruptions, brush fires, or gas and oil seepages. Hunters may have camped near fire, which was a natural resource as were game, water, and shelter. When they moved they may have taken smouldering embers with them; each band may have had a fire-bearer responsible for keeping the flame. From the beginning fire may have been used to keep predators away. Perhaps we became regular cave dwellers only after we learned to use fires to drive predators from the cave.

Fire for Hunting. Fire was used in hunting and Torralba strongly suggests that hunters used fire to stampede their prey. Fire may also have been used to produce more effective spears; Australian aborigines, for example, fire-harden the tips of their digging sticks. Fire hardens the core and makes the outer part crumbly and easier to sharpen. A possible fire-hardened spear from Germany dates to approximately 80,000 years ago.

Results of Fire Use. Psychological changes may have accompanied the use of fire; cooking may have produced behavioral restraint, that is, control of a tendency to do things on

Table 18-1. Review of *Homo erectus* Sites

Geographical Area	Remains	Pleistocene Dating
Asia		
Lan T'ien, China	Human remains	Middle Pleistocene
Java (Djetis, Trinil faunal beds)	Human remains	Middle Pleistocene
Chou Kou Tien, China	Human remains, artifacts, fire	Middle Pleistocene
India (?), Malaysia (?)	Possibility of tools	Middle Pleistocene
Solo, Indonesia	Human remains	Middle Pleistocene (?)
Africa		
Lake Turkana, Kenya	Human remains	Lower Pleistocene
Olduvai Gorge, Bed II, Tanzania	Human remains, artifacts	Lower Pleistocene
Omo, Ethiopia	Human remains	Middle Pleistocene (?)
Olorgesailie, Kenya	Artifacts, living site	Middle Pleistocene
North Africa (Morocco, Algeria, Tunisia)	Human remains, artifacts	Middle Pleistocene
Afar, Ethiopia	Human remains, artifacts	Middle Pleistocene
Bodo, Ethiopia	Human remains	Middle Pleistocene
Swartkrans, South Africa	Human remains, artifacts	Lower Pleistocene
Broken Hill, Zambia	Human remains, artifacts	Middle Pleistocene
Saldanha, South Africa	Human remains, artifacts	Middle Pleistocene (?)
Europe and Balkans		
Přezletice, Czechoslovakia	Artifacts, human molar crown (?)	Middle Pleistocene
Vértesszöllös, Hungary	Human remains, artifacts	Middle Pleistocene
Mauer or Heidelberg, Germany	Human remains	Middle Pleistocene
Petralona, Greece	Human remains	Middle Pleistocene
Torralba/Ambrona, Spain	Artifacts, fire, hunting	Middle Pleistocene
Terra Amata, France	Artifacts, dwelling structures	Middle Pleistocene
Arago (Tautavel), France	Human remains, artifacts	Middle Pleistocene
Bilzingsleben, Germany	Human remains, artifacts	Middle Pleistocene

the spur of the moment. Inhibition is a mark of evolutionary advance. Cooking of meat suggests that less food is eaten on the spot and more carried back to the camp. If the assumption that food sharing requires elaborate social rules is correct, it follows that the more there was to share, the more rules were needed. A continuing elaboration of the communication matrix would be in order.

Introducing fire into the living spaces created an artificial day independent of the sun's movements for light and heat; evening hours could be illuminated and one's attention turned to productive pursuits. Extra time could be used to think about complex hunting plans and migration routes. There is also the role of fire in the early religious ceremonies. Prehistoric hunters carrying torches entered the deepest cave recesses and here performed religious acts; these are recorded as early as 30,000 years ago. Fire obsession may be of ancient origin; fire may be a stimulant as potent as drugs in arousing visions and as such it would have served early religious functionaries.

We can raise a number of unanswerable questions at this time. What did early cave dwellers think of shadows dancing on dark cave walls as they sat about their fires? Did the willowy shapes cast on the walls lead the cave dwellers to thoughts that may have had magical or ritual overtones? Were any of the shadows construed as foes or as friends, as animals of the hunt? Did the place that fire holds in many of the world's religions have such inauspicious beginnings as these?

Homo erectus cultural associations are elaborations of earlier Lower Pleistocene activities. Some morphological features distinguishing H. erectus from earlier hominids, for example, changes in brain size, facial morphology, and dental structure, may be correlated with cultural elaboration. If culture is the basis of the hominid adaptation, natural selection furthered a more efficient culture. An enlarged brain is related to increasing capacity for complex cultural skills and behavior. Cultural and physical evolution went hand-in-hand.

In contrast to preceding hominids, H. erectus was distributed throughout the Old World. The H. erectus grade represented a level of cultural adaptation that allowed its possessors to expand into new, once inhospitable environments. It has been suggested that because of geographical spread and because of varying environmental conditions, the origin of modern racial groups can be dated to Middle Pleistocene hominid expansion. However, this suggestion lacks proof.

During the Middle Pleistocene temperature conditions appear to be less important to hominid evolution than a rich and relatively dependable supply of big game. The glacials opened large areas of light woodland or parkland in mid-latitude Europe, substantially increasing the biomass of large herbivores, a major source of food of H. erectus. The warmer interglacials, in contrast, witnessed the return of closed forests and a low biomass. This probably decreased the human carrying capacity of the environment. Deserts and rain forests were largely unfavorable and there is no record of human activity to speak of from these areas. Butzer (1977:50) feels that the "... Acheulian perspective of an optimal environment was predicated on open habitats with high animal biomass."

Homo erectus is probably the intermediate evolutionary grade between the Lower Pleistocene hominids and H. sapiens. Evidence in Africa and Europe shows that H. erectus and earlier H. sapiens forms were evolving contemporaneously. The best evidence suggests that H. erectus arose in Africa or Java. The line from H. erectus to

H. sapiens is hazy, but fragments can be seen in Africa, China, and Europe. In Europe, for example, it is suggested that the Mauer jaw belonged to a representative of an *H. erectus* population that perhaps gave rise to a population such as Vértesszöllös, and then to Steinheim and Swanscombe. The latter two or three may be *H. sapiens* subspecies.

Bibliography

Black, D. 1931. On an adolescent skull of "Sinanthropus pekinensis" in comparison with an adult skull of the same species and with other hominid skulls. *Paleontologia Sinica,* Series D7.

Bordes, F., and de Sonneville-Bordes, D. 1970. The significance of variability in paleolithic assemblages. *World Archaeology* 2:61-73.

Butzer, K. 1964. Environment and archeology. Chicago: Aldine.

_____. 1977. Environment, culture and human evolution. *American Scientist* 65:572-84.

Campbell, B. 1966. *Human evolution: an introduction to man's adaptations.* Chicago: Aldine.

Chance, M., and Jolly, C. 1971. *Social groups of monkeys, apes and men.* London: Cape.

Chang, K. 1962. New evidence on fossil man in China. *Science* 136:749.

_____. 1979. Chinese paleoanthropology. *Annual Review of Anthropology* 6:137-59.

Clark, J. 1976. African origins of man the toolmaker. In *Human origins: Louis Leakey and the East African evidence,* edited by G. Isaac and E. McCown, pp. 1-53. Menlo Park, Calif.: Benjamin.

Coon, C. 1962. *The origin of races.* New York: Knopf.

Day, M. 1971. Postcranial remains of *Homo erectus* from Bed IV, Olduvai Gorge, Tanzania. *Nature* 232:383.

de Lumley, H. 1969. A Paleolithic camp at Nice. *Scientific American* 220:42-50.

de Lumley, H., and de Lumley, M. 1973. Pre-Neanderthal human remains from Arago Cave in southeastern France. *Yearbook of Physical Anthropology* 17:162-69.

Eiseley, L. 1954. Man the fire-maker. *Scientific American* 191:52-57.

Fejfar, O. 1969. Human remains from the early Pleistocene in Czechoslovakia. *Current Anthropology* 10:170.

Garn, S. and Block, W. 1970. The limited nutritional value of cannibalism. *American Anthropologist* 72:106.

Hemmer, F. 1972. Notes sur la position phylétique de l'homme de Petralona. *L'Anthropologie* 76:155-62.

Howell, F. 1960. European and northwest African Middle Pleistocene hominids. *Current Anthropology* 1:195.

_____. 1965. *Early man.* New York: Time-Life Books.

Howells, W. 1966. *Homo erectus. Scientific American* 215:46-53.

_____. 1973. *Evolution of the genus Homo.* Reading, Mass.: Addison-Wesley.

Isaac, G. 1968. Traces of Pleistocene hunters: an East African example. In *Man the hunter,* edited by R. Lee and I. DeVore, pp. 258-61. Chicago: Aldine.

_____. 1969. Studies of early cultures in East Africa. *World Archaeology* 1:1-28.

_____. 1975. Stratigraphy and cultural patterns in East Africa during the middle ranges of Pleistocene time. In *After the australopithecines: stratigraphy, ecology and culture change in the Middle Pleistocene,* edited by K. Butzer and G. Isaac, pp. 495-542. The Hague: Mouton.

_____. 1977. *Olorgesailie: archaeological studies of a Middle Pleistocene lake basin in Kenya.* Chicago: University of Chicago Press.

Jacob, T. 1967. Recent "Pithecanthropus" finds in Indonesia. *Current Anthropology* 8:501.

Jacob, T., Soejono, R., Freeman, L., and Brown, F. 1978. Stone tools from mid-Pleistocene sediments in Java. *Science* 202:885-87.

Jelinek, A. 1977. The Lower Paleolithic: current evidence and interpretations. In *Annual Review of Anthropology* 6:11-32.

Jolly, C., and Plog, F. 1976. *Physical anthropology and prehistory.* New York: Knopf.

Klein, R. 1973. Geologic antiquity of Rhodesian man. *Nature* 244:311-12.

Kretzoi, M., and Vertés, L. 1965. Upper biharian (intermindel) pebble-industry occupation in western Hungary. *Current Anthropology* 6:74.

Leakey, M. 1971. Discovery of postcranial remains of *Homo erectus* and associated artifacts in Bed IV at Olduvai Gorge, Tanzania. *Nature* 232:380.

Mann, A. 1971. *Homo erectus.* In *Background for man,* edited by P. Dolhinow and V. Sarich, pp. 161-81. Boston: Little, Brown.

Oakley, K. 1955. Fire as a Paleolithic tool and weapon. *Proceedings of the Prehistoric Society* 21:36.

_____. 1961. On man's use of fire, with comments on tool-making and hunting. In *Social life of early man,* edited by S. Washburn, pp. 176-93. Chicago: Aldine.

Pfeiffer, J. 1969. *The emergence of man.* New York: Harper & Row.

_____. 1971. When *Homo erectus* tamed fire he tamed himself. In *Human variation,* edited by H. Bleibtreu and J. Downs, pp. 193-203. Beverly Hills, Calif.: Glencoe Press.

Pilbeam, D. 1975. Middle Pleistocene hominids. In *After the australopithecines: stratigraphy, ecology, and culture change in the Middle Pleistocene,* edited by K. Butzer and G. Isaac, pp. 809-56. The Hague: Mouton.

Poirier, F. 1981. *Fossil evidence: the human evolutionary journey.* St. Louis: Mosby.

Rightmire, G. 1979. Cranial remains of *Homo erectus* from Beds II and IV, Olduvai Gorge, Tanzania. *American Journal of Physical Anthropology* 51:99-116.

Sartono, S. 1972. Discovery of another hominid skull at Sangiran, central Java. *Current Anthropology* 13:124.

Sauer, C. 1961. Sedentary and mobile bents in early societies. In *Social life of early man,* edited by S. Washburn, pp. 256-66. Chicago: Aldine.

Semenov, S. 1964. *Prehistoric technology.* London: Cory, Adams and McKay.

Shapiro, H. 1971. The strange, unfinished saga of Peking man. *Natural History* 80:74.

Stringer, C. 1974. A multivariate study of the Petralona skull. *Journal of Human Evolution,* 3:397-404.

Tobias, P. 1971. *The brain in hominid evolution.* New York: Columbia University Press.

Vleck, G. 1978. A new discovery of *Homo erectus* in central Europe. *Journal of Human Evolution* 7:239-52.

Walker, A., and Leakey, R. 1978. The hominids of East Turkana. *Scientific American* 239:54-66.

Weidenreich, F. 1943. The skull of "Sinanthropus pekinensis." *Paleontologia Sinica,* New Series D 10.

Wolpoff, M. 1977. Some notes of the Vértesszöllös occipital. *American Journal of Physical Anthropology* 47:357-64.

_____. 1980. *Paleoanthropology.* New York: Knopf.

Woo Ju-Kang, 1964. Mandible of "Sinanthropus lantianensis." *Current Anthropology* 5:98.

Chapter 19

Early *Homo sapiens* and the Neanderthals

When, where, and how did the transition from *Homo erectus* to *H. sapiens* occur? The closer one comes in time to modern *Homo*, the easier it should be to find the answer; this has not, however, been true. The ancestral line, or lines, leading to modern populations become hazy approximately 300,000 years ago.

Wolpoff (1980) notes that the main morphological differences between the early *H. sapiens* and late *H. erectus* lineages are found in changes in the cranial size and morphology and, to a lesser degree, in the face. Dental changes conform to continued trends for posterior reduction and anterior expansion. There is a continuity between the earliest members of *H. sapiens* and the latest *H. erectus* sample in areas where the samples are large.

The Middle Pleistocene fossil record is rather complete both in fossil materials and conflicting interpretations. This fossil record is often divided into Second interglacial forms, including Swanscombe and Steinheim, Third interglacial forms from France, Italy, and Germany, and the third glacial inhabitants, the Neanderthals.

The Neanderthals' role in subsequent hominid evolutionary history has always been disputed. Some rule them out of our lineage while others make them direct ancestors; and there are other viewpoints. The argument one follows rests with one's interpretation of Second and Third interglacial fossil remains. This chapter discusses the controversy.

Environmental factors may have played a basic role in the evolution of *H. sapiens* (Butzer, 1977). One of the prerequisites to the appearance of *H. sapiens* was the unequal distribution of resources at the subcontinental scale. Subcontinental regions included several areas of intermediate size providing a sufficient density and productivity of resources to support sizeable clusters of human groups while large intervening areas were completely unoccupied. A second prerequisite to the rise of *H. sapiens* is the long-term cyclic variation of resources that both creates sufficient ecological stress to promote natural selection and also sets in motion alternating movements of dispersed breeding populations, thus favoring genetic drift and gene flow. Genetic drift and gene flow provide the potential for rapid local change in peripheral areas.

Second Interglacial Hominids

Swanscombe. The fossil record from approximately 200,000 to 300,000 years ago is rather meager. However, during the second interglacial period, about 200,000 to 250,000 years ago, tantalizing remains appear in England and Germany. The site at Swanscombe, England, is now a gravel pit along the Thames River located not far from London. Swanscombe, however, seems once to have been a favorite hunting site for prehistoric populations. Several hundred thousand tools were recovered from the site. The first hominid remains appeared in 1935 when a local worker uncovered an occipital bone. This began a series of lucky happenings associated with Swanscombe. A second lucky find occurred the following March. This time a left partial **parietal** bone was uncovered; the fragment, against overwhelming odds, belonged with the 1935 occipital. The parietal was recovered during excavation of hundreds of tons of gravel as part of a harbor project. Nineteen years later, in 1955, a third skull fragment, the right parietal, was uncovered 75 feet from the original find. By remarkable coincidence, this belonged to the same individual as the two other fragments.

Deposits yielding the Swanscombe hominid remains are of Second interglacial age (Table 19-1). Associated faunal and archaeological materials are referred to the Mindel-Riss interglacial of the Middle Pleistocene. This dating was confirmed by fluorine analysis, making the Swanscombe material one of the best-dated fossil hominid remains.

Morphology. The three skull fragments (occipital and two parietals) were well preserved and articulated perfectly (Figure 19-1). The cranial sutures were open, indicating, by modern comparison, an age at death of between 20 and 25 years. The inferred cranial capacity of 1275

Table 19-1. Middle Pleistocene Fossil Record[a]

Third (Würm) Glacial Forms

Form	Location
Western European ("Classic") Neanderthals	France, Spain, Southwestern Europe
Central and Eastern European Neanderthals	Czechoslovakia, Hungary
Eastern ("Progressive") Neanderthals	Israel, Lebanon, Turkey
Saccopostore	Italy
Quinzano	Italy

Third (Riss-Würm) Interglacial Forms

Fontéchevade	France
Ehringsdorf	Germany
Krapina	Yugoslavia

Second (Mindel-Riss) Interglacial Forms

Swanscombe	England
Steinheim	Germany

Includes only forms discussed in this chapter.

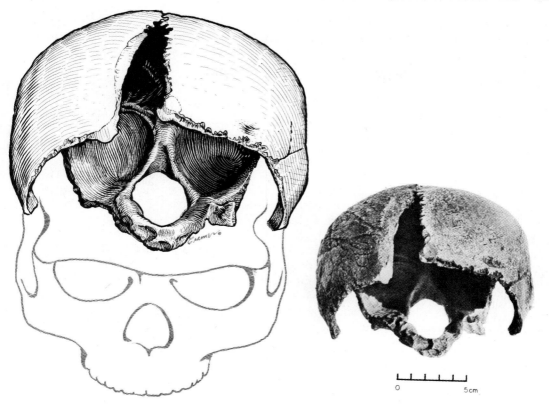

Figure 19-1. Swanscombe partial cranium.

to 1325 cc falls within the range of modern populations. Two major features of distinguishing Swanscombe from modern *Homo sapiens* skulls are its thickness (based on forms both preceding and following it) and an indication of heavy brow ridges. Because a frontal bone is lacking, however, this cannot be confirmed.

Taxonomy. The "advanced" characteristics of Swanscombe, especially the rather modern cranial capacity, have led to some taxonomic confusion. Swanscombe represents an evolutionary advance over *H. erectus;* its large brain and the general suggestion of a rounded and expanded skull contour approach conditions of modern populations. Conversely, the relatively low braincase height suggests that the specimen may be a less advanced form intermediate between *H. erectus* and modern *H. sapiens* populations. Swanscombe appears to represent a somewhat primitive variety of *H. sapiens* and is often referred to as *H. sapiens swanscombensis.*

Steinheim. Swanscombe's taxonomic position is clarified somewhat by the discovery of contemporaneous material from Steinheim, north of Stuttgart, West Germany. Steinheim has been dated with great care to the Mindel-Riss interglacial, roughly 250,000 years ago. Swanscombe and Steinheim are very similar. The Steinheim skull was alone; it lacked a mandible. Badly damaged behind the left eye, it evidenced a sizeable hole in the skull base indicating cannibalism. The skull, found in 1933, came from 25 feet deep in a gravel pit, capping a 25-year search by H. Berckhemer. The hominid skull bones were associated with many faunal remains; no tools were recovered.

Owing to the weight of the wet earth covering it, the skull was warped and crushed; however, with some reconstruction, we can obtain an idea of how the skull and face looked (Figure 19-2). The rear of the skull resembles Swanscombe, but the cranial capacity seems smaller and it has been estimated at 1150 to 1175 cc. This is similar to the larger-brained *H. erectus*. However, it significantly differs from *H. erectus* in the back of the head and possibly the face.

Facially, Steinheim possessed heavy brow ridges and a low forehead, but these traits were not as marked as in *H. erectus*. Steinheim's face seems shorter than that of "Sinanthropus," but is prognathic in comparison with modern populations. The nose is rather broad; the brow ridges, although large and heavy, were slightly separated above the nose. Although lacking front teeth, these were probably rather large, and the back teeth appear modern. The teeth are moderately **taurodont** (i.e., there is a tendency toward an enlarged pulp cavity and perhaps fusion of the molar roots). Except for taurodontism, nothing notable distinguishes Steinheim's teeth from those of modern Europeans.

Steinheim shows a combination of "advanced" and "primitive" traits. The cranium is small (1150 to 1175 cc), the skull is low, and brow ridges are large. Along with these features typical of *H. erectus*, however, are features of a more modern aspect. The face is relatively small and

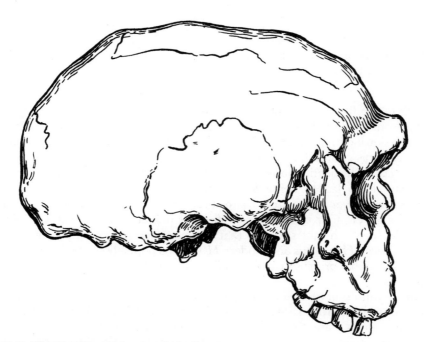

Figure 19-2. The Steinheim face and skull.

does not protrude in the jaw region, that is, there is minimal prognathism. The skull also appears to be tucked under at the brow ridges. The maximal skull breadth is higher than in earlier *H. erectus,* indicating that although the skull is small, it approaches that of *H. sapiens* in morphology. The teeth are small and the M3 is reduced, both relatively modern features. The occipital is rounded without a sharp angle.

The derivation of Swanscombe and Steinheim is still being questioned. The most direct answer would be that they arose in Europe and are descendent from populations similar to those at Vértesszöllös According to another theory, they were European immigrants who evolved in the Far East, perhaps from a stock such as "Peking man" or else in central Asia.

Third Interglacial Hominids

Preceding European "Classic Neanderthals," a number of European skeletal remains were recovered dating to the Third, or Riss-Würm interglacial. These, along with Second interglacial material from England, Germany, and France, are often referred to as pre-Mousterian (referring to the Neanderthal cultural assemblage) *H. sapiens.* Third interglacial forms come from France, Germany, and Italy. Although fragmentary, they play a major role in the taxonomic controversy as to the place of subsequent Neanderthal populations in our evolutionary history.

Fontéchevade. The Fontéchevade cave was excavated by G. Henri-Martin; in 1947 she broke through the "cave floor" to find seven more meters of deposits containing tools and warm-weather fauna that belonged to the Third interglacial period. Parts of two other skulls came from the same deposits; these included a patch from the brow area of one skull, about the size of a silver dollar, and most of the top of another, exhibiting signs of charring. Beneath this layer, Henri-Martin found another tool assemblage but without associated skeletal remains. Fluorine tests were conducted to establish contemporaneity of the human and non-human material. The antiquity of the Fontéchevade skull bones seems well assured.

Morphology and Taxonomic Debate. A furor was caused by assertions that Fontéchevade is not demonstrably different from modern *H. sapiens,* and is more "advanced" than subsequent Neanderthals. Fontéchevade cranial capacities are estimated at about 1450 cc. The most complete skull, number 2, consists of a left parietal, upper half of the right parietal, and an upper portion of the **frontal.** Because of the scanty nature of the frontal bone, there is some disagreement over whether the Fontéchevade material exhibited brow ridges. It seems, however, that Fontéchevade did, in fact, possess brow ridges. Some charge that the smaller fragment is from an immature individual in whom the large ridges claimed to be characteristic of European Neanderthals have not developed. The "nonbrow ridge" proponents counter that the skull is from a mature individual, and, in any case, the young Neanderthal boy from Teshik-Tash (Uzbekistan, USSR) possessed brow ridges.

Fontéchevade is distinguishable from modern populations. It most closely approaches Swanscombe in cranial thickness and in breadth across the back of the skull. There are two alternatives: (1) Fontéchevade is simply an ancestor of later European populations, or (2) it is a member of a separate evolutionary line, commonly called the Presapiens.

Ehringsdorf. The Ehringsdorf skull is a Third interglacial form found in 1925 near Weimar, Germany. It comes from a depth of 54 feet and was associated with warm-temperature forest floral and faunal remains. The major osteological material consists of a parietal and broken faceless braincase.

The cranial capacity was large, 1450 cc according to one estimate. The brow ridges were heavily built, as in Steinheim, but somewhat thicker and show some degree of approximation to subsequent Neanderthals. The braincase is low and archaic looking with a well-developed **occipital bun** (a bony protruberance at the rear of the skull) and the greatest width low on the occipitals. Ehringsdorf closely approximates Steinheim and Swanscombe; most consider it an archaic member of *H. sapiens.*

Krapina. These remains come from the floor of a rock shelter in northern Croatia, Yugoslavia. The material was excavated between 1895 and 1906; the remains consist of some 649 shattered pieces of skull, skeleton, and teeth. Some bones are charred and may be relics of cannibalism.

More than 1,000 flint implements were removed from the hominid-bearing level at Krapina. The osteological material includes postcranial remains from practically every part of the body, and more than 270 teeth. All the adult skulls have strong brow ridge development. In some skull and jaw features these materials approximate later Neanderthal skulls, but the frontal region of some skulls closely resembles *H. sapiens.*

Quinzano and Saccopastore. These remains were found in cave deposits near Verona, Italy, and from a river deposit on the bank of a small tributary of the Tiber River just outside the walls of Rome. At Saccopastore two skulls were recovered; one found in 1929 may belong to a 30- to 35-year-old female; the other, a male aged about 35, was found in 1936. The female skull is nearly complete, but the male skull lacks the skullcap.

The Saccopastore skulls (now dated to the early Würm) are not large; the female has a cranial capacity of 1200 cc, close to the Steinheim figure. The male probably had a capacity close to 1300 cc. The skulls have supraorbital ridges, some cranial flattening, and a rather massive lower jaw, features that resemble subsequent Neanderthals. In other features—the position of the **foramen magnum,** rounded contour of the rear of the skull, and dental arcade—they resemble modern populations. Because of the curious combination of modern and archaic features of the Saccopastore skulls, they are often referred to as transitional. Some suggest that the skulls represent a population in an initial phase of a progressive development leading to the European Neanderthals.

Summary. Second and Third interglacial fossil hominids are structurally interesting; in some respects they resemble subsequent European Neanderthals; in others they seem very modern. A number of phyletic schemes have been proposed to account for variation within these populations. They reduce to the following: (1) These forms are simply ancestral to European Neanderthals. (2) The fossils are the basis of a separate evolutionary line with little or no genetic connection with subsequent European Neanderthals. (3) Steinheim may be ancestral to European Neanderthals while Swanscombe and Fontéchevade are the basis of a separate evolutionary line leading to modern populations. Each scheme is based on the importance one attaches to the range of variation within these limited population samples.

Neanderthals: How Many Evolutionary Lines?

The Problem: Fantasy, Romanticism, Truth. The so-called "Neanderthal problem" has long plagued anthropologists, and until those fairly numerous remains are arranged in some order and the temporal, geographical, and cultural boundaries delineated, confusion will reign. The appearance of what some investigators feel are more modern-looking hominids in Europe predating the European Neanderthals raised the spectre of evolutionary reversals and multiple (or **polyphyletic**) evolutionary lines. What many visualized as the overnight disappearance of western European Neanderthals and their replacement by anatomically modern populations smacked of catastrophism, a process akin to the Biblical flood. Fanciful notions of savage warfare between brutish Neanderthals and modern contemporaries were commonly presented.

> Of all the different kinds of prehistoric peoples, certainly the one who projects the clearest image is Neanderthal man. For most of us he *is* Stone Age man, the squat, shaggy, beetle-browed fellow that inevitably comes to mind when we think of our ancient relatives. We see him standing in the mouth of a cave—stone axe in hand, a few rough furs over his shoulder, some mammoth bones piled in the background—staring out over a snow-choked landscape as he ponders the ever-present problems of the ice age and the giant cave bear (Howell, 1965:123).

Besides the romantic aspect, this image persists because there is some truth in it. In some respects, Neanderthals were more primitive morphologically than we; sometimes they lived in caves, wore skins, and inhabited cold climates. The first fossil skull positively identified as belonging to ancient hominids was a Neanderthal; with nothing to compare it with but skulls of modern populations, scientists were struck by the divergence between them. Today the reverse is true.

Neanderthal fossil remains and their cultural assemblage (the **Mousterian**) have been traced from Near Eastern, African, Asian, and European sites (Figure 19-3). One of the problems with discerning their true nature is that we have so many Neanderthal skeletal remains, and we know so much of their culture from undisturbed cave deposits. If we know so much, why so much trouble interpreting the data? It may be that we know too much, that is, we may be too accustomed to analyzing limited population samples.

If the concept of the Neanderthal population is to have justification, it must be limited in time, space, and culture. Most anthropologists accept the following criteria as diagnostic of this stage of hominid evolution. The time span was from about 75,000 years ago to about

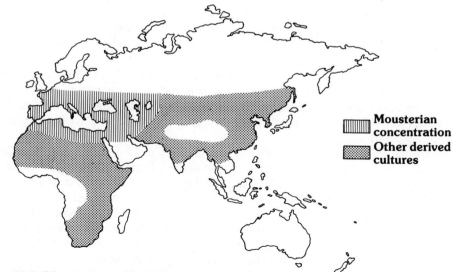

Figure 19-3. Mousterian and derived cultures.

35,000 years ago. Neanderthals inhabited Europe and the Near East. Their culture was the Mousterian, itself a complex derivative of earlier toolmaking complexes.

To appreciate some of the problems of interpretation, a word on the scientific climate of the times is needed. The discovery of the first Neanderthal remains preceded only slightly the publication of Darwin and Wallace's evolutionary theory. Because of the timing of their discovery, the remains drew more attention than they might have otherwise. People were searching for a "missing link": the Neanderthals were characterized as big, burly, and hairy, with a sloping head and back, a club-wielding creature dragging its mate to its cave by the hair.

The term "Neanderthal" itself refers to a quiet valley in the heart of western Germany which seventeenth-century Germans favored as a picnic spot. This spot was especially admired by the Dusseldorf organist and composer Joachim Neumann. He signed some of his works "Neander," the Greek translation of his name, and after his death, local inhabitants began calling the valley, then spelled "Thal" in German, Neanderthal. The valley has since lent its name to a major group of human fossil remains.

The first-described Neanderthal find came from Germany in 1856. It was first mistaken for animal bones and immediately discarded, but at the last moment the owner of the excavation site saved the bones and turned them over to a local teacher. He passed them on to the anatomist Schaffhausen who termed the material "ancient," a pronouncement pleasing to the budding group of evolutionists. Antievolutionists, however, felt the material represented some pathological freak.

One of the most amusing of the many interpretations of the Neanderthal populations, as exemplified by the original discovery, was based on the following traits: (1) evidently the left elbow had been broken early in life and healed in such a way that movement was restricted; (2) the individual was presumed to suffer from rickets, so it was suggested that pain from the elbow and the rickets caused the person to knit its brows in a perpetual frown. This supposedly led to large brow ridges. A Bonn professor suggested that the bowed femurs might testify to a lifetime of horseback riding. Another suggested that the Neanderthal was a deserter from the Russian army that chased Napoleon's army back across the Rhine in 1814. More specifically the fossil was of a rickety Mongolian Cossack who crawled into the cave for refuge. Another interpretation reflected the prejudices of the nineteenth century—a French scholar referred to the form as a robust Celt resembling "a modern Irishman with low mental organization."

Further finds came to light in 1866 when a jaw accompanied by a Mousterian cultural assemblage was recovered from a Belgian cave. The associated rhinoceros, mammoth, and bear bones provided clues to the specimen's age. In 1871 Darwin described this find in *The Descent of Man*. In 1886 two additional skeletons appeared from Spy Cave in Belgium; now talk of pathological freaks was minimal.

The years prior to World War I witnessed the recovery of much European Neanderthal material, most from the Dordogne region of southwestern France. Other finds came from Spain, Italy, southeastern Europe, Russia, and Turkey. The late French paleontologist M. Boule described them in detail but erroneously noted what he considered to be their highly uniform, specialized nature. Until the 1930s it was assumed that European Neanderthals were slowly driven to extinction by subsequent populations. Then discoveries of hominid remains not quite the same as those of either their European contemporaries or modern *Homo* came to light in the Middle East mandate area of Palestine. At the same time, recovery and reexamination of Second and Third interglacial forms continued.

Western European (Classic) Neanderthals

European classic Neanderthal remains are limited to southwestern Europe. A number of sites are located in sheltered and well-watered valleys of southern France and similar parts of the Spanish and Italian peninsulas, regions outside the main zone of frozen ground and tundra vegetation. It should be noted that the numerous remains from the area result not only from high population concentrations but also from good preservation conditions coupled with much archaeological exploration. There was, however, at least sporadic penetration, perhaps seasonally for hunting and collecting, into adjacent areas.

Cultural Remains. The name of the Neanderthal cultural assemblage, Mousterian, is derived from the French village of Le Moustier where the type site (the site to which others are compared) is located. The functional tool categories (scrapers, points, and knives) tell us something about the life and concerns of their manufacturers. The archaeological record from the French village of Les Eyzies reveals much about how European Neanderthals adapted to their physical surroundings. There are 200 prehistoric sites within a 20-mile radius of Les Eyzies. Most sites are in caves, rock shelters, and open-air locations within a mile or so of well-traveled routes.

New stone-working techniques began to appear in Europe and Africa about 100,000 years ago. As in the preceding Acheulian, the Mousterian tradition in its European form gradually replaced earlier stone-working techniques. By 30,000 to 40,000 years ago the Mousterian tradition was being supplanted. Perhaps the most important change in material culture associated with the change from the Acheulian to the Mousterian is the increase in the number of traditions. Five Mousterian traditions have been identified in Europe (Jolly and Plog, 1976:178-79)):

1. Mousterian of the Acheulian tradition. This tradition is characterized by the presence of at least a small percentage of hand axes.
2. Typical Mousterian. This tool kit contains 50 percent or fewer side scrapers, some Levallois flake tools, carefully shaped points, and usually no hand axes.
3. Quina Mousterian. This assemblage has a high proportion (50% to 80%) of scrapers, few or no hand axes, few denticulated tools, and many notched flakes. This is basically a non-Levallois tool kit.
4. Ferrassie Mousterian. This tradition is almost identical to that of the Quina Mousterian. Both have more than 50 percent side scrapers; however, the Ferrassie Mousterian includes some Levallois flakes.
5. Denticular Mousterian. This tradition has a large proportion (35% to 55%) of denticulated tools and notched flakes. The Levallois technique may or may not have been used.

The Mousterian witnesses the development of prepared core techniques for tool production. Toward the end of the Middle Paleolithic, and characterizing the Upper Paleolithic, tools were prepared by striking off thin, fine flakes of predetermined size and shape with greater precision. In this Levallois technique, a core was prepared by removing a large number of flakes to produce the desired shape. The core from which the flake was removed was not the tool, as was the case in all prior periods of hominid tool making.

The Levallois technique is not invariably found in all Mousterian assemblages. The Levallois technique goes back much further in time and was associated with the Acheulian percussion technique. A Levallois-Mousterian version of the Old Levallois technique also developed at this time.

The Mousterian appears to be the only Middle Paleolithic industry to be derived without major discontinuities from the preceding Acheulian. The Mousterian in the strict sense is a set of stone-tool assemblages suggesting greater versatility and sophistication in applying the overall technology mastered in the Acheulian. Hand axes appear to be replaced in importance and are represented by smaller versions. A new range of tools made from prepared flakes appears. At their best, these tools were meticulously prepared and trimmed, suggesting a special purpose rather than the multipurpose tools of preceding times.

Most Mousterian tools are characterized by careful manufacture. Butzer (1977) suggests the possibility that this is due to an increasing number of good craftsmen producing new artifactual types to accommodate a wider range of activities than previous hominids had. Although similar tools are found in northern Africa and the Near East, the true Mousterian of Europe includes a greater proportion and diversity of highly refined tools. The classical range of Mousterian implements is limited to Europe and the Near East.

The Mousterian Tradition

The Mousterian tradition is essentially a chipped-stone technology typified by a number of different types of tools. The Levallois technique, characteristic of the Mousterian, enabled the tool makers to extract thin, fine flakes of predetermined size and shape with considerable precision. Levallois blades are relatively long and have a sharp cutting edge.

In Europe alone prehistorians distinguish what many feel are five distinct tool traditions in the Mousterian stage, but not all agree on what these different traditions signify. Some argue that the different traditions belong to different time periods, others argue that the different traditions belong to different cultural groups, and still others argue that they merely represent differentiation of task activities.

Neanderthals were big-game hunters and it has been suggested that animal meat provided the bulk of their caloric intake. Evidence from an open-air site such as Lebenstedt, Germany, supports the assumption that during the summer some Neanderthals followed herds of grazing animals northward into the open tundras. Some Neanderthals may have adapted to an existence of seasonal movement, following herds into the forest-tundra in winter and returning with them onto the broad tundra expanse in summer. Some members of the Neanderthal population were also sedentary; some sites in southwestern France were probably occupied year-round. It has also been suggested that the complex nature of the Mousterian assemblage in southern France precludes anything but well-established territoriality and semipermanent settlements. Migration was probably not a general pattern; perhaps it was confined to marginal populations inhabiting tundra fringes. Groups in less severe climates and where good shelter was provided basically remained sedentary. Seasonal movement seems to be a localized adaptation to certain environmental stresses.

Faunal remains associated with Neanderthal assemblages indicate that Neanderthals were efficient hunters. Wooly mammoth and rhinoceros were hunted successfully; the presence of fish and fowl remains at the Lebenstedt site underscores the Neanderthals' hunting efficiency. They overcame either the great cave bear or the brown bear, which must have been a formidable foe. The killing and eviction of the cave or brown bear must have been a cooperative group effort. At the Drachenhöhle site (Dragon's Cave) at Mixnitz, Austria, it appears that hibernating bears, including females with young, were attacked and killed on numerous occasions.

Certain Neanderthal implements suggest use for skin working and butchery. "Points," broad, triangular, retouched flakes, may have been tied (hafted) to a wooden spear or used as dart heads, improving the penetrating power of the plain wooden implement. Stone balls may have been used as bolas. Familiarity with fat-dressed skins could have led to the use of rawhide lashings and thongs. Neanderthals may have trapped their prey; evidence from the Shanidar Cave area in Iraq suggests that animal remains were caught by either running grazing herds over cliffs or by running them into a blind canyon and slaughtering them.

Combe Grenal is an exceptionally interesting French cave site, located in a little valley 14 miles from Les Eyzies. It was originally dug by F. Bordes, who expected to complete the excavations in short order; however, excavations covered a period of roughly 11 years. When work terminated, Combe Grenal was huge 40-foot hole with 64 separate layers of geological and archaeological deposits. The first occupants of Combe Grenal left no fossil remains. The richest and most important layers yield an almost continuous occupation record from about 40,000 to 90,000 years ago. Groups of 30 or 40 individuals may have lived and died here over many generations.

The Combe Grenal site includes an empty grave so small that it must have contained the remains of a young child. Three smaller ceremonial pits near the grave, which are also empty, may have held food and clothing for the dead child. Another interesting discovery is the uncovering of a posthole that may have been one of several at the cave mouth where stakes were driven into the ground to support skins or woven branches to provide shelter from wind, rain, and snow. Or, they might have supported a meat-drying rack.

Combe Grenal is especially rich in Neanderthal tools. Bordes was able to collect and classify 19,000 tools. Bordes feels that differences in manufacture reflect differences in use; he feels that some tools were used to help scrape bark from narrow branches to make stakes and/or spear shafts while others were used to clean hides or make clothes. Sally and Lewis Binford have suggested that the tool types at Combe Grenal represent different everyday activities. One kit was used for "maintenance activities" such as working wood and bone— perhaps to make such items as shafts, ax handles, and tent pegs. A second kit suggests activities associated with killing and butchering meat and a third kit indicates activities associated with food processing, especially meat preparation. A fourth kit was used for shredding and cutting wood and/or other plant materials; a fifth for more specialized killing and butchering.

The Binfords further tried to discern whether some of the tool kits could be associated with men's or women's tasks, speculating that since women are more likely to stay close to the base camp to care for children, they should tend to make their tools from local, readily available materials. Tools fabricated from local flint were predominantly denticulate or notched items commonly associated with food processing, which might have been woman's work. Tools generally considered to be used for hunting, for example, spear points and scrapers, were made from remote sources. The use of a variety of materials for hunting tools shows that men were away from the base camp and had ready access to available suitable materials.

Further evidence of Neanderthal cultural ways comes from burials and other indications of ritualistic behavior (Table 19-2). Quoting Howell (1965:130), "In keeping with the growing complexity of his life, and the greater variety of his possessions, and his talents, Neanderthal man also apparently stood on the edge of becoming both an esthete and mystic. For the first time in human experience faint signs of decoration and artistic appreciation appear." The Neanderthals recognized death as a special social phenomenon; they buried their dead,

Table 19-2. Evidence of Neanderthal and Preneanderthal Ritualistic Behavior

Year Discovered	Evidence and Site
1970	Deer ceremony in Lebanese cave.
1965	Smashed and charred skulls at Hortus, France.
1960	Crushed skull and burial with flowers at Shanidar, Iraq.
1939	Mutilated skull at Monte Circero, Italy.
1938	Skull surrounded by goat frontlets at Teshik-Tash, USSR.
1931	Solo skulls evidence cannibalism, Java.
1930	Jaw bones of bear at Mount Carmel burial, Israel.
1925	Evidence of cannibalism at Ehringsdorf, Germany.
1924	Kiik-Koba burials, USSR.
1917	Bear ceremony remains at Drachenloch, Switzerland.
1912	"Family cemetery," La Ferrassie, France.
1908	La Chapelle-aux-Saints burial with artifacts, France.
1899	Smashed and charred skulls at Krapina, Yugoslavia.

Adapted from B.G. Campbell, *Humankind emerging*, p. 359. Little, Brown and Company, Boston © 1976.

suggesting an awareness of the transitoriness of life and perhaps concern for the future. Burials have been found in western and eastern Europe, Iraq, and central Asia. The French sites of Le Moustier, La Ferrassie, and La Chapelle-aux-Saints yield Neanderthal burials. At Le Moustier a young boy (between 15 and 20) was buried in a cave; he was lowered into a trench on his right side, his knees slightly drawn and his head resting on his forearm reminiscent of a sleeping position. Several stone implements and number of charred animal bones that may be relics of a roasted meat funeral offering were also buried.

One of the most interesting of the many Neanderthal burials is Shanidar Cave, the excavation of which is described in R. Solecki's book *Shanidar: The First Flower People.* One Shanidar skeleton, number 4, was buried on a bed of flowers—the first evidence of prehistoric floral remains. Not all anthropologists accept this interpretation (see, for example, Brace, 1971). The floral remains are represented by small, brightly colored wild flowers that may have been woven into the branches of a pinelike shrub. Evidence of the latter is found in the soils. Leroi-Gourhan studied the floral remains and concluded that someone in the last Ice Age ranged the mountainside in the mournful task of collecting floral offerings.

Another example of Neanderthal ritual practices, some suggest, is a bear cave cult. Although probably a formidable foe, the cave bear was hunted. At the Swiss site of Drachenlöch a number of bear skulls may have been stacked in a stone chest and may have been among the first hunting trophies. Another possible cult symbol from the same site is the skull of a 3-year-old cave bear with a leg bone of a younger animal piercing its cheek. This rests on two bones from still two other bears (Figure 19-4). A mountain cave in eastern Austria contained a rectangular vault holding seven bear skulls, all facing the entrance. There appears to be an elaborate cave bear burial at Regourdo in southern France that includes a complete skeleton, minus the skull (which may have been stolen), stone drains, a rectangular pit covered by a flat stone slab weighing almost a ton, and the remains of more than 20 cave bears.

In a very interesting book entitled *The Cave Bear Story,* Kurtén reviews evidence from such supposed burial sites as Drachenlöch Cave, Switzerland, Petershöhle, Germany, and

Figure 19-4. A symbol of the cave bear cult at Drachenloch, Switzerland. A bear skull is pierced by the leg bone of a younger bear.

Mixnitz, Austria. He dismisses the bear remains as the result of natural forces (1976:91): "I believe that we must conclude . . . that there is no real evidence for a cave bear cult among the Neanderthal men who inhabited Europe in the last interglacial and the earlier part of the last glaciation. There may have been a bear cult—but we have no proof." He also notes that the bear that was the object of other cults was the brown bear and not the cave bear.

These apparent findings mark a new stage in hominid evolution; life and death seemingly held new values. Burial implies concern for the individual; further evidence of concern is recovery of individuals who survived serious injuries and who must have been cared for by their contemporaries. Supportive evidence comes from Shanidar, where one individual was apparently recovering from a spear or knife wound in the ribs when he was killed by a rock fall. Another Shanidar individual had his lower right arm amputated prior to death and showed healed wounds above the eyes and right parietal. Survival from these injuries means that such individuals were possibly kept alive, nursed, and supported because of some concern for the individual. Perhaps such individuals had special knowledge of magic, rituals, or hunting techniques that indicate a more complex, extensive social organization.

Osteological Remains. The following characteristics are representative of European or Western Neanderthals. European Neanderthals were a heterogeneous population. Wolpoff (1980) attributes much of this systematic variation to sexual dimorphism. Cranial capacities were large, ranging from 1525 to 1640 cc in six male skulls and 1300 to 1425 cc in three females. The skulls were more capacious than those of modern populations, accommodating a larger brain than common to modern *Homo*. The skull was shaped differently; it had a lower crown and achieved its interior shape by bulging on the side and back. A fairly consistent trait is an occipital bun at the rear of the skull (Figure 19-5).

Four major features distinguish the Neanderthal face: a receding chin, or lack thereof, large cheeks, prominent brow ridges curving over the eyes and connected across the bridge of the nose, and a rather large nose. The rather large nose may be a functional adaptation to severe climates, serving perhaps to warm and moisten inhaled air, for in cold climates the brain can be endangered by inhalation of cold air. European Neanderthal jaws and teeth also manifest some distinguishing traits. The jaws are large and give evidence of strong muscle attachments, and certain dental traits suggests use of the teeth as tools. Neanderthal incisors are broader than those in modern populations and may have been important tools in environmental manipulation. As such, they required robust roots and supporting structures, features readily seen in the fossil record.

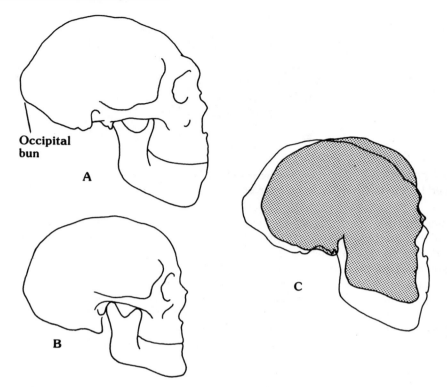

Occipital bun

A

B

C

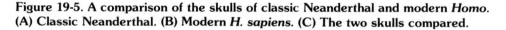

Figure 19-5. A comparison of the skulls of classic Neanderthal and modern *Homo*. (A) Classic Neanderthal. (B) Modern *H. sapiens*. (C) The two skulls compared.

European Neanderthal postcranial skeletons mark them as short, powerfully built individuals just over 5 feet tall. Their extremities were short; the hands and fingers were short and stubby. Their feet were similar to ours, for we have a remarkably preserved Neanderthal footprint cast in the wet clay of an Italian cave. Howell (1965) suggests that a Neanderthal "would have been a formidable opponent in a college wrestling tournament." They may have weighed 160 pounds or more. It has been suggested that classic Neanderthals were incapable of erect bipedalism; however, this is based upon faulty reconstruction.

Cold Adaptations? Although it is being debated, many European Neanderthal characteristics are seen as cold adaptations. Nasal prognathism, for example, is seen as an adaptation to the cold conditions throughout southwestern Europe. The postcranial skeleton, with short, stubby limbs and phalanges, is similarly cold-adapted. There is a rough gradient of what are considered classical Neanderthal traits; the most extreme expressions are prevalent in the cold regions of Europe and tail off to the south and east into the Middle East. Western European Neanderthal populations are most readily identified, for here climatic selection was maximized.

Nasal morphology and associated features are the most distinctive features of the Neanderthal face. There is an adaptive explanation for this morphological complex; one of the primary functions of the nose is to warm and moisten inspired air. The size and shape of the nose are related to this function. Nasal breadth is also related to breadth between the canines, because the roots of these teeth run along the sides of the nose. Among Neanderthals, the breadth across the canines is large because of the large anterior teeth. This feature probably accounts for the large nasal breadths in *early H. sapiens* samples. Thus, as Wolpoff (1980) points out, before the emergence of cold-adapted Neanderthals, there was a background of broad nasal openings in *H. sapiens*.

Wolpoff (1980) notes that the development of facial prognathism, expansion of all nasal dimensions, and the other features of the face are part of a general Neanderthal cold adaptation. This adaptation could have evolved because of features that were present in the ancestral hominid populations of Europe.

La Chapelle-aux-Saints: A Mistake Compounded

The La Chapelle-aux-Saints remains (Figure 19-6) and fine Mousterian tools were recovered on 3 August 1908 from a grotto in the commune of La Chapelle-aux-Saints, in the valley of a tributary of the Dordogne River. The first written report of the find was presented to the French Academy of Sciences on 21 December 1908. The fossil material was entrusted to M. Boule for study and only now is his report being seen in proper perspective after having confused our picture of the Neanderthals for many years. Pfeiffer (1969:162) notes that the study of the La Chapelle-aux-Saints remains was ". . . one of the most amazing phenomena in the history of man's efforts to downgrade his ancestors."

Boule's original report was presented orally (by E. Perrier) to the French Academy of Sciences on 14 December 1908. Excerpts of this report follow.

> The state of the cranial sutures and of the dentition proves that this skull is that of an elderly man. It strikes me first by its very considerable dimensions, keeping in mind meanwhile the small stature of its ancient possessor. Next it strikes us with its bestial appearance, or, to put it better, by the general collection of simian (ape) or pithecoid (monkey) characteristics.
>
> It seems to me no less certain that, from the collection of its characteristics, the group of Neanderthal . . . represents an inferior type closer to the apes than to any other human group.
>
> Finally, I will point out that the human group of the Middle Pleistocene, so primitive from the point of view of physical characteristics, is very primitive from an intellectual point of view.

In other places, Boule speaks about a slumped posture and supposed monkeylike arrangement of certain spinal vertebrae. He even suggests that the feet may have been grasping like those of apes.

As recently as 1957 this study was cited as a major source; several museums still display Neanderthals as slumped-postured brutes. La Chapelle-aux-Saints was restudied in 1957 and this study showed that La Chapelle-aux-Saints was hardly typical. The bones were from a rather old individual (40 or 50 years old) who suffered from arthritis of the jaws, spine, and perhaps lower limbs. Any stooped appearance was caused by arthritis.

Central and Eastern European Neanderthals

Although less numerous than remains from western Europe, Neanderthal remains from East and Central Europe are nevertheless very important. Some argue that the sudden appearance of modern populations in western Europe suggests that they originated elsewhere in the East. Fossil evidence from eastern and central Europe lends some credence to this. New finds from this area have filled some of the geographical and chronological gaps in the fossil record; they have also blurred the boundary between classical European Neanderthals and fully

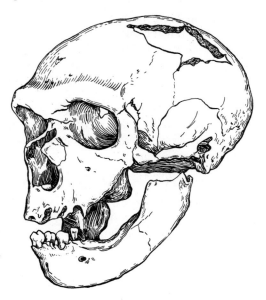

Figure 19-6. The face and skull of La Chapelle-aux-Saints.

modern *H. sapiens* populations. Major eastern and central European materials come from Czechoslovakia and Hungary. Some refer to them as transitional specimens, that is, transitional between modern and Neanderthal populations.

   Taxonomic Significance. The transitional status of these materials suggests that hominid evolution in eastern and central Europe was proceeding towards modern *Homo*. The transitional forms are important because: (1) To varying degrees, they display many traits found in anatomically modern populations. (2) Chronologically they extend to the time period in which the oldest finds of fully modern *H. sapiens* appear. (3) Even forms designated fully modern *H. sapiens* exhibit some cultural and morphological links to the past. Such findings indicate that the appearance of *H. sapiens sapiens* in central and western Europe (and perhaps other regions) need not be explained in terms of a sudden east-to-west migration, but rather as local evolution in populations sharing basic traits but differing in intensity and detail. Such a situation permits relatively rapid morphological change.

Middle Eastern (Progressive) Neanderthals

Some Middle Eastern populations of this period appear to be transitional. Some, such as Quafzeh 6 and Skhūl 5, closely approach modern *Homo sapiens* anatomically; others, such as Tabūn and Shanidar I, which date to an earlier time, closely approach western European classical Neanderthals save for extremes of cold adaptation. Some consider the Middle Eastern forms members of a late noncold-adapted Neanderthal group imperceptibly grading into fully modern *H. sapiens sapiens*. The most complete finds come from Israel and Iraq; other remains come from Lebanon and Jordan. Israeli remains come from six caves: Zuttiya near the Sea of Galilee, Tabūn and Skhūl at Mount Carmel, Jebel Qafza near Nazareth, Shukba, 17 miles northwest of Jerusalem, and Amud near Lake Tiberias. Although from the same geographical area and dating from approximately the same time period, the skulls differ from one another.

The Middle East has long been a crossroads of humanity; many consider the Middle Eastern corridor, stretching along the Mediterranean and Lebanon Mountains, as an evolutionary focal point. Many factors contributed to making the Middle East an important evolutionary pocket. Game has always been abundant, and the concentration of game seems to have produced rather heavy local human population centers. There was a climatic shift to somewhat drier conditions at approximately 40,000 to 45,000 years ago that led to local concentrations of grazing animals and their hunters. The richest and deepest fossil sites are in areas where vegetation and game were most abundant, for example, in the valleys along the western slopes of the coastal ranges. Mount Carmel lies in such a valley.

Mount Carmel. The two major sites at Mount Carmel are the Cave of et-Tabūn (Cave of the Oven) and the Cave of es-Skhūl (Cave of the Kids). A third cave, el-Wad, has yielded fragmentary remains. Mount Carmel, 12 miles from Haifa, was located as a by-product of efforts to build the port of Haifa. Skulls from both caves show pronounced brow ridges; however, they display a remarkable variability in the degree of development of other features typically associated with classic Neanderthals and in some respects they rather closely resemble *H. sapiens sapiens.*

et-Tabūn. Tabūn Cave yielded a male mandible and a female skeleton. Tabūn woman had the low skull, arched brows, and the heavy continuous ridges of her western European contemporaries. She lacked an occipital bun; her cranial capacity is estimated at 1270 cc and her mandible lacks a chin. The male mandible is large, deep, and rather square in front. Morphologically the Tabūn material falls between the central and western Neanderthals and possesses some traits seen at Skhūl. The Tabūn materials may, in fact, be ancestral to Skhūl.

es-Skhūl. The es-Skhūl Cave site, containing 10 skeletons in differing states of preservation, was one of anthropology's great finds. Originally thought to be contemporaneous to Tabūn, es-Skhūl seems to be about 10,000 years later in time and following some climatic interval that witnessed the local disappearance of hippopotamus and rhinoceros. The Tabūn group manifests some classic Neanderthal traits, but those from Skhūl show a general similarity to modern *H. sapiens* (Figure 19-7). The Skhūl braincases are similar to ours in size and shape. They are high, flat-sided, and round and lack an occipital bun. The frontal of the skull is reminiscent of earlier Neanderthals; the brows are marked, but they are not heavy or bulbous as in earlier Neanderthals. The mandible has a chin.

Interpretation of Mt. Carmel Remains. A host of explanations has been offered to explain the variation at Mt. Carmel. A recent explanation based on new dating shows that Skhūl is subsequent to Tabūn by about 10,000 years. Tabūn lived approximately 60,000 years ago, the Skhūl population thousands of years later. We have, fairly late in time, a Neanderthal population (Tabūn) giving way to an almost modern form as typified by Skhūl (especially skull number 5). The Skhūl remains morphologically and temporally crowd toward modern *H. sapiens;* it has been suggested that a population such as Tabūn was replaced by a population such as Skhūl. Assuming the date at Skhūl is correct, modern populations arose from local stocks, and not necessarily in the Middle East. Transitional central and eastern European remains may be remnants of such groups.

Shanidar Cave. Shanidar Cave is an extremely interesting Middle Eastern Würm site. Shanidar, a huge cave in the Western Zagros mountains of northern Iraq, has been occupied from early Mousterian to present times. Solecki had to ask local Kurdish inhabitants to leave

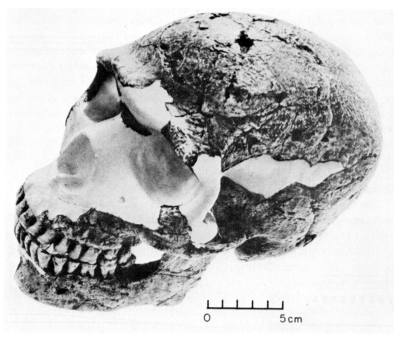

Figure 19-7. Es-Skhūl V skull.

the cave before he could excavate the site. Now and then, due to local earthquakes or formation of ice on the ceiling, limestone slabs plummeted from the cave roof, killing many inhabitants. Luckily for an inquisitive anthropologist, the remains of a number of victims are available for study. In 1953 Solecki uncovered a baby's skeleton, in 1957 three adult skeletons, and in 1960 three more skeletons.

The Shanidar remains lay in Mousterian culture-bearing deposits. Shanidar 1 is radiocarbon (C-14) dated to 46,000 ± 1,500 years ago. Shanidar 3 was perhaps a few hundred years older and Shanidar 2 and the baby were close to 60,000 years old. Shanidar 1 and 2 were males. Shanidar 3 appears to have been killed by a projectile point embedded in his ribs and was subsequently buried against the cave wall. Shanidar 1 met death at about age 40. His skull may prove to be one of the largest fossil skulls found—the cranial capacity is estimated at more than 1700 cc. Shanidar 1 manifests signs of having come under the scalpel (probably a flint knife) of a caveman surgeon and survived an operation amputating his right arm. He was also severely wounded by blows of some sharp instrument around and above the left eye and may have been blinded in this eye. He has a healed bone lesion from a blow on the right parietal. Despite these infirmities, which surely affected his food-getting abilities, he survived and was subsequently crushed by a slab of falling limestone, apparently while standing erect.

The flower burial (Figure 19-8) was an unexpected Shanidar find. To quote Solecki (1971:250): "With the finding of flowers in association with Neanderthals, we are brought suddenly to the realization that the universality of mankind and the love of beauty go beyond the boundary of our species. No longer can we deny the early men the full range of human feelings and experience."

It is difficult to generalize about the skeletal characteristics of Near Eastern and central Asian populations contemporaneous with the Neanderthals of Europe. Some specimens, for example, Tabūn, Shanidar, Amud, and perhaps Teshik-Tash, shared more features with western Neanderthals than did Skhūl. Kennedy (1975) suggests that physical differences in the populations of the Near East and central Asia may be of the order of subspecific or racial variation. These populations may constitute one part of the species range that had more ties with the western European Neanderthals and another variety with closer ties to populations in the direct line to Upper and post-Paleolithic *H. sapiens*.

The So-Called Neanderthaloids

The category of the so-called Neanderthaloids has always been suspect and of limited use, and it is all the more so following the recovery of more information and the reanalysis and redating

Figure 19-8. Shanidar flower burial. The bones are supposedly buried on a bed of flowers, but only pollen grains (not visible in the photograph) remain.

of some of the material. The taxonomic position of some forms placed within this group has been clarified within recent years, particularly the Broken Hill and Saldanha forms, both of which are now included in *H. erectus.*

Presently, the only material that might still be referred to this nebulous category is the Ma-pa skullcap from Kwang Tung Province, China. The Ma-pa skullcap was recovered in a limestone cave in 1958. Unfortunately the dating is quite vague; it might be contemporaneous with the Neanderthals or it might be considerably earlier.

The Ma-pa skullcap consists of the frontal, parietal, and nasal bones and the lower border of the right eye socket. The fragmentary nature of the material complicates taxonomic allocation. In a number of details the Chinese skullcap approaches the Neanderthals, even though its taxonomic position is not clear.

Interpretations

How Many Ancestors and Who? The "Neanderthal problem" has circulated for years. The major questions are: (1) What is the taxonomic position of the classic or western European Neanderthals? (2) How does one interpret the variability of these populations? (3) What led to the demise of western European Neanderthals? (4) In which area or areas of the world did anatomically modern populations evolve? Some answers become clearer with the recovery of new forms and the reexamination of others; other questions become harder to answer. Some of the problem is semantics.[1]

There are conflicting viewpoints as to the taxonomy of the western group. Some designate it a separate species, that is, *H. neanderthalensis;* others include it in the species *H. sapiens* and recognize a subspecific designation, *H. sapiens neanderthalensis.* One of the major reasons for this taxonomic reshuffling is the recognition of transitional forms that cannot be assigned to either the Neanderthal or anatomically modern *H. sapiens* group. What can be said with assurance about these populations? They were geographically widespread and characterized by a great deal of morphological variability. The gene pool as a whole evolved from *H. erectus.* Some populations (i.e., classic Neanderthals) died out, lending few of their genes to modern populations. Others, that is, transitional forms in eastern and central Europe and the Middle East, became fully modern *Homo.*

Unilinear School. Various possibilities have led to various interpretations, which are illustrated in Figure 19-9. Variations of these theories are endless; they are constantly being revised and rejected. Howells (1967:241) aptly states, ". . . they sometimes generate more heat than light." The first-offered Neanderthal theory of unilinear evolution dates to a time when few fossils were available and dating was inaccurate or unavailable. This theory argues that modern *Homo* arose directly through a number of simple evolutionary stages including a Neanderthal phase. A. Hrdlička was the principal advocate of this theory, which many reject as too simplistic. C. Loring Brace has taken up the cudgels and vigorously argued that

---

[1]C. Loring Brace, long an opponent of the theory that the Neanderthals were too primitive to be included in our ancestral lineage, notes the misusage of the term "Neanderthal." The term itself is now so familiar, specifically its implications of an archaic form, that it describes things quite unrelated to its original meaning. As Brace notes, modern writers are not averse to referring to ultraconservatives and out-dated social attitudes as "Neanderthal," and occasionally call those with whom they disagree "Neanderthals" in thoughts or action. Similarly, "Neanderthals" in politics are regarded as human fossils, with the implication that they are outmoded and possessing long-past untenable ideas.

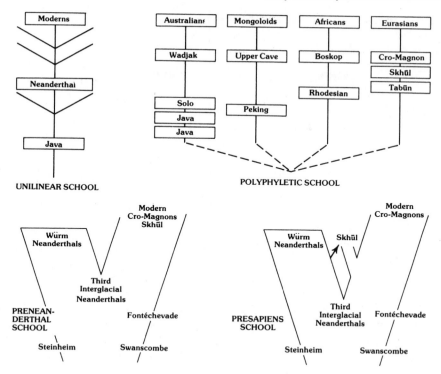

Figure 19-9. Different interpretations of human descent.

Neanderthals, as typified in western Europe, formed a large part and parcel of our genetic ancestry.

The two other points of view, the Preneanderthal and Presapiens schools, have much in common. Both split the main stem of hominid evolution back to the time of Steinheim and Swanscombe and both consider classic Neanderthals evolutionary dead ends, becoming extinct as climatic conditions to which they were adapted ameliorated.

Presapiens School. The Presapiens school is rather old; it originally argued that *H. sapiens* in essentially modern form reached back into the Pleistocene as a separate evolutionary branch. Both theories use the same evidence differently. Some adherents of the Presapiens school split the trunk at Swanscombe and Steinheim, arguing that Steinheim led to the Neanderthals, and Swanscombe, through Fontéchevade, to modern populations. Its major proponents were found among some members of the paleontological schools of Italy, Germany, and France.

Preneanderthal School. Adherents of the Preneanderthal school, the viewpoint to which most subscribe, see Steinheim and Swanscombe as leading to another Third interglacial stem (i.e., Ehringsdorf and Quinzano), of basically Neanderthal type. This group was ancestral to the western Neanderthals and to the eastern varieties, which led to modern *Homo*. In this view, there is a broad, variable population. One segment of this population is the isolated, western European, cold-adapted group (western Neanderthals); the other segment inhabited the Near East and became modern *H. sapiens*.

Is There Another Explanation? Perhaps modern *H. sapiens* arose from a stock such as Steinheim and Swanscombe through a number of intermediate populations. There seems to have been in situ transitions of both hominids and their tool industries throughout the Old World during the last glaciation (Brose and Wolpoff, 1971). These transitions do not preclude the possibility of western European Neanderthal genes being incorporated into modern populations. In fact, the possibility is strong that some of their genes did find their way into modern populations. The evidence for such genetic exchange would fulfill the criteria for containing the Neanderthals and *H. sapiens* in a single biospecies, separate at the subspecies or racial level.

Without much doubt classic Neanderthals were greatly reduced by the end of the Würm I; there is evidence, however, that segments of the general population survived. Perhaps the population became extinct through absorption by anatomically and culturally more advanced immigrants, although we have no evidence to support this. Climatic amelioration probably allowed populations to meet more frequently along the glacial fringes; perhaps emigrating populations simply bred with the Neanderthals. Or, populations with more advanced technologies swamped the classic Neanderthals, a process known as cultural exploitation. Old tools and methods give way to newer, finer, and better adapted technologies and less technologically advanced cultures are slowly forced to extinction in contact with technologically advanced neighbors.

Wolpoff (1980) feels that differences between contemporary Würm populations are not due to one group's being more advanced than another. Rather, these differences may result from the same kinds of evolutionary forces that lead to differences between living populations. Those evolutionary forces causing regional differences between Würm populations were a combination of climate-related differences in selection, local differentiation (microevolution), and local genetic continuity. Wolpoff feels that the presence of local morphological continuity extending into the Neanderthal time span and characterizing different parts of the world provides one of the strongest arguments for a "Neanderthal phase" in European hominid evolution.

This chapter supports the argument that there is nothing in Second and Third interglacial hominid assemblages suggestive of a modern *Homo sapiens* population preceding the Neanderthals. The evidence arguing for a separation of Steinheim and Swanscombe and for an advanced status for Fontéchevade seems dubious.

The Neanderthal controversy is unsettled. The viewpoint adopted here is that the Neanderthals are part of our evolutionary heritage, for it seems likely that we share some of our genes with the European Neanderthals. We need a clearer definition of what the term "Neanderthal" means and a closer investigation of the importance and distribution of eastern and central European "transitionals" and their tool assemblages.

Bibliography

Bada, J., Schroeder, R., Protsch, R., and Berger, R. 1974. Concordance of collagen-based radiocarbon and aspartic acid racemization ages. *Proceedings of the National Academy of Sciences* 71:914-17.

Binford, L, and Binford, S. 1966. A preliminary analysis of functional variability in the Mousterian of Levallois facies. In *Recent studies in paleoanthropology* (*American Anthropologist* special publication), pp. 238-95.

Binford, S. 1968. Early Upper Pleistocene adaptations in the Levant. *American Anthropologist* 70:707.

Bordaz, J. 1968. *The Old Stone Age.* New York: McGraw-Hill.

Bordes, F. 1972. *A tale of two caves.* New York: Harper & Row.

Bouyssonie, A., Bouyssonie, J., and Bardon, L. 1908. The discovery of a human Mousterian skeleton at La Chapelle-aux-Saints (Correze) (a note by the authors to the French Academy of Sciences). In *Adam or ape,* edited by L. Leakey, J. Prost, and S. Prost, pp. 177-78. Cambridge, Mass.: Schenkman, 1971.

Brace, C. 1962a. Cultural factors in the evolution of the human dentition. In *Culture and the evolution of man,* edited by A. Montagu, pp. 343-54. New York: Oxford University Press.

——————. 1962b. Refocusing on the Neanderthal problem. *American Anthropologist* 64:729.

——————. 1964. The fate of the "classic" Neanderthals: a consideration of hominid catastrophism. *Current Anthropology* 65:3.

——————. 1968. Ridiculed, rejected, but still our ancestor. Neanderthal. *Natural History* 77:38-45.

——————. 1971. Digging Shanidar. *Natural History* 80:82.

Brose, D., and Wolpoff, M. 1971. Early upper Paleolithic man and late Paleolithic tools. *American Anthropologist* 73:1156.

Butzer, K. 1964. *Environment and archaeology.* Chicago: Aldine.

——————. 1971. *Environment and archaeology: an ecological approach to prehistory,* 2nd ed. Chicago: Aldine.

——————. 1977. Environment, culture and human evolution. *American Scientist* 65:572-84.

Campbell, B. 1966. *Human evolution.* Chicago: Aldine.

——————. 1976. *Humankind emerging.* Boston: Little, Brown.

Clark, W. Le Gros. 1964. *Fossil evidence for human evolution.* Chicago: University of Chicago Press.

Coon, C. 1962. *The origin of races.* New York: Knopf.

Cornwell, I. 1968. *Prehistoric animals and their hunters.* New York: Praeger.

Day, M. 1965. *Guide to fossil man.* Cleveland: World.

Ewing, J. 1960. Human types and prehistoric cultures of Ksar 'Akil, Lebanon. *Fifth International Congress of Anthropological and Ethnological Sciences,* pp. 535-39.

Flint, R. 1971. *Glacial and quaternary geology.* New York: Wiley.

Howell, F. 1951. The place of Neanderthal man in human evolution. *American Journal of Physical Anthropology* 9:379.

——————. 1957a. Pleistocene glacial ecology and the evolution of "classical Neanderthal" man. *Quarterly Review of Biology* 32:330.

——————. 1957b. Pathology and posture of Neanderthal man. *Quarterly Review of Biology* 32:360.

——————. 1960. European and Northwest African Middle Pleistocene hominids. *Current Anthropology* 1:195.

——————. 1965. *Early man.* New York: Time-Life Books.

Howells, W. 1967. *Mankind in the making.* Garden City, N.Y.: Doubleday.

——————. 1974. Neanderthals: names, hypotheses, and scientific method. *American Anthropologist* 76:24-38.

——————. 1976. Explaining modern man: evolutionist versus migrationist. *Journal of Human Evolution* 5:477-95.

Jelinek, J. 1969. Neanderthal man and *Homo sapiens* in central and eastern Europe. *Current Anthropology* 10:475.

——————. 1976. A contribution to the origin of *Homo sapiens sapiens. Journal of Human Evolution* 5:497-500.

Jolly, C., and Plog, F. 1976. *Physical anthropology and archeology.* New York: Knopf.

Keith, A. 1925. *The antiquity of man,* 2nd ed. London: Williams and Norgate.

Keith, A., and McCown, T. 1939. *The stone age of Mount Carmel,* Vol. 2. Oxford: Clarendon Press.

Kennedy, K. 1975. *Neanderthal man.* Minneapolis: Burgess.

Kolata, G. 1974. The demise of the Neanderthals: was language a factor? *Science* 186:618-19.

Kurtén, B. 1976. *The cave bear story.* New York: Columbia University Press.

Luguet, G. 1930. *The art and religion of fossil man.* New Haven: Yale University Press.

Maringer, J. 1960. *The gods of prehistoric man.* London: Weidenfeld & Nicolson.

Marschack, A. 1972. *The roots of civilization.* New York: McGraw-Hill.

McCown, T., and Keith, A. 1939. *The stone age of Mount Carmel,* Vol. 2. *The fossil human remains from the Levalloiso-Mousterian.* Oxford: Clarendon Press.

Morant, G. 1938. The form of the Swanscombe skull. *Journal of the Royal Anthropological Institute* 68:67.

Pfeiffer, J. 1969. *The emergence of man.* New York: Harper & Row.

Poirier, F. 1972. Reply to teeth wear and culture: a survey of tooth functions among some prehistoric populations (by S. Molnar). *Current Anthropology* 13:519.

_____. 1981. *Fossil evidence: the human evolutionary journey.* St. Louis: Mosby.

Proetz, A. 1953. *Essays on the applied physiology of the nose,* 2nd ed. St. Louis: Annals.

Santa Luca, A. 1978. A re-examination of presumed Neanderthal-like fossils. *Journal of Human Evolution* 7:619-36.

Sergi, S. 1967. The Neanderthal palaeanthropi in Italy. In *Selected essays 1949-61,* edited by W. Howells, pp. 500-506. New York: Atheneum.

Solecki, R. 1971. *Shanidar: the first flower people.* New York: Knopf.

Steegman, A. 1972. Cold response, body form, and craniofacial shape in two racial groups of Hawaiians. *American Journal of Anthropology* 37:193-221.

Straus, W., and Cave, A. 1957. Pathology and the posture of Neanderthal man. *Quarterly Review of Biology* 32:340.

Trinkaus, E. 1973. A reconsideration of the Fontéchevade fossils. *American Journal of Physical Anthropology* 39:25-35.

_____. 1978. Hard times among the Neanderthals. *Natural History* 87:58-63.

Vallois, H. 1952. Monophyletism and polyphyletism in man. *South African Journal of Science* 49:69.

_____. 1954. Neanderthals and presapiens. *Journal of the Royal Anthropological Institute* 84:11.

_____. 1961. The social life of early man: the evidence of skeletons. In *Social life of early man,* edited by S. Washburn, pp. 214-35. Chicago: Aldine.

Weiner, J., and Campbell, B. 1964. The taxonomic status of the Swanscombe skull. In *The Swanscombe skull,* edited by C. Overy. London: Royal Anthropological Society of Great Britain.

Wolpoff, M. 1968. Climatic influence on the skeletal nasal aperture. *American Journal of Physical Anthropology* 29:405.

_____. 1971. Vértesszöllös and the presapiens theory. *American Journal of Physical Anthropology* 35:209.

_____. 1979. The Krapina dental remains. *American Journal of Physical Anthropology* 50:67-113.

_____. 1980. *Paleoanthropology.* New York: Knopf.

Chapter 20

Appearance of Modern
Homo sapiens sapiens

In the last chapter we traced hominid evolutionary history until approximately 40,000 years ago. This chapter completes that history with the colonization of the New World and some of the Pacific Islands. No single Pleistocene cultural group emerges so clearly as Late Paleolithic European hunters. During this time there is a noticeable acceleration of cultural and technological innovation and a flowering of artistic expression.

Where the transition to modern *Homo sapiens* occurred is still arguable. Current evidence is skewed toward Europe because this is where most work has been done. We know a lot about some early European *H. sapiens* populations, especially in France, and comparatively little about those residing in other parts of the world. It is not questioned, however, that other parts of the world were inhabited; late Paleolithic inhabitants moved into North and South America and into Australia. During the time period from 10,000 to 40,000 years ago *H. sapiens* lived as small-band hunters and gatherers. *H. sapiens* spread across the world and met with a variety of environmental conditions.

Development of Modern *Homo sapiens*

Wolpoff (1980) has argued that the reasons for the evolutionary development of modern *Homo sapiens* can be best understood in terms of worldwide changes in selection acting on already differentiated local populations of archaic *H. sapiens*. Wolpoff feels that these developments relate to the cultural and technological changes that were truly worldwide, for example, the appearance of Middle Paleolithic industries and the development of the prepared-core technique of tool manufacture.

Wolpoff (1980:300) argues that selection changed existing archaic *H. sapiens* gene pools in the direction necessary to account for the appearance of modern *H. sapiens:* "I believe the model is credible because every feature said to characterize these modern populations is present, although at lower frequency, in the earlier populations of Europe and elsewhere."

Wolpoff (1980) reminds us that the most important thing about the earliest modern *H. sapiens* populations is that they did not look especially modern. These early *H. sapiens* populations were probably as different from living populations as they are from the preceding archaic *H. sapiens* samples. They are recognized as modern *H. sapiens* because they show a higher incidence of what are considered to be modern *H. sapiens* traits and a lower incidence of what are considered to be archaic *H. sapiens* traits.

Modern *H. sapiens* samples are distinguished from previous samples by anterior tooth reduction, facial and brow-ridge reduction, and increasing cranial height. In all early modern *H. sapiens* samples, these attributes are less marked than in today's populations. However, these morphological changes occurred at different rates in various parts of the world. For example, the brow ridge in the east African sample was already largely reduced, while in the contemporary European sample, especially in those individuals designated males, the brow-ridge region was large and well developed (Wolpoff, 1980).

Upper Paleolithic Lifeways

Dietary Patterns. Upper Paleolithic economies varied according to the habitat, but the people were primarily big-game hunters with hunting techniques comparable to those of preceding times. The offensive weaponry included spears, javelins, harpoons, clubs, stone missiles, bow and arrow, and boomerangs or throwing sticks. Bolas were probably slung at the legs of animals, snares and pitfalls almost certainly trapped big game, and gregarious herds were run off cliff faces. Some French and Spanish cave drawings have been interpreted as depicting snares, traps, pitfalls, and enclosures.

Although fishing long preceded Upper Paleolithic peoples, the technique underwent refinement. Harpoons and fish gorges were used during the Upper Paleolithic. Aquatic foods may have formed a sizeable part of some local diets.

Reindeer played a large role in the hunting of some later Upper Paleolithic populations. It has even been suggested (on scanty evidence) that reindeer were semidomesticated and that some form of reindeer nomadism occurred during the terminal Paleolithic. Some Upper Paleolithic sites indicate that the human inhabitants relied almost entirely on reindeer for food. The reindeer/hominid relationship seems to have been very close. Clark (1967:64) notes that "by establishing close association with a reindeer herd a group of hunters was able to secure what was in effect a walking larder and a source of supply of raw materials needed in technology."

Reindeer supplied their hunters with raw materials for clothing and tents, sinews for thread and line for hunting gear, bones and antlers for tools and weapons, and teeth for ornaments in addition to animal protein. There is abundant evidence of reindeer antler being fashioned into harpoons at the German sites of Schleswig-Holstein. The frequency of bone sewing needles, bodkins, and belt fasteners suggests that elaborate wearing apparel, presumably of tanned hides and furs, was common.

Group hunting economies may have been specialized for certain animals. While the reindeer was certainly the most important food item in France and Germany, the wooly mammoth was important to folks farther east. Horses were locally important. If the game animals were seasonal migrants, their predatory hunters presumably followed the same pattern. If the gregarious herds were sedentary, semipermanent dwellings were possible.

Group Organization. Although Upper Paleolithic groups probably still lived in bands, larger social organizations may have begun. A tribal structure, an association of many bands cemented by marriage and economic bonds, may have been developing. Upper Paleolithic populations may have developed rituals for coming and remaining together. To reduce friction they may have elaborated on previous social and behavioral patterns. Incest taboos and mating and kinship rules may have been formulated to create an intricate and cohesive relationship among large numbers of individuals.

Reliance on reindeer as a food source played a large role in sustaining the rather sizeable communities common to Upper Paleolithic populations. Some summer reindeer hunting sites cover as much as 5 acres; the rather large continuous string of rock shelters stretching along the Dordogne River Valley may have housed communities of 300 to 900 persons. This, of course, assumes the total site was simultaneously occupied, for which there is no supportive evidence. The sizeable communities probably instituted new forms of social controls to make life more bearable and organized. These societies were probably more complicated and stratified than those of their predecessors.

Despite technological achievements, Upper Paleolithic populations had high mortality rates; the mortality pattern is similar to preceding Neanderthal populations. Less than 50 percent of the 76 Eurasian skeletons were from individuals attaining 20 years of age. Only 12 percent were past 40. Practically no female reached the ripe old age of 30.

Dwellings. Upper Paleolithic populations inhabited a great variety of dwellings (Figure 20-1); rock shelters (i.e., rock overhangs as distinguished from deep caves) were widely used. Trees were felled and propped against the rock face, perhaps trellised by branches and skins. Large caves were inhabited; huts or tents built inside caves were heated with wood or bone fires. Where rock shelters are rare, as in central and eastern Europe, we find remains of permanent dwellings. At Pushkari, USSR, there are long-shaped huts that are sometimes sunk into the ground. One hut measures 39 feet by 13 feet. At the Kostenki I site there are traces of two dwellings, each 120 feet by 49 feet. There are also nine hearths situated on the long axis, and numerous silos of varying shapes and heights. It is unlikely that this complex was accommodated under one roof.

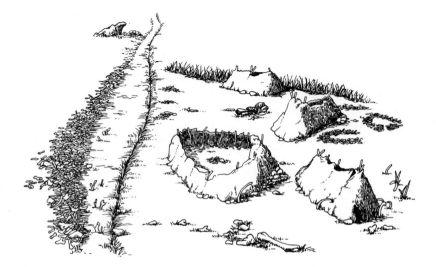

Figure 20-1. A reconstruction of the 23,000-year-old Dolni Vestonice site.

An Example of an Upper Paleolithic Living Site: Kostenki-Borshevo

The Kostenki-Borshevo sites are located in the Don Valley of Russia. Human occupation layers date to 25,000 years ago; however, most occupation layers have a C^{14} date of 12,000 to 15,000 years ago. The last occupations are from about 11,000 years ago.

The inhabitants of this region in late Würm times were successful big-game hunters who used the meat and bones of their quarry. They built rather permanent structures; the spectacular size and nature of some dwellings suggest that some settlements were rather large. Cultural activity, through trade or movement, extended over distances greater than 100 miles. Evidence for ritual practices and perhaps religious life is manifested in burial practices and in the presence of numerous art objects.

Vast quantities of faunal remains found in association with cultural levels furnish direct evidence of subsistence patterns. The most prevalent animal remains are of large herbivores, especially horse and mammoth; wild cattle are rare and reindeer not especially abundant. Wolf and fox skeletons are the most frequent carnivore remains. Although they may be remnants of a meal, it is likely that they were caught for their pelts, which subsequently became clothing. Furthermore, perforated canine teeth seem to have been popular decorative items. Hare remains also occur and hare pelts could have been used for clothing.

The numerous habitation ruins exhibit much variability in size, shape, and state of preservation. In some cases all that remains is a large ground depression; in others there is a considerable accumulation of nearly intact mammoth bones (which may have been used in construction). Others are simply a roundish or oval area where cultural materials accumulated. The framework of these habitations was probably wood and/or bone covered with skins and hides. Most structures seem to have contained hearths and pits used either for storage or cooking.

Fire was known to the site occupants. Besides the ordinary usages of providing warmth, light, and protection from predators, fire also seems to have been an important aid in artifact manufacture. It may have been used to harden spear tips, to prepare some types of flint for working by careful preheating, and to obtain (from iron ore) a red, ochreous pigment. Perhaps as part of a reburial or delayed burial ritual, this pigment was rubbed on bones of the deceased. Bone and stone artifacts compose the most abundant tool remains; a number of these artifacts probably represent elements of weaponry. Some stone and bone points may have armed throwing or thrusting spears. A large number of different tool types was probably used to process animal remains, especially to prepare skins. A wide variety of bone implements have been recovered including possible mattocks or hoes (for digging holes), "clothes fasteners," "hairpins," and a large array of unexplainable objects. Bone was used in house construction and may have been used for fuel.

Four burials were uncovered, and each was associated with some kind of burial ritual. In one instance, the deceased was accompanied by a quantity of goods. There are burials at some sites, but none at others. Some of the Kostenki-Borshevo people may have disposed of their dead away from the living sites.

Aesthetic Expressions of Upper Paleolithic Populations

One reason Upper Paleolithic populations, especially in Europe, are so vividly recalled is because they left numerous traces of their artistic works that tell much about their daily life, ritual practices, and concerns. Upper Paleolithic populations were inclined to animal worship. They left many provocative assortments of animal bones and skulls.

Table 20-1. Leroi-Gourhan's (1967) Chronology for the Development of Cave Art

Period IV	(10,000 to 15,000 years ago). Late Magdalenian Period. Fine modeling, increase in mobilary art and conventional symbolism.
Period III	(15,000 to 19,000 years ago). Mastery of painting techniques, relief sculpture, and depiction of movement. Solutrean and early Magdalenian cultures.
Period II	(19,000 to 25,000 years ago). Upper Perigordian and Gravettian cultures. Animal silhouettes on cave walls. Engravings common.
Period I	(25,000 to 32,000 years ago). Early Perigordian and Aurignacian. Mobilary art predominates.

Adapted from A. Leroi-Gourhan, *Treasures of Prehistoric Art*, pp. 206-15. Harry N. Abrams, Incorporated, New York, © 1967.

Cave Art. Leroi-Gourhan (1967) assigns Upper Paleolithic art to four periods (Table 20-1). The art can be divided into two categories: mobile art, that is art applied to small objects normally found in archaeological deposits (Figure 20-2), and cave art, that is, art restricted to the walls, roof, and occasionally floors of cave and rock shelters. France alone has more than 70 cave art sites dating from 10,000 to 28,000 years ago, most of which depict animals of the hunt. Cave art took the form of engraving and painting, either separately or together. Reliefs were made by cutting away the rock to varying depths and there are examples of doodling on clay films on cave walls, ceilings, and floors, and modeling of clay figurines. Coloring consisted of various kinds of ocher, manganese, and charcoal.

Art and Magic? Upper Paleolithic art seems strongly related to spiritual life; much of this is placed on walls deep in relatively inaccessible caves and much is very difficult to see. Caves were probably entered by people using artifical light (torches or fat-burning lamps). The French priest Henri Breuil devoted much of his life to the study of prehistory and he noted that much of the art is in areas badly situated for viewing—in narrow niches, behind rock bumps, and sometimes in areas that must have been dangerous for both artist and viewer to enter. The art is apparently not to enhance the beholder's life but for some mysterious ritual.

Some view Upper Paleolithic art as related to the food quest, as magical rituals bound to the hunt. Another group interprets much of the art as representative of sexual symbolism. No matter what interpretation one accepts—the time-honored theory that representations were made to gain control over the food supply by sympathetic magic, or as representing in some way the antithesis between male and female principles—much of the art is zoomorphic (i.e., concerned with animal representations). So close seems the tie between humans and animals that some are depicted as masked figures with animal heads, antlers, and skins strapped over human forms.

Upper Paleolithic art is not so much an attempt at amusement or self-expression as an adjustment to daily life. Much of the artistic expression reflects concerns with food procurement. Many of the animal figures are painted with spears in them or marked with blows from clubs. The French cave of Font-de-Gaume has several drawings of traps or enclosures with animals suggestively caught in them. One depicts a mammoth in a pitlike trap.

Many paintings are superimposed one atop another; some of the paintings in the magnificent cave at Lascaux, France, are four layers deep. If these paintings are magical manifestations, that is, a way of ensuring a good hunt, were there also magicians? There are

Figure 20-2. Examples of Upper Paleolithic mobile art.

some 50 paintings of strange-looking persons, human figures clad in animal skins, sometimes wearing animal heads or horns. Many of these are depicted in the midst of a dance (Figure 20-3).

Figure 20-3. A portrait of a possible Cro-Magnon sorcerer.

Sculpture and Engravings. Upper Paleolithic inhabitants also engaged in sculpture and engraving; there are incised animal outlines on cave walls, some produced in bas relief. At Cap Blanc, near the French village of Les Eyzies, there is a set of horses carved in bas relief; the natural rock curves accentuate the sides of the horses' bodies. Female statuettes of bone, stone, and ivory of varying design and merit are widely distributed throughout Europe. Their most obvious trait is emphasis on the torso, focusing on the stomach, breasts, and buttocks to the exclusion of head and limbs. These resemble tiny earth goddesses or fertility figurines, and so they have been interpreted. A prime example is the so-called "Venus of Willendorf," a 4-inch limestone statuette, with a wavy hairdo and accentuated female curves (Figure 20-4).

Tool Inventory. Upper Paleolithic populations produced a culture that far exceeded anything of its predecessors in variety and elegance. Upper Paleolithic groups made fine stone tools and delicately worked bone. The Eurasian Upper Paleolithic was essentially a blade-tool assemblage characterized by an abundance and variety of long, parallel-sided implements called "blades" (Figure 20-5). The blade-tool industry was partially devised for working bone and wood. Of the functional tool types, burins (chisel-shaped blades) were probably used for engraving and working wood, bone, or antler that may have been employed as handles or shafts. Various types of scrapers may have been used to scrape wood or hollow out wood or bone. Laurel-leaf blades were carefully made into thin, sharp-edged knives or arrowheads.

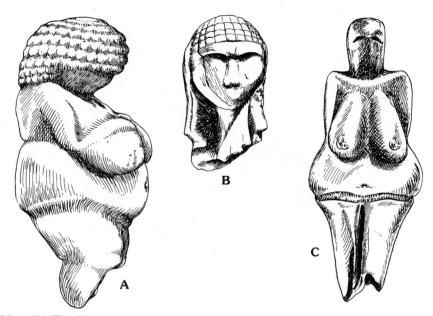

Figure 20-4. (A) The Venus of Willendorf, carved in stone, Austria. (B) The Lady of Brassempouy, carved in ivory, France. (C) The Venus of Vestonice, modeled in clay, Czechoslovakia.

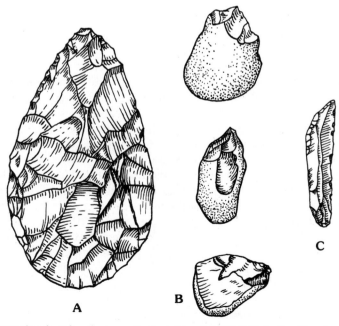

Figure 20-5. Successive levels of stone tool-making skills. (A) Acheulian hand axe. (B) Oldowan tools, East Africa. (C) Upper Paleolithic blade implement.

The Upper Paleolithic Traditions

A number of different tool types characterized the European Upper Paleolithic. There was a rapid increase in efficiency of tool manufacturing during this time. The basis of many of the tools is the blade, a thin parallel-sided flake whose greatest dimension is usually its length. Blades were produced using **percussion flaking,** whereby flakes were taken from a prepared core. More commonly used was punch flaking, an indirect percussion method. The punch, an intermediate tool, was placed between the hammer and prepared core. This allowed more direct and precise placing of the blow. Blades were also manufactured using pressure flaking, in which the tool maker attached a punch to a wooden handle and leaned against the handle. Upper Paleolithic tools were among the most sophisticated and aesthetically pleasing stone tools ever manufactured.

The **burin** was a basic Upper Paleolithic tool. Burins were used for incising and cutting wood and bone. They were used extensively thereby extending the range of raw materials available for use. Bone tools were particularly abundant during the Upper Paleolithic, probably as a result of more refined tool-making capabilities. Bone seems to have replaced stone as a more efficient tool for certain tasks.

Upper Paleolithic tool traditions had much the same character as the preceding Mousterian. For example, both the **Aurignacian** and **Perigordian,** the two earliest European Upper Paleolithic traditions, contained Mousterian-like tools. Bone tools characterize the Aurignacian; however, Perigordian assemblages have few bone implements. A characteristic tool of the Perigordian assemblage was the **Chatelperronian** knife, a pointed blade with a curved back blunted by retouching.

The Solutrean was a short phase geographically limited to southwestern France and Spain and was associated with laurel-leaf flakes of superior workmanship. The **Gravettian** was contemporaneous with the Solutrean and was distinguished by highly developed bone- and ivory-working techniques. The economic activity of Gravettian tool users and makers is related to mammoth hunting, the source of the ivory.

The Magdalenian tradition is associated with sites throughout Europe. Tool kits of this tradition are diverse and contain the first microliths, small blades an inch or less in length.

New Tools and Weapons. New items such as polished pins or bone or antler awls are found in Upper Paleolithic tool kits. New types of points were probably hafted to sticks. The later **Magdalenian** inventory (a cultural complex from western Europe dating from about 12,000 to 17,000 years ago) included hooked rods employed as spear throwers, barbed points and harpoons for fishing, fish hooks, needles with eyes, bone and ivory bodkins (large-eyed blunt needles), belt fasteners, and tools of undetermined use. Many of these tools were highly decorative, depicting hunt animals, and may have served as ceremonial items.

The use of the bow and arrow is first verified for the latter part of Late Paleolithic. Some 100 wooden arrows have been recovered at the Mesolithic Stellmoor site, a former lake near Hamburg, Germany, dating to about 10,500 years ago. About 25 percent of the arrows were designed for use without a tip; one such untipped arrow was found in situ in a wolf vertebra. These arrows were probably fire-hardened. The flint-tipped arrows may have been used for large game only, the untipped types for small game.

Osteological Evidence

There is a rather large sample of European Upper Paleolithic populations (Table 20-2). Because of the practice of burying their dead, a number of almost complete skeletons is known. The stature of the populations varied, but the males attained a height comparable to modern males. Women seem to have been somewhat shorter. Their bones indicate a robust

Table 20-2. The Upper Paleolithic of Southwestern France

Divisions of Würm Glaciation	Radiocarbon Dates	Cultural Tradition
Würm IV	9,500	Magdalenian
Würm III/IV	15,000 17,000	Magdalenian
Würm III	19,000 29,000	Solutrean Perigordian, Aurignacian
Würm III/II	32,000	Perigordian, Aurignacian
Würm II	37,000	Mousterian

Adapted from F. Bordes, *The Old Stone Age*, p. 222. McGraw-Hill, Incorporated, New York, © 1968.

build, but not as robust as preceding Neanderthals. Upper Paleolithic populations had large heads with modern cranial capacities, wide faces, prominent chins, and high-bridged noses.

Distribution. The geographical distribution of these populations reveals that places too cold during the Würm I were also difficult to inhabit during the Würm II and III and subsequently. Southern France again appears a favorite living spot, although the remains from here probably reflect the amount of work in the area. As were their predecessors, Upper Paleolithic populations were big-game hunters; perhaps Upper Paleolithic *Homo* was being shaped by the creatures hunted. To be a more effective hunter, *H. sapiens* became a herd animal. "He invented crowds to become a better predator" (Pfeiffer, 1969:198).

Upper Paleolithic populations learned to live successfully in all environments except high barren arctic regions and true deserts. Cultural and ecological adaptations to the diverse habitats are everywhere evident in housing structures and the clothes-making kits.

French and Italian Remains. Europe yielded many Upper Paleolithic hominid remains; they first appeared in the nineteenth century and were discarded as simply modern burials. Close to 90 individuals are known from European Upper Paleolithic sites. The famous Cro-Magnon shelter located in the limestone cliffs by Les Eyzies yielded some of the first remains. The remains (six skeletons: three males, two females, and one fetus) were uncovered in 1868 while workers were building a railroad through the valley. The Upper Paleolithic sample is indistinguishable from modern populations. They had small, nonprojecting faces; broad, high foreheads; protruding chins; and a cranial capacity estimated at 1590 cc. Their height has been variously estimated as between 5 feet, 4 inches and 6 feet.

Other traces of the French Upper Paleolithic population come from the Combe Capelle and Chancelade sites. The Combe Capelle individuals had a long face and a long, high, narrow forehead. They seem to have been of medium to small body size. The Chancelade remains belong to a later Upper Paleolithic stage than Combe Capelle and Cro-Magnon. Chancelade apparently lived when cool weather prevailed in Europe and their tools and reconstructed way of life originally led to suggestions that they were ancestral to the Eskimo. Chancelade was short (about 4 feet 11 inches in height), had wide cheek bones, and had a heavy jaw, indicating heavy chewing stress. The skull was long and narrow, the nose narrow. The Eskimo-like traits may simply be responses to heavy chewing stresses and to the use of the teeth as tools.

A pair of interesting skeletons, possibly a mother and teen-aged son, come from the Grotte des Enfants, one of the Grimaldi caves on the Riviera. These skeletons were originally called the "Grimaldi Negroids" because they supposedly exhibited African traits such as narrow heads, prognathic jaws and gracile body builds. However, the most likely explanation is that the resemblance is a coincidence due to a limited population sample and reconstruction errors.

Central European Remains. There is a host of central eastern European representatives of Upper Paleolithic populations. Three of the major finds come from Czechoslovakia: Předmosti, Brno, and Lautsch. Předmosti is a common grave containing eighteen individuals which may date more than 30,000 years ago. Two other individuals were recovered at the site. Some of the skulls show primitive traits; for example there is evidence of brow ridges among Upper Paleolithic populations. The material is associated with more than 1,000 mammoths; obviously, the Predmosti inhabitants were big-game hunters. The Brno skull, an adult male, manifests some primitive traits. In comparison with the French remains, it had more accentuated brow ridges and other skull features resembling the classic Neanderthals.

Asian Hominid Remains—China and Java. Asian Upper Paleolithic remains are not especially prevalent; the major material comes from Chou Kou Tien, China, and Wadjak, Java. The Chou Kou Tien remains, consisting of the skeletal parts of at least seven individuals, have been dated to approximately 10,000 years ago. Skull fractures indicate that they died an unnatural death, but while they may have been killed in a mass murder, they were not cannibalized. One of the seven was killed by an arrow or small-headed spear piercing the skull. Two of the females seem to have been killed by a stone dropped on the side of their heads. Other fragmentary materials also date to the Upper Paleolithic of China, and some argue that this material is ancestral to modern Chinese populations.

Africa

African Upper Paleolithic remains are scarce and much of the material, as a result of being blasted out of quarries, is of disputed dating. Most remains come from East and South Africa. A human mandible from Makapansgat, South Africa, is dated to 40,000 ± 10,000 years ago. Another South African find, the long and narrow Cape Flats skull, is from a site near Capetown. It has a cranial capacity of 1230 cc. Coon (1962) suggests that the skull may be ancestral to some modern black African populations; however, his evidence is questionable. A final Southern African skull is the Boskop braincase found in 1913. The cranial capacity of the skull is estimated between 1800 and 1900 cc. Along with other remains, known as Fish Hoek, the Boskop material is often considered ancestral to the modern South African Bushman.

In a recent study of the Border Cave remains, Rightmire (1979) claims there is metric evidence linking the Border Cave adult cranium directly to modern African black populations. He also claims an age of approximately 48,700 years. If this holds true, the age is unexpected for relics of fully modern *H. sapiens*. The skeletal remains of modern *H. sapiens* at this date in South Africa suggest the presence of earlier populations.

There are a number of Upper Paleolithic remains from East Africa, a crossroad open to access from many directions. With marginal success, many have searched here for the origins of a number of modern populations. Rather late remains, spanning the range between 5,000 and 10,000 years ago, include material from Gamble's Cave and the Singa skull from the Sudan. The Asselar skeleton was found in 1927 in a dry Sahara river bed north of Timbuctu and was associated with remains of freshwater molluscs, fish, crocodiles, gazelles, and antelope. A few contend that Asselar is one of the earliest representatives of modern black populations. This assumption is based on skull shape and size, tooth dimensions, and overall skeletal size. However, such assessments, without benefit of a large population sample, are questionable.

Perhaps the best evidence for the early appearance of *H. sapiens* in sub-Saharan Africa comes from the Omo River Valley. In 1967 R. Leakey recovered parts of three skeletons, including two broken crania and some postcranial bones, plus skull fragments of a third individual. The two incomplete crania have been described by Day (1969, 1971). Omo I and Omo II show some variation; however, Rightmire (1975) feels that they should be grouped together for now. Omo II, which unfortunately lacks a face, is quite heavily built and has a long low cranial vault. There is a well-developed ridge of bone across the back of the occiput. Omo I is more modern in appearance; it lacks frontal flattening and has a more rounded occiput. Both skulls are fairly clear representatives of *H. sapiens*.

The dating of this material is still questioned. Associated faunal remains may be of Middle Pleistocene derivation, and an age of 130,000 years has been obtained for the geological formation containing the crania. However, the thorium-uranium method used for the date is considered doubtful. According to Day, the Omo II cranium shows a general resemblance to the Rhodesian fossils, and Rightmire maintains some resemblance to the Florisbad material.

Australia

Dating. The colonization of Australia poses a number of problems such as: When and how did humans first enter Australia? With what Asian forms were they related? What are the relationships between Australia, Tasmania, and New Guinea on the one hand, and Indonesia on the other? Lately, the dating of when humans first entered Australia has undergone considerable alteration. New discoveries suggest a much earlier colonization date than once considered.

Australia's original colonizers arrived by boat and foot via two major island routes: (1) Java and Timor or (2) Borneo, the Celebes, and the Moluccas. The widest distance to be crossed over water was about 50 miles; crossing was probably managed in small rafts or boats. Which route was selected is unknown; however, there are broad anatomical relationships between modern Australian aborigines and the fossil materials from Ngandong and Wadjak, Java; Aitape, New Guinea; and Niah, Borneo. Once in Australia, humans crossed the Bass Strait and colonized Tasmania. Prior to 10,000 years ago, a broad, level causeway linked the two land masses. A period of approximately 9,000 years was available to cross the 150-mile causeway. One site in Tasmania dates back to 7,200 years ago.

The earliest indisputable date for human occupation of Greater Australia (including New Guinea, Tasmania, and other islands on the Sahul Shelf) is 32,750 ± 1,250 years ago at Lake Mungo. Other dates from the same unit are older, 34,000 to 38,000 years ago, but less certainly associated with human activity. Slightly more recent human occupation, 24,000 to 30,000 years ago, is well documented. Extensive searches have failed to produce human occupation in the underlying Golgol unit of 70,000 to 120,000 years ago. The earliest settlers may have arrived about 50,000 years ago, but continent-wide occupation is clearly demonstrated only within the 20,000- to 30,000-year-ago range. The most controversial claims for occupation prior to 50,000 years ago come from several sites in northwestern Victoria and adjacent parts of New South Wales. The remains here are from *H. sapiens,* but they bear a strong resemblance to *H. erectus* in certain features of cranial morphology, especially overall cranial size, vault thickness, and form of the face and mandible (White and O'Connell, 1979).

Green Gully. Until recently only three major finds were available in Australia: Keilor, Talgai, and Cohuna. New and exciting material has recently come to light, however. One of the major new remains is the Green Gully site located 2 miles south of the Keilor site and 9 miles northwest of Melbourne. The Green Gully bones were accidentally uncovered during a commercial excavation in August 1965. Various charcoal samples yielded dates of between 8,000 and 9,100 years ago.

The Green Gully material is largely fractured and is a mixture of male and female bones. The distortion of the bones, and the mixture of male and female remains, suggest that this is not a simple burial. It is quite likely a delayed burial; the skeletal remains were buried some 12 months after death and after most flesh had rotted away. Delayed burial is still practiced by some Australian aboriginal bands. This is a good example of the strength of cultural conservatism.

Reconstruction of the Green Gully remains was a horrendous task. A normal skeleton contains but 236 bones—the Green Gully material consisted of 3,900 pieces. Only 730 of these pieces could be identified and used for restoration. The unexpected discovery of male and female bones confused restoration. This mixture probably resulted from a male and a female body being adjacently exposed awaiting their delayed burials. The bones were mixed and dispersed by predatory birds and mammals. During actual burial, the skeletal material was gathered and buried in one grave, some two-thirds of the female and one-third of the male.

Keilor, Talgai, and Cohuna. The Keilor skull has been variously dated from 7,400 to 16,500 years ago; the later date is gaining respectability. The face is not projecting; the cranial capacity is estimated between 1464 and 1593 cc. It has been argued that there is a strong resemblance between this skull and the Wadjak material from Java. The Talgai skull, found in 1884, is apparently of a male, 14 to 16 years old. It is smaller than Keilor; the cranial capacity of 1300 cc falls within the range of modern Australian aborigines. The Cohuna skull was uncovered in 1925. The skull was mutilated; immediately after death the skull case was dislodged, apparently to get at the brain.

Lake Mungo. The Lake Mungo area is one of a chain of lakes in southwestern New South Wales. Five shoreline sites contain evidence of prehistoric populations dating back 32,000 years. One of the sites contains a human cremation; the others are typical aboriginal fireplaces. The Lake Mungo remains are among the most significant in Australian prehistory. Based on the number of teeth erupted, muscle markings on the bones, and the state of the cranial suture closure, the remains belong to a fragmented skeleton of a young, adult female. Before burial in a shallow grave, the body was burned and the charred bones extensively smashed. Reconstruction shows the female's skull to be full *H. sapiens*. Charcoal and shells near the site yield a date ranging from 30,000 to slightly older than 32,000 years.

The Americas

Dating. The date of entry of human populations into the New World has long been disputed. There is also a dispute as to how human populations arrived, that is, by crossing the Bering Straits into Alaska and moving south, or by floating across the ocean to South America and migrating north.[1] A superabundance of caution characterized the early outlook. When the first **Folsom point** (Figure 20-6) dating from about 11,000 years ago was discovered in

---

[1]For example, Thor Hyerdahl's Kon Tiki and more recent Ra I and II expeditions.

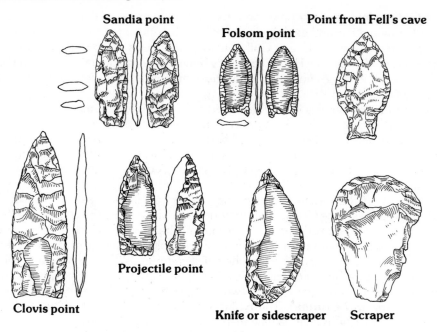

Figure 20-6. Paleo-Indian implements from America.

New Mexico in 1926, in association with extinct bison, it took three expeditions and discovery of several in situ points among faunal remains to convince many. Yet, nothing a priori argues against a Paleolithic entry into the New World.

The pendulum is now full swing; some, notably Louis Leakey, suggest a very old and very unlikely date for a New World entry. The Calico site is a very controversial site in San Bernardino County, California. This site has been subjected to much publicity and continuing intensive study, the results of which are contested. A major feature at Calico is a supposedly hearthlike feature uncovered at a depth of about 22 feet. The site has been variously dated from 30,000 to 500,000 years ago. The issue as to age, and in fact as to whether the supposed artifacts are fabricated or naturally flaked, is not yet resolved. However, it seems highly unlikely that the American continent was ever trodden on by the feet of *H. erectus* or its immediate successors.

Migration Routes: Bering Land Bridge. Most plausible theories concerning New World colonization are based on late Pleistocene sea levels and glaciations. It is generally agreed that populations passed from the Old to the New World by way of an emergent Bering land platform and moved southward through central Canada. Since vast continental glaciers grew at the expense of sea waters, sea levels were lowest when glaciation was at its maximum. During glaciation the emergence of the Bering land platform made Alaska part of the Asian continent. North America and Asia were one, creating a Siberia-to-Alaska migration route.

The maximum depth of the Bering Strait is now 180 feet. On a clear day one can see across the Strait from the heights of Cape Prince of Wales to Cape Dezhev in Siberia. Several small intermediate islands form stepping stones. The Wisconsin glacier that covered much of North

America reached its maximum about 40,000 years ago and lowered the sea by as much as 460 feet. As the glacier grew, oceans receded and a broad highway was created at the Bering Strait. A sea-level drop of only 150 feet created a 200-mile wide corridor connecting Alaska and Siberia. A drop of 450 feet would have created a corridor 1,300 miles wide for the flow of biological traffic between the joined continents.

Some argue that a smooth and unbroken land bridge wider than present-day Alaska joined the Old and New Worlds during much of the Pleistocene and large animals may have crossed it during the 80,000 years of the Wisconsin glaciation. The first humans probably crossed the bridge before the end of the Wisconsin period in pursuit of game slowly spreading out of Asia into Alaska. We may yet find New World hominids back 40,000 to 50,000 years.

Some suggest, in contrast, that the bridge first appeared 25,000 to 28,000 years ago. After a period it closed and reopened again at between 8,500 and 14,000 years ago. The bridge may have opened and closed several times in conjunction with the retreats and advances of ice during deglaciation. Resolution of the dating of the opening and closing of the Bering bridge is of major importance to settling the story of New World colonization. Whatever the nature of the migration, it probably occurred as two major waves. A first wave may have moved from Asia along the Pacific shores about 40,000 years ago.

One thing we do know is that humans were present in the western United States and northern South America by 15,000 years ago at the very latest. Besides the glacial ice barrier, there seems to have been no impediment to movement in the New World. No doubt the emptiness of the American continent speeded dispersal, as did the abundance of game. The estimated time for the journey from Alaska south to the tip of South America at Tierra del Fuego has been estimated as 8,000 to 9,000 years. The rather rapid southern expansion must have meant similar rapid loss of interaction between various groups, leading to cultural and genetic isolation. This could help explain the dissimilarities in modern American Indian languages.

Early Paleo-Indian Period. The easiest way to view the New World situation is to divide it into three relative periods: the Early, Middle, and Late Paleo-Indian. The most difficult period to define is the Early period, which began prior to 30,000 years ago. There are scant remains from this time, except for some flints of questionable workmanship. Sites are few, the most intriguing being Calico. Most possible Early Paleo-Indian sites do not meet the minimal criteria for inclusion as early hominid sites. Although the geological age of possible Early Paleo-Indian sites is reasonably well understood, either the association or nature of possible artifacts is questionable.

Some possible Early Paleo-Indian sites follow. The Lewisville site, near Lewisville, Texas, yielded 19 hearths with elephant, extinct bison, horse, and camel remains, as well as those of various small animals such as a coyote, prairie dog, and rabbit. The largest hearth contained a **Clovis point** (a fairly large dartlike, grooved point, Figure 20-6) and pieces of charred wood C^{14} dated at 37,000 years ago. The date may be in error, even though a second date is similar. Clovis points from other sites consistently fall within a range of 8,000 to 15,000 years old. One hearth at the site is believed to have been a camel cookery. Four samples of charred bone from Santa Rosa Island, off southern California, yielded dates averaging $29,650 \pm 2,500$ years ago.

California yields many interesting finds. In the years between 1926 and 1929, several skeletons were excavated at two sites near La Jolla. The first site was discovered in 1926 when a steam shovel working on a development project unearthed several skeletons. These materials received little attention until Bada et al. (1974) attempted to date them using the aspartic acid racemization method. According to their analysis the material is very old. The first individual, a rib and miscellaneous rib fragments that had olivella beads cemented to them, yielded a date of 28,000 years ago. The second individual, found at a lower level and consisting of a frontal bone, yielded a date of 44,000 years ago. The last individual, a skull and mandible plus long bones and a scapula fragment, yielded a date of 48,000 years ago. These are the oldest dates directly obtained from New World skeletal material. Although the dating technique is new and reliability may be questioned, a control sample of materials from a shell midden C[14] dated at from 5,000 to 7,500 years yielded an aspartic acid racemization date of 6,000 years (Bada et al., 1974).

Middle Paleo-Indian Period. The Middle Paleo-Indian period dates from 11,500 to 28,000 years ago. The earliest sites yield crude scrapers, flakes, and blade points. Human bones are generally lacking from the Middle Paleo-Indian period and no Middle Paleo-Indian site has yielded any quantity of cultural material. But, it seems simply a matter of time before the existence of this period is firmly established.

A rather recently described Paleo-Indian site producing a rich assemblage of Pleistocene fossils comes from the Yukon at the Old Crow River locality (Irving and Harington, 1973). A bone implement and a number of bone artifacts that were broken or considered to be otherwise modified were uncovered in 1966. Additional materials were uncovered in excavations through 1970. The single implement that can be identified is made from an excellently preserved caribou tibia. The proximal end of the tibia was chopped or broken and then whittled to a spatulate form; a regular series of notches was carved into the convex working edge to provide a row of subrectangular "teeth." Bone from the implement was dated to 27,000 +3,000 –2,000 years ago. Since attempts to establish the contemporaneity of this bone to two other large mammoth fragments (Figure 20-7) has proved fruitless, the dating must be considered questionable.

Figure 20-7. Bone core made from a thick section of mammoth bone from Old Crow site.

Recent digging along the Old Crow River at a site called Dry Creek has yielded a human jawbone with a single tooth intact dating to at least 20,000 years old and bone tools dated up to 29,000 years old. Some of the implements at the site represent an Asian-Siberian stone technology and suggest the possible source of these hunters.

In 1936 a group of workers working on a WPA project of digging a storm drain along the Los Angeles River near Los Angeles at a depth of 12 to 13 feet from the surface found a partial human cranium and seven other bone fragments. Less than 2 months after the original find workers discovered bones of large animals in the same geological stratum as the human remains. I. A. Lopatin of the University of Southern California explored the area and found some teeth and bone fragments identified as belonging to an Imperial Mammoth. The site was considered to be of Pleistocene age. The cranium was so badly crushed that little could be said beyond the fact that it may be from a female (Wormington, 1957). It was impossible to date the material when first discovered because it could not be shown to be undisturbed. In recent years, however, several dating methods have been applied. Heizer and Cook's (1953) chemical components analysis of the human and mammoth bones indicated that the human bone was slightly older than that of the mammoth. There is some confusion as to a recently obtained C^{14} date, and Stewart (1973) cites it as being less than 23,600 years ago. Bada et al. (1974), however, used aspartic acid racemization and found a date of 28,000 years ago.

In 1970, Morlin Childers of Imperial Valley Museum uncovered what may be the oldest complete New World fossil hominid. The remains come from 30 miles south of El Centro in the Yuha Desert, southern California. The fossil is christened "Yuha man"[2] and preliminary C^{14} dating suggests an age of 23,600 years (Figure 20-8). The Yuha material was found beneath a cairn of boulders and in a stratum of coarse-grained calcareous alluvium. The bones were partly covered and cemented into the material by caliche (a crust of calcium carbonate found on sandy soil in arid areas). Two samples were radiocarbon dated. The first, from caliche scraped from the bones after their excavation, yielded a date of 21,500 +2,000 −1,000 years ago. The second was on caliche scraped from one of the overlying cairn boulders and yielded a date of 22,125 ± 400 years ago (Childers, 1974). The newest date for Yuha, 23,600 years ago, is consistent with C^{14} and thorium^{230} (Th^{230}) dating. Final evaluation of this find will have to await the release of further and more detailed information. Two possible stone tools of the type Childers labels "Ridge-back" were uncovered with the burial.

Other sites dating to the Middle Paleo-Indian period follow. The Tule Springs site, Nevada, yielded charcoal dated to more than 23,800 years ago. A south-central Idaho cave yielded stone artifacts and cut bone assigned dates of 14,500 to 15,000 years ago. A C^{14} date of 13,200 ± 170 years ago (from a charcoal sample reportedly associated with a projectile point) has been obtained from Fort Rock cave, Oregon. The Midland skull from western Texas may be older, that is, about 18,500 years old.

Some of the most recently discovered, and exciting, finds in the New World are from the Meadowcroft Rockshelter about 25 miles southwest of Pittsburgh. Radiocarbon dating of charcoal from the site has yielded a date of 14,225 years ago; an earlier attempt at dating in 1974, on two pieces of charcoal, yielded a date of 17,000 years ago. The dig, under the supervision of J. Adovasio of the University of Pittsburgh, began in 1973. The first findings from the site established it as the earliest for human habitation in the eastern United States.

---

[2]An indication that most paleontologists are male is in the fact that most fossils are called "such and such" man.

Figure 20-8. The Yuha burial.

The newest discoveries from Meadowcroft include more than 50 cutting tools. These artifacts, plus another 100 found in the previous excavation season, make this site the richest and most securely dated collection of tools in North and South America. Scientists in charge of the dig feel that Meadowcroft was used as a temporary shelter for wandering bands.

Because of the number of projectile points, knives, and faunal and floral remains, it has been concluded that the rockshelter was continuously used until European contact.

Adovasio is hopeful that continued digging will reveal evidence of earlier settlement at Meadowcroft. Another firepit has been discovered below that yielding the 14,225-year-old date. This site lends credence to the argument that human migration to the New World will probably date back at least to 20,000 to 30,000 years.

Mexico and South America yield a number of Middle Paleo-Indian sites. The Mexican sites near Puebla and Tlapacoya constitute some of the strongest proof of a Middle Paleo-Indian occupation. A blade and hearth have been uncovered at Tlapacoya, near Mexico City, dating to 23,150 ± 950 years ago and 24,000 ± 4,000 years ago, respectively. A site of questionable dating of 21,850 ± 850 years ago was excavated in the Valsequillo reservoir area. There is also a C^{14} date of 16,375 ± 400 years ago from Venezuela.

Some interesting material was found in Peru in 1969 and 1970 (MacNeish, 1971) from an area near Ayacucho. All the sites from Ayacucho lie within a mountain-ringed valley, and most come from elevations of 6,500 feet above sea level. The valley in which Ayacucho sits is situated some 200 miles southeast of Lima and is rich in prehistoric remains. Two of the major caves at Ayacucho are Pikimachay (Flea) Cave and Jayamachay (Pepper) Cave. Flea Cave is situated 9,000 feet above sea level; the cave mouth is 40 feet high in places. The cave is 175 feet wide and 80 feet deep at the deepest end.

Excavations from the Ayacucho area reveal a series of remains representative of successive cultures in an unbroken sequence spanning an age from 20,000 years ago to A.D. 150. This sequence documents the progression from early hunter to incipient agriculturalist to village farmer and finally to the role of subject during imperial rule. The early strata at Flea Cave reveal a succession of stone tool types that appeared about 20,000 years ago and continued until about 10,500 years ago. The oldest level from Flea Cave, Zone K, revealed four crude stone tools made from volcanic tuff and a few flakes.

Late Paleo-Indian Period. The most complete evidence comes from the Late Paleo-Indian period dating from 11,500 years ago. Such sites are common and show increasing cultural sophistication. Humans were now well established in the New World, where hunting sites and camps appear from Tierra del Fuego to Nova Scotia. The earliest part of this period is characterized by the remains of technologically advanced and highly skilled hunters using a distinctive projectile point known as the Clovis point for killing mammoth and other big game. The transition from the Clovis to Folsom point about 11,000 years ago coincides with the extinction of mammoths, horses, camels, and several other members of the Pleistocene megafauna.

Clovis Points. Clovis remains predominate in the American Southwest. Clovis points take their name from an early site located between Clovis and Portales, New Mexico. Work has been conducted here since 1932. The most important discoveries were made in 1936 and 1937 when artifacts were found in a sand deposit in unmistakable association with mammoth remains. Two important polished bone pieces were also found. One lay near the foreleg of one of the mammoths, the other by a tusk. Similar finds come from Alaska, California, Washington, and Florida.

Folsom Points. A discovery of far-reaching impact on American archaeology was made in 1926, at a site 8 miles from Folsom, New Mexico. While excavating a fossil bison, a party uncovered two pieces of chipped flint. A third piece was later found embedded in clay surrounding an animal rib. This discovery of manufactured objects in association with the articulated bones of a long-extinct fauna, in undisturbed deposits, suggested a far greater human antiquity in North America than previously assumed. At first most rejected the evidence. After three field seasons, 19 flakes, and proof-positive of Pleistocene geological age, the date of Folsom points gained acceptance.

Folsom points are pressure flaked, about 2 inches (5 centimeters) in length, thin, more or less leaf-shaped, and have concave bases; a long flake was apparently removed from each side. This flake removal gives a fluted character. Grooves or channels extend from one-third to almost the whole length of the flake. Why they were fluted is debatable. However, there are three suggestions: (1) Grooves may have lightened the point so it carried further. (2) The points were grooved to facilitate hafting. (3) They were designed on the principle of the bayonet; the fluting permitted greater blood flow from the wound and faster downing of the prey. Hafting is most likely, according to some.

Since their original discovery, Folsom points, and their derivatives, have been found in many locales. These are often surface finds uncovered by wind and/or water erosion. The greatest concentration of Folsom points is in the High Plains, extending along the eastern slopes of the Rockies. Elsewhere finds are less frequent, although there are examples in Alberta and Saskatchewan, Canada. Examples of Folsom sites include the Lindenmeier and Kersey sites, Colorado; the Lubbock site, Texas, dated between 9,100 and 10,000 years ago; the Liscomb Bison Quarry site in Texas; and the MacHaffie site in Montana.

The **Plano tradition** overlaps the Clovis and Folsom traditions and continues later. The Plano tradition dates to the period of 6,000 to 10,000 years ago and occurs from the Rockies to the Atlantic and Mexico to Canada. Plano points are not fluted—instead they bear parallel pressure-flaked scars. The oldest Paleo-Indian housing remains date to Plano occupations at the Hell Gap site, in Wyoming. The houses seem to have been circular and from 6 to 8 feet in diameter. The most recent structure is dated to between 8,000 and 8,400 years ago. Manufacturers of the Plano points were big game hunters specializing on forms that exist yet today.

A number of important early finds come from South America. One of the most important is the 10,000- to 11,000-year-old Fells Cave site in Tierra del Fuego, where bone and stone artifacts were found associated with skeletal remains of extinct game animals.

Subsistence patterns. Usually located near bogs or marshes, sites of Clovis tradition hunters contain implements manufactured from materials whose source was as far as 200 miles away from the site. This indicates a large nomadic range. The Clovis tradition is closely related to kill sites. Because of their location and size, these sites appear to be adaptations to hunting these people's favorite prey, the mammoth.

The most feasible hunting strategy of the Clovis mammoth hunters would be to ambush their prey along the route of one of its feeding areas. Feeding areas would be close to water. Once wounded, the mammoth would head for the nearest water source, where the hunters would complete their kill.

Folsom tradition hunters took advantage of a distinct behavioral trait of their favorite prey, the bison. The extinct bison is judged to have behaved much the same as its modern descendent. Although having poor eyesight, these animals have a keen sense of smell. When frightened they close ranks and stampede. Adapting to this behavior, Folsom hunters used the jump and surround kill-hunting techniques. Using the jump technique, hunters stationed themselves downwind from the animals and stampeded them toward a high cliff where the animals would blindly fall to their death. Many kill sites associated with the Folsom tradition are located at the base of such cliffs. In the surround kill, animals are herded into a canyon, or other enclosed area, where they are then slaughtered.

Folsom settlement patterns are geared toward bison hunting. Camp sites are located on ridges that provided excellent lookout stations overlooking bison grazing areas. Camps were also located near closed areas such as canyons or arroyos. Sites of the Folsom tradition are most densely spaced just east of the Rockies in areas where the bison may have wintered. The dense settlement patterns in the Great Plains and the higher western elevations may be explained as an adaptation to the bison's seasonal migrations (DeGarmo, 1970).

Hunters of the Plano tradition also used the jump and surround kill techniques. Most big game hunted by the Plano tradition people belonged to modern species. At the Plainview site in Texas hundreds of bison skeletons are found at the base of a cliff associated with Plano tools.

Not all Paleo-Indian groups were hunters. Because of the ages of these sites, more perishable food items, such as many floral forms and small faunal remains, may have been destroyed or decayed. The remains of larger, more durable bones may give a skewed impression of the dietary pattern. There are good data from southern Arizona, for example, suggesting that Paleo-Indians were gatherers and hunters. Two types of early sites located in different environmental zones are found in Arizona: kill sites and sites containing ground stone tools used for woodworking and plant processing (Duncan, 1972). Some have suggested that these sites were seasonal settlements within a single subsistence-settlement system.

Where populations of fully modern *Homo sapiens* evolved is debatable, but it is likely they appeared in various places during the Upper Pleistocene. Upper Pleistocene populations were largely migrating hunters and gatherers; however, there is substantial evidence at some sites of a sedentary life style. The Upper Paleolithic provides many examples of artistic expression: cave paintings, engravings, and sculpture. Upper Paleolithic groups probably lived in larger groups than their predecessors, and their social organizations may have been more complex.

During the Upper Paleolithic, at about 30,000 years ago, populations moved into Australia that were ancestral to modern Australian aborigines. Ancestral American Indian populations moved out of Asia and entered the New World across the Bering land bridge. Although the date of entrance into the New World is debated, it is unlikely to have happened prior to 40,000 years ago.

Early New World populations were big-game hunters; in fact, they may have entered this virgin territory in pursuit of migratory game. The tool technology seems to have been "homegrown," despite some attempts to trace it to Europe.

Bibliography

Bada, J., Schroeder, R., and Carter, G. 1974. New evidence for the antiquity of man in North America deduced from aspartic acid racemization. *Science* 184:791-93.

Bada, J., and Helfman, H. 1975. Amino acid racemization dating of fossil bone. *World Archeology* 7:160-73.

Barbetti, N., and Allen, H. 1972. Prehistoric man at Lake Mungo, Australia, by 32,000 years B.P. *Nature* 240:346-48.

Bischoff, J., and Childers, M. 1979. Temperature calibration of amino acid racemization. Age implications for the Yuha skeleton. *Earth and Planetary Science Letters* 45:172-80.

Borden, C. 1979. Peopling and early cultures on the Pacific Northeast. *Science* 203:963-71.

Bordes, F. 1968. *The Old Stone Age.* New York: McGraw-Hill.

Bowler, J., Thorne, A., and Polack, H. 1972. Pleistocene man in Australia: age and significance of Mungo skeleton. *Nature* 240:348-50.

Brothwell, D. 1961. Upper Pleistocene human skull from Niah Caves, Sarawak. *Sarawak Museum Journal* 9:323.

Bryan, A. 1969. Early man in America and the late Pleistocene chronology of western Canada and Alaska. *Current Anthropology* 10:339.

Bushnell, G., and McBurney, C. 1959. New World origins as seen from the Old World. *Antiquity* 33:93.

Chard, C. 1959. New World origins: a reappraisal. *Antiquity* 33:44.

Childers, W. 1974. Preliminary report on the Yuha burial, California. *Anthropological Journal of Canada* 12:1-9.

Clark, C. 1967. *The stone age hunters.* New York: McGraw-Hill.

Coon, C. 1962. *The origin of races.* New York: Knopf.

Cornwall, I. 1968. *Prehistoric animals and their hunters.* New York: Praeger.

Cressman, L., with collaboration of Frank C. Baker, Henry P. Hansen, Paul S. Conger, and Robert F. Heizer. 1942. *Archeological researches in the northern Great Basin.* Washington, D.C.: Carnegie Institute of Washington. Publication 538.

Day, M. 1969. Omo human skeletal remains. *Nature* 222:1135.

_____. 1971. The Omo human skeletal remains. In *The origin of* Homo sapiens, edited by F. Bordes, pp. 31-35. Paris: UNESCO.

DeGarmo, G. 1970. Big game hunters: an alternative and a hypothesis. Paper presented to 35th Annual Meeting of the Society for American Archaeology, Mexico City.

Duncan, R. 1972. *The Cohise culture.* Master's thesis. University of California at Los Angeles.

Eiseley, L. 1955. The Paleo-Indians: their survival and diffusion. In *New interpretations of aboriginal American culture history,* pp. 1-11. Anniversary volume of Anthropological Society of Washington.

Fladmark, K. 1979. Routes: alternative migration corridors for early man in North America. *American Antiquity* 44:55-69.

Galt, J. 1970. Calico conference. *The Piltdown Newsletter* 2:1.

Griffin, J. 1960. Some prehistoric connections between Siberia and America. *Science* 131:801.

Haag, W. 1962. The Bering Strait land bridge. *Scientific American* 206:112-23.

Hallam, S. 1977. The relevance of Old World archaeology to the first entry of man into new worlds: colonizations seen from the Antipodes. *Quaternary Research* 8:128-48.

Haynes, C. 1969. The earliest Americans. *Science* 166:709.

Heizer, R., and Cook, S. 1953. Fluorine and other chemical tests of some North American human and animal bones. *American Journal of Physical Anthropology* 10:289-304.

Hrdlička, A. 1923. The origin and antiquity of the American Indian. *Annual report of the Board of Regents of the Smithsonian Institution,* pp. 481-94.

Hulbert, K. 1975. Hominoid-hominid heterography and evolutionary patterns. In *Paleoanthropology, morphology, and paleoecology,* edited by R. Tuttle, pp. 153-62. The Hague: Mouton.

Irving, W. 1971. Recent early man research in the North. *Arctic Anthropology* 8:68-82.

Irving, W., and Harington, C. 1973. Upper Pleistocene radiocarbon dated artifacts from the Northern Yukon. *Science* 179:335-40.

Jelinek, J. 1969. Neanderthal man and *Homo sapiens* in central and eastern Europe. *Current Anthropology* 10:475.

Jennings, J. 1978. Origins. In *Ancient native Americans,* edited by J. Jennings, pp. 1-41. San Francisco: Freeman.

Leakey, L., Simpson, R., and Clements, T. 1968. Archaeological excavations in the Calico Mountains, California: preliminary report. *Science* 160:1022.

Leroi-Gourhan, A. 1967. *Treasures of prehistoric art.* New York: Abrams.

Macintosh, N. 1967. Fossil man in Australia. In *Yearbook of Physical Anthropology* 15:39.

MacNeish, R. 1971. Early man in the Andes. *Scientific American* 224:36.

_____. 1976. Early man in the New World. *American Scientist* 64:316-27.

Martin, N. 1967. Pleistocene overkill. In *Pleistocene extinctions: the search for a cause,* edited by P. Martin and N. Wright, pp. 75-120. New Haven: Yale University Press.

Pfeiffer, J. 1969. *The emergence of man.* New York: Harper & Row.

Poirier, F. 1981. *Fossil evidence: the human evolutionary journey.* St. Louis: Mosby.

Protsch, R. 1978. *Catalog of fossil hominids of North America.* New York: Fischer.

Rightmire, G. 1975. New studies of post-Pleistocene human skeletal remains from the Rift Valley, Kenya. *American Journal of Physical Anthropology* 42:351-70.

_____. 1979. Implications of Border Cave skeletal remains for later Pleistocene human evolution. *Current Anthropology* 20:23-35.

Roberts, F. 1935. A Folsom complex: preliminary report on investigations at the Lindenmeier site in northern Colorado. *Smithsonian Miscellaneous Collections* 94.

Stewart, T. 1960. A physical anthropologist's view of the peopling of the New World. *Southwestern Journal of Anthropology* 16:259.

_____. 1973. *The people of America.* New York: Scribner.

Thorne, A., and Macumber, P. 1972. Discoveries of Late Pleistocene man at Kow Swamp, Australia. *Nature* 238:316-19.

Vallois, H. 1961. The social life of early man: the evidence of skeletons. In *Social life of early man,* edited by S. Washburn, pp. 214-35. Chicago: Aldine.

White, P., and Allen, J. 1980. Melanesian prehistory: some recent advances. *Science* 207:728-33.

White, P., and O'Connell, J. 1979. Australian prehistory: new aspects of antiquity. *Science* 203:21-28.

Wolpoff, M. 1980. *Paleoanthropology.* New York: Knopf.

Wormington, H. 1957. *Ancient man in North America.* Denver Museum of Natural History.

Chapter 21

Trends in Hominid Evolution

Before proceeding, we pause briefly to review six major trends apparent in hominid evolution. We are principally concerned with (1) mechanisms resulting in size reduction and differentiation of the anterior teeth, (2) anatomical modifications permitting postural uprightness, (3) exploitation of the habitat, (4) increasing brain size, (5) tool use and manufacture, and (6) adoption of an essentially omnivorous-carnivorous diet.

Trend 1: Tale of the Teeth—Reduction in Canine Tooth Size

It has been argued that there was a marked size reduction of the incisor, canine, and pre-molar teeth in *Ramapithecus*. Remember, our sample is so small that any discussion, no matter how tenuous, may be premature. The passage of time and additional information led to an assault on the traditional idea that canine reduction and tool use are related. For example, the study of the subfossil form (e.g., a form that has recently become extinct) *Hadropithecus* (Figure 21-1) from the Malagasy Republic shows that *Hadropithecus* had small canines, a most puzzling reduction given any validity to the canine reduction-tool use hypothesis. *Hadropithecus*, a clear-cut arboreal lemur in all but its chewing apparatus, could never have used tools. Yet the fact remains that it possessed small canines. Tattersall (1972) along with Every (1970), suggests that the human canine assumed its present size and form to comple-ment the incisor teeth and make the biting complex at the front of the mouth more efficient.[1] The argument is still to be resolved. If, however, the view of hominid evolution eventually supports a tie with forms possessing small canines, a number of more cherished theories concerning certain aspects of hominid evolution must change.

---

[1]It should be noted that canine reduction can come about by a number of means. When large canines are not used for fighting, there is no selection pressure for them; primates living in groups in which there is minimal intragroup aggression tend to have small canines. Canine reduction is also characteristic of primates in which the canines are not specialized for some feeding behavior. Tools are behavioral substitutes for large canines, but they may not be the only ones.

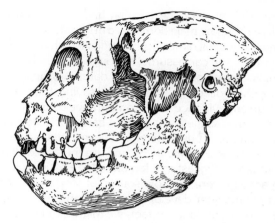

Figure 21-1. *Hadropithecus stenognathus*, **a subfossil form from the island of Madagascar.**

Trend 2: Moving Erect—Skeletal and Muscular Modifications Permitting Postural Uprightness and Erect Bipedalism

A number of morphological traits differentiate the hominid and pongid pelvis. Since hominid characteristics appear in a rather advanced state among Lower Pleistocene hominids, it is assumed that they were appearing among their ancestors.

Erect bipedalism was permitted by such morphological changes as a rearrangement of the pelvic structure (especially the **ilium**); shifts in the size and arrangement of **gluteal** (buttocks) muscles; and changes in the foot skeleton and its supporting musculature, all allowing the foot bones to assume full body weight and passage of the weight stress through the medial part of the foot; changes in the heel and ankle bones; and shifting in the spinal column. Correlated changes occurred in the upper limb structure as the limbs were freed from weight-bearing for periods of time. The lower limbs now assumed that duty. The relaxation of weight-bearing in the upper limbs led to changes in the shoulder structure. Rearrangements in the neck musculature followed changes in head balance (Figure 21-2). There is also the possibility that upending the body and changing the line of sight resulted in a reorientation to the environment.

Trend 3: Effective Exploitation of the Terrestrial Habitat

Behavioral adjustments as well as morphological changes were needed to cope with the terrestrial habitat. Major adjustments were probably reflected in the social group[2]. Based on comparative evidence and the archaeological record, early hominids were group-living forms, 25 members probably being an average, and there was sexual division of labor. It has been

[2]Group living is not a new adaptation. But for few exceptions, mostly nocturnal creatures, primates are group-living. In fact most mammals are group-living. However, primate groups differ from those of many other mammals in two basic features: they are year-round social groups and they are bisexual. Of all primate groups, those of the chimpanzee are probably most comparable to those of the early hominids (van Lawick-Goodall, 1967, 1971; Sugiyama, 1972). This behavioral manifestation is consistent with their taxonomic position in relation to hominids.

suggested that males did most of the hunting and females collected other edibles. Early hominid societies were probably male dominated in social control. In most nonhuman primate societies in which there is sexual dimorphism, and in which the male is the larger of the sexes, males dominate the troop. We can assume, although we may be wrong, that the same applies for the early hominids. Based on comparative data, it is hypothesized that males did the hunting and females the collecting. This is not saying that females were relegated to a peripheral role, for current evidence from comparative sources such as nonhuman primates and some social carnivores suggests that these early societies may have been female-focal. Current nonhuman primate studies strongly suggest that females play a key role as the purveyors of troop traditions (Poirier, 1973), and are the stable element of the group. Studies of modern hunter-gatherers suggest that females play a major role as food suppliers, and that if the male hunting activity were the sole source of food, many groups would soon starve. Perhaps it was not until the later development of organized hunting that male hunters of big game provided the bulk of the food. In fact, we might argue that because of cultural biases many of our evolutionary theories are focused too strongly on the role of males.

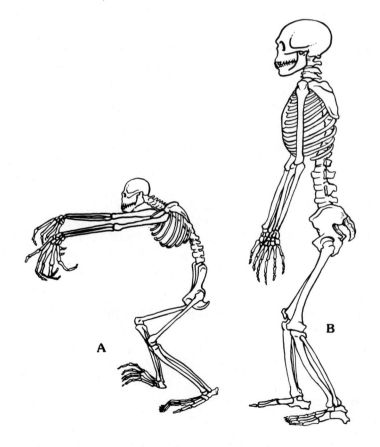

Figure 21-2. The upright posture and bipedal gait of (A) a running gibbon and (B) a walking *Homo*.

Most important in regard to role differentiation is the onset of the sexual division of labor. Among nonhuman primates each animal is its own separate subsistence unit. Even infants once they are weaned must depend on their own guile for survival as concerns food intake. Among humans, however, the weaned young still depend on the adults for food. Lancaster has postulated that because of this long-term dependence on adults for nourishment, the roles of both male and female humans have greatly expanded and much of the time during the day is spent in activities that provide food for the young. "Because of the long-term dependence of children, a division of labor evolved in which the adventurous, wandering male became the hunter and the female developed the less mobile role of gatherer and mother" (Lancaster, 1975:78-79).

Females give birth and bear the major responsibility for the early care, feeding, and rearing of the young. Therefore, any sexual division of labor, by increasing the reproductive fitness of the individuals, is beneficial for the survival of the group and the species. The human infant is born at a stage of relative immaturity and is generally unable to fend for itself. Furthermore, the human mother lacks the body hair (common in nonhuman primates) to which the infant can grasp and allow the mother the usual range of movement. The human mother must carry the infant. Both conditions, relative immaturity at birth and lack of body hair, may have characterized early hominids and necessitated that mothers give extensive care to their infants. Given the long period of immaturity characteristic of the human infant, there was no other way, once hunting and gathering developed as a way of life, than for a division of labor to have occurred except between males and females.

The division of labor that developed concomitant with the hunting and gathering way of life provided a flexible system of joint dependence on plant and animal foods. The division of labor provided an efficient coping strategy quite different from that characterizing the nonhuman primates. The human hunting-gathering pattern provided great flexibility in terms of coping, for it allowed adjustments to daily, seasonal, and cyclical variations in food supplies and geographical and habitat variants. Lancaster (1975) argues that this system permitted our ancestors to cover the earth without speciating.

There is no archaeological evidence to support the contention that the early hominids and their immediate successors exhibited a sexual division of labor. However, the adaptive advantages provided by this system suggest the likelihood that such a division existed. A division of labor may be useful in helping explain why early hominids were able to compete so successfully and establish themselves in their new habitat.

Isaac (1978) suggests that there was sexual division of labor among hominids less evolved than *Homo sapiens,* with the males doing the hunting and the females doing the gathering. All the food was brought back to a "home base" for some kind of ordered dispersal through the group. This pattern of behavior is the same as that of modern hunter-gatherers and different from the behavior of any known nonhuman primate. Isaac also suggests that the early hominids were becoming recognizably human while they remained biologically subhuman.

The concept of the "home" was probably developed early in hominid evolution as an important survival mechanism. A home base provided a location at which injured or sick individuals could remain and to which other group members could return at night. Among savanna-living baboons, with no home base to which they return daily, sick or injured members must move with the troop or be left behind to die or be killed by one of the many savanna predators. A home base also became important because of the human infant's slower maturation rate (or, put another way, longer growth period); extended maternal care was required to assure survival. Such care, although an imposition on the care-taker (presumably the mother), required longer mother-and-infant contact, allowed more time for infant socialization, and placed a premium on learning.

The acquisition of tool use, with all its concomitant muscular and neural requirements, helped bring about other adaptations for effective environmental exploration. Tool use and terrestriality probably placed a premium on the development of an effective signaling network. Language acquisition may be a partial response to continuing pressures to communicate effectively about increasing complexities of life—for example, how to make tools or where to find food.

Trend 4: Reign of the Brain—Increasing Brain Size

Throughout the hominid fossil record there is a trend toward increasing brain size and complexity (Figure 21-3 and 21-4). The trend was neither steady nor consistent; the increase was slight during the approximately 4 or more million years of *Australopithecus,* but rapid during the Middle Pleistocene with *H. erectus* and *H. sapiens.* The increase in brain size was probably related to various factors such as tool use, increasing environmental challenges, more complex social groups, and complex, organized hunting behavior.

If one takes a long-term evolutionary look, it seems that a larger brain may once have been vitally important in aiding survival in a world of predators and devoid of controlled fire. Consequent hominid development seems to have placed decreasing importance solely on brain size. Beyond a certain size increase, there is no evidence that further increases in brain size improve our adaptive abilities. Furthermore, there is also no evidence that brain size always correlates with intelligence in modern *Homo.* There is a shared feeling among many scientists that our brain (Figure 21-5) has reached its maximum size and one may speculate that pressures will not be for larger cranial capacities but for more efficient use of the brain we now possess.

Culture as normally defined has as a major component the proposition that it is characterized by learned behavior generationally transmitted. One prerequisite for culture is thus an adequate memory storage facility allowing relatively complex learning (Tunnell, 1973). In hominid evolution there was a three-fold increase in cranial capacity from early Pliocene-Pleistocene forms to modern *Homo.* This increase is likely to have enhanced the capacity for information storage and the ability to learn. An actual physiological change in the brain accompanies learning. Hyden and Egyhazi (1964) and Agranoff (1967) have shown that when a

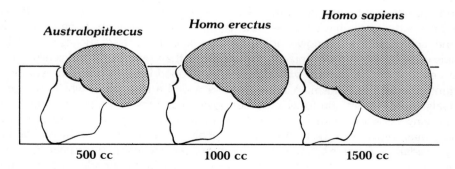

Australopithecus   *Homo erectus*   *Homo sapiens*

500 cc   1000 cc   1500 cc

Figure 21-3. Relation of brain size to face size.

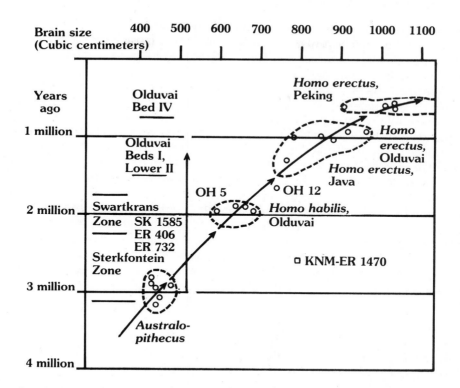

| Brain size (Cubic centimeters) | 400 | 500 | 600 | 700 | 800 | 900 | 1000 | 1100 |

Figure 21-4. Increasing brain size. This chart illustrates the increase in brain size from *Australopithecus* through *Homo habilis* to *H.* erectus. Individual fossils are shown as small circles. In most cases both date and brain size are estimates only. The chart is therefore not as exact as it may appear. Estimates of brain size are mostly those made by Holloway and Tobias in various writings.

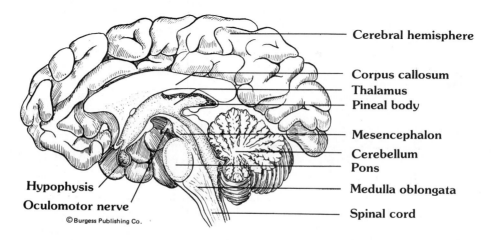

© Burgess Publishing Co.

Figure 21-5. Side view of bisected modern human brain.

behavior is learned there are accompanying permanent physiological changes; a protein synthesis occurs in which RNA is created and stored. Rosenzweig et al. (1972) found that experience directly influences the brain, causing an increased amount of cortex that is probably due to the creation of messenger RNA.

Anthropologists have long speculated on the feedback between increasing brain size and complexity and tool use and manufacture in hominid evolution (Krantz, 1968; Washburn, 1960, 1967; Washburn and Hamburg, 1965). Although some of the components of this interaction have been severely questioned (i.e., Holloway, 1967), there is little doubt as to the importance of this feedback. Figure 21-6 shows how the feedback may have occurred. Tool use and manufacture is best understood as a factor of cerebral specialization, especially brain lateralization (e.g., the specialization of the right and left hemispheres for different functions). We cannot say which appeared first—hemispheric specialization in the brain or manual skill. However, the whole complex of increasing verbal ability, skilled tool use and fabrication, and lateral cerebral specialization likely evolved together. Materials for tools were selected according to a classification system that was the result of experience and perhaps social learning. The system may have therefore consisted of a cognitive scheme (Figure 21-7).

Tunnell (1973:29-30) envisions the manufacture of tools as being accomplished according to the following scenario:

1. Material is selected according to a system that results from experience and perhaps social learning.
2. Material is selected based on its size and shape. The right hemisphere may contribute to this decision with its "feel" for the ideal size and shape of the product. This decision results from kinesthetic learning and perception of dimensions and angles.

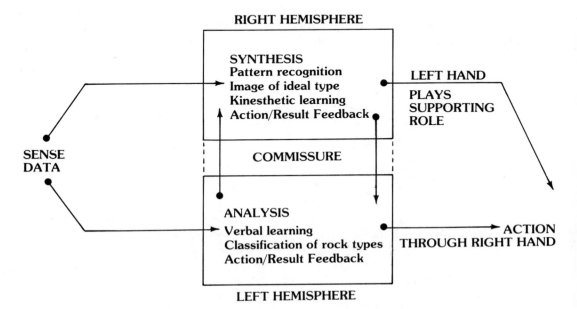

Figure 21-6. Tool use flow chart showing interaction of cerebral hemispheres in normal functioning.

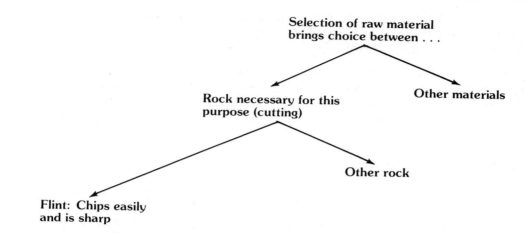

Figure 21-7. Tool manufacture accomplished through a possible cognitive classification system.

3. Then, perhaps, there is a "running commentary" between the hemispheres in the selection of the manufacture procedure. After the choice is made, both hemispheres supplement each other during the actual manufacture of the object.
4. The left hand holds the object and the right hand begins the action necessary for manufacture, controlled principally by the action-oriented left hemisphere. Both hemispheres contribute to the decisions in producing the final shape.

From this outline it is apparent how important the evolution of the brain is for the basic development of cultural forms. However, we are unsure of the full significance of the specializations of the brain hemispheres. We do not yet know how the specializations appeared or how they have been important in cultural development. We can only assume that these specializations were important in forming culture.

Hallowell (1961) expands on this theme, and wonders about the sociopsychological by-products of prolonged immaturity and other factors such as delayed reproduction and increasing life spans. With continuing increase in brain size and complexity, and with a continuing and perhaps heightened awareness of the surroundings, Hallowell argues that all distinctive features of a protocultural stage were being elevated to a new level of sociopsychological integration. In time, this new level of psychological organization would affect every aspect of the earlier modes of protocultural adaptation. This led, according to Hallowell (1961:272) to ". . . more inclusive, complex, and diversified sociocultural systems."

Hallowell goes on to state that psychological factors became paramount in the functioning of sociocultural systems because the socially sanctioned values characterizing them were linked to cognitive processes, motivations, and need satisfactions. This linkage occurred ". . . through the formation of a new and distinctive personality organization molded in the socialization process" (1961:272). The psychological reconstruction that Hallowell speaks of occurred in a primate in which a system of action existed, and not only allowed for a more advanced level of social existence but also laid the basis for subsequent cultural change.

Trend 5: The Hands Work—Extensive Manipulation of Natural Objects and the Development of Motor Skills to Facilitate Tool Making

This trend is an outgrowth of effectance motivation. Extensive manipulatory behavior was facilitated by hands freed of locomotor activities, stereoscopic vision, increasing brain size, and more effective hand-eye coordination. The pressures for extensive object manipulation probably derived from increasing tool use, which was, in turn, related to increasing survival problems.

One of the major advantages of the primate hand is that it permits detachment of objects from the environment (Campbell, 1966). Knowledge about our environment stemmed from, among other things, just naturally picking up objects and examining them. This behavioral curiosity appears to be a natural outgrowth of the process of effectance motivation, one component of which is play and exploratory behavior.

As primates we had another behavioral tradition that necessitates the use of the hands and hand-eye coordination; this was grooming. The pattern of one animal picking through its own hair or that of another requires sophisticated hand-eye coordination. Most nonhuman primates that engage in this behavior can oppose the thumb to the forefinger. Such opposability is important in holding and handling objects. From these seemingly inauspicious beginnings, play and grooming behavior, we were preadapted to picking up and examining objects. This possibly led, in time, to tool use and manufacture.

Let us return to our original proposition that the ability to detach objects from the environment is a major advance that was most important for the development of primate perceptual skills. We owe recognition of different kinds of objects to primate visual acuity and tactile examination. With the upright sitting position of nonhuman primates, vision gained strict control of manipulation. As Sphuler (1957:41) notes, "...it became a supervision, a guide and control of fine manipulation." The relation between the evolution of keen vision (which was possibly an adaptation to locomoting through the trees and grasping at swift insects [Cartmill, 1975]) and fine manipulation is two-dimensional.[3] Polyak (1957) suggests that vision became more refined and intellectual absorption and mental use more long lasting as skilled movements became more complex and efficient.

Nonhuman primates extract objects from the environment with their hands to smell and taste, visually and factually examine them, relish their feel, and then perhaps to replace them. If the reader has a pet dog or cat, the limitations of its abilities in such matters is readily apparent. As Campbell (1968:129) notes, " . . . in this way the higher primates have come to see the environment not as a continuum of events in the world of pattern but as an encounter with objects that proved to make up these events and this pattern."

Trend 6: Addition of Meat Protein to a Largely Vegetarian Diet

Most nonhuman primates are vegetarian, although some (especially the chimpanzee) kill and eat other vertebrates. The time when meat first assumed importance in the hominid diet is

---

[3]It should be noted that while other arboreal animals have some of the same adaptations as the nonhuman primates, rarely do any approach the fine manipulative abilities and the hand-eye coordination characteristic of the primates.

Table 21-1. Trends in Cultural Evolution

Pongids	Sporadic and unsystematic implemental activities; most widespread implemental use is among chimpanzees; limited problem-solving applications of implemental behavior; implemental use is not necessary for survival; implemental use limited to wooden and plant materials; no evidence of using tools to make tools.
Australopithecus[a]	Versatile array of implemental activities; implements primarily fashioned from stone, although possible use was made of bone, teeth, antlers, and perhaps wood; little workmanship witnessed in the tool fashioning; tool use of definite survival value; long traditions with relatively little change.
Homo habilis	Perhaps the first systematic tool manufacturers; tools made to set patterns; tool use and manufacture of definite survival value; tool traditions lay the basis for subsequent traditions.
H. erectus	Many cultural remains are present; tools of higher quality, more extensively worked, made from more materials, and perhaps used in a wider range of activities than H. habilis; sustained continuity of cultural development; first evidence of fire using and habitation of places such as caves and constructed shelters; survival value of culture is maximized.
H. sapiens	All significant trends of cultural hominization are emphasized; culture continues to affect biological evolution; survival depends on technology, complex ritual life.

[a]Some argue that the earliest tools were not made by creatures known as the australopithecines but by a more advanced group known as H. habilis. This chart avoids that issue and lists both forms.

Adapted from P. Tobias, *The Brain in Hominid Evolution*, pp. 137-38. Columbia University Press, New York © 1971.

conjectural; however, we assume that it was probably during the later stages of Lower Pleistocene hominid evolution. Consistent meat eating required a number of behavioral and anatomical changes. Once meat became basic to the diet, means would be developed whereby it could be most effectively obtained. Methods for carrying meat, rules for sharing (perhaps one of the first sets of rules for a society), and means for butchering meat would have appeared.

A carnivorous diet, and the advent of big-game hunting, had a marked impact on hominid evolution. In an article entitled "The Evolution of Hunting," Washburn and Lancaster (1971:83) note: "The agricultural revolution, continuing into the industrial and scientific revolutions, is now freeing man from the conditions and restraints of 99 percent of his history, but the biology of our species was created in the long gathering and hunting period. To assert the biological unity of mankind is to affirm the importance of the hunting way of life.... The biology, psychology, and customs that separate us from the apes—all these we owe to the hunters of time past . . . for those who would understand the origin and the nature of human behavior, there is no choice but to try to understand man the hunter." This theme is elaborated in such books as Morris' *The Naked Ape* and *The Human Zoo*. Elements of this argument appear in Ardrey's *African Genesis* and *The Territorial Imperative* and we should not skip Lorenz's *On Aggression*. A whole host of other authors have followed this line; unfortunately, many in their rush to "jump on the bandwagon" have completely missed the point.

Table 21-2. Review of Hominid and Cultural Evolution

Hominid	Cultural Stage	Industry	Hunting	Extension and Control of Environment	Arts and Beliefs
Homo sapiens	Upper Paleolithic	Composite and specialized tools, blades, burins, bone needles, regional specialization.	Many hunting and fishing techniques.	Reliable means of firemaking, clothes, elaborate artificial shelters, lunar notations.	Painting, engraving, sculpture, personal adornment, elaborate burials, elaborate hunting ritual, animal sacrifice, musical instruments.
Neanderthals (*H. sapiens neanderthalensis*)	Middle Paleolithic (Mousterian)	Flake tools, points, sidescraper, specialized core tools, incipient blade technology.	More elaborate hunting techniques, for example, use of pitfalls.	Increasing use of fire and firemaking, increasing use of improved shelters.	Aesthetic craftsmanship, first deliberate burials with some treatment, ritual cannibalism, hunting rituals and initiation.
Early *H. sapiens*	Beginning of Middle Paleolithic (?)				
H. erectus	Lower Paleolithic	Simple core and flake tools.	Missile stones and spears used for hunting.	First use of fire, use of natural shelters with little modification, building of temporary shelters.	Some symmetrical artifacts and some aesthetic craftsmanship, cannibalism possible.
Pliocene/Pleistocene hominids		Pebble tools.	Scavenging (?) and hunting.	Some use of natural shelter, for example, trees, possible modification.	

Adapted from S. L. Washburn, *Social Life of Early Man*, pp. viii-ix. Aldine Publishing Company, Chicago © 1961.

Although the hunting way of life has been stressed as an important factor in hominid evolution, we must caution that too much emphasis may have been placed on it. With most interest focused on the hunting half of the hunter-gatherer complex, gathering has been disproportionately underemphasized (McGrew, 1978). Many have ignored the probable evolutionary importance of gathering or dismissed its results as "casually collected foods" (Laughlin, 1968:319). Coon (1971) has also referred to the primacy of hunting and he contends that it had more impact on social structure than did gathering. However, Lee (1968), among others, has criticized this one-sided viewpoint. Food sources other than those offered by hunted meat were most important and it is very unlikely that any hominid group ever relied solely on meat for its food source.

Careful empirical studies of extant human foragers demonstrate the importance of gathering in daily nutrition. Some anthropologists are now suggesting that modern human foragers be called "gatherer-hunters" rather than "hunter-gatherers" to show that they obtain more food by gathering than by hunting and to suggest (on the basis that human foragers of the past lived similarly to those of the present) that hunting may be overemphasized in current theory building. How this shifting emphasis will eventually modify existing theories of hominid evolution awaits futher examination.

Views as to the adaptive mechanisms for some of the morphological traits discussed in this chapter are being challenged. The classic argument linking the adoption of tool use with consequent reduction of the front teeth has been challenged. Many still hold to the view, originally offered by Charles Darwin, that the adoption of tools had much to do with our subsequent evolution, for example, bipedalism. Some writers argue that once we became big-game hunters, predators, we established a behavioral pattern leading to what some consider to be our excessive aggressive behavior. There are many faults in this argument; however, it can be argued, as Washburn and Lancaster do, that much of what separates us from our pongid relatives we owe to a hunting way of life dominating much of our evolutionary history.

Bibliography

Agranoff, B. 1967. Memory and protein synthesis. *Scientific American* 216:115-22.

Campbell, B. 1966. *Human evolution: an introduction to man's adaptation.* Chicago: Aldine.

——————. 1976. *Humankind emerging.* Boston: Little, Brown.

Cartmill, M. 1975. *Primate origins.* Minneapolis: Burgess.

Coon, C. 1971. *The hunting peoples.* Boston: Little, Brown.

Every, R. 1970. Sharpness of teeth in man and other primates. *Postilla* 143:1.

Hallowell, A. 1961. The protocultural foundations of human adaptation. In *Social life of early man,* edited by S. Washburn, pp. 236-85. Chicago: Aldine.

Holloway, R. 1967. Tools and teeth: some speculations regarding canine reduction. *American Anthropologist* 93:63.

Howells, W. 1973. *Evolution of the genus* Homo. Reading, Mass.: Addison-Wesley.

Hyden, H., and Egyhazi, E. 1964. Changes in RNA content and base composition in critical neurons of rats in a learning experiment involving transfer of handedness. *Proceedings of the National Academy of Sciences* 52:1030-35.

Isaac, G. 1976. The activities of early African hominids. In *Human origins: Louis Leakey and the East African evidence,* edited by G. Isaac and E. McCown, pp. 483-514. Menlo Park, Calif.: Benjamin.

——————. 1978. The food-sharing behavior of protohuman hominids. *Scientific American* 238:90-109.

Krantz, G. 1968. Brain size and hunting ability in earliest man. *Current Anthropology* 11:176.

Lancaster, J. 1975. *Primate behavior and the emergence of human culture.* New York: Holt, Rinehart and Winston.

Laughlin, W. 1968. Hunting: an integrating biobehavior system and its evolutionary importance. In *Man the hunter,* edited by R. Lee and I. DeVore, pp. 304-20. Chicago: Aldine-Atherton.

Lee, R. 1968. What hunters do for a living, or how to make out on scarce resources. In *Man the hunter,* edited by R. Lee and I. DeVore, pp. 30-48. Chicago: Aldine-Atherton.

McGrew, W. 1978. Evolutionary implications of sex differences in chimpanzee predation and tool use. In *The great apes,* edited by D. Hamburg and E. McCown, pp. 441-64. Menlo Park, Calif.: Benjamin/Cummings.

Moscovici, S. 1976. *Society against nature.* New York: Humanities Press.

Poirier, F. 1972. Introduction. In *Primate Socialization,* edited by F. Poirier, pp. 1-28. New York: Random House.

_____. 1973. Socialization and learning among nonhuman primates. In *Culture and learning,* edited by S. Kimball and J. Burnett, pp. 3-41. Seattle: University of Washington Press.

_____. 1981. *Fossil evidence: the human evolutionary journey.* St. Louis: Mosby.

Polyak, S. 1957. *The vertebrate visual system.* Chicago: University of Chicago Press.

Radinski, L. 1972. Endocasts and studies of primate brain evolution. In *The functional and evolutionary biology of primates.* edited by R. Tuttle, pp. 175-84. Chicago: Aldine-Atherton.

Rosenzweig, M., Bennet, E., and Cleeves, M. 1972. Brain changes in response to experience. *Scientific American* 226:22-29.

Shapiro, J. 1971. I went to the animal fair: a review of the imperial animal. *Natural History* 80:90.

Sphuler, J. 1957. Somatic paths to culture. *Human biology* 31:1-13.

Sugiyama, Y. 1972. Social characteristics and socialization of wild chimpanzees. In *Primate socialization,* edited by F. Poirier, pp. 145-64. New York: Random House.

Tattersall, I. 1972. Of lemurs and men. *Natural History* 81:32.

Tobias, P. 1971. *The brain in hominid evolution.* New York: Columbia University Press.

Tunnell, G. 1973. *Culture and biology: becoming human.* Minneapolis: Burgess.

van Lawick-Goodall, J. 1967. *My friends the wild chimpanzees.* Washington, D.C.: National Geographic Society.

_____. 1971. *In the shadow of man.* Boston: Houghton Mifflin .

von Bonin, G. 1963. *The evolution of the human brain.* Chicago: University of Chicago Press.

Washburn, S. 1960. Tools and human evolution. *Scientific American* 203:62-75.

Washburn, S., ed. 1961. *Social life of early man.* Chicago: Aldine.

Washburn, S., and DeVore, I. 1961. The social life of baboons. *Scientific American* 204:62-71.

Washburn, S., and Hamburg, D. 1965. Implications of primate research. In *Primate behavior,* edited by I. DeVore, pp. 607-22. New York: Holt, Rinehart and Winston.

Washburn, S., and Lancaster, C. 1971. The evolution of hunting. In *Background for man: readings in physical anthropology,* edited by P. Dolhinow and V. Sarich, pp. 386-405. Boston: Little, Brown.

Washburn, S., and Moore, R. 1974. *Ape into man—a study of human evolution.* Boston: Little, Brown.

Chapter 22

Alternative Viewpoints of Hominid Evolution

There is no unanimity among paleoanthropologists as to how hominids evolved, due to such factors as the scarcity and limited nature of paleontological material, the vast time spans over which evolution occurred, and the personalities and academic backgrounds of the investigators. There is much disagreement as to the classification of various osteological remains and as to the total evolutionary scheme. This chapter reviews some hypotheses of hominid descent: the (1) tarsioid hypothesis, (2) pithecoid hypothesis, (3) brachiating hypothesis (recently modified to include a knuckle- or fist-walking stage), (4) immunological hypothesis, and finally, for diversity's sake, the (5) aquatic viewpoint.

Nonanthropoid Ape Hypotheses of Human Origins

The orthodox theory of hominid origins claims a particularly close relationship between hominids and pongids; it has not lacked critics, however. The late French paleontologist M. Boule was one of the first to doubt a close hominid-pongid link. Boule chided anthropologists for comparing hominids with only the anthropoid apes and for regarding pongids as those primates closest to the hominid ancestry. Boule emphasized that in the extremities humans approximated monkeys rather than apes. He believed that the hominid evolutionary line was independent of other primate branches, especially that leading to pongids. Boule suggested that we might be related to Old World primates at a level prior to the departure of the anthropoid ape stock, or even at the level of the divergence of New and Old World monkeys.

Tarsioid Hypothesis. The **tarsioid** (or *tarsian*) **hypothesis** was expounded by the anatomist F. Wood Jones and elaborated in his 1929 book entitled *Man's Place Among the Mammals.* The tarsioid hypothesis vigorously denies our kinship with the anthropoids. It claims instead that our phylogenetic line stems directly from a primitive tarsioid form. Our only living near-relatives are of the form *Tarsius,* today represented by the nocturnal *T. spectrum* inhabiting forested regions of Southeast Asia. If we accept Jones's argument, the hominid line became independent from the general primate evolutionary branch very near the base of the divergence from the mammalian stock.

The basis of the rejection of an anthropoid ape-hominid ancestry is rooted in the assumption that modern pongids are far too specialized to have given rise to hominids. Jones felt that the brachiating apes' lack of a developed thumb, while we have one, and the fact that the brachiators' arms are longer than the legs, while the reverse is true in hominids, remove hominids from the anthropoid ape lineage. The tarsioid adherents contend that supporters of the anthropoid ape theory of hominid descent advocate evolutionary reversals to derive a short-armed, long-legged form with a highly developed thumb from a form with long arms, short legs, and a poorly developed thumb.

Jones characterized the ancestral hominid stock as small, active, and agile animals that were erect and moved bipedally along the branches. Thus they were prepared for a terrestrial, bipedal life. This ancestral stock was also characterized as having a large head, small teeth, and moderately large eye orbits. If one accepts this viewpoint, then, with the possible exception of *Propliopithecus* from the Fayum in Egypt, there are no fossils in the hominid record between the Paleocene-Eocene tarsioids and the Pleistocene hominids.

Pithecoid Hypothesis. The **pithecoid hypothesis** was expounded by the anatomist W. Straus. Straus (1949) argued that the most likely evolutionary scheme should derive hominids from some sort of generalized Old World monkey, at a reasonably early date, rather than from an anthropoid ape stock. In Straus's view the major problem with the brachiator theory of hominid derivation is that it ignores a considerable number of hominid characters that can only be derived from an essentially generalized primate stock. Straus argues that the hominid phylogenetic line became independent of the Old World monkey stock prior to there being actual anthropoid apes.

Straus visualized the ancestral hominid stock as generally resembling Old World monkeys. Accordingly, the presumed earliest representatives of the hominid line may be visualized as essentially unspecialized quadrupeds, capable of both arboreal and terrestrial life, possessing expanding brains, short tails, and generalized extremities. Straus argues that they avoided specializations of brachiation (e.g., long arms, short legs, short thumbs) and early became terrestrial bipeds.

This argument centers on the crucial point of whether ancestral hominids were brachiators. Straus rejects the contention that outright, habitual brachiation was a necessary prelude to hominid terrestrial bipedalism. He argues that the major features wherein hominids and pongids show special affinities are due to parallelism through the inheritance of detailed characters or genes from a common pool. That is, the shared traits do not necessarily constitute a close phyletic relationship. Straus feels that the hominid line may have diverged from the evolving Old World monkey line between 32 million and 50 million years ago, probably no later than the end of the Oligocene.

Arguments Against Nonanthropoid Ape Derivation

Locomotor Patterns. The major arguments against nonanthropoid ape hypotheses of hominid evolution are based on the expanding fossil record and the fact that ancestral pongids lacked specialized adaptations for brachiation common to their modern descendants. F. Wood Jones formulated his idea when the fossil record was meager; much of the Fayum material was not yet recovered, let alone analyzed. The same is true for the dryopithecine, *Ramapithecus,* and *Australopithecus* material. Straus had access to more material, but the dryopithecines, *Ramapithecus,* and *Australopithecus* were still controversial. The major problem with both arguments rests on their insistence that fossil pongids were already brachiators by the time of the hominid divergence; dryopithecine remains contradict this.

The East African dryopithecine fossils and the humerus from France strongly suggest that habitual brachiation developed no earlier than the late Pliocene. Prior to the Pliocene, primates revealed a variety of limb characteristics; no fossilized limb structures show more than incipient brachiation as a mode of locomotion. Brachiation is now considered to be a late secondary acquisition, occupying perhaps as little as one-fortieth of the total primate evolutionary history. Perhaps feeding at the terminal ends of branches, where competition from other primates is less severe, led to brachiation. The early anthropoid apes manifested a range of locomotor behaviors providing a more promising point of departure for the development of bipedalism than the quadrupedal monkey.

Most paleontologists reject nonanthropoid ape hypotheses of hominid evolution. However, such hypotheses have served a very useful function, for they have forced rethinking of the problem and caused it to be modified.

Anthropoid Ape Derivation

Most paleontologists subscribe to some version of the anthropoid ape theory of hominid descent. There is considerable controversy, however, as to how early, or late, in time hominids and pongids diverged. There is also much contention as to which fossil materials, if we now possess them, were the first hominids.

Four years after Darwin's *On the Origin of Species* appeared in 1859, T. H. Huxley published his group of essays entitled *Evidence as to Man's Place in Nature*. In these essays he argued for a close relationship between hominids and two anthropoid apes, the chimpanzee and gorilla. Although the anthropoid ape theory of human origins was vaguely perceived by certain eighteenth-century philosophers such as Buffon, Huxley seems to have been the first to express it in modern, scientific form. In his later book entitled *The Descent of Man* (1871) Darwin supported Huxley's contentions.

The orthodox theory has had a long history and has been incorporated into many texts and popular treatises. Sir A. Keith, primarily an anatomist, produced a plausible explanation of how arm-swinging (brachiating) apes could have evolved into upright, bipedal hominids. Keith developed his thesis in a series of publications beginning in 1891. He argued that an apprenticeship of brachiating erectness, such as exhibited by modern anthropoids who habitually hang and progress by their arms, with an essentially erect trunk, was an evolutionary prelude to bipedal, terrestrial hominid erectness. Those accepting Keith's viewpoint, or something closely akin to it, claim the dryopithecines as the supposed common ancestral stock of hominids and pongids. William King Gregory contributed much to the development and popularity of this theory.

Anatomical Evidence. Serological and paleontological evidence suggests that a very early separation of the hominid line is unlikely. Our ancestors were probably behaviorally similar to pongids until the late Miocene or very early Pliocene; however, the approximate time of divergence of the hominid from the pongid line is currently a matter of major controversy. The Sarich and Wilson immunological viewpoint suggests a divergence on the order of 5 million to 8 million years ago.

Anatomical evidence for a brachiating behavioral stage among hominid precursors lies primarily in the trunk and arms of living species. Such traits as arm length, breadth of the trunk, and shortness of the lumbar region show similarities in humans and apes. More detailed examination shows that the similarity extends to the sternum (breast bone), clavicular length (which keeps the shoulders off to the side), and many details of the bones, joints, and muscles. Hominids and pongids share major structural features of the trunk and motions making possible such actions as stretching to the side and hanging comfortably by the arms. The structure of our trunk and arms is remarkably apelike; one way of illustrating this is the ease with which one can use a human anatomical atlas to dissect a chimpanzee arm.

A Knuckle- or Fist-Walking Stage. Some anthropologists have recently modified the brachiating theory of hominid origins to include an intermediate stage of either **knuckle-walking,** that is, walking on the knuckles as do chimpanzees and gorillas (Figure 22-1) or **fist-walking,** that is walking on the closed fist as orangutans usually do (Figure 22-2). Washburn, or example, envisions the following sequence of behavioral stages: quadruped (monkey)—knuckle-walker (modern pongids)—biped (modern hominids). The possibility that hominids passed through a knuckle-walking stage stems from the fact that brachiation is an infrequent behavior among our closest pongid relatives, the chimpanzee and gorilla. Recognizing this, Tuttle tried to ascertain if hominids were knuckle-walkers before becoming bipeds. Tuttle contends that there are no features in the hominid hand bones indicating a knuckle-walking stage.

Tuttle feels that the hominid upper limbs indicate that our ancestors engaged in some form of suspensory posturing. He argues that they assumed a bipedal posture soon after coming to the ground without passing through a knuckle-walking stage. Tuttle feels that the initial divergence between hominids and pongids resulted from a differential use of the hind limbs such that the center of gravity shifted more toward the pelvis in hominid ancestors. In contrast, pongid ancestors frequently used the forelimbs in foraging and locomotion; their center of gravity remained in, or perhaps moved higher in, the chest. When the respective populations shifted to the terrestrial habitat, pongids became semierect knuckle-walkers, and hominids became bipeds.

Another advocate of an intermediate stage preceding bipedalism is Mary Marzke, who suggests that hominid ancestors passed through a fist-walking rather than a knuckle-walking stage. She argues that certain traits of the human hand indicate that it was specialized for supporting the body on the back of the flexed (curled) fingers before bipedalism became the rule. She suggests that fist-walking is more advantageous for incipient tool-carriers than knuckle-walking. In fist-walking the fingers better enclose objects and bring them within the range of the thumb, which can then secure the grip. Perhaps our ancestors were more specialized fist-walkers than modern fist-walking orangutans. As does Washburn, she affirms the fact that our ancestors first went through a suspensory locomotor stage.

Washburn discounts Tuttle's argument against a knuckle-walking stage prior to erect bipedalism. The difficulty of deciding the argument rests with the fact that some anatomical adaptations to knuckle-walking occur in the ligaments. These are not likely to be determined from fossil materials.

In sum, it is still too early to say with certainty whether hominid ancestors went through a fist-walking or knuckle-walking stage, if either, before becoming bipedal.

The terms used to label a behavioral, locomotor stage do not represent absolute, exclusivistic categories. Animals obviously do many other things than just move quadrupedally or brachiate. For example, the knuckle-walking chimpanzee climbs, swings by its arms beneath branches (brachiates), and walks bipedally; ideally, its behavior would be characterized by a profile of all these activities. Since there are no carefully delineated natural boundaries, it is unreasonable to expect that every fossil will fit into a "locomotor stage." Furthermore, contemporary forms have evolved and there is little reason to believe that actual ancestors were identical with any living relatives. If both fossil skeletons and data on living forms were available, there would be a greatly reduced chance of reconstruction error, but

Figure 22-1. A male gorilla with right hand in knuckle-walking position.

Orangutan

Chimpanzee

Figure 22-2. Fist-walking in a young orangutan compared with knuckle-walking in a young chimpanzee.

there are no living prebrachiators with an anatomy comparable, for example, to the dryopithecines.

Immunological Time Scale

The rather recent discovery of a surprisingly close genetic relationship between humans and African apes (identical DNA sequence of 99%) has stimulated interest in molecular evolution. Although humans and apes are morphologically and behaviorally rather distinct in a number of critical factors, they are genetically extraordinarily close.

It is crucially important in the study of hominid evolution that the correct phylogenetic relationship of extant and extinct members of the Hominoidea be known. Molecular evidence from immunological and protein amino acid sequence data and from DNA hybridization data has shown that *Pan* and *Gorilla* are more closely related to *Homo* than to *Pongo* and *Hylobates*. (In fact, so close is the relationship between the gorilla and chimpanzee that many now argue for their inclusion in the same genus, *Pan*). There is a hint from these data that *Homo* and *Pan* may have separated from one another only after the divergence of *Gorilla*.

Recently Sarich and Wilson raised serious questions as to the time of the separation of hominids and pongids. They originally suggested a time of divergence of approximately 4 million to 5 million years ago as most consistent with their analytical method termed the immunological approach. They have now pushed this back to 8 million to 10 million years. The immunological date (or the "protein clock") provides a figure appreciably different from some interpretations of the paleontological record.

Wilson et al. (1977: 632) state:

> The molecular clock came as a surprise and is having a major impact on evolutionary biology. It allows the properties of organisms, even those with a poor fossil record, to be viewed easily from a time perspective. That is, rate of evolutionary change can be calculated whether the properties are chromosomal, morphological, or behavioral. By comparing these various rates, one can identify important evolutionary parameters at different levels of organization. It is on this basis that regulatory evolution is postulated as being at the basis of morphological evolution.

The immunochemical approach permits precise measurements with very small amounts of antigen, the substance produced when one animal is injected with serum from another animal. It has long been known that humans and other animals generally produce antibodies against foreign substances entering the bloodstream. If human serum is injected into a rabbit, the rabbit will accumulate the antihuman antibodies to counteract the foreign "invader." Repeated injections strengthen the reaction. Some blood may then be drawn from the rabbit and the serum used to test the serum of other animals. Because the test serum is antihuman, that is, reacts against human serum, the closer an animal is to us, the stronger the anti reaction will be.

In many tests Sarich and Wilson injected rabbits with human albumin (a blood protein) and tested the antihuman antibody obtained against a wide variety of other primates. The albumin results were expressed in terms of "immunological distance" (ID) units. Sarich and Wilson also studied the immunological distances between primates and nonprimates. By making the assumption that albumin has evolved at a constant rate in all lineages, an assumption that some reject, and that this rate can be measured, they calculated the times of divergence of various lineages. In contrast with the fossil record, Sarich and Wilson originally estimated that hominids, chimpanzees, and gorillas separated on the order of 4 million years ago, orangutans 7 million years ago, and gibbons 10 million years ago. If one accepts their data, hominid evolution is a recent event.

According to the immunological approach the numerous branches of the Miocene dryopithecines left a single surviving lineage owing its unique evolutionary success to the development of brachiation. Modern hominids and pongids, as products of the adaptive radiation following this development, show similarities in basic pattern but differences in detail. The unity of the Hominoidea is based on the relatively short time period during which a major adaptation evolved. Diversity between members is based on the relatively long time during which the lines independently evolved. The immunological approach places our ancestors as functionally monkeys until 10 million to 15 million years ago and brachiating apes until about 6 million years ago. Six million years ago a terrestrial adaptation began; Sarich feels that knuckle-walking would be a perfect transitional stage from full brachiation to bipedalism.

Human proteins differ from those of African apes (chimpanzees and gorillas) by an average of 0.8 percent in amino acid sequence (King and Wilson, 1975), and the unique sequences of human DNA differ from those of African apes by about 1.1 percent (King and Wilson, 1975). Sarich and Wilson (1967a, b) have suggested that if protein and nucleic acids evolved at a measurable rate in higher primates, the divergence time of the hominid-pongid line would then be on the order of 5 million years ago. They, along with some others, have suggested that the fossil record of human evolution is consistent with a hominid-pongid split anywhere between 4 million and 30 million years ago (Wilson et al., 1977).

The evolutionary clock hypothesis is reviewed in Wilson et al. (1977) and we will turn to that review. The authors state that published evidence (as of the publication date of their article) of indisputable hominids goes back only 3.1 million years. They do not include the new data from Laetoli, Baringo, and other possible sites dating prior to that time. They question the possibility that protochimpanzees and protogorillas may have lived 20 million years ago (that is, as the dryopithecines). "The hard fossil evidence is, therefore, easily reconciled with the divergence time of five million years between the human and African ape lineages" (Wilson et al., 1977:588).

Wilson et al. note the difficulty of assessing the phylogenetic relationship between hominoid fossils older than 5 million years. Noting the controversy revolving about the taxonomic position of *Ramapithecus,* the authors suggest that it may be unwise to tout *Ramapithecus* as a 14 million-year-old hominid or as the common ancestral lineage for African apes and humans. "Experiences like these serve as a reminder that while it is relatively easy for paleontologists to date fossils, it is far harder for them to date divergence events objectively and reliably, especially when the fossil record is as sparse as that for primates older than five million years" (Wilson et al., 1977:589).

The dating that the immunological scheme suggests was once unacceptable to paleontologists. However, there is growing acceptance of the time dimension suggested by this approach. Theories based on immunological and fossil evidence both agree that higher primates arose from an original insectivorous stock, but they differ as to the time of divergence of the hominid and pongid lines. The immunological adherents suggest that these lines diverged 8 million to 10 million years ago; the scenario based on the fossil record suggests that they diverged as early as 20 million years ago (Figure 22-3).

Aquatic Stage Suggestion

This final suggestion is not to be taken as a serious possibility. This idea suggests that the original terrestrial hominid went through a long aquatic stage before becoming a carnivorous biped. Our ancestors are envisioned as moving to the tropical seashores in search of food. There they found shellfish and other creatures in comparative abundance; the food supply was richer and more attractive than that on the open plains. This form first groped around the rock pools and shallow water; gradually it began to swim to greater depths and dive for food. During this process it supposedly lost its hair as did other mammals that returned to the sea. Only the head, protruding above the surface, retained a hairy coat to protect it from the sun. When their tools (originally developed for cracking open shells) became sufficiently advanced, our ancestors left the seashore and ventured into the open plains.

This idea supposedly explains why we are so nimble in water and why our closest relatives, the great apes, quickly drown. The aquatic idea explains that hair on our back points diagonally backward and inward toward the spine, following the direction of the flow of water over a swimming body. Our layer of subcutaneous fat is supposedly a compensatory insulating device.

A recent very delightful updating of this idea is found in Elaine Morgan's book *The Descent of Women* (1972). She argues that we were aquatic during the Pliocene as the seas provided us refuge from carnivorous predators. What is the evidence in support of this suggestion? Besides what has been mentioned here, which could be better explained by alternate means anyway, there is no evidence of importance to substantiate this idea. Unless some spectacular evidence is uncovered, the aquatic idea is merely an oddity.

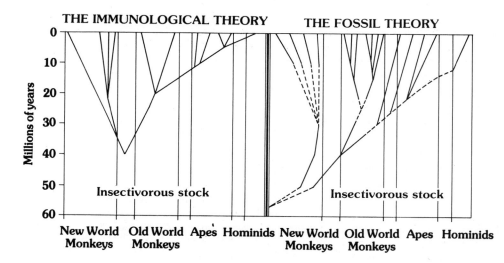

Figure 22-3. A comparison of two theories of the course of higher primate evolution based on different data sources.

The various suggestions mentioned are the major alternative views of hominid evolutionary history. The orthodox viewpoint is that we evolved from a pongid ancestry; few support the contention that hominids are derived from nonanthropoid apes. The brachiating theory is being questioned and modified and it may eventually include a prebipedal stage of fist-walking or knuckle-walking. While some paleontologists support a Miocene divergence of the hominid-pongid line, Sarich and Wilson support a divergence on the order of 5 million years ago. With the growing rejection of hominid status for *Ramapithecus,* the time scale of the "protein clock" is gaining wider acceptance.

Bibliography

Avis, V. 1962. Brachiation: the crucial issue of man's ancestry. *Southwest Journal of Anthropology* 18:119.

Buettner-Janusch, J. 1966. *Origins of man.* New York: Wiley.

Cartmill, M. 1972. Arboreal adaptations and the origins of the order Primates. In *The functional and evolutionary biology of primates,* edited by R. Tuttle, pp. 97-123. Chicago: Aldine-Atherton.

Dunn, F. 1966. Patterns of parasitism in primates. *Folia Primatologica* 4:329.

Erikson, G. 1963. Brachiation in New World monkeys and in anthropoid apes. *Symposium of the Zoological Society of London* 10:135.

Fitch, W. 1976. Molecular evolutionary clocks. In *Molecular evolution,* edited by F. Ayala, pp. 160-78. Sunderlands, Mass.: Sinauer Associates.

Goodman, M. 1963. Man's place in the phylogeny of the primates as reflected in serum proteins. In *Classification and human evolution,* edited by S. Washburn, pp. 204-35. New York: Viking Fund Publications.

Goodman, M., Tashian, R., and Tashian, J., eds. 1976. *Molecular anthropology: genes and proteins in the evolutionary ascent of the primates.* New York: Plenum.

Gregory, W. 1922. *The origin and evolution of human dentition.* Baltimore: Williams & Wilkins.

————. 1927a. How near is the relationship of man to the chimpanzee-gorilla stock? *Quarterly Review of Biology* 2:549.

————. 1927b. The origin of man from the anthropoid stem—when and where? *Proceedings of the American Philosophical Society* 66:439.

————. 1928. Were the ancestors of man primitive brachiators? *Proceedings of the American Philosophical Society* 67:129.

Haeckel, E. 1869. *The evolution of man.* New York: Appleton.

Hubrecht, A. 1897. *The descent of the primates.* New York: Scribner.

Huxley, T. 1863. *Evidence as to man's place in nature.* London: Williams & Norgate.

Jones, F. 1923. *The ancestry of man.* Brisbane: Gillies.

————. 1929. *Man's place among the mammals.* New York: Longmans, Green.

Jukes, T., and Holmquist, R. 1972. Evolutionary clock: nonconstancy of rate in different species. *Science* 177:530.

Keith, A. 1925. *The antiquity of man,* 2nd ed. London: Williams & Norgate.

Klinger, H., Hammerton, H., Nuston, D., and Lange, E. 1963. The chromosomes of the Hominoidea. In *Classification and human evolution,* edited by S. Washburn, pp. 235-42. New York: Viking Fund Publications.

Kohne, D. 1970. Evolution of higher organism DNA. *Quarterly Review of Biophysics* 3:327.

Lewis, O. 1972. Osteological features characterizing the wrist of monkeys and apes, with a reconsideration of this region in *Dryopithecus* (Proconsul) *africanus. American Journal of Physical Anthropology* 36:45.

Marzke, M. 1971. Origin of the human hand. *American Journal of Physical Anthropology* 34:61.

Morgan, E. 1972. *The descent of women.* New York: Stein & Day.

Morris, D. 1967. *The naked ape, a zoologist's study of the human animal.* New York: McGraw-Hill.

Nei, M. 1975. *Molecular population genetics and evolution.* New York: American Elsevier.

Oxnard, C. 1969. Evolution of the human shoulder: some possible pathways. *American Journal of Physical Anthropology* 30:319.

Pilbeam, D. 1972. *The ascent of man.* New York: Macmillan.

Poirier, F. 1981. *Fossil evidence: the human evolutionary journey.* St. Louis: Mosby.

Read, D., and Lestrel, P. 1970. Hominid phylogeny and immunology: a critical appraisal. *Science* 168:578.

Sarich, V. 1971. A molecular approach to the question of human origins. In *Background for man,* edited by P. Dolhinow and V. Sarich, pp. 60-81. Boston: Little, Brown.

——————. 1972. Hominid origins revised. In *Climbing man's family tree,* edited by T. McCown and K. Kennedy, pp. 450-60. Englewood Cliffs, N.J.: Prentice-Hall.

Sarich, V., and Wilson, A. 1967. An immunological time scale for hominid evolution. *Science* 158:1200.

Schultz, A. 1936. Characters common to higher primates and characters specific for man. *Quarterly Review of Biology* 11:259.

Simons, E. 1972. *Primate evolution: an introduction to man's place in nature.* New York: Macmillan.

Straus, W. 1949. The riddle of man's ancestry. *Quarterly Review of Biology* 24:200. Reprinted in *Ideas on human evolution—selected essays,* edited by W. Howells, 1967, pp. 69-105. New York: Atheneum.

Tuttle, R. 1969. Knuckle-walking and the problem of human origins. *Science* 166:953.

Uzell, T., and Pilbeam, D. 1971. Phyletic divergence dates of hominid origins. *Science* 166:953.

Washburn, S. 1971. The study of human evolution. In *Background for man,* edited by P. Dolhinow and V. Sarich, pp. 82-117. Boston: Little, Brown.

Chapter 23

Continuing Problems and Biological Relics

We have embarked on a long journey over time to recount an exciting tale of the attainment of our present condition. We began approximately 60 million years ago during the Paleocene, when hominids were an unknown among the primitive mammalian stock. During the Oligocene, as witnessed in the Egyptian Fayum, there are signs of the florescene of the pongid stock. Some argue that, during the Miocene, hominids were still a part of a general hominoid stock known as dryopithecines. Still others argue that hominids and pongids diverged only 5 million to 8 million years ago.

Questions on Hominid Evolution

My scheme was presented with minimal complication; however, the picture of hominid evolution is not simple. It is an abstract piece, at times a collage. The hominid evolutionary line becomes blurred in a myriad of forms, many with distinctive claims to fame. The hominid evolutionary line, or lines, resembles a three-dimensional model for which we do not presently have all the pieces, and probably never will. The present scheme has not been without its opponents, with various individuals championing different forms and theories. Some ideas are plausible, others can be forthrightly rejected. Some may argue that since questions can be raised about parts of the scheme, the scheme itself should be summarily discarded. This is an overreaction. If part of the scheme is wrong, the total scheme is not necessarily invalid. Current controversies, rather than negate the fact that hominid evolutionary history is closely related to that of the other primates, only strengthen it. The schemes currently presented are not 100 percent correct, but neither are they 100 percent wrong.

Between 4 million and 1 million years ago there is an expanding record of hominid evolution in Africa and in Eurasia. These hominids were bipeds with reduced canines and their brains, although small, were somewhat larger relative to their body size. After approximately 2 million years, the record stands in sharp contrast to preceding times; the archaeological record is now a major source of evidence regarding development and adaptation and the fossil record of at least one hominid line shows a clear trend of brain expansion. Lower Pleistocene hominids are succeeded by the Middle Pleistocene *Homo erectus* group and finally by members of our own species, *H. sapiens.*

Major Unanswered Questions. The major unanswered questions are: (1) What is the date of the hominid-pongid split?[1] (2) What is the true nature of Lower Pleistocene hominid evolution? (3) When and where did modern *H. sapiens sapiens* appear? These questions will be answered; the finds recovered in the last 10 years exceed those made in the last 100 years. Possibly finds made next year may exceed those of the last 10.

Dates may change and schemes be altered, but the basic fact remains—we are and were of the primates; their evolutionary development and ours are inextricably joined. Are we simply another primate, slightly bigger than most, lacking a tail, living, in contrast to our monkey cousins, outside nature's jungles in concrete jungles built by human hands? Or, are there major differences? We are primates and share many aspects of our behavioral and social repertoires with our relatives. However, we are also different. We are the products of a unique feedback between culture and biology (Figure 23-1). The feedback is manifested in anatomical, social, or technological traits usually assumed basic to hominids, that is, large brains, symbolic speech, bipedalism, consistent tool use and modification of tools with other tools, use of fire, and life within large complex social groups.

Appearance of Major Hominid Traits. When did those traits considered so important in hominid evolution first appear? For some traits such as speech there is no answer in the early fossil record, save for educated speculation. Hints as to brain size and bipedalism are fossilized, at least since the Lower Pleistocene. Other traits such as tool use and manufacture, use of fire, evidence of big-game hunting, and larger, complex social groups can also be identified in the fossil record.

Lower Pleistocene hominids present evidence of an increasing brain size, bipedalism, and somewhat complex social groups. However, we can do little but suggest the possibility of language, report no evidence of fire, and assume they were, to some degree, hunting creatures. By the Middle Pleistocene and *H. erectus,* we see increasing brain size, use of fire, tools, and shelters, evidence of big-game hunting, and the likelihood of complex social groups. There is still no evidence of language, but it is possible, given the economic (hunting) situation of these hominids. With early *H. sapiens,* and after, we see further increase in brain size, more complex hunting practices, more efficient tool use, continual use of fire, and large complex social groups. Again, language would be adaptive.

In addition to these still unanswered and partially answered questions, there exist a number of still-to-be-filled gaps.

---

[1]It should now be clear that the term "hominid" has had different meanings to different interpreters of the fossil record and that its meaning shifts according to the time period in which the fossil form lived. The very earliest forms (i.e., *Propliopithecus* and *Ramapithecus*) are (were) given hominid status by some paleontologists by virtue of their dental traits (such as parabolic arch, short face, bicuspid premolars, nonprojecting canines). Later forms, such as *Australopithecus* and *Homo,* are considered hominids on the basis of their overall morphology. In these forms, however, emphasis is placed on locomotor adaptations (i.e., evidence for bipedalism or incipient bipedalism), cranial capacity, and dental and facial structure. To the biological traits, we often add that these are culture-bearing, tool-using, and tool-manufacturing animals. However, no one claims that on this basis they are hominids or should be considered as such. One of the factors that clearly separates human from nonhuman primates is the possession of a symbolic means of communication, language. (This statement may have to be altered somewhat in light of claims that some of the fossil hominids, such as Neanderthals, lacked the ability for more than rudimentary speech. However, more evidence is needed before this view can become credible.)

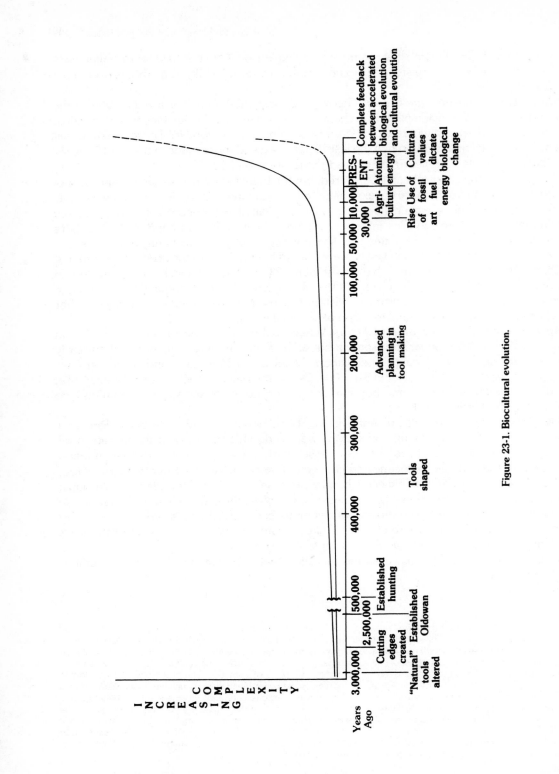

Figure 23-1. Biocultural evolution.

1. Late Miocene hominoid fossils are virtually unknown between 4 million and 8 million years ago, a time when species of *Australopithecus* first appear. Research in several areas, for example, Libya, Kenya, Tanzania, Ethiopia, Iran, Pakistan, India, Burma, and China, may fill this gap.
2. There is a paltry record of pongid evolution, especially of African pongids. One way of resolving the issue of the hominid-pongid split would be to fill this gap. Investigation should proceed in west and central Africa, Burma, Indochina, and China.
3. During the late Pliocene, by 2 million years ago or more, at least two species of hominids appear to coexist in Africa. Focusing on strata dated to 2 million to 3 million years in such areas as Kenya, Tanzania, and Ethiopia may expand our understanding of the evolutionary processes.
4. The Middle Pleistocene presents a challenge of trying to understand the nature of the biocultural feedback as expressed among *H. erectus* and *H. sapiens*.
5. The time period from 120,000 years ago to the first appearance of modern *H. sapiens* presents the problem of trying to determine whether the evolutionary change from more archaic to modern-looking hominids was gradual or abrupt, widespread or localized. The many determinants of that transition are still poorly understood.

Tool Use and Big-Game Hunting

What initiated these trends? Much has been written in an attempt to relate tool use and manufacture and hunting behavior with a large brain size, bipedalism, symbolic communication, domestication of fire, and life in complex social groups. In a classic article published in 1960 entitled "Tools and Human Evolution," S. L. Washburn argues that the anatomical structure of modern *H. sapiens* results from changes in natural selection connected with the tool-using way of life. Washburn suggests that use of tools, hunting, use of fire, and increasing brain size developed together to form the genus *Homo*. Then the brain evolved under pressures of a more complex social life. Washburn argues there was a circular evolutionary system in which the hand-eye coordination needed for effective tool use selected for a larger brain, especially the cortex. A larger brain allowed more effective tool use, which selected for a larger brain, and so on. Following Darwin, Washburn suggests that tool use led to effective bipedalism. Even limited bipedalism freed the hands from locomotor behavior so they could do other things. Hand-carried objects conveyed an advantage that led to more and more efficient bipedalism and more efficient tool use. (Doubts have been raised about parts of this scheme, especially the link between tool use and canine reduction.)

Big-game hunting has been of utmost importance to hominid evolution. *H. erectus* and its successors until about 6,000 years ago were primarily big-game hunters. It has been argued that our intellect, emotions, and basic social life are evolutionary products of the success of the hunting adaptation. It is argued that the success of the hunting adaptation dominated the course of human evolution for hundreds of thousands of years. Agriculture only began to replace hunting as an economically feasible pursuit about 8,000 years ago or somewhat earlier. The common factors dominating our evolutionary history and producing anatomically modern *H. sapiens* were preagricultural; they occurred during the hunting stage of hominid evolution. More effective tool use, selection for developing a more complex communication system, more efficient bipedalism, beginnings of movement over large ranges (compared to other primates), cooperation, and food sharing may all be related to big-game hunting. According to Washburn and Lancaster (1968), the agricultural revolution, continuing into the industrial and scientific revolutions, only now frees us from conditions characteristic of 99 percent of our evolutionary history. Our biology as a species was created during the hunting apprenticeship; asserting the biological unity of humanity affirms the importance of the hunting way of life.

It is worthwhile to mention something about the evolution of hunting behavior as this can be reconstructed from current evidence among nonhuman primates (for details of such hunting behavior see Chapters 11 and 12). The following information is drawn primarily from Harding (1975) and Suzuki (1975). As Harding notes, the nonhuman primate data support observations among human groups which show that meat eating is something more than simply a way of obtaining dietary protein because meat is a high-priority item no matter what portion it composes of the total diet (see Woodburn, 1968).

At least two nonhuman primates are known to include various portions of meat protein in their diet, the chimpanzee (Teleki, 1973; van Lawick-Goodall, 1967, 1968, 1971) and some baboon troops (Altmann and Altmann, 1970; Dart, 1963; DeVore and Washburn, 1963; Harding, 1975; Marais, 1939; Strum, 1975). This practice of catching and consuming small animals is done without any particular anatomical specializations. Nonhuman primates possess the brains for cooperative hunting, the communicative matrix to allow for group hunting (as among chimpanzees), the locomotor skills suitable for catching small prey, teeth capable of preparing meat protein, and a digestive system capable of receiving the masticated meat.

Harding notes that while it is possible to use nonhuman primate data to construct models for the evolution of human hunting behavior, these models are speculative. "The real importance of this information lies elsewhere; that is, the demonstration that at least two species of nonhuman primates, specifically the two species most often used as hominid surrogates in theories of human evolution, have a lively interest in meat eating and an ability to acquire substantial amounts of meat blurs the line dividing human and nonhuman primate behavior. Because it does so, it is less likely that predatory behavior was a major shaping force in human evolution . . ." (Harding, 1975:255-56). This statement is, of course, contrary to that of Washburn and Lancaster and of such popular writers as Robert Ardrey and Desmond Morris. Harding suggests that the characteristic human diet of a mixture of meat protein and vegetable matter is probably a continuation of an ancient primate diet.

Suzuki (1975) notes that there are three factors considered fundamental for the human pattern of hunting on a large scale: (1) the ability for long distance locomotion, (2) a high level of social relationships within the group and a division of labor, and (3) a high level of technical skills such as the making and using of tools. Chimpanzees today have the first two skills and also the ability to produce certain types of implements. Chimpanzees do share food (e.g., hunted meat) and have a flexible social organization and large-sized groups; furthermore they can and do travel long distances to exploit their habitat. As Suzuki sees it, the origins of human hunting behavior are related to a developing mental organization, which preceded an erect bipedal posture. The second stage required the release of the hands, and was one of the forces leading to the evolution of bipedalism, a larger brain, and consistent tool use.

Biological Relics

David Hamburg (1963), a psychiatrist, argues that although most of us no longer live as hunters, we are still physically (and emotionally) hunter-gatherers. The point has been made that we are biologically equipped for one way of life, hunting, but live in another. Is there some

Table 23-1. Review of the Pleistocene: Glacial Periods, Cultural Stages, and Selected Fossil Hominids

Geological Stage	Cultural Stage	Hominid Grade	Fossil Examples
Upper Pleistocene			
Recent 10.000 years ago	Upper Paleolithic	*Homo sapiens sapiens*	Cro-Magnon
Würm 70,000 years ago	Mousterian	*H. sapiens neander-thalensis*	Neanderthals
Middle Pleistocene			
Riss-Würm interglacial (3rd interglacial forms)	Acheulian	*H. sapiens*	Fontéchevade Ehringsdorf Saccopastore? Quinzano
Mindel-Riss interglacial (Second interglacial forms)	Acheulian	*H. sapiens steinheimensis swanscombensis*	Steinheim Swanscombe
Mindel 300,000 years ago	Acheulian	*H. erectus*	North Africa Arago Torralba-Ambrona Terra Amata
Günz 500,000+ years ago	Early Acheulian	*H. erectus*	Chou Kou Tien Trinil Heidelberg Vértesszöllös Olduvai Přezletice
Lower Pleistocene			
Villafranchian	Oldowan	*Australopithecus Homo*	Olduvai Omo Lake Turkana Afar Triangle, Ethiopia Laetoli

link between an emotional reaction such as aggression, which is most useful to a hunter, and some killing ailments of modern society, for example, heart disease? Strong emotions mobilize cholesterol. If cholesterol plays a role in heart disease, if our way of life no longer allows an efficient release of pent-up cholesterol, and if high levels of cholesterol are bad, then the point is made: modern *H. sapiens* is not equipped for modern life but is emotionally still in the Stone Age. (This is the biological correlate to the statement that we are technologically on the moon but culturally and socially still on earth.) Hunters have little problem dissipating cholesterol that they release during the hunting process. Adrenalin accumulation is also a problem;

adrenalin is increased during states of high tension. The rise in adrenalin increases blood flow to the heart, lungs, and central nervous system, but decreases the flow to the abdominal organs. This is advantageous to the hunter who has the chance to dissipate the effects of increased adrenalin levels during stalking, chasing, and killing the prey. However, in a modern society that frowns on violent outbursts, increased adrenalin and blood flow can have dire effects. We retain physiological adaptations making us effective hunters, but we have lost a major safety valve (the actual hunting behavior and its concomitants) that allows dissipation of the increased flow of cholesterol and fatty acids. Although hard physical labor helps dissipate increased adrenalin, frustrating desk jobs do not seem to do so.

Meaning of the Terms *Homo* and Hominid

From the standpoint of understanding human evolution, few points are more crucial than understanding the mechanisms leading to the appearance of the first hominids and to members of our genus, *Homo*. Nevertheless, few issues have raised more controversy than determining these points in our evolutionary history. To use a phrase of the late Albert Einstein, " . . . this huge world stands before us like a great eternal riddle."

As noted, there are many reasons for disagreement as to when, how, and why hominids diverged from the common pongid-hominid stock and as to when, how, and why the genus *Homo* appeared. Disregarding fossil remains for a moment, one useful means for understanding problems of interpretation is to refer to a "thought experiment" designed by the physicist John Archibald Wheeler. Reworking his experiment into terms to fit our situation, imagine, as the paleoanthropologist must do, that an evolutionary world exists whose major components can be comprehended. Yet, the development of and the arrangement of forms in that evolutionary world relate to the kinds of questions the scientist raises about that world. If the scientist, or scientists, ask different kinds of questions, the order of that world may then change. If the scientist performs different kinds of experiments a different world of realities may emerge. Since the nature of the evolutionary world does not usually reveal itself in anything more than bits and pieces, and since it does not reveal itself until it emerges from the questions the scientist asks, no conceptual scheme is the correct scheme until the correct questions are raised. We must come to terms with the fact that disagreement will, of necessity, always appear when interpreting the fossil record.

Let us now turn to the point of our concern, recognizing the first hominids and the first members of the genus *Homo*. What are the decisive traits by which a hominid, and ultimately the genus *Homo*, are to be recognized?

Birds and kangaroos are bipeds of a sort, whales and dolphins have relatively large brains, and some nonhuman primates exhibit behaviors designated as "protocultural" by some anthropologists. Some nonhuman primates and other animals use tools. However, few include many of these in the direct hominid line. Leslie White stated that the symbol is the universe of humanity, yet some have argued that chimpanzees and gorillas have at least the rudimentary ability to symbolize. Among insects, the dance of the honeybee can communicate such things as direction, distance, and quantity of food. Even such abstract emotions as love can be possibly identified among nonhumans. Without giving further examples, it should be clear that it is often difficult, if not impossible, to say which traits are purely human and which are not. Conversely, in everyday life, even the nonscientist can distinguish between human and nonhuman animals. The reason for this is simple—we distinguish between different forms on the basis of a combination of several traits.

It is highly unlikely that one trait can be used to distinguish the first appearance of hominids or of the genus *Homo*. Instead, we must recognize that several distinctive traits, when combined, will give an independent but mutual testimony to hominid and *Homo* status. Three traits seem to be germane to all our basic concepts of defining ourselves: bipedalism, a large brain, and a cultural way of life. Yet, except for bipedalism, these traits did not characterize the first hominids. Malinowski noted that humans are the only animals that do not lead a hand-to-mouth existence; they are totally dependent on their culture for all biological and psychological needs. This argument, however, is culture-centric and cannot be shown to be true in the human fossil record.

Bipedalism, a large brain, and culture all appear even in our stories and cartoons as indications of a human character. When we attempt to humanize animals we have them walk on two feet, give them a mental ability similar to our own, and bestow on them our own cultural attributes and motives. Babies are urged to locomote bipedally because nonhumans move on all fours. The recent controversy over the use of life-support machines has centered about the common belief that when the brain stops functioning, the individual no longer exists. The supposed absence of culture leads to such common folk tales as the "wild man of Borneo" or the so-called "wolf children."

Whatever theoretical or philosophical approach we take, if we ignore the three basic attributes of bipedalism, increasing brain size, and the appearance of a cultural life style, we ignore a construct that both consciously and unconsciously permeates our daily activities and attitudes. However, these criteria cannot be forced into a strict interpretative framework; they exhibit a wide range of variability. For example, even in shows such as Star Trek, we can accept aliens with pointed ears, green blood, and a host of other strange traits as equal to us so long as they exhibit bipedalism, culture, and advanced intellectual abilities.[2]

There are many unanswered questions concerning the primate fossil record. With luck and much hard work, the major controversies as to primate evolution may be solved. We badly need a fuller fossil sample, representing both sexes and various ages, from certain time spans and geographical areas.

A second set of questions asks about the appearance of hominid traits such as bipedalism, speech, tool use, and an increasing brain size. Unfortunately, the fossil record is not always helpful; we do not know when fully articulate speech appeared. The fossil record suggests a relationship between big-game hunting and more complex social groups, increased brain size, increased tool use, greater social coordination (and perhaps control), manipulation of fire, and increased pressures for efficient bipedalism.

Some biologists and psychiatrists working in the field of stress biology argue that emotionally and physically we remain hunters, regardless of our cultural pursuits. It is intriguing to try to relate modern ailments, like heart disease, to stresses linked to our failure to adjust to the decline of hunting and the rise of agriculture. However, the evidence is not conclusive.

---

[2]The discussion of what the terms "hominid" and "*Homo*" signify was originally developed by a student, Mr. Nigel Brush, in one of my seminars. The present discussion was formulated by myself and used with Mr. Brush's permission.

Bibliography

Altmann, S., and Altmann, J. 1970. *Baboon ecology.* Basel: Karger.

Dart, R. 1963. Carnivorous propensities of baboons. *Symposium of the Zoological Society of London* 10:49-56.

DeVore, I., and Washburn, S. 1963. Baboon ecology and human evolution. In *African ecology and human evolution,* edited by F. Howell and F. Bourliere, pp. 335-67. Viking Fund Publications in Anthropology 36. New York: Wenner-Gren Foundation.

Freud, S. 1951. *Psychopathology of everyday life.* New York: New American Library.

Hallowell, A. 1961. The protocultural foundations of human adaptation. In *Social life of early man,* edited by S. Washburn, pp. 236-55. Chicago: Aldine.

Hamburg, D. 1963. Emotions in the perspective of human evolution. In *Expression of the emotions in man,* edited by P. Knapp, pp. 300-17. New York: International Universities Press.

Harding, R. 1975. Meat-eating and hunting in baboons. In *Socioecology and psychology of primates,* edited by R. Tuttle, pp. 245-58. The Hague: Mouton.

Hockett, C., and Ascher, R. 1964. The human revolution. *Current Anthropology* 5:135.

Holloway, R. 1967. Tools and teeth: some speculations regarding canine reduction. *American Anthropologist* 69:63.

Krantz, G. 1968. Brain size and hunting ability in earliest man. *Current Anthropology* 9:450.

_____. 1970. On brain size and behavior in early man. *Current Anthropology* 11:176.

Laughlin, W. 1968. Hunting: an integrating biobehavior system and its evolutionary importance. In *Man the hunter,* edited by R. Lee and I. DeVore, pp. 304-20. Chicago: Aldine.

Lieberman, P. 1975. *On the origins of language.* New York: Macmillan.

Marais, E. 1939. *My friends the baboons.* London: Methuen.

Selye, H. 1956. *The stress of life.* New York: McGraw-Hill.

Strum, S. 1975. Primate predation: interim report on the development of a tradition in a troop of olive baboons. *Science* 187:755-57.

Suzuki, A. 1975. The origin of hominid hunting: a primatological perspective. In *Socioecology and psychology of primates,* edited by R. Tuttle, pp. 259-78. The Hague: Mouton.

Teleki, G. 1973. The omnivorous chimpanzee. *Scientific American* 228:32-42.

van Lawick-Goodall, J. 1967. *My friends the wild chimpanzees.* Washington, D.C.: National Geographic Society.

_____. 1968. The behavior of free-living chimpanzees in the Gombe Stream Reserve. *Animal Behavior Monographs* 1:161-311.

_____. 1971. *In the shadow of man.* Boston: Houghton Mifflin.

Washburn, S. 1959. Speculations on the interrelations of the history of tools and biological evolution. *Human Biology* 31:21.

_____. 1960. Tools and human evolution. *Scientific American* 203:62-75.

_____. 1965. An ape's eye view of evolution. In *The origin of man* (Symposium transcript), edited by P. DeVore, pp. 89-96. New York: Wenner-Gren Foundation.

Washburn, S., and Lancaster, C. 1968. The evolution of hunting. In *Perspectives on human evolution,* edited by S. Washburn and P. Jay, pp. 213-30. New York: Holt, Rinehart and Winston.

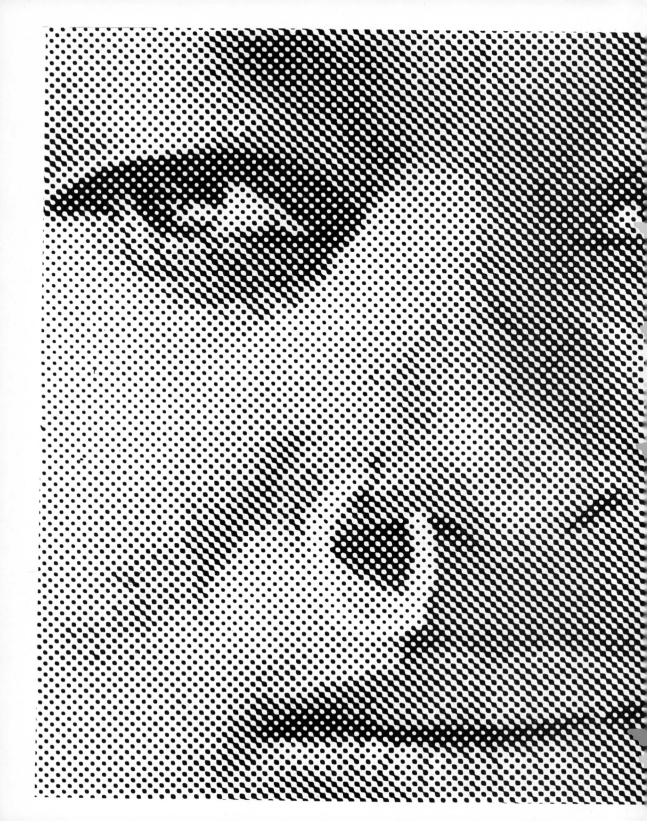

Part Five

Human Diversity

One day the master potter decided it
might be amusing to make men. So, he
scooped up some clay, molded it into a
man and put it into his kiln to bake.
However, while it was baking something
else attracted his attention, and he left it
in the kiln too long. When he took it out,
it had been blackened by the heat. Thus
was born the black man. Realizing his
mistake, the master potter fashioned
another man and tried again. This time
he took it out too soon, before it was
fully baked, and thus was born the white
man. Being a patient artisan, the master
potter tried again. This time he was
successful. There emerged from the kiln
the perfectly formed, golden founder of
the Chinese people.

A Chinese folk tale. From M. Klass and
H. Hellman. 1971. *The Kinds of
Mankind.* New York: J. P. Lippincott.

"UNDERSTANDING is a thirteen-letter
word — perhaps the length of the word
itself keeps us apart." (Poirier)

Chapter 24

Studies of Living Populations

One way of differentiating the interests of physical anthropologists is to distinguish between what can be termed evolutionary events and what can be termed evolutionary processes. George Gaylord Simpson has discussed this dichotomy and he separates historical studies of human evolution, based mostly on morphological information, from the study of evolutionary processes, that is, those phenomena causing evolution to occur. Evolutionary events are witnessed in the fossil record, whereas evolutionary processes such as mutation, drift, gene flow, and selection can be studied in living populations. This chapter introduces the reader to the study of evolutionary processes.

Humans as Research Subjects

Sanctions and taboos surrounding our own mating behavior effectively inhibit the required procedures for laboratory manipulation of humans. Even if this were not so, few would be interested in beginning an experiment that might not be concluded until long after the investigator's death. We are poor and impractical experimental animals for genetic studies; fortunately, however, we can obtain genetic information about ourselves without benefit of laboratory breeding stocks. By closely observing the effects of human mating, even outside the laboratory, we have added enormously to our knowledge about human genetics. Hospital records, genealogical records, and animal experimentation data have all contributed to a better understanding of human genetics.

Although information on human genetics is rapidly accumulating, much of it is concerned with genetic deviations, information that is of supreme importance to the physician but not so important for the physical anthropologist. Fortunately, most inborn metabolic errors are very rare. Few suffer from Wilson's disease, the inability to synthesize the proper quantity of a blood protein called ceruloplasmin, which contains copper. If ceruloplasmin is not formed, copper atoms, ingested as normal parts of food, are deposited in the liver and brain, among other organs, producing tissue degeneration. Few are afflicted by **phenylketonuria** (PKU), wherein the lack of an enzyme required for normal biochemical transformations within the body leads to excretion of large amounts of phenylpyruvic acid and severe mental deficiency. Each of these afflictions results from recessive alleles.

During the past 20 or 30 years, more attention has focused on the study of genetically based traits exhibited by a proportion of humans, normal or otherwise. However, our knowledge is still woefully inadequate. It is still difficult to design human chromosome maps, and attempts to demonstrate linkage between different genes have not been totally successful. Human genetic research is a very active field, however, and an understanding of our own complexities is rapidly increasing. Genetic engineering, that is, the ability to correct defects on the genes or chromosomes, is not simply a future dream; it is rapidly becoming a reality. The issues to be faced in the near future will be as much moral and philosophical as scientific.

The Mendelian Population

Living human populations offer a wide range of physical characteristics worthy of investigation. The focal point of an evolutionary study, the Mendelian population, is a spatial-temporal group of interbreeding individuals sharing a common gene pool, that is, sharing all the genes of all members of the population. Although the individual is indispensable to the evolutionary process as the carrier and transmitter of genetic matter and the source of all mutations, genetic changes within an individual are not looked on by the population geneticist as constituting evolution.

It is far easier to define a Mendelian population theoretically than to delimit it accurately from the totality of humanity. Our tendency to join other individuals and populations through, for example, trade, war, migration, and travel, has usually prevented genetic isolation of any human group for extended time periods. Human populations are not totally closed genetic systems; to varying degrees their gene pools are shared by individuals from other populations. Actual populations are thus less "pure" than those found in theoretical constructs.

The Deme. Theoretically, the concept of the Mendelian population may be extended to include the entire human species; all members of our species share in the common gene pool of *H. sapiens sapiens*. Modern *Homo* constitutes a population and can be considered the proper unit of genetic study, but only for the purpose of understanding the cohesive forces binding the total human species. Because the term "population" can refer to all of humanity, or to lesser constituent parts, the study of **demes** is often substituted. A deme is a relatively self-sufficient small endogamous group isolated from other such groups. Demes are the smallest basic population units studied by the population geneticist.

Obviously **panmixis (random mating)** does not occur within the total species of modern *Homo sapiens*. To the argument that populations are partially open breeding systems must be added the qualification that they are also partially closed. To the extent that one population's gene pool is closed to genes from another, they are considered genetically isolated from one another. The boundaries may be geographical or social and may be effective to varying degrees.

How to Identify the Breeding Population

An accurate definition of a human Mendelian population is complicated by the fact that one population segment in a social grouping may or may not serve as a biological breeding unit. One might mistake any American city as a Mendelian population, whereas the true structure of the city is a political unit subdivided into smaller subgroups. Some of these smaller subgroups may be distinct breeding units, but only careful preliminary demographic investigation of the structure and dynamics of a group will distinguish between social and political units and the true biological breeding units.

The population geneticist's first task before undertaking an analysis of the breeding population and the forces acting on it is to identify and describe the breeding unit. In small, isolated communities—on islands for example—this is a relatively simple matter, and this is one reason why population geneticists work with such groups. In these circumstances the social rules and regulations determining mating behavior (not simply marriage, for extramarital and premarital procreation also affect the gene pool) must be clearly understood. To infer the composition of a gene pool at any given time, one must first enumerate and describe the actual progenitors, that is, the parents in the population, for they constitute the breeding populations. The breeding population is always smaller than the total number of individuals actually living in the group. The breeding number cannot be obtained by census alone, for all individuals capable of breeding do not breed. Individuals that are incapable of contributing genes to the next generation because they have either not yet achieved reproductive maturity or are past reproductive age are not members of the actual breeding population. The breeding population can only be defined by documenting mating behavior and by eliciting reproductive records. This is difficult for many reasons, not the least of which is the fact that some societies (such as the Toda of South India) recognize sociological and not biological paternity.

After completing a demographic survey and defining the breeding population, genetic analysis is still in the future. The breeding population must be further defined. To determine the ideal population, that is, a population in which there are equal possibilities of genetic influences coming from any parent, with all parents unrelated, you must delete related individuals. Such individuals, to the extent they are related, do not reflect the size, composition, and heterozygosity of the ideal population. The actual number and type of unrelated gametes available to the next generation is less than the actual total number of (related and unrelated) present. Because of the presence of related individuals, the effective breeding size of any human population is generally smaller than its actual breeding size.

Population Structure and Dynamics

Vital Processes. To understand the dynamics of genetic evolution, it must be appreciated that every population has its own structure. The evolution of a population can be understood and studied only in terms of its structure and dynamics. This structure can be partially described in terms of distribution, size, and age and sex composition. A population's structure is determined by the vital processes of fertility, mortality, morbidity, and migration responsible for structural dissimilarities existing between populations at any given time and within a population through time. For example, the age composition of Americans of African descent in the cities is more youthful than that of Americans of European descent and, therefore, more conducive to high rates of increase through fertility. Likewise, the Amish population (descended from the seventeenth-century Mennonite Jacob Amen or Ammann) is characterized by a high fertility rate and consequent rapid growth. While the general U.S. population doubled, that of the Amish multiplied fivefold.

Changes in vital processes through time also account for historical changes in the population's structure. As a country undergoes rapid industrialization, population distribution is radically altered by migration from rural to urban centers. Migration is often accompanied by other changes in vital processes. Because urbanization intensifies certain environmental elements that are, or can be, unfavorable to fertility (such as the cost of raising children), fertility tends to drop in urbanized societies. The reduction of fertility in the United States since 1800 has been dramatic; the average number of children dropped from seven to slightly less than two per couple. Pronounced changes in the vital processes of a population markedly affect its structure and gene pool. However, genetic consequences on a gene pool may not be easily detectable or predictable.

Mechanisms of Evolution Within a Population

In Chapter 8 we noted that static populations are often eventually doomed to extinction and that variability within a population is some insurance against extinction. Populations in genetic equilibrium are populations that are not evolving. To understand how gene pools change we will discuss a number of factors that have been identified as a source of change: mutation, gene flow, natural selection, and genetic drift. Another process, that of nonrandom mating, is discussed in Chapter 26. Any circumstance that causes gene frequency changes is an important evolutionary factor.

Microevolution refers to changes in gene frequencies and patterns of distribution within a species. The causes of microevolution are departures from Hardy-Weinberg conditions (see p. 426). With such departures, population genetics shifts its focus from static to dynamic processes. These departures and their resultant evolutionary forces are listed in Table 24-1.

Mutation. A mutation is the spontaneous appearance of a new gene expression, that is, any change in the chemical organization of a gene or structural or chromosomal changes (Chapter 7). Because the stimuli activating the chemical changes in genes act randomly, mutations are considered to occur randomly (Table 24-2). Most mutations are harmful to the organism. However, mutation, whatever the cause, is the only means whereby genetic material can be altered.

Gene Flow. Gene flow is a process whereby genes of one gene pool or population of a species are introduced into another population (Table 24-3). The resulting process of hybridization changes the frequency of genes already existent within local populations of the species. Hybridization does not produce new genes, a process reserved to mutations. Nevertheless, gene flow can have significant effects on the genetic composition of a population.

Gene flow is expressed as the amount of genetic mixture from two parental populations in a descendent population. The mathematical calculation is rather simple if we know the following four frequencies: (1) the frequency of the allele in the three populations (two parent and the

Table 24-1. Departures from Hardy-Weinberg Conditions and Their Evolutionary Effects

Departure	*Resultant Evolutionary Forces*
Mating across population boundaries	Gene flow
Nonrandom mating	Phenotypic assortative mating and inbreeding
Unequal fertility or mortality	Natural selection
Finite population size	Genetic drift and consanguineous mating
Molecular changes in genes	Mutation

From R. Reid, *Human Population Genetics,* p. 17. Burgess Publishing Company, Minneapolis, © 1978.

Table 24-2. Human Mutation Rates for Several Traits

Trait	Population	Mutations per Million Gametes
Autosomal Dominants		
Retinoblastoma, an eye tumor	—	15 to 23
Retinoblastoma	England	14
Retinoblastoma	Michigan	23
Chondrodystrophy, dwarfism	Denmark	43
Chondrodystrophy, dwarfism	Sweden	70
Palmaris longus muscle	United States whites	32
Palmaris longus muscle	United States Afro-Americans	7
Huntington's chorea (involuntary uncontrollable movements)	United States whites	5.4
Autosomal Recessives		
Infantile amaurotic idiocy, (Tay-Sachs disease)	Eastern European Jews	38
Infantile amaurotic idiocy	Japan	11
Albinism	United States whites	28
Albinism	Japan	28
Cystic fibrosis of pancreas	—	0.7 to 1.0
Phenylketonuria	United States whites	25
Sex Linked		
Hemophilia	—	25 to 32
Hemophilia	England	20
Hemophilia	Denmark	32
Muscular dystrophy	—	43 to 100

Adapted from Stephen Molnar, *Races, Types and Ethnic Groups: The Problem of Human Variation,* © 1975, p. 33. Reprinted by permission of Prentice-Hall Inc., Englewood Cliffs, New Jersey.

Table 24-3. Levels of Gene Flow into Telaga-Kapu Populations of Six Villages in Southern India

Village	Kapu Population in 1968	Gene Flow into Village
Vella	2,433	.376
Utrumilli	291	.475
Vatripudi	280	.490
Pedda Palla	264	.469
Adampalli	182	.478
Kapavaram	92	.531

From R. Reid, *Human Population Genetics*, p. 23. Burgess Publishing Company, Minneapolis, © 1978.

descendant populations), (2) the frequency of the allele in the population into which gene migration is considered to have occurred (one parent population), (3) the frequency of the allele in the population from which the migrating genes derived (second parent population), and (4) the frequency of the allele in the descendant population. Three assumptions are made in calculating admixture: (1) the flow of genes is entirely from one population to another, (2) there is no assortative mating (see Chapter 27) with respect to the allele being considered, and (3) those zygotes produced by the admixture of the two parental populations are fertile. If this third condition were not met, admixture could not occur. If the hybrids could not reproduce, there would be no gene flow from one population to another regardless of the amount of hybridization. The effect of gene flow on gene frequencies in the recipient population is a function of the amount of genetic difference between the two populations. Williams (1973) provides the following example for calculating gene flow. If population C is composed of indigenous individuals plus arrivals from population B, then m, the rate of gene flow, is merely the proportion of members of population C who are immigrants.

A major problem in trying to calculate gene flow under these conditions is determination of the ancestral population. The amount of the calculated admixture depends on the frequency of the particular allele in each of the three populations. A mistake in choosing the ancestral or founder population could produce a considerable error in the calculated amount of admixture. An understanding of gene flow requires a knowledge of population structure, inbreeding, movements in and out of the population, mating practices, and the effect of other evolutionary processes on the population and any of its subunits.

Inbreeding. Inbreeding and outbreeding are major deviations from random mating. Due to the importance of animal and plant breeding in the development of population genetics, more is known about the mechanisms of inbreeding. The effects of outbreeding are assumed to be opposite those of inbreeding. An organism is considered to be inbred when its parents are related. A population is inbred when more such consanguineous mating occurs than expected under the assumptions of randomness. Inbreeding serves to increase the frequency of homozygous loci in the inbred individual or population as compared to expectation under the Hardy-Weinberg law.

Inbreeding can make recessive genes more available to selection by increasing the frequency of homozygous recessives. An immediate effect of an increase in inbreeding is a rise in mortality due to deleterious recessives becoming homozygous. A new equilibrium may eventually be reached when deleterious alleles are eliminated to the point at which they account for no more mortality than before close inbreeding began. If random mating returns, this "relaxation of inbreeding" will result in a period in which deleterious genes exist in the earliest lower frequencies and seldom manifest themselves in homozygous form as deleterious traits. Because they are not expressed, selection against them is lacking and these alleles may again increase in frequency (Williams, 1973).

Genetic Drift (Sampling Error). The mechanism known as genetic drift may explain apparent peculiarities in the extent to which gene frequencies are shared by different populations. When, for example, two or more populations believed to be distantly related are found to share gene frequencies, this similarity can be explained as due to genetic drift (chance). Genetic drift may also be used to explain differences between populations believed on other grounds to be closely related. Thus, differences between Micronesians and Polynesians may be explained by invoking drift.

Special circumstances such as accidents, natural catastrophes, or minor fluctuations in mate selection exist in small populations and can produce rapid changes in the population's gene structure. These changes may be completely independent of natural selection and mutation. Generally, the larger the population, the more resistant is its genetic structure to accidental or chance change. Conversely, the smaller the population, the more likely its genetic structure will be influenced by chance. Genetic changes due to genetic drift bear no relationship to the adaptive requirements of the organism. The change is random and entirely due to chance.

Take, for example, a population of 1,000 in which a specific mutation occurs in one individual per generation. Chance events may prevent this individual from reaching reproductive maturity, or from producing viable, fertile offspring, and thus the mutant gene is lost regardless of its potential adaptive value. However, with the same mutation rate a population of 1 million would produce 1,000 individuals per generation with the mutant gene, and it is much less probable that chance alone would control the fate of this gene. Instead, in a large population, natural selection would be the most important factor determining the survival and expression of the mutant form.

Because genetic drift is effective only in small populations, it may have played a major role in our early evolutionary stages. Genetic drift was possibly a more potent evolutionary force early in our history than it is today. Although the magnitude of drift is hard to assess, it seems certain that at one time our ancestors lived in exactly the situation conducive to drift— small, isolated groups. With the introduction of agriculture and sedentism, population size and density increased, thus decreasing the potential effect of drift on subsequent evolutionary history.

In 1931 Sewall Wright, one of the founders of population genetics, developed a mathematical model of the population as a finite evolutionary unit. He proposed that under certain conditions a population is subjected to special evolutionary forces that he labeled genetic drift. This process, the **Sewall Wright effect,** refers to the random fluctuation, or drift, of gene frequencies from generation to generation in relatively small isolated populations. Due to drift, a number of local populations, although originally derived from the same parental population, may eventually differ from one another to varying degrees. Genetic drift and mutation are both examples of processes of natural selection that occur randomly and exert a systematic pressure on the gene pool. Genetic drift exerts nonsystematic pressures, and gene frequency changes are indeterminate in direction. Genetic drift leads to a net loss of heterozygosity within a total population subdivided into small isolates (the so-called decay of variability).

What constitutes a small population within which drift is effective depends on the interrelations between the number of breeding individuals, selective value of the alleles, mutation pressure, and gene flow. It is often stated that drift is effective in small populations (numbering in the hundreds) and inoperative in larger populations, but this is an oversimplification.

The measurement and demonstration of genetic drift is difficult. It is doubtful if any human population was ever subject to the ideal conditions requisite for the application of mathematical models of drift. However, within limits imposed by the population, there are various means of measuring drift; one is by noting the variance in gene frequency between local populations and the offshoot and parental populations. Unless strong selection pressures account for gene frequency differences, they are probably due to drift.

Founder Principle. The **founder,** or bottleneck, principle refers to a change in the genetic composition of small breeding populations often accompanied by a reduction in total population size. The process is best defined as the total genetic impact experienced by a population due to the combined events of (1) drastic size reduction, (2) rapid expansion, and (3) relative isolation with little genetic admixture. With all three conditions present, the effects of the original size reduction persist, and, in accumulation, shape the profile of ancestral contributions to the present gene pool.

The initial event of the founder principle, drastic size reduction, occurs in two major ways: (1) death of a large number of the population and (2) migration. In the first instance, the remaining population constitutes the "founder population" for future generations, If, in the second case, the net mass migration results in leaving behind only a small group, this group is considered the founder population. If, however, the migration consists of only a small number of people who form a new community after leaving the majority, the emigrants are considered to be a founder population because they do not contain all the genes present in the parent population.

One oft-cited example of the founder principle is the absence of the gene for the B blood type in the ABO system among American Indians. It is quite likely that American Indian populations were descended from small groups of migratory hunters and gatherers who crossed the Bering Straits during the Late Pleistocene and migrated into the Americas to later form a rather large population. The original migrants came from a population that probably had relatively low frequencies of blood group B. The founding groups of the new populations may have had no B alleles. It is also possible, however, that natural selection, working on the ABO phenotypes, was operative. This is discussed in Chapter 27.

Two Examples of the Founder Principle. The island population of Tristan da Cunha[1] grew from 15 to 270 between 1816 and 1961. However, this overall growth was marked by two separate major population reductions that influenced the genetic pattern of subsequent growth. The first fluctuation was due to mass migration, the second to the combined effects of a boating accident that claimed most adult males and the subsequent migration of widows. The population twice passed through a "bottleneck" whereby some individuals were extracted and others left. Those who remained formed the founder population and they disproportionately contributed to the genetic structure of subsequent populations.

Our second example is the Amish living in a number of local endogamous communities ranging from 1,000 to 9,000 people. The focus of many genetic studies, the Amish provide a classic example of the results of inbreeding, genetic drift, and the founder effect. The present Amish population was founded by successive small waves of European immigrants between 1720 and 1850 who primarily settled in Pennsylvania, Ohio, and Indiana. Each Amish deme is descended from a very few founders, reflected in the relatively few sets of family names accounting for the majority of individuals within each deme. In three demes, three different sets of eight names account for approximately 80 percent of the Amish families. Extensive genetic and demographic studies show that the limited occurrence of certain rare recessive genetic syndromes and unique gene frequency distributions are best explained by the founder effect.

In addition to having been founded by relatively few individuals, both the Amish and Tristan da Cunha populations fulfill two other conditions of the founder effect: (1) rapid expansion in

---

[1]A group name for three small islands belonging to the United Kingdom, located in the South Atlantic midway between South Africa and South America. Of the three islands only Tristan is inhabited. The island is remote and is periodically evacuated because of volcanic action.

relative isolation and (2) rare interjection of genes from outside the breeding population. Tristan da Cunha's population grew from 15 people in 1851 to 270 in 1961 in extreme geographical isolation, interrupted only rarely by immigration. The Amish population grew from 8,200 people to 45,000 in the 1960s and remained socially isolated.

Drift and the Founder Principle: Forces in Evolution. Both genetic drift and the founder effect may have played a role, perhaps major in some cases, in determining the composition of early hominid populations. If early hominid populations were composed of relatively small, endogamous, and geographically distributed groups, this would have affected their breeding structure. The same situation may have produced some of the population diversity in the world today.

Isolated populations provide valuable information for the human geneticist in the form of aberrant gene frequencies, rare recessive diseases, and demographic data. Although unchallengeable proof of genetic drift in human populations is not readily available, isolated populations continue to be the human population geneticist's laboratory.

An Example of an Isolated Community: Roman Jewish Population

An example of a study of an isolated community is provided in the data that the geneticist L. C. Dunn and his anthropologist son Stephen collected on the small Roman Jewish community.[2] The Roman Jewish community is interesting because of its long documented history and because its members have retained their group identity. If there is a cultural or social unity in Jewry as a whole or in any single community, are there also biological effects? Do traditional rules prohibiting marriage outside the Jewish community provide effective genetic isolation from surrounding non-Jewish communities? If so, if this Jewish community is genetically isolated, then we have ways of evaluating some of the biological effects of social and cultural development and thought.

Until recently the typical European Jewish social unit was a small community. In northern and eastern Europe this community is known as the shtetl, the little town. In Italy the community is the *università*, a secular organization recognized by the state as representing the Jewish inhabitants of a town or region. Christianity culminated in the enclosure of many Jewish communities in walled ghettos. Palestinian Jews settled in Rome in 160 B.C. This ghetto was closed in 1554 and it remained closed for some 300 years. The intent was to isolate the Jewish community socially and reproductively. This was strenghtened by prohibitions against intermarriage, curfew laws, and forbidding the employment of those of Jewish origin in Christian homes. Garibaldi's troops eventually opened the ghetto to the outside world in 1870.

The Dunns were able to identify the Roman Jewish community readily because descendants of the ancient community were recognized by a group of families with "ghetto names," a residence pattern centering in ghetto areas, and use of the community's social facilities. Marriage and birth records showed them to be families of Roman Jewish origin, marrying among themselves. This was an endogamous community numbering about 4,000 persons with a high degree of reproductive isolation. The Dunns tested the blood, saliva, and urine of 700 individuals, about one-fifth of the community. The following characteristics were uncovered.

[2]Another fascinating example is discussed by Neel, 1970.

1. The B blood group was proportionally twice as great in the Jewish community as in the Italian Catholic community: 27 percent of the Jewish community was group B; in the Italian Catholic community the percentage was 10 or 11 percent. These percentages indicate that there was little interbreeding between the groups. If there had been interbreeding the B frequencies would tend toward similarity in both groups.
2. Some other Jewish communities showed similar high incidence of B in relation to surrounding communities, suggesting that the ancestral Jewish population showed a high percentage of group B. If so, it also suggests retention by separate Jewish populations of an ancestral genotype.
3. The proportion of B among Roman Jews is high compared to other Jewish communities. This may reflect the effect of population size, that is, we may be witnessing the effect of genetic drift.
4. One of the Rh alleles, Rh-negative, which is usually rare in Europe, is higher than in any other Jewish population. In the Roman Jewish community Rh-negative composes 5 percent of the population. This figure is much higher than the percentage of Rh-negative in Italy generally and may be due to genetic drift.
5. The above information suggests that social isolation has had its genetic effect.

Genetic Model of Natural Selection

Genetics has provided the explanatory vehicle of how living things adapt to their environment. Natural selection continually eliminates ill-adapted individuals; if poor adaptation results from genetic features, the deleterious allele is eventually eliminated from the breeding population. A store of "hidden" alleles may be retained, phenotypically invisible as it were, in the heterozygous individual. Deleterious genes tend to be removed over time, but some ailments may not appear until past reproductive age after the gene is transmitted to succeeding generations.

This simplistic method of genetic selection depends on the assumption that a given allele produces only adaptive or nonadaptive phenotypic traits, but such a situation is not always true. Many genetically based ailments serviced by the physician fit into this model, but many cases of genetic polymorphism that interest the anthropologist do not. The model inadequately explains these cases.

There are many genetic differences between members of any breeding population. In but a few cases is the possession of one allele rather than another at a given locus advantageous in any obvious way. Many times the selective advantage of a genetically determined trait is unknown. Some interpret this uncertainty to mean that natural selection ceases to be a factor under the conditions of modern life; but there are other alternative explanations. One popular view is that many, if not most, ways in which human populations differ result from genetic drift, or chance variation. Examples uphold each argument and statistical models supporting each can be created. Neither model explains all the available data and it is quite likely that modern variability is due in part to both these factors and many others.

From the standpoint of the gene pool, the product of natural selection may be a gradual reduction of population variation to conform to the requirements of selection. From the viewpoint of selection, the only measure of fitness within a species is the number of viable offspring produced that survive until sexual maturity. This perspective can be understood directly on a population level. It provides an explanation for the origin of species by means of natural selection. With respect to genotype distributions, natural selection exerts its influence in the following ways, considering one locus and two alleles: selection against (1) one or the other homozygote, (2) one or the other homozygote and the heterozygote, (3) both homozygotes, and (4) the heterozygote (Kelso, 1974).

Differential reproduction and mortality are usually combined in one measure of selection, the relative representation of genotypes in the offspring generation after the effects of mutation, migration, genetic drift, gene flow, and recombination are removed. One means of representing these differences is to let the most fit genotype or genotypes have a fitness value of 1.00 and express the fitness of the remaining genotypes as some fraction of 1.00. Williams (1973) provides the following example:

Genotypes	AA	Aa	aa
Fitness values	1.00	0.90	0.80

In this example the genotype *Aa* is intermediate in fitness between the two homozygotes. The definition of fitness, as reflected in this example, means that the ratio of *Aa* offspring to parents will be only 90 percent of the ratio of *AA* offspring to parents. The ratio of *aa* offspring to parents will be only 80 percent of the ratio of *AA* offspring to parents.

Natural Selection at the Gene Level. A new argument regarding the applicability of natural selection to evolution at the gene level has recently been proposed. At issue is the application of Darwinian evolutionary theory to genes, the fundamental units of heredity. Some researchers suggest that mere chance plays a bigger role in evolutionary change than previously suspected. The controversy does not threaten the basic premise of evolution, however. Scientists on both sides of the argument agree that natural selection determines most adaptations of an organism, although some question whether the same process occurs on the molecular level.

As with many other developments, this argument was born out of technological and methodological advances, in this case a process known as electrophoresis. The process of electrophoresis allows researchers to identify proteins, the large molecules that conduct most of the basic life processes. Electrophoresis works as follows: when a protein is placed in a gel between two electric terminals, it tends to drift toward one or the other at a speed determined by its electrical charge. The structure of a protein reflects the molecular code of the gene that originally created the protein—thus electrophoresis provides a means of identifying and analyzing individual genes.

Electrophoresis has revealed a wide variation of protein structures that conduct the same tasks in different individuals of the same species. This phenomenon is known as polymorphism, and polymorphic genes are the result of mutation. Most mutations are deleterious and disappear from the gene pool. According to Darwinian evolutionary theory, all genes that survive do so because they benefit the species in some way. In recent years, however, some scientists (primarily molecular biologists) have argued that the number of genetic polymorphisms is simply too great to be accounted for in this way.

Molecular critics of the Darwinian scheme offer an alternative and suggest that many of the polymorphic forms of genes neither increase nor decrease an individual's chances of survival. Rather, they suggest, such polymorphisms are neutral and become established simply by chance. Proponents of this view are often called "neutralists." In support of their argument they suggest that rates at which similar genes evolve in different species seem to be remarkedly constant—a fact they feel cannot be accounted for by natural selection. Two of the foremost proponents of this neutralist viewpoint are King and Jukes (1969).

Scientists who allow that Darwinian principles are still valid on the molecular level—often called "selectionists"—argue that this constancy is largely illusory and that Darwinian principles are still applicable on the molecular level. Studies by Ayala show that certain polymorphic genes appear with the same frequencies in a variety of different groups within the same species of fruit fly. Ayala argues that chance alone would not account for this (Ayala, 1974).

A third group of molecular biologists is casting doubt on the role of simple genetic mutations in major evolutionary changes. Using a method of analysis known as protein sequencing, these scientists have discovered considerable genetic similarities between living forms. For example, the proteins of humans and chimpanzees differ by no more than 1 percent. It has been argued, for example by Wilson and King (1975), that a small number of genes could be responsible for major evolutionary adaptations in shape, size, and behavior. This group of scientists assailed the interpretation of the primate fossil record, arguing that the hominid-pongid divergence occurred more recently in time than the paleontological record suggests. This was discussed in Chapter 22.

Relaxed Selection and Genetic Load. The first statements on relaxed selection date to the early eugenics movement, which had an unsavory political and social flavor. Early statements concerning relaxed selection argued for the so-called "survival of the fittest" in social terms. For example, various forms of social welfare were attacked because they supposedly preserved less fit individuals.

Genetically, however, the concept of relaxed selection is debatable. If the fitness of one genotype is increased, by definition the fitness of alternatives is decreased. One can only speak of relaxed selection in terms of specific genotypes and not as an overall phenomenon. This proposition then means that relaxed selection is only a change in fitness values of specific genotypes due to environmental changes. An example of this is the apparent rise in frequency of red-green color blindness (see Chapter 7 for the transmission of this X-linked trait). Studies suggest that the frequency of red-green color blindness is proportional to the length of time a society has depended on hunting as a way of life (Post, 1962, 1965). Post tabulated data on populations in which red-green color blindness was investigated. He classified these populations into three groups, presumably on the basis of how long it had been since their ancestors were hunters and gatherers. Averaging the frequency of red-green color blindness in each catagory, he arrived at the following figures:

Economic Pursuit	Frequency of Color Vision Defect
Hunters and gatherers	0.020
Intermediates	0.033
Long-time agriculturists	0.080

There is the possibility that a number of rare genetic defects may increase in frequency due to relaxed selection precipitated by medical intervention. Phenylketonuria, inherited as a recessive defect in the metabolism of phenylalanine, is an example. Since in the past children with PKU seldom survived to become adults and reproduce, the condition appears to have been maintained in the population solely by mutation. In most populations the frequency of PKU is one in 10,000 or less, a gene frequency of 0.01 or less. New tests can detect a PKU infant and a special dietary regime has been employed to try to mediate any occurrence of severe defects, often without success.

The PKU example serves to highlight a current controversy among social thinkers, namely the issue of genetic load. The issue of genetic load also serves to highlight the interaction between culture and biology and illustrates how modern culture can affect future evolutionary trends. Genetic load refers to the frequency with which deleterious genes are maintained within a population. The greater the number of deleterious genes, the heavier the genetic load. Some geneticists feel that populations have limits as to the number of deleterious genes they can tolerate. They fear that preventing the natural death of an organism, that is, neutralizing the deleterious gene, will result in genetic weakening of the population. The issue is a moral as well as a genetic problem. Which traits do we preserve within a population and which do we eliminate or permit to die out? Furthermore, what are today genetic malfunctions may tomorrow seem quite insignificant. For example, all individuals who today wear glasses for nearsightedness would, during the days of total reliance on hunting, have been deemed genetically unfit. Imagine trying to stalk an animal that you could not see!

In many societies the problem of genetic load is met by genetic counseling. Individuals exhibiting some genetic disorder can be helped to lead a "normal" life through medical intervention, and such individuals are often advised against reproducing. Some states in the United States have on occasion taken the extreme measure of sterilizing severely mentally impaired persons to prevent them from having children, but this was often done without the consent of the individuals concerned and was therefore illegal. It should be made quite clear that genetic counseling is as much a debatable topic as is genetic load. The fear that genetic counseling could be manipulated for social, political or economic means is quite apparent.

Genetic Engineering

Attempts at altering a population's gene pool are not new. In the *Republic,* Plato suggested that, "The best of both sexes ought to be brought together as often as possible, and the worst as seldom as possible." Today, the process of genetic intervention is called **eugenics,** and this will become increasingly a factor in future human evolution. Eugenics can be applied to use various methods to improve the inherited qualities of a species. Leaving aside the numerous political, moral, and ethical questions, for that is for each reader to ponder on his or her own, we will discuss eugenics.

The goal of eugenics, improving the genetic composition of a population, can be accomplished by both negative and positive means. Negative eugenics attempts to eliminate deleterious genes from the population. Positive eugenics, by contrast, attempts to encourage reproduction by those having what are considered to be desirable traits. It must be realized, however, that what are considered to be desirable traits are culturally biased. Since each culture emphasizes different traits as being desirable, a eugenics program must be consistent with the culture or subculture in which it is operative.

Three major means of eugenics exist, at least theoretically. (1) It has been suggested that the sperm and ova of individuals possessing desirable traits be frozen and used repeatedly to produce offspring through the process of artificial insemination. Remember, however, that the sperm and ova both contain a significant amount of genetic variability. All individuals produced from the sperm and ova of two donors would differ genetically from each other. Identical individuals would not be produced and it is quite possible that the selected traits might not be obtained. Furthermore, the total variability of the population would be reduced; (2) A second means of selection would attempt to alter the genetic material itself. Using this method, one could eliminate or repair deleterious alleles and change certain alleles to more advantageous types. This is genetic engineering. (3) Cloning is a third method of genetic manipulation. A clone is a group of offspring produced asexually by using a body cell instead of a normal fertilized egg. Cloning has been accomplished with plants and amphibians.

Gene Transplants. One of the most interesting and certainly most controversial, forms of genetic engineering is gene transplants (see Freifelder, 1978; Grobstein, 1979). Proponents and opponents make many statements attesting to reasons why or why not such experimentation should continue. Research on gene transplants began in the early 1970s and was confined to the laboratory. Now, however, the subject has been broached in the city council of Cambridge, Massachusetts, and by several federal agencies. Scientists themselves seem divided over the wisdom of this procedure.

The anxiety stemming from gene transplants is related to the fact that researchers who change (recombine) the gene sequence of DNA are creating new forms of life, that is, organisms nonexistent in nature. There is the risk of the unknown; what if some new pathological organism were created? What effect would its creation have on the human population? Scientists recognize these fears. They assert that past work with dangerous disease-producing organisms has been well contained by simple laboratory safeguards. Furthermore, some scientists argue that transplantation of genes from one species to another may actually occur in nature. It has long known that different species of bacteria can exchange genes. Furthermore, certain bacteria seemingly harbor genes similar to human genes regulating the production of a substance known as chorionic gonadotropin. This suggests a transfer between humans and bacteria, and suggests that such hybrids may not be as dangerous as had been feared.

Recombinant research is sophisticated surgery on DNA strands (Figure 24-1). Researchers remove plasmids[3] from bacteria using chemicals that cause the bacteria to split apart. Enzymes are then applied, opening the closed loops of the plasmids and allowing insertion of small stretches of DNA to represent one or more alien genes. The newly created plasmids then close and are reinserted into the bacteria of the type from which the original plasmids were removed. The transplanted foreign genes act as if they are "at home," and reproduce normally.

Recombinant research has the opportunity to achieve some interesting effects. For example, a forerunner of the recombinant technique has been employed to create a new organism for cleaning oil spills. One drug company is eyeing recombinant technology to help mass produce insulin and other rare medications.

Recently a team of scientists for the first time manipulated bacteria to produce a human hormone. This work was done with the common bacteria *Escherichia coli.* Researchers transferred to *E. coli* the hereditary information to produce a hormone called somatostatin. This hormone was discovered in 1972 by Roger Guillemin of the Salk Institute, who shared a Nobel Prize for his work. The bacterial production of somatostatin follows work that for the first time placed an insulin-producing gene in bacteria. This experiment, however, failed.

The bacterial production of a hormone produced by the brain is significant. Somatostatin is known to control the release of growth hormones from the pituitary gland. It is also believed to affect a number of other hormones. Eventually, somatostatin may have a role in the treatment for some hormonal disorders. The significance of this research lies in the clear demonstration that all the genetic information required to make a protein that is normally made in a cell of a higher organism can be transferred to a bacterium and there operate as in its former environment.

---

[3]Plasmids are extra genetic elements found in bacterial cells. Plasmids are capable of autonomous self-replication.

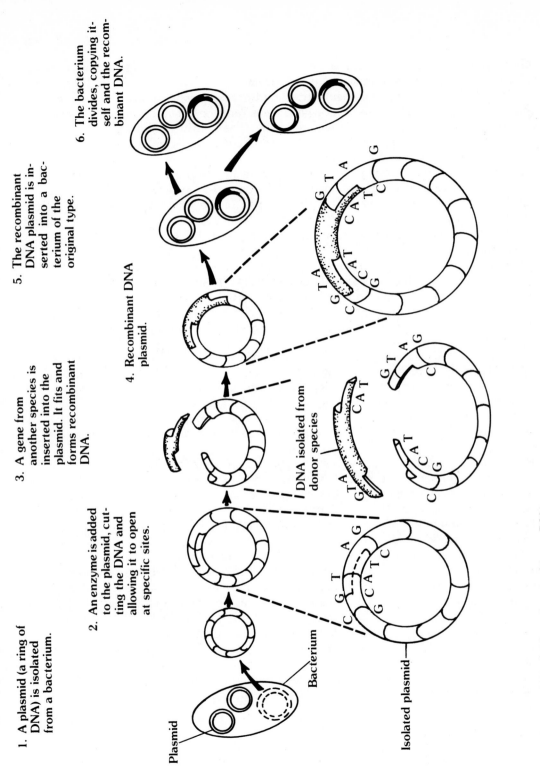

1. A plasmid (a ring of DNA) is isolated from a bacterium.

2. An enzyme is added to the plasmid, cutting the DNA and allowing it to open at specific sites.

3. A gene from another species is inserted into the plasmid. It fits and forms recombinant DNA.

4. Recombinant DNA plasmid.

5. The recombinant DNA plasmid is inserted into a bacterium of the original type.

6. The bacterium divides, copying itself and the recombinant DNA.

Plasmid

Bacterium

DNA isolated from donor species

Isolated plasmid

Figure 24-1. Action of recombinant DNA.

There are many problems with eugenics, not the least of which have been the sordid attempts to prostitute a so-called eugenics program for political ideals, as was done in Hitler's Germany. Some problems of implementing a eugenics program are:

1. *Who makes the choices?* Who, what person or group of persons can be entrusted with making the decisions? What system of accountability will be built into the nature of choosing? What methods of appeal? Many of the other problems noted are easier to solve than this one.

2. *Racism and elitism.* These are related to the first caveat. There are various forms of racism and elitism, all of them dangerous. However, the spectre of using a eugenics program as a guise for racism and elitism is insidious. What if racists and elitists are in power and decide, under the guise of improvement, to practice eugenics on people they are prejudiced against? The creation of a biological elite is also a danger. Groups of persons could conceivably be created who, for their own purpose, maintain power over the "drones" and others. Huxley's *Brave New World* and Orwell's *1984* could become realities.

3. *Dysgenic effects.* What genetic diseases should be arrested or cured? Where should one intervene? If a trait is eliminated by culling the alleles causing it, a eugenic effect—an improvement in the gene pool-has occurred. If, however, the trait is simply phenotypically controlled, the genetic component may be relatively untouched. This is a **dysgenic effect**, and has a tendency to increase the frequency of the trait. Under this program of intervention there would tend to be an increase of the so-called genetic load, perhaps impairing a population's ability to survive.

4. *Reduction of population variability.* Earlier we noted the importance of population variability as a long-range factor in survival. One of the dangers of a eugenics program would be an eventual reduction of variability. What traits are to be eliminated? While it may be easy to decide on certain traits, others, such as some of the malarial protectors, would cause considerable controversy. Although a homozygous individual might be at a disadvantage in some environments, the heterozygote would be at an advantage in malarial regions. If eugenics reduced the frequency of the allele for the malarial protection, what would happen if techniques for malarial control suddenly become ineffectual? This is a distinct possibility because there are now strains of mosquitoes resistant to such insecticides as DDT. Because of the disappearance of the protecting alleles, the population would then lack the malarial protection conferred by the allele.

Euthenics

Eugenics may be called genetic engineering and **euthenics** may be called environmental engineering. Because the phenotype is determined partly by the organism's environment, environmental changes can affect an organism's biology. Creation of a therapeutic environment has been a major feat of the last century. In many societies, the environment has been virtually sanitized, allowing many to live longer and healthier lives. Many human ills are now cured by simply changing the environment or by advocating movement to another environment.

A dysthenic effect is environmental manipulation that increases the frequency of disease and discomfort. For example, while modern agricultural methods have allowed the feeding of many more people, they have also contributed to a rise of population numbers and concentrations in some areas to the danger point. Urbanization, while it has many advantages, also creates in its wake excessive noise, pollution, and alienation for some. Industrialization, while raising the living standards of many, has also created noise and water and air pollution, led to personality disorders on the assembly line, and created a spectrum of industrial disease, endangering the very lives of those whom it promised to enrich.

A Model Population: Hardy-Weinberg Law

The frequency of a gene is its numerical incidence in the gene pool. In humans, for example, the dominant allele for pigment production has a frequency of 99 percent. The recessive allele for lack of pigment production that,when homozygous, causes the condition called albinism, has a frequency of 1 percent. Thus, 99 out of every 100 alleles for pigment production is a dominant allele and only 1 out of 100 is recessive. These values are generally expressed as the decimal equivalent of the percentage value; the frequency of the dominant allele is 0.99 and of the recessive is 0.01.

Population geneticists use symbols to represent all of a particular allele present in a particular gene pool. The symbol p is commonly used to represent all dominant alleles and the symbol q is used to represent all recessive alleles for the same trait. In the case of albinism, p (the dominant allele) = 0.99 and q (the recessive allele) = 0.01. The total of p and q for any pair of alleles must equal 1.0, or 100 percent (Table 24-4). The equation

$$p + q = 1$$

is a generalized statement representing the frequency of any two alleles in a two-allele system in a gene pool. In the case of albinism

$$
\begin{aligned}
p &= 0.99 \\
q &= 0.01 \\
\hline
p + q &= 1.00
\end{aligned}
$$

If the numerical value of either gene allele is known, the frequency of other alleles can be calculated by simple arithmetic:

$$
\begin{aligned}
&\text{if } p = 0.4 \text{ and } p + q = 1.0, \text{ then} \\
&q = 1.0 - p \\
&q = 1.0 - 0.4 = 0.6
\end{aligned}
$$

Genotype determines phenotype, and the symbols p and q by themselves convey no information concerning the number of individuals of different genotypes in a population. If the frequencies of individual alleles are known, however, one can determine the frequency of genotypes. The equation used to determine genotype frequencies in a population is the fundamental tool of population geneticists.

The goal of population genetics is to understand the distribution of inherited characteristics and the processes by which such distributions change through time. The basis of theoretical population genetics is a series of mathematical models that attempt to abstract from nature the essential features affecting genetic distribution. Population genetics models compose a series of assumed features of hypothetical populations. These models attempt to predict the logical consequences of Mendelian principles when mating occurs in a population character-ized by a given set of features. The population geneticist must compromise and choose a set of assumed conditions that closely reflects the nature of real populations yet does not become mathematically unmanageable.

Table 24-4. Distribution of Alleles in Genotypes in a Population if p = 0.99 and q = 0.01

Gene Frequencies	Genotype Frequencies
$p = 0.99$	$p^2 = (0.99)^2 = 0.9801$
$q = 0.01$	$2\,pq = 2\,(0.99)\,(0.01) = 0.0198$
	$q^2 = (0.01)^2 = 0.0001$[a]
	$p^2 + 2\,pq + q^2 = 1.000$

[a]If the frequency of the recessive allele, q, = 0.01, the frequency in the population of individuals homozygous for this allele is $q^2 = (0.01)^2 = 0.0001 = 1$ individual in 10,000. Albinism is an example of a recessive trait to which the figures shown here apply closely.

Most basic models in population genetics assume that not only populations, but generations, are discretely bounded. Actually, in humans there is a continuous distribution of ages, and we rarely find breeding populations defined by clear boundaries. Moreover, mating within a breeding population may be influenced by such things as socioeconomic status, rather than by discrete subdivision. Thus, theoretical models may be either too simplistic to account for natural phenomena or too complex to be useful.

Just as the phenotype of an individual is partly determined by the genes he or she carries, so the collective phenotype of a population is partly determined by its gene pool. To describe the composition of a gene pool, geneticists use the concept of gene frequency. The frequency of a particular gene is simply its abundance relative to all of its alleles in a population.

If we can determine gene frequencies at many loci for a particular population, we can describe its gene pool in some detail. To describe its collective phenotype, however, we need to know not so much the gene frequencies as the genotype frequencies; that is, the proportion of different genotypes in the population.

Is there any pattern in the relationship between gene frequencies and genotype frequencies? There is a predictable relationship stated in the Hardy-Weinberg formula, which is the cornerstone of population genetics.

The **Hardy-Weinberg Law** assumes a single, infinitely large, static panmictic population. When Mendel's principles were rediscovered in 1900, biologists began to seek explanations for genotype frequencies observed in total populations. Yule (1902) pointed to an apparent conflict between expected Mendelian ratios and observed frequencies in natural populations. Although Castle (1903) provided a partial solution to the discrepancy, it was Hardy (1908) and Weinberg (1908) who independently provided a theoretical basis for understanding genotype distributions within a total population. The Hardy-Weinberg Law applies the algebraic formula known as the expansion of the binomial to problems of population genetics. The formula is written as $p^2 + 2\,pq + q^2 = 1$.

Theoretical Assumptions. The Hardy-Weinberg Law, as it came to be known, is valid given a set of circumstances. The list of assumptions is such that all of them are seldom realized in a "real" population. However, the optimism underlying the use of such a set of simplifying assumptions is justified.

1. *Closed population.* All mates are selected from within the population.
2. *Random mating.* All mating is considered to be random. The probability that an individual of one sex of a particular genotype will mate with a person of another particular genotype is

equal to the frequency of that genotype within that generation. The age structure is ignored and parents are assumed to be replaced by their children.

3. *Equal fertility.* The number of offspring born to an individual is not influenced by the individual's genotype.
4. *Infinite population size.* Each generation within the population is infinitely large.
5. *Nonexistence of evolutionary forces.* No evolutionary forces (i.e., genetic drift, natural selection, migration, or mutation) exist.
6. *The numbers of males and females in the population are equal.*

Given these conditions, the Hardy-Weinberg Law shows a mathematical relationship between gene frequencies in the parents' generation and genotype frequencies in the offsprings' generation. To understand the Hardy-Weinberg Law, you must imagine a genetic locus with two alleles, *A* and *a*, having frequencies within the parental generation of p and q, respectively.

As an example of the workings of the Hardy-Weinberg Law, we refer to a study conducted by Frederick Hulse, a physical anthropologist at the University of Arizona. With a colleague, Hulse studied the Quinault Indians (a Northwest coast group) for the incidence of the MN blood group. Hulse found that 77 individuals were homozygous for type M (i.e., carried only the *M* allele), 101 were heterozygous for MN (i.e., carried one *M* and one *N* allele), 23 were homozygous for N (i.e., carried only the *N* allele). Each individual for *M* and *N* was homozygous for these alleles. Each individual heterozygous for *MN* contained one *M* and one *N* allele. The total number of *M* alleles is 77 + 77 (because of the homozygous state of M) + 101 (one allele in the *MN* heterozygote) = 255. The total number of the *N* alleles is 23 + 23 (because of the homozygous state of *N*) + 101 (there being one *N* allele and one *M* in the MN genotype) = 147. The population of 201 individuals has a total of 402 alleles at this locus. To obtain the allele frequency of *M*, you divide 255 by 402 (402 is the total number of alleles; 255 is the total number of *M* alleles). The answer is 63 percent. Likewise, to obtain the allele frequency of *N* you divide 147 (the actual number of *N* alleles) by 402 (the total alleles at the locus). The answer is 37 percent. We can then decide if the Quinault are a breeding population in genetic equilibrium by applying the Hardy-Weinberg Law.

Using the formula $p^2 + 2pq + q^2 = 1$, we let p stand for the allele *M* and q for the allele *N*. Since the phenotype M is only produced in the homozygous state, by receiving *M* from both parents, the frequency will be $M \times M = p^2$. Likewise, N is only phenotypically expressed in the homozygous state. N results from receipt of one *N* allele from each parent; thus $N \times N = q^2$. The heterozygous state is produced by receiving *M* from one parent and *N* from the other; the cross-fertilization of *M* and *N* is pq. Since it is equally likely that the egg or sperm be either *M* or *N*, the equation is given as 2 pq. To apply the formula we multiply $.63 \times .63$ (p^2, the percentage of *M*), which equals .397; we multiply $.37 \times .37$ (q^2, percentage of *N*), which equals .137; and then we multiply $.63 \times .37$ (pq, percentage of *MN*) and double it to equal .466. The total of 1.000 represents 201 individuals. Continuing, we compute the expected allele frequencies as follows: p^2 or .397 of 201 is 80 persons who are expected to have M. The observed number was 77. The 2 pq of .466 of 201 persons is 94 persons expected to have MN. The observed number was 101. The q^2 or .137 of 201 is 28 persons expected to have N. The observed number was 23. These values are applied to a chi-square test to determine if this tribe is in a state of equilibrium as concerns the MN blood types (Table 24-5).

This exercise tells the investigator if the particular traits being investigated are under selective pressure or are affected by other evolutionary processes. When a population is in

---

Table 24-5. The Hardy-Weinberg Law as Applied to the Quinault Indians

Step 1: The incidence of MN in the real population

M:	77
MN:	101
N:	23
	201

Step 2: Computing allele frequencies
M: 77 + 77 = 154 alleles + M 101 = 255 M alleles
N: 23 + 23 = 46 alleles + N 191 = 147 N alleles

Total alleles in the population: 402

Step 3: Computing the actual allele frequencies in percentage

$$M: \frac{255}{402} = 63\%$$

$$N: \frac{147}{402} = 37\%$$

Step 4: Computing expected genotype frequencies
Using the formula $p^2 + 2 pq + q^2 = 1$
we substitute $M^2 + 2 MN + N^2 = 1$
Given the figures above, the formula then reads:
p^2 (0.63 × 0.63) + 2 pq (2 × 0.63 × 0.37) + q^2 (0.37 × 0.37)
Which equals
0.397 + 0.466 + 0.137 = 1.000

Step 5: Comparing the expected frequencies to the observed phenotype frequencies:

	Expected		*Observed*
M:	80 persons		77 persons
N:	28		23
MN:	94		101

These figures are computed by multiplying the figure 201 (the actual number of persons) by the expected allelic frequencies of each allele. Thus for M we multiply 201 by 0.397 (80), for N we multiply 201 by 0.137 (28), and for MN 201 we multiply by 0.466 (94).

Step 6: Apply the observed frequencies to a chi-square test.

Step 7: Decide whether the population is in equilibrium or if selection of some other force is occurring at this locus for or against certain allelic expressions.

---

equilibrium for some trait, it can be assumed that there is no strong positive or negative selection. Other explanations such as genetic drift or the founder principle might then be entertained.

The basic evolutionary unit is the population. Evolutionarily the Mendelian population is the focal point of genetic studies. Because of the difficulties of working with large, relatively undefined populations, population geneticists restrict their research to small breeding units referred to as demes. A number of complicating factors impinge on the genetic study of populations; prime among these are

definition of vital processes, the Sewall Wright effect, and the founder principle.

The genetic model of gene frequency is based on a number of theoretical assumptions. One of these assumptions is that mating is random within a breeding population and that genetic stability is generationally maintained. This assumption is mathematically expressed in the Hardy-Weinberg Law. Application of this law tells the investigator whether or not the trait being studied is under selective pressure.

Gene frequencies within populations change primarily through the action of mutation, drift, flow, and selection. These mechanisms are discussed. Scientific methods now allow the tampering with the basis of cell life, DNA. Various kinds of genetic manipulations are possible, creating the possibility of great promise or disaster. The various possibilities and viewpoints are discussed.

Bibliography

Ayala, F. 1974. Biological evolution: natural selection or random walk? *American Scientist* 69:692-701.

Ayala, F., and Anderson, W. 1973. Evidence of natural selection in molecular evolution. *Nature: New Biology* 241:274-76.

Buettner-Janusch, J. 1968. *Origins of man.* New York: Wiley.

Castle, W. 1903. The laws of heredity of Galton and Mendel and some laws governing race improvement by selection. *Proceedings of the American Academy of Sciences* 39:233-42.

Crow, J. 1972. The dilemma of nearly neutral mutations: how important are they for evolution and human welfare? *Journal of Heredity* 63:306-16.

Davis, B. 1974. The recombinant DNA scenarios: Andromeda strain, Chimera, and Golem. *American Scientist* 65:542-55.

Dobzhansky, T. 1959. *Evolution, genetics and man.* New York: Wiley.

_____. 1962. *Mankind evolving: the evolution of the human species.* New Haven: Yale University Press.

Dunn, L., and Dobzhansky, T. 1960. *Heredity, race and society.* New York: Atheneum.

Ford, E. 1965. *Genetic polymorphism.* Cambridge, Mass.: M.I.T. Press.

Freifelder, D., ed. 1978. *Recombinant DNA.* San Francisco: Freeman.

Glass, B., Sacks, M., Jahn, E., and Hess, C. 1952. Genetic drift in a religious isolate; an analysis of the causes of variation in blood group and other gene frequencies in a small population. *American Naturalist* 86:145-59.

Grobstein, D., ed. 1979. *A double image of the double helix. The recombinant-DNA debate.* San Francisco: Freeman.

Hardy, G. 1908. Mendelian proportions in a mixed population. *Science* 28:49-50.

Hulse, F. 1971. *The human species.* New York: Random House.

Kelso, A. 1974. *Physical anthropology,* 2nd ed. Philadelphia: Lippincott.

King, J. 1974. *The biology of race.* New York: Harcourt Brace Jovanovich.

King, J., and Jukes, T. 1969. Non-Darwinian evolution. *Science* 164:788-98.

King, M., and Wilson, A. 1975. Evolution at two levels in humans and chimpanzees. *Science* 188:107-15.

Klass, M., and Hellman, H. 1971. *The kinds of mankind.* Philadelphia: Lippincott.

Lasker, G. 1952. Mixture and genetic drift in ongoing human evolution. *American Anthropologist* 54:433.

Livingstone, F. 1967. The founder effect and deleterious genes. *American Journal of Physical Anthropology* 30:55.

Mayr, E. 1970. *Populations, species and evolution.* Cambridge: Harvard University Press.

McKusick, V. 1969. *Human genetics.* Englewood Cliffs, N.J.: Prentice-Hall.

Molnar, S. 1975. *Races, types, and ethnic groups.* Englewood Cliffs, N.J.: Prentice-Hall.

Morris, L., ed. 1971. *Human populations, genetic variation and evolution.* San Francisco: Chandler.

Neel, J. 1958. The study of natural selection in primitive and civilized human populations. *Human Biology* 30:43.

───────. 1970. Lessons from a "primitive" people. *Science* 170:815.

Post, R. 1962. Population differences in red and green color vision deficiency: a review and a query on selection relaxation. *Eugenics Quarterly* 9:131-46.

───────. 1965. Selection against "colorblindness" among "primitive" populations. *Eugenics Quarterly* 12:28-29.

Racle, R. 1979. *Introduction to evolution.* Englewood Cliffs, N.J.: Prentice-Hall.

Reid, R. 1978. *Human population genetics.* Minneapolis: Burgess.

Weinberg, W. 1980. Über den Nachweis der vererbung beim menschen. *Naturkunde Württemberg* 64:368-82.

Williams, B. 1973. *Evolution and human origins.* New York: Harper and Row.

Wright, S. 1968. *Evolution and the genetics of populations.* Vol. 1. *Genetic and biometric foundations.* Chicago: University of Chicago Press.

───────. 1969. *Evolution and the genetics of populations.* Vol. 2. *The theory of gene frequencies.* Chicago: University of Chicago Press.

Yule, G. 1902. Mendel's laws and their probable relation to intra-racial heredity. *New Phytologist* 1:192-207, 222-38.

Chapter 25

An Outlook:
The Seeds of Controversy

Human populations have been the object of various means of classification. A major problem confounding the understanding of population diversity is finding a means whereby population variations can be accurately assessed, and then finding criteria that most agree are useful. The problem of establishing meaningful criteria whereby populations can be said to vary as a result of multitudinous factors is complicated by a combination of the following: (1) there is much disagreement as to what are "meaningful criteria" (what is meaningful to one researcher may be less so to another), (2) there are various assessments of physical types in the folk evaluation of various cultures (the recognition of "you" and "us") and (3) the subject of human variation is loaded with emotionalism. To appreciate the diversity of opinion and research outlooks, this chapter reviews the history of attempts at racial classification and some of the problems that have led to various classification schemes.

Classification Schemes

Various traits have been used since the fifteenth century to classify human populations.

Fifteenth and Sixteenth Centuries. During the fifteenth and sixteenth centuries efforts were made to order newly discovered human populations.[1] Attempts were made to explain morphological diversity, especially skin color, as being related to climatic factors. Jean Bodin (1530-1596) attempted to classify humanity in the following manner:

[1]For a most interesting brief review of the development of various explanations of human diversity, the reader might refer to Kennedy, 1976.

... the people of the South are of contrarie humor and disposition to them of the north: these are great and strong, they are little and weak; they of the north hot and moist, the others cold and dry; the one hath a big voyce and greene eyes, the other hath a weake voyce and black eyes; the one hath a flaxen haire and a faire skin, the other hath both haire and skin black; the one feareth cold, and the other heate.

Objective and systematic classification of natural phenomena such as plants and animals—and humans—began in the sixteenth century with the new philosophy of scientific observation and inductive reasoning under principles formulated by Francis Bacon. Previously, few classification schemes existed for any natural phenomena; the view of the world was about as subjective as Augustine's in the third century when he classified animals into three groups; helpful, hurtful, and superfluous. After Bacon, far-reaching explorations of the next two centuries from the South Pacific to the Arctic provided a vast array of previously unknown plants and animals. Samples and descriptions brought to Europe provided a wealth of material for scientific examination.

Seventeenth Century. During the seventeenth century the influence of the Old Testament's account of human history substantially handicapped biological research, especially that concerned with human origins. Despite this, polygenesis, that is, the notion of multiple human origins, not necessarily related to God's creation, cautiously began to emerge. Such ideas, however, remained isolated cries in the wilderness. In 1695 an anonymous author expounded on the polygenesis viewpoint, citing as evidence cultural differences between the Old and New Worlds, geographical difficulties of migration, and floral and faunal differences between the Old and New Worlds. Earlier investigators bold (or foolish) enough to expound heresies were burned at the stake.

Eighteenth Century. The Swedish botanist Carolus Linnaeus brought order to studies of the plant and animal world; in his work *Systema Naturae* he devised a hierarchical classificatory scheme for plants (1735) and animals (1758). In 1735 he proposed four living human races—Europeans, Africans, Asiatics, and American Indians—whose differentiation was largely based on pigmentation and a subjective judgment of each group's behavioral traits (Table 25-1).

Table 25-1. Early Racial Classifications

Linnaeus (1735)	Buffon (1749)
American (Reddish)	Laplander
European (White)	Tartar
Asiatic (Yellow)	South Asiatic
Negro (Black)	European
	American

Blumenbach (1781)	Cuvier (1790)
Caucasoid	Caucasoid
Mongoloid	Mongoloid
Negroid	Negroid
American Indian	
Ethiopian	
Malayan	

From Stephen Molnar, *Races, Types and Ethnic Groups: The Problem of Human Variation,* © 1975, p. 7. Reprinted by permission of Prentice-Hall, Inc., Englewood Cliffs, New Jersey.

Johann Friedrich Blumenbach (1752-1840) was the last influential eighteenth-century systematist; he might have been the first to use comparative anatomy to study different populations. In his 1770 book, whose title is roughly translated as "The Variety of Man," he divided *Homo* into four races. In the second edition, published in 1781, he divided *Homo* into six races on the basis of head shape. His six divisions were Caucasoid (a name coined on the basis of a skull from the Caucasus region, which Blumenbach felt typical of this "race"), Negroid, Mongoloid, Malayan, Ethiopian, and American Indian; he adhered to this scheme in all subsequent works. According to this theory, morphological differences were attributable to climate, diet, mode of life, hybrid generation, hereditary peculiarities of animals from a diseased temperament and perhaps mutilations, and other factors that may contribute to differences in native varieties. Blumenbach's classification avoided Linnaeus's subjective behavioral characteristics and more or less took into account basic differences in skin pigmentation.

Why Classify? The question often arises as to why early scientists (and pseudoscientists) and their heirs apparent were interested in classifying people into races. Early scientists were concerned with cataloging the human diversity rapidly being thrust on them by explorations. When Linnaeus published his classification in the mid-eighteenth century, Europe still was dividing the legendary from the real. Many still considered the unicorn real, and orangutans and chimpanzees were considered subhumans. In the zoological naiveté of the time they represented human creatures whose existence was sworn to by travelers, missionaries, and traders. "Scientific" descriptions of different human groups were another way of adding to one's knowledge about the environs.

During the period between Linnaeus and Darwin, individuals were measured and described; racial groupings were created and rearranged in an endless procession of descriptions. Behind attempts at constructing racial categories was the implicit, and sometimes explicit, belief that persistence would eventually reveal a divinely inspired pattern. An aura of theological fervor, the search for the "racial holy grail," pervaded. A certain dogmatic tenor characterized this work. Nothing could be more inaccurate; there is not now, and could never have been, anything akin to a "pure" race. Racial formation and breakdown is a dynamic process, occurring whenever populations meet and exchange genes with one another.

Problems with Early Attempts. Early classifiers worked in complete ignorance of what are today considered two fundamental concepts necessary for studying modern population variability—the principles of evolution and population genetics. Once we accepted our place within the evolutionary scheme, studies of population differences radically changed. Instead of seeking a divine pattern, students of human diversity asked questions such as: What is the evidence for natural selection in this group? What kinds of adaptations have certain populations made with their environment? How recent is this group's ancestry? Within this evolutionary framework, new questions were raised and new techniques developed.

Twentieth Century. The first two or three decades of the twentieth century witnessed much interest in population diversity and human adaptation. Unfortunately early twentieth-century workers shared much of their outlook with their preevolutionarily oriented predecessors. Ernest A. Hooton was among the last of the physical anthropologists to present a detailed classification of living populations based on comparative physical and pregenetic evolutionary formulations. Hooton's sorting criteria were primarily phenotypic features (Tables 25-2 and 25-3), many of which continue to be used in conjunction with other criteria. Hooton's scheme recognized three races—Caucasoid, Mongoloid, and Negroid—that were

Table 25-2. Racial Criteria Based on Blood Groups

System	Gene	Caucasoid (European)	Negroid (African)	Mongoloid (Asiatic)
ABO	A^2	Moderate	Moderate	Essentially absent
	B	Low	Intermediate	High
Rh	R	Low	High	Low
	r	High	Intermediate	Essentially absent
Duffy	Ry^a	Intermediate	Low	High
	Fy	Absent	High	High
Diego	Dr^a	Absent	Absent	High
Sutter	Js^a	Absent	High	Absent

From R. H. Osborne, *The Biological and Social Meaning of Race*, p. 169. W. H. Freeman and Company, San Francisco, © 1971.

then divided into primary subraces and then into morphological types. This system provided for different levels of intermixture and some races were considered to be the result of intermixture with other races. Soon some proposed a blender effect—mix two parts Negroid and one part Caucasoid to produce "subtype A," or what have you. This led to some ludicrous schemes.

Individuals were first differentiated one from another by measurement of phenotypic traits, outward manifestations of genetic combinations that were thought to be easily measured and described. The problem with using these traits, besides the fact that we are unsure of their genetic base, is that they do not segregate easily, making them hard to measure. Early attempts at distinguishing populations from one another were largely based on anthropometric measurements (i.e., measurements of the human body) made with the caliper (Figure 25-1). For example, head shapes were measured and divided into three types, according to a so-called cephalic index: dolicocephalic (narrow headed), mesocephalic (medium headed), and brachycephalic (round headed), obtained by calculating a ratio of skull breadth to skull height from fixed points on the skulls. The major problem with calculating skull shape is that skull shape changes with environment and diet. In the early part of the twentieth century it was shown that head shapes of American immigrants' children differed from those of their parents. This was probably due to dietary changes.

Early students often established classifications on the basis of other readily observable traits. Prime among these was skin color, measured by holding a paint chart against the skin and noting the nearest match. In addition to other invalidating points, charts used were not standardized. Hair form and distribution on the body were two additional traits used as an early basis for distinguishing populations.

The Present Outlook

Theoretical Stance. Hooton's scheme is still used today; however, new questions limit its value. His scheme has been greatly modified and is now part of a larger list of sorting criteria. Ideas about modern population diversity have been greatly altered by the impact of population genetics. The application of population genetics and new laboratory techniques

Table 25-3. Racial Criteria Based on Phenotypic Features

Sorting Criteria	Caucasoid	Negroid	Mongoloid
Skin color	Light brown to white, pink, or ruddy.	Dark brown to black.	Yellow or yellow-brown.
Eye color	Never black, all lighter shades.	Dark brown, all black.	Medium to dark brown.
Hair color	Rarely black, all lighter shades.	Black.	Black.
Hair form	Wavy to straight, sometimes loosely curled.	Wooly to frizzy.	Straight, coarse texture.
Nasal form	Usually high and narrow, index[a] under 70.	Usually low and broad, tip and alae thick, index 85 and over.	Root very low, top short, tip and alae medium, index intermediate to Caucasoid and Negroid.
Malars (Cheek bones)	Small.	Variable, usually larger than Caucasoid.	Strong forward and lateral jut, usually covered with a flat pad.
Beard and body hair	Usually medium to heavy, highly variable.	Medium to sparse.	Less than Caucasoid or Negroid.
Membranous lip	Medium to thin, little eversion.	Usually thick, everted, marked lip seam.	Medium, variable.
Skull	Greater development of brow ridges than in Negroids and Mongoloids, mastoid processes.	Rounded forehead, long skull, prominent occiput (back of skull).	Brow ridges poorly developed, round skull, flat occiput with marked ridge; vault (top of the skull) often with a keel.
Face	Straight face; small jaws and prominent chin; high narrow nasal bones and well-developed nasal spine.	Prognathism (forward protrusion of upper jaw), small chin, low broad basal bridge and broad nasal aperture; long narrow palate.	Malars (cheek bones) prominent; root of nose flat and broad; nasal aperture narrow, palate short and wide, lower jaw wide.
Long bones	Thick; joints large and muscle markings prominent.	Slender; shin and forearm bones long relative to upper segments.	Not remarkable; intermediate to Caucasoid and Negroid.

[a]As proposed by Hooton and others and customarily applied when race classification is based on surface features, this index is equal to Breadth × 100/height.

From Richard H. Osborne, *The Biological and Social Meaning of Race*, pp. 166-167. W. H. Freeman and Company, San Francisco, © 1971.

have added important dimensions toward better understanding population variability. Two ideas having the greatest impact for understanding human diversity are the genetic definition of the species and the concept that populations, not individuals, are being classified. Under the

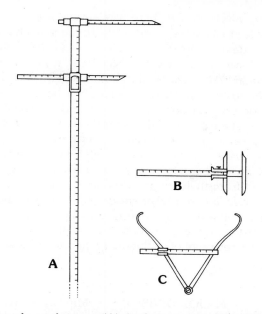

Figure 25-1. Anthropometric equipment. (A) Anthropometer. (B) Sliding caliper. (C) Spreading caliper.

old system even individuals of the same genetic family sometimes found themselves members of different races. We now recognize that a great deal of intrapopulation variability exists; there is no "pure" racial type to which all members of one group must strictly conform. With these realizations, new questions have been raised, such as: What is the nature of the distribution of genetic traits within and between populations resulting in observed population differentiation? Which population differences are genetic, which environmental, and which result from both?

From the Linnean system to the present, using multiple techniques, all attempts to classify human populations have consistently drawn lines at major geographic boundaries. This underlines the fact that these boundaries are fundamental to human diversification. Usually the greater the geographical distance between groups, the greater the genetic distance; geographically intermediate populations tend toward genetic intermediacy. We have moved from a nonevolutionary, threefold classification of "pure" stocks to an evolutionarily oriented genetically based classification. Today's questions—and today's answers—are different; furthermore, today's research techniques vary. There is, however, one basic conclusion: the world is composed of many different human populations and our task is to find out why.

Population diversity was traditionally described by racial subdivisions of the species. The species was divided into major races on the basis of such traits as skin color, hair form, and eye form. The major divisions were subdivided into minor racial groupings on the basis of other traits, such as head shape. Inevitably, populations not fitting the scheme were listed separately, sometimes to be explained away in terms of ancient racial hybridization (Figure 25-2).

In the years following World War II there was a rapid accumulation of genetic data on human populations that led to a reassessment of the traditional scheme. Population biologists anticipated that the new data and new approaches would allow them to construct the "correct" racial taxonomy. However, they soon realized that they were incapable of describing all the complexities of population affinities. While taxonomies emphasizing anthropometry (body measurements) were able to differentiate between the Northern and Southern hemispheres of the Old World, blood group data drew a sharp contrast between the West (Europe and Africa) and the East (Asia, Oceania, and the Americas). Boyd (1953, 1963) found that some populations placed in the same or closely related races in traditional taxonomies (e.g., Asians and American Indians) were genetically quite different from each other. Furthermore, populations described as mixed races (e.g., Australian aborigines) were found to be genetically quite different from their supposed parental populations.

Population and Racial Historical Approaches. Because of the problems with all these schemes, new approaches emerged. One alternative, the population approach, emphasizes variability within local groups rather than descriptions of the average or typical members. This is appealing from the viewpoint of evolutionary theory, because variability is the basis of

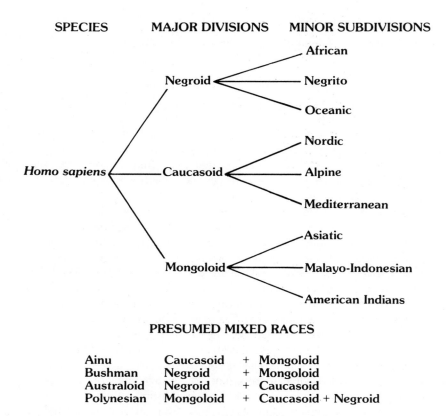

PRESUMED MIXED RACES

Ainu	Caucasoid	+ Mongoloid
Bushman	Negroid	+ Mongoloid
Australoid	Negroid	+ Caucasoid
Polynesian	Mongoloid	+ Caucasoid + Negroid

Figure 25-2. One method of racially classifying the human population.

evolution. The population approach also suggests that former racial taxonomies have little sensible empirical foundation and are more misleading than useful.

The racial-historical approach is the oldest. It considers races fixed and unchanging entities. The primary aim of this approach is to derive a group's evolutionary history by listing certain physical traits that are then compared to other possibly related populations. Under this scheme populations are classified into pure and mixed races, the latter being formed when two or more primary races meet as a result of large-scale migrations. The racial-historical approach renders only token credit to natural selection as the source of population differentiation. Most of the credit goes to historical derivations. The assumption is therefore inherent that races evolved separately.

Zoogeographic Approach. The zoogeographic approach attempts to integrate population genetics with evolution and classification; the major emphasis is on the relationship of physical traits to one's habitat. Adherents of this scheme are concerned with the role of environmental or geographical variation in influencing human diversity.

Clinal Approach. On the opposite end of a continuum of approaches on human variation in which Hooton's typological approach represents one scheme, we have the clinal, or genetic distance, approach, in which attention is paid to the distribution of individual traits and gene frequencies. Since the real variation of any particular genetic trait is limited at any given time, the distribution of identical forms can be grouped into zones and separated from other areas by boundaries determined by the ranges over which a particular trait may be found to have a common expression. Adherents of this approach deny that so-called races actually exist— only clines occur. The assumptions behind the clinal approach stem from evolutionary theory and population genetics. The major cornerstones of the clinal approach are blood group genes and abnormal hemoglobins, and population relationships are determined according to the frequencies of shared genetic traits. Clinal analysis has several assumptions: (1) traits vary, (2) trait variations are due to systematic forces that may relate to some evolutionary mechanism, that is, selection or migration, or to other factors, (3) the two kinds of systematic forces are, in principle, separable, and (4) trait distributions offer an alternative means of relating human diversity to evolutionary theory (Kelso, 1974). Four main alternatives for interpreting human diversity are shown in Table 25-4.

Table 25-4. Four Main Alternatives for Interpreting Human Diversity

Method of Classification	Unit of Analysis	Names Applied
Typological classifications	Trait clusters	Races and other "types"
Population	Mating systems, demes Mendelian populations	Breeding populations
Clinal approach	Individual trait distribution	Clines
Zoogeographical approach	Population genetics, physical traits adapted to habitats	Races

Adapted from A. Kelso, *Physical Anthropology,* 2nd ed., p. 307. J. B. Lippincott Company, Philadelphia, © 1974.

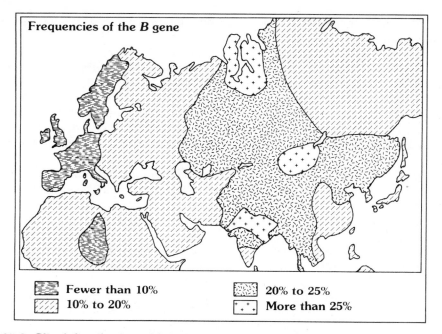

Figure 25-3. Clinal distribution of frequencies of the gene for the B blood group in Europe, Asia, and northern Africa.

With the mapping of clines in the clinal approach one gets a progressive change in allele frequency across space. Clinal maps (Figure 25-3) are similar to temperature maps or barometric pressure gradients. This approach does not assume that species are divided into discretely bounded populations. Clines have both the advantage and disadvantage of considering only one trait at a time. Similarities between a cline and the distribution of some environmental variable such as sickle-cell anemia and falciparum malaria, for example, may be a clue to the genetic system (pages 487-92). One disadvantage of this approach is that a single allele may give a distorted view of the overall degree of similarity or difference between two populations. between two populations. High frequencies of sickle-cell anemia in central Africa and some tribal societies in India indicate only that these populations both face the selective pressure of falciparum malaria, not that there is a genetic link between the populations.

Biological Distance Approach. Another approach to describing biological similarities or differences is to use various measures of biological distance. As in traditional racial taxonomies, distance measures use data from many characteristics. Differences between populations or localities for many traits are put into one of the various formulae which quantify the degrees of similarity or divergence between the populations. The biological difference is selective agents acting on the genetic system (pp. 487-92). One disadvantage of this approach is that a single allele may give a distorted view of the overall degree of similarity or difference then arrange the populations in a dendrogram, a branching diagram showing degrees of similarity or difference (Figure 25-4). Although superficially similar to a racial taxonomy, the dendrogram differs in that the same characterisitics are used at all levels of the branching dendrogram. Measures of biological distance overcome some of the limitations of both racial taxonomy and clines. Since the identity of individual alleles is lost in the process of calculating

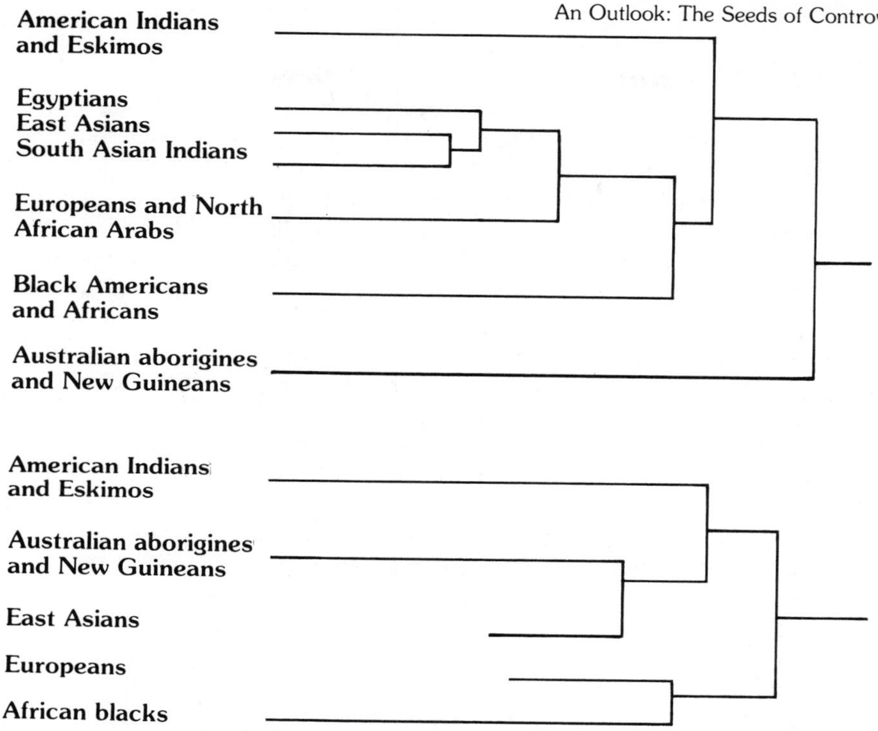

American Indians
and Eskimos

Egyptians
East Asians
South Asian Indians

Europeans and North
African Arabs

Black Americans
and Africans

Australian aborigines
and New Guineans

American Indians
and Eskimos

Australian aborigines
and New Guineans

East Asians

Europeans

African blacks

Figure 25-4. Two dendrograms based on genetic distances between various human populations. That on top is based on ABO, MN, and Rh frequencies. The bottom example is based on 58 genes. Note the striking differences in which populations are grouped together. These two examples are not only based on somewhat different genetic data, but also employ different measures of genetic distance.

distance, the dendrogram is not useful in searching for selective agents. Small distances between populations may be the result of a recent separation of those populations or of gene flow between them over a long time period. Biological distance is unlikely to be a reliable indicator of the time depth separating various populations of a species.

Important Concepts

Polytypism and Polymorphism. The Mendelian population is a reproductive community of sexual and cross-fertilizing individuals among whom mating regularly occurs and who thus contribute to the gene pool and is the focal point for determining population affinities. *Homo sapiens sapiens* is a **polymorphic** and **polytypic** species. The term "polymorphic" refers to traits that occur in one habitat in such proportions that the rarest of them cannot be maintained merely by mutation. "Polytypic" refers to the fact that *H. sapiens sapiens* contains different varieties of subpopulations. Both these traits are natural to any species.

Homo sapiens sapiens is also considered to be panmictic. Theoretically, in a panmictic population, gene flow is nonrestrictive; each population segment has the same or similar gene frequencies as other parts. In truth, however, restrictions exist; there are reproductive barriers. Cultural norms are among the most effective barriers to true panmixis; linguistic, cultural, or historical differences have all prevented panmixis from becoming a reality.

Race versus No Race

The concept of race arose in mercantile Europe, when Europeans awoke with renewed awareness to the fact that many different peoples and cultures existed in various parts of the world. The race concept emerged in an effort to assimilate this new information and the term "race" was introduced into common usage and scientific taxonomies. Soon, racist ideologies evolved, as much a result of economic, social, and religious exploitation as anything. Eighteenth-century scientists debated whether races had separate origins and they argued over whether God independently created each so-called race.[2] In the first decades of the twentieth century, especially during and immediately after World War II, most scientists and educated persons shifted to a position of equalitarianism. Now, anthropologists argue whether in fact there is such a phenomenon as race (Lieberman, 1968; Livingstone, 1964).

Lumpers and Splitters. The subject of population diversity, human races, elicits emotional and often passionate responses. Freed from the emotional situation, what posture should the scientist adopt? Two extreme attitudes emerge. One is to leave the problem in abeyance because of the risk that scientific findings will be prostituted to political or social ends. The alternative is to adopt a make-believe detachment. Some believe racial groups are discernible, that human races exist, that there is enough human diversity to separate populations.

Another viewpoint is that of the clinist school. Clinists believe that the causal mechanisms of variability between populations are what is important, not the magnitude of the variation. Clinists argue that human differences result from natural selection operating within ecological zones and that such forces and zones do not necessarily coincide with population boundaries.

Both sides do agree on a definition of race as a population distinguishable from others on the basis of inherited physical characters. Beyond this there is disagreement as to where one group ends and another begins. The various antagonists contend over the issue of whether one can locate boundaries; the argument hinges on the significance of the gradation of genetically based physical characters. The race-exists school argues that these genetic gradations are intergradations between races. The no-race adherents, clinists, hold that the gradations are not intergradations but overlapping gradients not confined to boundaries or a particular population.

Inhabitants in different parts of the world are often visibly different; these differences are in part genetic and this is the essence of the biological conception of race. Surely, any two persons, even brothers or sisters, differ; however, racial differences are genetic differences between Mendelian populations, not between persons. Yet traits considered to be racial differentiators are also traits that differ between persons. The difficulty arises when a group is given a name; at this time one is likely to assume that all individuals composing that group are the same in each trait. This is typological thinking, and modern biologists should abandon this notion.

Race Defined

What then are these so-called races and what constitutes a race? Those who believe races can be distinguished define a race as any population containing a genetic constellation differentiating is from adjacent populations. A race is characterized not so much by the

---

[2]The argument pitting monogenesis against polygenesis.

absolute presence or absence of some hereditary trait; rather racial differences are compounds of individual differences. This relativity, this lack of hard and fast dichotomies in racial differences, is disappointing to adherents of old-fashioned racial typologies.

New concepts as to what constitutes a taxonomic species have had an important influence on the race concept. The lowest category generally recognized in formal zoological nomenclature is the subspecies. These are not closed breeding units, as species normally are, although they represent distinct breeding populations. Such breeding units have been reproductively isolated from one another (for whatever reason) for a sufficient time to have developed a degree of genetic similarity rendering them distinguishable from adjacent populations. Some biologists, such as Ernst Mayr, consider subspecific differences to be equivalent to racial differences (Table 25-5). One widely accepted definition for establishing races is that they are breeding populations differing in the frequency of one or more genetic variants. Races are simply populations within which a significant number of individuals share a particular variant of a gene, or genes, common to the population.

Except for identical twins, everyone is biologically, genetically different; this diversity must not and cannot be confused with inequality. Equality and inequality are sociological, political, economic concepts, whereas identity and diversity are biological phenomena. Diversity is an observable fact whereas equality is an ethical concept. Societies may, and unfortunately many do, withhold equality from all their members, but at this stage they cannot make all their members genetically the same. It is very doubtful that eliminating diversity would be a good thing evolutionarily, for population diversity is a long-range adaptation for survival.

Table 25-5. Definitions of Race

Dobzhansky	Races are defined as populations differing in the incidence of certain genes, but actually exchanging or potentially able to exchange genes across whatever boundaries (usually geographic) separate them. (1944:252)
	Race differences are objectively ascertainable facts, the number of races we chose to recognize is a matter of convenience (1962:266)
Hulse	. . . races are populations which can be readily distinguished from one another on genetic grounds alone. (1963:262)
Boyd	We may define a human race as a population which differs significantly from other human populations in regard to the frequency of one or more of the genes it possesses. It is an arbitrary matter which, and how many, gene loci we choose to consider as a significant "constellation" . . . (1950:207)
Garn	At the present time there is general agreement that a race is a breeding population, largely if not entirely isolated reproductively from other breeding populations. The measure of race is thus reproductive isolation, arising commonly but not exclusively from geographical isolation. (1960:7)
Mayr	A subspecies is an aggregate of local populations of a species, inhabiting a geographic subdivision of the range of the species, and differing taxonomically from other populations of the species. (1963:348)

The IQ Controversy[3]

The Meanings of Intelligence. Out of data gathered in the nineteenth and twentieth centuries came the notion that races differ in intelligence. The concept of intelligence has been defined in various ways by psychologists without general agreement as to its precise meaning. In fact, there has never been any agreement among psychologists as to exactly what intelligence means. It has been defined by some as "the inseparable unity of affective and cognitive life." According to this perspective, intelligence, learning, and personality are inseparably linked (Piaget, 1950). It has also been defined in strictly neurological terms, in which it is said that intelligent behavior can be understood by understanding brain function. Another group, the psychometricians, construct various intelligence and special ability tests, apply them to young people, and assess the young people's performance (Horrocks and Schooner, 1968).

The construction of intelligence tests began early in the twentieth century. In 1904 the French government established a commission for the purpose of determining which children attending French public schools did not possess the intellectual capacity to profit from the usual academic instruction. Alfred Binet was asked to serve on this commission. The commission was instructed to devise a more valid instrument than the judgment of teachers for dividing French school children into special classes.

Binet and an associate, Theodore Simon, devised tests that were used with school children aged 3 to 11 years in an attempt to discover the mental capabilities of these children. In 1908, the tests were revised and test items organized in age groupings with specific tests for different age levels up to age 13. As a result, the concept of "mental age" was born. Mental age supposedly measured intelligence level independent of chronological age. Lewis Terman of Stanford University later translated these tests into English and subsequently standardized them on the white, middle-class population in the United States. The Stanford-Binet test of 1916 and its revisions in 1937 and 1960 became the standard measurement of intelligence in the United States.

Measurement of Intelligence. The Stanford-Binet Intelligence Scale and the several Wechsler intelligence scales for children and adults are now the most widely used intelligence tests in the United States. The Stanford-Binet test yields a score of intelligence called the Intelligence Quotient, or IQ. A child's IQ is the ratio of his or her mental age (MA) to his or her chronological age (CA), multiplied by 100, as in the formula

$$IQ = \frac{MA}{CA} \times 100$$

An IQ of 100, therefore, indicates that a child's mental age is identical to his or her chronological age. The Wechsler scales consist of a series of verbal and performance tests that also yield a measure of IQ.

Interpretation of IQ Scores. For several years the concept of IQ has been surrounded by controversy. The never-ending argument about whether intelligence comes primarily from the learning that takes place in an enriched environment or primarily from the genetic factors that are passed to children from parents remains unresolved. Obviously heredity and environment each play a major role in intellectual develpment. The specific proportions that each contributes remains in question. Many hours of debate have been devoted to this subject.

[3]The author thanks his colleague, Dr. E. O. Arewa, for providing the core of this discussion.

In 1969, Arthur Jensen published a controversial paper based on an extensive review of studies about the heritability (the proportion of the total phenotypic variance that is genetic) of IQ scores in a representative sample of British and American white populations. Jensen concluded that the heritability of IQ scores for the included populations in his sample was 0.80. The implication from this conclusion was that heredity plays a much greater role than environment in determining intelligence. Jensen concluded from this that the 15-point difference in the mean IQ scores of American whites and blacks may be genetic and not related to cultural differences. These conclusions are highly controversial since they could lead to the conclusion that compensatory education for black children would be futile as a means of increasing their IQ.

Heritability and Ability Differences Between Human Groups. Jensen claims that since IQ is highly heritable, observed IQ differences in blacks and whites are largely genetic in origin. He argues that the results obtained on within-group heritability for whites provides the basis for reaching a valid conclusion regarding between-group heritability for both blacks and whites.

From the perspective of population genetics, Jensen's conclusions are not supported. Population geneticists regard variations within and between populations as follows. The four evolutionary mechanisms of mutation, genetic drift, gene flow, and natural selection operate in opposite ways. Factors tending to increase genetic variation within populations also tend to decrease them between populations and vice versa (Lewontin, 1975). For example, mutation increases genetic differences within populations but decreases it between populations. Migration operates in a similar manner. Conversely, both genetic drift and natural selection decrease variation within populations and increase it between populations.

In view of the principle just stated, Jensen's conclusion of a high within-group heritability in white and black populations is unsound. There is no scientific basis on which within-group heritability can be equated with between-group heritability, as Jensen has done. Heritability estimates on the white population cannot be validly used to reach a scientific conclusion regarding the mental ability of blacks as a group or to make any valid comparative statements about the mental abilities of whites or blacks. In fact, variations within different ethnic groups in the United States are much more pronounced than differences between the groups. A more fruitful focus should, in the light of this fact, be on individual abilities and not on group averages in any investigation of ability differences.

Additional criticism of Heritability Studies.

1. Genetic studies by Glass and Li (1953) show that American blacks have about 28 percent nonblack ancestry, most of European derivation. Furthermore, it is estimated that 36 million whites share a genetic background with persons of African origin. There are no pure genetically homogeneous populations in the United States, as the heritability studies cited by Jensen imply.

2. It is not possible to find comparable groups for testing. We cannot accurately measure comparability. At present, we have no tools that will accurately minimize or adjust for the social, economic, and political privation of black Americans.

3. Brace and Livingstone (1973) have noted the effects of malnutrition on IQ, and this fact should affect the performance of many environmentally deprived children.

In short, there are numerous intervening environmental variables. Genetic inferiority has simply not been proven. In fact, one may make the opposite argument. If intelligence is in part defined as coping behavior, those blacks who survived centuries of privation and prejudice nhuman living conditions may be said to be more intelligent than those who have worked hard to exploit these conditions and have forced their fellow humans to live in these conditions. If every individual in a group were maturing and living in a uniform and nondiscriminatory environment, where equality existed, it would then be possible to determine with greater assurance that intergroup or individual differences were genetically based. In the absence of this condition, any explanation of differences solely on the basis of genes is not scientific.

Race and IQ: Is There a Relationship? To establish any significant relationship between any two variables, one needs an adequate understanding of the definitions and meanings of each variable. With regard to race, it has previously been shown that there is considerable confusion as to its meaning. Concerning IQ, there are a few myths about the intelligence that it presumably measures.

As does the concept of race, the concept of IQ has its own peculiar problems. Ginsburg (1972) has delineated several of the myths associated with the IQ test:

1. The IQ test measures an innate ability not affected by experience.
2. The IQ test measures a unitary mental ability called intelligence.
3. The IQ test is designed to measure intellectual competence.
4. Differences in IQ scores are a reflection of basic differences in fundamental intellectual ability.

All these statements are false because (1) human abilities are affected by experience, (2) intelligence consists of many kinds of ability, (3) IQ testing does not measure intellectual competence for a vast number of individuals, and (4) the definition of "fundamental intellectual ability" is both subjective and relative.

Given the various classifications of race, an association of race with IQ can have one of the following meanings:

1. In a typological classification of race, IQ can be linked with external visible differences such as skin color. There is no relationship between any physically visible human traits and IQ.
2. In a population classification of race, behavioral differences (such as IQ scores) between races can be considered genetic. Again, even though genetic differences between races for behavioral traits may exist, there is no sound evidence for such existence to date.
3. From a clinical perspective, IQ can be linked with clines. This classification is nonsense.

From this we can conclude that there cannot be a scientific relationship between biological race and IQ. The relevant variables with regard to IQ scores are not the genes but the socioeconomic variables producing differences in IQ. Investigations that attempted to link race and IQ have been built on invalid premises and are, therefore, scientifically unsound.

A Cultural Bias in Standardized Tests. The Stanford-Binet test and the Wechsler Intelligence Scale for Children were standardized on the U.S. white population. A major concern regarding the use of these tests has been whether they have taken into account subcultural differences in the background of the minority children on whom the tests have been administered even though such tests were not originally standardized on these children.

In addressing this problem, two opposing positions are taken. One position is that the standardized tests now being used are free of cultural bias and can therefore be validly and reliably used in a multicultural setting. The other position is that since these tests are standardized on a particular cultural segment in a multicultural environment, they are necessarily biased in favor of the cultural segment on which they are standardized.

Anthropologists as a group tend to support the latter position.

With particular reference to American blacks, the idea of a cultural bias in standardized tests has been closely linked to the significant question as to whether a distinct black subculture exists in the United States. If a distinct black subcultural entity exists and the various tests administered in schools are not standardized on such a subculture, but are in reality standardized on the larger Euroamerican culture, such tests are then culturally unfair to black children.

As used by anthropologists and sociologists, subcultures consist of groups within a larger sociocultural setting with a clearly recognized pattern of behavior. Such groups share the total culture of the society but their special cultural traits are numerous and unique to their members in such a manner that these traits cluster into distinctive and recognized subcultural patterns. Members of the various subcultures share meanings and symbols that differ from those held by the wider society of which they are a part.

Close examination shows that the prevailing approach whereby environmental and genetic effects are partitioned to determine which are more important in shaping human mental capability is extremely misleading. Environment and genes are significantly important, in fact, indispensable. All organisms are composed of genes and all inhabit environments. Without the latter, genes cannot act. This is why traits are both genetically and environmentally influenced. At present, science does not possess the tools to determine what portion of intelligence is determined by heredity and what portion is due to environment. It seems, therefore, that the appropriate question should be the extent to which certain observable differences in human groups are jointly conditioned by genotypic differences among the environments in which group members are born and mature.

There is considerable disagreement as to an effective means of defining populations and describing population diversity. Early attempts were frustrated by the Biblical injunction that all individuals were divinely created. In the fifteenth and sixteenth centuries populations were distinguished on the basis of readily observable traits such as skin color. Certain subjective statements were made about behavior according to morphological characteristics.

During the eighteenth century the work of Carolus Linnaeus received wide attention; he proposed that there were four living human races. Blumenbach, a well-known eighteenth-century systematist, based his racial classification on anatomy. Early twentieth-century anthropologists continued their reliance on easily measured traits and they distinguished populations on the basis of such things as head shape.

Today's theoretical outlook is different; the core of this new outlook is a reliance on the principles of population genetics. Today we prefer to study genetic traits with a known mode of inheritance. Basic to the study of population diversity is the understanding that *Homo sapiens sapiens* is a polymorphic, polytypic, and theoretically a panmictic population.

A debate rooted in social and political considerations has arisen in the study of population differences that opposes clinists to those arguing for the validity of race. Clinists contend that races cannot be differentiated, that there is a continuum of traits. Those arguing for the validity of race contend that there are clear-cut population differences. Neither set of proponents equates population differences with social discriminatory injustices.

The meaning of intelligence, its measurement, and its relation to race remain controversial issues. Performance on IQ tests reflects the experience of the individual, and studies that suggest that different levels of intelligence are characteristic of different races are invalid.

Bibliography

Anonymous. 1956. *The race question in modern science.* UNESCO Publications. New York: Morrow.

Baker, P. 1967. The biological race concept as a research tool. *American Journal of Physical Anthropology* 27:21.

Barnicot, N. 1964. Taxonomy and variation in modern man. In *The concept of race,* edited by A. Montagu, pp. 180-227. New York: Free Press.

Binet, A., and Henri, V. 1895. La psychologie individuelle. *L'Année Psychologique* 2:411-65.

Bleibtreu, H., and Downs, J., eds. 1971. *Human variation: readings in physical anthropology.* Beverly Hills, Calif.: Glencoe Press.

Boyd, W. 1950. *Genetics and the races of man.* Boston: Little, Brown.

_____. 1963. Genetics and the human race. *Science* 140:1057-64.

Brace, C., Gamble, C., and Bond, J., eds. 1971. *Race and intelligence.* Washington, D.C.: American Anthropological Association.

Brace, C., and Livingstone, F. 1973. On creeping Jensenism. In *Man in evolutionary perspective,* compiled by C. Brace and J. Metress, pp. 426-37. New York: Wiley.

Coon, C., Garn, S., and Birdsell, J. 1950. *Races: a study of the problems of race formation in man.* Springfield, Ill.: Thomas.

Count, E. 1950. *This is race.* New York: Shuman.

Dobzhansky, T. 1944. On species and races of living and fossil man. *American Journal of Physical Anthropology* 2:252.

_____. 1962. *Mankind evolving: the evolution of the human species.* New Haven and London: Yale University Press.

_____. 1968. *Science and the concept of race.* New York: Columbia University Press.

Ford, E. 1965. *Genetic polymorphism.* Cambridge, Mass.: M.I.T. Press.

Garn, S., ed. 1960. *Readings on race.* Springfield, Ill.: Thomas.

Garn, S. 1971. *Human races,* 3rd ed. Springfield, Ill.: Thomas.

Ginsburg, H. 1972. *The myth of the deprived child: poor children's intellect and education.* Englewood Cliffs, N. J.: Prentice-Hall.

Glass, B., and Li, C. 1953. The dynamics of racial intermixture—an analysis based on the American Negro. *American Journal of Human Genetics* 5:1-20.

Goldsby, R. 1971. *Race and races.* New York: Random House.

Hiernaux, J. 1964. The concept of race and the taxonomy of mankind. In *The concept of race,* edited by A. Montagu, pp. 29-45. New York: Free Press.

Horrocks, J., and Schooner, T. 1968. *Measurement for teachers.* Columbus: Merrill.

Hulse, F. 1963. *The human species.* New York: Random House.

Jensen, A. 1969. How much can we boost I.Q. and scholastic achivevement? *Harvard Educational Review* 39:1-123.

_____. 1976. Test bias and construct validity. *Phi Delta Kappan* 58:340-46.

Kennedy, K. 1976. *Human variation in space and time.* Dubuque, Ia.: Brown.

Kelso, A. 1974. *Physical anthropology,* 2nd ed. Philadelphia: Lippincott.

King, J. 1971. *The biology of race.* New York: Harcourt Brace Jovanovich.

Klass, M., and Hellman, H. 1971. *The kinds of mankind.* Philadelphia: Lippincott.

Laughlin, W., and Osborne, R., eds. 1967. *Human variation and origins.* San Francisco: Freeman.

Lieberman, L. 1968. The debate over race: a study in the sociology of knowledge. Reprint from *Phylon,* the Atlanta University Review of Race and Culture. Atlanta, Georgia.

Livingstone, F. 1964. On the nonexistence of human races. In *The concept of race,* edited by A. Montagu, pp. 46-60. New York: Macmillan.

Mead, M., Dobzhansky, T., Tobach, E., and Light, R., eds. 1968. *Science and the concept of race.* New York: Columbia University Press.

Molnar, S. 1975. *Races, types, and ethnic groups.* Englewood Cliffs, N.J.: Prentice-Hall.

Montagu, A. 1964. Discussions and criticism on the race concept. *Current Anthropology* 5:317.

——————. 1965. *Man's most dangerous myth: the fallacy of race.* New York: Macmillan.

Myrdal, G. 1944. *An American dilemma: the Negro problem and modern democracy.* New York: Harper and Brothers.

Osborne, R. 1971. The history and nature of race classification. In *The biological and social meaning of race,* edited by R. Osborne, pp. 159-70. San Francisco: Freeman.

Piaget, J. 1950. *The psychology of intelligence.* New York: Harcourt, Brace and World.

Ryan, J. 1972. I.Q. and the illusion of objectivity. In *Race and intelligence,* edited by K. Richardson and D. Spears, pp. 36-55. Baltimore: Penguin Books.

Slotkin, J. 1965. *Readings in early anthropology.* New York: Wenner-Gren Foundation.

Spuhler, J., ed. 1967. *Genetic diversity and human behavior.* Chicago: Aldine.

Stanton, W. 1960. *The leopard's spots: scientific attitudes toward race in America, 1815-59.* Chicago: University of Chicago Press.

Valentine, C. 1971. Deficit, difference, and bicultural models of Afro-American behavior. *Harvard Educational Review* 41:137-57.

Washburn, S. 1963. The study of race. *American Anthropologist* 65:521.

——————. The study of race. In *The concept of race,* edited by A. Montagu, pp. 242-60. New York: Macmillan.

Chapter 26

Climatic Adaptations

This chapter discusses the differences between the mechanisms of adaptation, acclimation, acclimatization, and habituation. The chapter focuses on adaptations requisite for life in humid, hot environments; life on the desert; life in extreme cold; and life at high altitudes. We are also concerned with possible explanations for differences in skin and eye color.

Important Concepts

At this point it is important to define a number of concepts applicable to the understanding of how an organism meets environmental pressures. Functional adaptation is accomplished through changes in organ system function, histology, morphology, biochemical composition, anatomical relationships, and body composition, either independently or integrated in the organism as a whole. These changes can occur through acclimation, acclimatization, or habituation (Figure 26-1).

Adaptation. The scientist trying to understand human diversity studies the problem of short-term adaptation (or acclimatization) and long-term adaptations related to survival in a particular environment. Garn (1957) has stated that it is one thing to prove that a given trait may be beneficial, and quite another to show its survival value. Individuals possess enough plasticity to adapt to new conditions in the short run, for example, tanning in high-light conditions. However, this plasticity is very different from the adaptive capacity of individuals living in an environment over a long period of time. As an example, individuals living in low altitudes can make some of the requisite adjustments to high-altitude living (such as life in the high Andes), but they will probably be unable to work and reproduce with the same efficiency as populations long-adapted to this environment. Both long- and short-term adaptations are of interest to the human biologist trying to ascertain evolutionary processes.

In humans, as well as among other animals, climatic adaptations are achieved through at least four different mechanisms: genetic changes, growth changes, physiological changes, and behavioral changes. Genetic changes are the slowest of the group and behavioral changes are

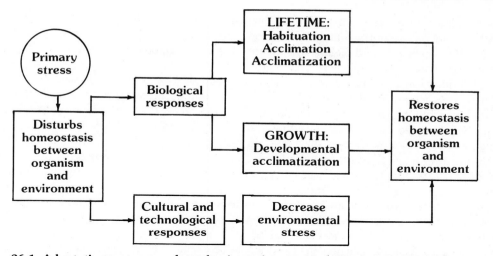

Figure 26-1. Adaptative process and mechanisms that enable individual or population to maintain homeostasis in the face of primary disturbing stress.

normally the most rapid. Genetic changes are intergenerational changes occurring between successive generations of a population. Growth changes refer to ontogenetic changes, that is, relatively irreversible changes occurring within an individual's lifetime. Physiological changes are, for the most part, reversible. An example of this is menstrual disorders experienced by females who move from low to high altitudes and back to low altitudes.

The problem with this scheme is that genetic, growth, and physiological changes are not mutually exclusive categories. The demarcation between growth and physiological response is often hazy. The same is true for the dividing line between physiological and behavioral responses. These categories of response are sometimes designated by the terms adaptation, acclimation, acclimatization, and habituation.

Our behavioral response takes on a greater importance than is the case with any other animal. Because of our culturally patterned ways of responding to environmental stresses, much of behavior, although capable of rapid alteration, usually manifests itself in quite stable patterns that are nongenetically generationally transmitted. This has proven to be a highly efficient means of responding to environmental stress, permitting *Homo sapiens* to explore many possibilities for moving into and inhabiting an array of environments. Although cultural adaptations have sometimes replaced genetic responses, the possibility of cultural adaptations to environmental stress has not totally excluded genetic adaptations. There are real differences among populations in their respective abilities to adapt to certain stresses. Technological adaptation has, however, opened many areas for human habitation that might not now be available if we relied solely on biological and genetic mechanisms.

Despite methodological problems brought about by the possibility of acclimatization, cultural adaptation, and small sample sizes, there are studies whose results indicate real differences in a given population's ability to adapt to certain stresses. Before we proceed to discuss some of these differences, we should note that climatic adaptations are not clear-cut. An adaptation often carries with it some disadvantageous side effects. Adaptation is a game of probabilities, of balancing the adaptive against the nonadaptive. If the bad side effects, the detrimental nature of the adaptation, are outweighed by its good effects, we may expect that adaptation to be retained. Balanced polymorphisms, discussed in the next chapter, are a good example of this process.

   Acclimation. Acclimation refers to short-term physiological changes in response to stress. These responses are relatively modest and use resources already present to reduce stresses that lower functional efficiency. For example, some problems encountered in high altitudes can be corrected by acclimation. In most cases the complaints of sea-level dwellers due to high-altitude stresses such as dizziness, nausea, shortness of breath, and inability to sleep subside after a few days as a result of short-term physiological adjustments. The capacity to endure new environmental stresses may be increased by repeated exposures until one attains a state resembling acclimatization.

   Acclimatization. Acclimatization refers to an adjustment to a situation that lasts for a relatively extended period of time, as when one makes a permanent move to a significantly different climatic condition. Acclimatization may also occur in response to conditions that last for only a few months, as when one experiences seasonal changes. Acclimatization consists of changes occurring within the organism's lifetime that reduce the strain caused by stressful changes in the natural climate or by complex environmental stresses. If adaptive traits are acquired during the organism's growth period, the process is termed either developmental adaptation or developmental acclimatization

   The changes that occur through acclimatization are useful for coping and they are reversible. Stini (1975:10) notes that acclimatization provides an example "of an unexpressed genotypic capacity being exploited in the face of a new set of demands and might be viewed as a temporary reordering of priorities, which may persist as long as the conditions evoking it persist."

   Habituation. Short-term responses to stress might be included in the category of habituation. Habituation may be viewed as reduction in the level of physiological responses to a stress situation. This process allows an organism to maintain a normal state despite potentially disruptive stimuli and cushions an individual from adverse secondary reactions of its own response system (Stini, 1975). Habituation may fall into two categories: "specific habituation" and "general habituation." The former refers to a process such as reduction in pain experienced in a specific region, as in chilling one finger. Using the same example, "general habituation" refers to the reduction in the overall intensity of a physiological response, such as vasoconstriction (reduction of the blood flow) to the entire periphery while the chilling of the single finger is experienced. Habituation is concerned with preventing damage to the organism as a result of its own overreaction to stress, whereas acclimation refers to a graded adjustment to the stress itself.

   Habituation relies on learning and conditioning, which enable the organism to transfer an existing response to a new stimulus. The extent to which nonphysiological responses are important in maintaining homeostasis depends on the severity of environmental stress (Frisancho, 1979).

Some General Rules of Adaptation

Attempts to link our physical features with environmental factors are not new. Hippocratic medicine viewed humans in their environmental context and attempted to explain observed physical differences in terms of climatic factors. In the *Historia Animalium,* Aristotle commented on the correlation between human skin pigmentation and latitude. Poseidonius suggested that hot climate was responsible for skin pigmentation, nasal flatness, thickening of the lips, and frizzled hair. Du Muller argued that in hot climates the amount of oxygen inspired is insufficient to change the carbon to carbonic acid and the unconsumed carbon is deposited in the pigment cells of the skin to produce dark pigmentation (Roberts, 1978). With this brief historical background, we can now look into modern research on the relationship between environment and human appearance.

Roberts (1978) notes that climatic factors can be expected to influence the form of the organism in various ways:

1. Climatic factors may influence an organism's genotype directly and indirectly. Direct influences include (a) promoting morphological and physiological features that provide greater organic efficiency in a given environment and (b) affecting cytological processes; indirect influences include (c) influencing the size of the population a region can support and (d) influencing the degree of accessibility of a population, that is, its degree of isolation.
2. Climatic factors may also influence the organism's phenotype. This can be accomplished directly by (a) modifying gene expression through such factors as temperature and humidity, and indirectly by (b) conditioning the amount and quality of materials necessary for existence, growth, and development.

Allen's and Bergmann's Rules. The human body comes in various shapes and sizes. Some variation is undoubtedly due to nutrition; but some is a response to long-standing adaptations to certain habitats. Two rules, **Bergmann's rule** (formulated in 1847) and **Allen's rule** (formulated in 1877), are generalizations that are often used to explain the diversity in body size and shape in animals. The climatic factor in the case of both rules is cold or heat. According to Allen's rule, shape changes to achieve an optimal volume-to-surface ratio (Figure 26-2). This rule states that extremities and appendages (ears, limbs, tail, fingers, and toes) tend to be shorter in cold climates than in warmer climates. Because they expose less body surface and are closer to the body's core temperature, shorter extremities conserve heat. Longer extremities expose greater body surface and offer additional surface for dissipating heat in

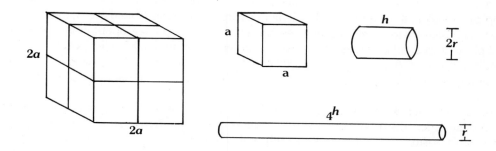

Figure 26-2. A change in the ratio of surface area to volume resulting from a change in size without a change in shape. (The large cube differs from the small by a factor of 2 in linear dimensions but by a factor of 8 in volume.) A change in the ratio of surface area to volume from a change in shape. (The long cylinder has twice the circumferential area of the short cylinder but an equal volume.)

warm climates. According to Bergmann's rule, body size changes to achieve an optimal volume-to-surface ratio. This rule states that body size tends to be greater (heavier) in cold than in warm climates. A low surface area to high body volume is efficient in heat retention, and a high surface area and low body volume proportion is efficient in heat dissipation.

Body surface area may influence heat exchange in two ways. Under conditions in which the ambient temperature is lower than that of the skin, a large surface area per unit of body weight can be advantageous for dissipating heat. However, when the ambient temperature is higher than that of the skin, as in the desert, such a ratio can be a disadvantage because it increases the amount of heat that can be gained from the larger surface area exposed. Increasing absolute size increases both metabolic heat production and the capacity to store heat, each being a function of body volume.

Tolerance to cold stress is affected by the size and shape of the body. When expressed as per unit of body weight, the heat required to maintain a constant internal body temperature is greater in a small individual than a large individual. This is because surface area exposed to the environment, all other factors being constant, is greater per unit of body weight if the total body is small. For this reason, in a cold environment, all factors being constant, a small individual must produce relatively more heat than a large individual to maintain homeostasis (Frisancho, 1979). According to Fourier's Law of Heat Flow, the rate of heat loss per minute is directly proportional to body surface and to the difference between body core temperature and that of the environment, and inversely proportional to the thickness of the body shell.

Allen's rule and Bergmann's rule were relatively unknown as explanatory vehicles of human diversity until 1950. Even now no one argues that these rules can be strictly applied to animal populations in all cases; they are, however, possible explanatory models for various adaptive traits. For example, the short limbs and minimum surface-to-mass ratio in the Eskimo illustrate Allen's rule at one extreme. These are adaptations to conserve heat. The increased limb length and a maximum surface-to-mass ratio characteristic of the African Nuer are oft-quoted examples of Allen's rule working where heat loss is adaptive. Overall, however, there is less evidence for Allen's rule than there is for Bergmann's in human populations. There is evidence, for example, for shorter lower extremities in cold climate populations, but not especially for short upper extremities.

Homo sapiens sapiens has inhabited diverse habitats since its first appearance in the tropical areas of Africa and Asia. Settlement in previously uninhabited areas, many of which presented new environmental pressures, required a number of new adaptations. Anatomical and physiological adaptations accompanied settlement in humid, hot climates, in dry desert conditions, in cold Arctic and semi-Arctic regions, and in areas of high altitude. What general adaptations might we expect to find in each of these different habitats? What are the adaptive pressures?

An environmental stress causes a disturbance in the normal functioning of an organism. Eventually, such disturbance causes disruption of internal homeostasis, for example, the organism's ability to maintain a stable internal environment despite diverse and disruptive environmental influences. Functionally, all adaptive responses of the organism are made to restore internal homeostasis. These controls operate in a hierarchy at all levels of biological organization.

Humans living in hot or cold climates must undergo some functional adjustments to maintain thermal balance. In the same manner, humans exposed to high altitudes must adjust through physiological, chemical, and morphological means. Failure to activate the functional adaptive processes may result in failure to maintain homeostasis. This failure, in turn, results in poor adaptation and eventual incapacity.

Homeostasis is a function of a dynamic interaction of feedback mechanisms whereby a given stimulus activates a response aimed at restoring the original equilibrium. Several mathematical models of homeostasis have been proposed. Generally, they show that when a primary stress disturbs the homeostasis between an organism and environment, to function normally the organism must resort to biological responses, or in the case of humans, to both biological and cultural-technological responses. Through biological responses, the organism overcomes the environmental stress and its physiological activities occur either at the same level as before the stress or take place at another level (Frisancho, 1979).

Bear in mind that the following discussion concerns only biological responses to stress. We will not discuss cultural adaptations to environmental stresses, although one factor separating us from the rest of the animal world is our capacity to adapt culturally to stress situations, as we have done so many times in our evolutionary history.

Heat Adaptation. The fundamental problem for all warm-blooded (homoiothermic) animals exposed to heat stress is heat dissipation. Therefore, most of the physiological responses to heat stress are aimed at dissipating heat. Successful tolerance of heat stress requires the development of synchronized responses permitting the organism to lose heat in an efficient manner and maintain homeostasis.

Humans encounter heat stress not only in tropical equatorial regions, but also during the summer in many of the areas in the temperate zones. Generally, hot climates are classified as either hot-dry or hot-wet. Hot-dry climates are found in desert regions such as those of the southwestern United States, the Kalahari, the Sahara, and other regions of the world. The hot-wet, or hot-humid, zones are typical of the tropical rain forest usually located within the latitudes of 10° to 20° Fahrenheit (F) above or below the equator.

As you may know from personal experience, hot-humid environments may be enervating. With moisture-laden air, the body becomes bathed in a continuous layer of sweat in an effort to reduce the heat load. However, this heat-reducing mechanism introduces the danger of excessive salt loss. If the body temperature rises too high, death due to circulatory collapse becomes possible. Hot-humid climates favor individuals who can maintain a moderate work load in the water-saturated atmosphere.

There is both direct and indirect evidence for the existence of heat adaptations in humans. Baker (1958), for example, compared the tolerance of American black and white subjects to humid heat. These subjects were carefully matched and acclimatized, and it was found that the American blacks were better adapted to humid heat.

Assuming that long-term tropical inhabitants are the product of evolutionary adaptations to humid heat, what mechanisms are at least theoretically operative? Darkly pigmented skin, by raising the surface temperature, could bring about perspiration at an early stage. Perspiration would induce cooling. A low rate of salt loss is another possible adaptive mechanism, along with the ability to tolerate increased heat loads.

Heat tolerance among humans is a complex adaptation achieved through genetic, physiological, morphological, and behavioral adjustments. Heat tolerance is a universal human adaptation and appears regardless of a population's distance from hot climates. Heat tolerance among humans is regulated by a unique pattern of high-capacity sweat glands widely dispersed over the body's surface. These glands total about 1.6 million with a wide regional variation in density (Hanna and Brown, 1979).

Human heat tolerance is due not only to the presence of high-capacity sweat glands, but to the wide dispersal of these glands over the skin. This dispersal assures rapid and effective heat dissipation. Although other mammals have sweat glands, the glands are not of the type found in humans. In other mammals, thermal sweating is produced by apocrine sweat glands associated with hair follicles, while in humans thermal sweating occurs via the eccrine glands. Eccrine glands are more effective for thermal regulation. In humans and other primates, the shift from apocrine to eccrine glands was a major evolutionary event resulting in heat tolerance (Hanna and Brown, 1979).

Human populations show a relative homogeneity in heat tolerance limits. Comparative studies of Europeans, Africans, and residents of hot regions have failed to document any significant population-specific biological adaptations to heat. It appears as if all human populations can respond to heat stress in an adequate manner. Physiological studies of heat adaptation in humans indicate that genetic selection for mechanisms of heat adaptation has not occurred in specific populations. Perhaps the human species as a whole is so well adapted genetically that further selection within the specific populations did not occur, or human cultural adaptations have been so effective that there is no genetic selection for specific population differences (Hanna and Brown, 1979). Furthermore, living in a hot climate for a long time only has a minor impact on heat tolerance beyond that resulting from acclimatization.

There is a possible interaction between a hot environment and growth patterns. Children in hot climates may differ from those in cold climates in the number of active sweat glands or in body build. All else being equal, children from a warm climate tend to grow in a more linear manner than children from a cold climate (Stinson and Frisancho, 1978). Stinson and Frisancho (1978) have identified extremity length as of particular importance because it influences the rate and amount of heat dissipation, as stated by Allen's rule.

Cultural adaptations are important factors in combating heat stress, and these behaviors may have been adequate to reduce selective pressure toward genetic adaptation. Cultural adaptations for being comfortable in hot or cold conditions include activity scheduling, shading, reflection, insulation, ventilation, and evaporation. Specific strategies are influenced by available materials, local environmental factors, stress levels, technology, subsistence requirements, and sociocultural considerations (Hanna and Brown, 1979).

Desert Adaptation. Adapting to desert life is essentially a compromise requiring a tolerance for midday heat and night cold. Desert inhabitants must also tolerate high intensities of ultraviolet radiation (UVR) without dramatically increasing heat load. At the same time they must be able to dissipate heat by perspiration while saving precious water. Assuming adaptations to desert living are not cultural adaptations such as air-conditioned homes and cars, lightly colored clothing, and ready water supplies, what adaptations has nature provided?

Skin Pigmentation. There are several ways to approach the multifaceted problem of desert life; many animals escape the desert's heat by sleeping during the day in cool dwellings and moving about at night. The most usual human biological adaptations are a lean body build, moderation of skin pigmentation, and reduction of water loss. Modern desert dwellers tend to be leaner than inhabitants in other environments. Among the South African Bushmen, for example, there is loss of subcutaneous fat early in life, which may indicate its maladaptive nature. In theory, desert dwellers should have moderate skin pigmentation; the skin should be pigmented enough to protect deep skin layers from UVR damage but must not be so dark that it builds an intolerable heat load. Extremely dark skin is disadvantageous under hot-dry conditions; for example, it was found that U.S. black soldiers fared worse in desert tests than their lighter-pigmented counterparts in that they overheated more rapidly. However, there is a lack of uniformity in skin pigmentation among desert dwellers.

Water Conservation. Another important adaptive mechanism is some means of conserving water. The desert-dwelling kangaroo rat *Dipodomys,* for example, has the ability to conserve water by concentrating urine. If humans could follow this example, they could conserve one to two pints of water per day. There is, however, no evidence that modern human desert-dwellers concentrate urine.

Any person who has a genetic condition that prevents the body from concentrating urine to save water is obviously at a disadvantage on the desert. For example, the heterozygous carrier for sickle-cell anemia has a survival advantage in areas where malaria occurs (Chapter 27). This same heterozygote, however, lacks the capacity to concentrate urine and is therefore at a disadvantage where water is scarce (Keetel et al., 1956). The sickle-cell trait is rare in the relatively dry parts of Africa and Arabia, partly because the carrier of the trait is at a disadvantage in these areas.

Cold Adaptation. Of the climatic extremes into which *H. sapiens sapiens* moved, none is more quickly lethal (therefore more selective) than extreme cold. Winter temperatures from –40° to –90° F are reported for parts of the inhabited Arctic. Furthermore, as in the desert, some areas may be relatively warm during the day and cold at night. Adaptation to this latter situation is probably much more of a compromise than is adaptation to the extremely cold Arctic. Approximately 20 percent of the earth is below freezing (32° F); examples of groups inhabiting such areas are the Eskimo, Lapplanders, Ainu of northern Japan, Tibetan and Andean highlanders, and the Indians of Tierra del Fuego.

Failure to make the requisite adjustments to extremely cold temperatures results in many problems, including death. One of the first problems to be avoided is lowering of the body temperature to a point at which frostbite, and eventually death, occurs. Secondly, body temperatures must be maintained at relatively comfortable levels, for it would be maladaptive to shiver constantly to maintain body temperature. Of importance, especially in Arctic areas, is the ability to maintain skin temperatures at sufficiently high levels for normal functioning (Figure 26-3).

The body responds to cold stress by both producing and conserving heat. These adaptive mechanisms to cold stress are more complex than those to heat stress. Successful responses to cold stress require the synchronization of cardiovascular and circulatory systems as well as the activation of the metabolic process.

Besides low temperatures, several other environmental factors must be considered when discussing human responses to cold stress. Among these, the most important are wind velocity, humidity, and duration of cold exposure.

The degree of cold stress to which a person is exposed is classified as either acute or chronic cold. Acute cold stress refers to severe stress for short periods of time. Chronic cold stress refers to moderate cold stress over long periods of time, either seasonally or throughout the year (Frisancho, 1979).

Peripheral Temperatures. Some of the earliest studies of cold adaptation by non-Western groups were conducted in the 1930s on the Australian aborigines. At night, Australian aborigines sleep nude in temperatures at or below freezing. Their only cultural acquiescence to this situation is sleeping between small fires or curling up with their dogs. (The name of the rock group The Three Dog Night means, in the aborigine experience, a rather cold night. The

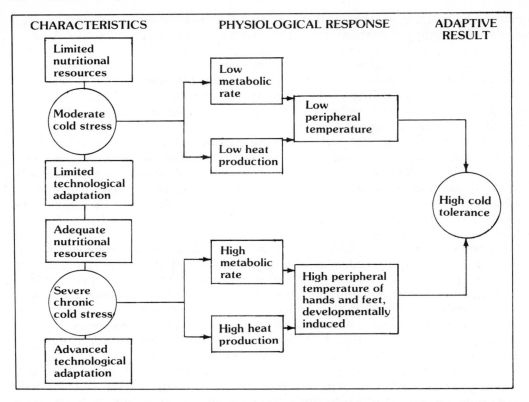

Figure 26-3. Adaptive responses to cold of indigenous populations in environments of moderate and severe cold stress. Populations have attained cold tolerance in environments of moderate and severe cold stress through specialized thermoregulatory responses that are intimately related to technology and access to food.

more dogs it takes to maintain warmth, the colder it is.) To test the aborigines' adaptation to the cold nights, some Western scientists attempted to sleep alongside them. The scientists remained awake most of the night, constantly shivering and thereby preventing anything other than intermittent sleep. The aborigines' major physiological adaptation for sleeping nude on cold nights is a marked drop in **peripheral temperatures** (that is, temperatures of the hands and feet). A reduction in the temperature gradient between the body and air conserves internal body heat and prevents cooling of the limbs when in contact with the air.

Despite warm arctic clothing, certain body parts such as the hands are often exposed to high winds and extreme cold. The hands must not only be protected from freezing, they must maintain their fine manipulative skills. It has been found that many cold-adapted peoples adapt to their environment by having high peripheral skin temperatures.

There are two fundamentally different mechanisms of cold adaptation. The first, characteristic of the Eskimo, increases the amount of heat near the skin by means of increased metabolic activity and peripheral blood flow (Figure 26-4). The second, found in Australian aborigines, is based on insulation of the vital organs. Unlike the Eskimo, the peripheral surfaces do cool, but as they do so, they further insulate the deep organs of the chest and

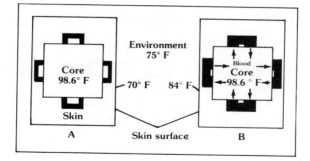

Figure 26-4. Relationship of skin's insulating capacity to its blood flow. (A) Skin acts as good insulator, that is, with minimal blood flow, the temperature of skin surface approaches that of external environment. (B) When skin blood vessels dilate, the increased blood flow carries heat to body surfaces, that is, reduces insulating capacity of skin, and surface temperature becomes intermediate between that of core and external environments.

abdomen. Whether these different mechanisms are due to different adaptive pressures, that is, rather continual cold for the Eskimo and primarily seasonal and night cold for aborigines, is not yet clear (Table 26-1).

Eskimos live in climatic conditions providing severe acute and chronic cold stress. Their material culture, in the form of housing and clothing, represents one important adaptation to such stress. Because of their subsistence economy, however, the Eskimos are still exposed to cold stress for prolonged time periods. The Eskimo's high fat diet and protein intake provide calorigenic effects (heating) and is an adaptive response to cold stress. All evidence confirms the Eskimos' increased metabolic rates, high peripheral temperatures, and remarkable cold tolerance. The Eskimos' ability to maintain high extremity temperatures and their ability to tolerate cold appear to be acquired during growth. The Eskimos' characteristic thermo-regulatory mechanisms reflect the influence of developmental adaptation or developmental acclimatization (Frisancho, 1979).

Body Shape. One of the most obvious biological adaptations to cold stress is minimizing the surface area/mass ratio (e.g., by having a heavy, small body). This body shape, coupled with short limbs and stubby fingers and toes, has a heat-preserving potentiality. There is a reduction of heat loss through blood flow to the body peripheries as these are brought closer to the center of the body. An increased thickness of the layer of subcutaneous fat is adaptive because it acts as a heat shield and thus conserves energy. Lastly, by raising the basal metabolism rate (BMR) to above-normal levels conversion of food to energy is accelerated, providing more heat.

Although some heat can be lost through breathing, most heat loss occurs through the skin. The size of an individual, which largely determines body surface area, is a factor in heat dissipation. Body mass consists of metabolizing tissues (which produce heat) and fat (much of it just beneath the skin where it may help insulate); hence, weight increases cause increased heat production and retention. Humans must maintain the temperatures of their brain, thoracic viscera, and abdominal viscera at approximately 98.6° F. Other tissues may have slightly lower "normal" temperatures. The temperate-climate individual produces at rest

Table 26-1. Population Differences in Response to Heat and Cold

Sample	*Results*
8 central Australian aborigines 6 control whites 9 tropical Australian aborigines	Small, important differences in temperature and metabolic responses to moderate nighttime cold while sleeping.
5 Australian whites 6 central Australian aborigines	Nonaborigines maintained body heat by increased muscle movement (i.e., shivering) during sleep.
2 unacculturated Bushmen 2 Europeans	No significant differences in response to moderate night cold.
9 Alacaluf	Marked increase in metabolic response to night cold, continued elevated BMR (basal metabolism rate).
7 Afro-American soldiers 7 white soldiers 6 Anaktuuk Eskimos	Systematic black-white Eskimo differences in skin temperatures and BMR during the 2-hour cold exposure.
17 white and 16 black volunteers matched for body size and composition	Fewer rewarming cycles and lower finger temperatures in black subjects exposed to moderate cold.
16 East Indians 16 U.S. blacks 23 Chinese 17 U.S. of European descent 8 Eskimos	Marked differences in plasma volume and blood volume for the Eskimo especially. Results of questionable value in terms of adaptive significance.
40 pairs of black and white soldiers matched for body composition and size	Blacks displayed higher physiological tolerance to hot, humid conditions, but less tolerance (in terms of building a heat load) in hot dry conditions.
8 African mine laborers compared with non-African white sample from literature	Africans had lower sweating rates, lower heart rates and lower rectal temperatures.

Adapted from Stanley M. Garn, *Human Races,* 2nd edition, p. 67, 1962. Courtesy of Charles C Thomas, Publishers, Springfield, Illinois.

approximately 39 calories of heat per square meter of surface area per hour. This is the "basal" metabolic rate (BMR). This rate is sufficient to maintain normal body temperature at temperatures only as low as 80° F for the nude individual resting in still air and with no proximate cold objects to absorb radiant energy. Any change of these conditions and additional heat-producing mechanisms, or heat-saving mechanisms, must come into play.

With cold acclimatization, some groups exhibit increasing BMR's. European test groups, for example, have been found to increase their BMR's a maximum of 8 percent with cold acclimatization (Williams, 1973).

Altitude Adaptation. Between 20 million and 25 million persons live permanently above 10,000 feet, mainly in the Ethiopian, Andean, Caucasus, and Himalayan highlands (Figure 26-5). Studies of high-altitude populations virtually provide a natural laboratory equipped with significant stresses of low humidity, low temperatures, low air pressures, high solar radiation, and often marginal diets. Large populations have resided at high altitudes for many generations.

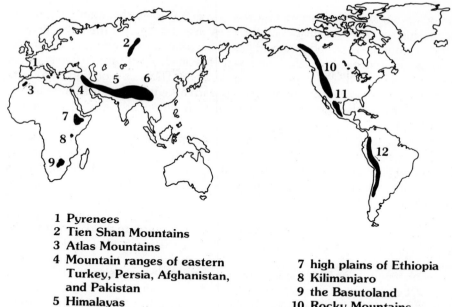

1 Pyrenees
2 Tien Shan Mountains
3 Atlas Mountains
4 Mountain ranges of eastern
   Turkey, Persia, Afghanistan,
   and Pakistan
5 Himalayas
6 Tibetan Plateau and
   southern China

7 high plains of Ethiopia
8 Kilimanjaro
9 the Basutoland
10 Rocky Mountains
11 Sierra Madre
12 Andes

Figure 26-5. Areas of the world that are more than 10,000 feet above sea level.

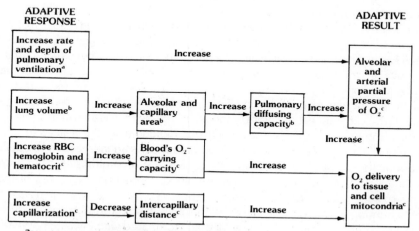

aUsed by sea-level sojourners at high altitudes.
bUsed by Highland natives.
cUsed by sea-level sojourners and Highland natives.

Figure 26-6. Adaptive pathways elicited by high-altitude hypoxia. Adaptation to high-altitude hypoxia results in coordinated mechanisms that help increase oxygen supply at tissue level. Lowland and highland natives use different means to acclimatize to high-altitude hypoxia. Although systems for increased oxygen-carrying capacity of the blood and augmented capillarization are operative in both lowland and highland natives, increased pulmonary ventilation is used mostly by lowland native.

The various adaptive mechanisms triggered by exposure to high altitude are directed toward increasing oxygen availability and the pressure of oxygen at the tissue level. This is accomplished through: (1) pulmonary ventilation, (2) lung volume and pulmonary diffusing capacity, (3) transport of oxygen in the blood, (4) diffusion of oxygen from blood to the tissues, and (5) use of oxygen at the tissue level (Figure 26-6). The study of high-altitude human adaptations provides an excellent opportunity to learn about the flexibility and nature of the homeostatic processes that permit an organism to function and survive under extreme environmental stress.

High altitudes present several stresses. The most important include: (1) hypoxia, (2) high solar radiation, (3) cold, (4) humidity, (5) high winds, (6) limited nutritional base, and (7) rough terrain. From a physiological viewpoint, **hypoxia** is the most important stress, because the other stresses are present in an equal or greater degree in other environmental zones. Hypoxia develops when tissues receive a deficient supply of oxygen. Hypoxia can result from any physiological or pathological condition that interferes with the oxygen supply to the tissues. High-altitude hypoxia is a pervasive and ever-present stress not easily modified by cultural or behavioral responses. Furthermore, all organ systems and physiological functions are affected by hypoxia.

The atmosphere contains 20.95 percent oxygen, and this is a constant figure up to 361,000 feet. However, because air is compressible, it contains a greater number of gaseous molecules at low altitudes. This is the fundamental problem of high-altitude hypoxia—the oxygen in the air at high altitudes is less concentrated and, consequently, is at a lower pressure than it is at low altitudes.

The effects of high-altitude hypoxia are considered to be either acute or chronic. Acute hypoxia results from reduced oxygen availability that lasts for a few minutes, hours, or perhaps several months. Chronic hypoxia is a continuation of this condition for months, years, or a lifetime. The distinction between the two forms of hypoxia results from the different mechanisms with which the organism responds to reduced oxygen availability.

Oxygen Debt. The main stress in altitude adaptation is that of low oxygen pressure. There is no effective, economical way to lessen oxygen deficiency culturally; thus populations living at high altitudes must biologically adjust to their surroundings. The oxygen debt is usually lessened by an increased production of red blood cells and a corresponding increase in hemoglobin (the substance that colors blood red). Hemoglobin is a protein substance carrying oxygen from the lungs to the tissues and carbon dioxide from the tissues to the lungs. Any increase in number and size of the red blood cells means an increase in the ability to move oxygen about the body. Another response to living at high altitudes is an increase in the capillary network of alveoli, resulting in more blood contacting the alveoli of the lungs and facilitating oxygen exchange and transportation. There is also an increase in capillary pressure, shunting oxygen-carrying red blood cells faster through the body and helping prevent oxygen debt. As might also be expected, compared with lowland populations there is as much as a 15 percent increase in the total lung volume of many high altitude dwellers.

Fertility Disorders. High-altitude living stimulates efficient oxygen exchange within the body, preventing oxygen debt, subsequent brain damage, and eventually death. However, there are some data suggesting that fertility disorders are more prevalent at high altitudes. For example, the number of miscarriages in Denver is higher than in most other parts of the United States and altitude is a likely cause. Female visitors to altitudes above 10,000 feet often experience menstrual disorders, that is, skipping of cycles or excessive flow. There is a

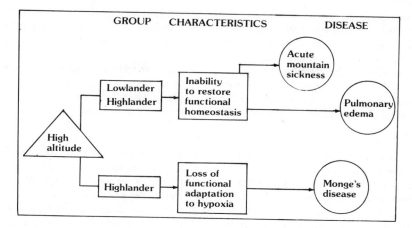

Figure 26-7. Group incidence and general characteristics of diseases associated with high-altitude environment. Acute mountain sickness and pulmonary edema occur mostly among sea level natives or highlanders returning from sea level. Both diseases are characterized by an inability to restore functional homeostasis when exposed to stress of high altitude. In contrast Monge's disease occurs mostly among highlanders who for some reason lose their functional adaptation.

tendency toward later onset of menarche (the age of first menstruation) among females native to high altitudes compared to inhabitants of low altitudes. Male visitors to high altitudes are also affected; after about 2 weeks the sperm level drops and becomes alkaline, a decrease in motility occurs, and a 40 percent increase in abnormal forms occurs. The sperm returns to normal with return to sea level.

Altitude Sicknesses. The inability to cope with altitude, primarily because of oxygen debt, causes a number of sicknesses such as pulmonary edema and mountain sickness (also called soroche). Mountain sickness is characterized by headaches, shortness of breath, and nausea. Acute cases of mountain sickness, often called Monge's disease, are further characterized by abnormal production of red blood cells and increased pulmonary hypertension (Figure 26-7).

Inhabitants of high altitudes show three modalities of coping: (1) short-run physiological changes, (2) modifications during growth and development, and (3) modification of the population's gene pool itself.

Climbing Mt. Kenya

Kenya, May 1975

We depart our camp at Met Station which is approximately 10,200 feet at 8:15 A.M. to begin our ascent to 14,000 feet and Teleki Hut. The climb takes us up a track which leads through the Cloud Forest and the Vertical Bog. Because of the foul weather, hail and rain, because we lose the trail, and because of physical fatigue the climb takes approximately ten hours and we arrive in cold darkness.

During our ascent we notice physical fatigue, due both to the strenuous nature of the hike and because of the altitude. We follow standard climbing procedures as concerns walking speed and gait and we constantly munch on our home-made gorp (a mixture of M and M's, peanuts, and dried fruits). We begin to notice that after a few hours most of us have lost our appetite (mine particularly for gorp). Clothing becomes a problem during the ascent, we turn hot and cold—not only with the weather but because of exhaustion.

Some of the problems we note when we finally reach our destination and camp within the shadows of the glacier follow. Temperature variations between the warm day sun and the night cold precipitate colds in some of the party. At night we have difficulty keeping warm—even though 13 of us are squeezed within a small tin hut. Most uncomfortable is the fatigue—although some of the party are well enough to do some exploring the day after arrival. Nighttime brings its own devilish problem—the inability to sleep. Most of the party sleeps in fits, if at all. Time hangs heavily on our minds and we all hope for an early sunrise to break the fight to go to sleep. The sleep problem remains for the three nights on the mountain. Another major problem is nausea and the lack of appetite. Many in the party are constantly sick to their stomachs and food rations go largely untouched. Irritability is also a problem for some—due to fatigue, lack of sleep, and nausea.

Within a day of our descent from the mountain the symptoms have alleviated, although some of the party still have troubles sleeping the first night and nausea is still with us. Within 48 hours everyone is readjusted.

Excerpt from my notes during my visit to Mt. Kenya.

Some Advantages and Disadvantages of Gross Body Size. Population variations in body size represent one of the important parameters in the study of ongoing human evolution. Considerable evidence indicates that variation in body size results from environmental and genetic factors at both the developmental and adult stages. One productive way to study possible variation in survival and mortality is under conditions of environmental stress. Poor socioeconomic conditions, because they are usually associated with limited nutritional levels, represent an environmental stress known to influence body size during growth and adolescence. A study in a "barriada" (poor section of a town) in southern Peru supports the hypothesis that small body size is more adaptive to poor socioeconomic conditions of dietary restriction than is a large body size (Frisancho et al., 1973). This is presumably due to lower caloric or nutritional requirements for growth and maintenance of the smaller body. It is possible that the high offspring survival effectiveness witnessed in this barriada (as indicated by the high percent of offspring survival), which is associated with small parental body size, may reflect developmental adaptive responses to poor socioeconomic conditions in the barriada. This particular study presents evidence of higher offspring survival associated with small parental body size; however, to advance these findings as an explanation of population variation in body size, further studies with larger samples are needed.

A disadvantage of a heavier body size is that it takes more calories to keep alive— Americans and Europeans in Asian prisoner-of-war camps soon learned this. Since larger body sizes usually require more calories for growth, genetically large children may be at a disadvantage when food is scarce. Famine is a most powerful selective force that can differentially eliminate massive individuals. Faced with continual caloric restriction, genetically small individuals might have more chance to mature and reproduce.

Climatic Correlations. Peoples of light weight tend to be found near the equator. Granting that our migration patterns cloud the picture, there nevertheless seems to be a correlation between mean annual temperature and body weight in a population long resident in an area. Moving southward in Europe, environmental temperature rises and body weight drops. The lowest average body weights (90 to 100 pounds) are associated with mean annual temperatures of 72° to 80° F; the highest average weights (in excess of 160 pounds) are associated with temperatures of 40° F and below. These correlations tend to hold true for U.S. Army inductees, for the warmer an inductee's state of origin, the greater the chances of thinner build and lower body weight compared to those of soldiers from colder states.

Skin Pigmentation

Of all traits used to differentiate populations, none has been more misused than skin pigmentation despite the fact that it is simply another biological adaptation to environmental stress. Regardless of what some may preach, the social, economic, religious, and political values associated with one or another pigmentation are nonbiologically based.

Skin is composed of two layers, the outer epidermis and inner dermis. The epidermis is composed of four layers; the deepest layer, the stratum germinativum (columnar layer), produces the **melanocytes,** amoebalike cells, that produce the **melanin** that gives skin its color. Above the columnar layer sits the prickle-cell layer; melanin from the melanocytes is injected into the prickle-cell layer. When this layer migrates to the skin's surface, melanain contained within the prickle-cells moves with it. Variations in skin pigmentation are not due to the number of melanocytes present; rather, skin pigmentation differences are due to the amount of melanin produced by the melanocytes. All individuals, even albinos (those lacking pigmentation in the skin, hair and eyes) have approximately the same number of melanocytes, but the melanocytes of albinos do not produce melanin.

In addition to melanin, oxyhemoglobin, reduced hemoglobin, and carotene contribute to pigmentation differences. The most useful measurement of these variables is by skin reflectance as measured by either a photoelectric reflectometer or a reflectance spectrophotometer. They both measure the amount of light reflected from a skin surface as compared with reflectance by a standard white magnesium surface, which gives 100 percent reflectance. Both have a photocell to measure reflectance and a galvanometer to record it, and with appropriate statistical adjustments, the values obtained by both are comparable.

Many ideas, each with its own proponents and merits, have been proposed to explain the distribution of different skin pigmentations. It is becoming quite obvious, however, that there are multiple causes for different skin pigmentations. Furthermore, there may be conflicting pressures on a particular skin pigmentation in any one environment (Figure 26-8).

Gloger's Rule. In 1833 an ornithologist named Gloger formulated a rule now applied to help explain variation in pigmentation of the skin, hair, and eyes. Simply stated, Gloger's rule says that animals living in wet tropical areas tend to be darkly pigmented, those in desert areas tend to be brown, and those in or near the Arctic tend to be lightly pigmented. This rule is generally true for *Homo*. Because we arose in tropical areas, it is conceivable that originally our skin was darkly pigmented; lightly pigmented skins may be a more recent adaptation to nontropical habitats.

Population differences in skin pigmentation are generally associated with two climatic and environmental factors. First, on each continent pigmentation is inversely related to latitude and temperature (Figure 26-9). The closer the population to the equator and the higher the temperature, the darker the pigmentation. Second, intensity of solar radiation is directly related to latitude and altitude. The closer the population to the equator and the higher the altitude, the greater the radiation intensity.

The general association of darkly pigmented skin and tropical habitats, especially in regions of intense solar radiation, has been known for a long time. However, the geographical distribution in terms of reflectance values is only now becoming known. More than 80 percent

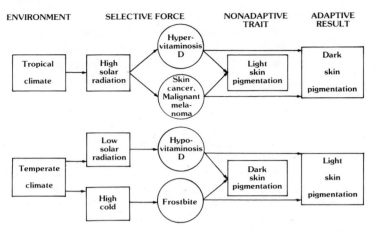

Figure 26-8. Selective forces in tropical and temperate climates that affect human variation in skin pigmentation. Population differences in skin pigmentation are viewed as result of evolutionary compromise to selective forces present in world climates.

of the total interpopulation variances in reflectance at each wavelength is attributable to climatic variables (Roberts and Kahlon, 1976).

Much has been made of the relationship between pigmentation and solar radiation (Blum, 1945). However, the relationship is not simple. Although UVR parts of the spectrum have some beneficial effects at minimum exposures, UVR at greater doses promotes injury in the form of sunburn and carcinogenesis. The carcinogenic wavelengths lie between 2537 and 3341 angstroms (Å), while erythema (reddening and swelling) is induced increasingly rapidly at wavelengths of less than 3200 Å, reaching a maximum at 2800 Å.

Vitamin D Production. One of the key explanatory means suggests a link between skin pigmentation and vitamin D production. This theory, first proposed in 1934, suggested that light skin pigmentation represents an adaptation to low levels of UVR where decreased melanin is necessary for maximal usage of UVR in synthesizing vitamin D. Accordingly, light skin pigmentation, as an adaptation to vitamin D synthesis, is adaptive in northern latitudes where sunlight is minimal. Light pigmentation allows maximal UVR absorption whereas darkly pigmented skin reflects UVR. Since a vitamin D deficiency can result in rickets (Figure 26-10) and scoliosis (abnormal spinal curvature), among other defects, which could interfere with the birth process, lightly pigmented individuals would be at an advantage in a low-light region because of the increased ability to absorb UVR and synthesize vitamin D. Because a darkly pigmented skin allows minimal penetration of UVR, causing improper bone growth, such individuals are selected against in low-UVR areas. Application of this rule to the modern situation is limited by the fact that we have vitamin-D enriched milk, bread, and other foods. If the vitamin D theory is applicable, the most darkly-pigmented individual today could still live in the lowest light situation without suffering from inadequate bone growth if vitamin D were artificially supplied.

What is the adaptation of darkly pigmented skin? Darkly pigmented individuals seem to be adapted to high-light conditions. While a vitamin D deficiency is harmful, too much vitamin D (hypervitaminosis D) results in bone resorption and pathological calcifications. Lightly

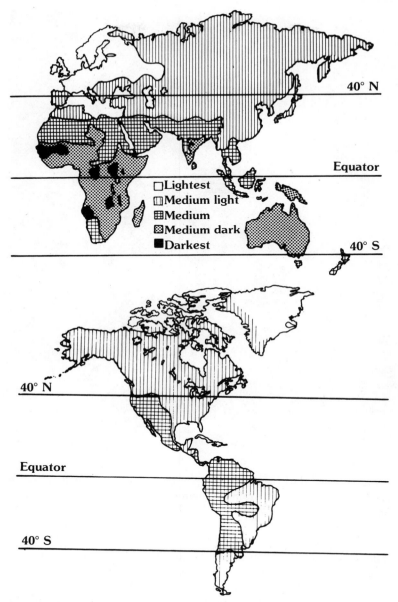

Figure 26-9. Distribution of human skin pigmentation according to latitude.

pigmented individuals may be at a disadvantage in high UVR conditions. Because darkly pigmented skins reflect UVR, darkly pigmented individuals may be selected for in high light areas.

Arguments Against the Vitamin D Theory. Selection against the dangers of rickets on the one hand and toxic doses of vitamin D on the other has been used to explain the worldwide

Figure 26-10. A case of rickets in a village in Nepal. The people in this village live in very narrow huts with tiny windows. During the rainy season of 5 to 6 months children are always kept indoors. Rickets develop from lack of sunshine, lack of vitamins, and from improper diet.

correlation of dark skin pigmentation with proximity to the equator. Although this theory has received much attention in standard anthropology texts, it has not been accepted without argument. One proponent suggested that lightly pigmented individuals inhabiting high-light areas are subject to toxic doses of vitamin D. However, there are no confirmatory reports suggesting a high incidence of hypervitaminosis D in the many lightly pigmented individuals living in Arizona, South Africa, and Australia. Another problem is that vitamin D is not stable to excess doses of UVR; there may be no naturally occurring toxic dosage such as can be laboratory produced.

A second qualifying statement about the relationship of dark skin pigmentation and tropical adaptations is that darkly pigmented individuals absorb more infrared light and thus the body heats faster. Light pigmentations reflect more heat, as everyone who wears a white shirt during the summer knows. However, overheating, while a subsidiary effect of skin color, is apparently not the "main" selective force influencing the evolution of different skin pigmentation.

   Disease Protection and Skin Injury. A second explanatory theory for skin pigmentation differences is that dark skin provides disease protection. Darkly pigmented tropic dwellers may reflect the selective forces of disease rather than climate. For example, darkly pigmented populations appear to have a greater resistance to certain tropical diseases such as the mosquito-borne filariasis.

   The supposed link between pigmentation and disease maintains that pigmentation is an indirect consequence of human adaptation to tropical disease. This hypothesis maintains that a single enzyme deficiency in the adrenal cortex may be the primary basis for variations in skin pigmentation. A major problem with this hypothesis is the assumption that infectious diseases were major selective factors during human evolution. Current data suggest that infectious diseases became prevalent and had a significant selective force only after the introduction of agriculture and a concomitant increase in population size. In an evolutionary perspective, this occurred too recently to account for skin pigmentation variations (Frisancho, 1979).

   Post (1971; Post et al., 1975) attempts to link skin pigmentation differences to cold injury. Using carefully documented epidemiological studies of U.S. Army personnel during the Korean War, it was found that soldiers of African origin were more susceptible to frostbite than those of European descent. A study conducted in Norway during World War II suggests that more darkly pigmented men had a higher incidence of frostbite than lighter-pigmented individuals. Considering the rather limited range of skin color among Norwegians, this observation is interesting.

   Post studied the effects of freezing skin patches on piebald (black and white) guinea pigs. By freezing small areas of the skin at overlapping points of white and black pigmentation, he tested the differential reaction to freezing and demonstrated that lightly pigmented skins are cold adapted by virtue of experiencing less cold-induced injury. Darkly pigmented skin, by contrast, sustained striking damage due to the freezing. These results make sense if our evolutionary past was originally tied to tropical areas, as we assume it was.

   One of the oldest explanations of skin pigmentation differences links the effects of UVR to skin damage. Mild sunburn produces erythema and mild discomfort. More severe sunburn causes increased sensitivity to pain, blistering, lowered resistance to further sunburn, susceptibility to infection, damage to the vascular beds in the dermis, loss of sweating in the damaged area, and skin cancers. Even a mild sunburn can significantly reduce perspiration; in turn, this can impair an individual's ability to lose excessive heat through evaporation. Repeated sunburn would affect an individual's fitness. Although few individuals die of skin cancers, and although skin cancers usually appear past reproductive age, they could be a secondary factor producing skin pigmentation differences.

   Skin pigmentation differences must be explained on the basis of selection acting on phenotypic variation leading to gene frequency changes. There were not one, but many, selective agents acting to produce the range of skin tones. Earlier selective pressures operating to produce skin pigmentation differences either are no longer important or are of reduced importance, given shelter, dietary vitamin D, central heating, and other technological changes. Most biological advantages of one or another skin pigmentation are things of the past.

   Explaining differences in pigmentation acknowledges that we arose in the tropical regions of the world. As we moved north out of the tropical zones, we began to meet lower light intensities. Because darkly pigmented individuals may have experienced difficulties in such situations—perhaps from rickets and cold damage, for example—more lightly pigmented individuals may have had an advantage and may have left more surviving offspring. As we continued to move north and encountered colder conditions where selection was stronger, we may assume that more lightly pigmented skins were selected for.

Eye Color. There is a correlation between eye color and skin color, for the same genes controlling skin color may also influence eye color; this is known as a **pleiotropic** effect. Generally, there is a correlation between visible skin color and the pigment of the optic fundus. Assuming an original darkly pigmented eye color, what are the selective advantages of lightly pigmented eyes? Lightly pigmented eyes are mostly found in conjunction with light hair and fair skin, traits primarily concentrated in cloudy, foggy northwest Europe, where we consider they had a long history. We should search here for selection pressures, for there may be advantages to lightly pigmented eyes in low light intensities. Because decreasing pigmentation of the fundus of the eye results in an increased sensitivity to long wavelengths of light, it has been postulated that this characteristic may have arisen in the cave-dwelling period of European prehistory as an adaptive response to low light levels. However, experimental studies indicate that variations in retinal and iris pigmentation under varying conditions of light stress are not related to visual acuity (Hoffman, 1975; Short, 1975).

In this chapter we introduced a number of important concepts. Adaptations are long-term biological adjustments related to survival in particular environments. Acclimation refers to short-term physiological responses to stress. These responses are relatively modest. Acclimatization refers to an adjustment to a situation that lasts for a relatively long period of time. However, acclimatization may also occur in response to conditions that last for only a few months, such as when one experiences seasonal changes. Habituation refers to a reduction in the level of physiological responses to a stress situation. Habituation may fall into two categories, specific and general.

Anthropologists have used a number of general rules of adaptation to help explain differences in body sizes, shapes, and skin pigmentation. Allen's rule states that the length of the extremities is related to climate—the colder the climate, the shorter the extremities. Bergman's rule states that body shape is related to climate—the warmer the climate, the more linear the body. Gloger's rule is used as an explanatory vehicle for skin pigmentation.

We have discussed some general adaptations of humans to various climatic stresses: to hot and humid climates; to desert life; to extreme cold; and to high altitudes. It is important to note that adaptations to various habitats are often balanced; that is, there may be elements of both adaptive and maladaptive features of an adaptation. Skin pigmentation differences are a good example of this proposition.

Of all animals, humans have occupied and now occupy perhaps the greatest diversity of habitats. To survive in this array of climates, we have adapted both culturally and biologically. Indeed, the success of our cultural adaptations allows us this freedom of movement and habitation.

Bibliography

Allen, J. 1877. The influence of physical conditions in the genesis of species. *Radical Review* 1:108.

Baker, P. 1958. Racial differences in heat tolerance. *American Journal of Physical Anthropology* 16:287.

_____. 1969. Human adaptation to high altitude. *Science* 163:1149.

Baker, P., and Little, M., eds. 1976. *Man in the Andes: a multidisciplinary study of high-altitude Quecha.* Stroudsburg, Pa.: Dowden, Hutchinson & Ross.

Baker, P., and Weiner, J., eds. 1966. *The biology of human adaptability.* London: Oxford University Press.

Barnicott, N. 1957. Human pigmentation. *Man* 57:114-20.

_____. 1959. Climatic factors in the evolution of human populations. *Cold Springs Harbor Symposia on Quantitative Biology* 24:115.

Blum, H. 1962. Does the melanin pigment of human skin have adaptive value? An essay in human ecology and the evolution of race. *Quarterly Review of Biology* 36:50-63.

_____. 1969. Is sunlight a factor in the geographical distribution of human skin color? *Geographical Review* 14:557-81.

Brues, A. 1959. The spearman and the archer—an essay on selection in body build. *American Anthropologist* 61:457.

Coon, C. 1962. *The origin of races.* New York: Knopf.

_____. 1965. *The living races of man.* New York: Knopf.

Coon, C., Garn, S., and Birdsell, J. 1950. *Races: a study of the problems of race formation in man.* Springfield, Ill.: Thomas.

Damon, A., ed. 1975. *Physiological anthropology.* New York: Oxford University Press.

Frisancho, A. 1975. Functional adaptation to high altitude hypoxia. *Science* 187:313-18.

_____. 1979. *Human adaptation: a functional interpretation.* St. Louis: Mosby.

Frisancho, A., Sanchez, J., Pallardel, D., and Yanez, L. 1973. Adaptive significance of small body size under poor socio-economic conditions in southern Peru. *American Journal of Physical Anthropology* 39:255.

Frisancho, A., and Revelle, R. 1969. Variations in body weights and the age of the adolescent growth spurt among Latin American and Asian populations, in relation to calorie supplies. *Human Biology* 41:185-212.

Garn, S. 1957. Race and evolution. *American Anthropologist* 59:218.

_____. 1971. *Human races,* 3rd ed. Springfield, Ill.: Thomas.

Hanna, J., and Brown, D. 1979. Human heat tolerance: biological and cultural adaptations. *Yearbook of Physical Anthropology* 22:163-86.

Hiernaux, J. 1971. Ethnic differences in growth and development. In *The biological and social meaning of race,* edited by Richard H. Osborne, pp. 39-55. San Francisco: Freeman.

Hoffman, J. 1975. Retinal pigmentation, visual acuity, and brightness levels. *American Journal of Physical Anthropology.* 43:417-24.

Keetel, H., Thompson, D., and Itano, H. 1956. Hyposthenuria in sickle-cell anemia: a reversible renal defect. *Journal of Clinical Investigation* 35:998-1007.

Kennedy, K. 1976. *Human variation in space and time.* Dubuque, Ia.: Brown.

King, J. 1970. *The biology of race.* New York: Harcourt Brace Jovanovich.

Loomis, F. 1967. Skin pigmentation regulation of vitamin D biosynthesis in man. *Science* 157:501-6.

Newman, R., and Munro, E. 1955. The relation of climate and body size in U.S. males. *American Journal of Physical Anthropology* 13:1.

Post, P. 1971. Pigmentation and its role in human adaptation. Ph.D. dissertation. Columbia University.

Post, P., Daniels, F., and Binford, R. 1975. Cold injury and the evolution of "white" skin. *Human Biology* 47:65.

Roberts, D. 1953. Body weight, race and climate. *American Journal of Physical Anthropology* 11:533.

_____. 1978. *Climate and human variability.* Menlo Park, Calif.: Benjamin/Cummings.

Short, G., 1975. Iris pigmentation and photopic visual acuity: a preliminary study. *American Journal of Physical Anthropology* 43:425-34.

Stini. W. 1975. *Ecology and human adaptation.* Dubuque, Ia.: Brown.

Stinson, S., and Frisancho, A. 1978. Body proportions of highland and lowland Peruvian Quechua children. *Human Biology* 50:57-68.

Williams, B. 1973. *Evolution and human origins: an introduction to physical anthropology.* New York: Harper & Row.

Chapter 27

Microevolutionary Studies and Human Variability

Whether or not one recognizes the term "race" as describing some actuality, such as a population exhibiting some trait(s) distinguishing it from other populations, everyone agrees that populations do differ. Some differences are easily recognizable with the naked eye, some take microscopic analysis. This chapter explores some differences and attempts to explain their occurrence. Some differences are genetically based, some are stable over time, and some change with diet and other influences.

Traits Used To Differentiate Populations

This chapter discusses traits that are used to differentiate populations one from another. It discusses both traits whose genetic inheritance is unknown or not clearly understood and traits of known genetic inheritance. Among the former are body shape and size, adaptations to such habitats as deserts and high altitudes, the advantages of gross body sizes, skin color, and eye color (all of which were discussed in Chapter 26), and bone densities and tooth size and shape. We shall also discuss various physiological and biochemical differences between populations. In the latter category, we shall discuss blood group distributions and disease correlates, in addition to exploring the occurrence of abnormal hemoglobins, polymorphisms, and population-limited diseases. The list is far from complete, and it is not even clear which of these traits are important in terms of a population's efforts to adapt to an environment and which ones appeared relatively recently.

Population Differences of Unknown Significance

Many traits appearing in various populations are of unknown adaptive value; presumably some were either once adaptive or appear in small isolated populations by drift or the founder principle (Chapter 24). For example, some interesting differences in the size, proportions, and form of bone have long been documented. There are population differences in the relative proportions of the limb bones, the relative length of the metatarsals of the feet, and in the heel bone.

Bone Densities. Recent bone density studies reveal marked population differences; the weight-to-volume ratio is high in African-descended populations. Members of this group seem to have a high mineral requirement for normal growth. Garn (1971) found that total bone apposition (i.e., growth around the perimeter of the bone) is greater in American blacks than in individuals of Asian and European descent. This is true in rural undernourished areas of the South and the northern city ghettos. During the period of adult bone loss (known as osteoporosis) American black women experience fewer femoral and radial fractures than women of Asian or European descent. Such differences have practical importance, especially after age 40 when progressive bone loss increases the possibility of fracture.

Dentition. Many population differences in dentition have been documented. Tooth size is variable; the largest crown sizes are found among Australian aborigines, New Guinea natives, and Pima Indians. Root length, a sexually dimorphic trait, also varies and is especially short in some Asiatic populations. Gross size differences exist in the canines, incisors, premolars, and molars. In some groups the anterior teeth are large, and in others the posterior teeth are large.

Tooth morphology also differs; for example, the rear surfaces of the upper mesial incisors of many American Indian and Asian populations are distinctive. This trait, shovel-shaped incisors, is one of the many traits used to historically link American Indians with Asian populations (Table 27-1)[1]. The number of molar cusps varies and is often reduced in Middle Eastern populations and increased in some Melanesian and Australian aborigine groups. The incidence of congenital tooth loss varies; while the last molar is rarely absent in East and West Africans, it is lacking in 12 percent of the Europeans, and 30 percent of some American Indian, Eskimo, and Asian groups.

[1]The inward folding of the incisors characteristic of shovel-shaped incisors increases the chewing surfaces without increasing their breadth in relation to the size of the dental arcade. To the extent that such an increase in chewing surface is desirable and improves tooth life, shoveling is an adaptive trait. Brace (1963) has suggested that shoveling is retained in those populations where the functions of the incisor teeth have not been superseded by such factors as food preparation and cutting tools.

Table 27-1. Shovel-Shape in Upper Mesial Incisors

Population	Percent Male	Percent Female
Chinese	66 to 89	82 to 94
Japanese	78	—
Mongolian	62 to 91	91
Eskimo	84	84
Pima Indians	96	99
Pueblo Indians	86 to 89	86 to 89
Aleut	96	—
American blacks	12	11
American whites	9	8

Adapted from J. Comas, *Manual of Physical Anthropology,* 1960. Courtesy of Charles C Thomas, Publishers, Springfield, Illinois.

Polymorphisms

Before discussing evidence for the existence of polymorphisms, it is well to briefly discuss the topic of polymorphism itself. A polymorphism can be defined as a trait that is controlled by two or more common alleles. Two types of polymorphisms are commonly recognized, transient polymorphisms and balanced polymorphisms. Transient polymorphisms are unstable systems; conversely, balanced polymorphisms are stable systems. Polymorphisms are maintained within a population by two processes: selection for the heterozygote and nonrandom mating. Commonly, selection is seen as a process that acts largely by limiting variation. In any favorable environment the prevailing conditions will create, for any gene, a favorable condition for one allele and thus either reduce the frequency of or completely eliminate its alternatives. Polymorphisms contradict selection in the sense that their existence proves that two or more alleles can be found and often are found together in the same population. Furthermore, they can be found in fairly high frequencies. If selection acts to favor one allele or genotype over another, then why are polymorphisms so frequent? The answer is that the heterozygote advantage results in a balanced polymorphism.

If heterozygous individuals are more viable and to some extent favored over individuals who are homozygous, the population is likely to achieve a state of balanced polymorphism. For example, if we take two alleles of a gene, which we will label Y and y, both alleles will be maintained within the population by selection for the survival of the Yy genotype. Since matings between two heterozygous genotypes ($Yy \times yy$) will produce roughly one homozygote (YY) and one homozygote (yy) for each two heterozygous (Yy) offspring, selection will continue every generation. Depending on selection pressures against both homozygotes, YY and yy, there will be some ratio of Y to y in the general population that will be maintained in equilibrium. In a state of balanced polymorphism there is a ratio of Y to y at which any increase in the relative frequency of either allele will tend also to increase the force of natural selection against that allele and tend to return the ratio to its former balance.

Balanced Polymorphisms. Both **thallassemia** and **sickle-cell anemia** are examples of **balanced polymorphisms;** there is strong selective pressure to maintain the heterozygote state in a certain proportion of the population. Thalassemic homozygotes (Th^2Th^2) die before reaching reproductive age due to severe anemia. "Normal" homozygotes, individuals without the thalassemia gene, are afflicted with malaria and frequently die early. The heterozygote is strongly selected for under such conditions. Heterozygotes experience milder forms of malaria than normal homozygotes and are not too incapacitated by the abnormal red blood cells (and consequent oxygen loss) characteristic of thalassemia. Malaria exerts strong selective pressures which help retain both "normal" and thalassemia genes within the population; selection pressure is for a balanced polymorphism (Figure 27-1).

Physiological and Biochemical Variations

BAIB. There are population differences in urinary excretion patterns. One of the normal urinary constituents (the nonprotein amino acid B-aminoisobutyric acid [BAIB]) shows a most interesting individual and population variation in the amount excreted. This acid is rarely excreted in large amounts by Australian aborigines or Europeans. However, a fair proportion of Chinese and Japanese excrete high amounts of BAIB; the same is true of many American Indian groups. High levels of BAIB excretion suggest an Asian origin. However, it is not yet clear how the BAIB polymorphism is maintained, or what population differences mean (Table 27-2).

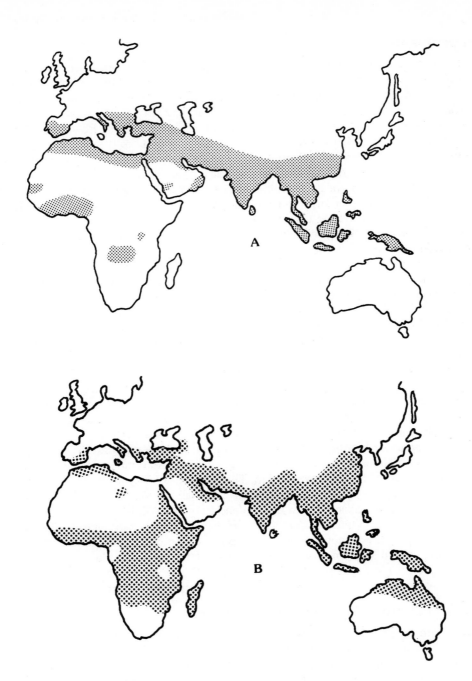

Figure 27-1. Distribution of (A) Mediterranean thalassemia and (B) falciparum malaria.

Table 27-2. Distribution of BAIB Excretors

Population	Number Tested	Percent of High Excretors
North America		
European descent		
Michigan	71	0.03
Texas	255	0.10
New York	218	0.10
New York	148	0.11
African descent		
Michigan	25	0.20
New York	38	0.15
Athabascan	25	0.56
Indians		
Apache	110	0.59
Apache	113	0.42
Eskimo	120	0.23
Chinese	33	0.45
Japanese	41	0.41
Central America		
African descent (Black Caribs)	285	0.32
Asia		
India	16	0
Thailand	13	0.46
Marshall Islands		
Rongelap	118	0.86
Utirik	18	0.83

Adapted from J. Buettner-Janusch, *The Origins of Man: Physical Anthropology*, p. 502. Copyright © 1973 by John Wiley & Sons, Inc.

Tasters versus Nontasters. Dietary differences have long been viewed with interest and numerous suggestions have been made that people who prefer the very hot, spicy foods differ in their taste acuity from those espousing culinary blandness. While conclusive evidence as to taste parameters is not yet available, there are some genetically determined differences in sensitivity. There are individual and population differences in the capacity to taste a laboratory-produced chemical compound known as phenylthiocarbamide (PTC) which does not exist in nature. This chemical was first discovered about 35 years ago when a chemist spilled some onto the laboratory floor. While the floor was being mopped, he and his coworkers tasted the substance and an argument ensued as to whether it was bitter or tasteless. Since then many monkeys and apes in zoos and humans have been tested. The procedure is easy; one simply slips a bit of paper treated with PTC into the mouth and waits.

The ability to taste PTC is controlled by allelic or multifactorial genes; *T* (for taster) is dominant, and *t* (for nontaster) is recessive. Those with genotypes *TT* and *Tt* are tasters. Asians and Africans have the highest percentage of tasters; Australian aborigines and some Pacific Islanders have the lowest percentage. Up to 43 percent of the population in India are nontasters.

What is the adaptive significance of being a taster or nontaster? The geographical distribution of the alleles shows no correlation with gross climatic conditions. Tasting may be nonadaptive in areas of scarce food sources where one must be able to consume anything. Since tasters probably have more food aversions than nontasters, tasting would be disadvantageous during food scarcity. There may be some disease correlates associated with tasting or nontasting. For example, one study showed that nontasters have a higher incidence of dental caries than tasters. Nontasters of European descent are more susceptible to glaucoma past age 40; they are also more susceptible to thyroid difficulties (such as goiter) than tasters. Tasters could be expected to have some advantage over nontasters in resisting nodular goiter by rejecting bitter-tasting thyroid-activity suppressors and it has been demonstrated that nontasters are more commonly victims of nodular goiter than would be expected by mere chance (Azevedo et al., 1965). While the relationship between tasting, thyroid function, and goiter is interesting, it fails to account for geographical variations in allelic frequencies.

Secretors. Some individuals show water-soluble antigens of the **ABO blood group** system in their saliva and other body fluids; others have alcohol-soluble antigens, which are found on the surface of the red blood cells. Almost everyone has alcohol-soluble antigens, but some do not have the water-soluble ABO antigens, and whether they do or do not is genetically determined. Those who have the water-soluble antigens are known as **secretors,** those who do not are **nonsecretors.** The secretor locus segregates independently of the ABO locus and can be occupied by either of a pair of alleles, *Se* or *se*. Secretors are either *SeSe* or *Sese*, and all nonsecretors are *sese*. Secretor is dominant to nonsecretor in such a way that:

Genotype	equals	Phenotype
SeSe		secretor
Sese		secretor
sese		nonsecretor

A person with one *Se* gene produces a water-soluble ABO substance, whereas the *sese* homozygote produces only an alcohol-soluble ABO substance. Because of this the ABO substance is found in many fluids of the secretor. The existence of ABO antigens outside the red blood cells was known as early as 1910, and the manner of inheritance has been known since 1932. Frequencies of *Se* and *se* were found to vary in no clear pattern.

In 1948 R. Grubb published a paper noting a relationship, a linkage, between the Lewis antigens (one member of the blood group system) and secretor. Grubb's findings are important because they provide an understanding of certain genetic principles (Kelso, 1970). It is clear that inherited traits result from an interaction among the loci as well as between genetic elements and the environment. As a practical consideration for physical anthropologists this suggests that a simultaneous consideration of allelic frequencies will be more informative than a consideration of each separately.

Blood Groups and Hemoglobin Variations

Blood groups are defined by the reactions of an individual's red blood cells to substances in the fluid (serum) portion of the blood. The surface of red blood cells contains antigens that react with antibodies in the serum (an antigen is a substance capable of stimulating the production of antibodies; an antibody is a substance produced in response to the presence of an antigen). The interest in blood groups originated with the practice of blood transfusions. Such experiments began in the seventeenth century and were frequently harmless; in a few cases, however, the recipient of the transfusion died. In 1900 Karl Landsteiner, who won a Nobel prize for his work, discovered why transfusions were fatal to some individuals. He noted that when red blood cells from some individuals are mixed with those from another individual, the cells may clump or agglutinate. Landsteiner and his students found that they could group humans into four types on the basis of these agglutination reactions. The four types are explained by the presence of either or both of two substances, the A and B antigens, in the cells.

The serum known to react with a specific antigen is called an antiserum to it. A and B antigens can be identified with tests using the two types of antisera containing antibodies called anti-A and anti-B. If a drop of anti-A serum is added to a drop of blood, the red cells may remain in normal suspension or they may clump together. If the blood clumps its red blood cells must contain the A antigen. If the blood reacts to anti-A but not to anti-B, it is called type A; if it reacts to anti-B but not anti-A, it is type B. If the red blood cells react to both anti-A and anti-B sera, it is called type AB, and if it reacts to neither it is called type O.

Although it was long believed that blood groups were inherited, it was the mathematician F. Bernstein who described the mechanism. Bernstein demonstrated that blood group inheritance could be explained as due to three alleles. The genes for antigen A (designated I^A) and for B (I^B) are equally dominant (codominant); the gene for antigen O (the universal donor), designated i, is recessive. Blood group O is homozygous; genotypes for A and B may be either AA or OA and BB or OB (Tables 27-3 and 27-4).

After the discovery of the ABO blood group systems, a number of other blood group systems were defined. A listing of these various blood group systems is found in Table 27-5. There are now about 80 known human blood cell antigens grouped into several systems. Each

Table 27-3. ABO Determinations

Genotype	Phenotype (Blood Type)	Antibodies
AA AO	A	anti-B
BB BO	B	anti-A
AB	AB	none
OO	O	anti-AB

Comparison of ABO types in families, sometimes for three generations, has shown the exact mode of inheritance. Given the parental genotypes, the probable genotypes of the children can be predicted.

	First	Second	Third
Parents	AB × OO	BB × OO	BO × AO
Children	AO BO	BO BO	AB AO BO OO

In mating 1, type O offspring are not possible, even though one parent has this blood type. Mating 2 produces only type B children. A mating of heterozygotes for type A and B produces four different blood types in their children, as shown in mating 3.

Adapted from Stephen Molnar, *Races, Types and Ethnic Groups: The Problem of Human Variation,* © 1975, p. 69. Reprinted by permission of Prentice-Hall, Inc., Englewood Cliffs, New Jersey.

Table 27-4. Matings and Offspring in Selected Blood Group Systems

Mating	Offspring Possible Phenotypes	Impossible Phenotypes
ABO system[a]		
O × O	O	A, B, AB
O × A	O, A	B, AB
O × B	O, B	A, AB
O × AB	A, B	AB
A × A	O, A	AB
A × B	A, AB, B	none
A × AB	A, B, AB	O
B × B	O, B	A, AB
B × AB	A, B, AB	O
AB × AB	A, B, AB	O
MNSs System[b]		
M × M	M	N, MN
M × MN	M, MN	N
M × N	MN	M, N
MN × MN	M, MN, N	none
MN × N	MN, N	M
N × N	N	M, MN

[a]Phenotypes defined by anti-A and anti-B antisera.
[b]Phenotypes defined by anti-M and anti-N antisera.

Table 27-5. Summary of Principal Blood Group Systems Distributions

System	Phenotypic Frequencies
ABO (including A_1 and A_2)	Type O most common, more than 50% of most individuals in a population. Type B nearly absent in American Indians and Australian aborigines. Type B present in up to 15% of Europe and 40% of Africa, Asia and India. A_2 limited primarily to Europe.
MNS-U	American Indians almost exclusively M; N most common in Australia and the Pacific. MS and NS absent in Australia. U-negative appears limited to Africa.
Rh (R_1, R_2, R_O, r', and others)	Rh negative (rr) rare or absent in most of world, but found in 15% of Europeans. R_O, almost exclusively of African origin, found in 70% of Africans.
Duffy (Fy^a, Fy^b, Fy)	Most Australians and Polynesians and 90% to 99% of Asian populations. Duffy positive (Fy^a) 90% in India, 85% to 90% in American Indians, 65% in England and America, 27% in American blacks. Fy^a very low in Africa, but Fy gene is very common to about 80%.
Diego (Di^a. Di^b)	Diego-positive (Di^a) limited to American Indians, 2% to 20%, and Asians. Diego-positive is absent in Europe and Africa, and much of the Pacific and among Eskimos.

Table 27-5. continued

System	Phenotypic Frequencies
Kidd (Jk^a, Jk^b)	Jk^a, Kidd-positive, is most common in West Africa and among American blacks, 90%. Also found in American Indians, 70% to 90%, Europeans, about 70%, and is least common among Chinese, 50% to 55%.

Adapted from Stanley M. Garn, *Human Races*, 2nd edition, p. 47, 1962. Courtesy of Charles C Thomas, Publishers, Springfield, Illinois.

Table 27-6. History of Discovery of Red Blood Cell Antigens

System	Year of Discovery	Number of Antigens Known
ABO	1900	6
MNS	1927	18
P	1927	3
Rhesus	1940	17
Lutheran	1945	2
Kell-Cellano	1946	5
Lewis	1946	2
Duffy	1950	2
Kidd	1951	2
Diego	1955	1
Xg	1962	1
Dombruck	1965	1

In addition to antigens of the major systems, there are also antigens found only in single families (private systems) or antigens which are common to most humans (public systems).

Private Systems		Public Systems
Levay	Romunde	1
Jobbins	Chr^a	Vel
Becker	Swann (Sw^a)	Yt
Ven	Good	Gerbich
Cavaliere	Bi (Biles)	Lan
Berrens	Tr^a	Sm
Wright (Wr^a)	Webb	
Batty		

Adapted from I. M. Lerner, *Heredity, Evolution and Society*, 2nd edition, p. 354. W. H. Freeman and Company San Francisco, © 1976.

major system is controlled by alleles at a different locus. Table 27-6 summarizes the history of the discovery of the major blood group systems.

Anthropologists have studied blood groups and other polymorphic blood factors as a means of reconstructing the history of human populations. Although first considered a taxonomic panacea for determining racial classification, blood groups have not produced very firm results, for each blood factor calls for another hypothesis to help explain its distribution. The discovery of the blood groups produced the biological version of the California Gold Rush. Anthropologists and geneticists searched the world for blood group distributions in the hope that by matching the blood groups of various populations they could discover their true relationships.

Modern blood group studies follow two paths: (1) Dividing the world into more or less discrete populations and deriving blood group frequencies for each separate system. This approach is used to measure population divergence. (2) Tracing the occurrence of each blood group system in an attempt to explain its distribution in terms of natural selection (Table 27-7). The most fruitful studies have followed the second course.

Early Results of Serology. Blood groups were considered ideal study traits because they are simply inherited. Thus, they qualify as ideal traits for population comparisons. They won further approval because samples are usually easy to obtain. (I qualify this statement because there are societies in which it is considered grossly inappropriate to take someone's blood. Although samples are not hard to obtain—you simply prick the fingertip—they are difficult to store and need refrigeration. More than one research project has been spoiled in the muggy heat of tropical areas).

Because millions of blood type samples are taken each year, the investigator has a ready backlog of data. In spite of the advantages of blood grouping, early taxonomies were fanciful at best. Totally unrelated populations were linked on the basis of comparative serology. Using the ABO system, India and Africa were lumped together and the American Indian and the Australian aborigine were considered members of the same group. Coupled with a refinement of the system was the belated serological confirmation that the American Indian and Asiatic populations were historically related and that Europeans were not the result of a blend between an Asiatic and Australian aborigine population. (Needless to say, this brought a sigh of relief from the stalwarts of European supremacy!)

The greatest contribution of **serology** (blood group genetics) is that it has provided a better basis for comparing populations than morphological studies, rather than establishing a racial taxonomy. For populations formed by the recent interbreeding of two populations, blood groups offer the possibility of precise quantification of genetic contributions. For example, genetic studies leave no doubt about the fact that American blacks have felt the considerable genetic influence from American white populations. Blood groups offer help in determining population relationships; however, some blood group genes are more sensitive than others as indicators of genetic interchange. While blood group distributions are not always consistent with other forms of evidence such as the fossil record, the blood group record serves as another independent line of evidence.

An additional problem with using comparative serological data is that blood groups themselves may be subjected to selection pressures. Contrary to what was originally thought, present gene frequencies do not provide a perfect indication of what they were in the past, making present distributions of limited value in solving ancient population distributions. The fact that there is some relationship between antigens in the ABO system and illness indicates that some blood groups may have been selected for or against (Table 27-8). This selection influences their current numbers. For example, individuals of group A tend to have a higher incidence of gastric cancer than those with the other ABO genotypes.

Blood Group Distributions. Type O is the most common blood group in the ABO system; among American Indians generally the incidence is more than 90 percent. However,

Table 27-7. Frequencies of ABO Blood Groups

Population	Place	Number Tested	Blood-Group Frequency			
			O	A	B	AB
Low A, virtually no B						
American Indians:						
Toba	Argentina	194	98.5	1.5	0.0	0.0
Sioux	South Dakota	100	91.0	7.0	2.0	0.0
Moderately high A, virtually no B						
Navaho	New Mexico	359	77.7	22.5	0.0	.0
Pueblo	New Mexico (including Jemez)	310	78.4	20.0	1.6	.0
High A, little B						
American Indians:						
Shoshone	Wyoming	60	51.6	45.0	1.6	1.6
Bloods	Montana	69	17.4	81.2	0.0	1.4
Eskimo	Baffin Land	146	55.5	43.8	.0	0.7
Austr. aborigines	South Australia	54	42.6	57.4	.0	.0
Basques	San Sebastian	91	57.2	41.7	1.1	.0
Polynesians	Hawaii	413	36.5	60.8	2.2	0.5
Fairly high A, some B						
English	London	422	47.9	42.4	8.3	1.4
French	Paris	1,265	39.8	42.3	11.8	6.1
Armenians	From Turkey	330	27.3	53.9	12.7	6.1
Lapps	Finland	94	33.0	52.1	12.8	2.1
Melanesians	New Guinea	500	37.6	44.4	13.2	4.8
Germans	Berlin	39,174	36.5	42.5	14.5	6.5
High A and high B						
Welsh	North Towns	192	47.9	32.8	16.2	3.1
Italians	Sicily	540	45.9	33.4	17.3	3.4
Siamese	Bangkok	213	37.1	17.8	35.2	9.9
Finns	Hame	972	34.0	42.4	17.1	6.5
Germans	Danzig	1,888	33.1	41.6	18.0	7.3
Ukrainians	Kharkov	310	36.4	38.4	21.6	3.6
Asiatic Indians	Bengal	160	32.5	20.0	39.4	8.1

After William C. Boyd, "Genetics and the human race," *Science*, Vol. 140, pp. 1057-64, 7 June 1963. Copyright © 1963 by the American Association for the Advancement of Science.

there are variations; 97 percent of the Utes and only 23 percent of the Blackfoot are of type O. In much of Europe the incidence of O is between 35 and 40 percent. Among Chinese, Japanese, and many African groups O is about 30 percent.

Following O, type A is the most frequent blood group. Type A is rare in some American Indian tribes; however, in other tribes it accounts for more than 75 percent of those typed. Type A is found in about 45 percent of the English population and in approximately the same proportion of Americans of Northwest European ancestry.

Table 27-8. Association Between Blood Group Phenotypes and Diseases

Disease	Associated ABO or Secretor Phenotype
Bronchial pneumonia	A
Filaria parasitic infection	A
Smallpox	A
Staphylococci infection	A
Streptococci infection	A and O
Typhoid	A
Stomach cancer	A
Pernicious anemia	A
Diabetes mellitus	A
Salivary gland tumors	A
Cervix cancer	A
Ovarian tumors	A
Cancer of pancreas	A
Influenza	probably 0
Plague	0
Duodenal ulcer	0
Gastric ulcer	0
Adenoma of pituitary	0
Rheumatic fever	excess of secretors[a]
Paralytic poliomyelitis	excess of secretors, B reduced[b]

[a,b]Evidence is inconclusive.

Adapted from J. Buettner-Janusch, *Physical Anthropology: A Perspective*, p. 428. Copyright © 1973 by John Wiley & Sons, Inc., and Stephen Molnar, *Races, Types and Ethnic Groups: The Problem of Human Variation*, © 1975, pp. 136-37. Reprinted by permission of Prentice-Hall, Inc., Englewood Cliffs, New Jersey.

Blood type B is the least common of the ABO system, and has the most interesting worldwide distribution. Type B appears to be totally absent in North and South American Indians and is rarely found in more than 2 percent of any American Indian population, a low percentage that may be the result of intermating. Type B is less common than type A in Europe; it is found in 9 to 25 percent of the population. The average for type B in Europe is about 15 percent. The percentage in Asia is between 35 and 37 percent and is a bit higher in Africa. Type B seems to be more an Asiatic and African rather than a European type. Although it is assumed that American Indians are historically related to some part of the Asian population, there is a surprising lack of evidence for that relationship in the B blood type. Again, assuming the ancestor-descendant relationship valid, type B may be a relatively recent phenomenon in Asia, appearing after the colonization of the Americas; it may have been lost or selected against in the American descendants, or its relatively low incidence in the Americas may be the result of the founder effect.

MNS-U System Other blood systems are helpful in determining population relationships; one is the **MNS-U system**. Most of the world is equally divided between M and N, rarely is either entirely missing. M is especially high in American Indians, N is slight or missing. In contrast, the incidence of N is especially high in Australia. The percentage of N dominates M throughout the Pacific area, and the high incidence of N in Pacific populations sets them off' from and probably precludes recent contact with America. The near absence of B separates Pacific area populations from those of Asia.

Because extreme percentages of M and N occur in populations formerly explained as having developed on the basis of admixture, it is notable that no combination of Asiatic populations could yield the current low values of both M and N common to Australian aborigines. Furthermore, no hypothetical mixture of "Caucasoid" with "Negroid" could yield the nearly M-free Australian aborigine population. Either the so-called three original races, that is, Caucasoid, Negroid, and Mongoloid, never existed, or subsequent evolution altered their genetic composition beyond recognition. The first possibility is the most likely.

The S gene was discovered in 1947 in England, where it is quite common. While the S gene is absent among Australian aborigines, it is present in New Guinea. Since there is strong fossil evidence of a relationship between the Upper Pleistocene New Guinea population (represented by the Niah skull) and the Upper Pleistocene Australian population (at Lake Mungo), it is possible that S was selected out in Australia or that it is a new arrival in New Guinea. Europeans are U positive; American blacks are about 1 percent U negative. A mismatch of positive and negative can lead to tranfusion complications.

Rhesus System. The **Rhesus (RH) blood group** was described in 1940 and shortly afterward the Rh system was identified as the cause of a hemolytic disease of the newborn due to isoimmunization of the mother (Levine, 1943). This process occurs when an incompatible pregnancy results from an incompatible mating. The consequences of this for a population depend partly on the frequency of the Rh+ and Rh– genes, leading to the Rh-positive or Rh-negative classification. Rh incompatibility, erythroblastosis fetalis, is characterized by an excessive destruction of fetal red blood cells and a compensatory overdevelopment of tissues in which such blood cells are formed. The skin may have a yellowish color, and the liver and spleen become enlarged.

The disease is usually due to a difference in Rh blood types between the mother and her infant. Various subtypes of the Rh factor are all inherited as dominants over the Rh-negative condition. In addition to sensitization by transfusion, an Rh-negative woman may become sensitized from an Rh-positive fetus carried in her womb. Although fetal blood does not freely cross the placenta to flow into the mother's veins, some antigen does cross, because Rh substances in the fetal red blood cells can produce antibodies in the mother's blood serum. Antibodies can accumulate in the mother and may then be carried in her serum to a subsequent Rh-positive fetus where they react with the red cells to the detriment of the fetus. Interestingly, erythroblastosis fetalis apparently occurs less often when mother and father are of different ABO blood groups. Incompatability in the ABO system appears to reduce the likelihood of erythroblastosis fetalis caused by development of Rh antibodies in the infant.

Erythroblastosis fetalis can be prevented by treating the Rh-negative mother after her first Rh-positive infant. Immediately after delivery the mother is given immunoglobulin with anti-Rh antibodies that prevent her developing them in her own serum and thus protect any future Rh-positive child. Furthermore, erythroblastosis fetalis can be treated by blood transfusions to the infant.

Most of you are aware that your blood types are given as positive (+) or negative (–). You are either rhesus positive (Rh+) or rhesus negative (Rh–). The proportion of Rh– ranges from about 12 to 15 percent in the United States and England. Among the Basques, a population primarily settled in France and Spain and who maintain considerable cultural and political autonomy, the percentage rises to 30 percent. Elsewhere the percentage of Rh– is rare.

Among Afro-Americans the incidence of Rh– is about half of what it is among Europeans. One gene, known as R_O, is common in Afro-Americans, running about 40 percent incidence. This is of some interest, for this gene appears in about 70 percent of the ancestral African populations. There appears to have been some loss of the R_O gene in New World African-derived populations. This loss may be explained in one of three ways, or as a combination of all three: (1) there is some advantage to the R_O gene in Africa, but none in the New World, (2) the separation of the African population because of the institution of slavery resulted in some drift among the New World group, or (3) there may have been a dissolution of the R_O gene in the New World as a result of the interpopulation matings.

Duffy System. The Duffy blood group derives its name from a Mr. Duffy in whose blood the antigen was discovered in 1950. There are two forms of Duffy, a positive allele Fy^a and a negative allele Fy^b. Since Fy^a (Duffy positive) is dominant over Fy^b, (Duffy negative), there are only two phenotypes. In England 65 percent of a test population was Fy^a. This amounts to a gene frequency of 0.40. Higher frequencies appear in Pakistan and India and among New York Chinese and the Australian aborigine, and far lower percentages appear in African populations. The extreme rarity of the Fy^a type in Africa and the relatively high frequency of its appearance in Europe make the Duffy system the most sensitive measure of European admixture with Afro-American populations. The incidence of Duffy among Afro-Americans is a good sign of mating with Europeans. Apparently the home of Duffy positive is in the Pacific area and East Asia; there is a decreasing frequency both southward into the Americas and westward into Europe and Africa.

Diego System. One of the most recently discovered blood groups consists of a pair of genes Di^a and Di^b, and two phenotypes, positive and negative. The positive phenotype is in the minority. The Di^a gene incidence clearly separates indigenous Australian and Pacific populations from American Indians and Asian populations. No Diego negative individuals have been found in New Guinea and among the Central Australian aborigines. Diego positive is found in about 25 percent of the Peruvian Indians.

Haptoglobins and Transferrins

Haptoglobins are serum proteins that are part of the alpha$_2$-globulins in serum. Haptoglobins can combine with free hemoglobin (that is, hemoglobin released into the plasma when a red blood cell disintegrates), and this ability prevents it from being lost through excretion in the kidneys. Three types of haptoglobin are known, each apparently under genetic control. While the occurrence of different haptoglobins varies widely, the adaptive significance of the various haptoglobins is unclear, although there may be some environmental selection.

Another type of serum protein variant is a beta-globulin fraction of serum that binds with iron. The transferrins transport iron to the tissues as needed, especially bone marrow, where hemoglobin is formed. There are at least 17 forms of transferrins and each appears to be under genetic control. Transferrin variants are arranged in three groups, TfC, TfD, and TfB.

These transferrins are distributed unevenly in populations; TfC is most common and TfB is not widely distributed. Since there may be a difference in binding capacity of the various transferrins, certain forms may be more efficient in some populations. However, as with haptoglobins, more study is needed.

Hemoglobins

Before discussing hemoglobin variations such as sickle-cell and thalassemia, it is well to discuss the qualities of hemoglobin itself[2]. Hemoglobin is found within the red blood cells and carries oxygen to the body's cells while it carries away carbon dioxide. Hemoglobin shows a good deal of genetic variability and is one of the proteins whose structure is known quite precisely. The most common adult hemoglobin molecule consists of four long amino acid chains, or, more accurately, two pairs of identical chains, two alpha and two beta. The amino acid sequences in both chains are well known. In the human fetus there is another hemoglobin, hemoglobin F. Hemoglobin F is replaced by adult hemoglobin, A, in normal individuals within 2 months of birth. Both hemoglobin F and hemoglobin A contain two alpha chains, but hemoglobin F contains two distinct chains in place of the two beta chains in hemoglobin A.

The most common type of hemoglobin is Hb A; however, there are now more than 100 known "abnormal" hemoglobins that have an hereditary basis. Hemoglobin variations can occur in three ways: (1) alterations in the amino acids in either the alpha or beta chains, (2) molecular modifications of the iron-bearing structures (the hemes) that serve as sites for oxygen attachment, and (3) quantitative differences in the production of the alpha and beta chains. A change in any of these is almost always harmful, varying in severity from mild anemias to fatal diseases.

Examples of hemoglobin variations follow in the form of a discussion of sickle-cell anemia and thalassemia.

Today malarial vectors are primarily concentrated in the New and Old World tropics. In the Old World they are spread from West Africa to Melanesia, and are especially prevalent in West African forest regions; only rarely does malaria extend into regions above 6,000 feet or above the winter frost line. We would expect populations long-resident in malarial regions to have some natural protection from one of the species of *Plasmodium* (parasites that cause malaria). The two principal malarial adaptations of which we are aware are thalassemia, major and minor, appearing primarily in the Mediterranean area and southeast Asia, and the sickle-cell trait.

Sickle-Cell Anemia. The hereditary antimalarial defense with which most of you are familiar is sickle-cell anemia, which is primarily (but not exclusively) African in its distribution (Figure 27-2). The sickling trait also occurs among Greeks and Italians, for example. It was also found that an individual could have both sickle-cell anemia or the trait and thalassemia. The disorder receives its name from the characteristic sickle-shaped appearance of affected red blood cells when they are placed in a saline solution (Figure 27-3). Sickling is inherited as a Mendelian codominant (incompletely recessive) trait. There are two forms: the mild sickle-cell trait (the heterozygotic state) and the severe sickle-cell disease (the homozygotic state).

James Neel confirmed the inheritance of sickling in 1949, noting that individuals with the sickle-cell disease were invariably offspring of parents who both carried the sickle-cell trait (Chapter 7). The individual homozygous for sickle-cell anemia (*SS*) produces hemoglobin (called hemoglobin S) that has less oxygen-carrying ability than the normal hemoglobin, A. There are three genotypes—homozygous normals (*AA*), homozygous for sickle-cell disease (*SS*), and heterozygous for the sickle-cell trait (*AS*).

[2]Three substances in the blood are known, or thought, to offer some disease resistance. These are hemoglobin, blood group antigens (the foreign particles stimulating antibody production), and the globulins (proteins that carry the antibodies).

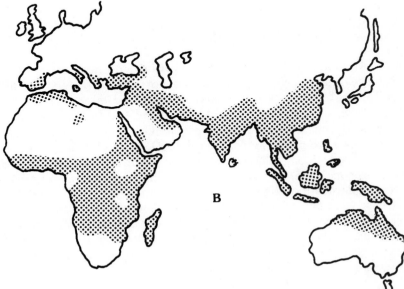

Figure 27-2. Distribution of (A) sickle-cell hemoglobin and (B) falciparum malaria.

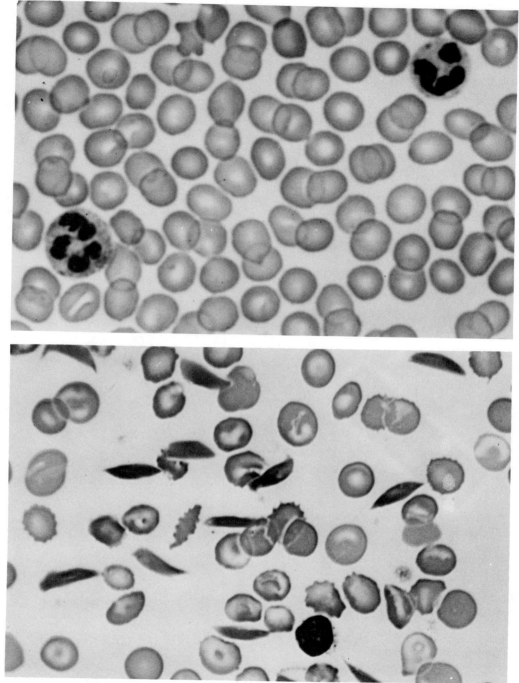

Figure 27-3. (A) Normal red blood cells (two white blood cells are also shown). (B) Sickled red blood cells.

Adaptive Significance. Table 27-9 shows the adaptive advantage of sickle-cell trait in malarial zones. In some African areas frequencies for the sickling trait vary from zero to as high as 40 percent and estimates as to the number of Americans of African origin carrying the trait range above 3 million. The disorder probably came to the United States when the first slaves were brought to Jamestown in 1619; it is now the most common hemoglobin disorder found in the United States. What is the advantage of such a trait? Since sickle-cell anemia (the homozygote) is usually lethal because of the hemoglobin's inability to hold and carry oxygen, and since there is some selection against individuals with the sickle-cell trait (the heterozygote) in nonmalarial areas, some selective advantage must maintain the sickling gene. Several workers have noted the geographical association between malaria and sickling, and have postulated a heterozygous advantage. In malarial areas individual homozygous normals develop malaria early and many die; the survivors have impaired vitality. Individuals heterozygous for sickling have increased protection against malaria because the malarial parasite, which spends part of its life cycle in red blood cells, fails to thrive on their blood. These individuals are at a relative advantage over both homozygotes in malarial areas. However, in essentially nonmalarial areas, such as the present-day United States, [3] some

[3]It should be kept in mind that malaria occurred in various of the swampy areas in the American South in the eighteenth and nineteenth centuries. It also occurred as far north as St. Louis and Evansville as late as the 1940s and is still found in some areas of the United States today.

Table 27-9. The Adaptation of Sickle-Cell Trait

Let S = the sickle allele
A = the normal allele

In a West African population there are both sickling and normal alleles.

SS	SS	SS	Homozygous sickling
AA	AA	AA	Homozygous normal
AS	AS	AS	Heterozygous

In each generation the sickling homozygote dies of sickle-cell anemia.

SS	SS	SS	These forms die because of lack of oxygen caused by sickle-cell anemia.

The normal homozygotes also die each generation.

AA	AA	AA	These forms die of malaria.

The heterozygotic condition survives.

AS	AS	AS	If these forms contract malaria, it is only a mild form. In malarial conditions, these individuals are selected for.

The surviving heterozygotes leave progeny which include the range of genotypes: homozygous sickler, normal, and heterozygous.

SS	SS	SS	As long as malaria remains a selective factor, the progeny are subject to the same evolutionary pressures as their parents. The cycle is repeated anew.
AA	AA	AA	
AS	AS	AS	

individuals with sickling may be at a disadvantage, for the trait sometimes causes pain and reduced vitality and can lead to other complications (Figure 27-4).

Culture, Malaria, and the Sickle-Cell Trait. The relationship between malaria and abnormal hemoglobins is quite clear in Africa and the Mediterranean; however, the existence of malaria poses a problem. Much of Africa is not naturally malarious; preagricultural Africa offered little to the malarial mosquito and only when rain forests were opened for agriculture did the mosquito have a chance to spread. The mosquito does not breed in the rain forest or the shaded forest floor, and malaria seems to be nonexistent in untouched African jungles. Frank Livingstone concluded that malaria is of recent origin in West Africa and appeared following the introduction of slash-and-burn (swidden) agriculture. With the opening of the forest floor and the appearance of stagnant, unshaded pools, a whole new habitat was provided for the carrier mosquito. Agriculture made Africa malarial by providing the mosquito

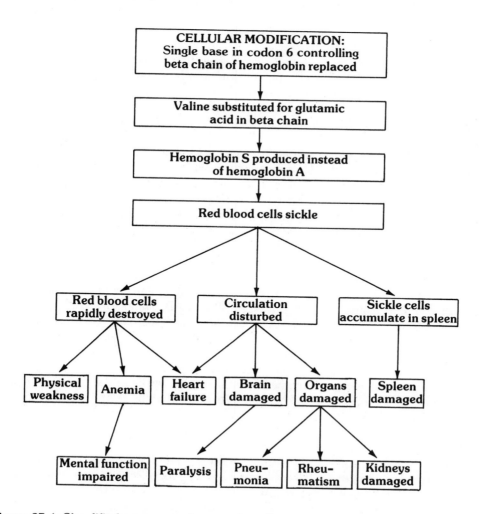

Figure 27-4. Simplified sequence of events in sickle-cell anemia.

a place to breed; malaria spread following the spread of slash-and-burn agriculture, and S hemoglobin became adaptive in its wake. Sickling frequencies, especially in West Africa, bear out this hypothesis; preagricultural peoples or those recently becoming agriculturalists have the lowest incidence of sickling.

The relationship Livingstone postulates between malaria and agriculture with the consequent change in genetic structure, is the first well-documented example of how culture can inititate genetic change. The demonstration of the mosquito-malaria relationship brought about a review of the situation in the Mediterranean. Here, human habitation did not create wet, humid, marshy areas; however, populations moved into them for the purpose of practicing lowland agriculture. Early agricultural civilizations developed along the rivers, with their seasonal floods and consequent stagnant pools and lowland marshes. Oasis villages (where malaria is a scourge) provided the basis for early stable populations; primitive means of irrigation—ditch irrigation and wheel bucket watering—caused seasonal flooding and created optimum areas for breeding malarial mosquitos. Consequent food surpluses made high population densities possible and vastly increased the numbers subjected to malarial selection.

Culture created malarial zones in Africa, and it is again changing the picture, for by the use of modern sprays, such as DDT and other mosquito sprays, technology is killing many malarial vectors. (It is also selecting for DDT-resistant strains of mosquitos.) This selection may again result in changed proportions of genotypes; one could expect a slow increase in the proportion of normal homozygotes and a slow decline in the heterozygote condition, depending on the mosquito's adaptation.

Thalassemia. One form of thalassemia (from the Greek *thalassa,* the Mediterranean Sea, and *haima,* blood) is known as "Mediterranean thalassemia" or Cooley's anemia (Figure 27-1). Clinical and geographical data on thalassemia raised important questions about the origin of the abnormal gene (and its seeming original restriction to malarial areas) and its survival. From its wide distribution on both shores of the Mediterranean, it was postulated that the gene was of ancient origin—perhaps dating to about 5000 B.C. However, the absence of the thalassemia trait in parts of Europe where Mediterraneans migrated remained a puzzling mystery.

Original explanations tried to link high regional incidences of thalassemia with increased fertility of heterozygous individuals. However, a high rate of fertility could not be found, nor could abnormally high rates for the thalassemic gene. Beginning in 1950, a number of workers pointed to the correspondence of thalassemia with the distribution of malaria. In those parts of the Mediterranean where malaria was a severe year-round problem, thalassemia frequencies were the highest. The current picture, confirmed by the sickle-cell pattern, is that thalassemia provides some malarial protection.

Table 27-10 shows the mechanism whereby thalassemia works in the three genotypes: homozygous normal, homozygous for thalassemia (thalassemia major), and heterozygous for thalassemia (thalassemia minor).

G6PD Deficiency

Hemoglobin is not the only protein in the red cell. About 5 percent of the total protein in the red cell is a heterogeneous mixture of several enzymes with specific functions. One of these enzymes is glucose-6-phosphate dehydrogenase (G6PD). This enzyme is a necessary catalyst in the metabolism of carbohydrates. The G6PD-deficiency disease was discovered when a

Table 27-10. Thalassemia Genotypes and Clinical Picture

Clinical Status	Genotype	Clinical Picture	Hemoglobins
Normal	Homozygote normal	Within normal limits for hemoglobin and cellular fragility	Normal, slight amount of fetal hemoglobin
Thalassemia minor	Heterozygote	Slight anemia, increased osmotic pressure of the red cells	Slight amount of fetal hemoglobin
Thalassemia major	Homozygote	Marked anemia, abnormal red cells fragile and increased osmotic pressure	Hemoglobin primarily of fetal type, little normal hemoglobin

From Stanley M. Garn, *Human Races,* 2nd edition, p. 71, 1962. Courtesy of Charles C Thomas, Publishers, Springfield, Illinois.

number of Americans of African and Asian descent were treated with certain antimalarial drugs, primarily primaquine. Primaquine produced a mild hemolysis (the rupture of the red blood cells and the freeing of their hemoglobin). Individuals exhibiting this reaction contain G6PD in very low amounts. A number of other drugs chemically related to primaquine produce hemolysis when given to G6PD-deficient individuals. **Favism** is a hemolytic condition produced by eating the fava bean (*Vicia fava*), which is commercially grown in southern Europe and the Middle East. Favism is connected with G6PD deficiency.

The G6PD deficiency is inherited as an X-linked trait that is apparently incompletely dominant. Females homozygous for the trait exhibit as marked a deficiency as males with the trait. Enzyme-deficient red blood cells contain very little glutathione, which malarial parasites depend on for growth. Some species of *Plasmodium* enter and live in old red cells rather than the young cells. Because old red blood cells are normally those deficient in glutathione, the parasites are poorly nourished in the bloodstream of anyone having this enzyme deficiency.

The distribution of G6PD deficiency parallels the distribution of falciparum malaria (Figure 27-5). Resistance to malaria is the suggested advantage of G6PD and is the factor maintaining the condition in various populations. Falciparum malaria is a good candidate for the selective agent in all protein abnormalities affecting red cells. The parasite *P. falciparum* lives on the proteins contained in the red cells. When the red cell is unable to support the parasite, the host is immune or resistant to malaria.

We have shown that there is a parallel distribution between sickle-cell trait, G6PD deficiency, and thalassemia. Buettner-Janusch (1966:589) states, however, that "arguments about distributions, parallel or not, are no longer apt to lead to further understanding of the evolutionary dynamics that produce relatively high frequencies of various red cell abnormalities in many human groups. . . . The exact physiological interaction of the parasite and the abnormal condition must be studied."

Population-Associated Diseases

A brief look at Table 27-11 shows that some populations and diseases are related. Since many populations are reproductively isolated from each other and therefore have had a somewhat

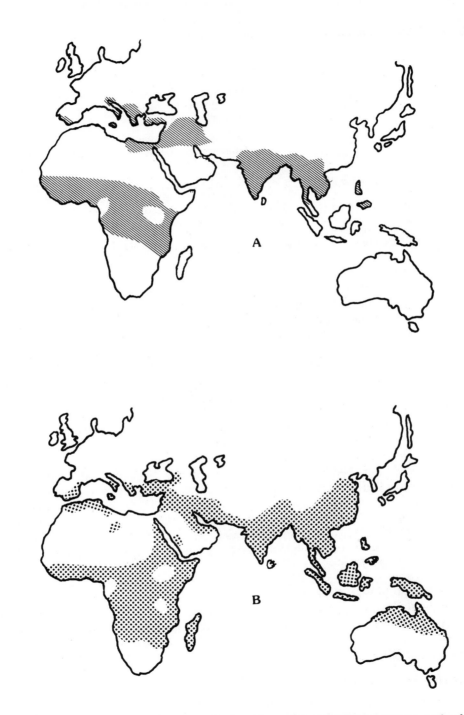

Figure 27-5. Distribution of (A) glucose-6-phosphate dehydrogenase deficiency in the Old World and (B) falciparum malaria.

Table 27-11. Populations and Their Diseases (Simply Inherited Disorders)

Population	Relatively High Frequency	Relatively Low Frequency
Ashkenazic Jews	Abetalipoproteinemia Bloom's disease Dystonia musculorum deformans Factor XI (PTA) deficiency Familial dysautonomia Gaucher's disease Niemann-Pick disease Pentosuria Spongy degeneration of brain Stub thumbs Tay-Sachs disease	Phenylketonuria
Mediterranean peoples (Greeks, Italians, Sephardic Jews)	Familial-Mediterranean fever G6PD deficiency Hemoglobinopathies (i.e., thalassemia)	Cystic fibrosis
Africans	G6PD deficiency (African type) Hemoglobinopathies	Cystic fibrosis Hemophilia PKU Wilson's disease
Japanese (Koreans)	Acatalasis Dyschromatosis universalis hereditaria Oguchi's disease	
Chinese	Thalassemia G6PD (Chinese type)	
Armenians	Familial Mediterranean fever	

Adapted from A. Damon, "Race, Ethnic Group and Disease." *Social Biology,* Vol. 16, 1969, p. 74.

separate evolutionary history, it is not surprising that we find certain diseases primarily restricted to some groups. Some diseases, rare in themselves, are also very rare in the populations exhibiting them. Population isolates such as the Amish have a high frequency of rare genetic diseases due to inbreeding or random genetic drift. There are a number of diseases in which inheritance may determine susceptibility but environment determines which individuals are afflicted. Some examples are diabetes mellitus, peptic ulcers, cancers, and pulmonary tuberculosis, and, if current research is correct, alcoholism, drug abuse, and schizophrenia can also be included. Mutations being what they are, no disease can be considered 100 percent population limited; the same abnormal hemoglobin protecting Italians from malaria also protects Burmese. Furthermore, common diseases may not always indicate common ancestry.

Kuru. **Kuru,** limited to the Eastern highlands of New Guinea, is one of the most remarkable population-associated diseases and was unknown to scientists until 1953 and unstudied until 1957. In pidgin English kuru is known as "skin guria," or shaking. Kuru is a progressive and incurable neurological disorder—the afflicted individual usually dies within a year. The first sign of the disease is uncoordination; persons begin to stumble and then are unable to walk. Involuntary tremors become more common and soon the victim cannot walk, sit, or speak intelligibly. The final stage comes when the victim cannot swallow food or control urination and defecation. The course of the disease is usually a year, but the victim may die within 3 months.

Kuru is limited to the Eastern New Guinea Fore and to some neighboring peoples married to Fore women. Women are more often afflicted than men, resulting in a sex ratio of 14 males to every female in later life. In some Fore hamlets the kuru death rate runs as high as 50 percent.

In an effort to discover the cause of the disease, C. Gajdusek (who won a Nobel Prize in 1976 for his work) and his colleagues began a search of such components of Fore society as food, water, and fires. No trace element or rare earth that could poison the nervous system was found and since Fore men outside the district living on government diets were also afflicted, nutritional sources were ruled out. The search was narrowed to some sort of slow virus.[4] When investigators found they produce kurulike disorders in chimpanzees inoculated with extracts of nerve tissue from kuru victims, they concluded that a virus was the cause.

How was the virus transmitted? Gajdusek suspected cannibalism as the primary means of transmission. The usual practice of cannibalism as a mourning rite had women and children disposing of the butchered bodies of dead relatives. They were thus covered with human tissue, including the brain and visceral tissue. Cannibalism was outlawed in 1957; since then the rate of kuru affliction has slowly declined.

The sex-limited nature of the disease, with females heavily predominating in terms of affliction, is due to the sexual division of labor. Dismembering a kuru victim is women's work. The familial nature of the disease is due to the fact that "one takes care of one's own." The lack of direct person-to-person transmission is explained by the fact that a slow virus causes the disease; the disease is infectious but not contagious. The men are aloof, engaging in cannibalism only when it is a very close relative, such as a mother. Even then they only sample muscle tissue.

Familial Mediterranean Fever. **Familial Mediterranean fever** is a cyclic disease; once the symptoms appear, they recur sporadically and unpredictably throughout life. In mild cases there is fever that lasts a day or so, joint pains, and chest and abdominal pains. In severe cases there is joint damage, bone decalcification, and kidney insufficiency. Most afflicted individuals are not permanently or seriously impaired; however, about 10 percent of the case studies have succumbed to renal complications.

Familial Mediterranean fever arose in the Middle East and appears to be of ancient origin. The disorder has a narrow distribution among Armenians and Sephardic Jews. Although its inception may be due to the founder principle, the high incidence suggests instead a heterozygote effect. The mutation may be 5,000 to 6,000 years old, and its concentration in the Mediterranean area suggests its origin there. The familial nature of the fever is apparent; about half of the siblings of index cases and about 50 percent of the offspring of index cases develop

---

[4]Similarly, slow viruses may be the cause of multiple sclerosis, Parkinson's disease, amyotrophic lateral sclerosis (Lou Gehrig's disease), and Legionnaire's disease.

familial Mediterranean fever, suggesting a Mendelian dominant. There is a slight excess of males over females among the afflicted.

Since the gene frequency for the disorder is low—well under .0001—the present limits may be due to chance. However, since the fever is associated with impaired fertility and since a certain portion of the genes is removed from the population each generation due to death, the maintenance of the frequency must be explained. The fact that Ashkenazic Jews (those in Europe and North America) rarely exhibit the trait while Sephardic Jews (those in the Middle East) do requires explanation. The heterozygote may be at an advantage in the Mediterranean region but not in colder northern climates.

Tay-Sachs Disease. **Tay-Sachs disease** is a rare disease that bears the name of its codiscoverers and is found primarily in Jewish populations. The disease is genetically determined and results in a neurological disorder that begins in infancy. The progressive nature of the disease usually results in death between ages 2 and 4. The disease has its highest incidence in European Ashkenazic Jewish populations, where it is about 100 times more common than in Sephardic Jews. The highest incidence is found in Jewish populations living in the provinces along the old Polish-Russian border near Vilna. Among non-Jews the incidence of the homozygote is one in about 500,000 live births. Since the disease is on the rise, there is the possibility of some selective advantage to the heterozygote; however, we do not yet know what it is.

Lactase Deficiency. The ability to digest the milk sugar lactose depends on the presence of the enzyme lactase in the lining of the small intestine. All human infants can readily produce lactase and can digest milk sugar. However, people in many populations cannot digest lactose after 4 years of age. Thereafter, no lactase is secreted, and milk consumption in any quantity leads to severe cramps and flatulence. Lactase deficiency seems to have a simple genetic base being determined by a pair of alleles. The allele for lactase production is dominant to that for nonproduction. Variations among populations in the frequency of lactase deficiency are closely correlated with the use of fresh milk by adults. Most adults of European ancestry and some African groups can readily digest milk. In West Africa, for example, populations with a low frequency of lactase deficiency live close by populations of farmers who drink little milk and have a high frequency of lactase deficiency.

Since the majority of the human population appears to be lactase deficient (Table 27-12), the nondeficient gene appears to represent a new mutation. It has been suggested that the gene for lactase production arose sometime in the past 10,000 years and was favored in populations practicing herding and dairying. In the case of lactase deficiency, we have an example of an enzyme activity that seems to have accompanied a major dietary change.

This chapter discussed some population differences and their significance. We have not exhausted the traits we could list, and we are unsure about the genetics and meaning of many of them. Whatever social meaning may be inappropriately attached to some of the traits, they are, by and large, reflections of a population's past or continuing struggles to adapt.

We do not know when and where many of the population differences discussed here arose. But such differences probably do not date very far back into the fossil record and many traits useful in modern classification cannot be obtained from the fossil record.

Table 27-12. Frequency of Lactase Deficiency

Group	Number of Subjects	Percent Deficient
Afro-American	137	74 (approx.)
Batutsi (Rwanda)	12	17
Bahina (Ankole)	11	9
Australian aborigines		
Papunya (all less than 15 years old)	25	90
Maningrida (age range 6 to 48 months; mean 22 months)	19	80
Greenland Eskimos	32	72
American Indian (Chami, Colombia)	24	100
American Indian	3	67
Chinese	20	85
Taiwan	(7)	
U.S.	(3)	
Philippines	(10)	
Baganda (Africa)	17	94
Bantu .	35	89
Thai	140	97
Thai	75	100

Adapted from R. McCracken, "Lactase Deficiency: An Example of Dietary Evolution." *Current Anthropology,* Vol. 12, 1971, pp. 483, 486-89.

Bibliography

Allison, A. 1954. Protection afforded by sickle-cell trait against subtertian malarial infection. *British Medical Journal* 1:290.

_____. 1955. Aspects of polymorphism in man. *Cold Springs Harbor Symposia on Quantitative Biology* 20:239.

_____. 1963. Malaria and glucose-6-phosphate dehydrogenase deficiency. *Nature* 179:609.

_____. 1964. Polymorphism and natural selection in human populations. *Cold Springs Harbor Symposia on Quantitative Biology* 29:137-49.

Allison, J., and Blumberg, B. 1959. Ability to taste phenylthiocarbamide among Alaskan Eskimos and other populations. *Human Biology* 31:352-59.

Angel, J. 1966. Porotic hyperostosis amnesias, malarias, and marshes in prehistoric eastern Mediterranean. *Science* 153:760-63.

Azevedo, E., Kreeger, H., Mi, P., and Morton, N. 1965. PTC taste sensitivity and endemic goiter in Brazil. *American Journal of Human Genetics* 17:87-90.

Bayless, T., and Rosenzweig, N. 1966. A social difference in incidence of lactase deficiency. *Journal of American Medical Association* 197:968.

Blumberg, B., and Gartler, S. 1961. The urinary excretion of B-aminoisobutyric acid in Pacific populations. *Human biology* 33:355.

Boyd, W. 1950. *Genetics and the races of man.* Boston: Little, Brown.

_____. 1963. Genetics and the human race. *Science* 140:1057-64.

Brace, C. 1963. Structural reduction in evolution. *American Naturalist* 97:39-49.

Brues, A. 1963. Stochastic tests of selection in the ABO blood groups. *American Journal of Physical Anthropology* 21:287.

Buettner-Janusch, J. 1966. *Origins of man.* New York: Wiley.

_____. 1973. *Physical anthropology: a perspective.* New York: Wiley.

Carbonell, V. 1963. Variations in the frequency of shovel-shape incisors in different populations. In *Dental anthropology*, edited by D. R. Brothwell, pp. 211-34. Elmsford, N.Y.: Pergamon Press.

Cavalli-Sforza, L., and Bodmer, W. 1971. *The genetics of human populations*. San Francisco: Freeman.

Comas, J. 1960. *Manual of physical anthropology*. Springfield, Ill.: Thomas.

Coon, C., Garn, S., and Birdsell, J. 1950. *Races: a study of the problems of race formation in man*. Springfield, Ill.: Thomas.

Damon, A. 1969. Race, ethnic group and disease. *Social Biology* 16:69-80.

Gajdusek, C. 1962. Kuru—an appraisal of five years of investigation. *Eugenics Quarterly* 9:69.

Gajdusek, C., and Zigas, V. 1959. Kuru. *American Journal of Medicine* 26:442.

Garn, S. 1957. Race and evolution. *American Anthropologist* 59:218.

——————. 1962. *Human races*, 2nd ed. Springfield, Ill.: Thomas.

——————. 1971. *Human races*, 3rd ed. Springfield, Ill.: Thomas.

Giblett, E. 1969. *Genetic markers in human blood*. Philadelphia: Davis.

Giles, E. 1962. Favism, sex-linkage, and the Indo-European kinship system. *Southwest Journal Anthropology* 18:286-90.

Grubb, R. 1948. Correlation between Lewis blood group and secretor character in man. *Nature* 16:933.

Harrison, G., Weiner, J., Tanner, J., and Barnicot, N. 1964. *Human biology: an introduction to human evolution, variation and growth*. New York: Oxford University Press.

Johnston, F. 1973. *Microevolution of human populations*. Englewood Cliffs, N.J.: Prentice-Hall.

Kelso, A. 1963. Dietary differences: a possible selective mechanism in ABO blood group frequencies. *Southwestern Lore* 28:48-56.

Landsteiner, K. 1945. *The specificity of serological reactions*. Cambridge: Harvard University Press.

Lerner, I. 1968. Heredity, evolution and society. San Francisco: Freeman.

Levine, P. 1943. Serological factors as possible causes of spontaneous abortion. *Journal of Heredity* 34:71-80.

Livingstone, F. 1958. Anthropological implications of sickle-cell gene distribution in West Africa. *American Anthropologist* 60:533.

——————. 1967. *Abnormal hemoglobins in human populations*. Chicago: Aldine.

——————. 1971. Malaria and human polymorphisms. *Annual Review of Genetics* 5:33-64.

McCracken, R. 1971. Lactase deficiency: an example of dietary evolution. *Current Anthropology* 12:479-500.

Molnar, S. 1975. *Races, types, and ethnic groups*. Englewood Cliffs, N.J.: Prentice-Hall.

Motulsky, A. 1960. Metabolic polymorphisms and the role of infectious diseases in human evolution. *Human Biology* 32:28.

Mourant, A. 1956. *The distribution of blood groups in animals and humans*. Springfield, Ill.: Thomas.

Myrianthropoulos, N., and Aronson, S. 1966. Population dynamics of Tay-Sachs disease. I. Reproductive fitness and selection. *American Journal of Human Genetics* 18:313.

Neel, J. 1949. The inheritance of sickle-cell anemia. *Science* 110:64.

Osborne, R., ed. 1971. *The biological and social meaning of race*. San Francisco: Freeman.

Otten, C. 1967. On pestilence, diet, natural selection, and the distribution of microbial and human blood group antigens and antibodies. *Current Anthropology* 8:209.

Race, R., and Sanger, R. 1962. *Blood groups in man*. Oxford: Blackwell Scientific Publishers.

Rosen, A., and Scanlan, J. 1948. Favism. *New England Journal of Medicine* 239:367.

Saldanha, P., and Nacrur, J. 1963. Taste thresholds for phenylthiouria among Chilians. *American Journal of Physical Anthropology* 21:113-20.

Stini, W. 1975. *Ecology and human adaptation*. Dubuque, Ia.: Brown.

Vogel, F. 1968. Anthropological implications of the relationship between ABO blood groups and infections. *Proceedings of the Eighth International Congress of Anthropological and Ethnological Sciences* 1:365-70.

Wiesenfeld, S. 1967. Sickle-cell trait in human biological and cultural evolution. *Science* 157:1134-40.

Williams, B. 1973. *Evolution and human origins: an introduction to physical anthropology*. New York: Harper and Row.

Chapter 28

Development of Human Diversity

How have population differences become established and perpetuated? Gene frequencies must change if changes are to occur in the gene pool; changes in gene frequency can be accomplished by migration, genetic drift, mutation, and natural selection. Once change occurs adaptation and natural selection play their role, separating adaptive from nonadaptive or maladaptive genes. Most differences in population genotypes result from natural selection, which acts by increasing the frequency of genes that improve adaptation and decreasing those lowering adaptation. Thus genotype differences are primarily adaptive responses to the environment.

The conclusion that population differences in genotypes result from natural selection must not be seen as proof that any given phenotypic characteristic is or has been adaptive to a specific environment. As discussed in Chapter 24, some traits may be neutral in their environment and appear to confer no apparent advantage. Most genes affect many traits, a condition known as pleiotropy. Even though there is a close relationship between genetic inheritance and phenotypic traits, the adaptive value of a gene need not be related to any one aspect of the phenotype to the exclusion of others.

Looking at the Fossil Record

The longer a population lives in an area, the greater the probability that any of its genetic eccentricities result from adaptation; ecologically stable populations are more likely to show genetic adaptations than ecologically unstable populations. Genetic differences are probably related to stable environmental stresses such as climate and disease rather than to the more changeable stresses produced by culture. We are, as were many of our ancestors, a geographically and ecologically diverse species. We live now, and did so in the past, in various climatic conditions; and any living thing (plant or animal) occupying an extended range is subjected to forces tending to divide it into smaller segments. Simple geographical isolation impedes random mating and gene flow. Among social animals, no matter how naturally and unconsciously they may be organized, social as well as geographical barriers to mating occur. Mutations in one group do not necessarily spread to another, regardless of how potentially useful they are. We might expect that as a species diffuses from Africa to Java to China and parts of Europe and North Africa, it will begin to differentiate.

An examination of living human populations shows that we are not exempt from the normal processes of local evolutionary change. Genetic differences between groups have accumulated throughout the thousands of generations during which such groups were at least semi-isolated from each other. What is of interest is not that we share such features with other animals but that we differ in one very significant respect. In contrast to many other animals that spread across the world, we did not divide into different species. One of the most widespread and evolutionarily successful members of the animal kingdom is still one species. Among modern human populations, none is so isolated that it is today a member of its own species; with modern transportation and the so-called "shrinking world," no population is likely to evolve into a different species in the future.

Since today we are all members of the same species, and since the hominid fossil record yields forms different from you and me, it is often assumed that population diversity postdates the appearance of modern *Homo sapiens*. Undoubtedly there are differences in fossil populations. The Middle Pleistocene form *H. erectus,* scattered throughout Europe, Asia, and Africa, was perhaps as variable as modern populations. Whether these differences were such that modern populations arose directly from different Middle Pleistocene groups is debatable.

Upper Paleolithic fossil populations are often placed into various racial groups; however, European skeletal remains indicate a lack of racial divisions among them, regardless of the fact that some are called Eskimo or Negroid. Yet, European fossil populations are distinguishable from those of Asia and Africa. The Upper Paleolithic witnessed populations adapted to different environmental conditions; therefore, what forces kept Upper Paleolithic populations and their predecessors from becoming different species? Obviously there was gene flow, but how much gene flow existed and how it was accomplished is not known. A hypothesis suggesting widespread population migrations as the reason behind assumed worldwide similarities is tenuous. A more cautious view suggests that gene flow occurred by mating between adjacent groups. Judging from western technological societies, and from modern hunters and gatherers, we assume that the average distance of movement was not very great. Gene transmission was probably quite slow when walking was the only means of transportation. We should not be surprised to find differences among fossil hominids; and we should expect differences among contemporaneous fossil populations from different geographic areas.

Role of Culture

Incest Taboo. As an influence on a population's genetic composition, culture is second only to geography as an isolating factor. Although it is difficult to assess the exact role culture played in the original diversification of populations, it certainly played a potent role in later hominid evolution. The incest taboo, as a characteristic of all human societies, has served to maintain genetic lines of communication. Although what constitutes incest varies from culture to culture, the taboo usually denies sexual access to persons who are culturally defined as close. Incest rules have reduced the incidence of consanguineous mating (i.e., matings between genetically related individuals). There is probably more gene flow among adjacent hominid groups than is true for any other primate. Such mating offers an opportunity for forming new genetic combinations and increasing heterozygosity and also causes the spread of new mutations from the point of origin.

Migration. Another factor maintaining genetic communication has been the migration of hunting groups. To what extent migration occurred, and to what extent hunters from different groups passed their genes to other groups is unknown. However, we can assume that geographical barriers impeded some movement. The persistence of different tool traditions separating East Asia and the rest of the Old World suggests minimal population movement between these areas. Culture again influences the direction of human evolution, for migration becomes easier as technology improves.

Assortive Mating Patterns. Culture has acted as a unifying influence in the evolution of the human species; however, particular cultures, or cultural ideals, often act as divisive forces. Ideals as to what constitutes a suitable mate vary from population to population. Darwin suggested that races developed as a result of sexual selection; while this is debatable, existing differences may have been at least partially maintained in this manner. Assortative or preferential mating patterns have probably had a major role in keeping segments of populations or populations themselves genetically isolated. Preferential mating patterns refer to mate choices according to certain cultural ideals; religious ties, class or caste affiliation, and standards of beauty all affect mating patterns. The upper class American male of European background will probably marry another upper class American of European background.

Positive assortative mating patterns that refer to the mating of individuals sharing certain traits can work for or against natural selection. There is strong positive assortative mating between individuals with abnormal genetic traits. The incidence of dwarfs marrying dwarfs, for example, is probably higher than the incidence of dwarfs marrying nondwarfs. Mating of this sort is reinforced by individuals (e.g., the blind and the deaf) attending special schools, clinics, and events.

Miss America: Cultural Ideals. As an example of these processes at work, let us take a brief look at what are considered to be "typical" American (of European descent) social ideals (Kurtz, 1971). Miss America in 1962 had measurements of 35-24-35. This was the ideal, and for some it has changed little. There is a tendency to romanticize the Hollywood image; the ideal man should be tall and muscular, the ideal woman proportioned in a certain way and not too tall. While there is a good deal of individual preference, the presence of the ideal can be tested by noting perceptions of one's body images. Do these images reflect cultural values? A test conducted in the early 1960s by a clinical psychologist attempted to answer this question using a young, white, middle-class student sample of 89 males and 80 females. These individuals were asked to judge their own bodies according to various dimensions using a seven-point rating scale. They were asked to judge the value of their body; was it considered good or bad? How good or how bad was it to be of one body type as compared to another? They were asked to rate their body according to potency; was their body strong or weak? Finally, they were asked to rate their body in terms of activity; was their body active or passive?

The following results are interesting. It must be remembered, however, that with so many dependent variables, inferences such as those noted here are tenous at best. Women tend to have global attitudes toward body shapes. Women have opinions about their bodies as good or bad, strong or weak, active or passive, and they are aware of body features in considerably greater detail than men. Could this result from the fact that our male-oriented society is far more conscious and admiring of the female than the male form? Women tend to like their own bodies more than men like their own bodies—they tend to value their bodies more.

Since muscular strength, aggression, and dominance are considered male virtues, males should rate their bodies higher in potency than women—they do. The large mesomorphs (Charles Atlas types) like their bodies best of all—so did the women. These men thought themselves more active and sexually potent than did men with other body builds. Large and small heavy-set men also considered their bodies potent, and men seemed to associate potency as much with sheer bulk as with physical strength.

Lean, tall women liked their bodies more than women with other types of builds. (Does this reflect the TV commercial and Hollywood ideal?) Broad-hipped, buxom women thought their bodies more potent, however. Large, heavy-set women were seen as the most potent, but tall, thin women felt themselves more desirable (and other women seemed to agree).

Height is also important; in American society height is often associated with dominance, self-confidence, and leadership. Were we to review the history of presidential elections we would find that in most cases the taller man was the winner. Did voters respond to height in casting their votes? It is commonly said that women admire tall men and consider them good mates. Men see shortness as a liability, as the elevator shoe industry well knows.

This exercise reflects certain values in some segments of American society.[1] Given an equal chance, certain individuals may be more apt to transmit their genes than others because of cultural conceptions of what makes a person an ideal mate. Those individuals deviating too far from cultural norms may have a slightly lower chance of passing their genes on to following generations.

Other Cultural Factors. Culture influences population differences in other ways. In certain areas population increases due to food production have led to a rapid spread of contagious diseases and the eventual selection of mutations providing immunity from one disease or another. Cultural devices, such as clothing, housing, and artificial means of warmth or cooling, have permitted individuals not biologically adapted to an environment to move into it. In many cases these late arrivals have replaced biologically adapted native populations.

Diversity as an Evolutionary Episode

This paraphrase of a statement by F. Hulse (1962) implies that population differences are not eternally stable and that selection causing evolution does not occur overnight. As conditions change, new selective forces replace old ones; individuals who might once have died out are now successful. The flow of genes from one population to another may accelerate or impede any shift of gene frequencies due to local adaptations.

Discrete populations, which some call races, are simply episodes in the evolutionary history of a widespread species. Without diversification in response to existing local circumstances over a wide geographical range and through time, species cannot be considered successful. (By most measures, *H. sapiens sapiens* has been successful, too successful in fact for most of the world's other flora and fauna. It is sobering to ponder that our successes may ultimately be the source of our doom.) Such diversification as witnessed among modern human populations is useful insurance against environmental changes bound to occur. Perhaps these environmental changes will occur at greater speeds as we continue to tamper with, and destroy, segments of the world surrounding us.

[1]See also Vandenberg, 1972.

A Taxonomy

Although clines (Chapter 25) occur, such gradations do not deny that gene clusters exist that some argue are of the magnitude to distinguish some populations from others. This does not deny that there is substantial and continuous overlap of genes from very diverse populations; but all populations are not exactly the same. We can deplore the social stigmas attached to certain groups, as any intelligent person should; but by denying that differences occur we do not reduce racial prejudices. Only major social and intellectual changes can do that and should such changes occur tomorrow, they will already be long overdue.

Geographical Race. Following Garn's (1971) taxonomy, many anthropologists recognize three major levels of racial groupings (Table 28-1), each of which may be divided into smaller units. The largest unit is a broad, geographically delimited population called a **geographical race.** Such populations coincide with major continental boundaries and their existence is largely due to such barriers. Each geographical race is a collection of populations whose similarities are due to long-continued confinement within set geographical limits. They are collections of breeding populations but are not genetically uniform units. The long-resident populations of Europe are an example of such a unit. We stress long-resident populations, for transportation, mobility, and cultural desires constantly disembark individuals whose evolutionary history is outside the sphere where they now reside.

Local Race. The second unit is the **local race,** which corresponds more closely to what we might designate breeding populations. Local races are largely endogamous groups that are most readily identified where populations are small and there is little doubt of their limits due

---

Table 28-1. Geographical Races of *Homo sapiens sapiens*

Geographical Race	*Geographical Range*
Amerindian	From Alaska, Northern Canada, throughout the Americas
Polynesian	Pacific Islands
Micronesian	Pacific Islands, limited to area from Ulithi, Palau, and Tobi to Marshall and Gilberts
Melanesian-Papuan	New Guinea and neighboring islands
Australian	Australia
Asiatic	Eastern continental Asia, Japan, Philippines, Sumatra, Borneo, Celebes, Taiwan
Indian	India
European	Europe, western Asia, Middle East, Africa north of Sahara
African	Africa, south of Sahara

Local Races of Homo sapiens sapiens *(Partial Listing)*

Eskimo	Northwest European
North American Indian	Mediterranean
Fuegian	Afro-American
Ladino	East African
Neo-Hawaiian	Bantu
Negrito	

After Stanley M. Garn, *Human Races;* 3rd edition, 1971. Courtesy of Charles C Thomas, Publishers, Springfield, Illinois.

to geographical separation or cultural strictures on marriage and/or mating. An example of such a group is the South African Bushman. Although clearly members of a geographical race that might be termed Africans, Bushmen are more likely to marry or mate with Bushmen than Nigerians or other Africans.

Microrace. Local races may not be demonstrable in densely populated areas, yet there are biological differences between groups that are maintained by regional or cultural differences. There are many microraces in Europe; the Basques and Lapps are two examples. Other possibilities include members of small, isolated villages in which endogamy is rather strongly enforced. Microraces are the smallest units of a breeding population; population geneticists normally refer to them as demes.

Population Rise and Fall. Why some populations are more numerous than others is difficult to explain, although historical and technological factors have had an impact. Given two populations, one a subsistence group of nomadic hunters and gatherers in which numbers are limited by food resources, the other a sedentary agricultural population, we might expect that the agriculturalists will eventually outnumber the hunter-gatherers. Because of a larger potential food supply, the agriculturalists' gene pool theoretically has a greater upper limit than does the hunter-gatherer gene pool. A population that moves into a rich habitat may soon outnumber its neighbors in poorer environments. In time one set of genotypes, one gene pool, may come to dominate. Given that both populations feel their way of life is best and thus might not mate with members of the other, we could expect disproportionate growth rates. These possibilities, and many others, may have influenced the sizes of different gene pools. Many of the original factors are still at work while new possibilities constantly appear.

The scheme presented here follows the suggestion of a number of anthropologists that the roots of modern population differences are yet unknown. The distribution of modern population density is due partly to evolutionary forces and partly to modern technology. The picture continually changes as more and more groups come into contact; but, given the current situation, we can assume that differences will remain. Differences will be maintained, if not due to geographical barriers, due then to cultural sanctions against cross-mating.

We have little more than leads as to when modern population differences first appeared. A few anthropologists argue that this occurred early, perhaps during the Lower or Middle Pleistocene. However, most anthropologists agree that modern differences are of rather recent origin and some give a figure of 10,000 years or so.

Culture has played a strong role in both maintaining and preventing population contact. The incest taboo and migration are two means whereby genetic intermixture is encouraged. As isolating mechanisms we mentioned a number of cultural expressions.

Bibliography

Chagnon, N., Neel, J., Weitkamp, L., Gershowitz, H., and Ayres, M. 1970. The influence of cultural factors on the demography and pattern of gene flow from the Makiritare to the Yanomomo Indians. *American Journal of Physical Anthropology* 32:339-50.

Coon, C. 1962. *Origin of races.* New York: Knopf.

Ehrlich, P., and Raven, P. 1969. Differentiation of populations. *Science* 165:1228-32.

Garn, S. 1963. Culture and the direction of human evolution. *Human Biology* 35:221.

_____. 1971. *Human races,* 3rd ed. Springfield, Ill.: Thomas.

Hulse, F. 1955. Technological advance and major racial stocks. *Human Biology* 27:184.

_____. 1962. Race as an evolutionary episode. *American Anthropologist* 64:929.

_____. 1972. *The human species*. New York: Random House.

Johnston, F. 1964. Racial taxonomies from an evolutionary perspective. *American Anthropologist* 66:822.

Kurtz, R. 1971. Body image—male and female. In *Human variation*, edited by J. Downs and H. Bleibtreu, pp. 102-106. Beverly Hills, Calif.: Glencoe Press.

Laughlin, W., and Osborne, R., eds. 1968. *Human variation and origins*. San Francisco: Freeman.

Mead, M., Dobzhansky, T., Tobach, E., and Light, R., eds. 1968. *Science and the concept of race*. New York: Columbia University Press.

Montagu, A., ed. 1965. *The concept of race*. New York: Free Press.

Newman, M. 1963. Geographic and microgeographic races. *Current Anthropology* 5:189-207.

Osborne, R., ed. 1971. *The biological and social meaning of race*. San Francisco: Freeman.

Vandenberg, J. 1972. Assortative mating, or who marries whom? *Behavior Genetics* 2:127-57.

Chapter 29

Conclusion

> **We shall not cease from exploration,**
> **And the end of all our exploring**
> **Will be to arrive where we started**
> **And know the place for the first time.**
> **From T. S. Eliot, "*Little Gidding.*"[1]**

We have attempted to answer some questions about our past. We began our task with a short history of physical anthropology, for the history of anything, either a people or a discipline, influences its future. Physical anthropology's past has strongly influenced its present. Some physical anthropologists once argued that primate behavior was outside the anthropological purview. Further arguments are apt to occur as other "nonrelevant," "nonanthropological" endeavors are undertaken by physical anthropologists.

For many the meat of physical anthropology is the study of fossil hominids and human diversity. It is safe to say that as these sections are here constituted, they would have been foreign to investigators only a short while ago. Time and methods have changed, and to be current today means to be left behind tomorrow. Few fields are more exciting than physical anthropology, especially if one is interested in knowing about himself or herself.

The importance of the behavioral approach in anthropology is likely to increase. Current studies indicate several trends in behavioral evolution. How far we can carry our studies, and in which directions, is not yet clear. One thing is certain, however—in our exhausting search for new explanations we will soon be on the edges of new horizons.

> **In the time when Dendid created all things,**
> **He created the sun,**

[1]From "Little Gidding" in *Four Quartets* by T. S. Eliot, copyright, 1943, by T. S. Eliot; copyright, 1971, by Esne Valerie Eliot. Reprinted by permission of Harcourt Brace Jovanovich, Inc.

And the sun is born, and dies, and comes again;
He created the moon,
And the moon is born, and dies, and comes again;
And the stars are born, and die, and come again;
He created man,
And man is born and dies, and does not come again.

Old Dinka song. From P. Matthiessen, *The Tree Where Man Was Born.*

Glossary

The terms defined here are boldfaced in the text.

ABO blood groups—The originally defined blood group system.

Acheulian tradition—Refers to Lower Paleolithic tool-making technique from the Old World. Name derives from Saint-Acheul, France, where tools were first defined.

adaptation—The means whereby an organism meets demands of its econiche.

adaptive radiation—Divergence from a basic form to meet diversified ecological niches. A basic feature of the early evolutionary stages of new forms.

allele—Alternate form of a gene, one of a series of genes with the same locus on homologous chromosomes.

Allen's rule—The tendency for animals living in cold places to have shorter appendages than their close relatives in warmer areas.

allopatric—Species or populations inhabiting exclusive areas that are often adjacent.

anagenesis (phyletic evolution)—The evolution of one species from another of the same lineage.

ancestral traits—Inherited adaptations from a form's ancestor.

aneuploidy—Lack of or addition of one or more chromosomes.

anthropometry—Measurement of the body.

arboreal—Tree-dwelling

Aurignacian—One of two earliest European Upper Paleolithic cultural traditions.

autosome—Any chromosome that is not a sex chromosome.

BAIB (beta-aminoisobutyric acid)—An amino acid usually excreted in small amounts. Because of genetic misfunctioning some individuals often excrete large amounts.

balanced polymorphism—Maintenance in a population of two or more alleles in such proportions that the rarest of them cannot be maintained merely by recurrent mutation.

Bergmann's rule—The tendency for animals living in cold areas to have greater body bulk than their relatives in warm areas.

bicuspid—Having two cusps, a characteristic of P_3, the hominid first lower premolar.

bipedal—Upright locomotion on two hind limbs.

brachiation—Locomotor mode, referring to arm swinging beneath branches.

burin—Chisel-edged artifact for incising and cutting wood, bone, and ivory.

canine diastema—Gap in the dental arcade to accommodate the projecting canines.

canine fossa—Anatomical term referring to the hollow in the cheekbone on either side of the nose. This is a characteristic of later hominids and appears with facial reduction.

catarrhines—The primate group including humans, apes, and the Old World monkeys.

catastrophism—A belief that earth's history consists of series of great catastrophes. Popularized by the Frenchman Georges Cuvier.

ceboids—New World monkeys.

cell—A small, complex unit, usually with a nucleus, cytoplasm, and enclosing membrane. All plants and animals are composed of one or more cells.

centromere—Spindle-fiber attachment region of a chromosome.

cercopithecoid—Pertaining to Old World monkeys.

cerebrum—The forebrain section that controls reasoning and learned hand movements.

Chatelperronian—Early phase of the Perigordian tradition.

chromatid—In prophase of mitosis, each chromosome appears to be two closely related filaments called chromatids.

chromatin—A protoplasmic substance in the nucleus of living cells; chromatin forms the chromosomes and contains the genes.

chromosomes—Microscopic bodies that carry the genes that convey hereditary characteristics and are constant in number for each species.

chronometric chronology—Determination of the age, in years, of a specimen or geological formation.

cladogenesis—The splitting of one lineage into two.

clavicle—Bone connecting the sternum, or breastbone, with scapula or shoulder blade.

cline—Gradient in the frequency of a biological trait that is common in one area but less so in another.

Clovis point—Fairly large dart point with a groove extending up the sides, dating to about 10,000 years ago in the New World.

codominance—A condition in which the phenotype reflects the influence of two alleles.

codon—A sequence of three mRNA nucleotides that specifies a single amino acid.

complementary bases—Those bases in the DNA molecule that bond together.

coprolites—Fossilized fecal material.

cranium—The part of the skull enclosing the brain, also called the brain case.

cranial capacity—Referring to the size of the brain. Often given in cubic centimeters (cc).

crossing over—A process inferred genetically by a new association of linked genes. It results in the exchange of segments between homologous chromosomes and therefore produces combinations differing from those characteristic of the parents.

cusp—Elevation on the crowns of the premolar and molar teeth.

DNA (deoxyribonucleic acid)—A nucleic acid based on the sugar deoxyribose. DNA is composed of sugar-phosphate chains to which organic bases are attached. DNA stores genetic information and is replicated to form two identical copies.

deciduous—Refers to the first set of temporary teeth, the "milk teeth."

deme—Usually the smallest identifiable breeding population.

dental formula—The count of the different teeth. Old World primates show a formula of 2, 1, 2, 3: 2 incisors, 1 canine, 2 premolars, and 3 molars in each half of each jaw.

dental hominid—A name commonly applied to *Ramapithecus*. The term refers to the fact that teeth are hominidlike, but judgment as to phyletic position should be reserved.

derived traits—Result of recent adaptations.

dietary hypothesis—A hypothesis proposed by John Robinson to explain the differences between *Australopithecus* and *Paranthropus*.

dimorphism—Two different forms in a group, as determined by such characters as sex, size and coloration.

diploid—The condition of having two full sets of chromosomes, the chromosomes occurring in homologous pairs.

diurnal—Day-living as opposed to night-living (nocturnal).

dominance hierarchy—A ranking of animals in relation to one another.

dominant—An allele that is expressed in the phenotype in either homozygous or heterozygous condition.

dysgenic effect—An effect detrimental to the breeding quality of the stock.

effectance motivation—Behavior, such as investigatory or play behavior, that does not serve an immediate end. An important mammalian trait.

endocranial cast—Cast of the skull interior. The cast represents the shape of the brain and, to some degree, the brain's surface.

enzyme—A protein controlling a chemical reaction is an enzyme. Each enzyme has the ability to mediate at least one chemical reaction.

Eocene—Second Cenozoic geological epoch.

evolution—Process of descent with modification.

eugenics—Attempts to improve the species by deliberate breeding (positive eugenics) or by discouraging breeding (negative eugenics).

euthenics—Environmental engineering.

extinct—A form that has died out, leaving no phyletic offspring.

familial Mediterrean fever—A recessive periodic disease, largely restricted to persons of Eastern Mediterranean origin, that causes high fever and muscle pain.

favism—An affliction caused by sensitivity to the fava bean.

femur—Upper leg bone, the thigh bone.

fibula—The smaller of the two lower leg bones.

fission-track dating—A method of dating volcanic substances. A chronometric dating method used at Olduvai, Bed I and elsewhere.

fist-walking—Walking on the clenched fist, as do orangutans.

fixity of species—A preevolutionary idea which states that forms, once created, do not change.

Folsom points—A cultural assemblage spread over the Great Plains area. A thin, leaf-shaped blade. Dates from 10,000 to 25,000 years ago in the New World.

foramen magnum—Opening at the base of skull through which the spinal cord passes.

founder principle—The chance effects of a small number of parents on the gene pool of their descendants.

frontal bone—The bone forming the forehead.

frugivorous—A fruit eater.

gamete—A mature male or female reproductive cell (sperm or egg).

gene—A structure occurring at a specific point on chromosomes by which hereditary characters are transmitted and determined.

gene flow—Genetic interchange between subunits in a population that tend to mate most often within themselves but which may, nevertheless, regularly mate with other members of the population.

generalized—An animal, or organ, that is not specifically adapted to any given environment or task. The ability to function in a number of ways or environments.

genetic drift—Shift in allele frequencies due to chance rather than selection. Most likely to occur in small, isolated populations.

gene pool (breeding population)—The group in which most breeding occurs and within which an individual is most likely to mate.

genotype—The genetic constitution of an organism. The complete set of alleles inherited from the parents.

genus—Taxonomic category between the family and the species.
geographical race—A geographically delineated collection of similar races.
Gloger's rule—The tendency for animals that live in hot, damp areas to have darkly pigmented coat colors.
gluteal muscles—Buttock muscles that function in walking and extending the trunk.
Gravettian—Upper Paleolithic cultural tradition dating from 17,000 to 27,000 years ago found mostly in eastern Europe.
grooming—A behavioral pattern whereby an animal picks through the hair of another animal with either or both hands and teeth (social grooming) or picks through its own hair (allogrooming).
G6PD (glucose-6-phosphate dehydrogenase) deficiency—A genetic disease also known as favism and primaquine sensitivity. Causes severe reaction to primaquine (an antimalarial drug) and the fava bean. Provides some protection against certain forms of malaria.

hand axes—Superficially flaked core-tools probably used as one of the first formal implements.
haploid—The condition of having a single set of chromosomes, such as is normally carried by a mature sex cell.
Hardy-Weinberg Law—A law which maintains that, under random mating and free from disturbing forces, genotype frequencies will be constant in successive generations.
herbivorous—Feeding on buds and leaves, eating vegetable matter only.
heterodontism—Differentiation of the teeth for different functions.
heterozygous—Plants or animals that have contrasting alleles at corresponding loci on homologous chromosomes and hence do not breed true to type for the particular trait being transmitted; a hybrid.
holandric—Term applied to traits determined by genes on the Y chromosome.
home range—The area in which an animal lives. The total geographical area covered in the normal course of events.
hominid—Any living or fossil member of the Family Hominidae.
hominoids—A group including apes and humans.
homoiothermy—The maintenance of constant body temperature. Warm-bloodedness.
homologous chromosomes—A pair of chromosomes that have identical genes or their alleles located at corresponding loci.
homozygous—Having identical alleles at the same gene locus.
humerus—The upper arm bone.
hunting and gathering—A way of life characteristic of most hominid evolutionary history. A way of life prior to agriculture.
hypoxia—A condition in which tissues receive a deficient supply of oxygen.

illium—Uppermost part of the innominate bone.
immunological theory—A theory associated with a late divergence of the hominid-pongid lines.
incest taboo—Sexual or marriage prohibition between individuals culturally considered related.
insectivorous—Feeding on insects.
interstitial wear—Wear between adjacent teeth.
ischial callosities—Hairless areas of the buttocks found on all Old World monkeys and gibbons.

karyotype—Classification of chromosome pairs according to number and pattern.
knuckle-walking—Walking on the knuckles as do chimpanzees and gorillas.
kuru—A progressive, incurable, and lethal neurological disease caused by a slow virus. Restricted to a New Guinea group called the Fore.

linkage—Genes traveling together on the same chromosomes are said to be linked, and the condition is called linkage.
living floor—Area of intense activity within a hominid fossil site.

local race—A breeding population or population isolate. Totally or largely endogamous population.

locus (plural, loci)—The area that a gene occupies on a chromosome.

macroevolution—Evolutionary changes resulting in the rise and divergence of discontinuous groups.

Magdalenian—The last level of the European Upper Paleolithic, characterized by an increase in antler and bone working.

mandible—The lower jawbone.

masseter muscle—A large muscle of the lower jaw important for chewing.

maxilla—The upper jawbone.

megaevolution—Major rapid changes usually occurring in small, isolated populations.

meiosis—The process whereby sex cells are produced. All cells produced by meiosis have the haploid number of chromosomes.

melanin—Pigmented substance deposited in the skin, hair, and eyes that gives them their color.

melanocytes—Melanin-producing cells contained within the prickle-cell layer in the skin.

Mendelian population—Genetically, a spatial-temporal group of interbreeding individuals sharing a common gene pool.

mesial drift—Movement of the teeth forward in the jaw.

microevolution—Small changes within potentially continuous populations.

Miocene—The fourth geological epoch of the Cenozoic Era.

mitosis—Ordinary cell division through which a cell gives rise to two cells that are the same as the original and each other in chromosome composition.

MNS-U system—One of the blood group systems.

modifiability of species—The concept that forms could and would change over time. In a way, the philosophical precursor to evolutionary theory.

monogenesis—Early view that all of humanity is descended from one pair of progenitors.

morphology—Structure or form.

Mousterian—The cultural assemblage commonly associated with the Neanderthals.

mutant—A changed gene.

mutation—A change in the structure of a gene or group of genes.

natural selection—Mechanism of evolution proposed by Charles Darwin.

neoteny—Evolutionary change in which young developmental forms persist into the maturity of adult forms.

neural—Referring to the brain structure.

nonsecretor—Individual who does not show water-soluble antigens in the ABO system in the saliva and other body fluids.

notochord—Rodlike structure running the length of the body, providing support and strength in chordate animals.

nuchal crest—Crest of bone on the occipital bone to which heavy neck muscles attach.

nucleolus—Site within the cell nucleus where a nucleic acid (rRNA) and ribosomes are processed.

nucleoprotein—General term for molecular structure of nucleus.

nucleotide—Basic unit of DNA molecule composed of phosphate, deoxyribose or ribose sugar, and a purine or pyrimidine base.

nucleus—Large, spherical structure within the cell that contains the chromosomes.

occipital bone—Rearmost portion of skull to which the neck muscles attach.

occipital bun—Projection of bone on occipital. A characteristic of classic Neanderthals. Also occurs in some living populations.

occipital condyle—Knob or joint surface on the occipital bone with which the first vertebra articulates.

Oligocene—The third geological epoch of the Cenozoic Era.

olfactory—Refers to sense of smell.

omnivorous—A method of feeding that includes ingestion of various foodstuffs. A diet not specialized for one food source.

orthagnathous—Reduction of face and jaws.

orthograde—Refers to upright body posture.

osteodontokeratic culture—Dart's claim for an australopithecine bone, tooth, and antler culture.

osteological—Refers to bone material, that is, osteological remains.

osteometry—The measurement of bone.

Paleocene—The first geological epoch of the Cenozoic Era.

Paleolithic—The first 99 percent of our evolutionary history, prior to the inception of agriculture.

palynology—Analysis of fossil pollens and spores. Very helpful in reconstructing paleoecological conditions.

panmixis (random mating)—Random, nonrestricted mating within a gene pool.

parabolic dental arch—A horseshoe-shaped dental arcade between the front teeth. The modern human arrangement.

parallel dental arch—Tooth rows diverge anteriorly. This is primarily a nonhuman primate trait.

parietals—The bones on either side of the top of the skull.

pebble tools—Crudely worked early stone tools associated with early hominid deposits.

pentadactyly—Having five fingers and toes.

percussion flaking—A technique in which a stone is used as a hammer to chip off flakes on one or two sides of another stone.

Perigordian—One of two oldest European Upper Paleolithic traditions.

peripheral temperature—The temperature of the digits, ears, and tail

phenotype—The observable characteristics of an organism that result collectively from both its heredity and its environment.

phenylketonuria (PKU)—A recessive disease, due to the inability to convert phenylalanine, that causes severe mental retardation.

phyletic tree—Branching diagram representing evolutionary relations of a group of a species.

pithecoid theory—The theory that we arose directly from monkeylike forms without passing through an ape stage. Associated with W. Straus.

Plano tradition—Late Paleo-Indian cultural tradition in the New World.

platycephaly—Flattening of the top of the skull.

platyrrhine—Referring to New World primates.

pleiotropy—Refers to a condition whereby a single gene produces multiple phenotypic expressions.

Pleistocene—The sixth of the geological epochs of the Cenozoic Era.

Pliocene—The fifth geological epoch of the Cenozoic Era.

pluvials—Periods of increasing rainfall. Study of pluvials is useful for dividing the African Pleistocene.

polygenesis—The hypothesis that different human groups arose from different ancestors. The opposite of monogenesis.

polymorphism—The maintenance of two or more forms in a breeding population.

polyphyletic—Multiple phyletic (evolutionary) lines.

polyploidy—A condition in which the chromosome number is a multiple of the haploid state greater than the diploid state.

polysome—A complex of several ribosomes plus attached mRNA.

polytypic—Occurring in several readily distinguishable forms.

pongid—A term that refers to apes.

Pongidae—The pongid taxonomic family.

postcranial—All the bones below the head or cranium.

postorbital bar—Bony enclosure at the rear of the eye orbit, a diagnostic primate trait lacking in some Paleocene forms.

postorbital constriction—Constriction of the cranium behind the brow ridges.

potassium-argon (K-Ar) dating—A method of chronometric dating. The method dates volcanically derived materials.

power grip—The grip used in wielding an object such as a hammer forcefully, in which the thumb and forefinger are not opposed.

preadaptation—A behavioral and/or morphological characteristic (determinable by hindsight only) useful for conditions in which an animal does not yet live.

precision grip—The grip used in holding small objects by opposing the thumb and forefinger.

presapiens—A theory which suggests that *Homo sapiens* originated as a distinct, completely separate line from that leading to the Neanderthals.

prognathism—Forward protrusion of lower face and jaws.

prosimian—One of the lower primates. Member of taxonomic suborder Prosimii, which includes all fossil and living lemurs, tree shrews, lorises, and galagos.

provisioned colonies—Artificially fed primate colonies.

punctuated equilibrium—Short bursts of evolutionary change.

quadrupedal—Locomotion on all fours.

race—A population within a species that can be distinguished from other populations within the same species.

radiocarbon (C¹⁴) dating—A chronometric dating technique. Dates the time when an organism died by measuring the amount of radioactive C¹⁴ that has disappeared.

radius—One of the two lower arm bones.

range of variation—Intrapopulation variability.

recessive—An allele that is not expressed in the phenotype except when the organism is homozygous.

recombination—The process whereby units of genetic information are shuffled, giving rise to a number of different genotypes.

relative chronology—Determination of the age, in years, of a specimen or geological formation in relation to another specimen or formation.

relative dating—Dating methods that establish a chronological sequence of latest to youngest.

rhesus (Rh) blood group—A blood group system named after the North Indian rhesus macaque.

ribosomes—Tiny structures in cell cytoplasm that seem to be the centers for protein synthesis.

RNA (ribonucleic acid)—An essential component in all living matter, present in the cytoplasm of all cells and composed of long chains of phosphate and sugar ribose along with several bases; one form is the carrier of genetic information from the nuclear DNA and is important in the synthesis of proteins in the cell.

sagittal crest—The strut of bone across the top of the skull from front to back to which the temporalis muscles attach.

scapula—The shoulder blade.

secretor—Individual who shows water-soluble antigens in the ABO system in the saliva and other body fluids.

sectorial—Unicuspid. A unicuspid lower first premolar (P₃), is characteristic of all nonhuman primates. The sectorial premolar accommodates the projecting canine from the opposing jaw.

selection—The differential survival of certain genotypes because they are better adapted than others.

serology—The comparative study of blood groups.

Sewall Wright effect—Nondirected changes in gene frequency, that is, genetic drift.

sex chromosomes—Chromosomes (*X* and *Y* in the human) that determine the sex of the individual.

sexual dimorphism—Marked differences in morphological characteristics of males and females.

sickle-cell anemia—A condition caused by presence of sickled red blood cells in the bloodstream.

socionomic sex ratio—The ratio of females to males in primate groups.

somatic cells—Referring to cells of body tissues; having two sets of chromosomes, one set normally coming from the female parent and one from the male.

soft hammer technique (soft percussion)—A technique in which wood, bone, or antler is used instead of rock to chip off flakes from a core.

speciation—The process through which species evolve into different species.

species—Total group of organisms capable of breeding and producing fertile offspring.

stereoscopic vision—The ability to merge visual images from both eyes. Stereoscopic vision allows depth perception.

subspecies—A subdivision of a species, consisting of individuals in a given geographical area, that differs slightly from, but can interbreed with, other subspecies of the same species.

supraorbital torus (brow ridges)—Development of heavy bony ridges above the eyes.

sympatric—Reproductively isolated populations inhabiting overlapping areas or the same area.

synapsis—The coiling of homologous chromosomes around each other during early prophase I of meiosis.

systematics—Scientific study of kinds of organisms and the relationships between them.

taphonomy—Study of the processes of burial and fossilization.

tarsioid theory—The theory that we arose directly from a primitive tarsioid stock without passing through a monkey or ape stage. Associated with F. Wood Jones.

taurodont—Term referring to enlarged molar root cavity and perhaps fusion of the molar roots.

taxonomy—Science of the classification of living forms in a manner best suited to show their genetic relationship to each other.

Tay-Sachs disease—A genetic neurological disease, limited primarily to those of European Jewish ancestry, that begins in infancy. Usually leads to early death.

"T-complex"—Dental traits which C. Jolly relates to an adaptation of a seed-eating diet.

territory—That part of the home range that is defended against others.

Tertiary—The earlier period of the Cenozoic Era. Includes the Paleocene through Pliocene epochs.

thalassemia—An inherited anemia. Its presence in some malarial regions suggests a selective advantage.

tibia—The larger of the two lower leg bones.

total morphological pattern—A concept stressing that the assessment of taxonomic status must be based, not on individual isolated traits, but on a combination of the total pattern.

transcription—The process during which mRNA, rRNA, or tRNA is formed from a DNA template.

ulna—One of the two lower arm bones.

uniformitarianism—The doctrine that geological strata can only be interpreted by assuming that they were formed by agencies operating in a uniform way and at a rate comparable with the action of contemporary agencies.

Villafranchian fauna—Faunal assemblage marking the beginning of the Pleistocene. Includes representatives of the modern genera of horses, elephants, and cattle.

viviparous—Giving birth to young rather than laying eggs.

zygomatic arches—The cheekbones.

zygote—A cell formed by the union of two gametes.

(Credits continued)

Chapter 3. *Figures 3-1, 3-2, 3-3, 3-5, and 3-6.* Courtesy of the American Museum of Natural History. *Figure 3-4.* Courtesy of the British Museum of Natural History. *Figures 3-7 and 3-8.* Racle, F., *Introduction to Evolution,*,1979, pp. 27, 28. Reprinted by permission of Prentice-Hall, Inc., Englewood Cliffs, New Jersey. *Figure 3-11.* Aus dem Bilderarchiv der Osterr. Nationalbibliothek.

Chapter 4. *Figure 4-1.* Courtesy of the American Museum of Natural History. *Figure 4-7.* From P. W. Sciulli, *An Introduction to Mendelian Genetics and Gene Action.* Burgess Publishing Company, Minneapolis, 1978. *Figure 4-8.* From C. Benjamin Meleca et al., *Bio-Learning Guide.* Burgess Publishing Company, Minneapolis, 1971.

Chapter 6. *Figure 6-3.* From P. W. Sciulli, 1978.

Chapter 7. *Figure 7-4.* From P. W. Sciulli, 1978. *Figure 7-5.* From Richard E. Dickerson and Irving Geis, *Chemistry, Matter and the Universe.* Copyright © 1976 by The Benjamin/Cummings Publishing Company (formerly Cummings Publishing Company), Menlo Park, California. *Figure 7-7.* From C. Benjamin Meleca et al., 1971.

Chapter 8. *Figures 8-1 and 8-2.* Racle, F., *Introduction to Evolution,* 1979, pp. 66, 67. Reprinted by permission of Prentice-Hall, Inc., Englewood Cliffs, New Jersey. *Figures 8-3 and 8-4.* Adapted from J. Savage, *Evolution.* Holt, Rinehart and Winston, New York, 1963.

Chapter 9. *Figures 9-1 and 9-2.* Courtesy of the American Museum of Natural History.

Chapter 10. *Figure 10-3.* Adapted from John E. Pfeiffer, *The Emergence of Man* (Harper & Row, 1969). *Figures 10-4 and 10-5.* Courtesy of the American Museum of Natural History. *Figure 10-6.* Courtesy of Laurence K. Marshall. *Figure 10-7.* Adapted from illustration, "New World and Old World Monkeys," from *The Emergence of Man,* Revised and Enlarged Edition, by John E. Pfeiffer (Harper & Row, 1972). *Figure 10-8.* Adapted from illustration, "Increasing Social Complexity," from *The Emergence of Man,* Revised and Enlarged Edition, by John E. Pfeiffer (Harper & Row, 1972).

Chapter 11. *Figure 11-1.* Adapted from J. Napier and P. Napier, *A Handbook of Living Primates.* Academic Press, London, 1967. *Figure 11-4.* Adapted from S. Eimerl and I. DeVore, *The Primates.* Time-Life Books, New York, 1972. *Figures 11-5 and 11-6.* Courtesy of Dr. Kenneth Glander.

Chapter 12. *Figure 12-1.* Adapted from R. Yerkes, 1971, *Great Apes, a Study of Anthropoid Life.* Reprint of 1929 edition. Johnson Reprints. *Figures 12-2 through 12-8.* Courtesy of Caroline Tutin. *Figures 12-9, 12-10, and 12-11.* Courtesy of the Columbus Zoo, Powell, Ohio. *Figures 12-12, 12-13, and 12-14.* Courtesy of Don Beimborn.

Chapter 13. *Figure 13-1.* Adapted from R. Moore, *Man, Time, and Fossils.* Alfred A. Knopf, New York, 1961.

Chapter 14. *Figures 14-1 and 14-2.* Adapted from W. Le Gros Clark, *The Antecedents of Man.* Edinburgh University Press, 1969. *Figures 14-3, 14-4, and 14-7.* From M. Cartmill, 1975. *Figure 14-6.* Adapted from E. Simons and W. K. Gregory, 1972, "On the structure and relations of *Notharctus,* an Ecocene primate," *Mem. Amer. Mus. Nat. Hist.* 3(2:49). *Figure 14-8.* Adapted from E. Simons, *Primate Evolution, an Introduction to Man's Place in Nature* (The Macmillan Company, New York, 1972) and I. Tattersall, *Man's Ancestors* (Murray, London, 1970).

Chapter 15. *Figure 15-1.* Adapted from B. Kurtén, *Not from the Apes.* Pantheon Books, New York, 1971. *Figure 15-2.* Courtesy of the Wenner-Gren Foundation for Anthropological Research, Inc.

Chapter 16. *Figure 16-1.* Drawn by H. L. Oyen and O. J. Oyen. *Figure 16-2.* Courtesy of P. Andrews and A. C. Walker.

Chapter 17. *Figure 17-1.* Adapted from G. Findlay, *Dr. Robert Brook: Paleontologist and Physician, 1866-1951.* A. A. Balkema, Capetown, 1972. *Figure 17-2.* Adapted from P. Tobias, "Early man in sub-Sahara Africa," in *The Functional Biology of Primates,* edited by R. Tuttle. Aldine-Atherton, Inc., Chicago, 1972. *Figures 17-3 and 17-4.* Courtesy of Wendy Lawrence. *Figure 17-5.* Adapted from M. D. Leakey, 1967. *Figure 17-6.* Adapted from J. Buettner-Janusch, *The Origins of Man: Physical Anthropology.* John Wiley and Sons, New York, 1966. *Figure 17-7.* Adapted from J. Bordaz, *Tools of the Old and New Stone Age.* Natural History Press, New York, 1970. *Figure 17-9.* Adapted from B. Kurtén, 1971. *Figure 17-10.* Adapted from C. Coon, *The Origin of Race.* Alfred A. Knopf, New York, 1962. *Figure 17-12.* Adapted from W. Howells, *Mankind in the Making.* Doubleday & Company, New York, 1967. *Figures 17-13, 17-14, 17-16, and 17-18.* Courtesy of the Wenner-Gren Foundation for Anthropolgical Research, Inc.

Chapter 18. *Figures 18-1 and 18-3.* Courtesy of the American Museum of Natural History. *Figure 18-2.* Adapted from E. White and editors, *the First Men.* Time-Life Books, New York, 1973. *Figure 18-4.* Adapted from F. Bordes, *The Old Stone Age.* World University Library Series, McGraw-Hill Book Company, New York, 1968. *Figure 18-5.* Adapted from J. E. Pfeiffer, 1969. *Figure 18-6.* Adapted from F. Clark Howell and editors, *Early Man.* Time-Life Books, New York, 1970. *Figure 18-7.* From "A Paleolithic Camp at Nice," by H. de Lumley. Copyright © May, 1969 by Scientific American, Inc. All rights reserved. *Figure 18-8.* Drawn by H. L. Oyen and O. J. Oyen. *Figure 18-9.* Courtesy of the Wenner-Gren Foundation for Anthropological Research, Inc.

Chapter 19. *Figures 19-1 and 19-7.* Courtesy of the Wenner-Gren Foundation for Anthropological Research, Inc. *Figures 19-2 and 19-6.* Adapted from C. Brace, H. Nelson, and N. Korn, *Atlas of Fossil Man.* Holt, Rinehart and Winston, New York, 1971. *Figure 19-3.* Adapted from C. Brace and A. Montagu, *Man's Evolution: an Introduction to Physical Anthropology.* The Macmillan Company, New York, 1965. *Figure 19-4.* Adapted from F. Clark Howell and editors, 1970. *Figure 19-5.* Adapted from J. Birdsell, *Human Evolution: an Introduction to the New Physical Anthropology.* Rand McNally and Company, Skokie, Illinois, 1972. *Figure 19-8.* Courtesy of Dr. Ralph S. Solecki. *Figure 19-9.* Adapted from W. Howells, 1967.

Chapter 20. *Figures 20-1 and 20-5.* Adapted from F. Clark Howell and editors, 1970. *Figure 20-2.* From G. Hewes, *The Origin of Man.* Burgess Publishing Company, Minneapolis, 1973. *Figure 20-3.* Courtesy of the American Museum of Natural History. *Figure 20-4.* Adapted from T. Prideaux and editors, *Cro-Magnon Man,* Time-Life Books, New York, 1973. *Figure 20-6.* Adapted from F. Bordes, 1968. *Figure 20-7.* Courtesy of R. Bonnichsen. *Figure 20-8.* Courtesy of W. M. Childers.

Chapter 21. *Figure 21-1.* From "The Early Relations of Man," by E. Simons. Copyright © July, 1964 by Scientific American, Inc. All rights reserved. *Figure 21-2.* Adapted from B. Kraus, *The Basis of Human Evolution.* Harper & Row, New York, 1964; and from E. Hooten, *Up from the Apes.* The Macmillan Company, New York, 1960. *Figure 21-3.* Adapted from J. Birdsell, 1972. *Figure 21-4.* Adapted from W. Howells, *Evolution of the Genus* Homo. Copyright © 1973 by The Benjamin Cummings Publishing Company (formerly Cummings Publishing Company), Menlo Park, California. *Figure 21-6.* From G. Tunnell, *Culture and Biology: Becoming Human.* Burgess Publishing Company, Minneapolis, 1973.

Chapter 22. *Figure 22-1.* Courtesy of the Columbus Zoo, Powell, Ohio. *Figure 22-2.* Adapted from F. Clark Howell and editors, 1970. *Figure 22-3.* Adapted from D. Pilbeam, *The Ascent of Man.* The Macmillan Company, New York, 1972.

Chapter 23. *Figure 23-1.* From G. Tunnell, 1973.

Chapter 25. *Figure 25-1.* From A. J. Kelso, *Physical Anthropology.* Reprinted by permission of the publishers, J. B. Lippincott Company, Copyright © 1970 and 1974. *Figures 25-2, 25-3, and 25-4.* From R. Reid, *Human Population Genetics.* Burgess Publishing Company, Minneapolis, 1978.

Chapter 26. *Figure 26-1.* Adapted from B. J. Williams, *Evolution and Human Origins: an Introduction to Physical Anthropology.* Harper and Row Publishers, Inc., New York, 1973. *Figures 26-2 through 26-8.* Adapted from A. R. Frisancho, *Human Adaptation: a Functional Interpretation.* C. V. Mosby Company, St. Louis, 1979. *Figure 26-9.* Adapted from C. L. Brace and A. Montague, 1965. *Figure 26-10.* Courtesy of the World Health Organization.

Chapter 27. *Figure 27-1.* Adapted from J. Buettner-Janusch, 1966. *Figure 27-3.* Courtesy of Carolina Biological Supply Company. *Figure 27-4.* From A. J. Kelso, *Physical Anthropology.* Reprinted by permission of the publishers, J. B. Lippincott Company. Copyright © 1970 and 1974. *Figure 27-5.* Adapted from A. C. Allison, "Abnormal Haemoglobin and Erythrocyte Enzyme-Deficiency Traits," in *Genetical Variation in Human Populations,* edited by G. A. Harrison. Pergamon Press, Oxford, 1961.

Index